Right or Wrong?

Right or Wrong?

40 Years inside Notre Dame

Charles E. Rice

ST. AUGUSTINE'S PRESS
South Bend, Indiana

Manufactured in the United States of America

1 2 3 4 5 6   19 18 17 16 15 14 13

Library of Congress Cataloging in Publication Data
Rice, Charles E.
[Works. Selections]
Right or wrong?: 40 years inside Notre Dame / Charles E. Rice. –
First [edition].
pages cm
Includes index.
ISBN 978-1-58731-705-7 (paperbound: alk. paper)
1. University of Notre Dame. 2. University of Notre Dame –
Anecdotes. I. Rice, Charles E. Reality of abortion. II. Title.
LD4113.R53 2013
378.772'89 – dc23   2012040209

ST. AUGUSTINE'S PFRESS
www.staugustine.net

To my wife, Mary, "the brains of the outfit,"
our children and grandchildren,
and especially to our daughter, Ellen,
whose editorial assistance and guidance
were indispensable.

TABLE OF CONTENTS

Table of Contents

Table of Contents

INTRODUCTION

When the University of Notre Dame invited President Obama to deliver the 2009 Commencement Address and receive an honorary degree, many alumni and others protested, including 83 Catholic bishops. In the summer of 2009, I wrote a book, *What Happened to Notre Dame?* (St. Augustine's Press, 2009), describing the Obama invitation as a product of the loss of Catholic identity which Notre Dame had permitted over the past four decades. That loss of Catholic character stemmed from the University's leading role in the Land O'Lakes Declaration by the major Catholic Universities in 1967. That Declaration asserted that "the Catholic university must have a true autonomy and academic freedom in the face of authority of whatever kind, lay or clerical, external to the academic community itself." Notre Dame thereby declared its independence from the Magisterium, or teaching authority, of the Catholic Church as the divinely appointed, authoritative interpreter of the law of God including the natural moral law.

That "autonomy" asserted by Notre Dame is a fake. It substitutes for the moral authority of the Church a counterfeit orthodoxy of political correctness, committed to the pursuit of money, prestige, and the approval of the ruling class of the secular academic and political establishment. In that context, the University's willingness to confer its highest honor on the most implacably pro-abortion public official in the world was predictable if not automatic.

That book, *What Happened to Notre Dame?*, offered a big-picture analysis of Notre Dame's gradual—and we hope, reversible—loss of its Catholic identity. This book, *Right or Wrong?*, has a different perspective. Its title is the title of the columns I wrote at the invitation of the editors of *The Observer* from 1992 until I refused to continue in 2010 when the editor that year insisted, contrary to prior practice, that my presentations of Catholic teachings on homosexuality and other topics could not be printed unless they were "balanced" by an opposing view. I would gladly accept such a restriction at Michigan State but not at a university that claims to be Catholic.

Those *Right or Wrong?* columns, and earlier columns I wrote for *The Observer*, beginning in 1970, are presented in this book as a complement to the earlier book's broader analysis of the changes in the University's identity. Those columns offer a sort of worm's-eye view of those changes as they played out on the ground. They offer the commentary of one member of the University community on those developments. Some of those columns are summaries of basic Catholic teaching where such presentations appeared to be useful to students. Because of the need for readability and brevity, those running commentaries are lacking in the heavy apparatus of "scholarly" writing.

I began writing columns for *The Observer* the year after I joined the Notre Dame Law School faculty in 1969. In 1992, those columns took on a regular bi-weekly character under the title, *Right or Wrong.* This book arranges the columns by decades from the 1970s to 2010. In each decade, the columns are arranged by year, with a subject title for each column. In a college setting the reading audience changes from year to year. The undergrad audience is totally renewed every four years. The columns are sometimes edited, or omitted, to prevent repetition of the content of previous columns. In light of the constantly changing audience, however, some repetition is unavoidable. And sometimes it is necessary in order to preserve the context of a column. With some columns, a brief update is added to note further developments on the issues raised in that column.

Permit me to make two final introductory points. First, I express my appreciation to the student editors of *The Observer.* As noted above, I discontinued the columns in 2010 because of what I saw as an unacceptable restriction imposed by the editor-in-chief at that time. That difference of opinion, however, does nothing to alter my conclusion that the Observer editors with whom I dealt over the years acted with professionalism and courtesy. I am grateful to them for the opportunity they provided to participate in that important enterprise.

Second, I acknowledge the pivotal role of the late Professor Edward J. Murphy in the development and inception of these columns. My relation with Professor Murphy preceded my joining the Notre Dame Law School faculty. During the 1964 Presidential campaign, I gave a speech on the Supreme Court school prayer decisions that was broadcast on radio. Ed Murphy heard it and wrote to me commending the talk and expressing the "hope that before too long I will have the opportunity to meet you." After I joined the Law School faculty in 1969, Ed Murphy became a very close friend and collaborator. We team-taught a religion course for ten years at Marian High School. We also taught together the required Jurisprudence course at the Law School for more than a decade. Ed's guidance and encouragement were indispensable in the inception and development of the columns in this book. In fact, when the Observer invited me in 1992 to write a regular column, it was Ed who came to my rescue with the very-appropriate title, *Right or Wrong?* If he were with us today, he would urge us to trust God and to pray for Notre Dame and our country. Ed Murphy, who died in 1995, was a real Notre Dame man. *Requiescat in pace.*

PART I
THE 1970s

1969–1970

THE REALITY OF ABORTION, April 23, 1970

"The basic principle of the abortion movement is . . . the principle that underlay the Nazi extermination of the Jews: [A]n innocent human being can be killed if his existence is . . . inconvenient or uncomfortable to others or if those others deem him unfit to live. The unborn child is . . . a human being from the moment of conception. . . . It is so clearly a scientific fact that we teach it as such in our schools. As the fifth grade sex education text in the New York City school system flatly says, 'Human life begins when the sperm cells of the father and cells of the mother unite.'. . .

Incidentally the fusion of the abortion and population control movements involves the implicit coercion of welfare clients and other poor persons to undergo abortion. . . . The idea seems to be to eliminate poverty by eliminating the poor. Of course this is a form of genocide. Instead of working . . . to alleviate poverty, the abortion proponents turn to the mindless and cruel solution of death for the helpless child in the womb. . . . People sometimes support abortion because they do not know what it is. Until the twelfth week after conception, a common procedure is dilation of the entrance to the uterus and curettage. Dr. Alan Guttmacher detailed this method in the *Clinical Obstetrics and Gynecology Journal*:

"'*A sharp curette is then inserted to the top of the fundus with very little force, for it is during this phase that the uterus is most likely to be perforated. Moderate force can be safely exerted on the down stroke. The whole uterine cavity is curetted with short strokes, by visualizing a clock and making a stroke at each hour. The curette is then withdrawn several times bringing out pieces of placenta and sac. A small ovum forceps is then inserted and the cavity tonged for tissue, much like an oysterman tonging for oysters . . . In pregnancies beyond the seventh week, fetal parts are recognizable as they are removed piecemeal.*' [Guttmacher, "Techniques of Therapeutic Abortion," *Clinical Obstetrics and Gynecology*, March 1964, 100, 103.]

"When Dr. Guttmacher mentions 'fetal parts,' he means an arm, a leg, a head and other parts of what moments before was a living, though small, human body. . . .

"If an innocent human being can be killed because he is too young, that is, he has not lived nine months from his conception, there is no reason in principle why he cannot be killed because he is too old. Or too retarded. Or too black. Or too politically undesirable. The philosophy is Nazi Germany's. And this nation is adopting it.

5

1973–1974

NOTRE DAME SHOULD STAND FOR THE RIGHT TO LIFE, OPEN LETTER, Oct. 31, 1973.

"This letter is open within the University community. I respectfully request the Board of Trustees to take a corporate position committing the University of Notre Dame to the proposition that all human beings, including unborn children, are entitled to the right to live guaranteed by the United States Constitution. . . . It is appropriate for the University of Notre Dame, as an institution, to take a stand against abortion. There is ample precedent for such a stand in the many and varied commitments made by the University to the cause of equal justice for racial minorities. . . . While the University has shown its corporate dedication to racial justice, it has not evidenced a corresponding institutional concern for this deprived minority, the innocent children in the womb who are deprived of their right to live. Unfortunately, a failure to show that concern can fairly be regarded as an implicit condonation of abortion by the University. . . . [I]t is indefensible for a Catholic university, as for an individual, to proclaim its advocacy of civil rights if it is unwilling to speak forcefully in support of the civil right to live of the most poor and defenseless of all minorities."

1975–1976

CONTRACEPTION IS THE KEY TO THE HOMOSEXUAL ISSUE, April 22, 1976.

"[T]he recognition that homosexual activity is objectively wrong does not involve a judgment as to the subjective culpability of any person involved. The wrongness of the act arises from its violation of the objective moral order, rooted in the unchangeable essence of human nature. . . . Subjective culpability, on the other hand, depends on factors of knowledge and will which are properly judged . . . by God and a confessor. . . . In *Humanae Vitae*, [Pope Paul VI] affirmed 'the inseparable connection, willed by God and unable to be broken by man on his own initiative, between the two meanings of the conjugal act: the unitive meaning and the procreative meaning.' The willful separation of the unitive and procreative aspects of sex is characteristic not only of contraception but also of homosexual [activity] as well as pornography and abortion. As Cardinal John Wright commented, 'What . . . distinguishes 'perversion—as homosexuality, lesbianism and bestiality—from the bisexual relationship is . . . its lack of relationship to the transmission of life.'. . . . The intrinsic connection between the unitive and procreative is rooted in human nature itself. The contraceptive society, however, rests upon the fallacy that the unitive or recreational aspect of sex is an . . . end in itself with no inherent relation to procreation.

"This is the essence of the Playboy philosophy, pursuant to which the partner, whether male or female, tends to become merely an instrument of one's own gratification. Once that contraceptive philosophy is accepted, there can be no coherent . . . opposition to homosexual activity. . . . [W]e have paid great attention to the views of our friendly neighborhood or campus theologians on these matters. It is time for us to listen to the . . . teachings of the Vicar of Christ."

1976–1977

FR. HESBURGH AND THE ROCKEFELLER FOUNDATION, April 20, 1977

"[Fr. Hesburgh] has been a member of the board of the Rockefeller Foundation since 1961. On January 14, 1977, he was elected chairman of the board of the Foundation. . . . [C]alls for his resignation. . . . were prompted by the Foundation's support of various pro-abortion organizations. Fr. Hesburgh. . . . denied that the Foundation supports abortion. 'The Foundation has nothing to do with abortion. In fact,' he said, 'you'll never find the word "abortion" in the report' of the Foundation. . . .

"I am not concerned with the issue of whether Father Hesburgh should resign from the Rockefeller Foundation. Father Hesburgh is personally opposed to abortion and I have a very high respect for him. . . . Rather, I write to avoid misunderstandings. . . . with respect to the Rockefeller Foundation itself. . . .[T]he Foundation has indeed quite a bit to do with abortion. [I]t is not true that, as Father Hesburgh is reported to have stated, 'you'll never find the word "abortion" in the report' of the Foundation. [Omitted is a list of grants by the Rockefeller Foundation to explicitly known pro-abortion groups.] While its pro-abortion grants can not be called the major activity of the Rockefeller Foundation, it can hardly be denied that Foundation grants have been materially helpful to significant pro-abortion groups. It is fair to say, for instance, that the Supreme Court's 1973 abortion rulings would probably not have turned out as they did had it not been for the activities of the James Madison Constitutional Law Institute and the Association for the Study of Abortion. . . . [T]hose groups were aided substantially by Rockefeller Foundation grants. . . .What is at issue here is the erroneous impression generated by Father Hesburgh's reported claim that the Rockefeller Foundation has 'nothing to do with abortion.' The claim is wholly at variance with the record. The Foundation has done good things. But with respect to abortion, its impact has been and continues to be substantial and demonstrably evil in its effect."

8

PART II
THE 1980s

1982–1983

The Impact of Contraception,
Letter to the Editor of *The Observer*, Jan. 18, 1983

"It was not until 1930, with the Anglican Lambeth Conference, that any Christian denomination said that contraception could ever be objectively right. . . . [T]he pro-contraception essays in *The Observer* justify the conclusion that their authors have not read the two basic documents on the subject, *Humanae Vitae*, Pope Paul VI's 1968 encyclical, and *Familiaris Consortio*, the Apostolic Exhortation issued by Pope John Paul II in December, 1981. . . . Beyond an apparent failure to grasp the essential reason why contraception is wrong, *The Observer* essays showed little awareness of the role of contraception as a root cause of other evils. The general acceptance of the morality of the act of contraception is a major factor in the following developments:

"Abortion. Contraception is the prevention of life while abortion is the taking of life. But both come from a common root: the willful separation of the unitive and procreative aspects of sex. Widespread contraception tends to require abortion as a backstop. And the contraceptive mentality of unwanting babies tends to reduce objections to abortion to the emotional or esthetic. There is a technological link, too, in that many so-called contraceptives, such as the IUD, are abortifacient.

"Euthanasia. The contraceptive ethic, because it denies that life is always good, prepares the ground for permissive abortion. Once abortion has accustomed people to the idea that burdensome lives are not worth living, the way is clear for euthanasia for the aged and the 'useless.'

"Pornography. Like contraception, which reduces sexual relations to an exercise in mutual masturbation, pornography is the separation of sex from life and the reduction of sex to an exercise in self-gratification. In the process, a woman becomes an object rather than a person. . . . Pope Paul, in *Humanae Vitae,* warned that contraception would cause women to be viewed as sex objects, that 'man, growing used to the employment of anti-conceptive practices, may finally lose respect for the woman and, no longer caring for her physical and psychological equilibrium, may come to the point of considering her as a mere instrument of selfish enjoyment, and no longer as his respected and beloved companion.'

"Homosexual activity. If sex has no inherent relation to procreation, why not let Freddy marry George? The legitimization of homosexual activity is predictable in a contraceptive society, which cannot say that homosexual relations

11

are objectively wrong without condemning itself. . . . [A] society in which it makes no difference whether boys marry girls or other boys is not only on the road to extinction, it is clinically insane.

"*In vitro* fertilization. Contraception is the taking of the unitive without the procreative. *In vitro* fertilization is the reverse. The . . . Church has warned against this as a perversion. . . . [R]efinements of this technique [include] proposals that spare embryos be frozen and then defrosted and given, or sold, to prospective 'mothers,' that the embryos be used for experiments or that they be used for spare parts for persons in need of new organs.

"Divorce and child abuse. The divorce rate soared during the years in which contraception became practically universal. . . . If sex and marriage are not intrinsically related to the generation of children, then marriage loses its reason for permanence. It tends to become an alliance for individual self-fulfillment—what Pope Paul called 'the juxtaposition of two solitudes.' The refusal to accept responsibility for others and to endure frustration is characteristic of the contraceptive mind. According to Dr. Edward Lenoski, director of pediatric emergency services at Los Angeles County Hospital, 90 percent of the battered children in a six-year study 'were planned pregnancies.' Since the introduction of the pill, child beating has increased threefold.

It would be a mistake, however, to say that a 'contraceptive mentality' is undesirable but that individual acts of contraception can be justified and even meritorious . . . This . . . distinction was flatly rejected by Pope Paul and Pope John Paul II. The . . . error is the idea that the deliberate separation of the unitive and procreative aspects of sex can ever be right. The contraception issue cannot be understood without a prayerful reading of *Humanae Vitae* and *Familiaris Consortio*. I have copies . . . for students who cannot find them elsewhere."

Theologians Who Mislead,
Letter to the Editor of *The Observer*, March 9, 1983

"[O]n Nov. 1, 1982, Pope John Paul II stated, 'One cannot believe in Christ without believing in the Church, the Body of Christ; one cannot believe with the Catholic Faith in the Church without believing in its inalienable Magisterium. Fidelity to Christ implies then faithfulness to the Church, and faithfulness to the Church brings with it fidelity to the Magisterium. . . . [W]ith the same fundamental freedom of faith with which the Catholic theologian adheres to Christ, he adheres to the Church and to its Magisterium. Therefore, the . . . Magisterium is not . . . alien to theology, but is rather intrinsically and essentially a part of it. If the theologian is first of all . . . a believer, whose

Christian faith is faith in the Church of Christ and in the Magisterium, his theological work must remain faithfully bound to his ecclesial Faith, whose authentic and definitive interpreter is the Magisterium.'

"My impression is that Notre Dame students—through no fault of their own—generally do not have any idea that the Church makes this claim upon them. They have been misled by teachers who, in [a] self-serving conflict of interest, tell them instead that papal teachings such as *Humanae Vitae* are to be weighed in the balance with, and qualified by, the views of theologians including perhaps the teachers who are so misinforming them. There is an element of flattery in thus inducing the students to sit in judgment on the papal teachings; and the receptivity of the students is enhanced because, at least in the areas related to *Humanae Vitae,* the views of the theologians which are advanced are invariably more permissive than the teachings of the pope. The classroom teacher comes across, to his own aggrandizement, as benign and respectful of the students while the teaching Church is implicitly presented as restrictive and authoritarian. And into this battle of wits Notre Dame students commonly enter unarmed because they are simply not taught the true nature of papal authority as outlined in the councils and teachings of the popes. It is a scandal which ought to be corrected.

"One letter to *The Observer* criticized my essay because of my 'narrow view of the teaching Church.' On the contrary, it is the councils and the popes who define that the 'teaching Church consists of the Pope and the Bishops in union with the Pope.' I am merely retelling the teachings of that Church. And your friendly campus theologian is not the teaching Church.

"Unfortunately, Notre Dame students, through no fault of their own, are deprived of the opportunity to make an intelligent choice as to whether they will accept the teaching of the Church because they generally are taught, at least by implication, that those teachings are found by weighing the teachings of the Pope in the balance with the views of theologians and by arriving at some sort of consensus or synthesis. It is not surprising that the students are confused. As the Catholic bishops of Australia said, in warning against the use of Father Richard P. McBrien's book, *Catholicism*, the book 'puts side by side two things which cannot be equated: the Church's authentic teaching; the opinions of theologians, some of them quite radical ones. The result can easily be confusion about what the Church really teaches.'

"The teaching of the Church on contraception is eminently reasonable and convincing. And *The Observer* is to be commended for opening its columns to . . . discussion of the contraception issue. But, as the Second Vatican Council clearly indicated, an authentic papal teaching, such as *Humanae Vitae*, is not an invitation to debate. We are bound to accept that teaching in the formation of our consciences, that is, to give to it what the Council described as 'religious submission of will and of mind,' whether we agree with it or not."

1986–1987

Notre Dame and Truth in Labeling, Feb. 3, 1987

"The comment of Bishop John M. D'Arcy of Fort Wayne-South Bend epitomizes the truth in labeling issue: 'It can never be the role of a Catholic theologian,' said Bishop D'Arcy, 'to teach in opposition to what the Church teaches. People send their children to Catholic colleges and universities to receive Catholic teaching. If a theologian calls himself or herself Catholic, and then teaches in opposition to the Church, the Church has not only the right, but indeed the obligation, to declare that that particular theologian cannot be considered a Catholic theologian because he is not only probing, analyzing and questioning, but claiming that in these areas the Catholic Church is wrong and I am right.'. . . As Cardinal Ratzinger [said], 'the faithful must accept not only the infallible Magisterium; they are to give the religious submission of intellect and will to the teachings which the Supreme Pontiff or the college of bishops enunciate on faith or morals when they exercise the authentic Magisterium—even if they do not intend to proclaim it with a definitive act.' The fact that the 'dissenter' is a professor gives him no special privileges. If a theologian at a Catholic university cannot bring himself to accept the teaching of the Popes and Councils, he ought to have the candor at least to present himself as a generic, rather than a Catholic, theologian. . . .

"The Catholic university, of course, does not . . . guarantee the spiritual formation of its students. But the university's claim to be Catholic [implies] an . . . assurance at least that the students will have a predictable opportunity to study the Catholic Faith as that Faith is taught by the Popes and Councils. Those students are entitled to assurance that they will have a chance to study theological subjects with a professor who agrees with the Church or is at least willing and able to present the teachings of the Church favorably as well as accurately. If not, whatever they learn of those matters may be filtered through the distorting lens of a professor whose teaching will be affected by his own dissent, agnosticism, etc. What is most regrettable . . . is the missed opportunity to provide the students with the intellectual background that would enable them to make intelligent choices in matters of faith and morals for the governance of their own lives.

"If the parents of an entering freshman paid top dollar for a brand new Mercedes . . . and then discovered that what was under the hood was not a Mercedes engine but an old Ford Model T motor, they would have a remedy at law based on the violation of the principle of truth in labeling, whether the

14

switch was innocent or fraudulent. Those parents and students have a moral right to protection against a similar switch with respect to education. The professor who presents, as authentically Catholic, positions which contradict the Magisterium is merely applying to education the commercial standards of the Mercedes dealer who puts the Model T engine under the hood.

"If a Catholic university cannot assure its students a chance to study the Catholic Faith as the Vicar of Christ intends it to be studied, let it drop the 'Catholic' from its solicitations and let it acknowledge that, however good it may be in other respects, it is not Catholic in the most important sense in which that term is used.

"It ought to be possible at least for Notre Dame and Saint Mary's to undertake . . . that students will have available at every level identifiable courses in which the Catholic heritage will be studied with professors who accept it as understood by the Popes and Councils. Only then will the students have a fair opportunity to make intelligent judgments in that matter."

A Phony Debate,
Letter to the Editor of *The Observer*, Feb. 5, 1987

"The . . . Theology Department will sponsor the . . . debate on abortion between Dr. Daniel Maguire and Fr. James T. Burtchaell. This sponsorship is a disgrace to Notre Dame.

"Daniel Maguire, a leader of Catholics for a Free Choice, presents his pro-abortion view as a legitimate Catholic position. . . . In fact, as the Pope and Bishop D'Arcy of this diocese have made clear, the pro-abortion or 'pro-choice' position is not a genuine Catholic position. . . . Notre Dame, in providing [Dr. Maguire] a forum to present his claim at a Catholic university, implicitly concedes that his view is at least a debatably legitimate Catholic position. Whether or not Fr. Burtchaell himself regards the Maguire position as authentically Catholic and no matter how eloquently he speaks against abortion, he will have lost the real debate the moment he steps on the platform. By the mere fact that the 'debate' is held under these auspices, Dr. Maguire will have gained the sanction of Notre Dame for the false claim that the Catholic position is defined not by the Vicar of Christ, the Councils and the bishops in union with him, but by individual theologians. . . . If the present leaders of the Theology Department had been around in 1943, perhaps they would have provided a forum for a 'Catholic' apologist for Auschwitz and Buchenwald.

"The Notre Dame Theology Department (with a few notable exceptions) and Dr. Maguire deserve each other. Both claim to be 'Catholic' and yet neither accepts the teaching authority of the Vicar of Christ. It is time for the Theology Department to institute a course on 'The Moral Imperative of Truth in Labeling.'"

1988–1989

AN IMPRUDENT INVITATION, Sept. 22, 1988

"Supreme Court Justice John Paul Stevens will be the featured speaker at the dedication . . . of the Courtroom at the Notre Dame Law School. . . . Stevens is one of the . . . Justices . . . who [continues to] uphold [*Roe v. Wade*] . . . against attempts by the states to regulate abortion. . . . [B]y this invitation we tell our students that abortion is merely one constitutional issue among others and that it really does not make all that much difference whether a lawyer or judge supports the depersonalization of innocent human beings. We imply that the important thing is to be a 'competent' lawyer; yet it hardly vouches for one's professional competence if he is unable to see the centrality of this issue as of *Dred Scott*. We encourage our students to show 'compassion' to the poor and helpless. Yet the poorest and most helpless victim of all is the child who is murdered in the womb; society's answer to the difficult pregnancy should be, not to kill the baby, but to help the mother and child, before and after the birth, as long as and as fully as necessary. We encourage our students to serve the cause of 'peace'; we would do well to remind them, as Mother Teresa has often said, that 'The greatest destroyer of peace in the world is abortion.' And we encourage our students to work to build a just moral order. We might remind them of what Pope John Paul II said at the Capitol Mall in Washington in 1979: 'If a person's right to life is violated at the moment in which he is first conceived in his mother's womb, an indirect blow is struck also at the whole of the moral order, which serves to ensure the inviolable goods of man. Among these goods, life occupies the first place.'. . .

"The invitation disserves our students and degrades the University."

A UNIONIZED FACULTY? May 5, 1989

"The Faculty Senate has voted to explore the issue of faculty unionization. . . . At both the April and May meetings of the Senate, I moved that the senate be dissolved. Any organization has the power to dissolve itself, if only by adjourning *sine die*. . . . The move toward unionization is intended to promote faculty governance of the University. . . . My service on the senate is a form of "jury duty." I have enjoyed the company of the senators and for each of them individually I have a very high regard. But I have no confidence in the ability of the

17

senate, as a corporate body, to govern anything. William F. Buckley once said that he would rather be governed by the first 250 names in the Boston phone book than by the Harvard faculty. My sentiments are similar. The discontent in the Faculty Senate, however, is a reflection of a more basic unease. The primary historical focus of Notre Dame has been the education of undergraduates, with research and graduate studies playing a balanced and important role in the overall mission of the University. Now, however, Notre Dame is pursuing prestige as a great "research university." While the official rhetoric emphasizes that teaching and research are equally important, the undergraduate students know better. And so do the faculty, especially those who are untenured and who realistically conclude that the procurement of grants and the generation of publications count more heavily for career purposes than time spent with students.

"The students pay the price for the pursuit of prestige in more frequent mega-sections, more reliance on teaching assistants and increased difficulty in gaining entrance to desired courses. . . . The one thing that students and their families can rely upon is that they will pay an escalating tuition, beyond the rate of inflation, every year. It is not fair to impose on students and their families the burden of paying for research prestige that bears only a marginal relation, if any, to the education of undergraduates.

"How does the move for faculty unionization fit into the picture? As at other universities, the senior faculty have gone along with the pursuit of research prestige as their pay has steadily increased. Sadly and... comically, the senate was roused from its torpor, not by any substantive issue but by the temerity of the administration in reducing the . . . benefits package. The bottom line in the unionization move is a money line. Unionization is a tactic to preserve and improve the economic position of the faculty. It would perpetuate the devaluation of teaching in the building of a 'great research university.' If anything, it would worsen the position of the students and their families.

We do not need a faculty share in the actual governance of Notre Dame. And we do not need a faculty union. Rather we need to recover our historical mission in various respects. We are, strangely, a "Catholic" university with a de facto orthodoxy of dissent. We are a residential university with policies that tend to drive even non-drinking students off-campus for social activities. The Holy Cross priests, whose predecessors founded and built this institution, have relinquished the principal offices controlling academics, theology and admissions. [W]e are worse off as a result. In the process, they may be squandering a heritage that was not theirs to diminish. . . . What matters is not what they think of us at Princeton or Yale, but the quality of the service we provide for our students. We are entitled to hope that the Holy Cross priests, who are 6 of the 12 Fellows of the University, will reflect on the history of this institution and return it to its primary function which is the education of students in the Catholic tradition."

1989–1990

THE LAST TEMPTATION OF CHRIST,
LETTER TO THE EDITOR OF THE OBSERVER, SEPT. 28, 1989

"By any coherent criteria, *The Last Temptation of Christ* is a blasphemous film. . . . The public showing of this film on September 29 and 30 is not for examination by a class in the context of a course. It therefore cannot be justified as an exercise of academic freedom. Rather, it is . . . a challenge, an open affront, to the divine founder of the Christian religion and those who claim to believe in Him. . . . Priests of the Congregation of Holy Cross hold several of the top administrative positions at Notre Dame. . . . One could hardly imagine their predecessors in Holy Cross sitting still for such a blasphemy at the University dedicated to the Mother of God. I have read the script of *The Last Temptation of Christ*. Its intellectual content can be described most favorably as moronic. . . . If it is not cancelled, one could be justified, unfortunately, in concluding that we are in the presence of anatomical marvels, a communications department without brains and an administration without guts."

ANOTHER STUPID INVITATION,
LETTER TO THE EDITOR OF THE OBSERVER, JAN. 29, 1990

"The invitation to psychologist Sol Gordon to speak at Notre Dame . . . is sponsored by four [University] centers. Dr. Gordon . . . is an advocate of contraception, abortion, homosexual activity and masturbation as morally legitimate and desirable. . . . In its Year of the Family, Notre Dame, a 'Catholic' university, presents Sol Gordon with the implication that his views are legitimate alternatives for the consideration of the University community. . . . Last fall the University could not summon the will to draw the line short of University sponsorship of a direct blasphemy of the person of Christ in *The Last Temptation of Christ*. If Notre Dame feels obliged to sponsor a blasphemy of Christ, the invitation to Sol Gordon is small change indeed. . . . One could hardly imagine the Holy Cross priests of an earlier day sitting still for University sponsorship of a Sol Gordon to speak on love and the family, just as one could hardly imagine them sponsoring a blasphemy of Christ. Notre Dame has become something different from what it was. In this respect, the change is not for the better.

"By all accounts, Dr. Gordon is an entertaining speaker. So, for those who are so inclined—enjoy the lectures. And be sure to write your mother and tell her what you are learning at Notre Dame in The Year of the Family."

PART III
THE 1990s

1990–1991

THE STRIVING RESEARCH UNIVERSITY
AND THE EDUCATION OF UNDERGRADS

April 16, 1991 (Part One of a two-part column)

"The most important construction project on campus this year is neither the peace center nor the classroom building. It is the two signs proclaiming Notre Dame as 'A National Catholic Research University.' One first might ask whether 'national' is descriptive of 'Catholic' rather than 'university' in light of the reality that Notre Dame is a 'Catholic' university with a de facto orthodoxy of dissent.

"Twenty years of teaching Notre Dame graduates lead me to conclude that. . . . [t]he ordinary Notre Dame graduate . . . tends, through no fault of his own, to be a functional illiterate with respect to knowledge of the actual teachings of the Catholic Church. . . .

"The primary historical focus of Notre Dame had been the education of undergrads in the Catholic tradition, with research and graduate studies playing a balanced and important role. . . . Research is a valid part of the academic enterprise. But research itself is not education. Now, however, Notre Dame is submitting to politically dominant trends in the pursuit of prestige as a great 'research university.'. . . While the official rhetoric emphasizes that teaching and research are equally important, the undergrad students [and] the faculty [know] that . . . publications count more for career purposes than time spent with students. . . . The education of undergraduates is moving toward the status of an afterthought at Notre Dame. The undergrads. . . . see a building program that will, for the first time, move major university buildings to the very edge of the campus (as they do at big urban universities which have prestige and, besides, someone paid 33 million dollars for the project.)

"The building program has already obliterated a very substantial part of the students' athletic fields (in a 'research' university perhaps they will be more interested in spectator sports and coffee houses). . . . One thing that students and their families can rely upon is that they will pay an escalating tuition, beyond the rate of inflation, every year. . . . The University emphasizes that its tuition is in the lower range of the 'leading' universities. However, the 'leading' universities' general practice of hiking tuition in pursuit of research greatness is itself unjust.

"There are worse offenders, but the question is whether Notre Dame ought to be riding even with the rear echelons of that pack of exploiters. In truth, it is deeply immoral to impose on students and their families the burden of paying for research prestige that bears only a marginal relation, if any, to the education of those students.

"Undergrads who are not from wealthy families or on special financial aid emerge from Notre Dame with a loan commitment so heavy that it impedes a free choice of graduate study and career options. This distortion of career choices occurs as well on the graduate level, especially with the law students. . . . Needless to say, the loan burdens caused by the University's pursuit of research greatness make it difficult for young married alumni to maintain in their marriages an openness to new life as required by the moral law.

"Advanced research is very expensive. And the focus on research tends toward a 'bottom line' preoccupation with grants and money in general. Notre Dame's endowment reached $605.6 million on June 30, 1990, 15th highest among American institutions of higher learning. It would be helpful if someone in the Administration would explain how it is morally sound to raise tuition substantially beyond the inflation rate every year to pay for the 'research' enterprise while the University continues to build a record endowment that is not used to reduce tuition. Of course, that is what the prestige universities do. And if we channel new donations away from endowment and into efforts to hold tuition in line, how can we ever become 14th highest?

"A preoccupation with 'research' greatness is one symptom of a university's pursuit of 'PC'—political correctness. . . . Notre Dame is no latecomer to the pursuit of . . . PC. For decades, the University has sought to be 'great' as well as 'Catholic,' implying wrongly that there is a tension between the two concepts. Notre Dame has sought acceptance as a 'great university' according to the standards of Harvard, Yale, Stanford and other institutions."

POLITICAL CORRECTNESS TRUMPS CATHOLIC IDENTITY

April 17, 1991 (Part Two of a two-part column)
"The 'academic community,' external as well as internal, long ago assumed the authoritative role formerly played by the teaching Church in the life of Notre Dame. At the Land O'Lakes conference in 1967, the presidents of the leading Catholic universities, including Notre Dame, declared that, 'To perform its teaching and research functions effectively, the Catholic university must have a true autonomy and academic freedom in the face of authority of whatever kind, lay or clerical, external to the academic community itself.' The Land O'Lakes concept tends predictably toward an institutional renunciation of the duty to affirm religious truth.

"Thus, in the fall of 1989, Notre Dame sponsored a public showing of a blasphemy of Christ, in the film 'The Last Temptation of Christ.' That event remains crucial in the history of Notre Dame. The University decided that the First and Second Commandments were superseded by the authority of the secular establishment. As Professor Dean Porter, Director of the Snite Museum, said, 'when (the museum) was built nine years ago, we decided that if a film could be seen at the Museum of Modern Art, it could be seen here.' (South Bend Tribune, Sept. 29, 1989, p. C1, col. 1). . . . A serio-comic example of Notre Dame's tendency to endorse almost anything 'politically correct' is the Academic Council's recent prescription for gender-inclusive language. Only in the [closing decades] of the twentieth century did academics . . . discover that such words as 'he,' 'man,' and 'mankind' caused women to feel inferior. Now, Dean Eileen Kolman of the Freshman Year of Studies believes 'it would be an absolute shame if any student leaves Notre Dame in 1991 without knowing that exclusive language is simply no longer acceptable.'

"More likely, Notre Dame graduates (will they have 'bachelor's' degrees?) will discover in the world outside academe a less than unlimited tolerance for the neologisms and ambiguities generated by the ideological corruption of language. Meanwhile, unfortunately, linguistic vandals will mutilate some treasures of the English language, including the Bible. Thus, 'An Inclusive Lectionary,' produced by the National Council of Churches, describes God as 'the motherly father of the Church who comes forth' and has St. John, in 3:16, tell us, 'For God so loved the world that God gave God's only Child, that whoever believes in that Child should not perish but have eternal life.'

"When the Faculty Senate bestirred itself to pass the gender resolution, Professor Paul Conway, Chairman of the Senate, said, 'We're 10–15 years behind the [other universities] in making this resolution.' (The Observer, Feb. 6, 1991). What next? And will we ever catch up? While the gender policy represents a minor and probably transitory feminoid triumph, it does manifest the other-directed bent of an institution unsure of its heritage and beliefs.

"The pursuit of PC can sometimes take priority even over the health of students. An example is the muted policy of the University on homosexual activity. The University commendably refuses to officially recognize homosexual groups on campus. The University also rightly emphasizes that the objective wrongness of homosexual activity does not warrant unjust discrimination against persons who have homosexual tendencies. Nor does the objective wrongness of the act confer a license to judge the subjective culpability of anyone.

"Homosexual activity, however, is the main factor in the onset of AIDS. One could reasonably think that if the University is going to say anything to its students on the homosexual issue, it ought to include a demand that homosexuals refrain from the objectively wrong behavior which is a menace to themselves and potentially to the health of the community. I have yet to see any such public insistence from any office of the University. See, for example, the statements of Campus Ministry and of 39 members of the Notre Dame community on National Coming Out Day (The Observer, Oct. 11, 1990). Justice to the homosexuals as well as to the rest of the community requires an insistence on the duty to refrain from homosexual activity. Political correctness demands instead an emphasis on the evil of homophobia and on the duty of others to exercise tolerance and compassion. And that is predominantly what we hear on the subject.

"The two 'Research University' signs can be fairly regarded as a public acknowledgment of the other-directed pursuit of PC which has been on the Notre Dame agenda for decades. The research preoccupation and other PC examples arise from good faith judgments made by administrators and others who act in what they see as the best interest of Notre Dame. My criticism is of policies, not persons.

"We ought to ask, however, where this PC trend is leading us in educational and spiritual as well as financial terms. We have lost sight of some basic realities: that undergraduate education is entitled to the primary focus at Notre Dame; that research is collateral, i.e., that Notre Dame exists mainly for the benefit of its students rather than of the government, industry, foundations or the publishing professoriate; that graduate education and attendant research are important to Notre Dame but that there, too, the interests of the students are paramount; that the Catholic character of Notre Dame entails a responsibility to help its students who are so minded to prepare for service to the community and the Church without having to incur prohibitive loans just to make it through college. . . . I hope, perhaps unrealistically, that Notre Dame will survive as a Catholic institution loyal to the Vicar of Christ and actively seeking the aid of the Mother of God. The pursuit of PC and of 'research' greatness, however, is leading us in the opposite direction."

1991–1992

CAMPUS MINISTRY ON "NATIONAL COMING OUT DAY," Oct. 29, 1991

"Campus Ministry's statement on National Coming Out Day, published in *The Observer* of Oct. 8th, properly emphasized that 'while homosexual orientation is not sinful, homosexual acts are,' and that, for heterosexuals as well as homosexuals, 'the only proper place for genital sex is within the permanent bond of marriage and in the context of the potentiality of new life.'

"The statement stressed the duty to avoid harassment of homosexuals and to 'examine our expressed and sometimes implicit negative attitudes toward those among us who are homosexuals.'

"The political gay rights movement . . . seeks to legitimize as normal and as even a preferred constitutional right, an activity which is destructive to society and contrary to the nature of a person as well as to the law of God.

"In response to this movement, it is essential to avoid harassment and wrongful imputation of culpability to those who act as well as to those who are merely oriented toward homosexuality. It is important, however, to avoid an implicit promotion of the erroneous conclusion that the homosexual orientation is itself neutral or benign.

"The Letter on Homosexuality issued by the Congregation for the Doctrine of the Faith, with the approval of Pope John Paul II, on Oct. 1, 1986, said, . . . 'the proper reaction to crimes committed against homosexual persons should not be to claim that the homosexual orientation is not disordered. When such a claim is made and when homosexual activity is consequently condoned or when civil legislation is introduced to protect behavior to which no one has any conceivable right, neither the Church nor society at large should be surprised when other distorted notions and practices gain ground, and irrational and violent reactions increase.' No. 10 . . . .

"'Although the particular inclination of the homosexual person is not a sin, it is a more or less strong tendency ordered toward an intrinsic moral evil; and thus the inclination itself must be seen as an objective disorder.' No. 3.

"The statements of the teaching Church on the subject have consistently affirmed that the homosexual orientation, while not itself sinful, is disordered even if it is not acted upon. And those statements have stressed the importance for young people of prayer, 'frequent reception of the Sacraments of Penance and the Eucharist,' and 'devotion to the Immaculate Mother of God.' *Declaration on Sexual Ethics*, no. 12.

"Campus Ministry's generally constructive statement should have made the same points. Instead, while the statement commendably noted the intrinsic wrongness of extramarital sex of any kind, it went on to devote its major thrust to a politically correct condemnation of harassment.

"Notre Dame students are entitled to a more complete exposition of what the Catholic Church actually teaches on the subject. I suggest it would better serve the Notre Dame community for Campus Ministry to offer every week, verbatim, a current statement of the Vicar of Christ on a moral issue.

"Perhaps Notre Dame students care too little about what Campus Ministry thinks. But, if they were given the chance, I think they would care very much what the Vicar of Christ thinks."

LAETARE MEDAL TO SENATOR MOYNIHAN, April 13, 1992

"Senator Daniel Patrick Moynihan (Democrat, N.Y.), the 1992 Laetare medal recipient, has a consistently pro-abortion voting record, as indicated by the following votes: [Details of 18 pro-abortion votes by Sen. Moynihan omitted here.]

"Senator Moynihan is relentless in his support for legalizing and funding the killing of unborn children. Why did Notre Dame award the Laetare Medal to such a man? 'His passion for scholarship,' said the President, Rev. Edward A. Malloy, C.S.C., 'has made him sensible to the realities of state, sensitive to the cry of the poor and commendably supportive of higher education. At Notre Dame, we share that passion, and with this year's Laetare Medal, we celebrate it as well.'

"One of the 'realities of state' to which Senator Moynihan, and apparently our University leaders, are 'sensible' is that the American state, with Moynihan's approval, legalizes the execution of more than 4,000 innocent unborn human beings every single day.

"The sensitivity of Moynihan and our leaders to 'the cry of the poor' is selective. The poorest and most helpless of the poor is the unborn child who is murdered before he can utter a cry. Mother Teresa reminds us that the poorest nations are those which murder their young by abortion.

"Finally, we are told, Moynihan is 'commendably supportive of higher education.' Senator Moynihan is in a position to expedite the allocation of taxpayers' money and other supports to 'higher education.' 'Sensible to the realities of state,' our 'national Catholic research university' is not deterred from honoring this important person by a little thing like his support for legalized baby killing. . . . The award of this medal to Senator Moynihan is contemptuous of the Catholic tradition of Notre Dame and reprehensible in its disdain for the victims of abortion. We 'celebrate' this year the 25th anniversary of the transfer of Notre Dame from the Congregation of Holy Cross to secular status.

"If the Laetare award to Moynihan is a sample of what secularization means, it may be time to give the place back to the Congregation—provided it would be administered by Holy Cross priests who would be willing to run it as a Catholic institution."

1992–1993

RELATION BETWEEN NOTRE DAME AND THE CHURCH, Sept. 14, 1992

"It would be helpful if those who are concerned about preserving the Catholic character of Notre Dame would read 'The Decline and Fall of the Christian College,' by Fr. James T. Burtchaell, C.S.C., in the April and May issues of *First Things* magazine.

"The secularization of the liberal Protestant universities in the period 1870–1910, Fr. Burtchaell notes, 'consisted of gradual modifications called for by professing Christians.'

"For example, when President James Kirkland set about to improve the Vanderbilt program, he saw the Southern Methodist Church as 'a hindrance, not a help,' in the pursuit of his academic goals.

"He worked to transfer control from the Methodist bishops to a lay board. 'His intention was that (Vanderbilt) be laicized,' comments Burtchaell, 'but it was secularized as well. . . . (I)t was no longer Christian or religious.'. . . . The desire to be free of the church 'was usually motivated by the belief that the Christian context and spiritual nourishment . . . would continue after the removal of any authoritative link with the church.'

"'The widely shared church membership and piety of the campus population led them to suppose that the inertial force of faith is such that it would carry them along after their relationship to the church became informal and inexplicit rather than legal.' Unfortunately, the secular tendencies prevailed.

"Beginning in 1967, the leading American Catholic universities, including Notre Dame, severed their juridical connection with the Church and became autonomous institutions.

"Fr. Burtchaell, to the contrary, maintains that '*The only plausible way for a college or university to be significantly Christian is for it to function as a congregation in active communion within a church.*' He suggests that 'secularization is rapidly bleaching the Catholic character out of that church's universities and colleges, with all the elements we saw typified in the Vanderbilt story.'

"Once autonomy is declared, the secularization process is gradual and, regrettably, familiar: '(A)s a century earlier (with the Protestant universities), the Catholic universities enjoyed an immediate honeymoon period wherein autonomy actually enhanced the institution as both a faith community and a house of liberal learning.

"'But then the slow and inexorable gravity pull of the secularism

30

dominant in the force-field of the academy begins to retard and then counteract the inertial momentum that has hitherto set the course of the Catholic college or university, until, after a period when the forms and symbols of
Christian identity are gradually evacuated of their conviction, the institution
finally emerges as a wraith of the Christian community it once was.'

"The twelve Fellows, six of whom must be Holy Cross priests, control
Notre Dame in fact. Yet the Congregation of Holy Cross has no formal responsibility for the University.

"The divorce of de facto power from responsibility violates elementary
leadership principles. And it never works in the long run. The Burtchaell article fairly raises the issue of whether it would promote the Catholic character
of Notre Dame for the Congregation of Holy Cross to resume formal, juridical responsibility for the University. That article evidences courage as well as
perception. Its author has earned the appreciation of all who value the cause of
integrity in education. His analysis merits full and open debate within the
Notre Dame community."

ABORTION AND PERSONHOOD, Oct. 5, 1992

"In *Planned Parenthood v. Casey*, this year, the Supreme Court upheld four
marginal restrictions on Pennsylvania abortion procedure while striking down
a requirement that a married woman inform her husband before she has an
abortion.

"More important, the 5-4 majority explicitly reaffirmed *Roe v. Wade*, the
1973 abortion ruling. That 5-4 margin has led some pro-life advocates to claim
that 'we are only one vote away from overturning *Roe v. Wade.*' That is not true.

"The four dissenters in *Casey* did say, in Chief Justice Rehnquist's words,
'that *Roe* was wrongly decided and that it can and should be overruled.'
However, when those dissenters (Rehnquist, White, Scalia, Thomas) say they
want to 'overrule' *Roe*, they mean they want to turn the issue back to the states
to let them decide whether to allow or forbid abortion.

"Such a states' rights solution would confirm, rather than overturn, the
bedrock holding of *Roe*, that the unborn child is a nonperson who has no constitutional rights and who can therefore be legally killed at the discretion of others.

"The *Roe* Court held that, whether or not the unborn child is a human
being, he is a nonperson. The ruling is therefore the same in effect as a frank
holding that an acknowledged human being is an nonperson.

"The court in *Roe* indicated that if the unborn child is a person, the states
would be constitutionally obliged to protect his or her life and could not allow
abortion in any case. . . .

31

"In his opinion in *Webster v. Reproductive Health Services*, in 1989, Justice Stevens stressed that '[e]ven the dissenters in *Roe* implicitly endorsed that holding [of nonpersonhood]by arguing that state legislatures should decide whether to prohibit or to authorize abortions. . . . By characterizing the basic question as "a political issue," . . . Justice Scalia likewise implicitly accepts this holding.' 492 U.S. at 568, n. 13.

"When the *Casey* dissenters argue for a states' rights solution, they confirm the nonpersonhood of the unborn child. If an innocent human being is subject to execution at the decision of another whenever the legislature so decrees, he is a nonperson with no constitutional right to live. . . .

"In any civilized society in which personhood is the condition for possessing rights, there is a necessary correspondence between humanity and personhood.

"The depersonalization of innocent human beings was the weapon an earlier Supreme Court used against the slaves in the *Dred Scott* case. And it was used to provide legal justification for the Nazi oppression of the Jews.

"Our Supreme Court is not narrowly divided on the basic issue of abortion. Instead, it is unanimous in its endorsement of the proposition that the law can validly depersonalize innocent human beings so as to subject them to execution at the discretion of others.

"On the contrary, a coherent legal response to permissive abortion would require a federal, state or constitutional amendment specifying that the unborn child is a person whose life is entitled to constitutional protection without exception."

NUTRITION AND HYDRATION, Nov. 16, 1992

"Involuntary euthanasia will soon be legalized by the courts as a response to the pressures of an aging population and rising medical costs.

"The law recognizes the legal right of a competent adult to refuse any and all forms of medical treatment, including food and water, at least where they are provided by 'artificial' means.

"With respect to incompetent patients, the courts generally allow withdrawal of artificially provided food and water based on the patient's previously expressed intent (whether by living will or otherwise) or based on the decision of the family or other health care agent that the patient would have wanted such withdrawal or that the withdrawal would be in his best interest.

"In the leading case of *Matter of Conroy*, in 1985, the Supreme Court of New Jersey allowed withdrawal of a feeding tube from an incompetent but 'awake and conscious' patient even in the absence of 'any evidence at all, that the patient would have declined the treatment,' if 'the net burdens of the patient's life with the treatment . . . clearly and markedly outweigh the benefits that the patient derives from life.'

"In *Cruzan v. Director, Missouri Dept. of Health*, in 1990, the Supreme Court held that Missouri could require, if it chose, 'that evidence of the incompetent's wishes as to the withdrawal of treatment be proved by clear and convincing evidence.'

"But *Cruzan* does not forbid the states to allow withdrawal of food and water on a lesser showing of the patient's intent or on the basis that withdrawal is in the patient's best interest in the absence of a showing of intent.

"In these 'right to die' cases: First, the patients are not dying; Nancy Cruzan would have lived for 30 years. Second, the courts allow withholding, not of therapeutic medical treatment but of food and water that is neither burdensome nor useless in keeping the patient alive; and Third, the withholding of food and water is intended to cause death.

"Once euthanasia is authorized by withholding food and water, the allowance of active killing by injection or other means is inevitable. In *Brophy v. New England Sinai Hospital* (Mass., 1986), Justice Neil L. Lynch remarked in dissent: 'The withdrawal of the provision of food and water is a particularly difficult, painful and gruesome death; . . . (T)he natural question is: Why not use more humane methods of euthanasia if that is what we endorse?'. . . .

"The next line of cases will authorize painless, lethal injections for incompetent as well as competent patients. We do as much for convicted murderers.

"Eventually, if a terminal patient, facing a lingering, painful death, were to decline a lethal injection, that decision could be a factor in determining that he is incompetent and that the decision should be made for him by others. The quick, painless injection is easier on the 'care givers.' And it is cost effective. . . .

"If the unborn child can be treated as a nonperson subject to execution at the discretion of others, so can an octogenarian on a feeding tube. . . .

"As John Cardinal O'Connor said in 1989, 'I predict that the 'right to die'—which really means that hospitals and doctors and other health care 'providers' will be *required* to kill—will dwarf the abortion phenomenon in magnitude, in numbers, in horror. As mothers have become legalized agents of the deaths of their children, so children will become legalized agents of the deaths of their mothers—and fathers."

DISCRIMINATION AGAINST HOMOSEXUALS?, Dec. 7, 1992

"Alumnus Paul Fisher's informative paid advertisement on homosexuality, in the Nov. 6 issue, drew fire from Campus Ministry and others.

"As Campus Ministry noted in its Nov. 12 response, that office has correctly explained to the Notre Dame community some basic elements of the homosexual issue.

"However, Campus Ministry has generally failed to inform the community on two aspects of the issue: on the intrinsic disorder of the homosexual inclination itself and on the justifiability of discrimination against homosexuals in some situations.

"Specifically, to the date of this writing, Campus Ministry has not publicized the recent observations communicated by the Congregation for the Doctrine of the Faith(CDF) to the American bishops on legislative proposals 'which would make discrimination on the basis of sexual orientation illegal.'

"Released to the public by the Vatican on July 23, the document was intended as 'a background resource' rather than 'an official and public instruction on the matter.'. . . . The CDF document first reviews basic elements of the issue. . . . The CDF letter then applies these principles to the proposed legislation:

"'Sexual orientation' does not constitute a quality comparable to race, ethnic background, etc., in respect to nondiscrimination. Unlike these, homosexual orientation is an objective disorder. . . . There are areas in which it is not unjust discrimination to take sexual orientation into account, for example, in the placement of children for adoption or foster care, in employment of teachers or athletic coaches, and in military recruitment.

"'Homosexual persons, as human persons, have the same rights as all persons, including the right of not being treated in a manner which offends their personal dignity. . . . Among other rights, all persons have the right to work, to housing, etc.

"'Nevertheless, these rights are not absolute. They can be legitimately limited for objectively disordered external conduct. This is sometimes not only licit but obligatory. . . . Including "homosexual orientation" among the considerations on the basis of which it is illegal to discriminate can easily lead to regarding homosexuality as a positive source of human rights, for example, in respect to so-called affirmative action or preferential treatment in hiring practices.' . . .

"The CDF letter incorporates much Church teaching on the subject. Although it is not itself an official teaching, Notre Dame students were entitled to be informed about it so that they could adequately form their judgments on the subject. That they were not so informed is one indication, among others, that, at this Prestigious Research University, the functionally official religion is Political Correctness.

"In general, and beyond the homosexual issue, Campus Ministry would serve the community if it would present every week in The Observer a current statement of the Pope on a moral or social issue. At this allegedly Catholic institution, the Pope ought to be entitled to at least equal time."

"BAIT AND SWITCH," Jan. 18, 1993

"[M]any at Notre Dame believe that adherence to Church teaching on moral issues is discretionary. One reason . . . is the failure of this 'Catholic' University to affirm the . . . clear obligations of Catholics toward the teachings of the Vicar of Christ.

"The . . . principle here is truth-in-labeling, with its corollary . . . of full disclosure. You rely on that principle every time you pay $2.98 a pound [1993 prices!] for what the label tells you is ground round instead of $1.29 for the lowly ground beef. If the seller pulled a 'bait and switch' by labeling hamburger as if it were ground round, you could have a legal as well as a moral complaint.

"[T]he recent history of American Catholic universities exemplifies the 'bait and switch.' Notre Dame attracts alumni donors and prospective students by affirmations of its 'Catholic character.' Yet Notre Dame professes an orthodoxy of openness which is inconsistent with that character. As the first sentence of the Notre Dame President's Sesquicentennial Declaration put it, 'Notre Dame's first commitment is to freedom of inquiry and expression.' In practice this . . . invites a process of endless inquiry, without norms of content, which obscures the obligatory character of teachings of the Magisterium.

"*Ex Corde Ecclesiae,* the Apostolic Constitution on Catholic Universities, affirms the importance of due freedom in the 'search for truth.' But it also enumerates as one of the 'essential characteristics' of the Catholic university: 'Fidelity to the Christian message as it comes to us through the church.' And, 'the institutional fidelity of the University to the Christian message includes a recognition of and adherence to the teaching authority of the church in matters of faith and morals.'

"Christ is God and the Pope is His Vicar, the visible head of His Church on earth. Vatican II's *Dogmatic Constitution on Divine Revelation* states: 'The task of authentically interpreting the word of God, whether written or handed on, has been entrusted exclusively to the living teaching office of the Church, whose authority is exercised in the name Jesus Christ.' (No. 10.)

"That teaching office is possessed by the Pope and the bishops in union with him. (Vatican II, Dogmatic Constitution on the Church, No. 25). In his 1987 address to the bishops of the United States, John Paul noted that 'there is a tendency on the part of some Catholics to be selective in their adherence to the Church's moral teachings. It is sometimes claimed that dissent from the Magisterium is totally compatible with being a 'good Catholic' and poses no obstacle to the reception of the sacraments. This is a grave error that challenges the teaching office of the Bishops of the United States and elsewhere.'

"More than two decades of teaching Notre Dame alumni in law school lead me to conclude that Notre Dame undergraduates are shortchanged in that they are not afforded a predictable opportunity to learn what the Catholic Church actually teaches about itself and about the binding character of its moral teachings. What they do learn in this area is likely to be filtered through the lens of a hostile professor.

"They can count on Campus Ministry to say some good things but rarely anything politically incorrect. And it is the maximum political incorrectness to assert that one agrees with the moral teaching of the Pope and that all Catholics are bound to give to that teaching a 'religious submission of will and of mind.' (Vatican II, *Dogmatic Constitution on the Church*, No. 25.) In truth, as John Paul II stated to the American bishops, there is no moral right for a Catholic to dissent from the teaching of the Magisterium.

"Notre Dame raises money on the strength of its Catholic pretensions. Yet Notre Dame's profession and practice implicitly legitimize and even exalt dissent from Church teaching. If its officials were held . . . to the labeling and disclosure standards that govern lesser mortals, including sellers of hamburger, they would need a lawyer.

"It would be a constructive move to retrieve *Ex Corde Ecclesiae* from the dead letter file and make it the focus of the . . . campus discussions of the 'Catholic' character of Notre Dame."

NORPLANT, Feb. 1, 1993

"In his State of the State message on January 14th, Governor William Schaefer proposed that Maryland offer free Norplant inserts to women on welfare and free vasectomies to men leaving prison. He suggested that such birth control measures be made mandatory in some cases.

"Norplant consists of six matchstick-sized capsules implanted under the skin of a woman's upper arm. It releases a hormone which operates to prevent fertilization, or, if fertilization does occur, to prevent implantation of the embryo in the womb. Therefore, although commonly described as a contraceptive, Norplant is also an abortifacient. The implant is effective for five years and cannot be removed by the woman herself but only by a physician. Norplant is covered by Medicaid in all 50 states and more than 500,000 women have received the implant since its introduction in 1991. . . .

"Norplant is the utilitarian weapon of choice against the welfare problem, especially among minority groups. The coercion is implicit but real. As Arthur Caplan, director of the Center for Biomedical Ethics at the University of Minnesota, said, 'Today, a welfare mother is coerced into using Norplant. Tomorrow, the state is in the parent licensing business.'

"This advent of legalized genocide should prompt us to recall that this is

the 25th anniversary of *Humanae Vitae*, the 1968 encyclical of Pope Paul VI.
. . . *Humanae Vitae* was greeted with scorn by clerics and laity of The Church
of Where It's At. But nobody in his right mind is laughing at Paul VI now.

"*Humanae Vitae* prophetically forecast that, if contraception were regarded
as legitimate in any case, the state would eventually impose it by coercion. . . .

"The 'birth control' mentality, in the words of Irish Cardinal Cahal Daly,
'means the abandonment of self-control over sexual urges; it implicitly authorizes sexual promiscuity. . . .

"' Society . . . makes it unnaturally difficult for people, particularly young
people, to be continent; and then offers a remedy, contraceptives, which merely increases the incontinence.

"' Promiscuity is the logic of birth control; but to have promiscuity with
impunity there must also be abortion and infanticide, sterilization and euthanasia.

"' The logical contraceptionist must insist that if these cannot be generalized by persuasion, they must be imposed by law. It has long been recognized
that there is a connection between eroticism and totalitarianism.'

"My impression is that many Notre Dame students know *Humanae Vitae*
only through professiorial and clerical caricatures of it. Its 25th anniversary is
not likely to be officially celebrated here. But perhaps we could commemorate
the encyclical by taking an anniversary poll, providing the members of the
Notre Dame Theology Department an opportunity to state publicly and individually whether they agree with and support *Humanae Vitae*. The students
and alumni might be interested in the results. On a more basic level, it would
be appropriate for each of us to read and reflect on *Humanae Vitae* and its
prophetic character."

THE SOCIAL IMPACT OF CONTRACEPTION, Feb. 15, 1993

"In *Humanae Vitae*, Pope Paul said this teaching 'is founded upon the inseparable connection, willed by God and unable to be broken by man on his own
initiative, between the two meanings of the conjugal act: the unitive meaning
and the procreative meaning.'

"Contraception is wrong because, as Pope John Paul II said in *Familiaris
Consortio* in 1981, 'When couples, by means of resource to contraception,
separate these two meanings that God the Creator has inscribed in the being of
man and woman and in the dynamism of their sexual communion, they act as
arbiters of the divine plan and they manipulate and degrade human sexuality
and with it themselves and their married partner by altering its value of total
self-giving.'

"It is a question, therefore, of dominion: who is in charge, man or God? (In *Humanae Vitae,* incidentally, Pope Paul also explained the legitimacy of partial abstinence from sexual relations during the woman's fertile period, provided that such partial abstinence is practiced for 'serious motives.')

"The general acceptance of the morality of the act of contraception is a major factor in the following developments:

"Abortion. Contraception is the prevention of life while abortion is the taking of life. But both involve the willful separation of the unitive and procreative aspects of sex. The contraceptive mentality tends to require abortion as a backup. And many so-called contraceptives are abortifacient in that they cause the destruction of the developing human being.

"Euthanasia. Once the contraceptive ethic and abortion accustomed people to the idea that burdensome lives are not worth living, the way was clear for euthanasia for the aged and the 'useless.' If man is the arbiter of when life begins, he will predictably make himself the arbiter of when it ends. Euthanasia is postnatal abortion, as abortion is prenatal euthanasia.

"Pornography. Like contraception, which reduces sexual relations to an exercise in mutual masturbation, pornography is the separation of sex from life and the reduction of sex to an exercise in self-gratification. Pope Paul, in *Humanae Vitae*, warned that contraception would cause women to be viewed as sex objects, that 'man, growing used to the employment of anti-conceptive practices, may finally lose respect for the woman and, no longer caring for her physical and psychological equilibrium, may come to the point of considering her as a mere instrument of selfish enjoyment, and no longer as his respected and beloved companion.'

"In vitro fertilization. Contraception is the taking of the unitive without the procreative. In vitro fertilization is the reverse. . . .

"Promiscuity. According to the natural moral law and the Commandments, sex is reserved for marriage because sex is inherently connected with procreation and the natural way to raise children is in a marriage. But if, through contraception, we claim the power to decide whether sex will have anything to do with procreation, why should we have to reserve sex for marriage?

"Divorce. In the natural order, marriage should be permanent because sex is inherently related to procreation and children should be raised in a home with parents permanently married to each other. But if it is wholly our decision whether sex will have any relation to children, why should marriage be permanent? If sex and marriage are not intrinsically related to new life, marriage loses its reason for permanence. It tends to become a temporary alliance for individual gratification—what Pope Paul called 'the juxtaposition of two solitudes.'

"Homosexual activity. If sex has no inherent relation to procreation, and if man, rather than God, is the arbiter of whether and when it will have that relation, why not let Freddy marry George and Erica marry Susan? The contraceptive society cannot say that homosexual activity is objectively wrong without condemning itself. Objections to the legitimization of the homosexual 'lifestyle' are reduced, as in the military controversy, to the pragmatic and the esthetic. Homosexual activity, like contraception, also frustrates the interpersonal communion which is intrinsic to the conjugal act. And where that act should be open to life, homosexual activity is a dead end. It rejects life and focuses instead on excrement, which is dead.

"In these and other respects, *Humanae Vitae* is a providential and prophetic call to reason and sanity. At this supposedly Catholic university, *Humanae Vitae*'s anniversary ought to inspire a prayerful celebration. But don't count on it. Anyway, students especially ought to read *Humanae Vitae*. And share it with your theology professor. He might be surprised."

The Research University, March 1, 1993

"The Report of the Committee on Academic Life to the Colloquy for the Year 2000 calls to mind the unfairness of life: the Sears Catalog disappears and the documents of Colloquy 2000 proliferate.

"However, the Report also reminds us of two disturbing aspects of Notre Dame's pursuit of research greatness: First, the escalation of tuition beyond the inflation rate has apparently become a permanent University policy. Second, the cadging of research grants is now a very major responsibility of the faculty. . . .

"It is deeply immoral for Notre Dame to use federal loan guarantees as a lever to force undergraduate students and their parents to borrow money to finance its pursuit of a research prestige that bears only a marginal relation, if any, to the education of those students.

"And even if the federal government steps in to absolve parents and students, in whole or in part, from their loan obligations, the result will be to transfer the burden of Notre Dame's pursuit of greatness to the taxpayers generally. Either way, it is a shabby game in which Notre Dame ought not to be involved.

"Notre Dame relies heavily, in its pursuit of greatness, on faculty foraging for federal research grants. . . .

"The Report states that 'The federal government . . . provides about three quarters of the University's sponsored-program support.' The Report urges 'a comprehensive strategic plan for enhancing research and scholarship,' one objective of which would be to increase 'the level of federal funding of research at Notre Dame.'

"At the recent winter meeting of the Notre Dame trustees at the Ritz-Carlton Hotel in Manalapan, Florida, the University president, Fr. Malloy, urged greater involvement by Notre Dame in graduate education: 'If Notre Dame can become more of an actor in graduate education,' he said, 'I think we might have more of a role in influencing government and other national organizations.' Fr. Malloy was reported as saying that Notre Dame's faculty members are being encouraged to apply for more research grants. 'We think we're capable of operating in the same world as the Ivys, Stanford, Vanderbilt, Duke, Southern Cal and Northwestern." (Observer, Feb. 15, 1993).

"Research is only marginally related to education. An apocryphal statistic puts the average readership of a 'scholarly' article at one and one-half persons.

"Professor Ralph McInerny writes in *The Fellowship of Catholic Scholars Newsletter* that 'Research is what professors do on their own, it enhances their own reputation, it is addressed to a dozen or so others interested in the same things. The results might trickle down into classroom teaching, but this becomes increasingly doubtful.' March 1, 1993.

"As David W. Lutz stated (*The Observer*, Feb. 17), 'emphasizing research causes Catholicism [as well as teaching] to be de-emphasized. This is true, not because there is any problem with doing excellent Catholic research, but because it is more difficult to publish such research in prestigious journals and with elite university presses than to publish the kind of scholarship respected by secular universities.'

"The architects of these policies act in what they regard as the best interests of Notre Dame. My criticism is of policies, not persons. However, in its pursuit of money and illusory prestige, Notre Dame has turned itself into a vassal of the government and a freeloader on its own undergraduates, their parents, and the taxpayers. These policies ought to be rejected."

EX CORDE ECCLESIAE: A DEAD LETTER? March 23, 1993

"With all the ink recently about the Catholic character of Notre Dame, has anybody seen any real discussion of *Ex Corde Ecclesiae*, the 1990 Apostolic Constitution on Catholic Universities? That document, in the development of which Fr. Malloy had a prominent role, was described by Pope John Paul II as 'a sort of magna carta' for Catholic universities.

"*Ex Corde Ecclesiae* declared that 'every Catholic university, as Catholic, must have the following essential characteristics:

"'1. A Christian inspiration not only of individuals but of the university community as such.

"'2. A continuing reflection in the light of the Catholic faith upon the growing treasury of human knowledge, to which it seeks to contribute by its own research.

"'3. Fidelity to the Christian message as it comes to us through the church.

"'4. An institutional commitment to the service of the people of God and of the human family in their pilgrimage to the transcendental goal which gives meaning to life.'. . . .

"That document specifies that 'one consequence of its essential relationship to the church is that the institutional fidelity of the university to the Christian message includes a recognition of and adherence to the teaching authority of the church in matters of faith and morals.'. . . .

"The pre-1967 Catholic universities were not afraid to maintain a formal, juridical connection with the Church. *Ex Corde Ecclesiae* neither requires nor forbids such a connection.

"Cardinal Newman, as Fr. Rutler notes, 'insisted that the Catholicity of a university is secured by more than teaching theology as a branch of knowledge: "hence a direct and active jurisdiction of the Church over it and in it is necessary lest it should become the rival of the Church with the community at large in those theological matters which to the Church are exclusively committed—acting as the representative of the intellect, as the Church is the representative of the religious principle."' It could be useful to reconsider the desirability of such a connection in light of the general principles of *Ex Corde Ecclesiae.*

"In any event, it would seem clear that any university which claims to be Catholic, especially in raising money, ought to acknowledge the Apostolic Constitution on Catholic Universities as its criterion for the meaning of the term, 'Catholic university.'"

"No Commitment," April 14, 1993

"An intriguing aspect of Notre Dame's pursuit of Research Greatness is its impact on the University's willingness, as an institution, to take positions and affirm the truth.

"In response to the demand of Collegians Activated to Liberate Life, that Notre Dame take a position against legalized abortion, the associate provost, Rev. Oliver F. Williams, C.S.C., said, 'Notre Dame doesn't take an official position on issues.'

On the one hand, taking 'no position' on whether the killing of innocent human beings should be legal is taking the position that the proposition is debatable or at least that Catholic institutions are not obliged to speak against it. On the other hand, the claim that Notre Dame 'doesn't take an official position on issues' is simply untrue.

"For example, could anyone seriously contend that Notre Dame's Center for Civil and Human Rights is a neutral institution? It stands at least for the proposition that such rights should be protected by the law. Why, then, does Notre Dame refuse to take a position that the right to life of the youngest human beings—4,500 of whom are legally executed each day—should also be protected by the law?

"The Notre Dame of the 1940s would not have suspended judgment on the Holocaust, the basic principle of which is that of legalized abortion, that innocent human beings can be declared to be nonpersons and executed at the discretion of others.

"Notre Dame's disinclination to take positions on issues is generally bounded by the parameters of its functionally official religion, political correctness. Beyond particular issues, such as abortion, the University will not even officially affirm the truths of the Catholic Faith. The latest effusion from Colloquy 2000, "The Mission Statement of the University of Notre Dame," takes more than 500 words to describe the 'Catholic identity' of Notre Dame, without once mentioning the Catholic Church.

"The pre-note of the statement does refer once obliquely to 'the church.' But the 'Catholic identity' of Notre Dame is abstracted from the Catholic Church. One goal of Notre Dame, it says, is to provide a 'forum' for 'free inquiry and open discussion.' However, Notre Dame makes no affirmations of content. Its mission is one of process, with an orthodoxy of what David Lutz described as 'the four cardinal values of openness, equality, tolerance, and diversity.'

"For example, the Notre Dame President's 1992 Sesquicentennial Declaration began with the statement: 'Notre Dame's first commitment is to freedom of inquiry and expression.' You will search that document in vain for an explicit affirmation of any content-based truth beyond the process of inquiry and reflection.

"Cardinal John Henry Newman, on the other hand, had no hesitation: 'A University, so called, which refuses to profess the Catholic Creed is, from the nature of the case, hostile both to the Church and to Philosophy.' Newman, "My Campaign in Ireland," Part I, in *Catholic University Reports and Other Papers* (1896), 270. . . .

"The refusal of this Research University to affirm the truths of the Catholic Faith and to take positions on issues such as abortion is a symptom of its subservience to the standards of the secular academic establishment. When the University stands for nothing except the process dictated by the essentially quantitative standards of that establishment, it is not surprising that a result is the deterioration and depersonalization of the undergraduate experience. This is so with respect to the quality and availability of courses, but also in more incidental but important respects.

"Parking is more remote and dangerous. About 2/3 of the intramural athletic fields have disappeared to provide room for buildings. Architecture, incidentally, reflects the spirit. The difference between an Alumni Hall and a DeBartolo is more than money. The former bespeaks a humane grace and purpose. The latter evokes an image of five half-pint milk cartons in a line. Alumni was the conception of educators; DeBartolo is the work product of technocrats, by whom we are governed.

"When Fr. Malloy met with the CALL students, 'The only thing they asked of me,' he said, 'was to pray at a location where abortions are being performed. I gave them no commitment.' That last sentence could serve as the unofficial motto of this National Catholic Research University. It is time to recall that it is no less true of institutions than of individuals, that those who stand for nothing will fall for anything."

1993–1994

WHY NOT KILL ABORTIONISTS? Sept. 6, 1993

"Michael Griffin will stand trial on September 20th for the March 10th murder of abortionist Dr. David Gunn in Pensacola. . . . Some have defended . . . attacks on abortionists as an exercise of the . . . right to defend the life of . . . the unborn child threatened by abortion. . . . The common law or statutory defense of necessity or justification includes the privilege to defend a third party from attack. . . .

"If you were in the room with an abortionist as he was about to perform an abortion, it could be fairly argued that you would have the moral right to use reasonable force to prevent that imminently threatened killing of the unborn child. It is inconceivable, however, that deadly force would be necessary or justified, even in that situation. In any event, the killing of Dr. Gunn [Griffin shot Gunn three times in the back outside Gunn's abortion clinic] was not an inescapably and imminently necessary act of justified defense. Rather, it was a privately decreed execution.

"Whatever the applicability of the privilege to defend others to the abortion situation, there can be no justification for a private citizen to set himself up as judge, jury and executioner of anybody. As recognized by Catholic teaching, the only situations in which anyone ever has the moral right intentionally and directly to kill anybody are capital punishment and just war.

"In both cases, the killing is by authority of the state, which derives its authority from God. . . .

"Whether in an otherwise just war or any other circumstances, moreover, no one ever has the moral right intentionally and directly to kill an innocent human being. Even in self-defense or defense of others, the defender's intent must be to defend, rather than to kill.

"*Roe v. Wade* has corrupted the law by defining the innocent unborn child as a nonperson who therefore has no constitutional rights and who may be executed at the discretion of his mother. The necessity defense, however, is not limited to the protection of persons; it authorizes the use of necessary and reasonable force for the protection of human beings as well as animals and other property. The Supreme Court could not change the reality that the unborn child, whom it defined as a nonperson, is a human being.

"The result is a conflict of entitlements: the mother is entitled, by Court decree, to kill her child; other persons are entitled to protect a human being in danger, which the unborn child is. . . .

44

"Despite the decree of the Supreme Court, abortuaries, which are murder factories, have no moral right to exist. However, it does not follow that any action, whatever, is justified if only it prevents abortions. The use of violence, whether lethal or non-lethal, against abortuaries and abortion 'providers' is unjustified on several prudential grounds.

"It is not the most effective way to save lives of unborn children threatened by abortion. It is counterproductive in that it distracts attention from the real nature of the problem and diverts pro-life efforts away from more useful approaches. And it accelerates the disintegration of the civil order with predictably harmful impact on the common good.

"The use of violence in the pro-life cause should be utterly rejected. If we attempt to combat the abortion movement with force, we oppose its strongest weapon, the coercive power of the state, with our weakest. Legalized abortion, moreover, is only marginally a legal or political issue. At root it is a spiritual problem, a symptom of a pagan, contraceptive culture in which the autonomous individual, liberated from objective moral standards, has made himself the arbiter of the ending as well as the beginning of life.

"The ultimate remedy for abortion is the re-conversion of the American people to respect for God and His law which mandates our special concern for the weak and defenseless.

"While the nonviolent rescue movement has done much to dramatize the reality of abortion, the most effective on-site pro-life activity is the legal, peaceful prayer vigil with sidewalk counseling and referral to pregnancy help centers. These efforts are not spectacular, but they do save lives. And, unlike illegal disruptive tactics, they can be carried on continuously. Overall, whether on site or elsewhere, the most effective, practical thing we can do to restore respect and protection for the right to life is to pray, especially the Rosary because the issue is life and Mary is the mother of Life."

NOTE: Michael Griffin was found guilty of murder, in March 1994, and was sentenced to life in prison.

WHOSE NATURAL LAW? Sept. 20, 1993

"The subject of natural law comes up frequently in The Observer as well as in classrooms. It may be helpful at the start of the year to try to get the concept straight. 'A just law,' wrote Martin Luther King in his *Letter from Birmingham Jail*, 'is a manmade code that squares with the moral law or law of God. . . . An unjust law is a code that is out of harmony with the moral law.' To put it in the terms of St. Thomas Aquinas: 'An unjust law is a human law that is not rooted in eternal law and natural law.' So, when Rosa Parks refused to give up her seat on the bus in Montgomery, Alabama, on Dec. 11, 1955, she made a natural law statement. Legally enforced segregation is unjust in light of the natural law and a civil law that mandates it is void.

"The idea of natural law is neither a merely sectarian Catholic teaching nor even a Christian invention. Aristotle and Cicero affirmed it. Everything is governed by a natural law according to its own nature. Thus a rock will sink and grass will grow. The natural moral law, which governs human conduct, can be known certainly by reason. The first principle of the practical reason is self-evident, that, in Aquinas' words, 'good is to be done and promoted, and evil is to be avoided.' The good is that which is in accord with the nature of the subject, whether a car or a man. It is good to feed gasoline to a car and not good to feed it to a man. It is not good, i.e., it is evil, for a man to steal since theft is contrary to the natural human inclination to live in community.

"However, to declare that theft, abortion, etc., is objectively wrong is not to judge the subjective culpability of the person who does it. To be morally culpable, one must know it is wrong and yet choose to do it. We generally have neither the right nor the capacity to judge the subjective culpability of anyone. Nevertheless, as Pope John Paul II said in Denver: 'Moral truth is objective, and a properly formed conscience can perceive it.' St. Thomas described the function of the natural law as the 'light of natural reason, whereby we discern what is good and what is evil.' The natural law is a rule of reason, promulgated by God in man's nature, whereby man can discern how he should act so as to achieve his end of salvation.

"But whose natural law are you going to apply? As Supreme Court Justice James Iredell said in 1798, 'The ideas of natural justice are regulated by no fixed standard: the ablest and the purest men have differed on the subject.' If Iredell is right, the natural law is indeterminate and relatively useless as a higher standard for law and as a guide for human conduct. Suppose you think abortion, or military service, or whatever, is wrong. But who are you to say? Even if we recognize that there is a natural law, how do we know for sure what it means?

"Reason can attain to the truth in moral matters. But if reason were our only guide we would find ourselves in confusion. Our intellects are weakened by original sin and sincere advocates can be found on both sides of most moral issues. Aristotle, who was a fair student himself, sanctioned infanticide. Some Christians in the last century upheld the morality of slavery. Today, people differ on the morality of abortion. They can't both be right. As St. Thomas tells us, 'If . . . we consider one action in the moral order, it is impossible for it to be morally both good and evil.'

"'It was fitting,' wrote St. Thomas, 'that the Divine Law should come to man's assistance not only in those things for which reason is insufficient, but also in those things in which human reason may happen to be impeded. . . .

Hence there was need for the authority of the Divine Law to rescue man from both these defects.'

"Everyone has a pope, in the sense that everyone recognizes an ultimate arbiter on moral questions. If that arbiter is not the real Pope, it will be a pope of the individual's own selection: Ann Landers, CBS News, the Supreme Court, or the individual himself. On the other hand, Christ is God, the Church is his and the Pope is his Vicar on earth. The institution of the papacy is a gift of God, permitting us to be certain that the teachings we follow are God's own truth.

"'Everyone can see' said Pope Pius XI in his 1931 encyclical on Christian marriage, 'to how many fallacies an avenue would be opened up and how many errors would become mixed with the truth, if it were left solely to the light of reason of each to find it out, or if it were to be discovered by the private interpretation of the truth which is revealed. And if this is applicable to many other truths of the moral order, we must pay attention all the more to those things which appertain to marriage where the inordinate desire for pleasure can attack frail human nature and easily deceive it and lead it astray.'

"The guidance of the teaching Church is essential if men are to achieve a consistently correct observance of the law written in their nature. The Church, however, is not an academic 'superteacher' of natural law. Rather, she incorporates the natural law and especially the teachings of St. Thomas, into her teaching of the truth, who is a person, Christ. And she teaches that truth by the direct authority of that divine person.

"In giving this direction, the Church is not merely seeking to persuade. Rather, although she desires that we be convinced of the reasonableness of her position, she is expounding the law. For this reason, when the authentic teaching voice of the Church, whether the Pope or the bishops in union with him, pronounces authoritatively on a matter of natural moral law, the pronouncement's binding force is not limited by the persuasiveness of the arguments advanced."

CARDINAL O'CONNOR'S AFTERNOON OF RECOLLECTION, Oct. 18, 1993

"ND/SMC Right to Life has invited John Cardinal O'Connor, Archbishop of New York, to give an afternoon of recollection to interested students from noon to five on Monday, March 21, 1994, which is in the week before Holy Week. O'Connor has generously accepted.

"Because O'Connor prefers a parish setting for such programs, it will be held at Corpus Christi Church, in South Bend. . . .

"O'Connor and his party will drive from the airport, without visiting the campus. O'Connor is making this trip solely to spend an afternoon of prayer and reflection with students. No faculty, administrators or other non-students will be allowed to attend. ND/SMC Right to Life will arrange transportation for students as necessary.

"O'Connor will be accompanied by two members of the Sisters of Life, Sylvia Jimenez and Sheila Duncan, who are Notre Dame graduates. O'Connor himself founded the Sisters of Life in 1991.

"Through prayer and apostolic works, the Sisters are dedicated to protecting human life and promoting awareness of the sacredness of all human life, 'beginning with the infant in the womb and extending to all those vulnerable to the threat of euthanasia.' The Sisters emphasize the provision of direct, practical help to mothers in crisis pregnancies and to families affected by abortion and euthanasia. . . .

"The afternoon of reflection on March 21 will include two conferences given by O'Connor and a presentation by the Sisters of Life. O'Connor and priests from the area will hear confessions throughout the afternoon. O'Connor and the Sisters of Life will be readily available for questions and discussion. Snacks, soft drinks and coffee will be available, free, throughout the afternoon. The event will conclude with the Sacrifice of the Mass offered by O'Connor.

"This afternoon of recollection presents an unprecedented opportunity for Notre Dame and Saint Mary's students. *No one but students will be allowed to attend.* No faculty. No administrators. Nobody. O'Connor and the Sisters of Life will make this trip from New York solely to be with the students. This reflects O'Connor's oft-stated conviction that young people are the hope of the Church and that pro-life activity will succeed only to the extent that it draws its power from prayer, reflection and the sacraments.

"'The culture of death spawned by the world,' O'Connor has said, 'especially threatens women, the babies, and the sick and the frail elderly. . . . To be countercultural today is its own form of martyrdom. But to be countercultural except for the love of Christ is a sheer folly.'"

CNDPOW: The Committee on Notre Dame's Position on the Ordination of Women, Nov. 22, 1993

"CNDPOW's recurrent agitation conveys the false impression that women's ordination is an open question of civil rights on which politicized pressure tactics are appropriate.

"CNDPOW, in fact, has no reason for being. If this university is secular, why should anyone care what 'Notre Dame's position' is on the ordination of women, any more than one should care about the position of General Motors or Burger King? If, however, Notre Dame is Catholic as it claims to be in a sense, and as CNDPOW claims it to be, that identity carries with it an obligation of fidelity to the clear position of the Vicar of Christ on the subject. . . .

"The teaching of the Church here is settled and the issue is closed. In his Sept. 16, 1987, address to the American bishops, Pope John Paul II stated that 'women are not called to the priesthood. Although the teaching of the Church on this point is quite clear, it in no way alters the fact that women *are indeed an essential part of the Gospel plan to spread the Good News of the kingdom.*' (Emphasis in original.). . . .

"The papal statements affirm that the church does not have authority to ordain women. It is not like meatless Fridays, communion in the hand, or celibacy of the clergy. . . .

"CNDPOW responds to this settled position by seeking to change it through pressure tactics appropriate to the political arena. The Church, however, is not a political organization. And it is not a democracy. . . .

"In his World Youth Day address in Denver . . . John Paul II said, 'So many problems arise when people think of the Church as 'theirs,' when in fact, she belongs to Christ.' He could have had CNDPOW in mind. Their cafeteria, pick-and-choose Catholicism symbolizes the receding tide of the sixties.

"By contrast, John Paul II represents the wave of the Christian future, especially in his appeal to youth. . . . The CNDPOW types are in a time warp. Instead of voicing tiresome complaints about what they cannot change, they would better serve the Church and the Notre Dame community by encouraging prayer for increased vocations to the priesthood and religious life. And it would be a refreshing change if the Holy Cross priests at Notre Dame would openly and actively support the teaching of the Pope on this and other issues."

DR. KEVORKIAN AND CONTRACEPTION, Jan. 13, 1994

"Dr. Jack Kevorkian is a cult figure. The Michigan pathologist, who allegedly has helped 20 of his patients commit suicide, 'has an organized fan club,' according to the December 6 *Newsweek*, 'and some of his supporters regard him as a living saint.' Dr. Kevorkian's unique notoriety, unfortunately, distracts attention from the reality that his crusade is a predictable outcome of a basic moral and cultural disorder. . . .

"The acceptance of active as well as passive euthanasia on request, i.e., assisted suicide, and of euthanasia for incompetent patients at the direction of others, is a foregone conclusion from the dominance of the contraceptive ethic in our law and culture.

"One cause for this is the financial pressure arising from an aging population—due to contraception and abortion—and a shrinking base of wage earners to support them. . . . More basic than demographics, however, is the contraceptive culture. . . .

"Contraception rests on the premise that man, rather than God, is the arbiter of whether and when human life shall begin. In his audience of September 17, 1983, John Paul II said that 'men and women are not the arbiters, are not the masters of [the procreative capacity], called as they are, in it and through it, to be participants in God's creative decision. When, therefore, through contraception, married couples remove from the exercise of their conjugal sexuality its potential procreative capacity, they claim a power which belongs solely to God: the power to decide, in a final analysis, the coming into existence of a human person. They assume the qualification not of being cooperators in God's creative power, but the ultimate depositaries of the source of human life.'

"If you claim the right to act as arbiter of when life begins, you will eventually claim the right to act as arbiter of when life shall end, through suicide or euthanasia as well as through abortion, which is prenatal euthanasia.

"A second premise of contraception is that there is such a thing as a life not worth living. Man, as the arbiter of life, will decide, according to utilitarian calculations, whether that is so in particular situations. Under those ground rules, the elderly infirm, the 'vegetative,' the retarded and the handicapped are predictable losers. . . .

The law now permits a legally competent adult to starve himself to death, apparently whether the nutrition and fluids he rejects are artificially or naturally provided. This is a form of legalized suicide. An incompetent patient may be starved to death if the family or other custodians conclude (subject to review by the courts), that he would have wanted it that way or, if there is no sufficient proof of the patient's desires, that it would be in his best interest to die. This issue presented by Kevorkian is whether the law should permit another person to kill, by active means, someone who consents to that killing.

"There is no durable distinction between active and passive measures. The painless injection is an obvious alternative to painful starvation and dehydration. Moreover, a patient's decision—say an AIDS patient—that he does not want feeding withdrawn will, in some situations, raise the question of whether he is incompetent so that the decision ought to be made by others in his 'best interest.' It is clear, therefore, that regulated assisted suicide, i.e., the legalized killing of persons who consent to that killing, would quickly open the door to involuntary active euthanasia for patients labeled as incompetent.

"The challenge of the Kevorkian phenomenon is not merely to limit the activities of one obsessed pathologist. It is rather to reexamine our national acceptance of contraception, which is a root cause of euthanasia as well as of

50

abortion and other social evils. The trajectory is a straight line from the [Anglican] Lambeth Conference [which approved contraception, in 1930] to the home of the late Donald O'Keefe and the 'suicide' sites of other Kevorkian 'patients.'"

MAKING THE ABORTED GIRL A MOTHER, Jan. 31, 1994

"The mad scientists appear to be working overtime to make the Pope look good. Consider the disclosure last month by British researchers of their technique to retrieve eggs (i.e., ova) from aborted female babies, fertilize them by *in vitro* fertilization and implant them in the wombs of infertile women. If the technique is approved by the British Medical Association and government authorities, it may be able to produce the birth of a baby within three years.

"This new technique is significant in several respects. Some hailed it as a providential breakthrough for desperately infertile couples. It does no harm to the unborn child, who had just been killed anyway, and it allows a new life to come into the world. Others, however, have raised questions. How do you tell the resulting child, when he grows up, that his mother was never born because she was deliberately killed in the womb by the child's grandmother, and that he himself is the product of a salvage expedition on his dead mother's body?

"The technique, of course, treats the unborn child—the mother—not as a human being but as an object, a repository of component parts. . . . 'If a fetus can be a mother,' asked columnist Alan Keyes, 'how can we deny that it is a human being?'

"The mad scientists make the Pope look good in another respect. John Paul II insisted that 'science and technology require, for their own intrinsic meaning, an unconditional respect for the fundamental criteria of the moral law: that is to say, they must be at the service of the human person, of his inalienable rights and his true and integral good according to the design and will of God.'

"This principle is light years removed from the ethic of the mad scientists. They have liberated themselves from the moral law. For them the unborn mother and her child are objects of utility, to serve the interests of others, rather than persons with a dignity conferred by 'the design and will of God.'

"The countercultural character of the Church's teaching in this area is seen in the Pope's insistence, on two points, <u>first</u> that no one has a 'right' to have a child, and <u>second</u>, that the child himself has a right to be conceived in a conjugal act within marriage: '*A true and proper right to a child would be contrary to the child's dignity and nature. The child is not an object to which one has a right, nor can he be considered as an object of ownership. Rather, a child*

51

is a gift, "the supreme gift," and the most gratuitous gift of marriage, and is a living testimony of the mutual giving of his parents. For this reason, the child has the right . . . to be the fruit of the specific act of the conjugal love of his parents; and he also has the right to be respected as a person *from the moment of his conception.'*

"The British scientists are merely carrying the contraceptive ethic to its logical conclusion. Through contraception, man separated sex from procreation and made himself, rather than God, the arbiter of when and how life would begin. He subordinated the creation of human life to technology employed according to utilitarian calculations.

"In 'Humanae Vitae,' in 1968, Pope Paul VI warned that contraception would cause man to regard woman as an object. He could not have been thinking of 'the woman' as herself an unborn mother. But, as with John Paul II, the British scientists have made Paul VI look good.

"Once contraception cut us loose from the divine plan for procreation as taught by the Magisterium of the Church, there could be no intrinsic limit to the treatment of persons as objects, to trafficking (even commercial) in the bodies of the living as well as the dead, and to the subordination of the person to the interests of utility as determined by the state.

"The new British technique provides a window on the future of our utilitarian technocracy. 'Science without conscience,' said John Paul II, 'can only lead to man's ruin.' It is time instead for us to turn and to accept 'the design and will of God.' Totally. The only coherent answer here lies in the moral and social teachings of the Catholic Church."

EX CORDE ECCLESIAE AND CONDOMS, Feb. 14, 1994

"Two recent events invite us to reflect. . . . The first event was 'the Official Response of Notre Dame' to the Ordinances proposed by the Catholic bishops to implement *Ex Corde Ecclesiae*. . . . [T]he proposed Ordinances are vague and toothless. They exhort cooperation rather than command compliance. And their loopholes are big enough to drive the ice rink's Zamboni through them. These symbolic Ordinances pose no threat to, and effectively require no action from, anybody. Nevertheless, Notre Dame objects. . . .

"Now consider the second recent event. In January, Carol Seager, director of university health services, sent to 'all faculty and staff' a memo and an 'educational brochure' entitled 'HIV and AIDS.' The brochure contains, among other things, a set of eight detailed instructions on 'How to use condoms (rubbers).' This column will spare the details. This is the second year in a row that Notre Dame has given these instructions to its employees. The practice, therefore, can hardly be dismissed as an oversight. . . . Incidentally, apart from morality, the use of condoms does not prevent AIDS. . . .

"Why does Notre Dame do this? According to the memo, 'Indiana Public Law 123–88 . . . requires all public and private schools and institutions of higher education to annually provide information regarding AIDS to all employees.'

"That law, however, requires only the provision of 'medical information on . . . (p)recautions that reduce the risk of contracting the disease.' It would not seem to require the promotion of condoms by a Catholic university, especially in light of the new federal Religious Freedom Restoration Act which increases protection for the free exercise of religion. Nevertheless, Notre Dame obeys the law without challenge and exceeds it by instructing its employees in detail on how to put on a condom. . . .

"Whether or not the practice continues, the incident illustrates the tendency of Notre Dame, in its pursuit of recognition as a great research university, to defer to the standards of the secular educational establishment and of the State.

"To stand against the State and against the orthodoxy of condomania would be politically very incorrect. And what would they think of us at Princeton or Harvard? Therefore, when the State commands, Notre Dame obeys with surpassing zeal. In contrast, when the Catholic bishops speak, not to command but to plead for compliance with norms established by the Vicar of Christ, Notre Dame discovers its courage and a principle of 'true autonomy,' the sham character of which is evident from its selective application.

"In fact, Notre Dame has not liberated itself from 'external' authority. For the limited, moral authority of the Church, it has substituted the peremptory and amoral authority of the State and the secular academic establishment.

"Our leaders reject the symbolic Ordinances proposed by the bishops. They accept, without asserting possible legal defenses, the dictates of the assorted politicians who comprise the Indiana legislature. Notre Dame interprets those dictates, beyond their expressed intent, to require condom instruction contrary to the law of God. Notre Dame cannot even bring itself to urge the 'further and expanded dialogue' which it urged on the bishops. When the State speaks, Notre Dame's response is one of dumb and excessive obedience, precisely as the 'good Germans' responded to the Nazi depersonalization of the Jews.

"The pathetic contrast between these two responses confirms the reality that the operative religion of Notre Dame is political correctness."

VERITATIS SPLENDOR, Feb. 28, 1994

"Perhaps contrary to the view of some, the most important event in the Catholic world this academic year was not Notre Dame's [student government] election of the Hungeling-Orsagh ticket. It was the release of *Veritatis Splendor* [*The Splendor of Truth*], the encyclical on Christian morality. An overlooked aspect of the encyclical is its exposition, in chapter three, of the legal and social consequences of the denial of objective moral truth.

"In his presentation of *Veritatis* to the press, Cardinal Joseph Ratzinger described that chapter as among 'the great texts of the Magisterium' and 'a fundamental text for the questions which concern us all.' As the school year enters its final phase, it may be useful to mention some aspects of that chapter which, I hope, will encourage students to read the entire encyclical.

"Have you ever wondered at the paradox that the twentieth century has produced more proclamations of human rights than any other century, and yet has also produced the greatest violations of those rights ever seen? Pope John Paul explains why. The denial of objective truth by today's jurisprudence reduces law to a function of raw, totalitarian power.

"'Totalitarianism arises out of a denial of truth in the objective sense. If there is no transcendent truth, in obedience to which man achieves his full identity, then there is no sure principle for guaranteeing just relations between people. Their self-interest as a class, group or nation would inevitably set them in opposition to one another. If one does not acknowledge transcendent truth, then the force of power takes over, and each person tends to make full use of the means at his disposal in order to impose his own interests or his own opinion, with no regard for the rights of others. . . . [T]he root of modern totalitarianism is . . . the denial of the transcendent dignity of the human person who, as the visible image of the invisible God, is therefore by his very nature the subject of rights which no one may violate—no individual, group, class, nation or state. Not even the majority of a social body may violate these rights, by going against the minority, by isolating, oppressing, or exploiting it, or by attempting to annihilate it.' (No. 99)

"Adherents of The Church of Where It's At, on this campus and elsewhere, criticize papal teachings as arbitrary and hostile to freedom. On the contrary, as John Paul put it, recognition of objective moral norms is essential for freedom and 'genuine democracy': '[T]here can be no freedom apart from or in opposition to the truth. . . . [O]nly by obedience to universal moral norms does man find full confirmation of his personal uniqueness and the possibility of authentic moral growth. For this very reason . . . [t]hese norms . . . represent the foundation of genuine democracy, which can . . . develop only on the basis of the equality of all its members, who possess common rights and duties. *When it is a matter of the moral norms prohibiting intrinsic evil, there are no privileges or exceptions for anyone.* It makes no difference whether one is the master of the world or the "poorest of the poor" on the face of the earth. Before the demands of morality, we are all absolutely equal.' (No. 96.)

"This is applied common sense. If we do not affirm objective norms that always prohibit certain conduct, how can we define any moral limits to what the state can do?. . . .

"Indeed, 'if there is no ultimate truth to guide and direct political activity, then ideas and convictions can easily be manipulated for reasons of power. As history demonstrates, a democracy without values easily turns into open or thinly disguised totalitarianism.' (No. 101)

"Ideas have social and legal consequences, even the ideas of professors and others who are absolutely sure they cannot be sure of anything. 'Pilate's question: "What is truth?", said John Paul, 'reflects the distressing perplexity of a man who often no longer knows *who he is, whence* he comes and *where* he is going. Hence we not infrequently witness the fearful plunging of the human person into situations of gradual self-destruction.' (No. 84). . . .

"In *Veritatis*, the Pope is not merely expounding abstract principles. Rather, the separation of freedom from truth 'is the consequence . . . of *another more serious and destructive dichotomy, that which separates faith from morality.*' (No. 88).

"John Paul affirms that 'the true and final answer to the problem of morality lies in [Christ] alone. . . . *[I]n the Crucified Christ . . . the Church finds the answer* to the question troubling so many people today: how can obedience to universal and unchanging moral norms respect the uniqueness and individuality of the person, and not represent a threat to his freedom and dignity?.... *The Crucified Christ reveals the authentic meaning of freedom: he lives it fully in the total gift of himself* and calls his disciples to share in his freedom.' (No. 85)

"Some describe this era as 'post-Christian.' Not so. *Veritatis* lends support to the conclusion that this is really a 'pre-Christian' era. The failure of the Enlightenment, in its effort to achieve freedom apart from the truth of Christ, is so clear that the answer presented in *Veritatis Splendor* is obviously the only alternative.

"The academic spin doctors will advise you on what this encyclical means and how they could have written a better one. This definitive and moving document, however, should not be taken at second hand. Read it for yourself."

Catechism of the Catholic Church, March 21, 1994

"Catechisms are for kids. Right? Why should any university student want to learn his religion from a catechism? Permit me to suggest a reason. In the February 28th Observer, this column described some aspects of *Veritatis Splendor*, the 1993 encyclical on morality. *Veritatis*, however, is part of a paired entry, with the *Catechism of the Catholic Church*, issued by Pope John Paul II in 1992. . . .

"*Veritatis* and the *Catechism* complement each other. 'Both documents,' said Cardinal Joseph Ratzinger in presenting *Veritatis*, 'are . . . distinct and each . . . has its proper task whereby one supports the other. The *Catechism* does not engage in argument, it testifies. It does not dispute but states the faith positively, the faith which has its own inner reasonableness. The Encyclical also bears witness, but it has, at the same time, a dimension of argument. It takes up questions and shows in discursive argument what the way of faith is and how it comes to be that there even is a way for man.'. . . .

"For more than three decades of law school teaching, I have taught graduates of Catholic colleges, including more from Notre Dame than from anywhere else. In my opinion, students at those institutions, through no fault of their own, tend to be shortchanged in the treatment by those colleges of the teachings of the Catholic Church. In some, an orthodoxy of dissent prevails.

"What the students learn about the Church is often filtered through the lens of a professor who has a distorted idea of the nature of the Church and is hostile to its teachings. The curricula tend to offer the student no predictable opportunity to study the rich Catholic tradition in its undistorted totality. . . .

"Unless they select exceptional courses or have unusual access to other sources, students in Catholic colleges frequently absorb a caricature of the Church and they emerge unequipped to make a coherent decision as to whether to accept or reject the teachings of the Church. . . .

"Until now, the students had no . . . concise and authoritative source for an up-to-date knowledge of what the Church teaches. Now, in *Veritatis* and the *Catechism*, students have a direct line, to measure their own understanding and that of their professors. . . .

"It would be a mistake to assume that the *Catechism* is a catalogue of rules. As Cardinal O'Connor put it, 'This Catechism, despite advance criticism of those who haven't yet seen it, is not a list of condemnations. We've had a lot of condemnation—some things deserve condemnation—but that's not what this Catechism is for. It's to strive calmly to show the strength and beauty of the doctrine of the faith. Having gone through the Catechism from cover to cover I can tell you it's serene reading'. . . .

"The Pope has gone over the heads of the professorial and clerical adherents of The New American Church. In *Veritatis Splendor* and the Catechism he offers to students, as to others, a chance to find out for themselves what the Church is and teaches, so that they can make an informed judgment for themselves. Some professors and trendy clerics and nuns will advise you, as students, that these documents were not intended to be read by mere people. They will urge you to let them, the experts, tell you what the documents mean, or would mean if the experts had their way.

"But don't let them kid you. Take it as a summer project to read both *Veritatis Splendor* and the *Catechism* for yourself. Pray about what you have read. And make up your mind as to where you stand."

THE RESEARCH UNIVERSITY AND RISING TUITION, April 25, 1994

"We ought to retrieve and reflect on 'The Decline and Fall of the Christian College,' by Fr. James T. Burtchaell, C.S.C., in the April and May, 1991, issues of *First Things* magazine. In what is probably the most important article on Catholic higher education in the past twenty-five years, Fr. Burtchaell traces the secularization of Vanderbilt, Harvard and other originally Protestant universities and the process by which the Catholic Universities are moving toward the same end. Fr. Burtchaell suggests, without mentioning any institution by name, that 'secularization is rapidly bleaching the Catholic character out of that church's universities and colleges, with all the elements we saw typified in the Vanderbilt story.' He sees the severance of the formal connection with the church as decisive: 'The only plausible way for a college or university to be significantly Christian is for it to function as a congregation in active communion within a church. . . . In Christianity, communities that float free are not viable. There is neither faith nor ecumenism ungrounded on church.'

Notre Dame insists that it is Catholic, yet its mindset is Protestant in that it defines 'Catholic' according to its own lights rather than according to the mind of the Church. The predictable result is the total secularization that overtook the formerly Protestant universities.

"[O]ne result of secularization is the devaluation of both undergraduate education and the interests of students. For the authority of the Church, Notre Dame has substituted that of the secular educational establishment. Universities seeking secular prestige emphasize graduate programs and research. And they . . . want to be players on the national and international scenes.

"At the 1993 mid-winter meeting of the Notre Dame trustees at the Ritz-Carlton Hotel in Manapalan, Florida, Father Malloy said, 'If Notre Dame can become more of an actor in graduate education, I think we might have more of a role in influencing government and other national organizations.' With reference to encouraging faculty to apply for more research grants, he said, 'We think we're capable of operating in the same world as the Ivys, Stanford, Vanderbilt, Duke, Southern Cal, and Northwestern.' Observer, Feb. 15, 1993.

"In the old Notre Dame, undergraduate education was valued on its own merits as a Catholic work and resources were used primary to keep it accessible to students. In 1950, Notre Dame Magazine stated that, 'Still, as always, Notre Dame refuses to turn down any more worthy applicants than necessary, even those in need of financial assistance. This is one reason why Notre Dame, unlike many other universities, never has known wealth—or even appreciable financial reserve.' Vol. 3, p. 5. . . .

"Notre Dame's endowment in 1949 was $4,077,587, 'the lowest among all major colleges and universities,' p. 10. Interesting. Notre Dame took its small endowment as a point of pride because it was using its income to lessen the burden on students.

"By contrast, on March 24, 1994, Chief Investment Officer Scott Malpass wrote in the Observer, 'It is truly exciting that we are on the verge of a major milestone in the history of the Endowment, the $1 billion mark, which has placed us as the 16th largest university endowment and one of the fastest growing.' But the money is not discernibly used to reduce the tuition cost to the students, whose welfare is emphasized in solicitations to acquire more money. As the endowment goes up, so do tuition and fees at multiples of the inflation rate. . . .

"The University, said Father Malloy, has made the increase of scholarship assistance 'the number one priority of our fund-raising efforts.' Observer, April 7, 1994. p. 1. However, scholarships and other forms of University financial aid, apart from special cases, generally click in only after a student has taken the maximum loans for which he is eligible. Notre Dame and other universities have lobbied Congress to increase the amount of loans for which students are eligible. As those eligibilities rise, so do the tuitions at the 'research' universities.

"The universities use federal loan programs as a lever to force graduate and law as well as undergrad students to borrow prohibitive amounts to finance the pursuit of a prestige that has little, if any, relation to the education of those students, and with detriment to the career and family options of the graduating students. The old Notre Dame would not have played that game to the disadvantage of its students. Our leaders act in what they see as the best interest of Notre Dame. However, I hope that they and other members of the Notre Dame community will read the Burtchaell article. It shows that the root error of our policy, which operates to the detriment of our students, is the effort to be Catholic without the Church.

"'I firmly believe that there is a uniqueness about what Notre Dame offers a young woman or a young man, a uniqueness that in the end makes their sacrifices and those of their parents worth the investment in Our Lady's University,' said Father Malloy recently. . . . The question arises . . . as to whether Notre Dame can rightly claim to be 'Our Lady's University' as long as it rejects any significant connection with the body of her Son, which is the Catholic Church."

1994–1995

KILLING ABORTIONISTS: THE DOUBLE EFFECT, Sept. 5, 1994

"To shoot an abortionist in the parking lot is not an imminently necessary defense of his intended victim against actual attack. It is a privately decreed execution for the purpose of preventing the abortionist from later attacking the unborn child. The killing would also involve excessive force since it would not have been necessary to kill him to prevent him from performing the abortion. . . .

"The *Catechism* does affirm a right of individuals to defend themselves and others: 'The legitimate defense of persons and societies is not an exception to the prohibition against the murder of the innocent that constitutes intentional killing. "The act of self-defense can have a double effect: the preservation of one's own life; and the killing of the aggressor. . . . The one is intended, the other is not."' No. 2263, quoting St. Thomas Aquinas.

"In the right to defend. . . . [t]he intent must be to defend, rather than to kill. The principle of the double effect governs here, as quoted above in . . . the *Catechism*. A familiar application of that principle is with respect to operations to remove the cancerous womb of a pregnant woman. Such operations can be justified because the death of the child is an unintended effect of an operation independently justified by the necessity of saving the mother's life. They do not involve the intentional killing of the child for the purpose of achieving another good—for example, the preservation of the mother's life.

"The only situations in which anyone ever has the right intentionally to kill anyone are the just war, capital punishment, and a justified rebellion (or what the *Catechism* calls 'armed *resistance* to oppression by political authority.' No. 2243). The just war and capital punishment are decreed by the state, which derives its authority from God. See *Catechism*, nos. 2266–67, 2307–17. Armed rebellion involves an assumption by private persons of that authority of the state. No one can reasonably conclude that such rebellion is justified in the United States today; therefore, the recent killings of abortionists cannot be justified on that or any other ground.

"Consider two cases. In the first, Able, an abortionist's assistant in the killing room suddenly has a change of heart moments before the abortion begins. He has a moral [but not a legal] right, and probably even a duty, to use reasonable force to defend the child. It is unlikely, however, that lethal force could be justified there. In the second case, Baker, an opponent of abortion, shoots the abortionist in the parking lot as he is approaching the building to perform abortions a few minutes later.

"One difference between the two cases is imminence. Able engages himself in the immediate defense of the child; his intent is to defend that child; he must have no separate intent to harm or kill the abortionist. Baker, by contrast, is not in the heat of a physical struggle to save the child. He thinks, 'I can get no closer than this. If I do not stop him he will go in there and murder babies. So I will shoot him in the head.' His purpose or motive is to save children. But his intent in the act he performs that moment is to blow the abortionist's head off to achieve that purpose. Baker is performing an intrinsically evil act to achieve a good end. He assumes the authority of God, to decide when that person will face the final judgment of God. St. Thomas, quoting St. Augustine, said that 'A man who, without exercising public authority, kills an evildoer, shall be judged guilty of murder, and all the more, since he has dared to usurp a power which God has not given him.'" *Summa Theologica*, II, II, Q. 64, art. 3.

"Some may argue that killing the baby-killer in the parking lot is defense of the child because that is as close as Baker could get. But if Baker may kill the abortionist when he is not actually performing an abortion, why does he have to limit himself to the parking lot? Why can he not conclude that the only way he can get a clear shot at him is to shoot him on the golf course? Or at the video store? St. Thomas speaks of the justified defender as one who 'repels force.' See *Catechism*, no. 2264. The moral right to defend the child must be restricted to the immediate performance of the abortion. Even then it is practically inconceivable that lethal force would have to be used.

"The use of violence, whether lethal or non-lethal, against abortuaries and abortionists is unjustified also on several prudential grounds. It is not the most effective way to save the lives of unborn children threatened by abortion. It is counterproductive in that it distracts attention from the real, and spiritual, nature of the problem, and it diverts pro-life efforts away from more useful approaches. Moreover, it accelerates the disintegration of the civil order with predictably harmful impact on the common good. Violence should be utterly rejected as a pro-life tactic. . . .

"In her address on February 3, 1994, to the National Prayer Breakfast in Washington, Mother Teresa said that 'the greatest destroyer of peace today is abortion, because it is a war against the child, a direct killing of the innocent child, murder by the mother herself. And if we accept that a mother can kill even her own child, how can we tell other people not to kill one another?'"

JOHN PAUL ON POPULATION CONTROL, Sept. 19, 1994

"'What would the world be like without him?' So commented Vytautas Landsbergis, first president of independent Lithuania, on the role of Pope John

Paul II in the freeing of Eastern Europe from Communism and on the part the Pope would play in future events. At the 1994 International Conference on Population and Development, in Cairo . . . John Paul moved on from his Eastern European success to confront a population control movement which has a totalitarian potential comparable to that of Communism. . . .

"As a University of Maryland demographer, Julian Simon, noted: 'In the 1980s, there was a u-turn in the consensus of population economists about the effects of population growth. In 1986, the National Research Council of the National Academy of Sciences almost completely reversed the worried view it expressed in 1971. Its report noted that there was no statistical evidence of a negative connection between population increase and economic growth. This shift has gone unacknowledged by the media, by environmental organizations and by the agencies that foster population control abroad.' (*New York Times*, Aug. 21, 1994)

"In the September 12, 1994, *Forbes* magazine, Malcolm S. Forbes, Jr., observed that, 'The real issue is the assumption that curbing population growth is critical for economic development. The premise is preposterous. A growing population is not a drag on economic development. When combined with freedom, it is a stimulant.'

"While there are major problems with the concentration of people in megacities and maldistribution of resources, it is simplistic to ascribe them to an overall excess of people. If you took the 5.7 billion people now on earth and gave each one six square feet to stand on, you could fit them all into Nassau and Suffolk counties on Long Island, with 420 square miles left over. Nobody would propose that expedient, least of all the people of Long Island, but the heated rhetoric can cause us to assume that there are more people on earth than there actually are.

"The impetus for population control lies in the declining proportion of people in developed nations. . . . Due to the contraceptive culture which has prevailed in Europe and North America since the advent of the pill in the 1960s, the developed nations are not even replacing their own populations. Faced with demographic suicide, they choose to suppress populations in developing countries rather than abandon the contraceptive ethic. Pat Buchanan, however, had it right when he asked, 'Why should the black, brown and yellow people who look to inherit the earth follow the example of self-indulgent Westerners who are committing suicide?'

"With reason, the Brazilian Catholic Bishops' Conference recently concluded that 'The desired result [of population control] is always the same: to reduce the growth of the countries of the Third World so that the industrialized nations can continue to exploit them and dominate them as they always have.'. . . .

"Vatican spokesman Joaquin Navarro-Valls noted the totalitarian implications of the population control movement: 'World population is set at some such figure as 7½ billion. Since that figure is said to represent the "carrying capacity" of the earth—something itself purely arbitrary—this end justifies the means to achieve it. . . . We thus need to impose a widespread system of control of the reproductive act's consequences. All activity that results in children will be subject to political scrutiny and, if need be, to force.

"'All essentially sterile acts, on the other hand, are said to be relatively insignificant. Homosexual or lesbian activity, contraception or sterilization, all are viewed in a positive light because they have no visible consequences. Sex becomes literally insignificant. The social and political freedom of homosexual activity is thus rooted precisely in its lack of any real existential purpose or consequence. Only sexual activity that has potential consequences in the conception of a child has any political importance. And this activity must be limited and controlled as much as possible by the eugenic state. This theoretical position has its own prior logic. Its premise is that there is no nature or principle of morality that is not subject to the state. The state cannot be itself limited by anything except necessity.' (*Wall Street Journal*, Sept. 1, 1994). . . .

"[Pope John Paul II said]: 'In defense of the human person, the Church stands opposed to the imposition of limits on family size and to the promotion of methods of limiting births which separate the unitive and procreative dimensions of marital intercourse, which are contrary to the moral law inscribed on the human heart or which constitute an assault on the sacredness of life.'. . . .

"Some, on this campus and elsewhere, disparage John Paul. But he stands alone in defending the absolute dignity and rights of the person and of the family against the State. Josef Stalin once mockingly asked, 'How many divisions does the Pope have?' His successors found out. In his conflict with the utilitarian New World Order, it would be a mistake to bet against the Pope. And what would the world be like without him?"

THE BENGALS EXPERIENCE, Oct. 3, 1994

"A few years ago a Notre Dame law student won a Bengal Bouts championship. 'This was the only thing,' he said, 'that made law school worthwhile.' He was kidding about law school—I think. . . .

"The Boxing Club, which conducts the annual Bengal Bouts in March, [runs] the only such program that directly saves the lives of people in need. . . . Initiated in 1931 by a Notre Dame legend, Dominic Napolitano, the Bouts derive their name from the fact that all net proceeds go to the Holy Cross Bengal missions in Bangladesh. . . .

"Apart from the benefit to people in need, the Boxing Club provides a unique experience to the participants. The student officers (this year, Jeff

Goddard, Eric Hillegas, Robert Nobriga, Chris Rosen, Mike Thompson) themselves run the program, with administrative help from student managers headed by Annette Putz. Tom Kelly and Rich O'Leary, of Recreational Sports, provide all that could be desired in guidance and safety equipment. And Bengal Bouts champs Terry Johnson (1974) and Tom Suddes (1971) donate their time to share the head coaching duties. All coaches are volunteers.

"Assistant coach Pat Farrell epitomized the benefits to the participants: 'At Notre Dame, boxing is . . . an extension of the classroom. The vast majority of our boxers have never before been in the ring. . . . They learned about themselves, their strengths, their weaknesses. They learned to deal with adversity under pressure. . . . You are on your own in the ring. No substitutions, no time outs. Above all, no excuses. No rationalizing that someone else's missed block or tackle may have altered the outcome.' As Bob Mohan, a Bengal champ, reflected, 'I've had ten years to mull over my boxing experience and I know that for me the victory was in getting myself to step through those ropes. The experience has made me more willing to attempt to reach goals that seem distant or nearly impossible. I reflect back on my Bengals experience and remember how impossible stepping through those ropes seemed. It doesn't really matter whether you win or lose.'. . . .

"Some might deride the Bengal Bouts as a brutal imitation of professional boxing. That claim is unfounded. In 1988, Stockholm's Karolinska Institute, which awards the Nobel Prize in medicine, reported on the most extensive neurological study ever conducted on amateur boxers. The four-year study found that amateur boxing presented no more risk than heading a soccer ball. Notre Dame's program is far more protective than even the scrupulous program in Sweden, so much so that there has never been a serious injury in the 65-year history of the Bengal Bouts. The objective is not to injure but to score points by technique. The preoccupation with safety pervades the program.

"In his eulogy in 1986 for Dominic Napolitano, Father Edmund Joyce, executive vice-president of Notre Dame, said of Nappy: '[W]hat [the boxers] learned had very little to do with the effectiveness of a left hook. It had much more to do with absorbing . . . Nappy's own philosophy of life, . . . which incorporated a genuine spirituality with . . . a competitive spirit, courage, self-reliance and a deep respect for one's fellow man. It has been a source of inspiration to me . . . to be reminded constantly by returning former students what a decisive influence Nappy had on their lives.'

"The Boxing Club maintains a living link to Nappy and to Knute Rockne, who began an informal Notre Dame boxing program in the 1920s, in 81-year-old Jack Mooney, who works every day coaching the boxers and whose primary concern is their safety and their personal development during and after the program. Jack instinctively embodies the spirit of Nappy as it was described by Tom Suddes: '[Nappy's] boxing instruction was not meant to teach just the "know how," but also the "know why." And not just the why behind the punches or ring strategy, but the why of "Strong bodies fight that weak bodies may be nourished."'

"Among members of the Boxing Club, I have noted [an] eagerness to help other participants, including potential opponents, and a remarkable awareness that the benefit to the needy in Bangladesh is more important than any personal benefit to themselves. These attitudes reflect a generosity of spirit we could all do well to emulate: Last year, Observer sports editor, Mike Norbut, summarized his experience after losing a hard fight with John Christoferreti, 'I knew I had lost unanimously, but it didn't matter. I was on my feet. I was proud to be wearing gloves and head-gear. I was proud of John for winning. I was proud to be a Bengal Bouter.'"

RESEARCH ON EMBRYOS, Oct. 17, 1994

"On Sept. 27, a National Institutes of Health panel urged federal funding of non-therapeutic experimentation on 'preimplantation embryos resulting from in vitro fertilization (IVF) or other sources.' Private laboratories in the United States already perform such research. Some states and foreign countries regulate it and some foreign countries forbid it.

"Why is this panel report such a big deal? First, it is the initial step toward funding and supervision of the field by the federal government, possibly within a year. . . . Second, the embryos are no less human beings than are their grandmothers. . . .

"The Panel rejected that reality: 'The preimplantation human embryo,' it said, 'does not have the same moral status as infants and children . . . because of the absence of developmental individuation . . . , the lack of even the possibility of sentience [ability to feel pain] and most other qualities considered relevant to the moral status of persons, and the very high rate of natural mortality at this stage.'

"Once we cut loose from the reality that the one-cell zygote, as the late geneticist, Dr. Jerome Lejeune, of the University of Paris, put it, is already and thereafter 'a tiny human being,' any effort to define the beginning of his humanity at a later point will be arbitrary.

"'The Panel agreed that, for public policy purposes, a clear time limit should be set' on experiments. But its limit was a political compromise. . . .'[F]or the present, research involving human embryos should not be permitted beyond . . . 14 days'. . . . The Panel . . . reserved for 'additional review' the question of 'Research [up to] the beginning of closure of the neural tube [17 to 21 days].'

"The Panel went beyond the Nazis by approving 'the use of oocytes [female eggs] fertilized expressly for research'. . . . At least in spirit, Dr. Frankenstein is alive and well in Washington. The Panel hopes that this will not result in assembly-line production of humans for research. It said that such created-for-research human beings should be used only where 'necessary for . . . a study . . . of outstanding . . . value.' . . . .If you bet on the enduring character of that limitation, let me take your money on the Chicago Cubs.

"The Panel also left open the possibility of funding experiments on embryos created from eggs harvested from aborted female children, i.e., of 'oocytes from aborted fetuses,' pending an exploration of 'the ethical implications . . . by a national advisory body'. . . . Female children in the womb already have all the eggs they will ever have. Do you want to bet that such a source of supply will remain untapped? With respect to research on embryos intended for transfer to a woman's womb, [i]f the child may have been injured by the research, the Panel thinks the researchers ought to destroy him rather than allow him to be born.

"Ideas have consequences. The contraceptive ethic attempts to take the unitive aspects of sex without the procreative. IVF, the main source of 'spare' embryos, is the reverse. In contraception, man makes himself the arbiter of whether and when life shall begin and of which lives are worth living. The NIH report does the same thing.

"The issue here is the dignity of the person. Pope John Paul's 1987 Instruction on Bioethics stated that, 'From the time that the ovum is fertilized, . . . the life of a new human being [is begun] with his own growth. It would never be made human if it were not human already . . . From the moment of conception . . . his rights as a person must be recognized, among which in the first place is the inviolable right of every innocent human being to life.'. . . .

"The Panel proposals are premised on a functional definition of the human person. The eugenic State claims the right to decide who are human persons according to their ability to function, e.g., to experience pleasure. If the youngest can be so excluded from the human family, so can those who, at the other end of life, are unable to experience pleasure sufficiently to satisfy the criteria of the State. This is a replay of the *Genesis* script, with man making himself God. And it is a replay of Nazi Germany. If you want to keep your focus here, read the *Instruction on Bioethics* and the *Catechism*. Share them with your theology professor. And pray for our country."

THE O'MEARA POLICIES, NOV. 7, 1994

"On June 30, 1996, Dr. Timothy O'Meara will leave the Office of Provost. . . .[H]is successive appointments for a total of 18 years will make Dr. O'Meara's term of office perhaps the most significant in the history of Notre Dame, second only to the 35-year service of Father Theodore Hesburgh as President.

"The Provost and other administrators have acted throughout in what they have honestly seen as the best interest of Notre Dame. Nevertheless, it is not unfair to suggest that four prevailing policies have negatively altered the character of Notre Dame and ought to be reevaluated before 1996:

"1. The Devaluation of Undergraduate Education. The primary focus of Notre Dame had been the education of undergraduates in the Catholic tradition, with graduate studies and research playing a balanced role. However, the defining mark of the past 16 years is the redefinition of Notre Dame as a National Catholic Research University. . . .

"Members of our family have been undergrads at Notre Dame every year from 1977 to 1994, in a . . . variety of disciplines. Our experience supports the conclusion, admittedly anecdotal and subjective but supported by the views of others, that, in terms of the variety of available courses, class size, quality of teaching, and the general recognition of students as persons, the quality of the undergrad experience at Notre Dame has significantly deteriorated since 1977.

"2. The Overbuilding of the Campus. Since 1978, at least 16 major buildings have been added to the campus. These additions are, of course, permanent and the end is not in sight. During that period, two-thirds, at least, of the intramural athletic fields have been paved over or built upon with new structures, including what may be the most superfluous stadium in the history of baseball. In a research university, presumably, students will be more interested in spectator sports and coffee house discussions than in participatory athletics. The growing impersonality of the undergrad experience is reflected in the architecture of some of the major additions, including DeBartolo, a rendering in brick of the concept of five half-pint milk cartons on line, which was described at its opening, by *Observer* editor Stephen Zavetoski, as 'a factory of learning and not an environment for reflection and contemplation.' *The Observer*, Sept. 18, 1992, p. 2.

"The overbuilding of the campus also creates problems of safety through the remoteness of parking. These problems will be aggravated by the inevitable multi-story parking garage, which will be the fitting monument to the policies of our leaders.

"3. The Pressure on Students to Mortgage their Futures to Finance the University's Pursuit of Research Greatness. Father Hesburgh recently noted that the University budget in 1945 was only $6.5 million, while today it costs about $1 million a day to operate. That increase is an accomplishment. So, too, is the increase in the room, board, and tuition package, which in 1945–46 totaled $1,909. That package in 1978–79, at the start of the O'Meara era, totaled $5,180. Adjusted for inflation, using the Consumer Price Index, the 1978–79 cost totaled $10,026 in terms of 1992 dollars. With the 1994–95 package at $21,000, Notre Dame students now pay more than twice, in real money, what students paid at the start of the O'Meara era.

"The federal student loan program has been the 'Big Rock Candy Mountain' for aspiring research universities. They, including Notre Dame, have urged Congress to increase the amount and availability of such loans. As the loan limits go up, so does the tuition. Notre Dame makes a commendable effort to provide financial aid, but such aid usually does not click in until the student has borrowed as much as he can. The University then will try to bridge the gap between the student's resources, including borrowed funds, and the cost. Provost O'Meara has described the Notre Dame budget as 'tuition driven.' And so it is. However, Notre Dame, as with other universities, finances its pursuit of research greatness by using the government as a lever to shift the burden to its students, inducing those who are not wealthy, or recipients of special aid, to incur loans that will distort their career, marriage, and family options. Though it is far from the worst offender, it is immoral—a betrayal of trust—for Notre Dame to play this exploitative game.

"Meanwhile, the Endowment approaches one billion dollars, with a balance of $879 million on June 30, 1994, and with little observable impact in relieving the financial burdens on students. We are, however, rising in the ranking of endowments among the major universities. . . .

"4. 'Roll-your-own' Catholicism as the Religion of Notre Dame. The ongoing debate on its 'Catholic character' assumes that it is up to the Notre Dame community to define the term, 'Catholic university,' and that the definition of that term by the teaching Church—defined by the Second Vatican Council as the bishops in union with the Pope—is not binding on Notre Dame. . . .

"As the end of the O'Meara stewardship nears, it will be useful to address the 'truth-in-labeling' issue presented by Notre Dame's claim, especially in fund-raising, to be a Catholic university while it is reluctant to accept the definition of that term by the person—the Pope—who has ultimate authority to define it. Indeed, Notre Dame's determination to define 'Catholic university' according to its own terms, is at the root of the other problems noted here. Notre Dame has substituted, for the authority of the Vicar of Christ, the more peremptory authority and criteria of the secular academic establishment.

"This is an appropriate time for reconsideration of all these policies."

THE CONTRACT WITH AMERICA, Nov. 21, 1994

"Do you fear the first 100 days of the new Congress? If so, it may serve to decrease—or perhaps increase—your apprehension to note some details of the *Contract with America*, which 340 Republican House candidates signed on the

Capitol steps. 'If we break this contract,' they said, 'throw us out. We mean it.' The Contract is significant for what it pledges and also for what it does not.

"On the first day of the new Congress, the Republicans pledge to reform procedures; force Congress to live under the same laws as every other American; hire a major accounting firm to audit Congress for waste and fraud; cut the number of committees; cut the staffs by one-third; and make Congressional documents available on computer networks. . . .

"[The] Contract proposals are debatable, especially on welfare. Some reflect the principle of subsidiarity, pursuant to which, as John Paul II views it, 'Neither the state nor any society must ever substitute for the initiative and responsibility of individuals and of intermediate communities at the level on which they can function, nor must they take away the room necessary for their freedom,' *Instruction on Christian Freedom and Liberation*, No. 73. The *Contract*, however, says very little about abortion, and nothing about assisted suicide, vouchers or other 'school choice' plans, homosexuals in the military, experimentation on embryos, and other 'social issues,' although Newt Gingrich, prospective speaker of the House, has added a commitment to a constitutional amendment on school prayer. The 'big tent' philosophy stresses economic issues while avoiding stands on 'social issues.' Those 'social issues,' however, will not go away. . . .

"The Republican party has an unexpected opportunity to define the public debate. If it ignores the issues beyond the economic, however, it may ultimately justify columnist Samuel Francis' description of it as 'The Stupid Party.'"

HOMOSEXUALITY AND COURAGE, Dec. 5, 1994

"The December 1st lecture at DeBartolo on 'Gays, Lesbians and the Law,' reflects a continuing campus interest in the status of homosexuals. . . .Unfortunately, the discussions do not reflect an accurate understanding of the teachings of the Church on this subject.

"'The Roman Catholic Church is now the counterculture,' says Father John F. Harvey, director of Courage, a support group for Catholic men and women—and their families—who try to live chaste lives in accord with Catholic teaching on homosexuality. The countercultural character of Church teaching on homosexuality is evident even at Notre Dame. While the Administration rightly denies formal recognition to homosexual student groups, an informal but pervasive orthodoxy of dissent leads many to regard this Church teaching as arbitrary, oppressive and not binding on individual Catholics or Notre Dame. It may be useful here to set the record straight.

"First, the Church's teaching is not merely advisory. . . . Second, the Church teaching . . . is neither arbitrary nor oppressive. . . . On 'homosexual acts,' the new Catechism describes them as 'intrinsically disordered. They are contrary to the natural law. They close the sexual act to the gift of life. They do not proceed from a genuine affective and sexual complementarity. Under no circumstances can they be approved.' No. 2357. Thus, when the European Parliament resolved that homosexual couples should be allowed to marry and adopt children, John Paul II replied that. . . . 'the attempt has been made to tell the inhabitants of this continent that moral evil, deviation, a kind of slavery, is the way to liberation, thus distorting the true meaning of the family. The relationship of two men or two women cannot constitute a true family; still less can one grant such a union the right to adopt children who lack a family. These children suffer great danger, grave harm, because in these "substitute families" they do not have a father and mother, but two fathers or two mothers. This is dangerous.' *Address*, Feb. 20, 1993. . . .

"Church teaching here . . . offers a hope-filled affirmation of the human person. As the Catechism states: '[M]en and women who have deep-seated homosexual tendencies . . . do not choose their homosexual condition; for most of them it is a trial. They must be accepted with respect, compassion and sensitivity. Every sign of unjust discrimination in their regard should be avoided. These persons are called to fulfill God's will in their lives and, if they are Christians, to unite to the sacrifice of the Lord's Cross the difficulties they may encounter from their condition.' 2358. 'Homosexual persons are called to chastity.' 2359. . . .

"The work of Courage reflects the hopeful yet practical character of this Church teaching. Founded by New York's Terence Cardinal Cooke in 1980 and now sponsored by the Archdiocese of New York, Courage has 27 chapters in the United States and Canada. Prayer and meditation open each Courage meeting, followed by discussion and reflection on the 12 steps of the Alcoholics Anonymous approach. 'The psychology,' says Father Harvey, 'is that some people can change, and if they can't, they can still lead a chaste life. The theology is that you've got to avoid this kind of activity. You can still lead a good Christian life as a celibate person. . . .

"Courage (424 W. 34th St., N.Y, NY, 10001; (212) 421–0426), welcomes inquiries from Notre Dame students, faculty and others. In this area, as elsewhere, the only fully coherent approach will be found in the moral and social teachings of the Catholic Church."

A TOUCHING INVITATION, Jan. 23, 1995

"The most touching present I received this Christmas was a personalized, first-name invitation from the Executive Vice President, Father Beauchamp, asking me to join the Sorin Society, which consists of those who 'make an unrestricted annual investment of one thousand dollars or more' in the University. Benefits include 'regional meetings and luncheons,' the President's newsletter, *Notre Dame Magazine*, and 'honorary membership in the University Club.' If I popped for $3,000, I could join the Society's Founder's Circle and receive also a 'quarterly compendium' of articles on Notre Dame, the 'Notre Dame: Year in Review' video, the University's Annual Fiscal Report, an 'ombudsman service' to assist with hotel reservations and 'tickets to non-athletic events,' and 'parking assistance for select home Notre Dame football games.'

"Obviously, this personal invitation could not have come because I happened to be on some mailing list. No, this was finally recognition that I am somebody, worthy of inclusion in the inner circle. I was flattered and felt a rush of self-esteem and self-actualization.

"But then reality intruded. If our leaders are digging so deep as to make this Sorin pitch to a guy like me, Notre Dame must be in worse shape than I thought. On the other hand, the President, Father Malloy, reported that 'the 1993–94 fiscal year closed with positive results.' 'This positive result,' he said, 'goes against the grain of the general climate in American higher education which is characterized by retrenchment, budget deficits, deferred maintenance and frozen salary scales. . . .

"Notre Dame is not likely to remain unaffected for long by those national trends. A few days after my self-esteem was raised by the Sorin invitation, two *New York Times* articles highlighted the precarious position of American universities. A front-page analysis on Christmas noted that 'increasingly discount merchandising is coming to academia.'. . . .

"The second *Times* article, an op-ed by David Lipsky on December 29th, explained the origin of the national problem. The federal Guaranteed Student Loan Act of 1965 had strict income limits and by the mid-1970s few students had used it. In 1978, however, largely in response to pressure from universities, President Carter signed the Middle Income Student Assistance Act. That Act removed the income restrictions, so that, as Lipsky says, 'A Kennedy kid could qualify for a guaranteed loan almost as easily as a Katzenjammer kid.' However, as *Fortune* magazine warned, 'Anything that makes it easier to pay tuition bills will also make it easier to raise tuition charges.' The main beneficiaries of the Act are the universities and the banks: 'Although the babyboom generation was very big, the "baby bust" generation—kids born from about 1964 to 1975—is very small. So colleges, which had expanded, have charged students more money, subsidized by Federal loans. As for banks, student loans are more profitable than home mortgages and car loans. Since the Government is a co-signer, it must make good on bad loans, immediately.' In 1992 the student loan default rate was 22 percent, twice what it was in 1977. President Clinton's proposed $10,000 tax deduction for tuition, and similar proposals, incidentally, would enhance the ability of the university to raise tuition.

"The 1978 Act coincided with the start of the O'Meara provostship, in which Notre Dame has sought recognition as a 'national Catholic research university' and has more than doubled its tuition, in real dollars, over what it was in 1978. Notre Dame, like other universities, has used the federal loan program as a lever to expand its plant and pursue research greatness while shifting the cost to its students through the exaction of tuition at multiples of the inflation rate. According to an April 1994 survey, the average graduate of Notre Dame Law School will have between forty and sixty thousand dollars in educational debt. Many law students, to my knowledge, have much more, with some over $100,000. It is a safe assumption that the indebtedness of undergraduates would present a comparable picture on a lower scale. It is immoral for the University to finance its pursuit of research prestige by compelling non-wealthy students to assume heavy loan obligations which deny them genuine freedom in choosing careers and starting families.

"Notre Dame's unique reputation and 'market niche' have so far preserved it from the crisis affecting most universities. But market limits are inexorable. Notre Dame's market niche was built on solid undergraduate education in the authentic Catholic tradition. If the devaluation of that unique character continues, the market will expose both the loss of our 'niche' and the immoral folly of the money-driven race for prestige in which we have engaged for decades.

"Maybe it was a premonition of these prospects that prompted Father Beauchamp to solicit even people like me to join the Sorin Society. I would like to join. Perhaps I could apply for financial aid to make it possible. Maybe there's even a federal loan program. . . ."

ABORTION PROTESTS, Feb. 6, 1995

"'Words kill,' said the heading of a full-page Planned Parenthood ad in the Jan. 5 *New York Times*. The ad, in response to the killing of two abortion employees by John Salvi in Brookline, Mass., pinned responsibility on 'leaders of the extreme religious right [who] are heedlessly using a war of words to inspire killing. They call abortion providers "baby killers.". . .

"The ad raises serious questions. Should abortion opponents cease their on-site protests? Should they stop describing abortion as murder? If one so describes abortion, does he incite the murder of abortionists? Or does he speak a truth that must be heard?

"For historical and technical reasons, abortion has not been defined in law as the crime of murder. However, without presuming to judge the subjective culpability of any individual, every abortion, as the direct, intentional killing of a human being without justification, may fairly be described as murder in the moral sense. . . .

"Even Planned Parenthood acknowledged abortion as killing when it was promoting contraception in the 1960s. It sought to distinguish contraception from abortion and stated, in *Plan Your Children*, a 1963 pamphlet, 'An abortion kills the life of a baby after it has begun. It is dangerous to your life and health. It may make you sterile so that when you want a child, you cannot have it. Birth control merely postpones the beginning of life.' Save this column. That may be the only time Planned Parenthood has ever told the truth on abortion.

"Over the past two years, FACE, the federal Freedom of Access to Clinic Entrances act, and other laws and injunctions have stifled peaceful protest at abortuaries. As this repression of legitimate speech continues, it is likely that more people will succumb to the delusion that murder can be a proper response to murder, with a widening range of potential victims. If one claims the 'right' to kill abortionists, why would he not extend that 'right' to include physicians who prescribe abortion pills, pharmacists who sell them, etc.?

"The root violence here is the legalized violence against the unborn. . . . Some abortion opponents do advocate violence against abortionists. Murder is wrong and so is incitement to murder. But the few who so misuse speech are not the real targets of Planned Parenthood and the media guardians of the culture of death. Their targets are those who peacefully speak the truth in any forum. Abortion can remain entrenched as public policy only by redefining itself and its victims and by compelling the rest of us to acknowledge its legitimacy.

"In his forthcoming book, *Dehumanizing the Vulnerable*, Prof. William Brennan of St. Louis University recounts the 'semantics of oppression' that have often been used to dehumanize target groups so as to justify their oppression, including American Blacks, North American Indians, Jews in the Third Reich and the unborn who are defined as nonpersons and whose killers are euphemized as 'abortion providers.' 'Today, in retrospect,' said Brennan, 'with the exception of unwanted preborn humans, [these groups] are now acknowledged as legitimate victims . . . But . . . not too long ago each group was viewed in the same way that contemporary abortion proponents view the unborn: as inconsequential non-victims or as dangerous aggressors.'

"The abortion culture is based on homicide but it seeks its own survival by verbicide, by redefining abortion and exerting social and even legal pressure to prevent any of us from describing abortion as what it is. One unnoticed casualty of legalized abortion is the truth. Thus, in 1970, a pro-abortion editorial in the journal of the California Medical Association foreshadowed this tactic: 'Since the old ethic has not yet been fully displaced it has been necessary to separate the idea of abortion from the idea of killing, which continues to be socially abhorrent. The result has been a curious avoidance of the scientific fact, which everyone really knows, that human life begins at conception and is continuous whether intra-uterine or extra-uterine until death. . . . [T]he semantic gymnastics . . . required to rationalize abortion as anything but taking a human life would be ludicrous if they were not put forth under socially impeccable auspices.'. . . .

"Murder is an abomination, whether of an unborn child or an abortionist. But those who generate violence against abortionists are not those who peacefully and prayerfully speak the truth about abortion, but rather those who have legalized the depersonalization of the innocent and those who execute them under cover of the lie that murder is a medical service. Is Planned Parenthood right? Do words kill? In a sense, yes. As Father Matthew Habiger, of Human Life International, which group strongly opposes violence, said, 'I think the words that really kill are, 'Turn on the abortion machine.'"

ROTC at Notre Dame, Feb. 20, 1995

"Should ROTC be thrown out of the University? Maybe this question surfaced in recent Observer discussions because January and February are a little slow around here. However, the moment ought not to pass without some effort to note the vacuity of the claim that ROTC is inconsistent with the mission of a university that claims to be Catholic.

"The honorable military service of one's country is in the highest Christian tradition. From the earliest days of the Christian era, the legitimacy of military service has been recognized by tradition and the teaching Church. When John the Baptist was asked by newly converted soldiers, 'And we—what are we to do?' he did not tell them to quit the army. He told them how to behave as Christian soldiers: 'plunder no one, accuse no one falsely, and (perhaps most important today) be content with your pay.' Luke 3:14. Similarly, St. Paul did not demand that newly converted Christians who were soldiers must leave that profession. Instead he said, 'Let every man remain in the calling of which he was called.' 1 Col. 7:20. The general understanding of the early Christians that military service was consistent with their Christianity is shown by the fact that they served in large numbers in the armed forces of Rome.

"Indeed, the Emperor Galerius, at the beginning of the fourth century, undertook to purge the army of Christians because, in his opinion, there were too many of them in it. There were Christian pacifists who drew support from such theologians as Tertullian, Origen, and Lactantius, but they reflected neither the dominant Christian view nor the teaching of the Church.

"Through the centuries, the Catholic Church has consistently taught that war can be justified under proper conditions and that therefore military service is consistent with Christian belief. . . .

"It follows from this duty of the state to defend the common good against external enemies that members of the armed forces, in the words of Vatican II, 'should regard themselves as agents of security and freedom on behalf of their people. As long as they fulfill this role properly, they are making a genuine contribution to the—establishment of peace.'. . . .

"This clear teaching of the Catholic tradition was included in the new *Catechism of the Catholic Church*, issued by John Paul II. It affirmed the position of Vatican II . . . that 'governments cannot be denied the right of lawful self-defense, once all peace efforts have failed.' No. 2308. '[T]hose holding authority have the right to repel by armed force, aggressors against the community in their charge.' No. 2266. See No. 2309 for the conditions for 'legitimate defense by military force,' i.e. the 'just war.'

"'Public authorities should make equitable provision for those who for reasons of conscience refuse to bear arms; these are nonetheless obliged to serve the human community in some other way.' No. 2311. However, '[P]ublic authorities [in a just war] . . . have the right and duty to impose on citizens the obligations necessary for national defense. Those who are sworn to serve their country in the armed forces are servants of the security and freedom of nations. If they carry out their duty favorably, they truly contribute to the common good of the nation and the maintenance of peace.' No. 2310.

"At Notre Dame, we tend to give uncritical respect to the pacifist position. Its proponents are sincere but their position is fatally flawed. The pacifist says that he would rather die at the hands of an aggressor than defend himself by force. But the nobility of that position fades when we realize that the pacifist would consign the helpless and innocent to death or servitude rather than come to their defense. *The New York Times*, on February 6th, reported that the Khmer Rouge rebels 'still torment Cambodia 20 years after their rampage' in 1975 killed at least 2 million Cambodians.

"If military force exercised by proper authority in 1975 could have saved the Cambodian people from two decades of Khmer Rouge oppression and terror, what would have been the Christian position—to use that force to protect their freedom against the unjust aggressor, or to stand by, let those people disappear into slavery and salve one's conscience later on by sending food packages to such of them as might still be alive? Not only is pacifism not a dictate of Christianity. Pacifism is an unworkable and base creed unworthy of any people, Christian or otherwise, who would remain free.

"The mission of ROTC is to prepare students to conduct the honorable and necessary defense of the common good. The ROTC not only is appropriate to the University of Notre Dame. It honors Notre Dame by its presence." Feb. 20, 1995.

GLND/SMC, March 6, 1995

"Symbolism Over Substance.' Rush Limbaugh's Description of the Clinton Administration could apply to Notre Dame's denial of recognition to GLND/SMC, the homosexual student group. Let's look at some basics first.

"The Catholic Church teaches that 'homosexual acts' are 'intrinsically disordered' (*Catechism*, No. 2357). The Church further teaches that the homosexual condition is itself a disorder. *The Letter on the Pastoral Care of Homosexual Persons*, issued with the approval of John Paul II in 1986, said, 'Although the particular inclination of the homosexual person is not a sin, it is a more or less strong tendency ordered toward an intrinsic moral evil, and thus the inclination itself must be seen as an objective disorder. . . . This does not mean that homosexual persons are not often generous and giving of themselves; but when they engage in homosexual activity they confirm within themselves a disordered sexual inclination which is essentially self-indulgent. . . . It is deplorable that homosexual persons have been and are the object of violent malice in speech or in action. Such treatment deserves condemnation. . . . But the proper reaction to crimes committed against homosexual persons should not be to claim that the homosexual condition is not disordered.' (Nos. 3,7,10). . . .

"It makes no sense to insist that homosexual acts are intrinsically evil while denying that the inclination toward those acts is disordered. If one denies that the inclination is disordered, he will predictably conclude that it may rightly be acted upon. . . .

"According to Vice President Patricia O'Hara, GLND/SMC's position is 'not consistent with the teaching of the Church' because the group 'addressed homosexual acts neutrally, and urged the University towards encouraging monogamous homosexual relationships.' (*The Observer*, Feb. 21, 1995, p. 1). The denial of recognition is correct. To recognize GLND/SMC would be roughly comparable to recognizing a chapter of the Aryan Nation or a student bestiality club. Nevertheless, the University's overall position is incoherent.

"The University denies recognition of GLND/SMC because of its refusal to affirm the wrongness of homosexual acts. But this is empty symbolism, belied by the substance of the University's own contrary message to its students that the homosexual inclination is not disordered. . . .

"To my observation, neither Campus Ministry nor anyone else with University authority has affirmed, with respect to this controversy, both of these aspects of the teaching: not only that homosexual acts are wrong but also that the homosexual inclination is itself disordered. The persistent omission of that affirmation raises an inference that the inclination is not disordered or that its status in that regard is irrelevant. Interestingly, the 1986 Vatican letter said, 'we wish to make it clear that departure from the church's teaching or silence about it, in an effort to provide pastoral care, is neither caring nor pastoral. Only what is true can ultimately be pastoral. The neglect of the church's position prevents homosexual men and women from receiving the care they need and deserve.' (No. 15) Vice President O'Hara's denial of recognition is correct, but the position of the University as a whole is deceptive. It claims to defend the Catholic teaching but then, at the very least implicitly, it conveys to its students the decisive message, contrary to that teaching, that the homosexual condition is not disordered.

"If the leaders of this University are serious about wanting to help homosexual students, they ought to urge those students to contact Courage, a nationwide support group sponsored by the Archdiocese of New York, which strives to help men and women to live chaste lives in accord with the Catholic Church's teaching on homosexuality.

"If our leaders can somehow bring themselves to affirm in its entirety the hopeful, constructive teaching of the Church, they will serve well the Notre Dame community and especially those of homosexual inclination, who will find in that teaching an affirmation of themselves as persons. . . .

"As persons, the first thing our students are entitled to is the truth. All of it."

COURAGE AT NOTRE DAME, April 3, 1995

"Vice-President O'Hara has appointed a committee to advise her on how 'we can do a better job of meeting the needs of our gay and lesbian students.' But that committee is a non-starter because the University has already capitulated on the decisive issue of whether the homosexual orientation is a disorder. . . .

"While it affirms Catholic teaching that homosexual acts are immoral, Notre Dame contradicts, in words and implications, the essential teachings on the disorder of the homosexual inclination. Vice-President O'Hara describes the Counseling Center as one of the 'valuable resources' available to homosexual students. But Dr. Patrick Utz, director of the Counseling Center, believes that 'being homosexual is not a disorder.' *The Observer*, Feb. 10, p. 11. Moreover, as far as I know, no public statement by the University affirms the Catholic teaching on both points, not only that homosexual acts are wrong but also that the homosexual inclination is disordered. This omission implies that the inclination is not disordered or that its status is irrelevant.

"Neither element of the teaching can be denied without undermining the other. If, as the Counseling Center says, the homosexual condition is not a disorder, there is no intrinsic reason why it should not be acted upon. Any student-client with even a single-digit LSAT could figure that one out.

"The University's message that the inclination is not disordered nullifies its professed adherence to the teaching that homosexual acts are wrong. Instead of fully presenting to its students the hope-filled teaching of the Church, Notre Dame leads them through an exercise in cognitive dissonance which will incline them to see the prohibition of homosexual acts not as rooted in nature and the wisdom of God but as an arbitrary edict of celibate clerical authority.

"This misdirection of the students takes on added significance in light of the cultural war in which the general homosexual movement uses the media, schools and churches to validate the homosexual condition and lifestyles. The 1986 Vatican *Letter on the Pastoral Care of Homosexual Persons*, issued with the approval of John Paul II, noted that 'increasing numbers of people today, even within the church, are bringing enormous pressure to bear on the church to accept the homosexual condition as though it were not disordered and to condone homosexual activity. Those within the church who argue in this fashion often have close ties with those with similar views outside it. These latter groups are guided by a vision opposed to the truth about the human person, which is fully disclosed in the mystery of Christ. They reflect, even if not entirely consciously, a materialistic ideology which denies the transcendent nature of the human person as well as the supernatural vocation of every individual. . . . The movement within the church, which takes the form of pressure groups of various names and sizes, attempts to give the impression that it represents all homosexual persons who are Catholic. As a matter of fact, its membership is by and large restricted to those who either ignore the teaching of the church or seek somehow to undermine it. It brings together under the aegis of Catholicism homosexual persons who have no intention of abandoning their homosexual behavior. One tactic used is to protest that any and all criticism of or reservations about homosexual people, their activity and lifestyle are simply diverse forms of unjust discrimination.' Nos. 8 and 9.

"In the context of this cultural war, Notre Dame, as the most visible 'Catholic' University, has a special duty to present to its students the full teaching of the Church.

"Let me offer a suggestion. In 1980, Father John F. Harvey, OSFS, founded Courage, a nationwide support group for homosexuals, sponsored by the Archdiocese of New York and endorsed by the Pontifical Council on the Family. Courage helps homosexual men and women to live in accord with the teaching of the Church. 'The psychology is that some people can change, and if they can't, they can still lead a chaste life,' Father Harvey says, 'The theology is that you've got to avoid this kind of activity.'

"Father Harvey spoke at Notre Dame in 1991 and said that any 'organization whose explicit purpose is to foster chaste friendships among homosexuals should be encouraged and recognized.' He said he would like to start a Courage Chapter at Notre Dame. *The Observer*, Nov. 6, 1991, p. 1.

"The Notre Dame position on GLND/SMC is fatally flawed. But we don't need another committee to assemble another unreadable report. Maybe we just need Father Harvey and Courage (in lower as well as upper case)."

LAETARE MEDAL TO SUZMAN, April 24, 1995

"The 1995 Notre Dame Award was conferred on Helen Suzman, who led the fight against apartheid as a member of the South African Parliament from 1953 to 1989. Established in 1992, the Award honors those 'whose deeds give witness to God's kingdom among us.'. . . .

"The parliamentary record, which I have read, confirms that Mrs. Suzman, over more than two decades, was a relentless advocate of permissive abortion. . . .

"The Abortion and Sterilization Act of 1975 first permitted abortion in South Africa. Mrs. Suzman attacked it as too restrictive and repeatedly sought to liberalize it. . . .

"Mrs. Suzman said, 'I would like to see abortion on request, though not on demand,' *The Citizen*, Mar. 9, 1982. As she stated in Parliament, 'we should not talk about "abortion on demand" because the right terminology is "abortion on request" when one discusses the whole idea of liberalizing abortion laws.' May 20, 1985, p. 5811.

"To Mrs. Suzman, abortion is a back-up family planning technique. She said that 'most contraceptive methods fall short of providing complete protection against unwanted pregnancy . . . [O]ne is not asking for legalized abortion, instead of family planning. It is in addition to family planning, because family planning often fails. . . .'

"Mrs. Suzman supported abortion as a population control device. 'I believe,' she said, 'that there is no way in which we are going to achieve the ideal 2.1 child family . . . unless [we] liberalize our abortion laws.' May 20, 1985, p. 5814. She emphasized that 'legalizing abortions for girls under the age of 16 . . . would be a vital step in reducing population growth . . . since postponement of the first pregnancy is an essential factor in achieving this objective.' May 20, 1985, pp. 5812–13.

"Abortion, of course, is not 'postponement' of a pregnancy. It is the termination of that pregnancy by the murder of the unborn child. As Pope John Paul II said in his new encyclical, *Evangelium Vitae*, 'The moral gravity of procured abortion is apparent in all its truth if we recognize that we are dealing with murder.'. . . .

"Notre Dame president Edward A. Malloy, C.S.C., called Mrs. Suzman a 'freedom fighter,' and said her 'political career has been driven by the hunger and thirst for justice which the Beatitudes celebrate.' However, Mrs. Suzman fought not only for freedom from the violence of apartheid but also for the freedom to inflict the ultimate violence on the most innocent and helpless victims of all. Perhaps only in today's Notre Dame could such a record be honored as exemplifying the hunger and thirst for justice commended by Christ in the Beatitudes.

"The Award to Mrs. Suzman confirms that the operative official religion of this 'Catholic' university is political correctness. On apartheid, the moral imperative and political correctness coincide. But it is difficult to imagine any position more politically incorrect than uncompromising opposition to abortion. If our striving-to-be-accepted leaders refused to honor as a humanitarian anyone who advocates the legalized execution of the pre-born, it would cost them political correctness points among the movers and shakers in academia, the media, foundations and government. Or maybe our leaders just don't see the pro-life issues as a big deal. The Vicar of Christ, of course, sees it differently: '[W]e are facing an enormous and dramatic clash between good and evil, death and life, the "culture of death" and the "culture of life." We find ourselves not only "faced with" but necessarily "in the midst of" this conflict: we are all involved and we all share in it with the responsibility of choosing to be unconditionally pro-life.' *Evangelium Vitae* (No. 28)

"On a final note, we should keep this Award in context. Since the bestowal of the 1992 Laetare Medal on the egregiously pro-abortion Senator Daniel P. Moynihan, Notre Dame honors don't mean that much anyway. And maybe we should be relieved that the Award went to Mrs. Suzman. Given the evident mindset of our leaders, it could have been Teddy Kennedy. Or Hillary."

1995–1996

PROFESSOR EDWARD J. MURPHY, Aug. 28, 1995

"Professor Edward J. Murphy, who served on the Law School faculty from 1957 until cancer forced his retirement in 1994, died this past July 24.

"Professor Murphy was the leading academic authority in the nation on contracts. An exceptionally competent teacher, he taught every student at the Law School from 1957 to 1994.

"These students and his faculty colleagues learned much from him. Among other lessons, he taught, by example, that we should do our work very well but should always keep the family as our first priority. We learned from him, too, that constructive change in the law and society, as in this University, is best achieved by organic development rather than by pretentious master plans.

"Less well known than his contracts achievements is the unique contribution Ed Murphy made to Notre Dame and to his students by teaching Jurisprudence. He taught that law involves the definition of ultimates, and that it makes no sense to talk about law without affirming its source.

"He reminded us that the ultimate source of the measure of all law is God, who guides us to our end of eternal happiness through his natural law, which is related to reason, and through his explicit Revelation, which is communicated through the Church, which is the body of Christ, who is God.

"In his 1993 encyclical, *Veritatis Splendor*, Pope John Paul II said, 'there can be no freedom apart from or in opposition to the truth. . . . [O]nly by obedience to universal moral norms does man find full confirmation of his personal uniqueness and the possibility of authentic moral growth. . . . These norms in fact represent the unshakable foundation and solid guarantee of a just and peaceful human coexistence, and, hence, of genuine democracy.' (No. 96).

"Professor Murphy's teaching embodied those truths. In his essay, 'The Sign of the Cross and Jurisprudence,' in the *Notre Dame Law Review* last year, he wrote, 'Every class I have taught in Notre Dame Law School has begun with the same action and the same words. I have made the ancient Sign of the Cross while saying, 'In the name of the Father, and of the Son, and of the Holy Spirit.' The trinity is *the central fact of all reality*. There is nothing more basic than this. It is a fact of such overriding significance that everything else must be seen in relationship to it. By affirming the Trinity as we begin a law class, we make a fundamental jurisprudential statement. We acknowledge God as sovereign, and we pledge to model our work in the law upon what we know of His law-order. We cannot escape reality. According to God's word, we obey and we are blessed; we disobey and we are cursed. His moral laws are just as objective as his physical laws. We may, of course, ignore a law of God or pretend that it does not exist. But we must still suffer the consequences of violation.

"'It is, however, precisely this objective character that provides encouragement and hope. For the judgments are themselves therapeutic; they can have a healing effect. In whatever we do, let it be with confidence in the name of the Father, and of the Son, and of the Holy Spirit.'

"In his teaching, Professor Murphy uniquely integrated faith and morality with the law. What he taught is needed by law students today, including those at Notre Dame. Moreover, he was gifted with an exceptional ability to communicate on varied levels.

"For ten years, he and I team-taught a senior apologetics course on a volunteer basis at Marian High School. His own book, *Life to the Full*, was his basic text. I still encounter students in that course whose spontaneous comments evidence the impact his teaching had on their lives.

"However, the most effective class I ever saw Ed Murphy give was not even in a classroom. It was on a September night in 1989, when he led a handful of others in reciting the Rosary outside the Snite Museum in protest of, and reparation for, Notre Dame's sponsorship of a public showing of *The Last Temptation of Christ.*

"Professor Murphy accurately described that film as 'a blasphemy of Christ' and its sponsorship by the University as an 'outrage.' His witness, though quiet and dignified, was politically very incorrect. Very few joined him in it. Yet I am sure he would have gone out there all by himself, even if no one had followed his lead. He knew it was the right thing to do. That night he was a great teacher at his best, for those who were there and for those who would later reflect upon his witness.

"After retirement, and while he was fighting cancer, Professor Murphy embarked on one of his most intriguing enterprises.

"He wrote and published, as a family project, a card collection of Catholic saints. 'When I noticed,' he said, 'that a trading card series was being issued featuring prominent criminals, I knew it was time to act.' The cards include a classic picture or photograph and a short biography meticulously researched and written by Professor Murphy himself.

"They range from the Apostles to St. Maximilian Kolbe. 'Most of the saints are kind of stereotyped, a little bit syrupy. We wanted a more realistic picture,' Murphy said. The second set of fifty cards was published the day before Professor Murphy's funeral.

"Incidentally, the numbers one through 50 in the series were reserved for cards relating to the Blessed Mother. 'She comes first,' said Murphy, who was preparing to start work on those cards when he died. The thought occurs that Mary said to this good man, 'Well done. Now come on home, and let me take care of the rest.'

"'The most glorious and desirable death,' wrote St. Vincent de Paul, 'is that which surprises us with arms in our hands for the service of the Lord.' That describes in detail the death of Ed Murphy.

"His death was not immediately expected. He had just picked up a very large number of orders for the saint cards. Ed regarded those cards, and his books and other writings on God's law and jurisprudence, as more important than all his excellent technical legal works.

"The saint cards are a novel idea: they are popular and they are timeless. Their impact will go on for generations, especially with the young. In a real sense, those cards were weapons, in Ed's hands for the service of the Lord, when he died.

"In a larger sense, Ed Murphy spent his entire life in service to Christ. He was more effective and frustrating to the opposition, because of his unfailing kindness and fairness. Some might disagree with him, but no one could resent him or accord him anything but the highest respect.

"He was informed and uncompromising in his support of all the moral and social teachings of the Catholic Church, in his insistence that a Catholic university ought to be unequivocally Catholic, and in his defense of the right to life of the innocent, including first of all the unborn child.

"Ed Murphy's commitment to Christ was total, especially through his dedication to Mary and the Rosary, which he prayed with his wife, Mary Ann, in the car, minutes before he died.

"It is fitting that Ed Murphy died a death which was, 'the most glorious and desirable,' because he died in 'the service of the Lord.' Eternal rest grant unto him, O Lord, and let perpetual light shine upon him. May his soul and the souls of all the faithful departed, through the mercy of God, rest in peace."

EVANGELIUM VITAE, Sept. 25, 1995

"*Evangelium Vitae* is 'meant to be . . . a pressing appeal addressed to each and every person, in the name of God: *respect, protect, love and serve life, every human life!*' No. 5. 'Every' human life even includes the life of the guilty.

"John Paul would protect society from crime partly through 'rendering criminals harmless' by confining them rather than killing them. No. 27. More important, he seeks to protect society through the building of 'a new culture of life,' no. 95, that would prefer the 'reform' of the criminal to his execution. No. 27. He notes that personhood has a 'relational dimension' so that we must be concerned for the life and spiritual welfare even of the murderer. No. 19. *'Not even a murderer loses his personal dignity.'* No. 9.

"And '[i]f such great care must be taken to respect every human life, even that of criminals and unjust aggressors, the commandment 'You shall not kill' has absolute value when it refers to the '*innocent person*.' No. 57. No one may ever intentionally kill the innocent and human law may never validly authorize the intentional killing of the innocent. 'Abortion and euthanasia are thus crimes which no human law can claim to legitimize.' No. 73.

"John Paul is nothing if not counter-cultural. In tracing the 'culture of death' to its roots, he describes abortion and contraception 'as fruits of the same tree.' He says, 'the pro-abortion culture is especially strong precisely where the Church's teaching on contraception is rejected. . . . The close connection that exists . . . between the practice of contraception and that of abortion is . . . demonstrated by the development of chemical products, intrauterine devices and vaccines which, distributed with the same ease as contraceptives, really act as abortifacients in the very early stages of . . . the life of the new human being.' No. 13. . . .

"Abortion and euthanasia are generally seen as 'liberal' causes and the death penalty as 'conservative.' However, those issues cut across liberal and conservative lines. In our pragmatic, individualistic culture, abortion, euthanasia and capital punishment all rest on 'the criterion of efficiency, functionality and usefulness.' No. 23. And '[i]f the promotion of the self is understood in terms of absolute autonomy, people inevitably [reject] one another. Everyone else is considered an enemy from whom one has to defend oneself. Thus society becomes a mass of individuals placed side by side, but without any mutual bonds. Each one wishes to assert himself . . . and . . . make his own interests prevail. . . . [A]ny reference to . . . a truth absolutely binding on everyone is lost and social life ventures onto the shifting sands of complete relativism. At that point, everything is negotiable, everything is open to bargaining; even the first of the fundamental rights, the right to life.' Nos. 19–20. . . .

"That sanctity of life depends on God, and the American State has officially declared its neutrality on the question of whether God even exists. In this established secularism, the autonomous individual lives out the contraceptive ethic to make himself, rather than God, the arbiter, employing utilitarian criteria, of the ending as well as the beginning of the life of the innocent as well as of the guilty.

"*Evangelium Vitae* summons us instead to a 'cultural transformation' reconnecting morality with faith and freedom with truth. 'The first and fundamental step towards this cultural transformation consists in *forming consciences* with regard to the incomparable and inviolable worth of every human life. . . . Only respect for life can be the foundation and guarantee of the most precious and essential goods of society, such as democracy and peace.' Nos. 96, 101.

"So why should Notre Dame students read *Evangelium Vitae*? Because 'we are facing an enormous and dramatic clash between good and evil, death and life, the "culture of death" and the "culture of life." We find ourselves not only "faced with" but necessarily "in the midst of" this conflict: we are all involved and we all share in it with the inescapable responsibility of *choosing to be unconditionally pro-life.*' No. 28. So read *Evangelium Vitae*—reflect and pray on it, and take your stand."

ESCALATING TUITION REQUIRES FULL DISCLOSURE, Oct. 9, 1995

"It would be useful for the Notre Dame Fact Sheet, issued each fall, to include four additional items to enable applicants and present students to make informed decisions about the financial aspects of enrollment at Notre Dame:

"1. The current tuition, room and board figure in real dollars, compared to the figure in 1978–79, before Notre Dame embarked on its quest to become a National Catholic Research University. The Fact Sheet gives the unadjusted figure for 1995–96: $17,830 for undergrad tuition and $4,650 for room and board for a total of $22,480. The 1978–79 total, in 1993 dollars, would be $10,330. In real money, therefore, the current costs are more than double what they were before Notre Dame began its pursuit of Research Prestige. . . .

"The average need-based grant of $7,065 to 26 percent of the students brings the total those students pay down only to $15,415, or $5,085 more than the pre-Research University figure in real money.

"2. The average and median student loan obligation of the graduates of the previous year who have such obligations. Student borrowing has increased 50 percent since 1992, largely because of increased eligibility under the federal loan program. . . .

"3. The year-by-year growth of the non-faculty University staff since 1978–79. . . .

"4. Specifics on how all of the income from the Endowment is used. This past summer, the Notre Dame Endowment topped $1 billion for the first time. . . .

"One can hardly blame students and their families for their lack of enthusiasm at the topping of the billion mark by an Endowment which has had little or no discernible impact in preventing the doubling of real tuition costs over the past 17 years. The Endowment seems to have taken on a life of its own. Fairness would be served by full disclosure in this matter."

THE NATURAL LAW, Nov. 7, 1995

"In his Oct. 5 address to the United Nations, Pope John Paul based his pleas for 'freedom' and 'solidarity' . . . on 'universal human rights, rooted in the nature of the person, . . . which reflect . . . a universal moral law written on the human heart.'. . . .

"Everything has a nature built into it by its maker. General Motors builds into a Chevy a nature and provides directions as to the law of that nature so that the car will achieve its purpose. So also our 'Manufacturer' has built a nature into us which we ought to follow if we are to achieve our final end of eternal happiness with God.

"The law of our nature can be known certainly, as Thomas Aquinas put it, by 'the light of natural reason, whereby we discern what is good and what is evil.' *Summa Theologica*, I, II, Q. 91, art. 2. And God has provided specific directions in Revelation, including the Ten Commandments, which express the 'principal precepts of the natural law.' *Catechism of the Catholic Church*, No. 1955.

"The first, self-evident principle of the natural law is . . . that 'good is to be done and promoted, and evil is to be avoided.' (S.T., I, II, Q. 94, art. 2). The good is that which is in accord with the nature of the subject. While it is good to feed gasoline to a car, it is not good to feed it to a man. And it is not good, i.e., it is evil, to steal or murder, because such acts are contrary to the natural human inclination to live in community. . . . We can know through reason the objective rightness or wrongness of acts, but we generally have neither the right nor the ability to judge the subjective moral culpability of the person who commits that act. To be culpable, one must know the act is wrong and still choose to do it.

"The natural law provides a standard for human law as well as for conduct. Martin Luther King echoed Aquinas when he said, in his *Letter from Birmingham Jail*, that 'An unjust law is a code that is out of harmony with the moral law.' As St. Thomas put it, if a human law 'deflects from the law of nature,' it is unjust and 'is no longer a law but a perversion of law.' (S.T., I, II, Q. 95, art. 2.). Unjust laws are 'acts of violence rather than laws.' We may be obliged to obey an unjust law 'to avoid scandal or disturbance,' but a law that is unjust because it would compel one to violate the Divine law must never be obeyed. (S.T., I, II, Q. 96, art. 4.)

"'Moral truth is objective,' as John Paul said in Denver two years ago, 'and a properly formed conscience can perceive it.' But our intellects are weakened by original sin and people do sincerely disagree on applications of the natural law. . . . But if you and I disagree on the morality, say, of racial discrimination or abortion, we cannot both be right. 'If . . . we consider one action in the moral order, it is impossible for it to be morally both good and evil.' (S.T., I, II, Q. 20, art. 6.) But who am I to say . . . that you are wrong? And vice versa. An authoritative interpreter is needed if the natural law is not to degenerate into grist for endless discussion and become practically useless as a standard for law and human conduct.

"John Paul offers the solution to this problem: 'Christians have a great help for the formation of conscience in the Church and her Magisterium.'. . . 'The authority of the Church, when she pronounces on moral questions, in no way undermines the freedom of conscience of Christians. This is so . . . because freedom of conscience is never freedom 'from' the truth but always and only freedom 'in' the truth. . . . The Church puts herself . . . at the service of conscience, helping it to avoid being tossed to and fro by every wind of doctrine proposed by human deceit . . . and helping it not to swerve from the truth about the good of man, but rather . . . to attain the truth with certainty and to abide in it.' *Veritatis Splendor*, No. 65.

"The teaching authority of the Church is possessed by the Pope and the bishops in union with him. The question is not whether we must recognize a moral authority but rather which one it will be. Everyone has a pope, in that everyone recognizes an ultimate visible authority on moral questions. If that interpreter is not the real Pope, it will be a pope of the individual's own selection: Ann Landers, Dan Rather, your friendly campus theologian or the autonomous individual himself.

"On the other hand, Christ is God, the Church is his and the Pope is his vicar on earth. It makes sense to recognize that we have only one Pope, not six billion, and that his name is John Paul because he is the successor of Peter to whom Christ gave the keys. Catholics are obliged to give 'religious submission of will and of mind' to the moral teachings of the Pope whether or not those teachings are technically infallible. (Vatican II, *Dogmatic Constitution on the Church*, No. 25.). . . .

"The papacy is a gift of God, affording us an opportunity for moral certainty on applications of the natural law. However, the obligation of Catholics to accept the teaching authority of the Pope does not diminish the importance of framing issues in terms of the 'universal moral law.' That law provides, as John Paul put it, the 'moral logic which is built into human life and which makes possible dialogue between individuals and peoples.' In his reminder of the reality of universal moral truth, he has rendered a service to us all."

THE RESEARCH UNIVERSITY AND LAND O'LAKES, Nov. 20, 1995

"Notre Dame ought to reconsider its adherence to the Land O'Lakes mandate that 'institutional autonomy' from the Church is one of the 'essential conditions of life and growth, and indeed of survival, for Catholic universities.' This is so because the severance of its formal link to the Church is a decisive cause of two defining trends in the Notre Dame of the past three decades:

"1. The overemphasis on research to the detriment of Notre Dame's historic primary mission of undergraduate education in the Catholic tradition.

"The old Notre Dame, owned by the Congregation of Holy Cross, defined its primary mission as part of the educational effort of the Church. That mission was to make available to students, even those of modest means, a sound undergraduate education in the Catholic tradition. Research and graduate studies played a balanced role in the enterprise, but undergrad education was valued on its own merits as a Catholic intellectual work and resources were used primarily to keep it accessible to students. As *Notre Dame Magazine* stated in 1950, 'Still, as always, Notre Dame refuses to turn down any more worthy applicants than necessary, even those in need of financial assistance. This is one reason why Notre Dame, unlike many other universities, has never known wealth—or even appreciable financial reserve.' Vol. 3, p. 5. Notre Dame's endowment in 1949 was $4,077,587, 'the lowest among all major colleges and universities.' p. 10. Interestingly, Notre Dame took its small endowment (they spelled it with a small 'e') as a point of pride because it was using its income to lessen the burden on students. And the quality and the breadth of the undergrad program counted for more than did the achievement of recognition by the secular 'academic community.'

"When the new Notre Dame liberated itself from juridical adherence to this intellectual and spiritual mission of the Church, it predictably came to measure itself by its attainment of a reputation as a great university according to the standards of 'the academic community.' 'The reputations of universities,' said the President, Fr. Malloy, in 1992, 'are driven by the research and graduate programs, not by the undergraduate schools.' *The Observer,* Feb. 12, 1992, p. 7. One consequence of this pursuit of a reputation as a Great Research University is the devaluation and overpricing of undergrad education. Notre Dame is not the worst offender in this respect. But there is cause for concern, for example, at the fact that: 'Within any given semester, approximately 15 percent of arts and letters courses, including Freshman Composition and Freshman Seminar, are taught by graduate students.' Report of Graduate Studies Committee to Academic Council, *Notre Dame Report*, Sept. 16, 1994, p. 29. If you were a Notre Dame parent, think how thrilled you would be at the prospect of paying a tuition more than double, in real dollars, what it was in 1978—for instruction by grad students.

"2. The dilution of the Catholic character of Notre Dame.

"The overemphasis on research it itself a cause of the dilution of Notre Dame's Catholic character. . . .

"Unfortunately, in the pursuit of Research Greatness, the Catholic character of the University tends to become a secondary concern. As Provost O'Meara stated in 1993, 'I personally am confident that Notre Dame will be a university first of all, and secondly a Catholic university, for a long time to come.' Interview, WNDU-TV, Oct. 5, 1993.

"The definitive analysis in this area remains that of Father James Burtchaell, C.S.C., in the April and May 1991, issues of *First Things* magazine. Burtchaell described the process by which originally Protestant universities like Vanderbilt, Harvard, Yale, Princeton and others have become secular, and the process by which Catholic universities are following suit. He sees the critical element as the severance of the authoritative, juridical link between the university and the church. Burtchaell's essay . . . is perhaps the most important article written in the last three decades on Catholic higher education. [It] will be discussed in detail in a later column. For now, it is worth noting that the severance of the formal connection with the Church is a cause not only of the erosion of Catholic character but also of Notre Dame's sterile fixation on Research."

CATHOLIC CHARACTER OF NOTRE DAME, Jan. 22, 1996

"In the April and May, 1991, issues of *First Things*, Fr. James T. Burtchaell, C.S.C., described the secularization of various Protestant universities once they had severed their juridical and authoritative link with their founding church. According to Fr. Burtchaell, that severance made total secularization inevitable. The article, without naming any institutions, also details the journey of Catholic universities along the same path. Let me try to explain why the Burtchaell article is relevant in 1996.

"In 1994, the American Catholic universities, including Notre Dame, rejected ordinances proposed by the American bishops to enforce *Ex Corde Ecclesiae*, the 1990 Apostolic Constitution on Catholic Universities. . . .

"The bishops are considering this year new ordinances to enforce *Ex Corde*. If they adopt them, Notre Dame's relation to the Church will be a hot topic again. So let's look at it in the context of the Burtchaell article.

"The Burtchaell analysis can be discomforting. For example, *Ex Corde Ecclesiae* mandates that 'the number of non-Catholic teachers should not be allowed to constitute a majority within the institution.' For the past several years, fewer than half the new faculty at Notre Dame have been Catholic, including as 'Catholic' all who checked that box on the form. The issue, however, is not merely statistical.

"Fr. Burtchaell does not name any institution, but we should consider whether his analysis could be applied to Notre Dame: 'The Catholic colleges . . . have begun, one century after the Protestants did the same, to welcome an increasingly diversified faculty in which the communicants of the sponsoring church are fewer, and often a minority. But statistics tell only part of the story. The opening to noncommunicants appears to reflect a spirit not so much ecumenical as indifferent. Non-Catholics are welcomed not as allies in a religious undertaking; instead, they are recruited, evaluated, appointed, and welcomed without *any* frank word about religious commitment, the college's or their own, unless by way of an apology. While the remaining believers of the sponsoring church may imagine that the newcomers are being incorporated into the traditional undertaking of the college, in fact the opposite seems to be happening. Instead of their even being asked to defer to the college's religious commitment, the college stands ready to defer to their many individual commitments or anti-commitments, out of what it calls hospitality but what may frankly be called a failure of nerve. The ancient tokens of hallmark faith are withdrawn, evacuated, or desecrated so as not to make anyone feel estranged.'

"Fr. Burtchaell suggests that 'secularization is rapidly bleaching the Catholic character out of that church's universities . . . with all the elements . . . typified in the Vanderbilt story. . . . As with the Protestant alienation a century earlier. . . . the Catholic institutions enjoyed an immediate honeymoon period wherein autonomy actually enhanced the institution as both a faith community and a house of liberal learning. But then the slow and inexorable gravity pull of the secularism dominant in the force-field of the academy begins to retard and then counteract the inertial momentum that has hitherto set the course of the Catholic college or university, until, after a period when the forms and symbols of Christian identity are gradually evacuated of their conviction, the institution finally emerges as a wraith of the Christian community it once was.'

"Fr. Burtchaell's suggested cure is strong medicine:

"1. *'The only plausible way for a college or university to be significantly Christian is for it to function as a congregation in active communion with a church. . . . '* In Christianity, communities that float free are not viable.

"2. *'[T]he academy must have a predominance of committed and articulate communicants of its mother church.* This must be regarded, not as an alien consideration, but as a professional qualification. . . .

"3. *'A Christian college or university must advise noncommunicant members . . . that the institution is constitutionally committed to its church in a way that must transcend and transfigure the commitments of individual members.* Similarly, any institution will decline to let its foundational norms of scholarship yield to the private and personal standards of each individual scholar. Though the appropriate freedom of inquiry and advocacy will be protected procedurally for all, it cannot be done with prejudice to the school's filial bond to the church.' (Emphasis in original.)

"In Colloquy 2000, Notre Dame claims its Catholic identity in a mission statement that does not even mention the Catholic Church. Having cut any authoritative tie with the Church, Notre Dame defines its 'Catholic' identity, as a Protestant would, according to its own lights. Before this issue comes up again, the Notre Dame community could well reconsider the Burtchaell article and reflect on whether Notre Dame is fated to verify by its own degeneration the accuracy of his analysis."

PARTIAL-BIRTH ABORTION, Feb. 5, 1996

"President Clinton [said he will] veto the Partial Birth abortion Act, which forbids such abortions except where necessary to save the life of the mother. . . . The Act defines a 'partial-birth abortion' (PBA) as 'an abortion in which the person performing the abortion partially vaginally delivers a living fetus before killing the fetus and completing the delivery.'

"A PBA is also called D&X (dilation and extraction). In another method, D&E (dilation and evacuation), the abortionist dismembers the child inside the womb and withdraws the parts. However, according to Dr. Martin Haskell, who runs abortuaries in Cincinnati and Dayton, 'most surgeons find dismemberment at twenty weeks and beyond to be difficult due to the toughness of fetal tissues.' D&E also involves a risk of perforating the uterus. The D&X method avoids these difficulties.

"In the D&X, or PBA, procedure, the mother's cervix, the entrance to the uterus, is dilated over a two-day period sufficiently to remove the child's body with the exception of the head.

"On the third day the abortionist, guided by ultrasound, grasps one of the child's legs with forceps and pulls the leg into the birth canal. He then delivers the rest of the body except for the head. The abortionist then inserts surgical scissors into the base of the baby's skull. He opens the scissors to enlarge the hole. He inserts a suction catheter, the brains are sucked out, the head collapses and the child is removed. . . .

"Drs. Haskell and McMahon told *American Medical News* (July 5, 1993) that 'the majority of fetuses aborted this way are alive until the end of the procedure.' Dr. Haskell told AM News that 'two-thirds' are not dead. After the PBA Act was introduced to make such abortions criminal, Dr. Haskell changed his mind and denied the babies are alive when the scissors are inserted into the brain.

"Although anesthetics are administered to the mother, none is administered to the child. As to the claim that the anesthesia given to the mother kills the baby 'before it comes down the birth canal,' Dr. Norig Ellison, President of the American Society of Anesthesiologists, testified before the Senate committee that the claim is 'entirely inaccurate' and 'contrary to scientific fact.'

"Dr. Pamela Smith, Director of Medical Education at Mt. Sinai Hospital in Chicago, stated that 'There are absolutely no obstetrical situations encountered in this country which require a partially delivered human fetus to be destroyed to preserve the health of the mother.' Up to the time the scissors are inserted into the skull, Dr. Smith found no real difference between a breech (feet first) delivery and the PBA procedure. She testified to the House committee that, 'if by chance the cervix is floppy or loose and the head slips through, the surgeon will encounter the dreadful complication of delivering a live baby. The surgeon must therefore act quickly to ensure that the baby does not manage to move the inches that are legally required to transform its status from one of an abortus to that of a living human child.'. . . .

"While the effort to ban partial-birth abortions will fail because of the veto, it has exposed the barbarity of the abortion culture. . . .

"In any civilized society, the issue must be whether innocent human beings may be legally murdered. Over the past two decades, however, the pro-life movement has sought to limit, but not wholly prohibit, abortion, thus framing the issue as which innocents may be killed. The PBA campaign is a further retreat, focusing on the issue of how innocents may be legally killed. That PBA strategy raises issues we can discuss in a future column.

"In any event, the murder of an innocent child by jamming scissors into his brain is qualitatively no different from murder by any other method, including morning-after pills and other abortifacients. The next time one of your professors extols the 'pro-choice' position, visualize the PBA and remember what that choice really is—regardless of the method of the murder."

ABORTION AND COMPROMISE, Feb. 19, 1996

"It must be tough to be pro-abortion when the issue is Partial Birth Abortion. How does one argue that the law should continue to allow the execution of a partially delivered infant by jamming scissors into his head and vacuuming out his brains? . . .

"The principles governing legislation on abortion were spelled out by John Paul II in *Evangelium Vitae*, where he said that 'a civil law authorizing abortion or euthanasia ceases by that very fact to be a true, morally binding civil law. . . . In the case of an intrinsically unjust law, such as a law permitting abortion or euthanasia, it is therefore never licit to obey it, or to 'take part in a propaganda campaign in favour of such a law, or vote for it.' Nos. 72–73. The Pope went on to examine the responsibility of legislators 'where a legislative vote would be decisive for the passage of a more restrictive law aimed at limiting the number of authorized abortions in place of a more permissive law already passed or ready to be voted on. . . . [W]hen it is not possible to overturn or completely abrogate a pro-abortion law, an elected official, whose absolute personal opposition to procured abortion was well known, could licitly support proposals aimed at *limiting the harm* done by such a law and at lessening its negative consequences at the level of general opinion and public morality. This [is] not in fact an illicit cooperation with an unjust law, but rather a legitimate and proper attempt to limit its evil aspects.' (EV, no. 73.)

"Note that the Pope says that a legislator 'could' licitly support such a proposal. He does not say that he 'should.' This leaves open the prudential question of whether pro-life support for such compromise measures might actually increase the 'negative consequences' of legalized abortion 'at the level of general opinion and public morality,' especially when such compromises are promoted by 'pro-life' advocates themselves.

"Since 1981, major elements of the pro-life movement have promoted incremental legislation that would allow abortion for the life or health of the mother and in pregnancies caused by rape or incest. They have urged the states' rights solution which would allow the states to allow or forbid abortion. Both the incremental and states' rights approaches however, affirm the nonpersonhood holding of *Roe*. If an innocent human being is subject to execution at the discretion of another whenever the legislature so decrees, he is a nonperson with no constitutional right to live.

"It is fair to suggest that these compromise approaches have increased the toll of lives from abortion. The enactment of a law requiring an unmarried minor to obtain parental consent before an abortion will predictably decrease the number of abortions from those under the previously unrestricted law. The proper comparison, however, would be between a situation where the law was either wholly permissive or required parental consent on the one hand, and on the other, a situation where the pro-life movement insisted that the murder of the innocent can never be rightly allowed. A law allowing abortion with parental consent treats the killing of an unborn child as qualitatively the same as getting one's ears pierced. Ideas have consequences.

"The dominant abortions of the near future will be effected by pills, implants or other devices. The only effective way that the law will be able to reach such early abortions will be by licensing and prescription restrictions and similar regulations. The only way to mobilize sufficient support for such restrictions will be to restore the public conviction that all life is sacred and must be protected. The incremental strategy which seeks to regulate rather than prohibit abortion undermines that conviction because it permeates the public with the message that even the 'pro-life' advocates agree that innocent life is negotiable.

"The 1992 election confirms that a pro-life strategy of compromise contributes to the institutionalization of the abortion ethic. . . . In the presidential campaign, Mr. Clinton took the totally pro-abortion position. The 'pro-life' candidate, President Bush, backed by the pro-life movement, supported legalized abortion in the life of the mother, rape and incest cases. The result? The public attitude shifted markedly in a pro-abortion direction in all categories. The post-election support for abortion was the highest ever in the history of that poll. And why not? When the 'pro-life' people claim that the right to life is inalienable and then they themselves support its alienation, why should people take seriously their rhetoric about the absolute sanctity of innocent life?

"If the campaign against the PBA is interpreted by the public as opposition only to the method of the killing, that campaign will reinforce the abortion culture.

"Pope John Paul summed up the choice that each of us must make: 'We are facing an enormous and dramatic clash between good and evil, . . . the "culture of death" and the "culture of life." We find ourselves in the midst of this conflict: we are all involved and we all share in it, with the inescapable responsibility of choosing to be unconditionally prolife.' *Evangelium Vitae*, no. 28."

ABORTION AND "HARD CASES," March 4, 1996

"We need one more column on abortion. Our last two, discussing partial birth abortions, urged that the law should forbid abortion in every case and by whatever method. Many abortion opponents, however, concede that it ought to be allowed in 'hard cases,' to preserve the life or health of the mother, when pregnancy results from rape or incest or where the unborn child is defective. To round out our discussion, let's talk about those 'hard cases.'

"The most difficult case is where the abortion is claimed to be necessary to save the life of the mother. First, we should remember that operations to remove the cancerous womb of a pregnant woman, or to relieve an extra-uterine pregnancy, can be performed even under Catholic teaching if they are imminently necessary to save the life of the mother, even though they cause the death of the unborn child. Morally, such operations are justified by the principle of the double effect, since the death of the child is an unintended effect of an independently justified operation. They do not involve the intentional killing of the child for the purpose of achieving another good. Legally, such operations are justified by the principle of double effect, since the death of the child is an unintended effect of an independently justified operation. They do not involve the intentional killing of the child for the purpose of achieving another good. Legally, such operations are not regarded as abortions at all. There is no need, therefore, to provide an exception for such cases in a law prohibiting abortion. Apart from cases such as the extra-uterine pregnancy and the cancerous uterus, there appears to be no medical or psychiatric justification for terminating the pregnancy.

"Bernard Nathanson, M.D., who himself had been responsible for 30,000 abortions, said that after he stopped doing abortions, 'we proposed a lengthy list of illnesses (including but not limited to heart or kidney disease) which would justify abortion. We regard that list now with a growing sense of disbelief: if women with heart and liver transplants can be carried successfully through pregnancy, we can no longer conceive of any medical condition which would legitimize abortion. In short, we have slowly evolved to an unshakable posture of no exceptions. . . . [W]orkable, morally acceptable legislation proscribing abortion can have no exceptions written into it—not even medical ones.' As Dr. Hymie Gordon, the Mayo Clinic geneticist, put it, 'A doctor who kills a preborn baby to save the mother should surrender his license.'

"Even if there were a case where it was necessary to save the life of the mother, abortion should not be allowed. If two people are on a one-man raft in the middle of the ocean, the law does not permit one to throw the other overboard even to save his own life. Otherwise, might would make right. In maternity cases, the duty of the doctor is to use his best efforts to save both his patients, the mother and the child. He should not be given a license to intentionally kill either of them.

"'Never and in no case,' said Pope Pius XII in 1951, 'has the Church taught that the life of the child must be preferred to that of the mother. It is erroneous to put the question with this alternative: either the life of the child or that of the mother. No, neither the life of the mother nor that of the child can be subjected to direct suppression. In the one case as in the other, there can be but one obligation: to make every effort to save the lives of both, of the mother and the child.'

"If an exception should not be made where the life of the mother is concerned, it should not be made for any lesser reason. To allow abortion to prevent injury to the mother's mental or physical health (where her life is not in danger) is to allow killing for what ultimately amounts to inconvenience. And to kill the unborn child because he may be defective is to do exactly what the Nazis did to the Jews whose lives they regarded as not worth living.

"Politically, the most appealing cases to allow abortion are for rape and incest. Rape is the broader category. Every act of intercourse by a minor, below the age of legal consent, is rape, whether forcible or statutory or both. The fact that the intercourse is incestuous does not change its character as rape. Pro-abortion literature misleadingly refers to 'rape or incest' as if they were totally separate categories. But the only case of pregnancy resulting from incestuous intercourse which would not fall within the broader category of rape would be that resulting from voluntary intercourse by an adult woman capable of consent. A victim of rape has the right to resist her attacker. But the unborn child is an innocent non-aggressor and should not be killed because of the crime of his father. Since the woman has the right to resist the rapist, she has the right to resist his sperm. Non-abortive measures can be taken, consistent with the law and Catholic teaching, promptly after the rape, which are not intended to abort and which may prevent conception. However, once the innocent third party is conceived, he should not be killed. In all cases of troubled pregnancy, the community, and in some cases, the state, have the duty to solve the problems constructively with personal and financial support through delivery and beyond. It is not enough merely to forbid the abortion without providing all necessary help. A license to kill, however, is never a constructive solution to a troubled pregnancy.

"In abortion, wrote John Paul in *Evangelium Vitae*, '[t]he one eliminated is a human being at the very beginning of life. No one more absolutely innocent could be imagined. In no way could this human being ever be considered an aggressor, much less an unjust aggressor! . . . The unborn child is totally entrusted to the protection and care of the woman carrying him or her in the womb. . . . [T]he decision to have an abortion is often tragic and painful for the mother, insofar as the decision to rid herself of the fruit of conception is not made for purely selfish reasons or out of convenience, but out of a desire to protect certain important values such as her own health or a decent standard of living for the other members of the family. Sometimes it is feared that the child to be born would live in such conditions that it would be better if the birth did not take place. Nevertheless, these reasons and others like them, however serious and tragic, can never justify the deliberate killing of an innocent human being' (No. 58).

"The governing principle here is that 'civil law . . . can never presume to legitimize . . . an offense against other persons caused by the disregard of so fundamental a right as the right to life. The legal toleration of abortion or of euthanasia can in no way claim to be based on respect for the conscience of others, precisely because society has the right and the duty to protect itself against the abuses which can occur in the name of conscience and under the pretext of freedom. Consequently, a civil law authorizing abortion or euthanasia ceases by that very fact to be a true, morally binding civil law' (No. 71–72)."

WOMEN PRIESTS, April 1, 1996

"CNDPOW is back. . . . The Committee on Notre Dame's Position on the Ordination of Women . . . sponsored a discussion on papal infallibility, in the context of Pope John Paul's 1994 apostolic letter, *Ordinatio Sacerdotalis*. In that letter the Pope stated: 'Although the teaching that priestly ordination is to be reserved to men alone has been preserved by the constant and universal Tradition of the Church and firmly taught by the magisterium . . . at the present time in some places it is nonetheless considered still open to debate, or the Church's judgment that women are not to be admitted to ordination is considered to have a merely disciplinary force. Wherefore, in order that all doubt may be removed . . . I declare that the Church has no authority whatsoever to confer priestly ordination on women and that this judgment is to be definitively held by all of the Church's faithful.'

"This teaching, it should be noted, does not reflect adversely on women. As John Paul said: 'The fact that the Blessed Virgin Mary, Mother of God and Mother of the Church, received neither the mission proper to the apostles nor the ministerial priesthood clearly shows that the non-admission of women to priestly ordination cannot mean that women are of lesser dignity, nor can it be construed as discrimination against them. Rather, it is . . . the faithful observance of a plan . . . of the Lord of the universe. The presence and the role of women in the life and mission of the Church, although not linked to the ministerial priesthood, remains absolutely necessary and irreplaceable.'

"CNDPOW, however, has no reason to exist. If Notre Dame is a secular institution why should anyone care what its position is on women's ordination any more than one should care about the position on that issue of K-Mart or General Motors? If Notre Dame is Catholic its position must be the position of the Church, as definitively stated by the Vicar of Christ. So who needs CNDPOW?

"On October 28, 1995, the Congregation for the Doctrine of the Faith replied to an inquiry: 'This teaching [of *Ordinatio Sacerdotalis*] requires definitive assent, since, founded on the written word of God and from the beginning constantly preserved and applied in the tradition of the Church, it has been set forth infallibly by the . . . magisterium . . . [T]he Roman pontiff . . . has handed on this . . . teaching . . . stating what is to be held always, everywhere, and by all, as belonging to the deposit of the faith. The sovereign pontiff John Paul II . . . approved this reply, . . . and ordered it to be published.'

"Is this teaching infallible? Is it binding whether infallible or not? What, or who, determines what is Catholic teaching? The *Catechism of the Catholic Church* (CCC), drawing frequently on the Second Vatican Council, states: 'The task of giving an authentic interpretation of the Word of God . . . has been entrusted to the living, teaching office of the Church alone. . . . This means that the task of interpretation has been entrusted to the bishops in communion with the successor of Peter, the Bishop of Rome.' (CCC, No. 85).

"Who can teach infallibly? First of all, the Pope 'enjoys this infallibility in virtue of his office, when, as supreme pastor and teacher of all the faithful

. . . he proclaims by a definitive act a doctrine pertaining to faith or morals.' CCC, No. 891.

"The Bishops, in union with the Pope, can also teach infallibly: 'The infallibility promised to the Church is also present in the body of bishops when, together with Peter's successor, they exercise the supreme Magisterium, above all in an ecumenical Council. When the Church through its supreme Magisterium proposes a doctrine for belief as being divinely revealed. . . . the definitions must be adhered to with the obedience of faith.' CCC, No. 891.

"'Although the individual bishops do not enjoy the prerogative of infallibility,' said Vatican II's *Dogmatic Constitution on the Church*, 'they can nevertheless proclaim Christ's doctrine infallibly . . . even when they are dispersed throughout the world, provided that while maintaining the bond of unity among themselves and with Peter's successor, and while teaching authentically on a matter of faith or morals, they concur in a single viewpoint as the one which must be held conclusively.' No. 25. However, 'the college or body of bishops has no authority unless it is simultaneously conceived of in terms of its head, the Roman Pontiff, Peter's successor, and without any lessening of his power of primacy over all. . . . For in virtue of his office, that is, as Vicar of Christ and pastor of the whole Church, the Roman Pontiff has full, supreme, and universal power over the Church. And he can always exercise this power freely.' No. 22.

"A teaching can be infallible in a third way: 'The whole body of the faithful . . . cannot err in matters of belief. This characteristic is shown in the supernatural appreciation of faith (*sensus fidei*) on the part of the whole people, when, from the bishops to the last of the faithful, they manifest a universal consent to matters of faith and morals . . . By this appreciation of the faith . . . the People of God, guided by the sacred teaching authority (*Magisterium*) . . . receives . . . the faith.' CCC, Nos. 92, 93. Note that this infallibility of the *sensus fidei* of the people requires that the 'whole people' consent to the teaching, 'from the bishops (which would include the Pope, the bishop of Rome), to the last of the faithful.' A consensus of the people cannot prevail over a teaching of the Magisterium. Rather, the people are guided by the Magisterium: 'By a supernatural sense of faith the People of God, under guidance of the Church's living Magisterium, unfailingly adheres to this faith.' CCC, No. 889.

"In the words of an explanatory article in *L'Osservatore Romano*, 'the definitive and infallible nature of this teaching did not arise with the . . . Letter *Ordinatio Sacerdotalis*. In the Letter . . . an act of the ordinary papal Magisterium, in itself not infallible, witnesses to the infallibility of the teaching of a doctrine already possessed by the Church.' Nov. 22, 1995.

"In an address on November 29, 1995, John Paul said: The 'authority [of the Magisterium] includes *various degrees of teaching* . . . However, this does not entitle one to hold that the pronouncements . . . of the Magisterium call for irrevocable assent only when it states them in a solemn judgment or definitive act.' As Vatican II put it, 'religious submission of will and of mind must be shown in a special way to be the authentic teaching authority of the Roman Pontiff, even when he is not speaking ex cathedra.' No. 25.

"The case is closed. Maybe someday CNDPOW, and maybe even the Theology Department will get it. But don't count on that."

HONORARY DEGREE FOR POPE PAUL VI? April 22, 1996

"[The recent] legalizations—of homosexual marriage and assisted suicide—have a common root in the contraceptive ethic. We tend to forget that the Anglican Lambeth Conference in 1930 was the first time that any Christian denomination had ever said that contraception could ever be objectively right. 'Lambeth has delivered a fatal blow,' said editor James Douglas of the *London Sunday Express*, 'to marriage, to motherhood, to fatherhood, to the family and to morality.'

"The trajectory is a straight line from Lambeth to [San Francisco] Mayor [Willie] Brown's [domestic partnership] ceremony [for nearly 200 gay and lesbian] 'virtual spouses.' The contraceptive ethic affirms that sex has no inherent relation to procreation and that man (including both sexes) is the arbiter of whether and when it will have that relation. If that is true, what objections, other than pragmatic or aesthetic, can be raised to Mayor Brown's 'marriage' ceremony?

"The reality, of course, is that '[t]he relationship of two men or women cannot constitute a true family,' as Pope John Paul II said in 1994 to the European Parliament's endorsement of homosexual marriage. '[T]he attempt has been made,' he said, 'to tell the inhabitants of this continent that moral evil, deviation, a kind of slavery, is the way to liberation, thus distorting the true meaning of the family.'

"The trajectory is also a straight line from contraception to assisted suicide by way of abortion (which is merely prenatal euthanasia). If man (the word includes both sexes) makes himself the arbiter, by his own active intervention and mandate, of when life begins, he will predictably make himself the arbiter of when life ends. 'The close connection . . . in mentality between . . . contraception and . . . abortion is . . . increasingly obvious. . . . [T]here exists in contemporary culture a certain Promethean attitude which leads people to think that they can control life and death by taking the decisions about them into their own hands.' *Evangelium Vitae*, Nos. 13, 15.

"In *Planned Parenthood v. Casey*, in 1992, the Supreme Court said that 'in some critical respects the abortion decision is of the same character as the decision to use contraception.' And a contraceptive society needs abortion as a backup. As the *Casey* Court said, 'for two decades . . . people have organized intimate relationships and made choices that define their views of themselves and their places in society, in reliance on the availability of abortion in the event that contraception should fail.'

"Once abortion is accepted, euthanasia, which is postnatal abortion, is not far behind. . . .

"The prevailing culture 'presents recourse to contraception, sterilization, abortion and even euthanasia as a mark of progress and a victory of freedom, while depicting as enemies of freedom and progress those positions which are unreservedly pro-life.' *Evangelium Vitae*, no. 17. When Pope Paul VI, in *Humanae Vitae*, in 1968, reiterated the constant teaching of the Church that contraception is always objectively wrong, that teaching was denounced by adherents of The Church of Where It's At, on this campus and elsewhere. . . .

"Few in their right minds are laughing at Paul VI now. Our experience with abortion, and now euthanasia, verifies that a 'truly human civilization' cannot endure if man, through the contraceptive ethic, makes himself the arbiter not only of the relation of sex to procreation but also, implicitly, of the ending as well as the beginning of life.

"Today, whenever Pope John Paul II affirms the teaching of the Church on sex and marriage, the media can usually count on some Notre Dame professor, perhaps wearing an unfamiliar collar, to tell us why we should ignore the Pope. This is a dead end and it is getting old. Instead, maybe Notre Dame ought to confer next year a symbolic honorary degree posthumously on Pope Paul VI in recognition of his prophetic affirmation of truth and life in *Humanae Vitae*. This would be pure symbolism, a gesture, but it would beat some of the usual stuff the media pick up from Notre Dame. But, then again, we would have to declare what side we are on."

1996–1997

WHAT SHOULD WE DO WITH FROZEN EMBRYOS? Aug. 30, 1996

"A curious event in England this past summer invites us to reflect on our selective devotion to human rights. It also illustrates a tendency of scientists and lawyers to make the Pope look good.

"On August 1st, British scientists opened glass tubes which had been stored in freezing nitrogen. The tubes contained 3,300 human embryos, each the size of a grain of sand. The embryos died within minutes. They had been conceived by *in vitro* fertilization, in which a woman who cannot conceive normally can have her ovum fertilized 'in vitro' (on glass) and then implanted in her womb. The practice is to fertilize extra embryos which are frozen to keep for implantation in case the first effort fails. Or they can be donated to another woman, or used for experimentation. The Human Fertilisation and Embyrology Act provided that frozen embryos must be destroyed after five years. The five-year period expired on July 31, 1996, for the first embryos affected. Last May Parliament extended the period for embryos whose parents so requested. On August 1, the 3,300 embryos were destroyed because the 900 couples who conceived them did not request an extension. . . .

"In the United States, no federal laws, and virtually no state laws, govern the disposal of frozen embryos. In *Roe v. Wade*, the Supreme Court held that the unborn child is not a legal person until birth. He therefore has no constitutional right to life and may be killed at the virtual discretion of his mother. In *Davis v. Davis*, in 1992, the Tennessee Supreme Court ruled that frozen embryos conceived by a couple who later divorced were property and not persons. Most American clinics obtain directions from the parents as to disposition of frozen embryos, including storage, destruction, donation to other infertile couples or use in research.

"This British episode is interesting because the destruction was mandated by law and because each embryo, frozen or not, is a living human being. The humanity of the human embryo is clear. . . . I have an 'embryo donor selection list' sent by a clinic in another state to an inquirer who was seriously considering 'adoption' by having a frozen embryo implanted in her womb. The list describes, with respect to the 'mother and father' of each embryo the following characteristics: Sex, Race, Blood Type, Ethnic Origin (of the mother and father of each parent), Height, Weight, Body Build, Skin Tone, Eye Color, Hair Color and Type, Years in College, Occupation and Special Interests. Do you want a child whose mother is Caucasian, blood type O+, of

Scots-Irish and German parentage, 5'3", 107 lbs., light body build, fair skin, blue eyes, blond and straight hair, with two years of college, a homemaker, and with special interests in jazzercise and sewing? The father of her child is Caucasian, AB+ blood type, of Swedish and German-English parentage, 5'8", 165 lbs., medium build, fair skin, brown eyes, brown and straight hair, with 4 years of college, a Senior Programmer and with special interests in running and sports.

"For $6,600 you can have three of those selected embryos implanted in your womb. The prices are similar for embryos sold for experimentation rather than 'adoption.' If federal funding for experiments on embryos is approved, the market for embryos will be strong. . . .

"One historical counterpart is the slave auction block in the pre-Civil War South.

"Against this subjection of the human being to technological utilitarianism, the Pope stands virtually alone. Last May, he asserted the 'inviolable rights of the human being from his conception on behalf of all the embryos which are . . . subjected to freezing . . . , in many cases becoming an object of sheer experimentation or, worse, destined to programmed destruction backed by law.' He urged 'that the production of human embryos be halted, taking into account that there seems to be no morally licit solution regarding the human destiny of thousands . . . of "frozen embryos" which . . . should . . . be protected by law as human persons.'

"The Church has not definitively decided whether 'adoption' is a moral solution here. It could be argued to be a licit rescue. On the other hand it might constitute illicit cooperation in the mass production of human beings *in vitro*. Apart from the adoption question, *in vitro* fertilization is itself wrong because it separates procreation from spousal union and violates the right of the child to be conceived through an act of 'personal love' in the conjugal act of his parents.

"The English mass destruction of embryos should prompt us, at the start of this school year, to ask if our devotion to human rights is consistent if it excludes any human beings, even the smallest. It should also lead us to reflect on the cogency of the Church's teaching that contraception is always objectively wrong. Contraception seeks to take the unitive while deliberately frustrating the procreative. *In vitro* fertilization is the reverse, effecting procreation without union. It reduces the human being to the status of a laboratory specimen. On the contrary, human life is meant to begin only in the way ordained by the wisdom of God.

"The pragmatic scientists and the positivist lawyers cannot help but make John Paul look good. All they can offer is a relativist and utilitarian 'culture of death' which treats human beings as things. The Pope invites us to build a 'culture of life' through concern for all, even the smallest among us."

SELECTIVE REDUCTION OF UNBORN HUMAN BEINGS,
Sept. 20, 1996

"I apologize for writing about the Brits twice in a row. Our last column recounted the destruction of 3,300 frozen embryos in England. But two other prenatal dramas, which ran concurrently in the British tabloids with the embryo affair, should prompt us to ask whether our concern for the disabled is a sham. First, Mandy Allwood, 31, took fertility drugs and became pregnant by her 37-year-old boyfriend. Miss Allwood had already had one child and an abortion. Both she and her boyfriend are on welfare and, strangely, she was given free fertility drugs by the National Health Service. The drugs caused Miss Allwood to conceive eight children—at once. Dr. Kypros Nicolaides, her obstetrician, who had not prescribed the fertility drugs, offered to abort all but two of the 13-week-old fetuses, to prevent the 'high chance that all the babies will die, or if they survive there is a high chance they will all be handicapped.' Miss Allwood refused to abort. Instead, she agreed that Britain's largest tabloid, *News of the World*, would pay her at least $530,000 for attempting to give birth to all the octuplets. The size of the payment would depend on 'how many babies were born.' Miss Allwood's publicist, who also handled O.J. Simpson's trip to Oxford, said his client could make $1.5 million this year.

Now let's look at the other case. On August 6th, the Society for the Protection of Unborn Children (SPUC) got a court order against Queen Charlotte's Hospital forbidding an abortion on one twin child of a 28-year-old unidentified unmarried woman. The case drew notice because both twins were healthy and the woman sought the abortion because of money problems. Dr. Vivienne Nathanson, of the British Medical Association, said it was the first case she had seen of abortion of a healthy, naturally conceived twin. 'I don't think there's really any difference,' she said, 'between performing an abortion to leave no fetus and reducing the twin to a singleton.' Phyllis Bowman, director of SPUC, said, 'one baby is being killed. It will be left in the womb, its brother or sister growing beside it . . . the whole prospect is horrifying.'

"Anti-abortion activists pledged to pay the mother $77,000 if she would allow both children to live. But the case became moot when the hospital announced that the woman had already aborted the twin a month before the furor arose. These cases are instructive in light of the reality of the 'selective reduction' at stake in each case. 'We probably are doing an average of one or two a week,' said Dr. Norman Ginsberg of Chicago's Illinois Masonic Medical Center. 'If one believes in prochoice,' he said, 'then this is just another aspect of that. The number of multiple pregnancies has increased as a result of fertility drugs and *in vitro* fertilization.' '[S]elective reduction to a smaller number of fetuses [can] increase [the] chances of delivering infants mature enough to survive without being irreversibly damaged by the sequelae of marked prematurity.' Berkowitz, et al, *Selective Reduction . . . ,* 318 *New Eng. J. Med.* 1043–44, 1046 (1988). That seminal article on the subject described what happens: 'Under direct ultrasonic visualization, . . . a 20-gauge needle was introduced into the thorax of one of the upper-most fetuses. Whenever possible, the needle tip was placed directly into the fetal heart. Two to seven mml of potassium chloride was then injected. . . . If cardiac activity persisted, five to ten ml of sterile saline was injected next to the heart in an attempt to disrupt cardiac function by extrinsic pressure.' The dead child is absorbed by the mother's body. The authors advise against delaying beyond the 12th week because delay may increase the psychological difficulty of making the decision: 'Candidates . . . undergo multiple ultrasound examinations that provide visual contact with their fetuses; this can evoke the type of emotional bonding that normally begins to develop after birth.'

"When the physician describes how the '20-gauge needle' by-passes one child to seek the heart of his brother or sister, it is time to admit that 'selective reduction' is the execution of an innocent victim.

"The basic principle, as enunciated by John Paul II, is that 'the direct and voluntary killing of an innocent human being is always gravely immoral.' *Evangelium Vitae* (EV) no. 57. If we allow such killing in any case, the primary targets will quickly become those who are defective or otherwise burdensome to the killers. The British outcry arose [in one case] because the mother chose to abort one of the two healthy twins. But, as one physician noted, if she 'chose to abort both twins, no one would have noticed.' Nor would there have been an outcry if she had killed a defective twin. And that is the key to both of these cases.

"The 3,300 British frozen embryos were killed because they were unwanted and useless. The selectively reduced twin would have had few defenders if he had been disabled. And Mandy Allwood was urged to kill six of her children primarily to avoid burdening society with more disabled children.

"In EV, John Paul said that in the 'materialistic perspective . . . [t]he criterion of personal dignity—which demands respect, generosity and service—is replaced by the criterion of efficiency, functionality and usefulness; others are considered not for what they "are," but for what they "have, do and produce." This is the supremacy of the strong over the weak.' Nos. 22–23.

"The next time you see a ramp for the disabled, check your warm fuzzies and ask yourself whether American culture is concerned for all the weak and disabled or only those who can vote. And ask yourself what you are doing about it."

NOTRE DAME ON HOMOSEXUALS:
INCONSISTENT AND MISLEASDING?, Oct. 4, 1996

"With respect to the University's denial of recognition to GLND/SMC and its creation of Notre Dame Lesbian and Gay Students, Vice President O'Hara merits appreciation for her effort to make the best of a difficult situation. On its merits, however, the University's position is a non-starter.

"In her open letter last April 2, O'Hara emphasized that the University found GLND/SMC's position 'regarding the range of ways in which gays and lesbians might live out their orientation to be inconsistent with official Church teaching.'

"Homosexual acts, however, are not wrong because 'official Church teaching' forbids them. Rather, the Church forbids them because they are wrong. . . .

"Of course, the fact that a homosexual act is objectively contrary to the natural law does not warrant any opinion as to the subjective culpability of the person performing that act.

"The University claims only that homosexual acts are contrary to 'official Church teaching.' It does not affirm, and inferentially denies or regards as irrelevant, the realities that the acts are intrinsically wrong in themselves and that the inclination toward those acts is itself a disorder. Since the acts are wrong in themselves as contrary to the natural law, how could the inclination to those acts be anything but a disorder? On the other hand, if the inclination to the acts is not a disorder, as the University implies, why may it not be acted upon?. . .

"The University's refusal to recognize a student-run homosexual group is . . . a form of discrimination. However, while the Catechism rejects 'unjust discrimination' it does not change the reality that some discrimination against homosexuals is justified. For example, Pope John Paul denounced in 1994 the European Parliament's approval of homosexual marriage and the adoption of children by homosexual couples, as an 'attempt . . . to tell the inhabitants of this continent that moral evil, deviation, a kind of slavery, is the way to liberation, thus distorting the true meaning of the family.'. . .

"Subject to the imperative to respect the dignity of homosexuals as persons, and to treat them with 'respect, compassion and sensitivity,' a prudential judgment must be made as to what discrimination is fair in light of the common good.

"It could be fair and desirable for the University to approve a student-run group of homosexual students premised on the realities of natural law and Church teaching in their entirety. Similarly, it could be legitimate to have student-run groups of alcoholics, bulimics, or compulsive shoplifters, premised on the reality that their inclination toward those acts is disordered. However, the nature of the group as founded on such a shared disorder would justify increased supervision by the University.

"The purpose of authorizing a student group, say, of alcoholics, is not so that they can celebrate their condition but so that they can confront it and cure it or control it. So it is with homosexuals. Vice-President O'Hara's decision not to recognize an independent, and unpredictable, student homosexual group was appropriate and just.

"The University's position, however, is incomplete and misleading. . . . [I]t would be politically incorrect for the University to affirm that homosexual acts are intrinsically wrong and to affirm that the inclination to those acts is itself a disorder. But the University's persistent omission of these affirmations invites interpretation as a denial of those realities. Students might reasonably infer from the University's position that the homosexual culture is a legitimate alternative, differentiated mainly by the arbitrary imposition, by 'official Church teaching,' of a ban on homosexual genital expression.

"This inference is strengthened by the fact that the University singles out homosexuals for intense and formal solicitude beyond that accorded the perhaps not insignificant number of students afflicted with other disordered inclinations. '[A]t Freshman Orientation,' stated Vice-President O'Hara in her Open Letter, 'I include . . . a reference to harassment based on sexual orientation with words of welcome and support to our gay and lesbian students. I will continue to do this in future years.'

"Perhaps Vice-President O'Hara could also include 'words of welcome and support' to 'our students with inclinations toward excessive drinking, fornication, drug dealing, arson, shoplifting,' and other illicit acts. It might restore some balance—and it surely would impress the tuition-paying parents.

"The University's intellectually and morally flawed position disserves all its students including homosexuals. The first step in formulating a coherent University policy is simple: Tell the students the truth. All of it."

TUITION AND STUDENT DEBT, Nov. 22, 1996

"Last year, this column suggested that the University's Fact Sheet should include four new items to help applicants evaluate the financial aspects of attendance at Notre Dame. When this year's Fact Sheet appeared, none of those items was included. Persistence, however, is supposed to be a virtue. So let me try again with a streamlined version, suggesting only that next year's Fact Sheet could be improved if it disclosed two new things:

1. What does it really cost to attend Notre Dame, compared to the pre-Research University days?

"In 1978–79, Notre Dame's undergrad tuition, room and board (TRB) totaled $5,180. In 1994 dollars, on the Consumer Price Index, that amounts to $11,758. In 1996–97, the Notre Dame total is $23,660. Given the estimated 3.5 percent inflation rate since 1994, the TRB this year is almost double, in real money, what it was before Notre Dame intensified its drive for Research Prestige. . . .

"2. For Notre Dame students who have to borrow, how much debt can they expect to have after graduation?

"Student borrowing for college has increased more than 50 percent since 1992. A 1978 law removed income restrictions on federal loans. But, as Fortune magazine warned, 'anything that makes it easier to pay tuition bills will also make it easier to raise tuition charges.' The major universities, including Notre Dame, have lobbied Congress to increase the loan limits. As the limits have gone up, so has the tuition, with the universities financing their research and expansion projects on the backs of the borrowing students. . . .

"Notre Dame commendably helps students bridge the gap between the student's resources, including loans, and the costs. . . . Notre Dame's aid, however, is ordinarily given only after the student has borrowed what he/she can. . . .

"Why should the fact sheet include the details of true cost and the probable loan burden? The answer is: Truth in Labeling. Notre Dame profits from its historic appeal to middle-class and wage-earning families. The 'Rudy' syndrome reinforces this appeal. But Rudy was here before this place defined itself as a Research University. The main impact of the escalating tuition and loan burden is the practical foreclosing of a Notre Dame education to middle class students, apart from ROTC, scholarship athletes, faculty and staff children and special scholarships. The practical doubling of the real cost of a Notre Dame education over the past two decades and the probable loan burden should be components in a non-wealthy student's decision as to whether enrollment at Notre Dame is a prudent choice. Other educational factors are difficult to quantify. But Notre Dame ought to make full disclosure of the quantifiable cost and loan factors.

"It would also help if the University would explain why the real cost of a Notre Dame education should be practically double what it was before the Research Greatness years. The 1996–97 Fact Sheet stated that the market value of Notre Dame's Endowment is 'more than $1.22 billion,' an increase in one year of $250 million, or $23,809 for each of the approximately 10,500 students at Notre Dame. In Fiscal Year 1995, cash contributions to the University totaled a record $70.2 million, or $6,685 per student. One can fairly ask: Why does tuition keep going up when money in such amounts is cascading into the University's coffers and when the Endowment is more than ten times the $113 million Endowment of 1978? '[S]tudent tuition and fees' said the 1996–97 fact sheet, 'generally account for about 45 percent of

[University] income.' As former Provost O'Meara put it, 'Notre Dame's budget is 'tuition driven.'

"In terms of variety, availability and quality of courses and quality of teaching, it can hardly be claimed that undergrads receive anything close to twice the value that students received two decades ago. Nor is it merely incidental that the formerly pastoral Notre Dame has been transformed into a crowded urban-style campus like those at the big Research Universities. As one senior professor in another college of the University said to me, 'A few years ago, professors normally taught three courses or sections. Now they teach one. So they have to hire more professors, or reduce the number of courses or overcrowd the sections, or use grad students to teach. And the professor, to do his research, needs research assistants and they need office space. That's why we have some of the new buildings.' This comment, though undocumented, has the ring of truth. . . .

"[T]he University ought to disclose the financial realities to its prospective and present students."

THE IRISH FAMINE, NOV. 22, 1996

"150 years ago, Ireland was in the grip of the Great Hunger. 'No one knows precisely how many people died in Ireland's Great Famine of 1845–52, but in a population of more than eight million people, the death count reached at least one million. Another million and a half emigrated. This occurred within the jurisdiction of the richest and most industrially advanced empire in the world.' Christine Kinealy, 'How Politics Fed the Famine,' *Natural History*, Jan. 1996, 33.

"One reason why the Famine remains a subject of interest is that it need not have happened. 'Potatoes were . . . the only produce which the Irish—75 percent of whom were feudal tenants of British landlords, fanatical preachers of "free trade"—were allowed to eat or feed their livestocks. . . . During 1846, Ireland exported enough wheat, barley, oats, oatmeal, pigs, eggs, and butter to feed its entire population. Many modern historians have noted outrage at this export, which was heavily guarded by British troops against starving crowds. But few note that under British free trade policies, even more wheat was imported into Ireland that year than exported; however, at least half the entire Irish population was without any means to buy food; "free trade" dictated that none be given—"no welfare"—and the rate of evictions was growing with their destitution.' Paul Gallagher, 'How British Free Trade Starved Millions in Ireland's Potato Famine,' *The New Federalist*, May 29, 1995.

"In 1847, 'Irish produce was still being sent to Liverpool on the very same ships that carried the emigrants, whom the English lawmakers claimed could not be fed, were redundant in their native land, and therefore had to go somewhere else.' Thomas Gallagher, *Paddy's Lament* (1982), 148–49. For those who chose, or were forced by British design, to emigrate on the 'coffin ships,' the predicament was hardly better. In a typical case, the British brig *Larch*, from Sligo, buried at sea 108 of its 440 passengers, and 150 of the rest were seriously ill when she reached Canada. *Ibid.* at 210–11.

"Dr. Christine Kinealy, of the University of Liverpool, will speak at Notre Dame Law School at 12:15 on Nov. 26. In her definitive study of the Famine, Dr. Kinealy marshals facts that implicate British officials in what we could today fairly describe as crimes against humanity and genocide perpetrated by culpable indifference:

"'As the Famine progressed . . . the government was using . . . an opportunity to facilitate . . . long-desired changes within Ireland. These included population control and the consolidation of property through a variety of means, including emigration [and] the elimination of small holdings. . . . This was a pervasive and powerful "hidden agenda." The government measured the success of its relief policies by the changes which were brought about in Ireland rather than by the quality of relief provided . . . The response of the British government to the Famine was inadequate in terms of humanitarian criteria and, increasingly after 1847, systematically and deliberately so. The localized shortages that followed the blight of 1845 were adequately dealt with but, as the shortages became more widespread, the government retrenched. With the short-lived exception of the soup kitchens, access to relief—or even more importantly, access to food—became more restricted. That the response illustrated a view of Ireland and its people as distant and marginal is hard to deny. . . . A group of officials and their non-elected advisors were able to dominate government policy . . . to manipulate a theory of free enterprise, thus allowing a massive social injustice to be perpetrated within a part of the United Kingdom. . . . Within Ireland itself, there were substantial resources of food which . . . could have been diverted, even as a short-term measure, to supply a starving people. Instead, the government pursued the objective of economic, social and agrarian reform as a long-term aim, although the price paid for this ultimately elusive goal was privation, disease, emigration, mortality and an enduring legacy of disenchantment.' Kinealy, *This Great Calamity* (1994), 353, 359.

"A New York law and the New Jersey Commission on Holocaust Education have recently mandated inclusion of the Famine as an example of genocide in the human rights curricula in the public schools of those states. . . .

"The Famine was an appropriate curtain-raiser on the inhumanities that have plagued the past century. A common theme in these events is the subordination of the person to the dictates of ideology. From 1928 to 1933, the

Soviets exterminated the Kulaks by starvation because they were bourgeois and landowners. The Nazis exterminated Jews because the reigning ideology defined them as sub-human and a threat to the Nazi order. And so on. 'In the five decades since World War II there have been well over 100 million fatalities due to war, genocide, democide, politicide, and mass murder,' writes Srdja Trifkovic of the Lord Byron Foundation for Balkan Studies.

"The Irish Famine, of course, did not involve the direct and bloody murder of innocents. Instead, it resulted from a culpable official disinterest born of inflexible adherence to non-interventionist ideology and compounded by disdain for the Irish on account of their religion and race. In 1846, Charles Trevelyan, the British treasury secretary, responsible for Famine relief, described the Famine as a 'cure' for the overpopulation of Ireland 'applied by the direct stroke of an all-wise Providence.' He said, 'The great evil with which we have to contend is not the physical evil of the famine, but the moral evil of the selfish, perverse and turbulent character of the people.' 'Esquimaux and New Zealanders,' wrote Lord Clarendon, the British Lord Lieutenant in Ireland, 'are more thrifty and industrious than those people who deserve to be left to their fate instead of the hardworking people of England being taxed for their support.' Kinealy, 'How Politics Fed the Famine,' at 34–35. . . .

"We ought to reflect upon the Famine, not in a spirit of recrimination, but because it can tell us something about the deadly combination of ideology and bigotry."

MURDER IS A MATTER OF TIMING, Dec. 6, 1996

"'How can I give my only boy to the state to kill?,' Mrs. Barbara Peterson said as her 18-year-old son, Brian, surrendered to Newark, Delaware police. Brian and his girlfriend, Amy Grossberg, also 18, are charged with first-degree murder for killing their baby boy after she gave birth to him on Nov. 12 at the Comfort Inn in Newark. Delaware law provides for the death penalty where the victim of an intentional homicide is under 14 years of age. . . .

"Their lawyer does not concede that Brian and Amy killed the baby, but they did put him in a plastic bag which they put in a trash container in the hotel parking lot. It is unclear whether the injuries to the baby happened before or after he was put in the trash bin. After the birth, Brian and Amy returned to their colleges. The incident came to light when she was hospitalized for complications from the delivery. The next day a search dog found the body of the 6 lb., 2 oz. boy in the trash bin.

"Mrs. Peterson's question has a point. On what reasoned basis can the State of Delaware claim the right to kill Brian and Amy? They are candidates for lethal injection, not because they intentionally killed a human being, but because they waited ten minutes too long and used the wrong method. Brian and Amy would have been in the clear if they had hired an abortionist to solve their problem, even during delivery, by a partial-birth abortion, which is legal thanks to President Clinton's successful veto of the ban enacted by Congress. The Supreme Court has decreed that abortion may not be banned, even in the ninth month, when it is sought to protect the mother's mental health as could be claimed in a case such as this. Had Brian and Amy exercised their 'right to choose' in this way, the abortionist would have dilated the entrance to the uterus sufficiently to deliver the baby's body, except for the head. He then would have inserted scissors into the base of the baby's skull and opened the scissors to enlarge the hole. He would have inserted a suction catheter and sucked out the baby's brain. The head would have collapsed and the abortionist then would have removed and disposed of the body. If they had chosen that course, Brian and Amy then could have gone back to college, not as targets of a homicide prosecution, but as vindicators of the preferred constitutional 'right to choose.'. . .

"Brian and Amy would seem to be more in touch with reality than are the Supreme Court and the State of Delaware. Their boy was no less a human being—and in truth, no less a person—during delivery, or at his conception, than he was when they killed him or put him in the trash bin. Yet the Court and the State would have mobilized the federal marshals to protect their right to kill him before birth and even during delivery. But because Brian and Amy waited for ten minutes and didn't use an approved method of killing, the State says that they themselves must be killed. So who's crazy? As columnist George Will put it: 'Could Delaware *choose* to execute (Brian and Amy) by inserting scissors into the bases of their skulls, opening the scissors, inserting suction tubes and sucking out their brains? Of course not. The Constitution forbids *choosing* cruel and unusual punishments.'

"This case drew attention because Brian and Amy are children of wealth who could have easily had an abortion. But their case reminds us that legalized abortion will inevitably lead to infanticide and euthanasia. All three are founded on the denial of personhood to the victim.

"In *Roe v. Wade*, in 1973, the Supreme Court ruled that the unborn child is not a 'person' at any time before birth and therefore has no constitutional rights. The Court declined to decide whether the unborn child is a human being. Rather, the Court decreed that, whether or not he is a human being, he is a nonperson. The ruling is therefore the same in effect as a ruling that an acknowledged human being may be treated as a nonperson and deprived of the right to live. Once that principle is adopted, it cannot be contained. Partial-birth abortion is one application. Brian and Amy made another. And euthanasia of burdensome and useless incompetents will predictably follow.

110

"Through the depersonalization of the innocent, our legal system fosters the 'culture of death,' described by John Paul II as 'a war of the powerful against the weak; . . . A person who, because of illness, handicap, or more simply, just by existing, compromises the well-being or lifestyle of those who are more favored tends to be looked upon as an enemy to be resisted or eliminated.' *Evangelium Vitae*, no. 12.

"To respond to the culture of death, we must insist that the right of the innocent to life is absolute, without exception, because it comes from God. Ironically, the tactics of some opponents of abortion have had the unintended effect of reinforcing the abortion culture. In any civilized society, the question must be whether innocent human beings may be legally executed. Some abortion opponents have proposed merely to regulate abortion or to allow it for the life of the mother, rape or incest. Such compromise tactics frame the issue in terms of which innocents may be killed. The campaign to ban Partial Birth Abortion was a further retreat, framing the issue not in terms of *whether*, and not even in terms of *which*, but in terms of *how* the killing may be done. That campaign did expose the depravity of the abortion culture. But it reinforced that culture by focusing on the method of killing rather than on the murder as such. Brian and Amy could fairly conclude that if the method is what counts, their method was more humane than puncturing their boy's head and sucking his brain out.

"Brian Peterson and Amy Grossberg, in a sense, are themselves victims of the culture of death. They will be tried according to fair procedures in a court of law. But the ultimate culprits are the judicial and other promoters of a system which sanctions the execution of the innocent in any case whatever."

NOTE: Brian and Amy pled guilty to negligent manslaughter. Brian served 18 months of a two-year prison sentence. Amy served 22 months of a 30-month sentence. Brian married and moved to Florida with his wife. Amy returned to her parents' home.

SURRENDER BY HOLY CROSS PRIESTS, Jan. 17, 1997

"At the Notre Dame retreat at Land O'Lakes, Wisconsin, in 1967, officials of the leading Catholic universities declared that: 'To perform its teaching and research functions effectively, the Catholic university must have a true autonomy and academic freedom in the face of authority of whatever kind, lay or clerical, external to the academic community itself.'

"Land O'Lakes remains the embodiment of Notre Dame's conception of itself as a Catholic university. . . .

"It is not surprising that, three decades after Land O'Lakes, the preferred status of Holy Cross priests at Notre Dame is eroding. As Fr. Malloy stated, 'we are quickly slipping below 50 percent in the percentage of the overall faculty who describe themselves as Catholics.' The principal offices relating to academics and student affairs are held by others than Holy Cross priests, as is the chairmanship of the theology department. In some quarters of this University, the Holy Cross priests, like Rodney Dangerfield, get little respect. But they brought that on themselves.

"Curiously, the Holy Cross priests have not relinquished actual control of the University. The governance of the University is ultimately in the twelve fellows, six of whom must be Holy Cross priests. The Fellows 'have and exercise all power and authority granted by' the State of Indiana to Notre Dame. The Fellows, 'a self-perpetuating body,' elect the trustees, amend the bylaws, approve any substantial transfer of University property and are responsible for maintaining the 'essential character to the University as a Catholic institution.'

"Through the six Holy Cross priests who are fellows, the Congregation may fairly be said to have the de facto power to run Notre Dame or at least to prevent any action of which those Fellows disapprove. But this power is divorced from any corporate responsibility of the Congregation. The separation of power from responsibility for its exercise violates basic principles of leadership and management. Why are we surprised that Holy Cross priests are treated here with something less than the deference they received when they had the fortitude, as a Congregation, to run the place they had founded? They owned the place and imprudently gave it away. They seek preferential treatment as members of the Congregation, but they have surrendered the right, as a Congregation, to ensure it. Nor is it wholly incidental that they tend to look like everyone else, except perhaps on football weekends and other alumni-intensive events. In the spirit of Land O'Lakes they have put themselves on the road to a marginalization which invites disdain.

"Notre Dame should reconsider Land O'Lakes. If the Holy Cross priests want the respect they ought to have, they should take back the juridical authority, as a Congregation, to run the University. The Faculty Senate might throw a tantrum. But I have an old motion lying around somewhere. . . ."

WHY BENGAL BOUTS? Jan. 31, 1997

"The Bouts this year will honor Father Edmund Goedert, C.S.C., who died last Nov. 3. Fr. Goedert served in the Bangladesh missions from 1945 to 1983 during turbulent times. . . . On his return to Notre Dame in 1984, he acted as a chaplain for the Bengal Bouts. He would talk with the boxers, at the practices and at Mass, about the impact of the contributions from the Bouts in relieving the poverty of the people among whom he had worked. 'For over a hundred years' he wrote, 'Holy Cross priests, brothers and sisters have been working in Bengal, the country which is now Bangladesh. . . . For more than six decades, proceeds from the Bouts have assisted the missionaries in maintaining schools, dispensaries, and feeding the hungry in the poorest country of the world.'. . .

"The Boxing . . . Club officers, John Christoforetti, President, Mike DeBiasi, Mike Manley, Lucas Molina, Ryan Rans, John Kmetz and Fred Kelly . . . run the program, with help from student managers Emily Schmidt and Molly and Kari O'Rourke. 'It's a great experience,' said Schmidt, 'to know the importance of helping the missions and to see how hard the boxers work to support that cause.' Rich O'Leary and the Recreational Sports office provide all that could be desired in support and safety equipment. All the coaches are volunteers. Columbus, Ohio, developer Tom Suddes, and Chicago lawyer Terry Johnson, who are Bengals champs from 1971 and 1974, are the head coaches. In January and February, Tom spends four days a week here and Terry travels four afternoons a week from Chicago for the practices. They provide the boxers a level of instruction as good as any in the country, with the primary emphasis on safety.

"The Bengal Bouts, of course, are light years removed from the world of professional boxing. Stockholm's Karolinska Institute, which awards the Nobel Prize in medicine, reported in 1988 on the most extensive neurological study ever conducted on amateur boxers. The four-year study found that amateur boxing presented no more risk than heading a soccer ball. Notre Dame's program is far more protective than even the scrupulous program in Sweden, so much so that there has never been a serious injury in the 67-year history of the Bengal Bouts. The objective is not to injure but to score points by technique. The preoccupation with safety pervades the program. Paramedics are present at every practice involving contact. University physician, James Moriarty, M.D., oversees every aspect of the program relating to safety. In the competition, a fight will be interrupted for medical inspection of the participants if any blood appears and the physicians at ringside have full authority to stop any contest. . . .

"On a minor historical note, Dan (Rudy) Ruettiger was a vice-president of the Boxing Club in 1975–76. 'As far as I'm concerned,' Nappy said, 'Rudy has been one of the greatest motivators in a dozen years.'. . .

"Archbishop Lawrence Graner, of Dacca, East Bengal, summarized the bottom line reason for the Notre Dame community to support the Bengal Bouts: 'I wish I could conduct you and the whole student body on a complete tour of the Bengal missions. I believe your enthusiasm for the Bouts and for the Bengal missionaries of Holy Cross would know a blessed closeness and intensity never before felt."

ABORTION AND CONTEMPT, Feb. 14, 1997

"U.S. District Judge John Sprizzo found not guilty of criminal contempt a retired Catholic Bishop, George Lynch, and a young Franciscan brother, Christopher Moscinski (whose Franciscan name is Brother Fidelis).

"In February 1996, Judge Sprizzo had enjoined Lynch and Moscinski from 'obstructing . . . any . . . form of ingress into, or egress from' an abortion facility in Dobbs Ferry, New York. . . .

"On Aug. 24, Lynch and Moscinski seated themselves on the clinic's driveway where they prayed the Rosary. They blocked access to the parking lot, but nearby street parking was available. No one was denied access to the clinic. . . .

"On Sept. 6, the federal prosecutor charged Lynch and Moscinski with criminal contempt, which carries a penalty up to $5,000 and six months in jail. In such cases the judge sits without a jury. Judge Sprizzo found them 'not guilty . . . Not only does their sincere religious belief render their conduct lacking in the willfulness which criminal contempt requires, but also [their] conduct, which is purely passive . . . is so minimally obstructive as to justify the exercise of the prerogative of leniency.'

"Judge Sprizzo discussed whether, under the theory of necessity or justification, 'it is a defense to a criminal contempt charge that a person act with a sincere religious belief that he is acting to save a human life.' He noted that he 'is not persuaded . . . that there . . . should not be any [such] defense . . . because the conduct at issue, i.e., abortion, is legal. . . . Were a person to have violated a court order directing the return of a runaway slave when *Dred Scott* was the law, would a genuinely held belief that a slave was a human person and not an article of property be a matter that the Court would not consider in deciding whether that person was guilty of a criminal contempt charge?'

"Sprizzo did not have to resolve that issue 'because neither Lynch nor Moscinski acted with . . . willfulness.'. . .

"As Moscinski's lawyer, Gabriel Kralik, a college and law school graduate of Notre Dame, noted, Lynch and Moscinski 'explained to the court the meaning of their prayer of the Rosary and how they relied on its power to change the hearts of people . . . As patients and workers walked by, unobstructed, the men simply prayed. They felt no ill will or contempt for the court or arresting officers.' They 'were also ready to accept the imprisonment penalty sought by the government.'

"Judge Sprizzo said that 'Lynch's and Moscinski's . . . conscience-driven religious belief precludes a finding of willfulness [which] means deliberate conduct done with a bad purpose either to disobey or to disregard the law . . . [E]ven [if their conduct were willful] the Court would still find [them] not guilty. The facts presented . . . clearly call for . . . exercise of the prerogative of leniency which a fact-finder has to refuse to convict . . . [T]he Court must . . . have the broadest possible discretion to determine whether . . . a finding of criminal contempt is necessary to vindicate its authority. . . .'

"When the National Council of Churches, in 1968, approved peaceable 'civil disobedience,' in the Vietnam draft context as 'a valid instrument' to correct injustice, the Council's definition covers the conduct of Bishop Lynch and Brother Fidelis: 'Civil disobedience [means] deliberate, peaceable violation of a law deemed to be unjust, in obedience to conscience or a higher law, and with recognition of the state's legal authority to punish the violator.'

"Protest against the Vietnam War was politically correct. But nothing is politically more incorrect than total opposition to abortion, which is the defining sacrament of what Pope John Paul calls 'the culture of death.' Bishop Lynch and Brother Fidelis remind us of what we would rather forget: that every abortion is a murder and that every abortuary is a miniature Auschwitz. In any sane society, Bishop Lynch and Brother Fidelis would be honored and the killers of unborn babies would be put behind bars. When future generations look back on our pagan culture of death, one of its redeeming points of light will be an elderly bishop and a young monk witnessing peacefully and prayerfully for life, and a judge with the wisdom and courage to count them as moral exemplars rather than criminals."

PROFFESOR JOHN J. BRODERICK, March 21, 1997

"Most readers of this column were not born when Jack Broderick left this University. So let me tell you about this great teacher whose story exemplifies what has gone wrong with Notre Dame.

"John J. Broderick, professor emeritus at Notre Dame Law School, died in South Bend on Feb. 28. Born in New York in 1910, he graduated *summa cum laude* from Washington and Lee and St. John's Law School. He practiced law in New York until World War II. Declining an officer's commission, he served as a Chief Petty Officer assigned to the Navy officers' training program at Notre Dame. In 1947, the 'Chief' joined the faculty of Notre Dame Law School to teach evidence, labor law, trial practice and legal ethics; he also served for several years as assistant dean. . . .

"The editors of the *Notre Dame Law Review* dedicated their 1975 volume to him, saying 'the Chief has been a concerned friend as well as a scholar and a teacher. His offers to help find part-time work for . . . students and his willingness to share a concern of any student are well known. . . . [T]he Chief has often sought out students to offer his aid when he hears they have difficulties of any kind. His presence has added a special dimension to our study of law, a dimension that will stay with all of us throughout our lives. [He is] a scholar, a teacher, but even more, a noble friend and truly the embodiment of the spirit of Notre Dame.'

"The Chief was faculty advisor to the Boxing Club, he was on the sidelines at every football game and he helped athletes in various sports with their problems. Occasionally, he would invite a football player or coach to speak to his class on Friday morning before a home football game. This practice took on a life of its own. As *Scholastic* said in 1975, 'Friday morning before a home football game, the Law School lounge is transformed from a haven of quiet chatter to a teeming throng of enthusiastic Notre Dame rooters. It is here that the Chief . . . conducts his traditional pep rallies which draw law students, alumni, and curious bystanders, all attracted by the sounds of the Chief's personal student band, which features a variety of instruments, ranging from kazoo to trumpet.'

"That sort of thing, in my opinion, may have contributed to Broderick's undoing. What would they think of us at Harvard and Yale if word got out that a professor of law was standing on the desk leading the fight song? Jack Broderick was an original. As the *Law Review* editors said, 'Many have been surprised to find that the shirt-sleeved lawyer with the nuts-and-bolts approach to law was a scholar of classics and history and has held scholarships for his work in Latin and Greek. However, his interests were never limited to academic study. Those who have witnessed the white-haired professor jogging around the golf course at dawn can easily appreciate that he was captain of his college track team. By the time he left Washington and Lee he was already the man generations of Notre Dame lawyers would come to know; fast thinking, fast moving, and as playful with words as Cicero.'

"Broderick did not fit the image of the stuffed-shirt research professor sought by academic leaders on the make. When he reached the then-mandatory retirement age of 65, he applied for a full-time post-retirement appointment for 1975–76, for which there was precedent. His request was unanimously endorsed by the Law School faculty, the Advisory Board, the Student Bar Association and the Law School dean. The University tendered only a half-time appointment which it was financially impossible for him to accept. . . .

"Unfortunately, Broderick reached age 65 as Notre Dame was striving to become a Great Research University. Broderick had published scholarly articles on evidence, labor law and legal ethics. But he was essentially a teacher and not a manufacturer of useless 'scholarship.' Somebody like him would never be hired, let alone receive tenure, at the Notre Dame of today.

"So Notre Dame fired Broderick out the torpedo tubes. But he surfaced and survived. The Chief received seven offers from other law schools. Spurning the big money offers from other schools, in 1976 he joined in the founding of the law school of Campbell University, a 100-year-old Baptist school in North Carolina. This man, whom our leaders considered not good enough for Notre Dame, became an institution at Campbell.

"When I lectured at Campbell at Professor Broderick's invitation, I saw the affection the Campbell students had for him. In 1985, they hosted a national conference, the Dr. John Broderick Civil Rights Symposium, to honor the man whom they described as 'a very special friend, Dr. Broderick—the Chief—is truly a student's professor. He has left behind him a collection of admirers that even the most esteemed of celebrities would envy.'

"The Baptists at Campbell were better judges of human worth than were the leaders of this National Catholic Research University. At Campbell they praise and honor the teacher. At Notre Dame, the response to declining teaching is to get funding for a new center to do research on teaching. When he retired in 1992, Campbell dedicated the John J. Broderick Seminar Room in his honor. Broderick and his wife, Louise, then returned to South Bend. Jack loved Campbell and its students. But his heart was always at Notre Dame, even when its movers and shakers gave him the back of the hand.

"On his retirement, the Notre Dame Law faculty resolved that 'the Chief embodies, in a way all his own, the ideals and spirit of our school. . . . No one within memory has touched so many minds and hearts, or endeared himself to so many students—not only law students, but students all over campus.'

"Well said and true. But it is a sad reflection on what our leaders have done to Notre Dame that we shall not see the likes of the Chief on this campus again."

CLONING, April 4, 1997

"'Human cloning will take place . . . in my lifetime,' says Sen. Tom Harkin (D-Iowa). If you want a safe bet, forget the Chicago Cubs. Put your money on Sen. Harkin.

"Dolly the sheep, the first verifiably cloned animal, was introduced to the world by Dr. Ian Wilmut in Edinburgh this February. Dr. Wilmut took from an adult 'donor' sheep a cell which he then treated so that all its genes could be activated to develop into a lamb. He electrically fused that cell with the unfertilized egg of a ewe, from which egg the nucleus containing the DNA of the ewe had been removed. The fused cell and egg interacted and developed into a lamb embryo. Since the ewe's DNA had been removed, the only DNA in the embryo was that of the 'donor.' The embryo was then implanted in a 'surrogate mother' sheep and carried to term. The result is Dolly, a sheep that is the genetic copy of the 'donor' sheep. . . .

"Sen. Christopher Bond (R-Mo.), introducing his bill to bar federal funding of research on human cloning, said: 'For plants and animals, it makes sense to clone your specimens to improve . . . human well-being. But . . . creating an entire human being, identical to another, [is] playing God, and that is where we must draw the line.' Sen. Harkin, however, said: 'I don't think we can stop the inevitable march of science.' He also said, 'I don't think cloning is demeaning to human nature.'. . .

"The Catholic Church condemns human cloning. The 1987 *Instruction on Bioethics* said that attempts 'for obtaining a human being without any connection with sexuality [through cloning are] contrary to the moral law, since they are in opposition to the dignity both of human procreation and of the conjugal union.'

"For two reasons it is unlikely that any effective prohibition of human cloning will be enacted. One reason is the prevailing liberation of technology from moral restraints. . . .

"The second reason why human cloning will not be effectively prohibited is the dominance of the contraceptive ethic. . . .

"Contraception, like cloning, *in vitro* fertilization and other technological modes of creating life, involves the deliberate separation of the unitive and procreative aspects of sex. Pope John Paul said that, in contraception, couples 'act as arbiters of the divine plan and they manipulate and degrade human sexuality and with it themselves and their married partner by altering its value of total self-giving.'

"The question is: Who is in charge? Man or God? As John Paul put it, in contraception 'men and women . . . claim a power which belongs solely to God: the power to decide, in the final analysis, the coming into existence of a human person. They [act not as] cooperators in God's creative power, but [as] the ultimate depositories of the source of human life. In this perspective, contraception is . . . so profoundly unlawful as never to be, for any reason, justified. . . . [T]o say the contrary is equal to maintaining that . . . it is lawful not to recognize God as God.'

"Human cloning is one of the numerous aberrations that share the premises of the contraceptive ethic. If we claim the right to act as arbiters of when life shall begin, we will predictably make ourselves arbiters of when it shall end, as in abortion and euthanasia. If we claim the right to separate deliberately the unitive and procreative aspects of sex, how can we criticize homosexual activity on any ground other than the esthetic or the practical? In *Humanae Vitae*, Pope Paul VI warned that through contraception, man 'may finally lose respect for the woman and . . . may [consider] her as a mere instrument of selfish enjoyment.' This is so because, with contraception, sexual activity is no longer total self-donation, but instead it becomes an exercise in mutual masturbation and the woman becomes an object. Cloning

118

would decisively confirm the status of woman as an object, an impersonal egg bank.

"It is futile to try to put the brakes on human cloning, or abortion and euthanasia, without restoring the conviction that God, and not man, is the arbiter of when and how life begins and ends. This requires a reassessment and rejection of contraception.

"In the meantime, don't bet against Sen. Harkin's prediction. But do yourself a favor. Read, and pray about, *Humanae Vitae* and John Paul's *Letter to Families* (1994) and *Evangelium Vitae* (1995). Share them with your theology professor. He or she might learn something and might even thank you for it. And we do have anonymous grading."

HOMOSEXUALITY AND COURAGE, April 18, 1997

"Fr. John Harvey, the founder of Courage, the Catholic support group for homosexuals, has written a new book, *The Truth about Homosexuality*.'. . .

"Fr. Harvey's insights could be helpful to some at Notre Dame who might otherwise be misled by the University's policy. He affirms the reality, as stated in the Catechism of the Catholic Church, that homosexual acts are 'intrinsically . . . contrary to the natural law.' He insists, as does the Church, that those with homosexual inclinations are entitled to respect. . . .

"Unlike the Notre Dame policy, Fr. Harvey recognizes that the inclination to homosexual acts is itself disordered, as would be an inclination to excessive drinking, shoplifting or any other disordered act. And he insists on a point about which the Notre Dame policy is reticent—that some with a homosexual inclination may achieve a change of orientation through prayer, group support and professional help.

"In his essay in the book, Fr. Jeffrey Keefe notes the 'progress in social attitudes toward persons burdened with alcoholism. Alcoholism is now widely viewed as a disease . . . We need a corresponding shift in attitude toward homosexual persons. Denying that homosexuality is a developmental anomaly or a disorder is not the way to accomplish this turnabout.'. . .

"Fr. Harvey discusses Dr. Charles W. Socarides' research into 'the politicization of American psychiatry,' in which 'Socarides describes . . . the manipulative manner by which a small group of psychiatrists in league with gay organizations succeeded in having the American Psychiatric Association remove the condition of homosexuality from the Diagnostic and Statistical Manual. . . . Henceforward, homosexuality would be considered a normal variant of sexual behavior. . . . Among the disastrous effects of [this] is the abandonment of those persons who want help to move toward heterosexuality as the natural and God-given state for men and women. Why should one seek therapy for a lifestyle now considered 'normal'?

"Perhaps Fr. Harvey's most important point is that 'from the . . . testimony of secular professional and religious counselors, one may draw the modest conclusion that some persons with a homosexual orientation can acquire a heterosexual one through a process of prayer, group support, and sound therapy. This is not to say that everyone who seeks such change is able to attain it. . . . I now see such change as a live option. . . . I insist, however, on two things: 1) this is an option, not an obligation; and 2) individuals who pursue a change of orientation should not be discouraged if after several years . . . they . . . are not able to develop a genuine attraction toward the opposite sex; they should then resign themselves to a life of chaste service to Christ in the world.'

"'[T]here is a great spiritual hunger,' says Fr. Harvey, 'not only for the truth of Catholic teaching on homosexuality . . . but also for the inspiration to live a new kind of life with Christ. . . .'

"Fr. Harvey's book could be useful in promoting a sound and fair resolution of this issue at Notre Dame. Unfortunately, the University sends confusing signals to its students, especially those with homosexual inclinations. The denial of recognition to GLND/SMC on the ground that its position is merely 'inconsistent with official Church teaching' raises the inference that the prohibition of homosexual acts is not rooted in the natural law but rather is an arbitrary Church edict. GLND/SMC, to the knowledge of the administration, holds regular meetings in O'Shaughnessy which are unofficially publicized. The University conducts forums and presents speakers who are at best ambiguous or incomplete on the issues.

"There is no official statement by the University acknowledging that the homosexual inclination is itself a disorder. If it is not a disorder, why may it not be acted upon? The University's remarkable solicitude for students with homosexual inclinations, far beyond that accorded to students with other disorders, could convey the impression to some that it is cool to question one's sexual identity. Nor does the University explicitly affirm that its purpose is to assist homosexually inclined people to try to redirect that inclination itself. Instead, the University's unbalanced position conveys the impression that the defining problem is 'homophobia.'

"If our leaders were serious and practical about this, they would invite Fr. Harvey to give a series of lectures, and to consider forming a Courage chapter at Notre Dame. But don't bet on it. Fr. Harvey's position is politically incorrect. However, if you are interested you can read his book and call Courage at (212) 421-0426. . . . "

NOTE: The Notre Dame Core Council on Gay and Lesbian Students now includes on its website an essay, "Catholic Teaching on Homosexuality,' by Fr.

David Burrell, C.S.C. It is "[b]ased on information found in 'Always Our Children,'" the statement issued by the National Conference of Catholic Bishops' Committee on Marriage and Family in 1998. The Burrell essay correctly quotes and discusses the Catechism, no. 2358, which describes the homosexual orientation as 'objectively disordered.'

1997–1998

KILL TIMOTHY MCVEIGH? Aug. 29, 1997

"Timothy McVeigh should not be executed. His case verifies the wisdom of Pope John Paul's 1995 encyclical, *Evangelium Vitae (EV)*, which restricted the use of the state's authority to impose the death penalty.

"A Catholic can rightly support the use of the death penalty, according to *EV*, only in cases of 'absolute necessity . . . when it would not be possible otherwise to defend society.' No. 56. This appears to refer not to the protection of society by deterring potential offenders, but rather to protection of society *from this convicted criminal. . . .* 'Modern society . . . has the means of effectively suppressing crime by rendering criminals harmless without definitively denying them the chance to reform." No. 27.

"Under the new criterion of *Evangelium Vitae*, one could still argue for the death penalty in very limited situations, such as that of a prisoner already serving a life sentence who murders a guard or another inmate. What sense would it make to give him another life sentence? Or would it be consistent with his dignity to wall him up permanently in a cell, with food and wastes passed through an aperture and with no direct contact ever with any other human being? The death penalty could be argued to be absolutely necessary in such a case, although even there it is debatable. Other cases could be argued, such as a condition of unrest in which the authorities would lack the means to keep a murderer securely imprisoned.

"There is no way, however, that the execution of McVeigh can be made to square with *Evangelium Vitae*. The federal government is not so lacking in effective security facilities that his execution is a matter of 'absolute necessity' because 'it would not be possible otherwise to defend society.'

"Despite public approval, the death penalty is a deceptive quick-fix. As Archbishop Charles J. Chaput, O.F.M. Cap. of Denver said in opposing the McVeigh sentences, 'Capital punishment is just another drug we take to ease other, much more deeper anxieties about the direction of our culture. Executions may take away some of the symptoms for a time (symptoms who have names and their own stories before God), but the underlying illness—today's contempt for human life—remains and grows worse.'. . . Nor is the acceptance in our culture of intentional killing as a 'quick fix' limited to cases where the person to be killed is guilty. The Supreme Court has found in the Constitution a right to abortion which requires the states to allow the intentional killing of the innocent unborn, who are defined by the Court as nonpersons.

. . . Since the 1990 *Cruzan* case the Supreme Court has held that the states may allow the withdrawal or withholding of treatment, including food and water, from a patient, even an incompetent, under circumstances where the withdrawal or withholding was clearly done with the intent to cause death. . . .

"'God did not make death, and he does not delight in the death of the living.' EV, no. 7. This is seen in John Paul's discussion of the first murderer, Cain, who is, if possible, even more notorious than Timothy McVeigh. 'After the crime, *God intervenes to avenge the one killed.*' No. 8. But he gives a special protection to the murderer's life: 'And yet God, who is always merciful even when he punishes, *"put a mark on Cain,* lest one who came upon him should kill him."' . . . He thus gave him a distinctive sign, not to condemn him to the hatred of others, but to protect . . . him from those wishing to kill him. . . . *Not even a murderer loses his personal dignity*, and God himself pledges to guarantee this. God, who preferred the correction rather than the death of the sinner, did not desire that a homicide be punished by the exaction of another act of homicide.' No. 9

"Before EV, I and others supported the use of the death penalty, among other reasons, because it restored the balance of justice with respect to some crimes and because it uniquely promoted respect for innocent life by inflicting a punishment for murder which was qualitatively different from the punishment for other crimes. But the Vicar of Christ has raised the discussion to a new level, making the old arguments obsolete. . . .

"What hangs in the balance here is more than the life of Timothy McVeigh. It is rather the issue: Who is God? The real God? Or the State?"

NOTE: Timothy McVeigh was executed on June 11, 2001, at the federal prison in Terre Haute, IN, for the bombing of the federal office building in Oklahoma City on April 19, 1995.

ASSISTED SUICIDE AND EUTHANASIA, Sept. 12, 1997

"If you live in Oregon you should get an absentee ballot. Oregon voters will decide in November whether to repeal their 1994 law that allows assisted suicide.

"This year, in *Washington v. Glucksberg*, the Supreme Court held that there is no constitutional 'right to die' that would require the states to allow assisted suicide. . . .

"In assisted suicide, the physician, by prescribing or administering a lethal drug or treatment, intentionally and actively helps the patient kill himself. . . . [A]ssisted suicide . . . is a sideshow. This is so because the Supreme Court already permits the states to allow the starvation and dehydration of the patient, where such is clearly done with the intent to kill the patient. In its 1990 *Cruzan* decision, the Supreme Court held that Missouri could require 'clear and convincing' evidence of Nancy Cruzan's intent not to be sustained on a feeding tube before it would permit removal of that tube. On rehearing, such evidence was found, the tube was withdrawn, and Nancy died. But *Cruzan* does not forbid the states to allow withdrawal of food and water on a lesser showing of the patient's intent or on the basis that withdrawal is in the best interest of an incompetent patient even without a showing of his intent.

"The law should not require that excessive treatment be given to impede the act of dying. There comes a time when nature should take its course, and the proper judgments of physicians and family should be respected, and the patient should be allowed to die a natural and dignified death. But the patient in the *Cruzan*-type case is not dying. Nancy Cruzan had a life expectancy of 30 years. Her feeding by tube was not painful. It sustained her life, even though it would not correct her underlying condition. Contrary to the Supreme Court's view, the removal of the tube causes death by starvation and dehydration and not by the 'underlying fatal disease and pathology.' The removal of her food and water was intended not to relieve pain, but to allow Nancy to starve and dehydrate to death. When the tube was removed, she did that. The purpose was to relieve her of a life considered burdensome or useless, but the intent was to achieve that purpose by means of intentionally killing her. . . .

"When a state protects innocent, non-aggressor persons in general by forbidding them to be intentionally killed, it should be held to deny equal protection of the laws for the state to exclude from that protection some such persons because they are terminally ill or because they have asked to be killed. . . .

"It is very difficult, if not impossible, for the law to distinguish cases in which pain-relieving palliatives and sedation are used for proper medical reasons from cases where they are used with intent to kill. The Supreme Court allows the states to decline even to try to make that distinction.

"We are not on a slippery slope towards euthanasia. We are there. The Court has invited the states to turn a blind eye to euthanasia committed under the guise of legitimate palliative care, sedation or withdrawal of treatment. Nor will such euthanasia be limited to consenting patients. Rising costs will induce families and physicians to opt for termination of life of the incompetent, the aged and the disabled. This is especially so in light of the aging of the population of the United States. . . .

"The Supreme Court should have drawn the line in *Cruzan* to affirm that the state may not constitutionally allow the intentional killing of the innocent. And the states should forbid assisted suicide. But the technological privatization of euthanasia has moved the problem beyond the effective reach of the law. The solution is to restore the conviction that 'God . . . is the sole Lord of this life; man cannot do with it as he wills.' *Evangelium Vitae*, no. 39.

"So if you live in Oregon, you should vote to repeal the assisted suicide law. But wherever you live, tell your grandmother to be careful when she chooses a doctor."

NOTE: In the 1997 referendum, Oregon voters reaffirmed their 1994 decision to allow assisted suicide.

WHY IS THE HOMOSEXUAL INCLINATION PRIVILEGED AT NOTRE DAME? Sept. 26, 1997

"The administration rates an 'A' for sincerity and effort on the homosexual issue. But our leaders . . . have now demonstrated that their policy is harmful to students.

"The University denies recognition to GLND/SMC because, said vice president of Student Affairs Patricia O'Hara, that group's 'value-neutral approach' and its approval of 'stable, monogamous (homosexual) relationships' are not 'consistent with official Church teaching.' Notre Dame intends, as O'Hara stated, 'to remain faithful to the teachings of the Catholic Church.' However, the Church teaches not only that homosexual acts are wrong but also that the inclination toward them is disordered, a reality which Notre Dame refuses to affirm. *The Letter on the Pastoral Care of Homosexual Persons,* issued with the approval of John Paul II in 1986, said, 'Although the particular inclination of the homosexual person is not a sin, it is a more or less strong tendency ordered toward an intrinsic moral evil, and thus the inclination itself must be seen as an objective disorder.'

"On Sept. 8, 1997, the Pope promulgated the 'definitive and normative' Latin text of the *Catechism,* originally issued in French in 1992. The final text revises No. 2358 to state explicitly that the homosexual inclination is 'intrinsically disordered.'. . .

"The final text reads: 'The number of men and women who have deep-seated homosexual tendencies is not negligible. This inclination, objectively disordered, is a trial for most of them.'

"The first Italian edition had said 'innate' instead of 'deep-seated.' This led to objections, said [Cardinal Ratzinger], 'that we made people think homosexual tendency was innate, that it was already present at the moment of birth or conception . . . Many competent experts said this has not been proven.' The Catechism recognizes that homosexual orientation is 'deep-seated' in the individual's subconscious and 'is not simply a matter of choice or will,' he said. At the same time, it makes clear the Church's teaching that 'homosexual acts are objectively disordered' because 'they do not correspond to the fundamental tendency of sexuality which between a man and a woman is ordered toward the birth of children.' *Catholic Courier*, Sept. 11, 1997, p. 6.

"In its statement, 'The Spirit of Inclusion,' the University commendably said, 'We value gay and lesbian members of this community. . . . We condemn harassment of any kind.' But the administration still refuses to affirm, and therefore implicitly denies or regards as irrelevant, the reality that homosexual acts, and the inclination to them, are 'objectively disordered.' If, as the administration implies, the inclination is not disordered, why may it not be acted upon? But if, as the Catechism states, the acts are 'objectively disordered,' how could the inclination to those acts be anything but disordered?

"Now, regrettably, the administration has moved from failing to give its students the full truth to actively opposing efforts to promote constructive discussion in the context of that entire truth. In the first Jacques Maritain Center lecture, Dr. Joseph Nicolosi, who heads the National Association of Research and Therapy of Homosexuality, discussed the evidence that homosexuality is a treatable 'psychological disorder.' In the second, speakers associated with Exodus International discussed 'their histories as homosexuals and their spiritual journeys away from that way of life.'

"Instead of welcoming these discussions, the director of Campus Ministry took a full-page Observer ad to say, 'I do not think the presentation will be helpful . . . nor are the topics . . . pertinent to where our community is at this time . . . [T]hese two presentations will cause unnecessary pain and a deepened sense of isolation on the part of some of our homosexual students. . . . If you are uncertain about your sexual orientation, or if you are gay or lesbian, and you want a safe and caring place to talk about it, please contact Campus Ministry. Our first goal will be to assure you that homosexual orientation in and of itself is neither sinful nor morally wrong in any way. Secondly, we will try to provide you with a pastoral support group in a confidential atmosphere where you can speak freely about your own situation and learn from the experiences of other students. If you are a Catholic or a member of a Christian denomination, we will try to help you find ways of living out your faith convictions with integrity.'

"Search that statement—and any other University statement—and you will find no indication that the homosexual inclination is disordered or that it is anything but a permanent unchangeable condition.

"So why is that a big deal? Because the administration's position could lead students of homosexual inclination to conclude that they are locked in to that condition permanently and that the homosexual lifestyle is not disordered and is therefore an otherwise legitimate alternative, prohibited only by an arbitrary 'official Church teaching.' This inference is strengthened by the intense and formal solicitude shown by the University to those with homosexual inclinations, far beyond that shown to students afflicted with other inclinations. The University Smoking Policy states that, 'The University . . . will provide access to smoking cessation programs to all members of the campus community who desire them.'

"To treat an inclination to smoking as a treatable disorder is politically correct. To do so with the homosexual inclination would be politically incorrect to the maximum. This disparity reflects the reality that the de facto official religion of Notre Dame is political correctness, rivaled, perhaps, only by the cult of the money god.

"Homosexual acts, and the inclination to them, are 'intrinsically disordered,' not because of 'official Church teaching,' but because they are contrary to nature. Not even the Faculty Senate could repeal that law of nature. The University's refusal to affirm it is a dereliction of duty. As the 1986 *Letter* said, 'departure from the Church's teaching or silence about it, in an effort to provide pastoral care, is neither caring nor pastoral. The neglect of the Church's position prevents homosexual men and women from receiving the care they need and deserve.'

"The administration ought to reconsider its position. If it will not offer its students the entire constructive and hopeful teaching of the church on this issue, it ought at least to get out of the way of those members of the University who are trying to do so."

MISIDENTIFICATION. LETTER TO THE EDITOR OF *THE OBSERVER*, Oct. 2, 1997

"Dear Sirs:

"Thank you for the complimentary story in the October 1st Observer detailing my litigation efforts as counsel for the inmates of the St. Joseph County Jail. I shall treasure that story and will submit it to the University as evidence of public service meriting a pay increase.

"However, as you already know, there was only one thing wrong with that story. You had the wrong guy. The attorney for the inmates is Charles P. Rice, a South Bend attorney. I know him well. He is a caring, compassionate man of the 90s. But he is also a very competent and aggressive lawyer. He might sue you for stealing his case and crediting it to someone else. You could all end up in St. Joseph County Jail. But then you would automatically be his clients. . . .

"I wish your reporters had written up the Michigan game. We would have won."

"Sincerely,

"Charles E. Rice, Professor of Law."

"CORRECTION: Due to a reporting error, an article in Wednesday's Observer, 'ND professor sues to build new prison,' misidentified the attorney representing the inmates. Charles P. Rice is a South Bend attorney with no affiliation to the University." Observer, Oct. 3, 1997.

EUCHARISTIC ADORATION: WHY NOTRE DAME NEEDS IT, Nov. 7, 1997

"Entirely on student initiative and with the assistance of Campus Ministry, Notre Dame now has round-the-clock Adoration of the Blessed Sacrament in the chapel of Fisher Hall. . . . Students, faculty and staff participate, usually in half-hour segments. Walk-ins are welcome.

"Why do such a thing? 'I make a holy hour each day in the presence of Jesus in the Blessed Sacrament,' said Mother Teresa. 'All my sisters . . . make a daily holy hour, as well, because we find that through [it] our love for Jesus becomes more intimate, our love for each other more understanding, and our love for the poor more compassionate'. . . .

"The first thing to remember here is the reality of the presence of Christ in the Eucharist. Surveys indicate that only 27 percent of Catholics believe in the Real Presence. But the *Catechism of the Catholic Church* spells it out: 'In the most blessed sacrament of the Eucharist "the body and blood, together with the soul and divinity, of our Lord Jesus Christ and, therefore, the whole Christ is truly, really, and substantially contained." This presence is called "real"—by which is not intended to exclude the other types of presence as if they could not be "real" too, but because it is presence in the fullest sense: that is to say, it is a substantial presence by which Christ, God and man, makes himself wholly and entirely present . . . The Eucharistic presence of Christ begins at the moment of the consecration and endures as long as the Eucharistic species subsist.'

"You might think, 'What am I going to do for half an hour, just sitting there? I'll just fall asleep.' Archbishop [Fulton] Sheen recounts the occasion in the Church of St. Roch in Paris when he knelt down, promptly fell asleep and 'woke up exactly at the end of one hour.' He wondered if he had really made his promised Hour until he realized 'that's the way the Apostles made their first Holy Hour in the Garden.' So falling asleep should not be a concern.

"It would make sense to take advantage of this opportunity. . . . Pray for yourself, exams, your family, whatever. And remember that there is no law against praying for the success of the football team, including even an undefeated season next year. God is omnipotent. He can do anything."

ANNIVERSARIES TO THINK ABOUT, Jan. 23, 1998

"If you are a student, call your mother tonight and thank her. You probably were not around a quarter century ago yesterday, when the Supreme Court, in *Roe v. Wade*, mandated abortion on request. The principle of *Roe* is that of the Holocaust, that innocent human beings can be defined as nonpersons and killed at the discretion of others. At least 37 million in this country have died by surgical abortions, and many more by early abortifacients. In partial-birth abortion, even the partially delivered child can have his brains sucked out and his head crushed to facilitate his removal. Your mother could have had you killed. But she let you be born.

"Why this bloodbath and what is the remedy? Two other anniversaries in 1998 point to the answers. July 29 will mark 30 years since Pope Paul VI issued *Humanae Vitae*. And Oct. 16 will be the 20th anniversary of the papacy of John Paul II.

"*Humanae Vitae* and John Paul help us understand that legalized abortion follows from the acceptance of contraception. Both actions deliberately separate the unitive and procreative aspects of sex. A contraceptive society needs abortion as a backup. And, as John Paul put it, contracepting couples 'claim a power which belongs solely to God: . . . to decide, in a final analysis, the coming into existence of a human person.' If man makes himself the arbiter of when life begins, he will make himself the arbiter of when it ends, through euthanasia as well as abortion.

"'[T]here exists in contemporary culture,' wrote John Paul, 'a Promethean attitude which leads people to think that they can control life and death by taking the decisions about them into their own hands.' In *Evangelium Vitae*, he noted that 'the pro-abortion culture is especially strong . . . where the Church's teaching on contraception is rejected. . . . [C]ontraception and abortion are often closely connected, as fruits of the same tree . . . rooted in a hedonistic mentality unwilling to accept responsibility [and] a self-centered concept of freedom, which regards procreation as an obstacle to personal fulfillment. The life which could result . . . becomes an enemy to be avoided at all costs.'. . .

"In *Humanae Vitae*, Paul VI warned that, if contraception were seen as legitimate, 'a dangerous weapon would . . . be placed in the hands of . . . public authorities.' Today, coerced contraception as well as abortion are part of the utilitarian solution to the minority welfare problem. Blacks are 12 percent of the nation's population, but have 31 percent of its abortions. 'When you're a minority,' says Rev. Johnny Hunter, 'you can't take that kind of hit and survive as a race.' The federal birth control programs, international as well as domestic, are weighted against non-whites. As the Brazilian Catholic Bishops recently said, 'The desired result [of population control] is always the same: to reduce the growth of the countries of the Third World so that the industrialized nations can continue to exploit them and dominate them.'

"The answer to the 'culture of death' will not be found in courts and laws. A 'culture of life' must be built on the principle that a person has transcendent rights only because he is made in the image and likeness of God with a destiny that transcends the state. Significantly, John Paul II will mark another anniversary on Dec. 9–12, in Mexico, where Our Lady of Guadalupe appeared to Juan Diego in 1531, leaving her image on his cloak. Less than a decade before, the Aztec temples of human sacrifice had been overthrown. In the next few years millions were converted from the Aztec cult to the Catholic Faith. John Paul calls for a similar conversion from our own cult of human sacrifice. In *Evangelium Vitae* he asked Mary to 'look down ... upon the vast number of babies not allowed to be born, of the poor whose lives are made difficult, of men and women who are victims of brutal violence, of the elderly and the sick killed by indifference or out of misguided mercy.'

"We can profitably reflect on these anniversaries in 1998. And don't forget to thank your mother for letting you stay around."

DR. MARTIN LUTHER KING, Feb. 5, 1998

"Martin Luther King's birthday has taken on a life of its own, abstracted from the realities of his life and his statements on issues. Dr. King's authority is claimed for opposite positions on various matters. On one question, however, Dr. King's own written position is not only clear but relevant today. That is the question of the moral limits of the human law and the moral obligation to obey that law.

"In his *Letter from Birmingham Jail*, Dr. King said: 'One has not only a legal but a moral responsibility to obey just laws. Conversely one has a moral responsibility to disobey unjust laws. I would agree with St. Augustine that, "an unjust law is no law at all". . . . An unjust law is a code that is out of harmony with the moral law. To put it in the terms of St. Thomas Aquinas: An unjust law is a human law that is not rooted in eternal law and natural law.'. . .

"[H]owever, as Aquinas makes clear, a willingness to accept the penalty is not an automatic justification for breaking even an unjust law. . . .

"St. Thomas explains that a law may be unjust in two ways: '[F]irst, by being contrary to the human good . . . either in respect of the end, as when an authority imposes on his subjects burdensome laws, conducive not to the common good . . . ; or in respect of the author, as when a man makes a law that goes beyond the power committed to him; or in respect of the form, as when burdens are imposed unequally on the community. . . . The like are acts of violence rather than laws; because . . . a law that is not just, seems to be no law at all. Wherefore such laws do not bind in conscience, except perhaps in order to avoid scandal or disturbance, for which cause a man should even yield his right. . . . Secondly, laws may be unjust through being opposed to the divine good; such are the laws of tyrants inducing to idolatry, or to anything else contrary to the divine law; and laws of this kind must nowise be observed, because . . . we ought to obey God rather than men.'. . . .

"If a physician were ordered to perform an abortion, Aquinas' concept of the law which is unjust as contrary to divine good would require that physician to disobey at all cost. However, where a law does not compel a person himself to violate the divine law but rather is unjust because it is 'contrary to human good' because it is beyond the authority of the lawgiver, is oppressive, or imposes burdens 'unequally,' Aquinas would say that such a law might still 'bind in conscience' where disobedience would create a greater evil of 'scandal or disturbance.' There can be a moral right, therefore, to disobey an unjustly discriminatory law if such disobedience would not create a greater evil. If disobedience would create a greater evil, our duty instead would be to expose the injustice and work to change the law. Only if such a law compels the individual himself to violate the divine law would Aquinas say that there is an absolute obligation to disobey it. Income tax laws, for example, are unjust in significant respects. Yet there is no moral right to refuse to pay taxes, because the general assertion of such a right would create a greater evil. And the misuse of tax funds by the government does not make the payment of taxes . . . itself a violation by the taxpayer of divine law so as to mandate disobedience. . . .

"In his 1965 address to the New York Bar, Dr. King said, 'wherever unjust laws exist people on the basis of conscience have a right to disobey those laws.' Dr. King's position that the individual has an unqualified right to disobey every unjust law would work against the common good. . . . Nevertheless, Dr. King's essential affirmation that a human law is unjust if it is 'out of harmony with the moral law' is a needed reminder of the reality that the State is not God."

MOTHER TERESA AND THE BENGAL BOUTS, Feb. 20, 1998

"Could Mother Teresa have had a connection to the Bengal Bouts? Surely not as a competitor. . . . [W]e have never had a weight class that went that low. Instead, the connection was, and is, more basic.

"Her life, her death, drew world attention to the efforts of her Missionaries of Charity in a part of the world where Holy Cross missionaries in Bangladesh do the same work with the support of the Bengal Bouts. . . .

"This thought was frequently echoed by Father Edmund Goedert, the 1997 posthumous recipient of the Bengal Bouts Award, who worked 38 years in Bangladesh and served as chaplain to the Boxing Club after his return to Notre Dame. 'Proceeds from the Bouts,' he said to the boxers, 'have assisted the missionaries in their work of maintaining schools, dispensaries and feeding the hungry in the poorest country in the world.'

"So the first reason we should support the Bengal Bouts is to participate in the efforts of the Holy Cross missionaries as they do the great work brought to the attention of the world by Mother Teresa. Dominic J. 'Nappy' Napolitano, director of the Bengal Bouts from 1931–1981, epitomized this purpose of the Bouts: 'Strong bodies fight that weak bodies may be nourished.'

"Beyond that, the Bouts themselves are a unique athletic phenomenon that could happen only at Notre Dame. . . . 'For anyone who has attended Notre Dame,' wrote Chicago sports columnist Bill Gleason, 'the words "Bengal Bouts" have only a little less meaning than "Fighting Irish." 'In the beginning,' wrote Gleason, 'one college kid said to another, "Let's have a team for the students." Somewhat later, a coach said, "Let's have students for the team." And that was the start of the kind of recruiting which led to the current scandal caused by phony transcripts of credit. Every now and then there is an event that reminds us of how campus sports were run in the time before athletic directors and huge coaching staffs. The Bengal Bouts are . . . as purely amateur as a sport can be.' . . .

"'Any member of the Club,' said president Ryan Rans, 'will tell you that participation in this program is the most memorable experience of his Notre Dame career.' The other officers are Lucus Molina, Sean Sharpe, Fred Kelly, Tommy Will, Mike LaDuke and Brian Gaffney.

"'Our primary emphasis,' said Molina, 'is on safety. We have never had a serious injury in the program and we mean to keep it that way.'. . .

"Jack Mooney, [the trainer and] 85-years-young, was with Nappy at the beginning. He was Knute Rockne's paper boy, and Rockne himself smuggled Jack onto the sidelines at home football games. Jack has been an inspiration to countless members of the Boxing Club.

"Junior Emily Schmidt is indispensable in her handling of the administrative details of the program. Assisted by Molly O'Rourke, Emily has the title of office manager, but she is really the brains of the outfit. Her dedication and ability explain why the Bouts netted a record $23,000 contribution to the missions in 1997. . . .

"We hope you will support this effort. Mother Teresa would approve."

U.S. NEWS AND THE FACULTY SENATE, April 3, 1998

"The Administration has notified parents of undergrads that tuition, room and board for 1998–99 will total $26,225, an increase of 5.7 percent over the current year, which is four times the 1.4 percent rise in the Consumer Price Index this past year.

"Apart from 'Catholic character,' the most persistent problem here is the transformation of Notre Dame into a school that can be attended by non-wealthy students only at the price of a debt burden that will paralyze their career and family options. As the University was preparing its tuition notice, The Observer offered a striking glimpse of the mindset that underlies that transformation.

"The Observer reported on the March 18th Faculty Senate meeting that 'pressure to increase Notre Dame's ranking in *U.S. News and World Report* . . . has captured the attention of the University's faculty. [The] senate meeting . . . focused on measures to bring Notre Dame, currently ranked 19th, into the top 10,' with emphasis on improving 'reputation, faculty and financial resources.'. . .

"The Academic Affairs Committee estimated that nearly $200 million would be needed . . . [The senate chairman] also said money is what will get the University into the Top 10. . . . Notre Dame's urgency to make the top 10 also involves . . . faculty space expansion. . . . 'Arts and Letters needs a building bigger than Flanner to meet its needs,' said [the Academic Affairs Committee chairman]. The committee also proposed . . . a new science faculty building. . . . 'At 60 million dollars, this would be the most ambitious building process ever undertaken by the University,' said the committee chair' (aka chairman). . . .

"The U.S. News ranking, of course, is not a reliable measure of a university's performance at any level. . . . The Faculty Senate . . . seeks to have the University perceived as better by an entity that ranks universities in order to sell magazines. More significantly, every item in the Senate proposal would benefit the faculty. Smaller class size would benefit students, but the proposal is to do it by hiring more faculty.

"An alternative would be for the present faculty to teach more and research less, but don't hold your breath waiting for that idea to take the faculty by storm.

"Between 1985/86 and 1996/97, the student body increased by 6.8 percent, with undergrads increasing by only 4.1 percent, while instructional faculty increased by 16.7 percent. Which brings up an old motion I have from my 'jury duty' as a Faculty Senator a decade ago. It would have requested the Provost to publish each year a position-by-position disclosure, without identifying faculty, of teaching loads including classroom teaching hours and numbers of students. It would be interesting to know how much teaching the faculty actually does.

"The student-cost problem was raised in the meeting of the Student Senate on the same night as the Faculty Senate meeting. A resolution 'challenged the University's priorities in spending, pointing out the continuous construction and renovation of buildings, despite Notre Dame's inability to provide total financial aid to students in need.' The proposal suggested a moratorium on building projects until 'every student with demonstrated needs has their needs met.'

"The motion was not the most elegantly crafted in parliamentary history, but at least it addressed the problem from the standpoint of those who pay the bills. Perhaps the Faculty Senate should adopt the minutes of the Student Senate instead of spending time on proposals which would involve major expense and which would, incidentally, primarily benefit the faculty.

"These remarks are not intended to disparage the Faculty Senate. As individuals, the 53 senators are dedicated professionals with the interests of the University and its students at heart. But congregate them in a pack, give one of them a gavel and a shop-steward mentality takes over. There may be empirical support here for the proposition that 52 plus one *can* equal zero. However, the Faculty Senate's other-directedness in pursuing the approval of *U.S. News* merely follows the mindset of the Administration in its pursuit of the approval of the secular academic establishment. . . .

"In the process, the interests of students are subordinate to those of prestige-hungry administrators, the research professoriate and the bureaucracy. The Faculty Senate merely illustrates the empire-building attitude that has placed the University beyond the reach of middle-class students.

"It is fair to ask whether the administration is already beyond the point of no return in its subordination of students' interests to the worship of the money god and research prestige."

NOTRE DAME, HOMOSEXUALS AND SCANDAL, April 21, 1998

"If you want a sure bet, don't waste your money on the Chicago Cubs. Put it on the proposition that every semester, the homosexual issue will boil over at Notre Dame. . . .

"The University denies recognition to GLND/SMC because, in the words of Vice President Patty O'Hara, that group's 'value-neutral approach' and its approval of 'stable, monogamous [homosexual] relationships' are not 'consistent with official Church teaching.'

"The *Catechism of the Catholic Church* states that 'homosexual acts are intrinsically disordered.' 'They are contrary to the natural law. They close the sexual act to the gift of life.' No. 2357. But it also affirms that the inclination to those acts is itself disordered: 'The number of men and women who have deep-seated homosexual tendencies is not negligible. This inclination, which is objectively disordered, constitutes for most of them a trial. They must be accepted with respect, compassion and sensitivity. Every sign of unjust discrimination in their regard should be avoided.' No. 2358.

"The 1986 *Letter to Bishops on the Pastoral Care of Homosexual Persons*, issued with the Pope's approval, said: 'Although the particular inclination of the homosexual person is not a sin, it is more or less a strong tendency ordered toward an intrinsic moral evil and thus the inclination itself must be seen as an objective disorder.'

"Why is this point important? The administration's position that homosexual acts are merely contrary to 'official Church teaching' conveys the impression that the wrongness of such acts is not objectively rooted in nature, but rather that their prohibition is an arbitrary imposition by Church authorities. This is compounded by the administration's effective denial that the inclination to those acts is 'objectively disordered' and especially by its efforts to discourage students even from hearing the contrary view.

"This year, the Maritain Center presented lectures to discuss the evidence that the homosexual inclination is a disorder, that it is not innate and that a change in that inclination can be achieved in some cases. The lecturers included Dr. Joseph Nicolosi, Dr. Jeffrey Satinover, Fr. Benedict Ashley, O.P., Fr. John Harvey, the founder of Courage, and others. Campus Ministry had a full-page *Observer* ad to discourage attendance at the presentations. The Counseling Center placed an *Observer* ad to affirm its position that 'homosexuality is not a mental disorder' and that '[g]iven the fact that there is no scientifically confirmed evidence that a person's sexual orientation is changeable through psychotherapy, we do not provide "conversion therapy," "reparative therapy" or any other similar reported treatment.'

"The Maritain Center speakers, who would not be at a disadvantage in a comparison of professional credentials with anyone on this campus, offered a contrary view. 'Homosexuality,' said Dr. Nicolosi, 'is a gender-related identity disorder. Gay, on the other hand, is a social political identity.' Dr. Nicolosi, who is director of The National Association of Research and Therapy of Homosexuality, said: 'Students at Notre Dame might be interested in learning more about homosexuality from a perspective they won't hear from their university professors. . . . You may be surprised . . . at what you learn. That . . . no "gay gene" has been found . . . and that many studies show that change is possible.' As Dr. Satinover said: 'Homosexuality is not genetic and not innate. It occurs over a number of years in a certain environment.'. . .

"Notre Dame's 'autonomy' is qualified by its acquiescence in the politically correct standards of the secular educational establishment. It would be very politically incorrect for the Administration to agree with the Church that the inclination to homosexual acts is 'objectively disordered.' Although the administration denies formal recognition to GLND/SMC, its denial that the inclination is disordered cedes to the homosexual movement the decisive point, and . . . plays into the hands of the secular establishment by implicitly conceding that Church teaching here, and presumably elsewhere, is an arbitrary dictate.

"In the process, students, especially those of homosexual inclination who are genuinely searching for personal answers, are misled by the Administration into regarding the matter simplistically as involving their discovery of an innate, unchangeable orientation which entails subjection to an arbitrary Church prohibition on the expression of that orientation. The word for this is scandal.

"The University bears responsibility for the lives that are distorted by its withholding from students of the hopeful, constructive teaching of the Church in its entirety. As long as the current policy endures, the homosexual issue will erupt again and again. The administration ought to redirect its policy in this area."

1998–1999

Archbishop Chaput on *Humanae Vitae*, Sept. 4, 1998

"What event started the collapse of modern culture? That question was recently posed on a radio talk show. My favorite was the guy who claimed the 55 mph speed limit pushed us over the edge. No one mentioned the most likely candidate.

"What brings this to mind is the Pastoral Letter recently issued by Archbishop Charles Chaput of Denver. . . . His subject is *Humanae Vitae*, Pope Paul VI's 1968 encyclical on birth control. . . . 'Paul VI,' said Chaput, 'cautioned against four problems:

1) '[W]idespread use of contraception would lead to "conjugal infidelity and the . . . lowering of morality." . . . [T]he cultural revolution since 1968 . . . . would not have been possible . . . without easy access to reliable contraception . . . Paul VI was right.'
2) 'Through contraception, "man would lose respect for woman [and] would consider her as a mere instrument of enjoyment." . . . [C]ontraception might be marketed as liberating for women, but the real "beneficiaries" . . . . would be men. *Humanae Vitae* . . . rejected sexual exploitation of women *years before that message entered the cultural mainstream* . . . Paul VI was right.'
3) '[W]idespread use of contraception would place a dangerous weapon . . . in the hands of . . . public authorities . . . The massive export of contraceptives, abortion and sterilization by the developed world to developing countries . . . as a prerequisite for aid . . . in . . . contradiction to local moral traditions . . . is . . . population warfare and cultural re-engineering. . . . Paul VI was right.'
4) '[C]ontraception would mislead human beings into thinking they had unlimited dominion over their own bodies, . . . [a]t the heart of contraception . . . is the assumption that fertility is an infection which must be attacked. . . . In this attitude, one can also see the . . . link between contraception and abortion. If fertility can be misrepresented as an infection to be attacked, *so too can life. . . . Paul VI was right.*' . . . .

"'[I]f Paul VI was right about . . . the consequences [of]contraception, *it is because he was right about contraception itself.* [W]e need to begin by revisiting *Humanae Vitae* with open hearts.'

"'The Catholic attitude toward sexuality,' Chaput continued, 'is *anything* but puritanical. . . . [I]t's . . . a source of great humor for me to listen . . . as people simultaneously complain about the . . . "bottled-up sexuality" of Catholic moral doctrine, and the size of many good Catholic families. (From where . . . do they think the babies come?) Catholic married love always implies the possibility of new life; and because it does, it drives out loneliness and affirms the future. And . . . it becomes a furnace of hope in a world prone to despair. . . .

"'When spouses give themselves . . . to each other . . . *that must include their whole selves*—and the most intimate, powerful part of each person is his or her own fertility. Contraception . . . denies this fertility and attacks procreation. . . . [I]t damages unity as well. It is . . . spouses saying: "I'll give you all I am—*except* my fertility; I'll accept all you are—*except* your fertility." This withholding of self . . . works to isolate and divide the spouses . . . often fatally for the marriage.'

"'[T]he Church is against *all* contraception. The notion of "artificial" . . . tends to confuse discussion by implying that the debate is about a mechanical intrusion into the body's organic system. The Church has no problem with science appropriately intervening to heal or enhance bodily health. Rather, . . . the covenant which husband and wife enter at marriage requires that *all* intercourse remain open to the transmission of new life. This is what becoming "one flesh" implies: complete self-giving, without reservation or exception, just as Christ withheld nothing of Himself from His bride, the Church, by dying for her on the cross.

"'Natural family planning (NFP) . . . is not contraception. *[I]t is . . . fertility awareness and appreciation.* . . . NFP does nothing to attack fertility, or block the procreative nature of intercourse. [W]hen, for good reasons, a husband and wife limit the intercourse to the wife's natural periods of infertility . . . they are simply observing a cycle which God . . . created in the woman. . . . The wife preserves herself from intrusive chemicals or devices. . . . The husband shares in the . . . responsibility for NFP. Both learn . . . self-mastery and . . . respect for each other. . . . [A]t the heart of Catholic ambivalence toward *Humanae Vitae* is . . . a question of faith: *Do we really believe in God's goodness?* The Church speaks for . . . Jesus Christ [and] shows married couples the path to enduring love and a culture of life. Thirty years of history record the consequences of choosing otherwise. . . .

"'[C]onscience . . . requires us to . . . understand Church teaching, and to . . . strive to conform our hearts to it. Disordered sexuality is the dominant addiction of American society . . . *But do not lose heart.* . . . No matter how often we fail, God will deliver us if we repent and ask for the grace to do His will. . . .

"'*[T]eaching the truth should always be done with patience and compassion.* . . . [T]he Church now must evangelize . . . adolescents and young adults raised in moral confusion, often unaware of their own moral heritage, who hunger for meaning, community, and love with real substance. . . . [T]he good news is that the Church today, as in every age, has the answers to fill the God-shaped empty places in their heart.'"

THE IMPEACHMENT PROCESS, Sept. 18, 1998

"The bumper sticker says: 'Impeach Clinton Now. Call 1-800-LEAVEDC.' The issue is a little more complicated than that. It may be helpful here to note a few points on the impeachment process.

Background
"The Constitution provides that the President and other civil officers 'shall be removed from Office on Impeachment for, and Conviction of, Treason, Bribery, or other high Crimes and Misdemeanors.' Art. II, Sec. 4. Conviction on impeachment requires concurrence of two thirds of the Senators present. On impeachment of the President, the Chief Justice presides at the trial. Judgment on impeachment can extend only to removal from office and dis-qualification to hold any office under the United States, but the person con-victed on impeachment remains 'subject to Indictment, Trial, Judgment and Punishment, according to Law.' The President's pardoning power does not extend to 'cases of impeachment.' Art, I, Sec. 3; Art. II, Sec. 2.

"While more than fifty impeachment proceedings have been initiated by the House, fourteen have resulted in a trial in the Senate; eleven of those were against judges.. . . . President Andrew Johnson was impeached in 1868 and was acquitted in the Senate by one vote. It is unlikely that members of Congress are subject to impeachment since both houses of Congress are sep-arately authorized, with the concurrence of two thirds, to expel a member. Art. I, Sec. 5. In 1797 the Senate dismissed impeachment charges against Senator William Blount on the grounds that a Senator is not impeachable.

Do you have to commit a crime to be impeached?
"Evidently not. Former President Gerald R. Ford said, as a Congressman, that 'an impeachable offense is whatever a majority of the House of Representatives considers it to be . . . conviction results from whatever offense . . . two-thirds of the other body considers to be sufficiently serious to require removal of the accused from office. . . . [T]here are few fixed principles among the handful of precedents.' Seven persons, all federal judges, have been impeached, convicted by the Senate and removed from office: John Pickering, drunkenness and senility, 1803–1804; West Humphreys, incitement to rebel-lion, 1862; Robert Archibald, bribery, 1912–13; Halsted Ritter, kickbacks and

tax evasion, 1936; Harry Claiborne, tax evasion, 1986; Alcee Hastings, conspiracy to solicit a bribe, 1988–89; Walter Nixon, false statements to a grand jury, 1989.

"Neither Judge Pickering's senility, nor his intoxication on the bench, was criminal. Judge Hastings was impeached for an offense on which he had earlier been acquitted by a jury in a criminal trial. Judge Nixon was impeached and convicted on two charges of testifying falsely. He was impeached, but not convicted, on a third, non-criminal, charge of bringing disrepute on the Federal judiciary.

"President Andrew Johnson was impeached on a charge, not voted on in the Senate, that he had on various occasions delivered, 'with a loud voice, certain intemperate, inflammatory, and scandalous harangues and loud threats and bitter menaces, as well as against Congress as the laws of the United States . . . amid the cries, jeers and laughter of the multitudes then assembled.' If this were now the standard, many of our political class would be in danger today. Professor Raoul Berger, in his classic 1973 work, *Impeachment*, describes the impeachment and trial of Johnson as an 'abuse . . . an attempt to punish the President for differing with . . . the policy of Congress.' (p. 295).

"The first article of impeachment against President Nixon charged him with the apparently non-criminal offense that he lied to the public by making 'false . . . public statements for the purpose of deceiving the people of the United States into believing that a thorough . . . investigation had been conducted' on Watergate. . . .

"*Impeachment as an inducement to resignation.* President Nixon, several judges and Secretary of War William Belknap (1876) resigned under impeachment, or the threat thereof, rather than face a Senate trial.

"*Judicial review.* In the impeachment of Judge Walter Nixon, the Senate appointed a committee of Senators to hear the evidence and report to the full Senate. The Supreme Court, in 1993, refused to hear Judge Nixon's appeal from his 1989 conviction in the Senate. The Court said that 'judicial review of the procedures used by the Senate in trying impeachments would expose the political life of the country to months, or perhaps years, of chaos. . . . This lack of finality would manifest itself most dramatically if the President were impeached. . . .

"The result in Judge Nixon's case indicates that if a President, rather than a judge, were convicted by a Senate on impeachment, the Supreme Court would be likely to decline to review any challenge, whether procedural or otherwise, to that conviction.

"In sum, the issue is not as simple as the bumper sticker makes it out to be. But maybe President Ford was right. Maybe an impeachable offense is whatever the House says it is. Unfortunately, we may be about to find out."

WHY HONOR SENATOR BRADLEY? Oct. 2, 1998

"The appointment of former Senator Bill Bradley as a visiting professor of public affairs is objectionable on grounds that reflect primarily on our Notre Dame leaders rather than on Sen. Bradley. . . . This is not a criticism of Sen. Bradley. He is what he is: a pro-legalized abortion politician and a prospective presidential candidate. Notre Dame ought not to provide a potential launching pad for any politician, especially one whose record persistently favors legalization of the murder of the unborn.

"In his Senate career, 1979–97, Sen. Bradley had a virtually unbroken pro-legalized abortion record. He even voted, on March 19, 1996, against a prohibition of governmental discrimination against medical schools that refuse to train students in performing abortions. This was not training in how to remedy damage done by botched abortions. Rather, the issue arose from complaints by the abortion industry that schools were turning out too few abortionists to keep up with demand. Sen. Bradley thus voted to open the door to compulsion of hospitals to train abortionists. He also voted against prohibiting partial-birth abortion (PBA) and voted, on Sept. 26, 1996, to uphold President Clinton's veto of that prohibition.

"Sen. Bradley was not invited to lecture on a specialized subject such as tax or trade. Rather, he was invited as 'one of our foremost national leaders,' as an exemplar of what a legislator and public figure should be. In announcing Sen. Bradley's appointment, Notre Dame mentioned his 'role in the areas of tax reform, international trade, pension reform, community building and improving race relations.' But the announcement said not one word about his relentless support of legalized abortion. The appointment tells the students that it is acceptable for a 'foremost national leader' to support the legalized execution of the innocent. Not only is that support not a disqualification for leadership, it is, in the eyes of our University leaders, so irrelevant as not even to deserve mention in the detailed description of the Bradley record. The appointment implies that one can be a 'community' builder although he supports the legalization of the murder of the most defenseless members of the community.

"In response to criticism of the appointment, our leaders have sought to cover their action by professing their opposition to abortion, stressing the need for openness, etc. The death toll from legalized abortion since 1973 is at least 37 million, not counting the larger and indeterminate number killed by pills and other abortifacients. Yet our leaders evidently regard this slaughter as not a big enough deal even to deserve mention—until complaints from alumni and others begin.

"Alumnus Joseph M. Scheidler objected to the Bradley appointment on the ground that, 'in a society steeped in a "Culture of Death," as Pope John

Paul II has called the 20th century, we cannot afford to overlook a public figure's position on the moral issues.'. . . . Some have criticized Mr. Scheidler for opposing the Bradley appointment. However, in a Notre Dame true to its mission, Joe Scheidler would be, not a target of recrimination, but a candidate for the Laetare Medal. That might make up for the bestowal of that medal on pro-abortion Sen. Daniel Patrick Moynihan in 1992. . . .

"Unfortunately, the de facto religion of this university is the pursuit of politically correct prestige, which is perhaps fueled in part by the old Catholic inferiority complex. One may fairly doubt that our striving-for-respectability leaders would have invited Sen. Bradley if he had played basketball for UNLV instead of Princeton."

VERITATIS SPLENDOR AND MONICAGATE, Oct. 16, 1998

"'So many lawyers, so little truth.' This heading of a column by Mark Levin, of Landmark Legal Foundation, sums up the 'spinning' of truth by lawyers defending the certified liar in the White House. The first casualty of Monicagate is the very idea that truth and morality are objective. If the polls are right, the American people have bought the idea that a lie is not wrong if it is 'only about sex,' adultery is all right if the adulterer's spouse tolerates it and the character of a liar, even if he is President, does not matter as long as he is 'doing his job,' etc.. . . .

"We can expect a moral rebound from the Clinton scandals. But that recovery will last no longer than the one after Watergate unless it is based on sound principles. We can find those principles in Pope John Paul's 1993 encyclical, *Veritatis Splendor*, the *Splendor of Truth*. 'That encyclical,' said University of California Prof. James Q. Wilson, 'is not a list of specific moral rules. It is about the universal law of nature that is discoverable by human reason; it exists in all people regardless of culture, and leads us inevitably to judge actions as right or wrong—whatever their intentions and whether or not they help or harm others.'

"'In the political sphere,' the Pope said, in words that belong in the Congressional Record, 'truthfulness . . . between those governing and those governed, openness in public administration, impartiality [and] the rejection of equivocal or illicit means . . . all these are principles . . . rooted in . . . the transcendental value of the person and the objective moral demands of the functioning of States. When these principles are not observed, the very basis of political coexistence is weakened and the life of society itself is gradually jeopardized . . . and doomed to decay.' No. 101.

"As John Paul put it: '[T]here can be no freedom apart from or in

142

opposition to the truth. . . . [O]nly by obedience to universal moral norms does man find full confirmation of his personal uniqueness and the possibility of authentic moral growth. . . . These norms . . . represent the . . . foundation . . . of genuine democracy.' No. 96.. . . .

"We have to recover the conviction that '[t]he *negative precepts* of the natural law . . . oblige . . . always and in every circumstance . . . without exception, because the choice of this kind of behavior is in no case compatible with the goodness of the will of the acting person, with his vocation to life with God and in communion with his neighbor. It is prohibited—to everyone and in every case—to violate these precepts. They oblige everyone, . . . never to offend in anyone, beginning with oneself, the personal dignity common to all. . . . [O]ne may never choose kinds of behavior prohibited by the moral commandments expressed in the Old and New Testaments.' No. 52.

"These principles apply not only to sex but to business and social justice: 'The seventh commandment prohibits actions or enterprises which for any reason . . . lead to the *enslavement of human beings*, disregard for their personal dignity, buying or selling or exchanging them like merchandise. Reducing persons . . . to use-value or a source of profit is a sin against their dignity as persons and their fundamental rights.' No. 100.

"'[I]f there is no ultimate truth to guide and direct political activity,' John Paul tells us, 'ideas and convictions can easily be manipulated for reasons of power.' No. 101. 'Totalitarianism arises out of a denial of truth in the objective sense. If there is no transcendental truth, in obedience to which man achieves his full identity, then there is no sure principle for guaranteeing just relations between people. Their self-interest as a class, group or nation would inevitably set them in opposition to one another. . . . [T]he force of power takes over, and each person tends to make full use of the means at his disposal . . . to impose his own interests . . . with no regard for the rights of others.' No. 99. . . .

"The moral norm, however, is not a set of abstract principles. It is a Person. '*[I]n the Crucified Christ . . . the Church finds the answer* to the question troubling so many people today: how can obedience to universal and unchanging moral norms respect the uniqueness . . . of the person, and not represent a threat to his freedom and dignity? . . . The Crucified Christ reveals the authentic meaning of freedom: he lives it fully in the total gift of himself* and calls his disciples to share in his freedom.' No. 85.

"We suffer from '[d]echristianization, which weighs heavily upon entire peoples and communities once rich in faith and Christian life. [It] involves not only the loss of faith or . . . its becoming irrelevant for everyday life, but also . . . *a decline . . . of the moral sense*." No. 106. 'Pilate's question: 'What is truth?"' said John Paul, 'reflects the distressing perplexity of a man who often no longer knows who he is, whence he comes and where he is going.' No. 84.

"'I have been a Protestant minister for nearly half a century,' said Rev.

Harvey Chinn of Sacramento, 'but . . . I am a better Protestant for having studied this magnificent Catholic document. *Splendor of Truth,*' Chinn said, 'is a witness that above and beyond our pretenses and intellectual sophistication there shines a moral north star that never changes. . . . The world needs to learn from this wise man, who speaks with clarity, understanding, compassion and authority.'

"If you want to keep your head on straight in the Clinton era, read *Veritatis Splendor.* Send a copy to Bill and Hillary Clinton and pray for them—and for your country."

HATE CRIMES AND MATTHEW SHEPARD, Oct. 30, 1998

"Although the accused murderers of Matthew Shepard in Laramie had a robbery motive, his homosexuality was a contributing factor. . . . *[T]he Shepard case is an example of depersonalization.* When Matthew Shepard was targeted with violence because he was a homosexual, he was treated as a nonperson. However, the law is an educator in its decree that the most innocent human beings are nonpersons subject even to death at the discretion of others. As Mother Teresa said at the 1994 National Prayer Breakfast, 'If we accept that a mother can kill even her own child, how can we tell other people not to kill one another?' In a 'culture of death' innocent life is cheap and murder, whether legal or illegal, becomes a casual means for the venting of hostility or the satisfaction of utilitarian ends. . . .

"*[T]he abhorrent character of the Shepard murder is no excuse for the death penalty.* That penalty is not an absolute necessity in this case because it is not 'the only possible way of defending human lives against the unjust aggressor.' This is so because 'nonlethal means,' such as life without parole, 'are sufficient to . . . protect people's safety from the aggressor . . . without definitively taking away from him the possibility of redeeming himself.' *Catechism,* no. 2267. God put a mark on Cain, not to make him a target for vengeance but to protect his life. 'God did not desire that an act of homicide be punished by . . . another act of homicide.' *Evangelium Vitae,* no. 9. . . .

"*[T]he Shepard murder does not justify the expansion of 'hate-crime' laws.* 'We should not use Matt to further an agenda,' his father told the Wyoming Governor. 'Don't rush into just passing all kinds of hate-crime laws. Be very careful of any changes and be sure you're not taking away rights of others in the process to race to this.'

"In 41 states, hate-crime laws provide increased penalties for crimes motivated by such factors as race, religion or ethnicity. 11 states explicitly include sexual orientation. Those laws have no direct impact on crimes already subject

144

to the maximum possible penalty, such as the Shepard murder or the racial murder in Texas last June of James Byrd, Jr., who was torn apart when he was dragged behind a pickup truck.

"The Supreme Court has upheld hate-crime laws. As the Court said, 'motive plays the same role' in such laws 'as it does under federal and state antidiscrimination laws.' And judges, especially in state courts, have latitude to consider motive in sentencing. On the other hand, those laws can chill speech because of the fear that politically incorrect statements might be evidence of 'hateful' motivation if one is later accused of any crime that is covered by the statute. In a *New York Times* column, Frank Rich came close to blaming the Family Research Council for Matthew Shepard's murder. Why? Because the FRC advanced the biblical position that the homosexual inclination, while not sinful, is a disorder. And the FRC had the nerve to present the evidence that some homosexuals can transcend the orientation. Rich accused the FRC of 'stirring up the fear that produces hate,' with the result that 'emboldened thugs take over.' If you care about freedom of speech, that ought to bother you.

"The hate-crime concept is dubious. Is not every deliberate crime of violence a 'hate-crime'? If we focus so intently on a discriminatory motive, do we not run the risk of minimizing the seriousness of the underlying crime? 'What if it could be demonstrated,' wrote columnist Stephen Chapman, 'that Mr. Shepard's killers hadn't known he was gay? Would that make what they did to him any more excusable?'. . . .

"[But] should the law impose enhanced penalties for crimes purposefully committed against anyone with an inclination to a morally disordered act, e.g., excessive drinking, shoplifting, etc.? Or only with respect to disorders favored by the agenda of political correctness? The rush to expand hate-crime laws has more to do with enforcing politically correct ideas than with achieving justice. . . .

"Gay activists will use the Shepard murder to argue ultimately in favor of requiring even private persons to validate homosexual activity as a legitimate alternative lifestyle. . . .

"The Shepard murder should not be used to legitimize activity contrary to nature and the divine law. Instead, that murder calls us to reaffirm the dignity of every person and the inviolability of every innocent human life."

A STUDENT-CENTERED RESEARCH UNIVERSITY? Nov. 13, 1998

"Is a 'student-centered research university' an 'oxymoron'? That question was asked in a Report . . . issued last April by the Carnegie Foundation for the Advancement of Teaching. The Report analyzed undergrad education in the nation's 125 research universities. . . .

"The Report said universities can be 'both student-centered and research-centered . . . through a synergistic system in which faculty and students are learners and researchers, whose interactions make for a . . . flourishing intellectual atmosphere.'

"The Report's positive proposals for integration of the undergrad and research functions merit serious consideration. Research is not of itself teaching, although in some areas, especially in some sciences, the research role does facilitate the improvement of undergrad education at Notre Dame and elsewhere. In general, however, as described in the Report, the emphasis on research has shortchanged undergrads, especially in the liberal arts. The Notre Dame experience may be instructive.

"Two decades ago, Notre Dame embarked on its pursuit of recognition as a Great Research University. The historic mission of Notre Dame had emphasized the education of undergrads in the Catholic intellectual and moral tradition, with research and graduate education playing important complementary roles. Part of that mission was to maintain Notre Dame's accessibility to non-wealthy students. One impact of the pursuit of Research Greatness is the doubling since 1978, in real money adjusted for inflation, of undergrad tuition, room and board. Another is the transformation of the formerly pastoral Notre Dame into a crowded, urban-style research campus that prompted one former professor to say on his return, 'It looks like Michigan State.' And courses tend to be less accessible.

"Are Notre Dame undergrads receiving double the value they received two decades ago? The Carnegie Report's general criticisms of undergrad education in research universities can be helpful to the Notre Dame community as a guide for an institutional examination of conscience.

"'Research Universities,' said the report, 'have too often failed, and continue to fail, their undergraduate populations. Tuition . . . from undergraduates is one of the major sources of university income . . . but the students . . . get, in all too many cases, less than their money's worth. An undergraduate at an American research university can receive an education as good or better than anything . . . in the world, but that is not the normative experience. . . . [U]niversities are guilty of an advertising practice they would condemn in the commercial world. Recruitment materials display . . . world-famous professors, the splendid facilities, and the . . . research that goes on within them, but thousands of students graduate without ever seeing [those] professors or tasting genuine research. Some of their instructors are likely to be . . . untrained teaching assistants . . . ; some others may be tenured drones who deliver set lectures from yellowed notes, making no effort to engage the bored minds of the students in front of them. . . . The standing of a university is measured by the research productivity of its faculty; the place of a department . . . is determined by whether its members garner more or fewer research dollars and publish more or less noteworthy research . . . ; the individual within that department is judged by the scholarship produced.

"'[I]t is in research grants, books, articles, papers, and citations that every university defines its true worth. When students are considered, it is the graduate students that really matter; they are essential as research assistants on faculty projects, and their placement as post-doctoral fellows and new faculty reinforces the standing of the faculty that has trained them. . . . The use of graduate students . . . has been treated as a necessity for . . . both research programs and undergraduate instruction. This . . . has often led to the importation of foreign students new to American education. The international graduate students . . . must be welcomed; they have added strengths to research programs and, after graduation, to university faculties and research institutes. But the classroom results of employing teaching assistants who speak English poorly, and who are new to the American system of education constitute one of the conspicuous problems of undergraduate education. . . . [T]he undergraduate . . . may have little or no direct contact with established scholar-teachers. Instruction very often comes through . . . the graduate student: the academic luminary featured in admissions bulletins appears rarely if at all in undergraduate classes, and then too often as the lecturer addressing hundreds of students.

"'They might claim otherwise, but research universities consider 'success' and 'research productivity' to be . . . synonymous terms. The typical department will assert that it does place a high value on effective teaching. . . . At the same time, . . . tenure and promotion are likely to focus almost entirely on research or creative productivity. . . . The reward structures . . . need to reflect the synergy of teaching and research—and the essential reality of university life: That baccalaureate students are the university's life blood and are increasingly self-aware. . . . [I]n the education of undergraduates the record of America's research universities has been one of inadequacy, even failure. . . . Baccalaureate students are the second-class citizens who are allowed to pay taxes but are barred from voting, the guests at the banquet who pay their share of the tab but are given leftovers. Captivated by the excitement and the rewards of the research mission, research universities have not seriously attempted to think through what that mission might mean for undergraduates.'

"The Report is optimistic. It concludes that 'the most important obligation confronting research universities is to define in more creative ways what it means to be a research university committed to teaching undergraduates.' A more basic question which ought to be considered at this university, is whether the drive to become a Great Research University is not inherently destructive of the undergrad education which was the focus of the historic mission of Notre Dame.. . . . The Report should prompt a constructive assessment of what our leaders, in their well-intentioned pursuit of Research Prestige and money, have done to the character of Notre Dame and what, if anything, can now be done about it."

THE NON-DISCRIMINATION CLAUSE, Dec. 4, 1998

"It is a daunting task to voice reservations about a proposal endorsed by such arbiters of culture as Phil Donahue and the *South Bend Tribune*. But it may be useful here to note some reasons that militate against the addition of sexual orientation to the University's nondiscrimination clause.

"In his 1997 statement explaining the University's position, President Edward A. Malloy, C.S.C., said, 'The phrase 'sexual orientation' sometimes . . . does not admit a distinction between sexual orientation and the manner in which people live out their sexual orientation—a distinction that is critical to us as a Catholic institution. . . . Institutional non-discrimination clauses are . . . legally binding. . . . To make the change . . . would mean that our decisions . . . would be measured by civil courts that may interpret this change through the lens of the broader societal milieu. . . . This . . . might jeopardize our ability to make decisions that we believe necessary to support Church teaching. . . . We choose not to change our legal non-discrimination clause, but we call ourselves to act in accordance with . . . a higher standard—Christ's call to inclusiveness, coupled with the gospel's call to live chaste lives. In some senses both of these messages are counter-cultural. It is this dual call that is so deeply rooted in our religious tradition to which we commit ourselves.'

"The legal issues possibly involved are not clearly defined. The proposal would invite . . . litigation, especially in light of the reality that homosexual activists tend to seek the validation of homosexual practice as a . . . lifestyle entitled to treatment as the legal and social equivalent of marriage.

"The proposal, for example, would probably require Notre Dame to treat the acknowledged homosexual orientation of an applicant as irrelevant in filling Resident Assistant and Assistant Rector positions in the residence halls. It would be very difficult to maintain the distinction between orientation and practice under the proposal. It may fairly be doubted that the University could legally deny any position to a person who concededly engages in homosexual practice, if the objection were made that the practice is an outcome of the orientation and therefore that the supposed denial on the grounds of practice is really a denial on the grounds of orientation. Similarly, it is not clear that the University could legally deny use of the Basilica or other chapels for a 'commitment ceremony' between two homosexuals. One might ask, So what? Why should the University discriminate on sexual orientation with respect to such matters? Let's go back to the basics.

"The *Catechism of the Catholic Church* states that 'homosexual acts are intrinsically disordered. They are contrary to the natural law. They close the sexual act to the gift of life.' No. 2357. But it also affirms, in its final text, that the inclination to those acts is itself disordered: 'The number of men and women who have deep-seated homosexual tendencies is not negligible. This inclination, which is objectively disordered, constitutes for most of them a trial. They must be accepted with respect, compassion and sensitivity. Every sign of unjust discrimination in their regard should be avoided.' No. 2358. (emphasis added)

"In 1992, the Congregation for the Doctrine of the Faith sent a letter to the bishops of the United States. It was a 'background resource' rather than 'an official and public instruction.' The letter, *Responding to Legislative Proposals on Discrimination against Homosexuals*, said: 'Sexual orientation' does not constitute a quality comparable to race, ethnic background, etc., in respect to non-discrimination. Unlike these, homosexual orientation is an objective disorder . . . ' '[I]t is not unjust discrimination to take sexual orientation into account, for example, in the placement of children for adoption or foster care, in employment of teachers or athletic coaches and in military recruitment.'

"The University has a right and an obligation to take into account, in appointing to sensitive positions, an applicant's acknowledged inclination toward morally disordered acts. The proposed amendment would require the University to foreswear that right and default on that obligation. It could hardly be argued that the University, in choosing Resident Assistants, Assistant Rectors, and other appointees, should not take into account an applicant's acknowledged inclination to other morally disordered acts such as thievery, excessive drinking, etc. Why should the inclination to homosexual acts be accorded privileged treatment? Moreover, for the University to accept such a limitation would convey to students the message that the homosexual inclination is not disordered and that homosexual acts are themselves not intrinsically disordered but rather are prohibited only by an arbitrary edict of an insensitive Church.

"The University, in denying recognition to GLND/SMC (now called OUTreachND), stated that homosexual acts are clearly contrary to 'official Church teaching.' But the University refuses to acknowledge that the inclination toward those acts is itself disordered. If, as the Catechism states, the acts are 'objectively disordered,' how could the inclination to those acts be anything but disordered? And if, as the Administration maintains, the inclination is not disordered, why may it not be acted upon? No wonder that students and others resent the Administration position as arbitrary and incoherent. If 'sexual orientation' were added to the clause, it would be likely to prevent Notre Dame from ever changing its position so as to affirm, in accord with the teaching of the Church, that the homosexual inclination is itself disordered. . . .

149

"The reasons advanced by Fr. Malloy for adopting the Spirit of Inclusion rather than accepting the legally binding proposal were valid when he stated them. And they are no less valid today."

WILLIAM BENTLEY BALL, Jan. 29, 1999

"Let me tell you about a great, but underappreciated, Notre Dame man. William Bentley Ball, who died on Jan. 10 at age 82, would be accurately described as the premier constitutional litigator of this century in matters of church and state. But he was more.

"A graduate of Western Reserve University, Bill Ball served in combat in the Navy in World War II and retired as a Lt. Commander in the Naval Reserve. He earned his law degree in 1948 from Notre Dame Law School where he was editor-in-chief of the *Law Review*. He practiced corporate law in New York until 1955, when he decided to devote his career to constitutional issues. He then joined the faculty of the new Villanova University School of Law as professor of constitutional law. In 1960, at the invitation of Philadelphia's Archbishop (later Cardinal) John O'Hara, a former president of Notre Dame, Mr. Ball became General Counsel to the Pennsylvania Catholic Conference. In 1968 he formed his own firm in Harrisburg to litigate in defense of religious freedom.

"Mr. Ball's major litigation achievements were in two related areas. First, he successfully fought for the principle that persons ought not to be excluded, on account of their religion, from public benefits generally available to others. . . .

"Mr. Ball's second area of litigation success was in his defense, in many cases, of often impoverished Evangelicals and other 'little guys' against oppressive state regulations of their schools and families. . . .

"Mr. Ball was especially effective in curbing the aggressions of public education bureaucrats. In *Wisconsin v. Yoder*, in 1972, Ball successfully defended Old Order Amish families against a decree of state bureaucrats that the Amish children must attend high school. The Amish educate their children at home after eighth grade. Ball showed that the products of Amish education had a crime-free and welfare-free record. He proved that to require the Amish children to attend high school would destroy the Amish culture and force that Amish community to leave Wisconsin. The case was as basic as it gets, involving the purpose of education, of the family and of life itself.

"'Sometimes,' said Ball, 'there is intense drama in something very quiet, like a witness' silence in the face of a critically important question. Such a moment came in the *Yoder* trial when a question from [the state's] lawyer drew silence from [Prof. Hostetler, the Amish parents' expert witness], who then, after perhaps half a minute, gave an answer which touched the very heart of the case:

"'Q. The principal purpose to attend high school is to get education, is it not?

"'A. Yes, but I think there is a great deal of difference what education means—education for what?

"'Q. To put it bluntly, education so that the child can make his or her place in the world. [Long pause].

"'A. It depends which world.'

"As defender of 'the little guy,' Ball stood up for the littlest victims, the unborn children whom the Supreme Court defined as nonpersons subject to execution by abortion. 'The consequences of that principle,' he said, 'are staggering . . . if the right to innocent human life is at risk, all lesser rights are at risk. The Rule of Law becomes the Rule of Utility, and we—like all materialist civilizations before us—abandon the glory of our tradition and move into the dark night of barbarism.' Bill Ball was devoted to Notre Dame—Our Lady as well as the University. But he saw the identity crisis that the leaders of major Catholic universities have brought on themselves.

"'Presidents of . . . prominent Catholic colleges and universities,' he wrote, 'had come to a consensus that their institutions' . . . Catholicity tainted them with mediocrity. The presidents, at a 1967 conference at Land O'Lakes, Wisconsin, concluded that Catholic higher education must divorce itself from episcopal authority. The Fordham study, in the late 1960s, . . . supported by the presidents, urged that the colleges take overt steps to rid themselves of vital aspects of their religious character. The motivation was [that] the presidents' keen desire to belong might be fulfilled: They could now be acceptable to the secular academic community and government grant administrators. Their catalogues, buzzing the words 'excellence' and 'relevance,' would show just enough of a Catholic face to attract youngsters of Catholic families, but present a message to all others that they were, in fact, progressively secular.'

"'One sees' in these institutions, Ball said, 'a propensity to cry to the world: "We are of the mainstream—believe that of us!" The Catholic "look" [starts] diminishing when one is mainstreaming it with the people who "count"—the accrediting teams, the staffs of prestige institutions, the mediums of the media.'

"The Beltway-type promoters looked down on Bill Ball. He was politically incorrect and too, well, honest and direct. But, in character as well as in ability, he was a giant among pygmies. I acknowledge my own heavy personal indebtedness to him, as an exemplar and a counselor of wisdom and grace. In a sane society, Bill Ball would have been on the Supreme Court. . . .

"The second accolade Bill Ball should have received is an honorary degree from Notre Dame, as frequently requested by Notre Dame faculty members. Kings College, an institution of the Congregation of Holy Cross, had the sense to recognize Mr. Ball with a degree on the ground that 'You provide a sterling example for our graduates . . . and for all of us, showing that it is possible to be at one and the same time a committed Christian and a distinguished professional of great integrity. In the fullest sense of the words, you are truly a Catholic lawyer.' The refusal of our leaders to recognize this great man is Notre Dame's loss. . . .

"'The death of the just,' said St. Alphonsus Ligouri, himself a lawyer, 'is a victory.' Bill Ball, a man of justice, courageously, spoke the Truth to Power. He was, in the ultimate sense, a Notre Dame lawyer. *Requiescat in pace*."

BENGAL BOUTS: A LINK TO ROCKNE, Feb. 15, 1999

"Why would 132 apparently normal young men return from Christmas break to commit themselves to thousands of pushups, sit-ups, etc., endless miles of running and the prospect of having their facial landscapes rearranged? Are they certifiable? Not really. Permit me to suggest that they may be the sanest guys in town.

"In the century's worst flood last year in Bangladesh, one of the poorest areas in the world, at least 353,000 homes were destroyed and at least 630 people lost their lives. The Holy Cross missionaries, including many Notre Dame and St. Mary's grads, responded to the needs of their people as they have for more than a century. They bring Christ and the Faith to those impoverished people by helping them in their need.

"Since 1931, the Bengal Bouts have been conducted by the student-run Boxing Club to raise money for the Holy Cross missions in Bangladesh. The Club now operates under the able guidance of Rich O'Leary, director of Club Sports. . . .

"This year, under the leadership of President Tommy Will and his fellow officers, Tom Biolchini, Brian Gaffney, Mike LaDuke, Mike Maguire, J.R. Mellin, Dave Murphy, and Mike Romanchek, the Club has set the goal of sending $50,000 to the missions. The boxers sell ads and tickets and they pay for their own personal equipment, sweatshirts, shorts, mouthpieces, etc., at prices above cost with the profit going to the missions. . . .

"In the Boxing Room you will meet people who typify what is best at Notre Dame. Tom Suddes, a Columbus developer, and Terry Johnson, a Chicago attorney, are the coaches, giving enormous amounts of their time and talent to work with the boxers. With them is Pat Farrell, the University pilot, who has a remarkable ability to bring boxers to a higher level. These coaches are all former Bengal Bouts Champions.

"The boxers are helped by extraordinary assistant coaches, including especially Sweet C. Robinson and recent champs Toby Biolchini, '96, Ryan Rans, '98 and Chip Farrell, '98. We even have the judiciary involved through Judge Roland Chamblee, '73, a four-time Bengals champ whom you will see helping in a corner between rounds.

"Perhaps the dominant feature of the program is its combination of purpose and friendship. As President Tommy Will put it, 'There are two great things about the Boxing Club. One is knowing that you are really helping people in need. The other is in the friends you make.' Brian Gaffney, a Club officer who will be trying to become only the ninth boxer to win four titles, is listed on the program as 'The Nutty Irishman.' Don't believe it. He has his priorities right: 'Four titles would be great. But I wouldn't have missed this if I had never won a fight. The guys are great. And the program, no kidding, does save lives.'

"It must be confessed, however, that the main cause of the amazing recent success of the Bengal Bouts is Emily Schmidt, a Howard Hall senior accounting major. Assisted by Meghan Kelley of Pasquerilla East, Emily has turned the administrative side of the Club from a successful but slightly chaotic operation into a smoothly functioning machine. Emily's efficiency has made the daily routine glitch-free in every respect. Why does she do it? 'Because I believe in what this is all about,' she said. 'And it's been fun. And these are great people working for a purpose beyond themselves.'

"Last year the boxers chose Jack Mooney, their 85-year-young trainer whose service to the Bouts extends over six decades, as the recipient of the Bengal Bouts Award, presented every year to someone who uniquely represents the meaning of the Bouts. One recollection by Jack epitomizes his own status and that of the Bengal Bouts as a vital link to the storied history of Notre Dame. 'When I was a newspaper boy,' Jack recalls, 'selling in front of the Station, I used to sell newspapers to Knute Rockne and his players as they returned from road games or went on the road. A newspaper cost three cents but Rockne gave me fifty cents each time. He was a beautiful man. Having gotten to know Rockne, I wanted to go to Notre Dame but I did not have the money. I had quit school in the ninth grade. Rockne knew about my affection for Notre Dame and used to ask me to come to the old Field House before home games. I sat outside the locker room while the players dressed. When the players ran from the locker room to Cartier Field, Rockne pushed me into the middle of the pack. In this way, I snuck into Cartier Field free of charge and watched the home games. . . . I worked on the side as an undertaker for a while and every time I went to Highland Cemetery where Rockne was buried, I put flowers by his grave. I put flowers by his grave every week to this day.'

"Jack later was an engineer for Studebaker and fought professionally, including bouts on the same card with Joe Louis and Tony Zale. Jack is more than a coach to the boxers. His example and his direct, friendly advice will be one of their most enduring memories from Notre Dame.

"The Boxing Club, in short, is about more than boxing. We even have our own Poet Laureate, Jack Zimmerman, our trainer, who has attracted capacity crowds to his readings in Barnes & Noble, Recker's and elsewhere.

"Ryan Rans, last year's captain who is now an assistant coach, was one of the foremost leaders in the history of the Boxing Club. He was prevented from defending his title last year when he suffered stress fractures in both hands in the semi-finals. The grace with which Ryan accepted this, and the concern exhibited by his fellow boxers, attest to the unique character of the program."

JOHN PAUL II ON THE DEATH PENALTY, March 5, 1999

"Darryl Mease, a triple murderer, had been scheduled for execution by the state of Missouri on Jan. 27, the day Pope John Paul II celebrated Mass in the Trans World Dome before 104,000 persons. Mease's execution was postponed because of the Pope's visit. After the Mass, the Pope walked over to Missouri Governor Mel Carnahan and said, 'Have mercy on Mr. Mease.' The Governor commuted Mease's sentence to life without parole. . . .

"The death penalty, legal in 38 states, is in trouble. One problem is numerical. 3,549 inmates were on death row in the United States at the start of 1999, including 17 condemned under federal law. About 300 more are sentenced to death every year. In 1998, 68 persons were executed. To eliminate the backlog would require the execution of one person every day for about 60 years.

"A perennial problem, of possibly executing the innocent, was brought to the fore by the release this February of Anthony Porter from Illinois' death row. Porter, who had come within two days of execution, was released when a Northwestern University journalism class investigated his case and obtained from another man a confession which exonerated Porter.

"A third problem is expense. The death penalty is at least three times more expensive than life imprisonment without parole. . . .

"The popularity of the death penalty reflects the cultural acceptance of the intentional infliction of death as a problem-solving technique. Capital punishment is one manifestation of the 'culture of death,' as are abortion and euthanasia. The victim in abortion and euthanasia, unlike the convicted criminal, is innocent. But in all three cases, the ending of the life of a human being is the result of an essentially utilitarian calculation. . . .

"In *Evangelium Vitae* (EV), John Paul affirmed that the State, which derives its authority from God, has the right to impose the death penalty. But he restricted the permissible use of that penalty to 'cases of absolute necessity . . . when it would not be possible otherwise to defend society.' This refers not to some generalized defense of society by imposing retribution or by deterring potential offenders. Rather it refers only to the protection of society *from this convicted criminal. . . .*

"A Catholic could still argue for the death penalty in exceptional cases, such as where a 'lifer' prisoner murders a guard. Should you give him another life sentence? Or would it be consistent with dignity to wall him up in a cell, with food and wastes passed through a slot and with no direct contact ever with any other human being? Other cases could be argued, such as a rebellion or other disturbance in which the authorities would lack the ability to keep a murderer securely imprisoned. Although the death penalty could be argued to be absolutely necessary in such cases, even there it is debatable. But the criterion is protection of society from this criminal.

"Before EV, I and others supported the death penalty as a necessary way to restore the balance of justice and to promote respect for innocent life by inflicting a punishment for murder which was qualitatively different from the punishment for other crimes. But the Vicar of Christ has made these arguments obsolete, raising the discussion to a new level. He authoritatively challenges the claim of the state to assume the jurisdiction of God over life and death. After discussing the death penalty, EV states, 'If such great care must be taken to respect every life, even that of criminals and unjust aggressors, the commandment, "You shall not kill" has absolute value when it refers to the *innocent person.*' No. 57. If we owe such respect to the life of the guilty, so much more, and absolutely so, with respect to the innocent. But this works the other way, too. If we would maintain the absolute inviolability of innocent life, we must begin by safeguarding even the life of the guilty from termination except according to the very restrictive law of God.

"'God did not make death, and he does not delight in the death of the living.' After Cain murdered Abel, God 'put a mark on Cain . . . not to condemn him to the hatred of others, but to protect and defend him from those wishing to kill him. . . . *Not even a murderer loses his personal dignity,* and God himself pledges to guarantee this. . . . God, who preferred the correction rather than the death of a sinner, did not desire that a homicide be punished by the exaction of another act of homicide.' EV No. 9."

EX CORDE AND THE BALL PROPOSAL, March 19, 1999

"Next November, the American bishops will consider a revised draft document to implement *Ex Corde Ecclesiae* (ECE), the 1990 Apostolic Constitution on Catholic Universities.

"The draft was prepared by a bishops' subcommittee to comply with Vatican insistence that the document include 'juridical elements' to make it effective. The disagreements between the universities and the bishops include the following areas, among others:

"**The mandate for theologians.** Canon Law requires that 'those who teach theological disciplines in any institute of higher students have a mandate from the competent ecclesiastical authority.' Canon 812.

"**Fidelity to the Magisterium.** ECE requires that 'Catholic theologians, aware that they fulfill a mandate received from a church, are to be faithful to the magisterium of the church as the authentic interpreter of sacred Scripture and sacred tradition.'. . . .

"**The requirement that a majority of the faculty be Catholic.** ECE provides that '[i]n order not to endanger the Catholic identity of the university . . . the number of non-Catholic teachers should not be allowed to constitute a majority within the institution, which is and must remain Catholic.'

"The bishops do not seem eager to enforce ECE in a compulsory way. Moreover, it is unlikely that the leaders of the major American Catholic universities will ever voluntarily accept any effective implementation of the norms of ECE.

"Rev. J. Donald Monan, S.J., former president of Boston College, and Rev. Edward A. Malloy, C.S.C., president of Notre Dame, said in the Jan. 30th *America* magazine: 'The portions of the subcommittee draft that threaten . . . havoc within Catholic universities . . . are . . . those that apply small sections of . . . Canon Law directed to individual Catholics. These canons have created conundrums since their publication in 1983. [They] prescribe that Catholic teachers of theological disciplines hold a mandate from ecclesiastical authority (Canon 812); that theology professors and some administrative officers make a profession of faith and take an oath of fidelity upon assuming appointment (Canon 833) and that colleges condition an individual's appointment on integrity of doctrine and good character (Canon 810). It is unfortunate that [the subcommittee draft tries] to breathe life into canons that, with the full knowledge of the U.S. hierarchy, and with good reason, had been lifeless for 25 years.'

"It is not unfair to note that any 'lifeless' character of the Canons is attributable to the disobedience of the universities, which now assert the 'lifeless' condition of the Canons they reject as a justification for their own further disobedience. Father Monan and Father Malloy said the Canon 812 mandate requirement 'is an instrument . . . to control what is taught and written. The authority competent to give, deny or remove the mandate is . . . external to the university. . . . Most Catholic professors . . . will not request such a mandate, and Catholic universities will take no steps to implement it because of its obvious threat to academic freedom.' Interestingly, their concept of selective obedience is not applied by the universities to their on-campus drinking policies, their stated tuition charge and other rules that they themselves establish.

"The universities and the bishops may be at an impasse. It may be time to reconsider a proposal made in the March, 1987 *Crisis* by William Bentley Ball, the great constitutional lawyer and Notre Dame Law School graduate, who died two months ago:

"'My suggestion,' Ball wrote, 'would . . . enable any institution which desired to meet Church criteria . . . to be accredited as a Catholic institution. The [universities tell] us that accreditation processes, by secular and government agencies, are . . . acceptable—even though they involve a great deal of monitoring, . . . inspection [and] record-keeping, . . . even [as to] "whether the institution is meeting its stated objectives." A . . . far less cumbersome accrediting process . . . could . . . be adopted by the Church [so] the Church [could] provide Catholics and the public in general a list, in each diocese, of Church-accredited colleges and universities. We would then all know who is who. If a student, or parents, desired higher education at a college of the faith, they would run no risk of being deceived. If a college desired to be all-out orthodox, it would not be subject to unfair competition by those who tell the government that they are nonsectarian and the Catholic market that they are Catholic. But what of the [secularizing universities]? Their problem with the Church would be over. They could label themselves anything they wished. . . . They could do their own thing. But now everyone would know that that thing is not the real thing.'

"Instead of forcing institutions to comply with standards they resist, the objective under the Ball approach would be to afford any institutions that do accept ECE, Canon Law and their implementations the opportunity to affirm that acceptance and to pledge to put it into effect. The burden would be on the university. If it accepts those requirements, it could say so. The bishops, including the bishop of the diocese in which the school is located, could publish a list of institutions that have made that commitment. If the institution reneges on its commitment, the bishops could remove it from the list. Any oversight by bishops on the universities would be limited. And juridical enforcement of the norms and ordinances would be greatly minimized if not eliminated.

"The governing principle is truth in labeling. If the 'Catholic' universities were selling meat instead of education and if they labeled generic hamburger as ground round, they could be in legal difficulty. The government properly sets binding standards for labeling food. The Catholic Church, speaking through the Vicar of Christ, properly sets binding standards for labeling institutions as Catholic. Canon 808 provides that 'Even if it really be Catholic, no university may bear the title or name *Catholic university* without the consent of the competent ecclesiastical authority.' In *Veritatis Splendor*, John Paul II, citing Canon 808, said: 'It falls to [bishops], in communion with the Holy See, both to grant the title "Catholic" to Church-related . . . universities . . . and, in cases of a serious failure to live up to that title, to take it away.'

"The criteria that make a university 'Catholic' are clearly defined by the Pope, who is the only person in the world with the ultimate authority to make that definition. If a university will not live by those criteria, it is a species of consumer fraud for it to claim to be 'Catholic.' The controversy over Catholic universities need not be an occasion to start World War III. But it involves a non-negotiable principle of truth in labeling. The way to vindicate that principle may be simply to consider an adaptation of Mr. Ball's proposal."

KOSOVO AND CONSCIENTIOUS OBJECTION, April 20, 1999

"'If they reinstate the draft, do I have to go?' In light of Kosovo, that question may occur to a few Notre Dame men (and 'liberated' women). Let's talk about it.

"Some regard the Kosovo campaign as a just war required to stop genocide. Others regard it as another 'Wag the Dog' to divert attention from the provision of missile technology to China and other embarrassments. Whatever the reality, you might ask, 'Why should I put my life on the line just because some politician says so?'. . . .

"Note three aspects of [Catholic] teaching: 1. The state has the 'right and duty' to require citizens to aid the 'national defense;' 2. The state should make 'equitable provision' for conscientious objectors; and 3. Those objectors are 'obliged to serve . . . in some other way.'

"The law of the United States exempts only universal pacifists, who object to all war and not merely to the war in question. The *Catechism* [states that] '[t]hose who renounce violence and bloodshed and . . . to safeguard human rights, make use of those means of defense available to the weakest, bear witness to evangelical charity, provided they do so without harming the rights and obligations of other men and societies.' No. 2306. . . .

"It can, of course, be a commendable 'witness to evangelical charity' for one to renounce force in defending *himself*. The universal pacifist, however, who denies that force can ever be justified in defense of the common good, refuses to defend others. And he would deny to others their right to have the state provide what the *Catechism* calls 'legitimate defense by military force,' no. 2309. Such pacifism is, whatever the sincerity of those who hold to it, objectively ignoble and unworkable.

"In his message for the 1968 Day of Peace, Paul VI said: '[I]t is to be hoped that the exaltation of the ideal of peace may not favor the cowardice of those who fear it may be their duty to give their life for the service of their own country and of their own brothers, when these are engaged in the defense of justice and liberty, and who seek only a flight from their responsibility, from the risks that are necessarily involved in the accomplishment of great duties and generous exploits. Peace is not pacifism: it does not mask a base and slothful concept of life, but it proclaims the highest and most universal values of life: truth, justice, freedom, love.'

"Universal pacifism raises a mostly theoretical question. Of more pertinence, the *selective* pacifist refuses to fight, not in all wars, but only in an unjust war. The just war theory involves two concepts. 'Jus ad Bellum' determines when recourse to war is permissible. 'Jus in Bello' relates to the conduct of the just war once it has begun. The *Catechism* (no. 2309) specifies the requirements for going to war: 'the damage inflicted by the aggressor on the nation or community of nations must be lasting, grave and certain; all other means of putting an end to it [are] impractical or ineffective; there must be serious prospects of success; the use of arms must not produce evils and disorders graver than the evil to be eliminated.'

"The 'Jus in Bello' criteria for conducting a war are proportionality and discrimination. Proportionality relates not only to the war itself, which must be for a proportionate good, but also to the use of tactics or weapons. Discrimination prohibits directly intended attacks on noncombatants and nonmilitary targets. *Catechism*, nos. 2312–14.

"So what happens if you think the Kosovo campaign, or some other war, is unjust? An unjust law, as St. Thomas teaches, may not be morally binding. The decision of the state on war, as on other questions, however, carries a strong presumption of validity. But there can be a moral duty, in exceptional circumstances, to refuse to serve in an armed conflict whether or not a legal exemption is granted: '[D]uring a just war,' wrote Father John Hardon, 'a citizen must aid his country to gain victory, but he may not voluntarily provide help if his nation's cause is evidently unjust. . . . [T]hose conscripted or in military service when war [begins] may, if they doubt the justice of the war, assume that their nation is right and so engage in the conflict. The reason is that they do not have complete knowledge of the facts to warrant making a contrary judgment.' *The Catholic Catechism* (1975) 349–50.

"As the *Catechism* (No. 2311) suggests, the state should make 'equitable provision' for selective pacifists, provided they 'serve the human community in some other way.' It may be practically impossible, however, to provide such an exemption without encouraging wholesale fraud. . . . [In any event], [we] are all obliged to be selective pacifists, reserving the right to submit, with prudence, any act of the state, even a war, to the higher standard of the natural law and the law of God. . . .

"With a certified liar in the White House, our government has embarked on foreign adventures of dubious constitutionality and dubious relevance to the defense of the common good of the American people or of anyone else. That government, too, has sponsored an extermination of the innocent unborn that has produced a body count at least six times that of the Holocaust. At some point, a citizen will have to face the issue of whether his duty to avoid proximate and unjustified cooperation with evil prevents his active participation in the military adventures, other than evidently genuine defense, of such a regime. So let us not be too severe in our judgment of the pacifist. We may have to share a cell with him someday."

1999–2000

COLUMBINE AND *ECCLESIA IN AMERICA*, Aug. 27, 1999

"'Our children need our help to deal with tough issues, like violence. Please, talk with your kids,' said President Clinton in a recent TV spot. But what are the parents supposed to say?. . . . [Let's try to] understand how our culture can spawn an Eric Harris and a Dylan Klebold, who killed 13 others and themselves at Columbine. . . . [One reason] was described by John Paul II as an '[i]ndividualism . . . in which the subject does what he wants, in which he himself is the one to "establish the truth" of whatever he finds pleasing or useful. . . . Individualism thus remains egocentric and selfish.' *Letter to Families*, no. 14. This 'notion of freedom . . . exalts the isolated individual in an absolute way and gives no place to solidarity, to openness to others and service of them.' *Evangelium Vitae*, no. 19.

"This individualism arises from secularism and relativism. In truth, you are your brother's keeper because you are both children of God made in his image and likeness. But 'when the sense of God is lost, there is also a tendency to lose the sense of man, of his dignity and his life.' EV, no. 21. Other people are seen as objects for use and possible disposal. When objective truth is denied through relativism, each person claims 'the prerogative of independently determining the criteria of good and evil and then acting accordingly. Such an outlook is congenial to an individualistic ethic.' *Faith and Reason*, no. 98. 'If the promotion of the self is understood in terms of absolute autonomy,' said John Paul, 'people inevitably reach the point of rejecting one another. Everyone else is considered an enemy from whom one has to defend oneself. Thus society becomes a mass of individuals placed side by side, but without any mutual bonds. Each one wishes to make his own interests prevail.' EV, nos. 19–20. As the sense of God, of an objective moral law and of one's inherent relation to others, diminishes, only force can keep the peace in the absence of those inner restraints. And even in a police state, forcible restraint cannot be fully effective.

"So what is to be done? Let me pass on an invitation from John Paul II. While acknowledging differences among countries, he spoke in Mexico City of 'America' in the singular, as 'a human and geographical unity from the North to the South Pole' with a 'unity of destiny unique in the world.' In *Ecclesia in America* (EA), he charted a program for 'the new evangelization of America.' EA shows that the moral teaching of the Church is an integrated

161

whole. '[I]f we accept,' said Mother Teresa, 'that a mother can kill even her own child, how can we tell other people not to kill one another?' The errors that can lead us to regard the unborn, or fellow students, as disposable objects, can foster an objectification of employees, immigrants and others. '[I]n America,' according to EA, 'a model of society [is] emerging in which the powerful predominate even eliminating the powerless: I am thinking of victims of abortion [and] euthanasia; and the many other people relegated to the margins of society by consumerism and materialism. Nor can I fail to mention the unnecessary recourse to the death penalty.' EA, no. 63.

"Ideas have consequences. In abortion, euthanasia and the death penalty, we use the intentional infliction of death as a problem-solving technique. In the pursuit of global free trade, employees on both sides of the border are treated, not as persons, but as interchangeable objects. The Illinois worker loses his job because the corporation can pay a 15-year-old girl in a maquiladora in Tijuana 16 cents to make the shirt it will sell for $25. 'In the absence of moral points of reference,' says EA, 'an unbridled greed for wealth and power takes over. [I]n many countries of America, a system known as 'neoliberalism' prevails; based on a purely economic conception of man, this system considers profit and the law of the market as its only parameters, to the detriment of the dignity of individuals and people. [T]he poor are becoming ever more numerous, victims of policies and structures which are often unjust.'. . . .

"'On a continent marked by competition and aggressiveness, unbridled consumerism and corruption,' John Paul urges lay people 'to embody values such as mercy, forgiveness, honesty, transparency of heart and patience.' EA, no. 44. He invites '[y]oung Christians' to 'become apostles to young people wherever they are found: in schools, universities, the workplace, the countryside.' EA, no. 47. He calls on Catholic universities to preserve their Catholic orientation. The education they impart should make constant reference to Jesus Christ and his message as the Church presents it in her dogmatic and moral teaching. Only in this way will they train truly Christian leaders.' No. 71.

"EA shows that the answer to violence lies in a conversion of mind and heart: '[T]he Church in America is called to proclaim that conversion consists in commitment to the person of Jesus Christ, with all the theological and moral implications taught by the Magisterium of the Church.' No. 53. John Paul II cannot be dismissed as if he were some Polish tourist living in Rome. Rather, the Vicar of Christ is 'the enduring principle of unity and the visible foundation of the Church' No. 33. We ought to follow him.

"I hope Notre Dame students will read *Ecclesia in America*. It puts a lot of things, including violence, in context. And it may be the lowest-priced item you will ever buy in the Bookstore."

162

ABORTION, AS DESCRIBED BY ABORTIONISTS, Sept. 10, 1999

"Sometimes the truth does come out in a lawsuit. This month, the full U.S. 7th Circuit Court of Appeals will hear arguments on Wisconsin and Illinois laws forbidding partial birth abortion (PBA) except to save the mother's life. In *Planned Parenthood v. Doyle*, Judge Richard Posner, writing for a 7th Circuit panel that held the Wisconsin law unconstitutional, described PBA: 'After the cervix (the mouth of the uterus) has been dilated, [t]he physician draws the fetus out feet first. When only the fetus's head remains in the uterus, the physician inserts its scissors into the base of the fetus's brain, inserts a tube in the hole made by the scissors, and removes the contents of the skull by suction, causing the skull to collapse. The physician then completes the extraction of the now-dead fetus.'

"The PBA prohibitions would prevent few, if any, abortions. The abortionist could evade the prohibition against killing a 'partially delivered child' by killing the baby while he is entirely in the womb. But the abortion industry has reacted fanatically against the prohibitions. And that is how the truth has come out in the PBA cases.

"In his dissent in *Doyle*, Judge Daniel Manion noted that the abortionists claim that the PBA prohibition 'would limit a woman's right to abortion' because 'they routinely perform the procedures' the PBA law forbids. To support this claim they 'graphically described in detail how routine abortions are performed.'. . .

"Dennis Christensen, M.D., said in his declaration in *Doyle*: 'In 1997, I performed 2,350 abortions in Wisconsin, 300 in the second trimester. . . . For abortions before fourteen weeks . . . I . . . use suction curettage [in which] the physician . . . dilates the cervix and removes the embryo or fetus and the other products of conception, either whole or in parts, through the cervix into the vagina using a suction tube or syringe.

"' In some cases, a part of the fetus may be removed while another part remains in the uterus and may be "living." For abortions [after] fourteen weeks . . . I use dilation and evacuation (D & E) when the fetus is too large to remove by suction curettage. Once the cervix is . . . dilated, I evacuate the uterus using forceps, curettes and suction. Frequently the procedure results in the disjoining of the fetus. In . . . a D & E . . . I usually do not know at what point . . . the fetus dies; however, at the beginning of the procedure, the fetus is alive in the sense of having living cells and a heartbeat. In the intact D& E (also known as "dilation and extraction"), the physician dilates the cervix and then removes the fetus from the uterus through the vaginal canal intact. . . . '

"The intact D&E, or D&X, is a partial birth abortion. . . . Several abortionists made similar declarations in *Doyle*. As Frederik F. Broekhuizen, M.D., described a suction curettage, 'At times I must make multiple passes through the uterus with suction before it is empty. Sometimes when part of the fetus is removed with the initial pass, the part remaining in the uterus still has a heart-beat.'

"When Dr. Christensen refers to 'disjoining of the fetus,' he means cutting or tearing the arms and legs off an unborn child. The abortion industry uses euphemisms to gain acceptance. The unborn child becomes a 'fetus' or 'the product of conception.' The attack becomes 'the termination of pregnancy' or simply 'the procedure.' If you favor such legalized killing, you are merely 'pro-choice.' We are supposed to overlook what that choice involves.

"But now, in the PBA cases, the abortionists themselves show us that every abortion is, in moral but not in legal terms, the deliberate murder of an innocent human being. . . .

"Abortion pills and other early abortifacients are making abortion a private matter beyond the effective reach of the law. What is ultimately needed is a reconversion of the American people to a respect for all human life as a gift from God. In any event, it is not merely enough to oppose abortion. It is important to provide alternatives, with needed material as well as spiritual help, to women who contemplate abortion and to women who have had abortions. In *Evangelium Vitae* no. 99, John Paul II offered 'a special word to women who have had an abortion. . . . [D]o not give in to discouragement and do not lose hope. . . . You will come to understand that nothing is definitively lost and you will also be able to ask forgiveness from your child, who is now living in the Lord. . . . [Y]ou can be among the most eloquent defenders of everyone's right to life.' Pray for abortionists, and for women who have had an abortion or who are considering it. And pray for our country."

NOTE: On October 26, 1999, the full 7th Circuit Court of Appeals, by a 5-4 vote, upheld as constitutional the Wisconsin and Illinois laws involved in *Doyle*. 195 F. 3d 857 (7th Cir., 1999).

CLASHMORE MIKE, Sept. 24, 1999

"Suppose an aggressive lawyer uncovered a descendant of Clashmore Mike? Years ago, Mike, an Irish terrier, was the mascot of the Notre Dame football team. His replacement by a series of capering leprechauns was unfair. Mike was treated like a dog. But he could do nothing about it. The last Mike has long since gone to the big stadium in the sky. But now his heirs may be able to seek redress. They can claim that Mike was a person and that he was illegally fired because of species-ism, discrimination against persons of other species, as racism is discrimination against persons of other races. They could find support for that view at Harvard, Princeton and other 'great' universities.

"Harvard, Georgetown and Northwestern University law schools are offering courses on animal rights this fall. Adjunct professor Steven Wise, who will teach the Harvard course, has compared the 'legal thinghood of chimpanzees' to 'the abomination of human slavery.'. . . .

"Princeton is further ahead. The new DeCamp Professor of Bioethics at the University Center for Human Values is Peter Singer, the Australian critic of 'speciesism' and father of the animal rights movement. Singer thinks that any 'rational and self-conscious being' is a person. In his view chimpanzees are persons, as are apes, whales, dolphins, dogs, cats, pigs, seals and bears. Some human beings, however, including 'newborn infants and some mental defectives,' are not persons. 'So it seems,' concludes Singer, 'that killing, say, of a chimpanzee, is worse than the killing of a gravely defective human who is not a person.' Singer thinks that chickens might be persons, in which case the greatest mass murderer in history was not Adolf Hitler but Colonel Sanders. . . .

"In his book, *Practical Ethics*, which he assigns for his Princeton course, Singer said, 'Killing a disabled infant is not morally equivalent to killing a person. Very often it is not wrong at all. When the death of a disabled infant will lead to the birth of another infant with better prospects of a happy life, the total amount of happiness will be greater if the disabled infant is killed. The loss of happy life for the first infant is outweighed by the gain of a happier life for the second.' Singer is featured at a prestigious Sept. 25 conference at the Association of the Bar of the City of New York on 'The Legal Status of Non-Human Animals.'

"According to Catholic teaching, man has a serious duty to God, but not to the animals, to make a right use of animals without being cruel or inflicting needless pain. The move to confer legal rights on animals themselves, however, is based on a denial of the special nature of the human person. Singer says that 'we can no longer base our ethics on the idea that human beings are a special form of creation, made in the image of God, singled out from all other animals, and alone possessing an immortal soul.'. . .

"[Our] culture has lost sight of the human person as a unique creation of body and spirit in the image and likeness of God. '[W]hen the sense of God is lost,' said John Paul II, 'there is also a tendency to lose the sense of man, of his dignity and his life.'. . .

"The intellectual and moral bankruptcy implicit in the advocacy of animal rights ought to cause our leaders to ponder the wisdom of using those 'great' secular universities as models for Notre Dame. . . . [W]hat results from their effort to, pardon the expression, 'ape' the Ivy League, is the devaluation of undergraduate education and the imposition of unconscionable loan burdens on non-wealthy students to finance the drive for research prestige. . . .

"These comments are prompted by conversations with law students whose career and family options are constricted by loans in the $100–150,000 range. It is no consolation that this burden results from the effort of our leaders, perhaps in a working out of the old Catholic inferiority complex, to emulate institutions where it is seriously in question whether there is an intrinsic difference between a chicken and a philosophy professor. Clashmore Mike, who did not go to any of those places, knew the difference."

RESPECT LIFE WEEK, Oct. 8, 1999

"Maybe you haven't heard that this is Respect Life Week on campus. Or maybe you dismiss it as a knee-jerk attack on abortion from the fever swamps of the Radical Right. The reality is different. Let me try to explain. . . .

"Abortion, euthanasia and the wholesale use of the death penalty are symptoms of a culture that has lost sight of God as the Lord of life. 'We are facing,' said John Paul, '[a] clash between good and evil, death and life, the "culture of death" and the "culture of life." We are all involved in it with the responsibility of choosing to be unconditionally pro-life.'

"The Respect Life effort makes that choice. While it seeks to prohibit abortion and euthanasia and to restrict the death penalty, it offers positive alternatives and help to women contemplating abortion or who have had an abortion, to single mothers and to the disabled or terminally ill. It reminds us that, as John Paul put it, 'not even a murderer loses his personal dignity.' And it is not afraid to address the root evil of contraception. If, through contraception, you make yourself, rather than God, the arbiter as to whether and when life shall begin, you will make yourself the arbiter of whether and when it shall end through abortion, euthanasia or the death penalty. The entire 'culture of death' is based on the idea that there is such a thing as a life not worth living and that the decision on that point is for us rather than God. . . .

"[T]he heart of the Right to Life effort is Eucharistic Adoration. 'Through Jesus,' said John Paul, 'man is given the possibility of "knowing" the complete truth concerning the value of human life. From this source he receives the capacity to "accomplish" this truth perfectly.' 'The Church and the world,' he said, 'have a great need for Eucharistic worship. Jesus awaits us in this sacrament of love. Let us not refuse the time to go to meet him in adoration, in contemplation full of faith and open to making amends for the serious offenses and crimes of the world. Let our adoration never cease.'

"We suffer from the scourge of having the '60s and '70s generations in power. But, like an oil slick on a river, this, too, will pass. One of the Pope's recurrent themes is that 'God is preparing a great springtime for Christianity, and we can already see its first signs.'

"Respect Life Week, run by students on their own initiative, is one of those signs."

EX CORDE AND SELECTIVE AUTONOMY, Oct. 29, 1999

"In November, the United States bishops will consider an Application of the norms of *Ex Corde Ecclesiae*, the 1990 Apostolic Constitution on Catholic Universities. Notre Dame and other universities have reservations about the Application as a threat to their 'institutional autonomy.' The universities claimed that autonomy in their 1967 Land O'Lakes statement:. . . .

"The autonomy issue is raised by the Application's insistence, as required by canon law, that 'Catholics who teach the theological disciplines in a Catholic university are required to have a mandatum granted by ecclesiastical authority. The mandatum is an acknowledgement that a Catholic professor of a theological discipline teaches within the full communion of the Catholic Church. . . .

"In *America* magazine last January, Notre Dame's president, Father Edward A. Malloy, C.S.C., and Father J. Donald Monan, S.J., former president of Boston College, objected that the mandatum would be granted by an authority 'external to the university.' [They] said 'Catholic universities will take no steps to implement it because of its obvious threats to academic freedom.'

"In the Spring 1999 *Journal of College and University Law,* Father James T. Burtchaell, C.S.C., said, 'The presidents [of the Catholic universities] have evidently not realized the absurdity of their repeated claim that no outside authority could hold their institutions answerable.'

"Father Burtchaell listed 55 'external authorities or agencies' to which a typical Catholic university 'is answerable for her various standards,' including federal departments and agencies, accrediting bodies, the NCAA and so on. Nor is it accurate, as Father Richard Warner, C.S.C., said in the current *Notre Dame Magazine,* that 'none of these agencies demand or require that individuals hired by institutions be subject to their prior approval.' Is that so? Try hiring an illegal alien for the faculty. And you could have an uncomfortable accreditation review if you hired a disbarred attorney for the law faculty. The universities accept mandates from secular authorities but they reject a limited oversight by the Church. To accept the right of the Church to define what it means to be Catholic would conflict with the political correctness which, perhaps second only to the cult of the money god, is the dominant religion of the American Academy. What would they think of us at Princeton and Harvard if we let the Pope tell us what it means to be a 'Catholic' university? The movers and shakers in the 'Catholic' universities resist the definition of that term by the Pope, who has the ultimate legal and moral authority to define it. Instead, they define it according to their own private judgment, as Protestants would. . . .

"[S]tudents also have a stake in the prompt implementation of *Ex Corde.* 'Catholic students,' said the Application, 'have a right to receive from a university instruction in authentic Catholic doctrine and practice. Courses in

Catholic doctrine and practice should be made available to all students.' A similar point was made by the Notre Dame Student Union Board in its October report to the Trustees. The Board noted that pre-college 'theological education has degenerated to making collages rather than concentrating on the basic elements of the faith. There is little understanding of the faith in successive classes of students. We recommend as a first course a modified form of catechesis, a serious study of Catholic dogma and doctrine, so that students can gain the perspective that they have so far not had available. Students at Notre Dame want and need an introductory course that shows them what we believe and why because no one has taken the time so far to give most of the students this foundation so essential to pursuing fruitful Catholic theology in the future.'

"This important interest of the students, recognized by both the Application and the Student Union, is obscured by our leaders' focus on protecting their own turf by rejecting even the modest and cooperative effort of the Application to recall the universities to a 'Catholic' identity. Our leaders mean well. But they seem more concerned about the sensitivities of complaining faculty—who want to teach their own brand of Catholicism as if it were the real thing—than they are about the rights of tuition-paying students who are entitled to truth in labeling."

JONATHAN POLLARD, Nov. 12, 1999

"Now that the Middle East is back at the top of the news, we can expect discussion of the case of Jonathan Pollard, the Navy intelligence researcher who pleaded guilty of giving secrets to Israel and was sentenced in 1987 to life in prison. The standard view is that Pollard is a 'traitor' who did great damage to the security of the United States; that he got off lightly and should have been shot; and that the proceedings against him were fair. The reality is different. While I wrote part of Pollard's brief in the Court of Appeals, I do not want to rehash the case. But let me note some strange aspects you may not hear about in the media.

"Pollard and his crime are reprehensible. But never before has an American citizen received a life sentence for spying for an allied nation; the usual sentences range from two to eight years. In 1992, the Court of Appeals, by a 2-1 vote, upheld the denial of Pollard's move to withdraw his guilty plea. '[I]t cannot be said,' concluded the court, 'that justice completely miscarried.' Judge Williams, in dissent, called the sentencing 'a fundamental miscarriage of justice.' We can mention here only one point.

"In the plea agreement, the government made three promises to Pollard, including an implicit one not to seek a life sentence. 'The government,' Judge

Williams said, 'complied in spirit with none of its promises; with the third, it complied in neither letter nor spirit.' In the agreement, the only reference to statements the government might make to the sentencing judge in camera, i.e., off the record, was that 'representations concerning [Pollard's] cooperation [with the government after his arrest] may have to be made to the Court in camera.' Instead, the Government submitted in camera a 46-page classified memo by Defense Secretary Caspar Weinberger which focused not on Pollard's 'cooperation' but on the claim that Pollard did great damage to the United States. Weinberger, who was indicted for perjury on Iran-Contra and pardoned by President Bush, claimed in September 1999 that the sentencing judge himself made a 'formal official request' that Weinberger submit that secret memo.

"Pollard's attorneys were not told that the judge requested that memo. They received only a censored version of it although both of his attorneys had full security clearances. Defense attorneys have no absolute right to see such sentencing materials. But the only reference in the plea agreement to in-camera submission was to information favorable to Pollard with respect to his cooperation.

"Would Pollard have signed the plea agreement if the government had said that it would present to the court in camera, not information on Pollard's 'cooperation,' but allegations about the damage Pollard did to national security, allegations which Pollard would have no real chance to rebut because he would not be allowed to see them in full? Pollard . . . betrayed his country's trust. But if they can blindside a Pollard, they can do it to any of us.

"Weinberger also submitted an unclassified statement which said it was difficult to 'conceive of greater harm to national security' than that done by Pollard and that his punishment 'should reflect the magnitude of the treason committed, and the needs of national security.'

"While Weinberger's statement, said Judge Williams, 'did not expressly endorse a life sentence [it] implied an appeal for the maximum. Weinberger's reference to treason took the point further. Whereas treason carries the death penalty and involves aiding the nation's enemies, Pollard was charged with espionage, carrying a maximum of life imprisonment and encompassing aid even to friendly nations.'

"The emphasis in this case through the signing of the plea agreement corresponded to the indictment's explicit charge only that the information Pollard conveyed 'would be used to the advantage of Israel.' Once the agreement was signed, the government shifted its emphasis from Israeli benefit to damage to the United States. It was a bait and switch. It was not illegal. But it is cause for concern because government officials have waged a media campaign to keep Pollard in prison on that basis, that his spying did great damage to the United States, an offense for which he was not explicitly indicted and against which he now has no real chance to defend himself.

"A *Washington Post* editorial last January asked, 'Cannot a way be found to pierce some of the secrecy and provide the public with a better means of judging whether fairness was achieved in this case? [Pollard] is in the position of having his fate determined in part by materials to which he had no access and proceedings of which he was not a part.'

"The test of a legal system is not how it treats the best among us but how it deals with the worst. Pollard's punishment is beyond the usual. He is kept in prison through leaked and unrebuttable media assertions that go beyond the charge on which he was explicitly indicted. This is a case of permanent imprisonment for undisclosed reasons of state security. The 20th century has seen too many examples of that practice. It should not be imported into the law of the United States."

BENGAL BOUTS: FOR THE "ULTRA-POOR," Feb. 4, 2000

"In less time than it takes to read this column, you could easily spend $200 in the Notre Dame Bookstore, especially on a price-inflated football weekend. In Bangladesh, many families among the 27 million 'ultra-poor'—one person in five in the entire country—live on less than that for an entire year. . . .

"Since 1931, the entire proceeds of the Bengal Bouts have been sent to the Holy Cross missionaries in Bangladesh. . . . The club officers—president J.R. Mellin, Tom Biolchini, Brian Hobbins, Mike Maguire, Mike Romanchek, Pete Ryan and Josh Thompson—actually run the program. . . .

"The coaches, all former Bengal Bouts champs, are Terry Johnson, a Chicago attorney; Tom Suddes, a Columbus, Ohio, developer; and Pat Farrell, the University pilot. They devote great blocks of time to the program. They are helped by exceptional assistant coaches, especially Sweet C. Robinson and recent Bengals champs Ryan Rans, '98, Chip Farrell, '98, and Toby Biolchini, '96. Roland Chamblee, '73, a four-time Bengals champ, adds a unique dimension as probably the only state court judge who also serves as a corner man in the ring.

"The program emphasizes safety. Dr. James M. Moriarty, University chief of medicine, carefully screens and oversees the boxers. No sparring is conducted without paramedics at ringside. We have never had a serious injury beyond an occasional redirected nose and similar inconveniences. Everyone in the program is intent on maintaining that record.

"The heart of the program is trainer Jack Mooney, a mere youth of 86 years. Jack, who was Knute Rockne's paperboy, assisted Bengal Bouts founder Dominic Napolitano in the early years. Jack prepares the boxers for their sparring sessions and debriefs them afterward. As any boxer will tell you, Jack is unforgettable. His assistant, Jack Zimmerman, is not only an effective trainer but also a poet and a professional accordionist. The boxing club . . . is utterly dependent on the administrative skills of Meghan Kelley, '02, of Pasquerilla East. Last year Meghan and Emily Schmidt, '99, brought the program to a new level of efficiency. Meghan, assisted by Claire Dampeer, '02, is carrying on this year without skipping a beat.

"I hope the members of the Notre Dame community will continue their exceptional support for the Bengal Bouts. You are welcome to visit the practices in the JACC Boxing Room. . . . [Y]ou will be favorably impressed.

FREEZE TUITION, Feb. 22, 2000

"Williams College will freeze tuition and other charges for 2000–2001 at $31,520. It is the first exclusive private college or university in decades to hold the line. '[I]n a low inflation cycle with our endowment increasing and our contributions from alumni very strong,' Williams president Carl Vogt said, '[t]his seems a logical move.'. . . .

"Over the past two decades, Notre Dame's leaders have shown a remarkable ability to raise and spend money and to build the Endowment toward the Top Ten. They have transformed the formerly pastoral campus into a crowded imitation of urban research universities. The opulent new Bookstore remains open for 11 hours on Sunday, which reduces the chance that any sheep will pass through this campus unshorn. We also seem about to vault to the top of the category, Largest and Most Expensive Campus Ministry Building. And the end of the building boom is not in sight. Undergrads are paying more than twice as much, in real money, than they did two decades ago. But, in terms of quality and availability of courses and teachers, they are short-changed. In the Fall of 1999, 56, or 23 percent, of 100 level Arts and Letters courses were taught by 'Student Instructors,' and 32, or 13 percent, by 'Non-Regular Faculty,' not counting lab courses and tutorials. Of Arts & Letters 200 level courses, 42, or 18 percent, were taught by 'Student Instructors,' and 40, or 17 percent, by 'Non-Regular Faculty.'

"The law of the market, however, may be catching up to the universities. Like used-car lots, Notre Dame and other universities offer discounts from their exorbitant sticker prices to attract students with very high test scores who will gain the approval of *U.S. News* and other arbiters of prestige. If present trends continue, the only non-wealthy students at Notre Dame will be scholarship athletes, ROTC students, a limited number of minority scholarship students, faculty and staff children, some of the students whose test scores brought them heavy discounts and a diminishing pool of non-wealthy students who opt for Notre Dame even at the price of assuming a crippling loan burden that will distort their career and family options. Notre Dame ought not to become 'a rich kids' school.'

"Our leaders ought to freeze tuition, room, board and fees for two years for openers. This would not confer a major advantage on present students. But it would signal that Notre Dame intends, at least in principle, to recover its traditional mission which included the provision of education to qualified students regardless of their financial status. And it would signal that Notre Dame is opting out of the shabby game by which the major universities have financed on the backs of non-wealthy borrowing students a pursuit of research prestige which benefits those students only marginally if at all."

AGING POPULATION AND EUTHANASIA, March 31, 2000

"In *Vacco v. Quill*, in 1997, the Supreme Court upheld state laws prohibiting assisted suicide. The Court said: "Just as a State may prohibit assisting suicide . . . it may permit palliative care . . . which may have the foreseen but unintended "double effect" of hastening the patient's death.' '[P]ainkilling drugs,' said the Court, 'may hasten a patient's death, but the physician's purpose and intent is, or may be, only to ease his patient's pain.'

"It can be very difficult, however, for the law to determine whether the sedating physician's intent was to relieve pain or to cause death, unless there is exceptional proof of intent to kill. Moreover, in the 1990 *Cruzan* case, the Court allowed the states, in effect, to permit intentional killing by physicians. In *Cruzan* the Court allowed Missouri to permit the removal of a feeding tube, pursuant to the patient's inferred desire, from an incompetent patient who was not dying, was not in significant distress, and had a life expectancy of 30 years. The removal was intended to cause Nancy Cruzan's death to relieve her of a life considered burdensome or useless.

'In *Cruzan* the Court invited the states to turn a blind eye toward intentional killing through withdrawal of food and water. It is fair to expect the law to be tolerant also of intentional killing by sedation and ultimately by lethal injection. Through legalized abortion, euthanasia and popular support for the death penalty, our culture accepts the intentional infliction of death as a problem-solving technique. Three of the 27 patients who died under Oregon's assisted suicide law in 1999 took over 11 hours to die from the orally ingested drugs and one took 26 hours. A lethal injection is more efficient. We use it on convicted murderers to spare them pain. Why not in these cases?

"Cultural and demographic trends make the ultimate legalization of active and even nonvoluntary euthanasia predictable. Contraception and abortion have reduced the number of working people available to support the elderly and disabled. The fertility rate in the United States has been below the replacement level for more than two decades. In 1900, there were 10 times as many persons under 18 in the United States as there were persons over 65. By 2030, there will be more people over 65 than under 18. Between 2010 and 2030, the number of persons over 65 in the U.S. will rise from 40.4 million to 70.3 million, but the working-age population between 20 and 59 will remain stationary at 160 million. Who will pay the bills for all those old folks? The aging of the population will generate pressure on the old and infirm to recognize what former Colorado Governor Richard Lamm called their 'duty to die and get out of the way.' We are paying the price for being on the wrong side of what social historian Allan Carlson calls, 'the contest between a vital faith that welcomes children and a secular individualism that does not want them.'. . . . The real solution, however, requires more than law. It requires the building of what John Paul II calls 'a new culture of life,' especially through prayer."

"YOU NEVER KNOW," May 2, 2000

"Let me tell you a true story about something that happened a few days ago.

"It was described by Mike Johnson, a lawyer in Baton Rouge and sent to me by one of his colleagues. Mike Johnson's account, which I quote with permission, is as follows:

"'A remarkable event took place at our law office yesterday. . . . Last week, a woman called one of our senior partners, Tommy Benton, to schedule an appointment to discuss the succession of a large, family estate. Though Tommy had no immediate recollection of this woman, she reminded him that she was an old client of one of our firm's former associates more than 20 years ago, and that she remembered Tommy as being a person whom her family could trust. He thanked her for her kind gesture, and scheduled her for an appointment early this week.

"'Yesterday [Monday, April 10th], the woman arrived at our office to discuss the necessary legal work. She was accompanied by her daughter, a bright, attractive 23-year-old, who sat in on and contributed to the routine meeting. Tommy enjoyed making the re-acquaintance with this old client of our firm, and particularly enjoyed the input and cheerful smile of the client's daughter. After the meeting, the woman and her daughter warmly thanked Tommy for his time and for agreeing to accept their case, and left our office.

"'About an hour later, Tommy came into my office with a rare, somewhat stunned expression on his face. 'The most . . . wonderful thing just happened,' he said, 'I just received a most remarkable phone call.' Less than an hour after she left their meeting, the woman had called Tommy to share with him a very moving story.

"'She explained that over 23 years ago, she was agonizing over a personal crisis. Because her circumstances at the time made her situation seem unbearable, she decided to terminate her unwanted pregnancy. When her female attorney (our former associate) learned that the woman had scheduled an abortion, she convinced the woman to make an anonymous phone call to an associate in her firm who had been extensively involved in various Christian pro-life efforts in the past. That associate was Tommy Benton, and the woman reported that it was because of the compassion and reason that he shared in that call, that she ultimately decided to keep her baby, the greatest blessing and joy of her life.

"'On the phone yesterday, Tommy realized before the woman finished her story that the beautiful young lady whom he had just met was the child that he had literally talked into existence over 23 years earlier.'

"That is the end of Mike Johnson's story. What can it tell us? When Tommy Benton took that anonymous call, he did not go into the attack mode. Nor did he start a debate about abortion. Instead he treated her as a person, with kindness and concern. He was ready to help. He spoke the truth, with 'compassion and reason.' And God took care of the rest.

"As Cardinal Edouard Gagnon described a conversation he had with Pope John Paul II, 'He told me truth has a grace attached to it. Anytime we speak the truth . . . there is an internal grace of God that accompanies that truth. The truth may not immediately enter in the mind and heart of those to whom we talk, but the grace of God is there and at the time they need it, God will open their heart and they will accept it.'

"Mike Johnson's account reminds us that the essential pro-life mission is to change minds and hearts with prayer and the truth, and to save lives one by one. But the point of Mike Johnson's story transcends abortion. As he summarized it: 'The lesson? Be ready. You never know when God might use you to change someone's life forever.' Something to think about."

Part IV
The 2000s

2000–2001

Ex Corde's APPLICATION TO THE UNITED STATES, Aug. 29, 2000

"The Catholic bishops' Application to the United States of *Ex Corde Ecclesiae*, the 1990 apostolic constitution on Catholic universities, will go into effect next May 3rd. In this academic year, the bishops and the universities will dialogue as to how to implement the Application.

"First, the Application requires that 'the university should . . . recruit and appoint Catholics as professors so that to the extent possible, those committed to the witness of the faith will constitute a majority of the faculty.'. . .

"Second, the Application says Catholic professors of theology 'have a . . . duty to be faithful to the Church's magisterium as the authoritative interpreter of sacred Scripture and sacred tradition [and they] are required to have a mandatum granted by competent ecclesiastical authority.' The mandatum, which is required by Canon Law, is 'an acknowledgement by church authority that a Catholic professor [of theology] is a teacher within the full communion of the Catholic Church.' . . . .

"According to the Application, 'the mandatum recognizes the professor's commitment . . . to teach authentic Catholic doctrine and to refrain from putting forth as Catholic teaching anything contrary to the Church's magisterium.' That makes sense. It is fair to say that, if Notre Dame will not ensure that its required courses in theology are 'faithful to the church's magisterium,' those courses (and required philosophy courses) should no longer be required. If the professors want to do their own thing, let them and the University abandon any claim that it is the 'Catholic' thing and let the students decide whether to take such courses.

"Third, the Application states that 'students should have the opportunity to be educated in the church's moral and religious principles and social teachings and to participate in the life of faith . . . Catholic students have a right to receive . . . instruction in authentic Catholic doctrine and practice . . . Courses in Catholic doctrine and practice should be available to all students.'

"The Application enumerates, among 'the essential elements of Catholic identity': 'Commitment to Catholic . . . attitudes in . . . all . . . university activities, including recognized student and faculty organizations . . . with due regard for academic freedom and the conscience of every individual; . . . Commitment to provide personal services (health care, counseling and guidance) . . . in conformity with the church's ethical and religious teaching and directives; Commitment to create a campus culture and environment that are expressive . . . of a Catholic way of life.'

"The principle here is truth in labeling. As the *Wall Street Journal* noted, 'The . . . secularizing trends that . . . erased the Protestant foundations of America's leading universities . . . threaten to do the same to the country's 235 Catholic . . . universities. Even non-Catholics would likely regard the [Application] as a tautology: that theologians advertised as Catholic actually teach 'authentic Catholic doctrine' and that a majority of a Catholic university's trustees and faculty be Catholic as well. From the outcry this has provoked you might think the bishops had called for reinstating the rack. . . . As former Notre Dame Provost James T. Burtchaell pointed out, 'the same administrators howling about autonomy submit without protest to authorities ranging from the NCAA to the Department of Education, who tell them what they can and cannot do, on everything from hiring and admissions to curricula and how they run their basketball programs. . . . All of which makes it hard to avoid the suspicion that what really bothers Catholic administrators is the fear not of censorship but of not being accepted by their colleagues at secular campuses. . . . And do not parents who . . . send their sons and daughters to Catholic . . . universities precisely because they are Catholic have the right to expect that their children will get what they paid for?'

"The dialogue over the next few months provides an opportunity for Notre Dame and other affected universities to define their identity in a spirit of cooperation. Perhaps we should recall Mother Teresa's advice to the Notre Dame class of 1986, that 'We need to be humble like Mary to be able to say 'Yes' to God, to accept God's law, God's teaching as given to us by His Vicar on earth, the Holy Father and the Magisterium of the Church.'"

WHAT'S LEFT OF CONSTITUTIONAL LAW, Sept. 12, 2000

"Three Supreme Court cases last June provide a look at what passes for constitutional law (or what is left of it) these days.

"First, in *Stenberg v. Carhart*, the Court held unconstitutional Nebraska's prohibition of 'partial birth abortion' (PBA). . . .

"The Court, by a 5-4 vote, struck down the PBA prohibition for two reasons. First, because it did not allow PBA to preserve the 'health of the mother.' '[T]he Court must know,' said dissenting Justice Antonin Scalia, 'that demanding a "health exception" . . . is to give live-birth abortion free rein.'

"The second reason the Court struck down the Nebraska law was because it could prohibit not only PBA but also 'dilation and evacuation' (D & E), the 'most commonly used procedure during the second trimester.' Concurring

Justice John Paul Stevens said he found 'no reason to believe that [PBA] is more brutal, more gruesome, or less respectful of "potential life" than the equally gruesome procedure Nebraska claims it still allows.'

"And concurring Justice Ruth Bader Ginsburg agreed that, 'the most common method of performing pre-viability second trimester abortions is no less distressing or susceptible to gruesome description.' Stevens and Ginsburg got that one right. . . .

"The PBA ruling confirms the Court will permit no law to prohibit any method of abortion at any stage. The PBA prohibition, incidentally, was symbolic. It would not have prevented a single abortion. It prohibited only the killing of a partially delivered, living baby; the abortionist could evade it by killing the child inside the womb.

"The PBA decision, however, shows the face of the culture of death. In the words of Scalia, 'The method of killing a human child—one cannot even accurately say an entirely unborn human child—proscribed by this statute is so horrible that the most clinical description of it evokes a shudder of revulsion.'

"The second case is *Hill v. Colorado*, where the Court upheld a statute restricting the right to 'knowingly approach' within eight feet of unconsenting persons to communicate with them within 100 feet of a health care facility. As the case confirms, abortion opponents are subject to greater restrictions on peaceful speech than are any other persons. . . .

"The third case is *Santa Fe Independent School District v. Doe*, where the Court forbade a public school district to allow a student-initiated and student-led prayer before a football game. In his dissent, Chief Justice William Rehnquist accurately said, 'The Court distorts . . . precedent [and] the tone of the court's opinion . . . bristles with hostility to all things religious in public life.'

"The three cases are related. The Court forbids the people to affirm in their public capacity that God is the source of inalienable rights. We ought not to be surprised at the result. The quote is wrongly attributed to Dostoevsky, but it remains true that 'If God does not exist, then everything is permitted.' Even the legal protection of baby killers as a privileged class."

EUCHARISTIC ADORATION, Sept. 26, 2000

"As our last column noted, the Supreme Court has made abortion, including even the killing of a partially-delivered baby, a privileged constitutional right. It is easy to be pessimistic about this. But that would be a mistake. John Paul II has told us about one practical and positive thing we can do on the life issue right here at Notre Dame. . . .

"In his homily closing the 2000 World Youth Day, attended by two million young people, John Paul . . . urged them 'to change direction and to turn to Christ.' 'Dear friends, when you go back home, set the Eucharist at the center of your personal life and community life. Love the Eucharist, adore the Eucharist and celebrate it, especially on Sundays, the Lord's day. Live the Eucharist by testifying to God's love for every person.' A continuing theme with John Paul, as he put it to the 1993 Eucharistic Congress, is his belief that 'the . . . surest and the most effective way of establishing peace on the face of the earth is through the great power of Perpetual Adoration of the Blessed Sacrament.'

"Which brings us back to Notre Dame. Many good things happen at Notre Dame from the bottom up. Students in ND/SMC Right to Life, with the cooperation of Campus Ministry, took the initiative in 1997 to establish Eucharistic adoration as an integral part of the pro-life effort. It is counter-cultural. But it is solidly based. As the *Catechism* states, 'The Eucharistic presence of Christ begins at the moment of consecration and endures as long as the Eucharistic species subsist. The Catholic Church has always offered . . . to the . . . Eucharist . . . adoration, not only during Mass, but also outside of it. . . . The Church and the world have a great need for Eucharistic worship. Jesus awaits us in this sacrament of love. Let us not refuse . . . to meet him in adoration, in contemplation . . . making amends for the serious offenses and crimes of the world. Let our adoration never cease.' Nos. 1377–80.

"So why should we rouse ourselves to give 30 minutes in this way? One reason is that it works. When Mother Teresa was asked, 'What will convert America and save the world?' she replied: 'My answer is prayer. What we need is for every parish to come before Jesus in the Blessed Sacrament in the holy hour of prayer.' Archbishop Fulton J. Sheen made a daily hour of adoration before the Blessed Sacrament every day of his priestly life. He said, '[T]he Holy Hour is not a devotion; it is a sharing in the work of redemption. In the Garden, our Lord contrasted two 'hours,'—one was the evil hour, 'this is your hour' with which Judas could turn out the lights of the world. In contrast, our Lord asked, 'Could you not watch one hour with Me?' He asked for an hour of reparation to combat the hour of evil. Not for an hour of activity did He plead but for an hour of companionship. . . .

"Each week has 168 hours. It is difficult to imagine a more practically effective way to spend 1/336th of our week. And while you are at it, remember that there is no rule against praying for the success of the football team."

HUMAN EMBRYONIC RESEARCH, Oct. 10, 2000

"Let's talk about your tax dollars at work. On Aug. 23, the National Institutes of Health (NIH) issued final guidelines on federal funding for research on

180

'human pluripotent stem cells derived from human embryos (technically known as human embryonic stem cells).' The studies will be funded 'only if the cells were derived (without federal funds) from human embryos that were created for the purposes of fertility treatment and were in excess of the clinical need of the individuals seeking such treatment.'

"The cells can be used to form any tissue of the human body except the placenta. Scientists hope the cells could play a role in curing Parkinson's, Alzheimer's, heart disease, diabetes, spinal cord injuries, burns and other ailments.

"There is just one catch. The human embryo, preserved by freezing, is not just a mass of cells. It is a human being. As Fr. Joseph C. Howard, Jr., of the American Bioethics Advisory Committee, put it, 'to obtain stem cells from a human embryo necessitates the removal of the inner cell mass which each and every time destroys a human life.'

"'Even if NIH doesn't grant funds to destroy human embryos,' said C. Ben Mitchell, senior fellow of the Center for Bioethics and Human Dignity, 'it is encouraging those who do by producing a 'market' for those cells.' In this process, human beings are reduced to objects of utility and ultimately commerce. A trade already exists in fetal tissue and we can expect one to develop in embryonic stem cells.

"It might be argued that these frozen embryos would be discarded and die anyway. But how is killing them for their cells different from what the Nazis did in harvesting the organs of Jews and other living inmates who were going to die anyway? And why not harvest the heart, kidneys, etc., of living persons on death row? And comatose patients whom nobody wants?. . . .

"Richard Doerflinger, of the National Conference of Catholic Bishops, said, 'The claim that embryonic stem cell research is needed for new medical advances has been rebutted by numerous breakthroughs in adult stem-cell research and other alternatives'. . . .

"'The Catholic Church is not opposed to adult stem-cell research or stem-cell research on umbilical cords because these procedures do not endanger life,' said Cardinal Anthony Bevilacqua of Philadelphia. . . . 'It is absolutely forbidden to directly destroy one innocent human being to help another.'

"In our pagan culture of death, we regard the intentional infliction of death as a legitimate and optional problem-solving technique. And law is a matter of will rather than reason. Whatever the State decrees is the law, unlimited by any higher standard of justice. In that culture of death, the human person is defined in functional terms. He is valued not for what he is, 'an immortal being endowed with unalienable rights by his Creator,' but for what he can do or for how he can be used for the benefit of others. We started down this road when, through the contraceptive ethic, we made man rather than God the arbiter of when and how life shall begin and, with abortion and euthanasia, of when and how it shall end. Tax-funded research on human embryonic stem cells is a predictable application of this utilitarian logic. And the end is not yet in sight.

"'Not since the exploits of German science in the earlier part of this century,' wrote columnist Paul Greenberg, 'have so many rationalizations been produced for experimenting on human tissue.' Don't think of it as a human being in embryo. And if all these sophisticated rationalizations still don't quite convince, then remember that they probably sounded a lot better in the original German. And ignore that still small voice in the back of your mind that keeps whispering: 'This is wrong.'"

THE ABORTION PILL, Oct. 31, 2000

"On Sept. 28, the Food and Drug Administration approved the marketing of mifepristone, or RU-486, the abortion pill used in France for more than a decade. . . .

"The drug will allow women to have abortions in the privacy of their own homes up to seven weeks after their last menstrual period. . . .

"Apart from the risk to the mother, a further legal complication in the use of RU-486 is the possible application to it of state laws that regulate abortion, including notice to parents of a minor, counseling and waiting periods, disposal of fetal remains, etc.

"Physicians already can terminate pregnancies by giving high doses of birth control pills, or the 'emergency contraceptive' pill, within 72 hours of unprotected intercourse. Human life begins at the fertilization of the ovum by the sperm. Such 'morning after' pills or 'emergency contraceptives' are therefore not truly contraceptives. They kill the unborn child by preventing his implantation in the wall of the womb from which he would otherwise draw sustenance until his birth.

"RU-486 allows the mother to kill by pill at later stages than such early abortifacients. . . . Technology is making abortion a truly private matter, beyond the effective reach of the law.

"Legalized abortion, whether surgical or chemical, is an outgrowth of the contraceptive ethic in which one makes himself or herself the arbiter of whether and when life shall begin and, predictably, of whether and when it shall end. In *Evangelium Vitae*, John Paul II described abortion and contraception as 'closely related, as fruits of the same tree.' '[T]he pro-abortion culture,' he said, 'is especially strong . . . where the church's teaching on contraception is rejected. [I]n . . . many . . . instances such practices are rooted in a hedonistic mentality unwilling to accept responsibility . . . and they imply a self-centered concept of freedom, which regards procreation as an obstacle to personal fulfillment. The life which could result from a sexual encounter thus becomes an enemy to be avoided at all costs, and abortion becomes the only possible decisive response to contraception. The close connection between . . . contraception and . . . abortion . . . is . . . demonstrated . . . by the development of . . . products, . . . which, distributed with the same ease as contraceptives, . . . act as abortifacients in the very early stages of . . . the life of the new human being.'

"It is fitting that the manufacturer of RU-486 . . . is Hua Lian Pharmaceutical Co. in Shanghai. RU-486 is used in China to implement its one-child policy which includes forced abortion and infanticide. China, of course, cares nothing for the life of the child nor for the health of the mother. Neither, it appears, does the Clinton Administration."

HOMOSEXUALITY AND COURAGE, Nov. 28, 2000

"At Notre Dame good things happen from the bottom up. For example, on Nov. 9 the Maritain Center, Knights of Columbus and St. Thomas More Society sponsored a presentation by Father John Harvey, OSFS, and David Morrison on Catholic teaching and homosexuality. . . .

"Father Harvey and Morrison put this issue in a personalized context. At the request of Terence Cardinal Cooke of New York in 1980, Father Harvey founded Courage, the growing international support group for men and women and a support group for parents, called Encourage.

"The Five Goals of Courage, written by the early members, are: '1. To live chaste lives in accordance with the Roman Catholic Church's teaching on homosexuality; 2. To dedicate our entire lives to Christ; 3. To foster . . . fellowship [to] ensure that none of us will have to face the problems of homosexuality alone; 4. . . . [T]o encourage one another in forming and sustaining [chaste friendships.] 5. To live lives that may serve as good examples to others with homosexual difficulties.'

"Courage members 'follow a plan of life that takes the person as far as possible from the gay milieu. . . . Since Courage is primarily concerned with helping individuals to live a life of interior chastity, it does not require that its members strive to get out of the condition itself. Courage, however, does encourage members who want to do so to seek counsel and group therapy in a context of prayer.'

"David Morrison, author of *Beyond Gay*, described his 'pilgrimage from being a homosexual-rights activist to living life as a chaste Catholic. I had a lover of five years, a condominium in a major urban area, a satisfying job, and a church life as an Episcopalian.' The writings of the Protestant, Dietrich Bonhoeffer, martyred by the Nazis, led Morrison to embark on what became his 'journey to the Catholic faith . . . [T]he Catholic Church is the only Christian institution that not only preaches the truth of chastity for homosexual people but offers practical, tangible help for achieving it.'

"'In the act of 'coming out," notes Morrison, 'one sacrifices individual personhood for identity in the group . . . Homosexual orientation is not a choice for most people, but being gay is and it is this choice which motivates homosexual groups ranging from Dignity to ACT UP.'

"It has not been proven that the homosexual inclination is genetic or otherwise innate. We do not definitively know what causes that inclination. Yet there is abundant evidence that persons of homosexual inclination can lead chaste lives committed to Christ. Neither Father Harvey nor Morrison makes any universal claim beyond that, although they affirm that some persons of homosexual inclination have been able, with counseling and therapy, to go on to marriage and successful heterosexual lives.

"The Administration misleads Notre Dame students here. The Administration refuses to admit that the homosexual inclination is disordered. Yet the Administration affirms that 'official Church teaching' mandates that the inclination may not be acted upon. This implies that the 'Church teaching' is an arbitrary restriction. If the inclination is not disordered, why may it not be acted upon? In truth, homosexual acts and the inclination toward them are 'objectively disordered' because they are contrary to the nature built into us by God. The recognition of this reality is the first step toward a coherent approach to this question.

"The Administration should invite Father Harvey to form a Courage chapter at Notre Dame. Students could benefit from the efforts of this admirable, perceptive and charitable priest. Political correctness ought not to stand in the way."

HIGH TUITION IN THE RESEARCH UNIVERSITY, Jan. 17, 2001

"Every Christmas I get a personal, first-name invitation to join the Sorin Society. If I pay $1,000, benefits include 'regional meetings' and the President's Newsletter. For $3,000 I could join the Founder's Circle and receive a video, an 'ombudsman service' for tickets to non-athletic events and other comparable perks. I have not been able to join, but every year I feel a rush of self-esteem. This is recognition that I am a somebody, worthy to be a player in the University's inner circle.

"One reason I would like to join is to ask the movers and shakers one question: With unprecedented sums cascading into the University's coffers, why does tuition keep rising beyond the inflation rate? . . . .

"Increasingly, colleges, like used car lots, discount their 'sticker price' through aid packages. But why should that process begin with a sticker price that rises every year above the inflation rate? And could not our fundraisers, the best in the nation, raise funds targeted to offset a freeze or even a rollback in tuition?

"Our leaders act in what they see as the best interests of Notre Dame. These comments are directed at policies not persons. But the rise in tuition beyond the inflation rate reflects a change in priorities over the past two decades. Notre Dame here is a follower, not a leader.

"In the nation generally, until the late '70s, tuition increased at or below the inflation rate. In 1978, in response to pressure from universities, Congress relaxed the income restrictions on federal guaranteed student loans. As *Fortune* magazine warned, 'Anything that makes it easier to pay tuition bills will also make it easier to raise tuition charges.' Since 1980, according to the College Board, median family income, adjusted for inflation, rose 20 percent while tuition at private four-year universities rose by 118 percent.

"The universities lobbied Congress for funding for student loans. But as loan availability went up, so did tuition beyond the inflation rate, with those universities financing their research and other expansion projects on the backs of the borrowing students. Notre Dame was far from the worst offender. But after proclaiming itself a National Catholic Research University in 1978, Notre Dame did play this shabby game. In 1978–79, when the Endowment was only $114 million, Notre Dame's undergrad tuition, room and board was $5,180. Today, adjusted for inflation, that total would be $13,468. In 2000–2001, the charge is $29,100, more than double, in real money, what is was in 1978–79. Notre Dame makes a strong effort to provide financial aid. . . . But the primary form of financial aid remains the student loan. . . .

"The historical mission of Notre Dame had been the provision of affordable education in the Catholic tradition to undergrads with research and grad programs in a complementary role. The relentless increase of tuition over the past two decades reflects a shift in emphasis to the pursuit of money and prestige as a Research University. A freeze or rollback in tuition could symbolize a redirection of that shift. Research is important, especially in the sciences. But Notre Dame ought not to have a regular faculty which teaches less and less to students who pay more and more.

"In the pursuit of prestige and money, the undergrad mission is devalued. Members of our family were Notre Dame undergrads every year from 1977 to 2000 in various majors. Our experience, admittedly subjective but supported by others, is that, in the variety of available courses, class size, quality of teaching, and the recognition of students as persons, the undergrad experience at Notre Dame has deteriorated since 1977. And our leaders are not even close to finishing the 'binge building' which has converted the formerly pastoral Notre Dame into a cramped, urban-style research campus.

"If I joined the Sorin Society perhaps I could raise these questions. Maybe there's financial aid to enable guys like me to join. Maybe I could get a federal loan. . . ."

DEATH ROW MARV, Jan. 30, 2001

"One of the hot toys this Christmas was Death Row Marv, a 6-inch doll complete with 'chair, wired helmet . . . and . . . switch.' Marv can move his neck, torso and arms. For $23.95, the ad urges the targeted 13-year-olds to '[f]eel the burn as the electric buzz fills the room and he starts to shake and convulse. Experience the pain as the shaking continues and his eyes start to glow bright red. Enjoy the torment.' As columnist Michelle Malkin noted, more than 65,000 were sold and there were 'waiting lists across the country.'

"What brings this to mind is the media frenzy building toward Timothy McVeigh's May 16 execution. McVeigh abandoned his appeals on his conviction of blowing up the Oklahoma City federal building in 1995, killing 168, including 19 children and injuring more than 500. . . .

"McVeigh's acceptance of execution does not avoid the question: Does the government have the right to kill him?

"The State, which derives its authority from God, has authority to impose the death penalty 'if this is the only possible way of . . . defending human lives against the unjust aggressor. If . . . non-lethal means are sufficient to . . . protect people's safety from the aggressor, authority will limit itself to such means, as these are more in keeping with . . . the common good and . . . the dignity of the human person. Today, . . . as a consequence of the possibilities which the state has for . . . rendering one who has committed an offense incapable of doing harm without . . . taking away from him the possibility of redeeming himself the cases in which . . . execution . . . is an absolute necessity are very rare if not practically nonexistent.' *Catechism*, no. 2267.

"That penalty cannot be justified as a means to retribution or to the protection of society by deterring other offenders. Rather it must be absolutely necessary to protect other lives from this convicted criminal. . . . The alternative to executing McVeigh is life without parole, which can be as onerous as execution. As the *Denver Post* editorialized, 'Death by . . . injection would be too quick and easy.'

"The death penalty . . . is a deceptive quick-fix. . . . As Archbishop Charles Chaput of Denver said in opposing the McVeigh sentence, 'Capital punishment is just another drug we take to ease other, much deeper anxieties about the direction of our culture. Executions may take away some of the symptoms for a time (symptoms who have names and their own stories before God), but the underlying illness—today's contempt for human life—remains and grows worse.'

186

"The death penalty kills the guilty rather than the innocent. However, as with abortion and euthanasia, mass bombing of civilians in Kosovo, etc., it reflects an acceptance of the intentional infliction of death as an optional problem-solving technique.

"There is cause for concern when the killing of a human being becomes a media event which will cater to the voyeurism characteristic of our culture of death. Video games, rap music and other amusements have accustomed many, especially the young, to seek pleasure in portrayals of the infliction of pain and even of death on others. Death Row Marv is the poster boy of such a culture.

"Cain was a more notorious murderer even than McVeigh. Yet God put a mark on Cain, 'to protect . . . him from those wishing to kill him. . . . Not even a murderer loses his personal dignity . . . God, who preferred the correction rather than the death of a sinner, did not desire that a homicide be punished by . . . another . . . homicide.' *Evangelium Vitae*, no. 9.

"'We must build a new culture of life,' said John Paul. 'The first . . . step [is] forming consciences with regard to the . . . inviolable worth of every human life.'. . . . In his challenge to our pagan culture of death, John Paul insists that God—not the individual and not the state—is in charge of the ending as well as the beginning of life."

NOTE: Timothy McVeigh was executed on June 11, 2001, at the federal prison in Terre Haute, IN.

BENGAL BOUTS: NOT THE XFL, Feb. 13, 2001

"Knute Rockne began an informal boxing program at Notre Dame in the late 1920s. Dominic (Nappy) Napolitano, the legendary director of non-varsity athletics, carried it forward to begin the Bengal Bouts in 1931. Every year, all proceeds go to support the Holy Cross missions in Bangladesh. . . .

"The Boxing Club provides a unique experience to its participants. 'At Notre Dame,' said assistant coach Pat Farrell, who is also the University pilot and a former Bengal Bouts champ, 'boxing is . . . an extension of the classroom. The vast majority of our boxers have never before been in the ring. They learned about themselves. They learned how to deal with adversity under pressure. You are on your own in the ring. No substitutions, no time outs. Above all, no excuses. No rationalizing that someone else's missed block or tackle may have altered the outcome.'

"The Club is run by the student captains: Brian Hobbins, Josh Thompson, Pete Ryan, Dennis Abdelnour, Rob Joyce, Mark Criniti and Matt Fumigalli. They run the practices, make the pairings and bring the younger boxers along effectively.

"Incidentally, visitors are welcome at the practices in the JACC. Throughout the program, safety is the primary concern. If you like the XFL—the Xtreme Football League—which signals our athletic culture's descent to a new level of violence and voyeurism, you won't like the Bengal Bouts. The practices and the bouts are tightly monitored by medical personnel under the supervision of Dr. James Moriarty, University chief of medicine. Entering our eighth decade, we have never had a serious injury. We pray and work that it will remain so.

"The Bengal Bouts' proceeds began their climb from the $10,000 range when Emily Schmidt, '99, took over the business end, including promotion, in 1996. Meghan Kelley, '02, who worked with Emily, now runs the show and has taken it to even greater heights. She is ably assisted by Ellen Quinn, '01, Dave Peloquin, '03, and Laura Anderson, '03. They are an impressive team.

"The Bouts are under the supervision of Rich O'Leary, director of Club Sports. Rich works through an exceptional group of volunteers. Columbus, Ohio, developer Tom Suddes and Chicago lawyer Terry Johnson, who are Bengals champs from 1971 and 1974, are the head coaches. In addition to coach Farrell, the assistant coaches include former Bengal champs Chip Farrell, '98, Ryan Rans, '98, and John Christoforetti, '97.

"We have a living link to Rockne and Nappy in 87-year-old Jack Mooney. Jack delivered papers to Rockne, who used to sneak him into football games. Every day at practice, Jack actively coaches the boxers; his primary concern is their safety and personal development during and after the program. Jack's assistant is former professional boxer Jack Zimmerman, who is also a poet of note. Coach Farrell works the corners at the Bouts, along with Judge Roland Chamblee, '73, of the Superior Court in South Bend who is a four-time Bengals champ and Sweet C. Robinson, a former police officer and professional kick-boxing champion. We also have an ecclesiastical bell-ringer in Monsignor John Hagerty, a Notre Dame man who takes his vacation from his duties as pastor of Notre Dame Church in Hermitage, Pa., to work on the Bouts.

"So why should the Notre Dame community support the Bouts? Let Archbishop Laurence Graner, of Dacca, answer. 'I wish I could conduct you and the whole student body on a complete tour of the Bengal missions,' he said. 'I believe your enthusiasm for the Bouts and for the Bengal missionaries of Holy Cross would know a blessed closeness and intensity never before felt.'"

ARE PETS PEOPLE? March 8, 2001

"If you live in West Hollywood and go home on break, be nice to that dog you used to own. The City Council has decreed that you are no longer a 'pet owner' but a 'pet guardian.' It's 'the latest ordinance,' said the *L.A. Daily News*, 'from a city . . . in the vanguard of liberal causes, from homosexual rights to condom distribution to animal cruelty laws.' 'The resolution,' according to Mayor Jeffrey Prang, 'has a symbolic purpose' as a reminder that animals have rights.

"Questions arise. Can a 'guardian' sterilize his or her ward without that ward's consent? A new breed of 'doggie lawyers' can be counted on to make something and contingent fees out of that. Harvard last year started the nation's first law school course in Animal Rights Law. Princeton's Peter Singer, the father (sorry, parent) of the animal rights movement, attacks 'speciesism,' which is prejudice against persons of another species. He defines a person as 'a rational and self-conscious being.' Singer regards 'newborn infants and some mental defectives' as nonpersons. But chimpanzees, dolphins, dogs, cats, bears and even chickens can make the personhood cut. For Singer, 'killing . . . a chimpanzee is worse than the killing of a . . . defective human who is not a person.'

"Thus he concludes that 'parents of severely disabled babies . . . should be allowed to kill a child whose prospects for a minimally decent life are very poor.' The animal rights movement has a lighter side. Flughund, a German 'canine travel agency,' specializes in dream vacations for pets, including doggie cinemas (Lassie films are the big favorite), dog restaurants and massage parlors. 'People would be surprised,' said Flughund's director, 'at the range of dog-related holidays . . . around the world.'

"Let's look at some basics. We know from reason that humans have a spiritual soul because we can engage in the spiritual activities of abstraction and reflection. The nature of a spiritual being is that it will not die, since death is the breaking up of a thing into its parts and a spiritual entity has no parts. Therefore we are immortal. Dogs, other animals and plants have souls because the soul is the life principle of something that is alive. The soul of a dog, however, is material. This means that the animal soul is dependent for its existence on the matter of which it is the life principle. We know by observation that animals have no spiritual intellect. They cannot form abstract ideas or reflect on themselves. Have you ever seen a bird on a tree branch scrutinizing a set of plans? Birds build nests according to the instincts programmed into them by their designer, i.e., God.

"In the nature of things and in God's design, animals themselves have no rights. We can own animals because they are things and not persons. As Thomas Aquinas noted, 'The rational plan of divine providence demands that the other creatures be ruled by rational creatures.' '[T]he order of things,' said Aquinas, 'is such that the imperfect are for the perfect. . . . [I]t is lawful both to take life from plants for the use of animals, and from animals for the use of man.' Vatican II described 'man' as 'the only creature on earth that God has wanted for its own sake.'

"'Use of the mineral, vegetable, and animal resources of the universe cannot be divorced from . . . moral imperatives. . . . [S]cientific experimentation on animals, if . . . reasonable . . . is . . . morally acceptable. . . . It is contrary to human dignity to cause animals to suffer or die needlessly. It is . . . unworthy to spend money on them that should . . . go to the relief of human misery. One can love animals; one should not direct to them the affection due only to persons.' *Catechism*, Nos. 2415, 2417, 2418.

"In short, man owes a duty to God to make reasonable use of animals. The animal rights movement, instead, in Singer's words, treats 'ethics as entirely independent of religion' and rejects 'the idea that human beings are a special form of creation, made in the image of God . . . and . . . possessing an immortal soul.' Our elites foster a culture that rejects God and therefore views man as nothing special. The implicit legitimization in our law of euthanasia of some patients by 'terminal sedation' validates a process that is really no different from putting a dog to sleep.

"'When the sense of God is lost,' said John Paul, 'there is also a tendency to lose the sense of man, of his dignity and his life.' (*Evangelium Vitae*, no. 21).

"Every culture has to have a god. Ours rejects the real God and deifies material nature, inanimate as well as animate. It is a new, but old, pagan religion. As an ideology, it tends to apply its principle with rigorous logic. In England the Animal Liberation Front has gone to war in defense of fish and cockroaches. This recently came to light when letter bombs packed with nails exploded in a fish-and-chips shop and in the offices of a pest-control firm.

"So when you go home, be nice to Wrecks, or whatever your 'ward' calls himself. He has friends. And if you are nice to him maybe he will take you along on his next vacation to Maui."

PARENTS AND SCHOOL VIOLENCE, March 20, 2001

"If your dog bit someone, you could be civilly and perhaps criminally liable even if the dog had never bitten anyone before. Is your duty to control your dog greater than a parent's duty to control his child? The question arises in the wake of the Santana High School shootings in Santee, Ca. Charles Andrew Williams, 15, will be tried as an adult for killing two students and wounding 13 with his father's revolver.

"At common law, the parent (or guardian) could be liable for injury caused by his child where the parent had notice of the child's dangerous tendency and failed to prevent the injury by reasonably controlling the child. Most states also impose parental liability by statute, up to a stated amount, for a child's torts, or, in some states, 'criminal gang' activity. Many states impose criminal liability on parents for crimes committed by their minor children, especially with firearms, if there is intent or criminal negligence on the part of the parent and the parent's act or failure caused the child's act.

"Parental liability laws are sound in principle but difficult to enforce. Their efficacy is debatable. . . .

"Stricter enforcement of parental liability would probably not have prevented the killings at Santana and other schools. Nor is it likely that those killings would have been avoided by stricter gun control, more police and metal detectors at schools and other measures which address symptoms. . . .

"But, as Education Secretary Rod Paige said, 'It's beyond guns. The guns may be the instrument of the violence, but they're not the cause of the violence.' One cause is the collapse of the American family. Marisa McFedries, director of the City of Santee teen center, said, 'Something's missing in these kids' lives. They're on their own. Their parents work all the time. Their peers have become family.'

"Former Education Secretary William Bennett states, in his Index of Cultural Indicators 2001, 'A child conceived in the United States today . . . has a 25 percent chance of not being brought to term, because of abortion. . . . If that child is born, there's a 33 percent chance he will be born out of wedlock. And for children who are not born out of wedlock, there's a 50 percent chance that their parents will divorce before they're 16.'

"'The scale of marital breakdown in the West since 1960 has no historical precedent,' he said. 'The breakup of the American family is the most profound . . . social trend of our time.'

"Two other causes were noted by Denver Archbishop Charles Chaput in his 1999 Senate testimony on Columbine: 'First . . . we've lost our common sense. . . . The reasonable person understands that what we eat, drink and breathe will make us healthy or sick. In like manner, what we hear and . . . see lifts us up—or drags us down. . . . Common sense tells us that the violence of our music, our video games, our films, and our television has to go somewhere, and it goes straight into the hearts of our children to bear fruit in ways we can't imagine—until something like [Columbine] happens.'

"'Second, . . . the real problem is . . . in us, and it won't be fixed by v-chips. . . . We've created a culture that markets violence in dozens of . . . ways, seven days a week. When we build our advertising campaigns on . . . selfishness and greed, and when money becomes the universal measure of value, how can we be surprised when our sense of community erodes? . . . When we answer murder with more violence in the death penalty, we put the state's seal of approval on revenge. When the most dangerous place in the country is a mother's womb and the unborn child can have his or her head crushed in an abortion, even in the process of being born, the . . . message . . . is that life . . . may not be worth much at all. . . . Certain kinds of killing we enshrine as rights and protect by law. When we live this kind of contradiction, why are we surprised at the results? I don't think [the Columbine murders] will be the last. . . . Nothing makes us immune from that violence except a relentless commitment to respect the sanctity of each human life, from womb to natural death.' Maybe it's time to pay attention. Mother Teresa, as usual, gave us the bottom line: 'If we accept that a mother can kill even her own child, how can we tell other people not to kill one another?'"

FAMILY DECLINE, April 4, 2001

"Is the 'traditional' family, based on the marriage of a man and a woman, on the way out? Maybe so. Consider two signs."

First, cohabitation without benefit of marriage is rapidly becoming the statistical norm. . . .

"Cohabitation, incidentally, increases despite evidence . . . that it does not work too well: 'Only about 1/6 of cohabiting couples endure for three years, and only 1/10 last 10 years or more. Couples who cohabit before marriage are almost twice as likely to divorce as those who do not. . . .

"The second sign is that seven states, numerous local governments, federal agencies and private employers have extended to unmarried couples—homosexual as well as heterosexual—pension, health and other benefits comparable to those extended to married couples. . . .

"Should the law exclusively favor the traditional marriage and family? The logic of the individualist contraceptive ethic would say no. In the natural order of things, one reason why sex is reserved for marriage and why marriage is between a man and a woman is because sex has an intrinsic relation to babies. But if it is up to the discretion of man (of both sexes) whether sex will have any relation to procreation, why should sex be reserved for marriage? And why should the law exclusively define 'marriage' as male-female?

"Last July the Pontifical Council for the Family issued a document, *Family, Marriage and De Facto Unions*, offering reasons why marriage is a 'natural' institution prior to the state and why the family must be favored by the law.

"The Council framed the issue as one of 'justice, which means treating equals equally, and what is different differently.' It would be unjust 'if de facto unions were given a juridical treatment similar . . . to the family based on marriage [because] society would take on obligations towards the partners in a de facto union [but] they in turn would not take on the . . . obligations to society that are proper to marriage.'

"Marriage, in the words of John Paul II, is entitled to a 'juridical status that recognizes the rights and duties of the spouses to one another and to their children. . . . Families play an essential role in society, whose permanence they guarantee. The family fosters the socialization of the young and helps curb . . . violence by transmitting values and . . . brotherhood and solidarity.'

"The traditional family, based on marriage, has been privileged by the law because it is the seedbed for future generations. The partners in a heterosexual de facto union make no comparable binding and public commitments to themselves, their children or society. 'Even more serious,' in the Council's view, is 'the grave error of recognizing or even making homosexual relations equivalent to marriage.'

"The Council quoted John Paul II on the point: 'The demand to grant marital status, to unions between persons of the same sex . . . is opposed . . . by the . . . impossibility of making the partnership fruitful . . . according to the plan inscribed by God in the very structure of the human being. Another obstacle is the absence of . . . that . . . complementarity between male and female willed by the Creator. . . . Lastly, de facto unions between homosexuals are a deplorable distortion of what should be a communion of love and life between a man and a woman in a reciprocal gift open to life. . . . The bond between two men or two women cannot constitute a real family and much less can the right be attributed to that union to adopt children without a family.' . . .

"A society in which it makes no difference whether boys marry girls or other boys is on a dead-end road to extinction. Society and the state cannot be neutral on the definition of marriage and on the moral question of whether the family based on marriage should be exclusively promoted by the law. The evidence is abundant that our 'Cultural Indicators' are moving in the wrong direction. We ought to think seriously about that."

EX CORDE: A STUDENT'S BILL OF RIGHTS, May 1, 2001

"*Ex Corde Ecclesiae*, the constitution on Catholic higher education issued by John Paul II in 1990, will go into effect in the United States this month. The Vatican and the American Catholic bishops have worked out an application of *Ex Corde* to the United States which emphasizes dialogue rather than confrontation. . . .

"*Ex Corde* and the application are really a students' bill of rights. The local bishop has a duty to 'watch over the . . . Catholic character of the university.' The bishops do not run the place but 'they should be . . . participants in the life of the Catholic university.' The bishop is concerned with the rights of all involved, including students: 'Catholic students have a right to . . . instruction in authentic Catholic doctrine and practice [and] to be provided with opportunities to practice the faith.' Students' rights are implicated also in the requirement that 'The university should strive to . . . appoint Catholic as professors so that, to the extent possible, those committed to the witness of the faith will constitute a majority of the faculty. All professors are expected to be . . . committed to the Catholic mission and identity of their institutions.'

"The most controversial point in the application is that 'Catholics who teach the theological disciplines in a Catholic university are required to have a mandatum granted by competent ecclesiastical authority.' . . .

"All these requirements protect students' rights through the principle of truth in labeling. . . .

"But what will be the effect of *Ex Corde*? It is fair to speculate that, in addition to the emerging technologies of 'distance education,' potential students will have four main alternatives:

"1. Some major Catholic colleges and universities will reject *Ex Corde* formally or in practice. Some will be committed to the model of the secular research university, especially in faculty and student recruitment. They may have a Catholic presence and student groups and individual faculty with Catholic interests. They will profess their 'Catholic' character, especially to potential Catholic donors. But the evidence of that character will become anecdotal and marginal because the institution will be cut off from active communion with the Church. Those 'Catholic Lite' universities will be pretentious and expensive. They will retain an upscale constituency. But for those who want the real Catholic thing, they will not be worth the money. As secular, they will never be among the best. As 'Catholic,' they will become irrelevant.

"2. Some Catholic colleges and universities, including some major research universities, will accept *Ex Corde* and will seriously try to implement it.

"3. Institutions such as Franciscan University of Steubenville, Christendom College, Ave Maria University, Thomas Aquinas College in California and others enthusiastically accept *Ex Corde*. They offer on a smaller scale an excellent Catholic liberal arts education at a much lower cost than the major institutions.

"4. Catholic centers at secular institutions may be a window on the future, enabling students to integrate their studies into a Catholic intellectual and spiritual life. For in-state students at state universities, this may be a way to achieve a sound Catholic formation without heavy debt. One example is the Newman Foundation at the University of Illinois at Champaign-Urbana, where 12,000 of the 35,000 students are Catholic. The Foundation includes St. John's Catholic Chapel, the Newman Library for research and study, residence halls for men and for women, with a dining hall, computer lab, and 350 students in residence, and four religion courses which students may take for university credit. The chapel seats 800, with six Masses on Sunday and three each weekday, including a Spanish Mass.

"Such centers fill a need, especially for non-wealthy Catholic students.

"'It is certainly easier,' said Father Hesburgh two decades ago, 'just to be a great university, and not to worry about being a Catholic university as well.' But the great universities were Catholic in their origin. Only a Catholic university can really be great, because, as *Ex Corde* put it, 'by its Catholic character a university is made more capable of conducting an impartial search for truth, a search that is neither subordinated to nor conditioned by particular interests of any kind.'

"This is a time for choosing, for truth in labeling, requiring every college or university that claims to be 'Catholic' to put up or shut up."

2001–2002

TUITION AND THE MOUSE, Sept. 4, 2001

"*Pariuntur montes, nascetur ridiculum mus.* The mountains will be in labor, and will bring forth a ridiculous little mouse.

"That line from the Roman poet Horace was brought to mind by the 4.9 percent tuition, room and board increase for 2001–2002, to $30,530. It was the lowest percentage increase since 1959 when there was no increase over the previous year.

"The increase satisfies the Trustees' mandate that tuition increases be held to about 5 percent. And the administration, especially through the excellent financial aid office, does make commendable efforts to increase scholarships and reduce student dependence on loans. Unfortunately, the primary form of financial aid remains the student loan.

"Given the good intentions of our leaders, why does the increase remind one of Horace's little mouse? Because the administration had an opportunity for leadership here and blew it. . . .

"Hope had flickered this spring that, just maybe, this would be the year our leaders would reverse the inexorable escalation of the 'sticker price' beyond the inflation rate. The tuition, room and board charge, in real money, has more than doubled since Notre Dame proclaimed itself a National Catholic Research University in 1978. Notre Dame's total charge in 1978–79 was $5,180. If it had kept pace with inflation, it would now be $13,468 instead of $30,530.

"Money continues to cascade into the University's coffers in record amounts from numerous sources, including the endowment and various contributions. The Generations Campaign, concluded last December 31st, raised $1,061,097,581 (that's $1.06 billion), or $98,249.76 for each of the 10,800 undergrad and grad students now enrolled at Notre Dame. So, some had hoped, perhaps 2001–2002 would be the year for this Research University to signal a shift in priorities by freezing tuition or at least holding any increase below this year's 3.7 rise in the Consumer Price Index.

"This, however, is where Horace comes in. After abundant publicity celebrating their fundraising successes, our leaders announced the 4.9 percent increase to $30,530, a rise of $1430. That 4.9 percent increase makes the total for 2001–2002 $83 less than the $30,613 total it would have been if last year's increase of 5.2 percent had been repeated. Our leaders labored mightily, at least in proclaiming the University's new wealth. And then they brought forth a ridiculous mouse, an $83 reduction in the increase of the gouge, a trifle that was raised to the level of insult when it became the launching pad for self-congratulatory statements by the administration.

"Notre Dame should be the national leader, not a timid follower, in making an authentically Catholic education accessible to non-wealthy, qualified students. A tuition freeze, or at least an increase below the inflation rate, would have symbolized a commitment in that direction. Our leaders evidently have other priorities, including principally the pursuit of money in the hunt for ranking and prestige. But we can continue to hope. Maybe next year. . . ."

RESPONSE TO 9/11, Sept. 18, 2001

"In light of the recent terrorist attacks, it may be useful to review some points on the legitimacy and conduct of war.

"First, and obvious: The government of the United States in this case, in defense of the common good, has the right and duty to use force, both to restore the balance of justice by punishing the perpetrators and their facilitators and to render them incapable, by death or otherwise, of again committing such an act.

"Provided, of course, that the responsible parties or nations, including aiders and abettors, are identified, the traditional elements of the just war, as stated in the *Catechism*, no. 2309, would appear to be satisfied here:

"1. '[T]he damage inflicted by the aggressor [is] lasting, grave and certain;'

"2. Other means of recourse 'are impractical or ineffective;'

"3. There are 'serious prospects of success;'

"4. '[T]he use of arms must not produce evils and disorders graver than the evil to be eliminated.'

"This last requirement, one of proportionality, leads to the second basic point: Two criteria, proportionality and discrimination, govern the conduct of a just war.

"Proportionality requires that tactics and weapons used must be proportionate to the situation. Discrimination, as the Catholic bishops of the United States said in their 1983 pastoral letter, 'prohibits directly intended attacks on noncombatants and nonmilitary targets.'

"In the words of the Second Vatican Council, 'Every act of war directed to the indiscriminate destruction of whole cities or vast areas with their inhabitants is a crime against God and man, which merits firm and unequivocal condemnation.'

"Cardinal John O'Connor of New York, for example, strongly expressed his doubt in 1999 that the NATO bombing of Serbia met this criterion of discrimination.

"The recent hijacking and bombings justify and even demand a conclusive military response. They were deliberate attacks on innocent civilians. They do not justify, however, a response in kind. This does not mean that a military response by the United States and its allies cannot legitimately kill innocent civilians. Pursuant to the principle of the double effect, it can be morally justified to attack a military target of sufficient importance even though the attacker knows, but does not intend, that innocent civilians will be killed in the attack. The key is the intent. No one ever has the moral right intentionally to kill the innocent. But the good act of attacking the legitimate target can be justified even though it has the unintended evil effect of killing the innocent, provided that the good effect of the attack is not obtained by means of the evil effect and provided there is sufficient reason for permitting the unintended evil effect.

"The third point of this essay is more basic. What good can come out of this atrocity? Nothing happens in this world except by the ordaining or permitting will of God. As Saint Maximilian Kolbe, martyred at Auschwitz, said, 'God permits everything in view of a greater blessing.' The innocent died here, as did the innocent victims in Oklahoma City. They are all in the care of a loving God. The most effective thing we can do is pray for them, the injured, the missing and all their families, as well as, it must be said, for the hijackers.

"For our part, the recent events may lead to good as a wake-up call, prompting us to reexamine some things. The *Magnificat* series of monthly prayer books offered, remarkably, for Sept. 12, the day after the terrorist attacks, a striking meditation from Father Walter Ciszek, S.J., who spent 23 years in Soviet prisons. Father Ciszek wrote, 'We begin to take things for granted, to rely on ourselves and on our own resources. . . . We go along, taking for granted that tomorrow will be very much like today, comfortable in the world we have created for ourselves. [We] give little thought to God at all. Somehow . . . God must contrive to break through . . . and remind us once again, like Israel, that we are ultimately dependent on him. . . . Then it is, perhaps, that he must allow our whole world to be turned upside down . . . to remind us that it is not our permanent abode . . . to turn our thoughts once more to him—even if at first our thoughts are full of questionings and reproaches.'

"Something to think about."

BUSH COMPROMISE ON EMBRYONIC STEM CELL RESEARCH, Oct. 2, 2001

"Should taxpayers pay for research on embryonic stem cells? The answer offered, with evident sincerity, by President Bush is neither moral nor capable of practical limitation.

"In its earliest days, the embryo is a living human composed of stem cells, each of which can develop into all or many of the more than 200 tissues in the human body. If stem cells are removed to a dish they can replenish themselves in 'lines,' perhaps indefinitely. Stem cells can also be obtained from adults, in bone marrow and other sources. Scientists hope that research on stem cells, whether from embryos or adults, can lead to relief for some diseases, including Parkinson's, Alzheimer's and others.

"No moral problems arise in the use of stem cells derived from adults. But to obtain stem cells from a human embryo requires the removal of the inner cell mass which terminates the life of that embryo.

"President Bush said: 'We do not end some lives for the medical benefit of others. . . . [T]hat life, including early life, is biologically human, genetically distinct and valuable. [We can] promote stem cell research without . . . ethical abuses. First, we can encourage research on stem cells removed from sources other than embryos. . . . Second, we can encourage research on embryonic stem cell lines that already exist. . . . Therefore . . . [f]ederal funding for research on existing stem cell lines will move forward; federal funding that sanctions or encourages the destruction of additional embryos will not. While it is unethical to end life in medical research, it is ethical to benefit from research where life and death decisions have already been made.'

"Bush approved funding on cell lines 'derived (1) with the informed consent of donors, (2) from excess embryos created solely for reproductive purposes and (3) without any financial inducement to the donors.' His policy differs from National Institutes of Health guidelines, issued in 2000, only in that he would not fund research on lines created after his August 9 announcement.

"One question is whether the parents of an embryo have standing to consent to the killing of their child so that his body can be used for research. And proper consent obviously is absent where embryos are created for the purpose of killing them to obtain their stem cells.

"Apart from consent, the decision to fund research on existing cell lines is not intrinsically wrong. With proper consent, one can morally use the body of a murder victim for research. But the Bush policy is immoral for circumstantial reasons.

"The policy 'encourages' scientists to kill more embryos by extracting their stem cells in the hope of persuading the government to fund research on them. And it 'encourages' the creation of embryos for the specific purpose of killing them and seeking federal funding for such research. Pressure for funding of new cell lines will be irresistible because the Bush policy already concedes the legitimacy of funding research on stem cells after embryos have been killed.

"The Bush policy involves the government in scandalous complicity in murder, both as to existing cell lines and especially as to any lines created in the future.

"Remember: Each of us is a former embryo. Each and every killing of a human embryo by removal of the stem cells is, in moral terms, a homicide. It is no defense that the victims were going to die anyway. Aren't we all? Nor is it a defense that the research will benefit older human beings, as when the Nazis and Japanese, in World War II, used prisoners in lethal experiments. And if we can kill innocent human beings to use their bodies to save lives, what conclusive objection can there be to killing them to make lampshades?

"Under *Roe v. Wade,* the unborn child is a nonperson until birth and therefore destruction of the embryo is a constitutional right. President Bush missed an opportunity to challenge that nonpersonhood of the youngest human beings. His focus only on funding implicitly concedes the legitimacy, under *Roe,* of the research itself, of homicide as a scientific technique. This carries us further down the path charted by the contraceptive ethic in which man makes himself (or herself) the arbiter of whether and when life shall begin (and, implicitly, end).

"The Bush policy, as the Pennsylvania Catholic Conference put it, puts America 'on a dangerous path in which government endorses the death of one for the potential cure of another. [Instead], scientific advancements that cooperate with God's plan for life and love are the surest means of alleviating suffering and building up the dignity of man and the sanctity of life.'"

WHAT CAN WE DO AT NOTRE DAME ABOUT 9/11?
Oct. 16, 2001

"What can we do in response to the terrorist attacks? Let me tell you about a constructive thing we can do right here at Notre Dame. First, however, we should consider the nature of the evil perpetrated on Sept. 11. Barbara Olson died when American Airlines Flight 77 hit the Pentagon. At her memorial service, Father Franklyn McAfee said: 'With amazing speed, we have identified the terrorists who took over the planes, and we probably know who masterminded it. But who is really behind it all? We are speaking of an enormity of hate and evil here, for these were evil acts. But evil is not something. Evil is someone. Satan.'

"'Love, however, is stronger than hate,' said Bishop John M. D'Arcy of Fort Wayne-South Bend. 'Truth is more powerful than lies. God is stronger than Satan. Life is stronger than death. . . . Evil will not have the last word.'

"We at Notre Dame have a special way to counter this evil with good. It is the weekly adoration of the Blessed Sacrament. Initiated by students and approved by Campus Ministry, Eucharistic Adoration takes place in Fisher Hall chapel from 11:30 p.m. Monday until Benediction at 9:45 p.m. Tuesday.

It also occurs in the Lady Chapel of the Basilica on Friday from noon to 5 p.m.

"'In times of great crisis and suffering,' wrote Bishop Raymond L. Burke of LaCrosse, 'Catholics rightly turn to prayer before the Most Blessed Sacrament exposed in the monstrance. The consecrated Host is the efficacious sign of the Father's love and mercy toward us. In prayer before the Blessed Sacrament, we place into the Heart of the Incarnate Redeemer all our cares and trials.'

"'In the most blessed sacrament of the Eucharist, the body and blood, together with the soul and divinity, of our Lord Jesus Christ and, therefore, the whole Christ is truly, really and substantially contained. This presence is called real, by which is not intended to exclude the other types of presence as if they could not be real, too, but because it is presence in the fullest sense . . . it is substantial presence by which Christ, God and man, makes himself wholly and entirely present.' (*Catechism*, no. 1374).

"John Paul II has called for 'the spread of Perpetual Adoration, with permanent exposition of the Blessed Sacrament . . . in all parishes and Christian communities throughout the world.' When he instituted such adoration at St. Peter's Basilica in 1981, he said, 'The best, the surest, and the most effective way of establishing everlasting peace on the face of the earth is through the great power of Perpetual Adoration of the Blessed Sacrament.'

"What do you do in your half-hour or 15 minutes of Adoration? There is no set format. You can stand, sit, kneel, whatever you think appropriate. You can read and meditate on the books provided there. You can pray the Rosary or other prayers. Or you can just remain in the presence of Christ, communicating with him. It would be good to pray for the United States, for peace, for the victims of terrorists, for the members of the armed forces, many of college age and younger, who are putting their lives on the line in defense of the common good. And pray for the hijackers and other terrorists; they, too, have immortal souls.

"In the words of Archbishop Fulton J. Sheen, 'The holy hour is not a devotion; it is a sharing in the work of redemption. He [Jesus] asked for an hour of reparation to combat the hour of evil; an hour of victimal union with the cross to overcome the anti-love of sin.'

"Personal benefits, too, flow from Eucharistic Adoration. Listen to Bishop D'Arcy: 'It must be said . . . with joy and thanksgiving that the periodic practice of exposition of the Blessed Sacrament is . . . rooted in faith, blessed by the church, linked to the Mass and a help in strengthening our faith . . . in the Real Presence. . . . [P]rayer in the presence of the exposed Eucharist has also been a great influence in my own spiritual life.'

"Now more than ever, we should consider this opportunity. As the *Catechism* states, 'The Church and the world have a great need for Eucharistic worship. Jesus awaits us in this sacrament of love. Let us not refuse the time to go meet him in adoration, in contemplation full of faith, and open to making amends for the serious offenses and crimes of the world. Let our adoration never cease.' (No. 1380)

"You can sign up for a period of Adoration. . . . Or just show up. Walk-ins are welcome and encouraged."

PACIFISM AND PATRIOTISM, Nov. 6, 2001

"'The Real Terrorists Are in the White House.' This sign, carried by a University of Michigan freshman, captures the spirit of one aspect of the vocal and growing anti-war movement. Such protests imply a moral equivalence between American foreign policy and the Sept. 11 attacks, implicitly viewing the latter as retribution for the former. Other anti-war activities, including peace vigils at Notre Dame, focus on prayer and a rejection of all violence.

"'For those of us,' said one Notre Dame participant, 'who understand that peace is in no way related to violence . . . [y]ou just can't be silent . . . not as Christians, not as human beings.'

"Last month this column examined the just war concept which recognizes a limited right of the state to engage in war for defense of the common good. A separate question, raised by the anti-war protest, is whether a Catholic is obliged in conscience to serve in such a war. Or is a Catholic obliged not to serve? This controversy is likely to continue. So let us note four points made by the *Catechism*:

"First: 'As long as the danger of war persists and there is no international authority with the necessary competence and power, governments cannot be denied the right of lawful self-defense, once all peace efforts have failed' (No. 2308). Such defense must be justified by the conditions for a 'just war.' 'The evaluation of these conditions . . . belongs to the prudential judgment of those who have responsibility for the common good.' (No. 2309).

"Second: Citizens are obliged to support a just war. 'Public authorities in this case, have the right and duty to impose on citizens the obligations necessary for national defense.' (No. 2310).

"Third: 'Public authorities should make equitable provision for those who for reasons of conscience refuse to bear arms; these are . . . obliged to serve the . . . community in some other way' (No. 2311).

"Fourth: 'Those who renounce violence . . . and, in order to safeguard human rights, make use of the means of defense available to the weakest, bear witness to evangelical charity, provided they do so without harming the rights and obligations of other men and societies. They bear . . . witness to the . . . physical and moral risks of recourse to violence.' (No. 2306).

"Pacifism is universal or selective. The universal pacifist refuses to take part in any and all wars because he denies that war can ever be justified in defense of the common good. A Catholic is clearly not obliged to be a universal pacifist. Nor is universal pacifism, which denies the right of the state ever to use force in defense, consistent with the teaching of the Church.

"The selective pacifist, on the other hand, refuses to take part, not in any and all wars, but only in a particular war he regards as unjust. The law of the United States allows exemption from military service only for universal pacifists and not for selective pacifists. The *Catechism* urges, but does not require, exemption for all conscientious objectors (No. 2311). It is difficult, however, to see how an exemption for selective objectors could be administered without inviting fraudulent evasion.

"It involves no reflection on the sincerity of universal pacifists to deny any claim of objective moral superiority for their position. One can well 'bear witness to evangelical charity' by renouncing force in defending himself. The universal pacifist, however, denies that force can ever be used in defense of the common good. He would refuse to defend not only himself but others, and he would deny to his fellow citizens their right to have the state provide what the *Catechism* calls 'legitimate defense by military force' (No. 2309). This sort of universal pacifism was aptly described by General Douglas MacArthur as 'a base creed.'

"Selective pacifism, on the other hand, is not only consistent with, but required by, the teaching of the Church. We all should be selective pacifists, insisting, with prudence, that any war—or any other act of the state—is subject to the higher standard of the natural law and the law of God. A strong presumption of validity attaches to the decisions and acts of those entrusted with the care of the common good. But that presumption is not conclusive.

"Patriotism is a virtue. And the present war on terrorism clearly satisfies the conditions of a just war. 'Our government,' said Anthony Cardinal Bevilacqua in his Oct. 16 letter to President Bush, 'has the right and the duty to defend its people against this modern plague upon mankind.'

"The conduct of that, or any, war, however, is subject to the principles of proportionality and discrimination. The latter forbids intentional attacks on innocent civilians. In this and in other respects the right of the state to wage war is never unlimited. Nevertheless, the exercise of that limited right can be, as in this case, a high duty of the state."

STUDENT VOUCHER PROGRAMS, NOV. 19, 2001

"Supreme Court edicts forbid voluntary prayer in government activities, including classrooms and even football games. Yet in the aftermath of

September 11, public officials, from the White House to the school house, have acted as if the Court's rulings do not exist. When Congressmen assemble on the steps of the Capitol to sing 'God Bless America,' we are entitled to wonder, Is this public religiosity only a passing nightmare for the American Civil Liberties Union? Or could it foreshadow a relaxation of the Court's prohibitions? That is unlikely. But it is interesting that, two weeks after Sept. 11, the Supreme Court decided to review three consolidated cases that could modify its doctrine on government aid to religion. . . .

"The cases involve the voucher program for Cleveland public school students, which a panel of the federal Court of Appeals, by a 2-1 vote, held unconstitutional. The vouchers, primarily for students from low-income families, may be used to pay tuition at private schools, including sectarian schools. The voucher check, payable to the parents, is mailed to the school selected by the parents, who then endorse the check to the school to pay tuition. The program forbids participating schools from discriminating against prospective students on the basis of religion. . . .

"As Judge James Ryan argued in his Court of Appeals dissent, 'the . . . categorical prohibition against direct grants to aid religious schools is no longer the law; and second, the criteria for determining when a statute has the forbidden 'primary effect' of advancing religion have been modified.'

"The First Amendment provides, in part, 'Congress shall make no law respecting an establishment of religion or prohibiting the free exercise thereof.' The Establishment Clause originally required Congress to maintain neutrality among religious sects. It had no application to the states, six of which had established churches at the time of the adoption of the Constitution. Since the 1940s, the Supreme Court has misinterpreted the post-Civil War 14th Amendment to hold that the Clause binds the states as well as the federal government. The Court developed a test, evolving from *Lemon v. Kurtzman*, in 1971, which required that, to pass muster under the Clause, a statute must have a secular purpose, its primary effect must neither advance nor inhibit religion and it must not foster an excessive entanglement of religion. Over the past 15 years most members of the Court have indicated their dissatisfaction with the so-called *Lemon* test.

"In *Mitchell v. Helms*, in 2000, the Court upheld a state program for the loan of computers to public and private schools including religious schools. Justice Clarence Thomas, in his *Mitchell* opinion, joined by Chief Justice William Rehnquist and Justices Antonin Scalia and Anthony Kennedy, said, 'nothing in the Establishment Clause requires the exclusion of pervasively sectarian schools from otherwise permissible aid programs and other doctrines of this Court bar it. This doctrine, born of bigotry, should be buried now.' The Cleveland voucher case could complete that burial.

"If you are a betting person, you ought to stick to the ponies and not bet on the outcome of a Supreme Court case. Nonetheless, few would be surprised if the

204

Supreme Court upheld the voucher on a theory along the lines of Judge Ryan's summary: 'The rule is now settled that a government program that permits financial aid ultimately to reach religious schools does not offend the Establishment Clause if the government's role in the program is neutral. Neutrality exists if the governmental aid that goes to a religious institution does so 'only as a result of the genuinely independent and private choices of individuals.'

"Even if the Court upheld the voucher, that ruling would probably have no direct impact on the Court's prohibition of official facilitation of prayers, religious activities, etc. Such a voucher ruling, however, in the aftermath of Sept. 11, could intensify efforts to relax that prohibition of prayer.

"Incidentally the constitutionality of vouchers is a separate question from that of their wisdom. Many, including this writer, are of the view that vouchers are constitutional but unwise. The basic natural law principle is TANSTAAFL: 'There ain't no such thing as a free lunch.' If religious schools feed at the public trough they will lose their independence and ability to carry out their mission."

NOTE: In *Zelman v. Simmons-Harris*, 536 U.S. 639 (2002), the Supreme Court, by a vote of 5-4, held that this Cleveland voucher program is constitutional.

CLONING, Dec. 4, 2001

"'We should not as a society grow life to destroy it.' In these words President Bush summed up the only civilized response to the recent cloning of a human embryo by scientists in Worcester, Mass. . . .

"Cloning is either therapeutic or reproductive. The [Worcester] cloning was therapeutic in that the embryos were created for the purpose of extracting their stem cells for possible use in treating Parkinson's and other diseases. Embryos are killed when stem cells are removed. In reproductive cloning, the cloned embryo would be implanted in a woman's womb and carried by her to birth.

"Various technical problems remain to be solved before efficient human cloning of either type becomes a practical possibility. . . .

"Cloning is not illegal, although federal law forbids the use of federal funds for human cloning. Advanced Cell Technology, which did the Worcester cloning, receives no federal funds. . . .

"What is the relation between cloning and embryonic stem cell research? Advances in research on stem cells derived from adults may render the use of embryonic stem cells unnecessary. Last Aug. 9, President Bush announced his support for federal funding of research only on embryonic stem cells which had already been harvested at that time. However, use of embryonic stem cells, or stem cells derived from other adults for transplant into a patient involves possible rejection of those cells by the patient's immune system. The rejection problem would be avoided by use of stem cells taken from an embryonic clone of the patient himself.

"This is one reason why therapeutic embryonic cloning will probably not be outlawed. Another reason is that 'therapeutic' cloning of human beings is a potentially profitable enterprise. . . .

"For a more basic reason, it is unlikely that either type of human embryonic cloning will be banned. Our culture tends to liberate technology from moral restraints. John Paul II insists that: 'Science and technology require . . . respect for the fundamental criteria of the moral law . . . [T]hey must be at the service of the human person . . . according to the design and will of God.' Unfortunately, as author Kirkpatrick Sale predicted, 'In a world that . . . commodifies gene-splicing, amniocentesis and *in vitro* fertilization, there cannot be any lasting legal restraints on . . . reproductive technology . . . [W]hen the Supreme Court found in 1980 that patenting genetically created life was legal, and thus that people could make profits from it, it opened a floodgate.'

"A further reason why human cloning will not be effectively prohibited is the dominance of the contraceptive ethic. In contraception, like cloning and *in vitro* fertilization, couples deliberately separate the unitive and the procreative aspects of sex and, as John Paul put it, they 'act as arbiters of the divine plan.' They 'claim a power which belongs solely to God: the power to decide, in the final analysis, the coming into existence of a human person'. . . .

"It is futile to try to put the brakes on human cloning, or abortion or euthanasia, without restoring the conviction that God, and not man, is the arbiter of when and how life begins and ends. This requires a reassessment and rejection of contraception."

CARDINALS NEWMAN AND DULLES, Jan. 15, 2002

"In announcing Notre Dame's plan to spend $500 million on new building projects, Vice President Timothy R. Scully said, 'We really feel a deep responsibility to build the world's leading Catholic university.' A worthy objective. But the Catholic Church alone has authority to define the 'Catholic university.' John Paul II did so in 1990 in *Ex Corde Ecclesiae*, the apostolic constitution on Catholic higher education.

"Notre Dame's focus on money and a veritable building binge might obscure an important question: If Notre Dame is to become a really Catholic university, what attitude must our leaders have toward *Ex Corde*?

"Fortunately, Avery Cardinal Dulles, the eminent Jesuit scholar, offered some guidance on that point in his recent address on John Henry Cardinal Newman, the great 19th century Catholic educator. To put Cardinal Dulles's advice in context, we ought to look at some basics.

"In Nov. 1999, the bishops approved an Application of *Ex Corde Ecclesiae* to the United States. The Application's emphasis on dialogue rather than on formal enforcement makes it likely that the implementation of *Ex Corde*, that is, whether a university will be truly Catholic or Catholic-lite, will be up to the choice of the university itself. . . .

"As the Application notes, 'Catholic students have a right to receive from a university instruction in authentic Catholic doctrine and practice, especially from those who teach the theological disciplines.' Universities that claim to be Catholic ought to conform their product to their fund-raising pitch.

"There is no mystery about what it takes to be a Catholic university. Read *Ex Corde* and the Application. And reflect on Cardinal Dulles's analysis: 'If Newman were alive today,' said Cardinal Dulles, 'he would enthusiastically embrace the principles set forth by John Paul II in *Ex Corde Ecclesiae.*'

"Describing Newman's position, Dulles said, 'because the university cannot fulfill its mission without revealed truth, and because the Church has full authority to teach the contents of revelation, the university must accept the Church's guidance . . . the higher authority of the Church was necessary to rescue freedom of thought from what Newman called its own "suicidal excesses."'

"'In the United States,' said Cardinal Dulles, 'Catholic universities have been very apologetic, almost embarrassed, by their obligation to adhere to the faith of the Church. For Newman and for John Paul II, any university that lacks the guidance of Christian revelation and the oversight of the Catholic magisterium is . . . impeded in its mission to find and transmit truth. It fails to make use of an important resource that God in His providence has provided. Surrounded by powerful institutions constructed on principles of metaphysical and religious agnosticism, the Catholic universities of this nation have too long been on the defensive. While making certain necessary adaptations to the needs of our own day, they should proudly reaffirm the essentials of their own tradition, so brilliantly synthesized by Newman in his classic work.'

"Cardinal Dulles's analysis should be instructive for our leaders, especially on the necessary relation between the Catholic university and the Magisterium, the teaching authority of the Church."

WHY BENGAL BOUTS? Jan. 29, 2002

"Seventy-seven thousand dollars is a lot of money, maybe even more than next year's Notre Dame tuition. Yet that is the record amount the Bengal Bouts raised in 2001 for the Holy Cross Mission in Bangladesh. In accepting the donation, Fr. Jose Peixotto, a 39-year veteran of the Mission, remarked that the conversion rate from the Bangladesh taka to the American dollar is 55 to 1. Seventy-seven thousand dollars will go a long way in a poverty-stricken country where many families live on less than $200 a year.

"Bangladesh has 200,000 Catholics in a population of 130 million, 89 percent of whom are Muslims. Joe Zilligan, a 2001 Notre Dame grad, described his visit on a research project to the Mission: 'I could write for days recounting the amazing tales of these men. Stories of men such as 'the peanut butter priest.' I call him that because I did not catch his name. I ran into him briefly during one of his quick stops in Dhaka to pick up some peanut butter at Notre Dame College, so that he may have some source of protein. He then continued to travel from village to village caring for and ministering to the sick, subsisting on bread, water and a little bit of peanut butter, as he has done for the last twenty or so years. I could tell stories of priests who have brought peace and understanding to villages consumed by hatred between Hindus and Muslims.'

"Knute Rockne initiated boxing at Notre Dame in the 1920s. The Bengal Bouts began in 1931. The program operates through the Recreational Sports office, headed by Rich O'Leary. The Boxing Club members themselves organize and conduct the daily training, fund-raising, ticket sales and promotion. The captains this year are: Matt Fumagalli, Mark Criniti, Rob Joyce, Brock Heckmann, Andrew Harms, Clay Cosse and Shawn Newburg. The recent success of the fund raising is due largely to the student managers, who this year are Mark Reynolds and Laura Anderson. . . .

"The emphasis throughout is on safety. Emergency medical technicians Terry Engel, Sharon Farrell and John Osborn are present at all sparring. University physicians James M. Moriarty and Patrick Leary are present at ringside at the Bouts and supervise the training. . . .

"The boxers undergo training that caused one new participant to voice the old boot camp aphorism, 'The first day I was afraid I would die. For the rest of that week I was afraid I wouldn't.'

"Why do intelligent and presumably sane students freely subject themselves to workouts including thousands of push-ups, sit-ups, jumping jacks, endless running and sparring that sometimes rearranges one's facial landscape? After all that, he has to enter a ring all by himself, except that his opponent is there with a contrary intent. As the T-shirt says, 'No substitutions, no time-outs, no excuses.'

"Why do it? As one boxer told me, 'I signed up to get in shape and to see if I could really do this thing. Once-in-a-lifetime. But there's more to it. We can be the difference between living and dying for some kid in Bangladesh."

CONTRACEPTION, PAT BUCHANAN, AND THE BIRTH DEARTH, Feb. 12, 2002

"On contraception, it may be time for a reality check. Contraception has gained nearly universal acceptance among Catholics, as well as others, as a moral alternative—the private choice of each individual. A new book, however, should make us think about the terminal social consequences of the contraceptive ethic.

"Patrick Buchanan may not be very popular on this campus. But his book, *The Death of the West*, exposes an undeniable reality: The first world, including not only Europe and North America but also Japan and Russia, is dying. For example, Muslim Albania is the only one of 47 European nations that has a birthrate that will replenish its population. . . .

"Buchanan analyzes cultural influences that have caused the West to refuse to renew itself, principally including the dominance of a self-centered and secular ethic. 'The new gospel has as its governing axioms: there is no God; there are no absolute values . . . ; the supernatural is superstition.'

"The defining reality is that 'we are creating,' in the words of Czech president Vaclav Havel, 'the first atheistic civilization in the history of mankind.'

"Buchanan offers debatable policy proposals, including major restrictions on immigration. While immigration laws are in need of revision, Americans of European origin are losing their dominance, not because of immigration, but because they practice the 'race suicide' of the contraceptive ethic. They have no right to exclude unjustifiably people of other backgrounds who share the right to the universal destination of the earth as of other goods. . . .

"The point of this essay is not to analyze Buchanan's policy proposals, but to note the demographic handwriting on the wall. As Australian demographer Peter McDonald explains, 'the problem with low fertility is that it reduces population size not at all ages but only among the young. Low fertility produces an age structure that creates a momentum for future population decline, a situation that must be stopped at some point if the population is to be demographically sustainable. Also, populations with low fertility can fall in size at an extremely rapid rate. The longer low fertility is maintained, the harder it becomes to reverse population decline.'

"That is one reason why contraception must be reconsidered. Until the Anglican Lambeth Conference in 1930, no Christian denomination had ever said that contraception could ever be objectively right. The Catholic Church maintains that unbroken teaching. Discussion of contraception in detail must await another day. Suffice it to say here that the contraceptive ethic is predictably a suicide pact. Any group that refuses to reproduce itself will disappear.

"Notre Dame rightly prides itself on the social activism of its students, which, we hope, they will continue to practice throughout their lives. But the demographics indicate that the most enduring future contribution those students can make to society is to cooperate in the procreation of new persons who will enrich that society and who, not incidentally, will live forever. Whatever your view, the Buchanan book will make you think."

HOMOSEXUALITY, Feb. 26, 2002

"The American Academy of Pediatrics recently announced its support for legislation to allow children born to or adopted by one member of a same-sex couple to be adopted by the other member of that couple. In light of this and other events, including the presentation of 'The Vagina Monologues' at Notre Dame and the emergence of the altar boy as a hazardous occupation in Boston and elsewhere, it may be useful here to recall some basics.

"Homosexual acts are intrinsically wrong. As the *Letter on the Pastoral Care of Homosexual Persons*, issued with the approval of John Paul II in 1986, stated: 'It is only in the marital relationship that the use of the sexual faculty can be morally good. A person engaging in homosexual behavior therefore acts immorally. To choose someone of the same sex for one's sexual activity is to annul the rich symbolism and meaning, not to mention the goals, of the Creator's sexual design.'

"The 'inclination' to commit homosexual acts is not a sin. But it is a 'tendency ordered toward an intrinsic moral evil, and thus the inclination itself must been seen as an objective disorder.'

"The *Catechism* incorporates this teaching and the entitlement of each person to respect and fairness: 'The number of men and women who have deep-seated homosexual tendencies is not negligible. This inclination, which is objectively disordered, constitutes for most of them a trial. They must be accepted with respect, compassion and sensitivity. Every sign of unjust discrimination in their regard should be avoided. These persons are called to fulfill God's will in their lives and, if they are Christians, to unite to the sacrifice of the Lord's Cross the difficulties they may encounter from their condition.'

"The 1986 *Letter* condemned the subjection of 'homosexual persons' to 'violent malice in speech or in action. . . . The dignity of each person must be respected. But the proper reaction to crimes against homosexual persons should not be to claim that the homosexual condition is not disordered. When such a claim is made and when homosexual activity is consequently condoned, or when civil legislation is introduced to protect behavior to which no one has any conceivable right, neither the Church nor society should be surprised when other distorted notions gain ground, and irrational and violent reactions increase.'

"In 1992, the Congregation for the Doctrine of the Faith sent to the United

States bishops a 'background resource' on *Legislative Proposals on Discrimination against Homosexuals*. 'Sexual orientation' [is] not comparable to race, ethnic background, etc. in respect to non-discrimination,' it said. 'Unlike these, homosexual orientation is an objective disorder. It is not unjust discrimination to take sexual orientation into account in the placement of children for adoption or foster care, in employment of teachers or athletic coaches and in military recruitment.'

"In response to the European Parliament's 1994 approval of same-sex marriage and the adoption of children by homosexual couples, John Paul II described it as an 'attempt to tell the inhabitants of this continent that moral evil, deviation, a kind of slavery, is the way to liberation, thus distorting the true meaning of the family. The relationship of two men or two women cannot constitute a true family; still less can one grant such a union the right to adopt children. These children suffer grave harm, because in these 'substitute families' they do not have a father and mother, but two fathers and two mothers. This is dangerous.'

"As Father John Harvey, the founder of Courage, a support group for men and women who try to live in accord with Catholic teaching on homosexuality, put it, 'The Roman Catholic Church is now the counterculture.' The homosexual culture has a privileged status in the media and other politically correct institutions, including universities.

"'I have often wondered,' said Chicago's Francis Cardinal George, 'why a supposedly heterosexual man, perhaps married and with children, is admired and celebrated when he declares himself homosexual, but a journey in the opposite direction is excoriated as repressive.'

"The Church insists on the dignity of the person while affirming that homosexual acts are an 'intrinsic moral evil' and that the homosexual inclination is a disorder as is the inclination to any other moral wrong. In the words of the 1986 *Letter*, 'Departure from the Church's teaching or silence about it, in an effort to provide pastoral care, is neither caring nor pastoral. Only what is true can ultimately be pastoral.' That truth is politically incorrect. But Notre Dame students are entitled to that truth from the administration without omission or equivocation."

THE VAGINA MONOLOGUES, March 19, 2002

NOTE: This column included quotations of some (but not the worst) sexually explicit material from the Vagina Monologues. The purpose of quoting X-rated content is not to magnify the scandal caused by the Monologues but to give the reader some idea of the actual content of that play. With the publication of that content in this Observer column, and elsewhere in more explicit detail, the responsible officials of the University cannot plead ignorance about the content of the play. Their choice to have this "Catholic" university permit the performance of that play takes on an exceptional gravity.

"One point still needs to be made on 'The Vagina Monologues.'. . . .

"The only issue I raise here is the judgment of the administration in permitting academic units to sponsor a public play which presents an act of pedophilia as a benefit to the child-victim. Sexual activity between an adult and a teenager or other post-pubescent minor is technically called by the unfamiliar term, 'ephebophilia.' This column uses the more familiar term, 'pedophilia,' which as commonly used today, includes adult-child sex, whether heterosexual, man-boy or woman-girl and whether or not the child is pre-pubescent. Each is an objective moral wrong because it is contrary to nature and the divine law of the Author of that nature. . . .

"Against this background, one would think that the administrators of any institution that claims to be Catholic would avoid any equivocation on pedophilia of any sort. Yet our leaders allowed Notre Dame to be used for a public play which presented pedophilia—child abuse—as a benefit to the victim. Our leaders acted here, as elsewhere, in what they saw as the best interest of Notre Dame and its students. The problem is a failure of prudential judgment. To put it in context let us consider the monologue in question.

"In 'The Little Coochi Snorcher That Could,' an adult 'Southern woman of color' describes, among other childhood sexual memories, her encounters at age 16 with a 'gorgeous' 24-year-old woman in the neighborhood. The child's mother agrees to the woman's request that the child spend the night with her. (I omit explicit details.) 'I'm scared but I really can't wait. Her apartment's fantastic . . . the beads, the fluffy pillows, the mood lights . . . She makes a vodka for herself and then . . . the pretty lady makes me a drink. . . . The alcohol has gone to my head and I'm loose and ready . . . as she gently and slowly lays me out on the bed. . . . Then she does everything to me . . . that I always thought was nasty before, and wow, I'm so hot, so wild . . . I get crazy wild. . . . Afterward the gorgeous lady teaches me . . . all the different ways to give myself pleasure. She's very thorough. She tells me to always know how to give myself pleasure so I'll never need to rely on a man. In the morning I am worried . . . because I'm so in love with her. She laughs, but I never see her again. I realized later she was my surprising, unexpected, politically incorrect salvation. She transformed my sorry-ass coochi snorcher and raised it up into a kind of heaven.'. . . .

"Why did our leaders offer Notre Dame—'the University of Our Lady'— as a forum for the public portrayal of an act of pedophilia as a 'salvation' for the child-victim? Perhaps our leaders did not know what was in the Monologues. If so, they were negligent. . . .

"Or maybe our leaders knew the play contained this favorable portrayal of child sexual abuse as a benefit to the victim and still approved of its public presentation. If so, their misjudgment rose to a new level beyond ordinary stupidity. Or maybe our leaders knew it was wrong but were unwilling to risk the ire of various activists. If so, one might understandably suspect that we are governed by anatomical wonders with neither brains nor guts. In any event, no amount of academic double-talk can justify this public presentation at a Catholic university, which is what Notre Dame claims to be. . . .

"The University has a duty to rectify this blunder. That rectification would be advanced by the resignation of all those responsible from their administrative positions."

CONTRACEPTION AND NFP, April 12, 2002

"The 19th century laws restricting contraceptives were passed by Protestant-dominated legislatures. No Christian denomination had ever held that contraception could be justified until the Anglican Lambeth Conference of 1930. The seismic effect of that rejection of millennia of moral teaching came in the 1960s with the advent of the pill. Does it make sense for the Catholic Church still to insist on that formerly unbroken teaching? Three questions are relevant:

"Why is contraception wrong? First, it breaks, in the words of Pope Paul VI, 'the connection—which is willed by God and which man cannot lawfully break on his own initiative—between the two meanings of the conjugal act: the unitive and the procreative.'

"Second, the contracepting couple makes themselves the arbiters of whether and when human life shall begin. They confer on themselves, as Pope John Paul II put it, 'a power which belongs solely to God; the power to decide in a final analysis, the coming into existence of a human person.'

"And, third, in contraception, instead of what John Paul II called the 'total reciprocal self-giving of husband and wife,' there is a withholding: I give you myself except for my fertility, I will accept you only if you are altered to cancel your fertility.

"In his 1994 *Letter to Families*, which could be read with profit by every engaged or married couple, whether Catholic or not, John Paul II explained that God, who is love, 'wills' that each human person ought to come into existence through a loving act of self-gift between spouses united in the 'communion of persons' modeled on the self-giving relation of the persons of the Trinity. Thus he noted the 'similarity between the union of the divine persons' in the Trinity and the marital union. (LF, no. 8).

"We, however, have free will. The contracepting couple, in effect, say to God, 'For all we know, it may be your will that through this act of ours a new person, who will live forever, will come into existence. But we won't let you do it.' In this light, we can see why John Paul said that, 'Contraception is . . . so . . . unlawful as never to be . . . justified. To think . . . the contrary is equal to maintaining that . . . it is lawful not to recognize God as God.'

"What about natural family planning (NFP)? In NFP the couple refrain from sexual relations during the fertile period. When they engage in relations during the rest of the month they may prefer not to have a child. But they have an accepting intent, in that they do nothing to destroy the integrity of the act and they are willing to accept the responsibility for a child. The contracepting couple may be willing to accept a child if one results from their act. But they take measures, by drugs or plugs, to destroy the integrity of the act to prevent a child. The privilege of procreation, however, is so important that NFP can be used only for 'serious motives,' which may include health, financial or other reasons. 'In destroying the power of giving life through contraception,' said Mother Teresa at the 1994 National Prayer Breakfast, 'a husband or wife . . . turns the attention to self and so destroys the gift of love . . . The husband and wife must turn the attention to each other, as . . . in natural family planning and not to self, as . . . in contraception. Once that living love is destroyed by contraception, abortion follows very easily.'

"What are the social consequences of contraception? If man (of both sexes) makes himself the arbiter of when life shall begin, he will predictably make himself the arbiter of when it shall end, in abortion and euthanasia. The contraceptive society needs abortion as a back-up. It cannot say that homosexual activity is wrong without condemning its own premise that man is the arbiter of whether and when sex will have any relation to procreation. As Paul VI predicted, the acceptance of contraception puts 'a dangerous weapon . . . in the hands of . . . public authorities' to reduce births among minorities. Promiscuity, divorce and cloning also follow from the contraceptive ethic. The growth of pornography, too, validates Paul VI's warning that contraception would cause women to be viewed as objects.

"As Francis Fukuyama observed in *The Great Disruption*, the pill and abortion liberated men from responsibility and put the burden on women, allowing 'many . . . ordinary men . . . to live out fantasy lives of hedonism and serial polygamy formerly reserved only for a tiny group of men at the very top of society.' (121) Women pay the price for the sexual revolution.

"The authentic Christian teaching on contraception does make sense."

THE 20TH HIJACKER, April 23, 2002

"The Justice Department has charged Zacarias Moussaoui, the so-called 20th hijacker, in federal court with six counts of conspiracy to commit murder and other crimes. Allegedly, he took flying lessons to participate in the September 11 attacks. On that day, he was in jail for visa violations. Attorney General John Ashcroft is seeking the death penalty.

"The government has constitutional authority to prosecute Moussaoui in a military tribunal for violation of the laws of war. In trying Moussaoui instead in federal court for violations of ordinary criminal law, the government is bound by the procedural limits on such prosecutions. It is not certain that Moussaoui will be convicted and it is less likely that the government will obtain the death penalty where the charge is conspiracy rather than actual commission of the murders.

"Does the restrictive teaching of Pope John Paul II on the death penalty apply to this case? The *Catechism* puts that teaching in the context of 'preventing crime.' If the government had prosecuted Moussaoui in a military tribunal, it might be argued that the papal teaching does not apply in such a tribunal which applies the 'laws of war' outside the usual criminal process. In a just war, the state has authority to kill intentionally, subject to the restrictions of proportionality and non-combatant immunity. Since the government, however, has prosecuted Moussaoui in the ordinary criminal process, John Paul's teaching applies.

"John Paul II reaffirmed the traditional teaching that the state has authority to impose the death penalty. He has given us a new development of the teaching as to the use of that authority.

"*Evangelium Vitae* (EV) and the *Catechism* affirm that retribution, the restoration of the balance of justice, is the primary purpose of punishment in general. But, because of the importance of the conversion of the sinner, neither retribution, deterrence of others nor any other reason can any longer justify, by itself, the use of the state's power to execute unless that execution is 'the only possible way of . . . defending . . . lives against the unjust aggressor,' that is, against this criminal.

"Whether execution is such an 'absolute necessity' depends on the ability of the prison system to confine this prison securely. That involves a prudential judgment. But the new teaching as to the use of the death penalty is universal and not a prudential teaching. It applies everywhere and to all states. Nor can it be dismissed as merely the Pope's personal opinion—he put it in the *Catechism*.

"Even under John Paul's teaching one could still argue for the death penalty in some cases: for example, if a life inmate, already in maximum security, murders another inmate, or where the state is unable to confine inmates securely. In a military tribunal case that teaching might not apply. Or it might be argued that even John Paul's criteria could justify execution of a terrorist leader if his continued existence in prison would incite further terrorist attacks. On the other hand, the martyrization by execution of such a leader might have the same inciting effect. Or, could a clandestine terrorist be regarded as a spy and rightly executed pursuant to the laws of war?

"Whatever the answer to such hypotheticals, John Paul's teaching fully applies to all prosecutions under ordinary criminal law, including that of Moussaoui.

"When Paul VI, in *Humanae Vitae*, affirmed the immorality of contraception, many liberal Catholics took a walk or began a sit-in schism. John Paul's teaching on the death penalty may become the *Humanae Vitae* of some politically conservative Catholics, including Justice Antonin Scalia and Patrick J. Buchanan. Scalia argues that because EV 'does not represent *ex cathedra* teaching . . . it need not be accepted by practicing Catholics.' Canon Law and the *Catechism*, however, agree with Vatican II that 'loyal submission of will and intellect must be given, in a special way, to the authentic teaching authority of the Roman Pontiff, even when he does not speak *ex cathedra*.'

"John Paul insists that the power of the state is subject to the law of the Lord of life. He seeks the protection of society and of innocent life, not through homicidal acts of the state, but through a 'cultural transformation' building a 'new culture of life,' recognizing 'the incomparable and inviolable worth of every human life' (EV, no. 95). I agree enthusiastically with his position. But even if a Catholic does not agree with it, he must support it because John Paul is the Vicar of Christ and not some Polish guest-worker in Rome. Under that teaching, Moussaoui should not be executed."

NOTE: Zacarias Moussaoui was convicted and sentenced to life imprisonment.

2002–2003

Bishops Cop-out on Sex Abuse, Sept. 3, 2002

"One flippant proof for the divine origin of the Catholic Church is that, in 2,000 years, the priests and bishops have been unable to kill it. . . . [T]he Vatican will decide on the 'sex abuse' norms for diocesan priests adopted by the [U.S.] bishops and on the less rigorous rules adopted by religious orders for their priests. The bishops at Dallas, however, gave us a virtual manual in how not to handle a crisis. We can note only a few points here.

"First, the bishops refused even to authorize a study of the relevance of dissent and clerical homosexuality to the abuse problem. Michael Novak, a former dissenter, described the reaction to Paul VI's *Humanae Vitae* in 1968: 'Immediately, a host of theologians, clergy and lay people publicly dissented. Then, more afraid of being called "conservative" than of being faithful to Catholic teaching, the bishops . . . refused to exercise their teaching authority. . . . Dissent-as-rebellion spread from one aspect of the Church's sexual teaching to others. It grew and grew. Soon enough, homosexual rings were operating freely in several important seminaries. Over the years, scores of . . . seminarians were seduced and corrupted.' As Father Richard John Neuhaus noted, 'The overwhelming majority of the [clerical] sexual abuse cases involve adult men having sex with teenage boys and young men, and by ordinary English usage we call that a homosexual relationship.' That subject is worthy of the bishops' attention.

"Second, the bishops imposed sanctions on their priests while they insulated themselves from any personal and financial accountability. . . . Nor did they put their own jobs on the line. Why did they not oblige every bishop who has knowingly authorized the continued ministry of a priest guilty of sexual abuse to submit his resignation to the Pope? The Pope would decide whether to accept that resignation. The bishops who caused this crisis should at least volunteer to get out of the way.

"Third, the bishops imposed a one-size-fits-all system of permanent separation from ministry—'for even a single act of sexual abuse . . . of a minor—past, present, or future.' That includes even elderly priests who might have committed one misdeed, many years before, and have served with distinction since. Impersonal 'zero tolerance' is a dubious Christian response, but it does play to the media.

"Fourth, the bishops painted a bull's-eye on the backs of their good priests, whom they exposed to permanent removal from ministry pursuant to vague criteria. The bishops' definition of 'sexual abuse' does not require any 'physical contact' or any 'discernible harmful outcome.' Such abuse can be found 'whether or not it was initiated by the child.' It applies to 'contacts or interactions between a child and an adult where the child is being used as an object of sexual gratification for the adult.' Neither a presumption of innocence nor a burden of proof is specified. How can a priest disprove an accusation framed in such vague terms? The potential for intimidation and blackmail is obvious.

"A priest's continuance in ministry after the adoption of the bishops' policies could expose him to tort liability on the theory that the priest had thereby assumed a duty to avoid the vaguely defined 'sexual abuse.' An 'alleged offender' will be relieved of his 'function' merely on the bishop's finding that the allegation is 'credible.' Evidently, only after he is so relieved will an 'investigation in harmony with canon law' begin. Good priests, subjected to this regime, may now be inclined to act with a caution inconsistent with the energetic performance of their ministry.

"Fifth, the bishops created uncertainty as to the terms 'minor' and 'child.' They generally describe the problem as 'sexual abuse of minors.' As amended in 2001, Canon 1395 § 2, cited by the bishops, authorizes punishment of a cleric who has sex with a 'minor' below the age of 18. But the bishops define 'sexual abuse' as activity between 'a child and an adult.' At common law, a 'child' is a person below 14. In most states, however, the age of consent is 16. Is a person above the legal age of consent a 'child' or a minor? Does the bishops' emphasis on the 'child' imply a tolerant minimization of sex between homosexual priests and males who are post-pubescent or above the legal age of consent? In its civil law implications, the bishops' work product at Dallas is replete with ambiguities and invitations to litigation.

"Neuhaus made the basic point: 'If bishops and priests had been faithful to the Church's teaching and their sacred vows, there would be no crisis. That is a fact quite totally evaded at Dallas.' However, as John Paul II said in his homily at World Youth Day in Toronto: 'Do not be discouraged by the sins and failings of some of [the Church's] members. . . . Think of the vast majority of dedicated and generous priests and religious whose only wish is to serve and do good.'"

UNICEF: TRICK OR TREAT? Sept. 20, 2002

"The U.N. Child Summit convened in New York last May to promote the welfare of children. Two intriguing concepts of child welfare emerged.

"First, only a coalition of the United States, the Holy See and various Muslim and African nations prevented the inclusion of a right to abortion in the

Summit's final action document, 'A World Fit for Children.' Abortion, of course, protects children by killing them because they are not fit for the world. . . .

"The second odd concept of child welfare surfaced when it was disclosed at the Summit that UNICEF, the U.N. Children's Fund, had financed the 1999 publication and distribution by the Mexican government of a book called 'Theoretic Elements for Working with Mothers and Pregnant Teens.' The book states: 'Reproductive health includes the following components: counseling on sexuality, pregnancy, methods of contraception, abortion, infertility, infections and diseases.'. . . .

"UNICEF is no stranger to controversy over such matters. Since at least 1966, UNICEF has promoted contraception, sterilization and other birth-reduction programs.

"In 1996, the Vatican Mission to the U.N. suspended its 'symbolic' contribution of $2,000 a year to UNICEF. 'The new involvement of UNICEF in the areas of concern' the Vatican Mission said, 'had forced the Holy See to take this visible step.' The Vatican charged that UNICEF had participated in the publication of a U.N. manual 'advocating' the distribution of post-coital contraceptives to refugee women in emergency situations and had become 'involved in advocacy work' on abortion legislation. 'Post-coital contraceptives' are not really contraceptives. They cause abortion early in pregnancy.

"The Vatican also said that UNICEF workers in various countries had 'distributed contraceptives and counseled people on using them.' Archbishop Renato Martino said the decision was made after UNICEF announced that it would distribute 'contraceptives and drugs to terminate pregnancies' to refugees in Rwanda and Zaire. The Vatican still refuses to contribute to UNICEF.

"In October of 2000, Archbishop Saenz Lacalle of San Salvador denounced from the pulpit an 'insinuating and grotesque' 170-page sex-education booklet designed by UNICEF and El Salvador's Ministries of Health and Education for training adolescents on sexuality issues including contraception, homosexuality and abortion.

"These comments are not meant to criticize the little kids carrying the UNICEF donation cans on Halloween and the many persons who send UNICEF 'holiday cards.' Last year in the United States, UNICEF enlisted 2.5 million 'Trick-or-Treaters' to forego asking for candy and instead to raise nearly $4 million for UNICEF. The 'holiday cards' raised in the United States another $13 million for UNICEF. The kids and the users of the cards want to help needy children, which UNICEF does in various respects.

"But it would seem to be time for truth-in-labeling, for full disclosure that UNICEF's idea of promoting 'A World Fit for Children' includes the prevention of children coming into existence and the distribution of abortifacients which kill children because somebody thinks they are unfit for the world."

MOOSE KRAUSE, Oct. 9, 2002

"Who is that big guy with the politically incorrect cigar on the bench outside the Joyce Center? Moose Krause. All-American, coach, athletic director and truly 'Mr. Notre Dame.'

"That is the title of Jason Kelly's excellent new book. If you have a Domer in your family, this takes care of one item on your Christmas list. Or you can find a miniature replica of Moose and the bench at the bookstore for only $1,500 (no kidding). Moose could not have afforded it on his salary, which never exceeded $30,000. He turned down job offers many times higher because he would not leave Notre Dame.

"Edward Walter Krauciunas was born in 1913 into a 'cash-poor but spirit-rich' family in Chicago's Back of the Yards. His high school coach, Norm Barry, a teammate of George Gipp, gave him the name 'Moose' and shortened Krauciunas to Krause. Krause entered Notre Dame in 1930, Rockne's last year of coaching, and was an All-American in football and basketball. He joined Frank Leahy's football staff in 1942 and was also head basketball coach.

"In World War II, Moose was a Marine Corps intelligence officer with an aviation unit in the Solomon Islands. He routinely did his own reconnaissance, squeezing into the nose turret of a B-25 with no parachute.

"One night, a Moro scout, Antoun, led Krause and the chaplain, Father James Gannon, to Rabaul to recover the remains of six Marines. They escaped capture because Antoun hid them in a leper colony that the Japanese feared to enter. Krause later collected over $2,000 from the Marines to finance Antoun's studies for the priesthood. Moose carried Notre Dame to the Solomons.

"At a tense briefing before an important raid, he brought in 20 Moro scouts. The Marines expected the usual message, that if they got lost the Moros would bring them back safely. This time Moose turned to the young Moros and they broke into the Notre Dame Victory March in their own language. 'The . . . 200 men went berserk,' Gannon says, 'laughing and cheering and whistling.' The raid was successful with not a man lost.

"During 1946–49, Krause was Leahy's assistant and head basketball coach. He served as athletic director from 1951 till his retirement in 1982. He built a program to serve all the students, emphasizing intramural and club sports.

"In January 1967, Moose's wife, Elise, suffered severe brain and other injuries when a car broadsided a taxi in which she was riding. She lost her rationality and control of her emotions. Moose Krause devoted himself utterly to the care of Elise until her death in 1990. He turned to alcohol but changed his life after a heart attack and pleas from his children. He became a leader in Alcoholics Anonymous.

"Jason Kelly concludes that Krause's greatest achievement occurred at Cardinal Nursing Home, where he spoon-fed meals and sang to his ailing wife.

Although he described it as 'a veritable crucifixion for both of us,' there was no self-pity in Moose.

"'There's really no place I'd rather be than in that room with your mother.' Krause said, 'I know a lot of people feel sorry for me, but I'm the lucky one. I'm in the fortunate position of being able to extend care. That's the easy part. Mother has the hard part.'

"'I call him Saint Edward,' said Ara Parseghian. '[I]f every person had that kind of compassion and . . . respect for his spouse, this would be a . . . lot better world.'

"Father Theodore Hesburgh concurred, describing Moose as, 'Absolutely the Rock of Gibraltar, the soul of integrity. If I ever met a saint, he was one of them.'

"Moose's son, Father Edward Krause, C.S.C., who teaches theology at Gannon University, calls *Mr. Notre Dame* the story of a whole generation who took God, the 10 commandments and their faith seriously. Moose, as Father Krause put it, had a special affection for John Paul II as fellow athlete and successor to Peter. In his funeral homily in 1992, Fr. Krause quoted his father: 'Unless my eyes are getting bad, the Bible doesn't say, 'Thou art Peter, and upon this teenie weenie pebble, I will found my debating society. [It doesn't say] take up a Gallup poll, and tell 'em what they want to hear.' Moose Krause knew what he believed and why.

"College sports are now a major business, driven by money, media and government regulation. Moose and his assistant, Colonel Jack Stephens, ran the show in a different, and, in various ways, a better era. The common wisdom has it that it took 23 people to replace Moose. The athletic department has new faces and new skills. But the important things have not changed, like character and commitment. Moose would be pleased.

"Notre Dame will never see the likes of Moose Krause again. So buy the book. You can sit on the bench and read it with Moose. You will learn something about the real Notre Dame. And about yourself."

KILL THE WASHINGTON SNIPERS? NOV. 8, 2002

"Should the Washington snipers be executed? Four states and the federal government want to execute John A. Muhammad. Lee Boyd Malvo, aka John Lee Malvo, who was 17 when the crimes were committed, could be executed in any of three states. The public favors the execution of both.

"Would the teaching of the Catholic Church permit the death penalty in this case? The answer is: No, unless the facts bring the case outside the scope of Pope John Paul II's teaching on the use of the death penalty.

"In *Evangelium Vitae* and the *Catechism*, John Paul affirmed the traditional teaching that the 'primary purpose' of punishment is retribution 'to redress the disorder caused by the offense.' He also affirmed that the state has authority to impose the death penalty. But he has developed the teaching on the use of that authority: Neither retribution, deterrence of others nor any other objective of itself will justify the execution of a criminal unless it is an 'absolute necessity' in the exclusive sense that it is 'the only possible way of effectively defending human lives against the unjust aggressor.' A criminal may be executed only if there is no other way to defend other lives from him. The horrendous character of the crime is immaterial on the use of the death penalty. This is not merely John Paul's personal opinion. He put it in the *Catechism* as the teaching of the Church.

"This new development of the teaching on the use of the death penalty arises from the importance of the conversion of the criminal. As Saint Augustine and Saint Thomas Aquinas taught, the conversion of one sinner is a greater good than the creation of the entire material universe. . . .

"In a penal system without adequate security, the death penalty could be argued to be absolutely necessary to protect others from that criminal. The system in the United States, however, is able to restrain Muhammad and Malvo from harming others, unless their mere continued existence in prison would motivate others to kill people. However, their martyrization by execution could have that same result. It would depend on the facts. John Paul's teaching is placed by the *Catechism* in context of 'preventing crime.' If Muhammad and Malvo were terrorists tried in a military tribunal under the 'laws of war,' it could be argued that John Paul's teaching is inapplicable. Similarly, if they are proved to be terrorist combatants they presumably could be executed under the 'laws of war,' just as captured spies can be executed. The authorities, so far, have not based their case on the 'laws of war.' Instead, they are prosecuting the snipers under the ordinary criminal process. John Paul's teaching would apply to that process so that, unless the facts show that execution is 'the only possibly way of effectively defending' others from them, the snipers should not be executed. This may be a 'hard saying.' But consider two points.

"First, while some oppose the death penalty because they reject the reality of life after death and, for them, death is therefore the greatest evil, John Paul has raised the discussion to a new level based on the immortal destiny of human persons, each of whom is created in the image and likeness of God. 'Not even a murderer,' he said, 'loses his personal dignity.' John Paul asserts the dignity of the human person over the claim of the modern state to final dominion over life and death. Every state that has ever existed or ever will exist has gone out of business or will do so. But every human being who has ever been conceived will live forever. That is why the conversion and salvation even of a serial murderer is so important.

"Second, this teaching is not the brainchild of some Polish tourist living in Rome. It is a serious teaching of the Vicar of Christ. . . .

"Maybe it is time . . . to start obeying the teaching of the Pope, not only on the death penalty but also on everything else, because of who and what he is."

NOTE: John A. Muhammad was executed in Virginia by lethal injection on Nov. 10, 2009. Lee Boyd Malvo is serving in a Virginia state prison a sentence of life imprisonment without the possibility of parole.

HOMOSEXUAL PRIESTS? Jan. 21, 2003

"In December, the Vatican released a response sent by Cardinal Medina Estevez, Prefect of the Congregation for Divine Worship and the Discipline of the Sacraments, to a bishop who asked if it is licit to ordain 'men with homosexual tendencies.' The response said: 'Ordination to the diaconate and the priesthood of homosexual men or men with homosexual tendencies is absolutely inadvisable and imprudent and, from the pastoral point of view, very risky. A homosexual person, or one with a homosexual tendency, is not, therefore, fit to receive the sacrament of Holy Orders.'

"The inquiry and response may have arisen from the fact that most cases in the clerical sex abuse scandal involve not assaults on young children but homosexual relations between priests and adolescents or young adults.

"Whether such a response to an individual bishop is authoritative is debatable. But the response raises an important issue. An implicit premise of the response is that the homosexual inclination is, as the *Catechism* puts it, 'objectively disordered.' That inclination is not itself a sin but it is disordered because it is a tendency toward 'intrinsically disordered' acts.

"The recognition of the homosexual inclination itself as disordered is important because the media and the academy have fostered a national brain cramp on every aspect of this issue. A cascade of laws and regulations is establishing a virtual parity between sodomitic relations and authentic marriage. The family, founded on marriage between a man and a woman, is the bedrock of civil society because it is the source of life and nurturing for future generations.

"The homosexual relation, by contrast, is a dead end with no future. If it were universalized, there would soon be no civil society. Homosexual acts are not wrong because they are prohibited by the Church. Rather, the Church merely affirms the reality, recognized by millennia of moral teaching, that such acts are contrary to the natural law and destructive of the person and the society that attempts to legitimize them."

BENGAL BOUTS: PURELY AMATEUR, Feb. 11, 2003

"Notre Dame students are supposed to be smart. Right? So why have 140 of them signed up for the Bengal Bouts? They do endless sit-ups, pushups, running and hurting. Additionally, they subject themselves to the controlled violence of sparring which can give them a new facial configuration. As a 'reward,' they are allowed to climb into a ring to run the risk of embarrassment, if not unconsciousness, before thousands of people.

"Those young men are not certifiably nuts. They do it for a reason. In 2002 they raised over $70,000 for the Holy Cross missions in Bangladesh, where the per capita income is $285 a year, and a family of five among the ultra-poor has to survive for almost half a year on the equivalent price of two Notre Dame football tickets.

"The Bengal Bouts have run without interruption since 1931. 'Bengal Bouts,' under Brother Alan McNeill, C.S.C., were held in 1920 and succeeding years. They were the predecessors of the Bengal Bouts which Dominic J. 'Nappy' Napolitano established in 1931 and directed for the next five decades. 'Every now and then,' wrote Chicago sportswriter Bill Gleason, 'an event reminds us of how campus sports were run in the time before athletic directors and huge coaching staffs. The Bengal Bouts are as purely amateur as a sport can be.'

"'The Bengal Bouts,' wrote Father David E. Schlaver, director of Holy Cross Missions, 'enable many to earn a living, provide medical care and housing for their families, and educate their children for life—and survival—in a difficult society.' The population of Bangladesh is 88.3 percent Muslim and 10.5 percent Hindu. . . .

"'I have seen,' wrote Father Joseph Sidera, 'men and women dedicating themselves to the very poorest of the poor in the name of the Lord and his church under the threat of political and religious persecution and with the threat of imminent disease—malaria, dengue fever, ebola, cholera and many others. For some this is their native land, for others it is their adoptive home. Among those who have made this choice to go there, one of the few characteristics that differentiate them from the local religious is a need to know the Notre Dame football scores.'

"The members of the Boxing Club themselves run the Bengal Bouts under the direction of Rich O'Leary of Rec Sports. The captains this year are Clay Cosse, Shawn Newburg, John Lynk, Andrew Harsmon, Tom Pierce, Pat Dillon, Tommy Denko and Tony Hollowell. The captains run the practices, under the guidance of the head coaches—Chicago attorney Terry Johnson and Columbus developer Tom Suddes. . . .

"The contributions from the Bouts to the missions have recently grown five-fold. This is largely due to the acumen of the business managers who now are Laura Anderson and Mark Reynolds and the promotional efforts of the Women's Boxing Club under co-presidents Laura Young and Shelley Skiba.

"So, apart from latent masochism, why do these allegedly smart guys enlist for this punishing regime?

"'Any member,' said coach and former captain Ryan Rans, 'will tell you that participation in this program is the most memorable experience of his Notre Dame career.'

"As captain Shawn Newburg put it, 'It's unique. We get in great shape, we make real friends and we can make a life-saving difference for people who need it halfway around the world.'

"Members of the Notre Dame community are encouraged to visit the practices every weekday. . . . Please support this effort which exemplifies the spirit of Notre Dame at its best."

PREVENTIVE WAR? Feb. 25, 2003

"The 'just war' theory is a method of moral reasoning to prevent war and to minimize its effects if it does occur. The requirements for *jus ad bellum*, justice in going to war, are: proper authority, just cause and right intention. The *Catechism* lists further details: '[T]he damage inflicted by the aggressor must be lasting, grave and certain;' war must be a last resort, with 'all other means impractical or ineffective;' 'there must be serious prospects of success;' and 'the use of arms must not produce evils graver than the evil to be eliminated.' *Jus in bello*, justice in fighting a war, requires proportionality and discrimination (non-combatant immunity from intentional attack.)

"Pope John Paul II has emphasized, with reference to Iraq, that war 'is always a defeat for humanity' and cannot be waged 'except as the very last option in accordance with very strict conditions.' On Nov. 13, the U.S. Catholic bishops opposed the Iraq war in a major but guarded statement. They affirmed the fact-dependent nature of the just war criteria and the deference owed to the government's evaluation. The bishops said 'We offer not definitive conclusions, but our serious concerns and questions. People of good will may differ on how to apply just war norms especially when the facts are not altogether clear. Based on the facts that are known to us, we find it difficult to justify the war against Iraq, lacking clear and adequate evidence of an imminent attack of a grave nature.' But then the bishops conceded: 'There are no easy answers. Ultimately, our elected leaders are responsible for decisions about national security.' Similarly, the *Catechism* notes that the 'evaluation' of the conditions for a just war 'belongs to the prudential judgment of those who have responsibility for the common good.'

"A preventive war is not intrinsically wrong, but it is more difficult to justify. It is debatable whether the administration has disclosed convincing evidence that Iraq aids, or is about to aid, the terror network or that Iraq is an imminent threat to the United States. But, as the bishops implicitly acknowledge, the public does not have a right to disclosure of facts where that would be contrary to national security. The governmental decisions here are entitled to the benefit of the doubt up to a point of incredibility that does not appear to have been reached in this case. One factor is that we no longer have an adjudicated liar in the White House.

"In any event, all this shows the wisdom of the framers of the Constitution in putting the decision on declaring war in the hands of Congress rather than in one man. The President has a war power, to enable him, as James Madison said, 'to repel sudden attacks.' Congress, unwisely but probably validly, has authorized the President to decide whether to make war on Iraq. So war or peace will be decided by one man.

"On a positive note, we at Notre Dame can do something real for the cause of peace. '[T]he surest . . . way of establishing peace on the face of the earth,' said John Paul II, 'is through Perpetual Adoration of the Blessed Sacrament.'"

MEGALOMANIA, March 18, 2003

"'Megalomania. That's what ails Notre Dame.' A now-deceased Holy Cross priest told me that, referring to Notre Dame's decision to abandon its historical mission in pursuit of 'big school' prestige. The mission of Notre Dame had been the provision of affordable education in the Catholic tradition to undergrads, with research and graduate programs, especially in the sciences, in an important but complementary role.

"'Megalomania' is an 'obsessive desire to do things on a grand scale.' The priest's comment comes to mind because this is the 25th anniversary of Notre Dame's Great Leap Forward, its definition of itself as a 'National Catholic Research University.'

"In the 1970s, the major universities went heavily into the 'research university' business. In 1978, income restrictions were removed on eligibility for federal student loans. The universities then raised tuition to finance their research programs and buildings. They then lobbied Congress to raise loan limits. As the limits went up, so did tuition and back to Congress went the universities to lobby for higher limits. And so on. The research empires were built on the backs of borrowing students. Notre Dame, while far from the worst offender, played this shabby game.

"Our leaders act in what they see as the best interest of Notre Dame and its students. It may be useful, however, to ask what price Notre Dame has paid for the greatness project.

"1. <u>Cost.</u> Notre Dame's tuition and fees make up 55 percent of the budget. The undergrad tuition, room and board charge for 2002–2003 is $32,020. In 1978–79, it was $5,180. If it had kept pace with inflation it would now be $14,245. Notre Dame, through its excellent financial aid office, tries to provide University aid to students. The student loan, however, remains the primary form of financial aid. Predictably, the only non-wealthy students at Notre Dame will soon be those whose test scores won heavy discounts, scholarship athletes, ROTC students, minority scholarship students, faculty and staff children and those non-wealthy students, diminishing in number, who choose Notre Dame even at a price of a crippling loan burden.

"2. <u>Diminution of the undergrad experience</u>. Notre Dame undergrads are paying more than twice as much, in real dollars, than they did in 1978, but they are getting less. Members of our family were Notre Dame undergrads every year from 1977 to 2000 in various majors. In the variety of available courses, class size, quality of teaching and the recognition of students as persons, the undergrad experience has deteriorated since 1977. Twenty-two percent of 100-level courses are taught by student instructors. The University's report on Graduate Education, 1996–2001, noted that Notre Dame needs 507 more grad students 'because the number of graduate students has not kept pace with the increase in faculty in Ph.D. granting departments.' In the Research University, you hire more and more researching faculty who teach less and less. The rhetoric puts teaching on a par with research. But everyone knows better. Notre Dame's answer to inadequate teaching is not to reward faculty as teachers but to get funding for a center to do research on teaching. As one tenured philosophy professor put it, 'You really don't need to have any impact on the undergraduates' to get promoted. 'You just need [to have written] a book.'

"3. <u>The campus</u>. Undergrad life is diminished by the 'binge building' which has transformed Notre Dame into a cramped, urban-style research campus, with at least 40 of the 90 buildings built after 1980. The economy has put some projects on hold, but no end is in sight. Which donor will have the most buildings named after him or her? Will the world-class parking garage be the crowning feature? In contrast to the more humane design of older buildings, the newer creations evoke technocratic images, such as the DeBartolo rendering of the concept of five half-pint milk cartons on line and the relentless triangular patterns of other new buildings. The open recreational spaces have given way to concrete. Social restrictions tend to induce undergrads to leave the campus, sometimes to their peril.

"4. <u>Catholic character</u>. Notre Dame accepts the authority of the federal government, the NCAA and many other entities, as well as the secular 'academic community.' The only authority it will not accept is that of the Catholic Church to define the meaning of a 'Catholic' university. The problem is truth-in-labeling. For reasons beyond our space limits, Notre Dame's 'Catholic' character erodes in proportion to its pursuit of secular prestige.

"We can fairly ask, 25 years on, whether Notre Dame's excursion into 'megalomania' has come at an unacceptable price. It is possible for a research university to maintain its Catholic character and a positive focus on undergrad education without the imposition of crushing student debt. Perhaps it is time to reconsider a few things."

CATHOLIC EDUCATION AS CONSUMER FRAUD, April 1, 2003

"A new study by the Higher Education Research Institute at UCLA raises the issue of whether, in terms of 'Catholic character,' the pricey education at Catholic colleges is worth it. The study tracked attitudes of students in 38 Catholic colleges and universities, including Notre Dame and Saint Mary's. In 1997, HERI surveyed 7,197 incoming freshmen, including 5,199 Catholics and 1,998 non-Catholics. In 2001, it surveyed again those same students.

"The percentage of students who agreed with the following statements changed as follows from 1997 to 2001: 'Abortion should be legal.' Catholic, 37 percent to 51 percent; non-Catholic, 62 percent to 71 percent.

"If two people really like each other, it's all right for them to have sex even if they've known each other for only a very short time.' Catholic, 27 percent to 48 percent; non-Catholic, 36 percent to 53 percent.

"Same-sex couples should have the right to legal marital status.' Catholic, 52 percent to 69 percent; non-Catholic, 60 percent to 73 percent.

"Of students who described themselves as 'Roman Catholic' as freshmen, 91 percent did so at graduation, while 11 percent of the non-Catholics became Catholic. As freshmen, 2 percent of the Catholics said they attended a religious service 'not at all,' compared to 12 percent four years later. Fifteen percent of the Catholics said their religious beliefs became 'much stronger' over the four years. As freshmen, 14 percent of the Catholics spent no time at all in prayer or meditation, compared to 25 percent four years later. The study does not claim to be representative of the 223 Catholic colleges and universities. It had no uniform standards for selection of the surveyed students. It released only aggregate data and not results for the students at each institution. Therefore, one cannot draw conclusions about a specific school from the study.

"Despite its limits, the HERI study is instructive but no surprise. The problem is not merely a failure of colleges. Rather, an apostasy overtook the Catholic educational system, from kindergarten to university, over the past few decades. The Catholic intellectual tradition, including Augustine, Aquinas, Bonaventure, Newman and others is a mine of wisdom, integrating faith with reason. The Catholic system transmitted and enriched that tradition until the 20th century. Regrettably, the teachings of Vatican II became something else at the hands of 'The Church of Where It's At.' '[M]ore than in any other historical period,' said John Paul II last year, 'there is a breakdown in the process of handing on moral and religious values between generations.' Several generations of Catholic grade and high school students wasted their religion classes making collages or mouthing politicized slogans. The Catholic universities did not cause that failure, but they do little to remedy it. In many cases they compound it.

"*Ex Corde Ecclesiae*, the 1990 constitution on Catholic universities, requires 'adherence' by the university 'to the teaching authority of the church in matters of faith and morals.' 'Catholic students,' said the Bishops' Application of *Ex Corde* to the United States, 'have a right to receive from a university instruction in authentic Catholic doctrine and practice. Courses in Catholic doctrine and practice should be made available to all students.'

"Notre Dame has a Catholic presence and offers abundant spiritual resources to students who want them. But no one can rationally claim that Notre Dame conforms to the *Ex Corde* requirements. As one Notre Dame sophomore was quoted in a news report on the HERI study, 'The required theology classes for all students don't necessarily cover Catholic teachings. Everyone has to take a Scripture class, but mine was taught by a Protestant graduate student who knew nothing about Catholic teaching. The second theology requirement can be completed by any of a wide variety of classes that don't normally pertain to Church teaching specifically.' The system is hit-or-miss and often hostile to Catholic teaching on morality and sex. The leaders of Notre Dame and other 'Catholic' universities reject the definition of that term by the Vicar of Christ who is the only person with ultimate authority to define it. Yet they are as obedient as serfs to decrees of the NCAA and a host of government and private regulators. . . .

"[T]he HERI study reminds us that the paladins of 'Catholic' education, especially at the higher levels, have practiced a form of consumer fraud for several decades. If they were selling hamburgers instead of education, their bait-and-switch could put them in need of a defense lawyer. The HERI study should prompt Catholic families to ask whether the 'Catholic' colleges and universities are worth the monetary and other costs. Maybe it will even prompt those institutions to reflect on the moral imperative of truth-in-labeling; but don't hold your breath waiting for that."

CONGRESS' WAR POWER: THE RULING CLASS RULES, Apr. 15, 2003

"'Military Mirrors a Working-Class America.'

"Question: What constitutional issue is raised by this March 30 *New York Times* headline? It titled a long analysis concluding that the armed forces resemble 'the makeup of a two-year commuter or trade school outside Birmingham or Biloxi far more than that of a ghetto or a barrio or four-year university in Boston.'

"Compared to civilian contemporaries, the armed forces have a higher proportion of minorities, high school grads and those with 'better reading levels,' but with 'the wealthy and the underclass essentially absent.' Although the nation's 'wealthy and more well-educated youth have shunned the military, others less privileged have gravitated toward it.' Minority members see the military as egalitarian and racially harmonious with prejudice trumped by merit, discipline and the need to get along to survive. Vietnam caused many in the nation's elite to disdain the military, 'leading their children to lose the propensity to service that had characterized earlier generations of America's privileged.'

"The embedding of reporters in Iraq brought home the edifying quality of the men and women who have carried out a war plan exceptional in its design to avoid civilian casualties and disproportionate damage. Those volunteers evoke the line from *The Bridges of Toko Ri*, 'Where do we find such men?!' The Times analysis, however, confirms the social—and potentially political—divide 'between those who fight and those who ask them to.'

"The answer to that divide is not to reinstate the draft, which would weaken the armed forces and send the draftable children of the elite into their protesting tantrum mode. One unlikely answer would be for the economically and socially privileged to recover the tradition of service established by their forebears.

"A more realistic answer involves the constitutional issue raised by the Times analysis. To see it, let's go back a few days to Aug. 17, 1787, when the delegates to the Constitutional Convention gave Congress the power to declare war, leaving 'to the Executive' the power to 'make' war 'to repel sudden attacks.' As reported in James Madison's notes, Roger Sherman said, 'The Executive [should] be able to repel and not to commence war.' Elbridge Gerry said he 'never expected to hear in a republic a motion to empower the Executive alone to declare war.' Oliver Ellsworth stated 'It [should] be more easy to get out of war, than into it.' George Mason 'was against giving the power of war to the Executive, because not [safely] to be trusted with it. . . . He was for clogging rather than facilitating war; but for facilitating peace.'

"The framers built wisely. Over the years, however, Congress has declared war only five times while the President has used his power to 'make war' more than 200 times, all apparently with explicit or implicit approval of Congress. Since Congress last declared war, in 1941, we have had three major wars by Presidential initiative.

"The Iraq war calls for a reconsideration of the abdication by Congress of its duty to decide whether this nation should go to war. . . .

"Whatever one's view of the Iraq war, it should be clear that any deliberate decision to go to war should be made by the elected representatives who are more immediately responsible to the people than is the President.

"And here is where the Times analysis comes in. The sons and daughters of the economically and socially privileged, who are the likely leaders of tomorrow, are under-represented in the officer corps as well as in the enlisted ranks. 'The number of veterans in the Senate and the House is dropping every year,' said Northwestern Professor Charles C. Moskos. 'It shows you that our upper class no longer serves.' It is no reflection on President Bush to suggest that if the choice of war or peace remains with one man, it could open the door to the future exploitation of non-wealthy volunteers by politicized decisions manipulated by influential—and in this context parasitical—elites who place neither themselves nor their children in harm's way. Instead, the power to decide on war or peace should be reclaimed by the branch of government closest to the people whose sons and daughters will fight that war. Unfortunately, that would require a backbone transplant for most members of Congress, especially the Senate. In any event, it is time to reconsider the process by which we go to war."

2003–2004

KILL ABORTIONISTS? Sept. 17, 2003

"'I expect a great reward in heaven,' said Paul Hill before his execution for the murders of abortionist John Britton and his escort, James Barrett. None of us is Deputy God Almighty, therefore we cannot judge Hill's entitlement to such a reward. But he did give us a wake-up call.

"Hill, Britton and Barrett were all victims of a utilitarian culture in which the intentional infliction of death is an optional problem-solving technique. . . .

"Hill's act was legally and morally unjustified. One has a legal right to use reasonable force, including lethal force if necessary, to defend his life or that of another. Courts deny this necessity defense to those who block abortuaries to stop the killing of unborn 'non-persons.' When his trial judge refused to allow Hill to raise the necessity defense, Hill offered no further defense. Hill shot Britton in the parking lot. Even if the necessity defense applied, it would not legalize Hill's act since he was not defending the unborn child from actual or sufficiently imminent attack.

"In moral terms, the only situations in which anyone ever has the right intentionally to kill anyone are the just war and capital punishment. Both are by the authority of the state which derives its authority from God who is the Lord of life. In a justified rebellion, private persons rightly assume the 'just war' authority of the state. We are clearly not in a condition of rebellion that could justify Hill's killing of Britton as a combatant in that rebellion.

"The moral right to defend oneself or others is governed by the principle of the double effect. An act can have two effects, a good one which is intended, and a bad one which is permitted for sufficient reason but not intended. If he had been in the abortuary killing room as Britton was doing an abortion, Hill would have had a moral (but not legal) right and perhaps a moral duty, to stop him by force, although it is inconceivable that lethal force could have been necessary. Hill's intent would have had to have been to stop Britton rather than to injure or kill him.

"In the parking lot, Hill killed Britton, not as he was killing an unborn child, but to prevent him from doing so later. Hill was not defending the unborn child from an actual or imminent attack. If Hill could morally kill Britton in the parking lot, why could he not kill him in the supermarket? Or in medical school?

"As a private execution, Hill's act was intrinsically evil. No private person ever has the right intentionally to kill anyone. 'A man who, without exercising public authority, kills an evildoer,' said Thomas Aquinas, is 'guilty of murder, and all the more, since he has dared to usurp a power which God has not given him.'

"Hill sent a false but important message. In our relativist, individualist culture, we assume the power to decide whether, when and how life will begin and end, as in contraception, abortion, euthanasia by sedation or by withdrawal of food and water, assisted suicide, embryonic stem-cell research, etc. In his private judgment usurping the authority of God, Paul Hill was a child as well as an opponent of that 'culture of death.' Far better is the position of Joseph Scheidler, head of the Pro-Life Action League and a Notre Dame graduate. 'We don't want to kill the abortionist,' he says, 'We want to convert him.' The League has had six national conferences of reformed abortionists. Joe Scheidler saves more lives by prayer and witness than Paul Hill and his followers ever did.

"Legalized abortion will be overcome daily through a reconversion of the American people to the conviction that the right to life is sacred because each human being is created in the image and likeness of God with an eternal destiny that transcends the state. Help to women in problem pregnancies and political activity are needed. But the most important step toward that reconversion is prayer, especially the rosary since Mary is the mother of life. Pray for Paul Hill, for his victims and for all those involved in the killing of unborn children, especially their mothers."

NOTE: Paul Hill was executed by lethal injection on September 3, 2003 at Florida State Prison in Starke.

THE TEN COMMANDMENTS, Oct. 1, 2003

"When Moses brought down the Ten Commandments, he carried them in his hands. When Alabama Chief Justice Roy Moore put the Commandments in the courthouse rotunda, he needed a 5,280 pound monument. The federal courts ordered it removed. When Moore refused, he was suspended.

"Now that the uproar has subsided, it would be good to reflect on what this case was really about. . . .

"Moore rendered a service by calling attention to a constitutional revolution perpetrated by federal judges. This revolution has two aspects:

"First, the Supreme Court wrongly interprets the Fourteenth Amendment to incorporate and apply against the states virtually all of the first eight amendments of the Bill of Rights, including the Establishment Clause. The protections of the Bill of Rights, as the Supreme Court held in 1833, restricted the Federal Government and not the states. For protection against state governments, the people relied on state constitutions and state courts. The Court today uses this Incorporation Doctrine to invent new rights and enforce them against every state and local government, as with abortion, pornography, criminal procedure, etc. The Establishment Clause was a demarcation of federal and state jurisdiction over religion rather than a protection of 'liberty' such as freedom of speech. So even if the Incorporation Doctrine were legitimate, it should not include the Establishment Clause.

"Second, the Court has re-invented the Establishment Clause. At the adoption of the First Amendment, six Anglican or Congregational churches were established. The last one was not ended until 1828. The Establishment Clause was to prevent Congress, not from recognizing God, but from interfering with those state establishments and from creating a national established church. On Sept. 22 to 24, 1789, the First Congress approved the First Amendment and called on the President to proclaim a national day of 'public thanksgiving and prayer.' The President did so, including a *Te Deum* service in an Anglican church. Would Congress have approved an amendment to forbid governmental promotion of prayer and recognition of God at the same time it requested the President to proclaim a national day of prayer? The Supreme Court has wrongly interpreted the Establishment Clause to require governmental neutrality, not only among theistic sects, but also between theism and non-theism. So 'under God' can stay in the pledge of allegiance, as Justice William Brennan put it in 1963, only if those words 'merely recognize the historical fact that our Nation was believed to have been founded 'under God." This suspension of judgment on the existence of God establishes in practice an agnostic secularism as the national religion.

"The Moore case reminds us that, in this and other respects, the Supreme Court has usurped the role of a continuing constitutional convention. Neither James Madison nor the framers of the Fourteenth Amendment would have walked out of the stadium when the high school football teams gathered on the 50 yard line for prayer."

SAME-SEX MARRIAGE, Oct. 15, 2003

"'We're leading the way for the rest of the nation,' San Francisco Mayor Willie Brown said in 1996 as he presided over a 'domestic partnership ceremony' for 200 gay and lesbian couples whom he anointed as 'virtual spouses.' Seven years later, the mayor looks like a prophet. . . .

"Why not allow those couples to marry? One reason is that in the nature of things, the family is founded, as Aristotle put it, on 'a union of . . . male and female, that the race may continue.' The law gives exclusive recognition to heterosexual marriage because it carries the future and common good of society and of the state. Despite exceptional cases to the contrary, heterosexual marriage is generally ordered to the procreation of new persons, to whose education and upbringing the spouses legally and socially commit themselves. Same-sex couples can make no such commitment. It would therefore be unjust to give such couples the legal status or rights belonging to marriage.

"As a June 3, 2003 Vatican statement, issued with the approval of John Paul II, put it: 'Homosexual unions are . . . lacking in the biological and anthropological elements . . . which would be the basis, on the level of reason, for granting them legal recognition. Such unions are not able to contribute in a proper way to the procreation and survival of the human race. The possibility of using recently discovered methods of artificial reproduction . . . does nothing to alter this inadequacy.'

"This conclusion of reason is confirmed by the laws of God. Through marriage, men and women are given the privilege of living in full and permanent communion and of sharing in the procreation of new persons. Where authentic conjugal love is open to new life, homosexual acts are a dead end with no future. They are intrinsically wrong and the inclination to them, while not sinful, is disordered just as would be an inclination to any other objectively immoral act. Their immorality is compounded by the fact that they are contrary to nature.

"As Thomas Aquinas said, 'it is most grave and shameful to act against things as determined by nature. Therefore, since by the unnatural vices man transgresses that which has been determined by nature with regard to the use of venereal actions, it follows that in this matter this sin is gravest of all.'

"Aquinas also insisted that the law should not attempt to enforce every virtue or forbid every vice, lest the law be ineffectual and held up to 'disrepute.' A law criminalizing private homosexual conduct could be so intrusive as to be harmful to the common good. But it does not follow that a homosexual relation should be given the legal status or incidents of marriage. The homosexual relation, in practice as well as in theory, tends to be a parody of authentic marriage. A study of homosexual men under age 30 in Amsterdam, sponsored by the Dutch AIDS project and published in *AIDS 2003*, found that single men acquire 22 casual partners a year, men with a steady partner acquire eight casual partners a year and 'steady partnerships' last an average of 18 months.

"When the European Parliament in 1994 approved same-sex marriage and the adoption of children by homosexual couples, John Paul II said that action 'does not merely defend people with homosexual tendencies by rejecting unjust discrimination . . . The Church agrees with that . . . What is not morally acceptable is the legal approval of homosexual activity . . . [T]he attempt has been made to tell the inhabitants of this continent that moral evil, deviation, a kind of slavery, is the way to liberation, thus destroying the true meaning of the family. The relationship of two men or two women cannot constitute a true family, still less can one grant such a union the right to adopt children . . . These children suffer . . . grave harm, because . . . they do not have a father and mother, but two fathers or two mothers. This is dangerous.'

"For the past three centuries and more philosophers and politicians have attempted to organize society as if God did not exist and as if there were no knowable, objective moral truths. The drive to legalize same-sex marriage is an outgrowth of this and especially of the dominance of the contraceptive ethic. If sex has no intrinsic relation to procreation and if it is entirely up to man (of both sexes) to decide whether it will have that relation, any objection to the equal treatment of heterosexual and same-sex 'marriage' will be reduced to the pragmatic and aesthetic.

"But a society in which it makes no legal and social difference whether boys grow up to marry girls or other boys is certifiably insane and is on the road to extinction. The lack of effective opposition to the same-sex marriage drive, especially in the trendy American Catholic Church, should cause us to ask whether we have become what G.K. Chesterton described as a 'people that have lost the power of astonishment at their own actions.'"

DEATH FOR PSYCHOTICS? Nov. 5, 2003

"If you favor the death penalty, you have to defend some pretty bizarre results.

"Before most readers of this column were born, Charles Singleton was sentenced to death in Arkansas in 1979 for murdering Mary Lou York by stabbing her twice in the neck during his robbery of her family's grocery store. In 1997, Singleton's claim that he was incompetent, and therefore ineligible for execution was denied because he was voluntarily taking anti-psychotic drugs that made him competent. The State of Arkansas then put him on a mandatory anti-psychotic drug regime on the ground that he was a danger to himself and others. When the state scheduled his execution in 2000, Singleton claimed that the state could not compel him to take drugs to make him competent enough to be executed.

"The Supreme Court has forbidden the execution of those who are so incompetent that they 'are unaware of the punishment they are about to suffer and why they are to suffer it.' The Court also held that a State may forcibly give anti-psychotic drugs to an inmate 'who has a serious mental illness. . . . If the inmate is dangerous to himself or others and the treatment is in the inmate's medical interest.' Singleton argues that while medication relieves his psychosis it is not in his 'ultimate best medical interest' because it would qualify him to be executed.

"The United States Court of Appeals said that 'Singleton presents . . . a choice between involuntary medication followed by execution and no medication followed by psychosis and imprisonment.' The court upheld the involuntary medication which relieves his psychosis and has no significant side effects. The State's compelling interest in punishing criminals, especially in capital cases, outweighed Singleton's interest and preference. The Supreme Court of the United States denied review; that denial is not a ruling by the Court on the merits of the case.

"If we have a death penalty this result makes sense. If Singleton were not a capital offender, no one could reasonably deny the State's right to medicate him involuntarily if necessary to prevent danger to himself and others. Apart from the fact that it would lead to his execution, Singleton himself preferred to be medicated and non-psychotic. He voluntarily took the drugs until his execution date was set. It would reduce the death penalty system to futility if he were able to avoid that penalty by not taking his medicine. Singleton argues that his execution should be stayed until he no longer needs medication to make him competent for execution. In the meantime, he would voluntarily take the drugs.

"This case illustrates how the death penalty, with its delay, complications and expense, has distorted the justice system. That penalty ought to be reconsidered. As the Church has always taught, the State, which derives its authority from God, has authority to impose that penalty. But, as John Paul II teaches, the death penalty has outlived its usefulness apart from special cases. It should no longer be used for retribution or deterrence of other potential criminals. As the *Catechism* states, it may not be used unless it is 'the only possible way of effectively defending human lives against the unjust aggressor'— i.e., defending them from that criminal (No. 2267). His opportunity for conversion may not be cut off unless absolutely necessary to prevent him from committing more murders. Such cases, at least in advanced penal systems, are 'very rare, if not practically non-existent.' An inmate under a life sentence who kills another inmate or guard might qualify. Or a system lacking means of secure confinement might use that penalty. And perhaps this teaching, which is offered in the context of 'preventing crime,' might not apply to trials in military tribunals for violations of the 'laws of war' rather than of the domestic criminal laws. . . .

"The forced medication of Singleton to make him lucid enough to be killed should give us pause. Why do we have to execute a person like that? The Singleton result fits a culture which in many ways endorses the intentional infliction of death as an optional problem-solving technique. Singleton was sentenced to death only a year after Karol Wojtyla became Pope. Singleton's game is almost over. But the bizarre result in his case should prompt us to question the use of the death penalty and to reflect on the alternative offered by John Paul II."

NOTE: Charles Singleton was executed by lethal injection in Arkansas on January 6, 2004. The Arkansas Governor denied a request for clemency filed by Singleton's lawyer; Singleton did not ask the Governor to intervene.

TERRI SCHIAVO, Nov. 19, 2003

"Since 1990, when she suffered a cardiac arrest, Theresa Marie (Terri) Schiavo has been in what a Florida court found to be a 'persistent vegetative state.' Other experts claim she is not PVS and can be rehabilitated. Terri's husband, Michael, obtained a court order to remove her feeding tube on the ground that Terri, before 1990, had orally said to Michael, his brother and his brother's wife that she would not want 'tubes' to keep her alive. Terri's parents deny that Terri would want to be starved to death. Six days after the tube was withdrawn, the Florida legislature authorized Governor Jeb Bush to prevent the withholding of nutrition and hydration 'from such a patient.' The Governor did so. Terri is receiving nutrition and hydration while the courts consider the case.

"The court granted Michael's request to end Terri's life despite a clear conflict of interest. In 1993 Michael recovered $1.1 million from doctors whose misdiagnosis resulted in Terri's PVS. An undisclosed part of that award has been used for Michael's legal fees in seeking to end Terri's life. 'This fund remains sufficient to care for Theresa for many years,' said the Florida Court of Appeals in 2001. 'If she were to die today, her husband would inherit the money. . . . If Michael . . . divorced Theresa . . . the fund remaining at the end of Theresa's life would . . . go to her parents.' Financially, Michael has much to gain from Terri's death. Also, Michael has been living for the past seven years with Jodi Cetonze; they have one child and she is pregnant with another. Michael has stated that he plans to marry Jodi after Terri's death.

"The law allows a competent adult to starve himself to death, which is a form of suicide. Because Terri is incompetent, the decision was made for her by others that she would want to be starved and dehydrated to death. In this light the event has the character not of suicide but of homicide. Which leads to a point that tends to be overlooked here.

"The only reason anyone has heard about this case is because Michael and Terri's parents disagree. He wants to kill her. They want to keep her alive. What Michael proposes happens every day without publicity in cases where the relatives and care-givers are in agreement that it is time for the patient to die.

"In 1990, the Supreme Court of the United States allowed the starvation of Nancy Cruzan at the request of her family on 'clear and convincing evidence' that Nancy would want that. In the 1997 case of *Vacco v. Quill*, the Court upheld New York's prohibition of assisted suicide but gave the green light to 'palliative care' including sedation which results in the unintended death of the patient.

"Except in a most unusual case, how can you tell that the doctor's intent in sedating the patient was to kill rather than to relieve pain? Euthanasia by withdrawal of feeding or by sedation, where the family or other care-givers are in agreement, is moving beyond the practical reach of the law. As the Florida Supreme Court said in the 1990 *Browning* case, the family or guardian can starve a patient to death 'without prior juridical approval' if the patient, when competent, made 'oral declarations' showing a desire to forego feeding.

"Under Catholic teaching a feeding tube may be withdrawn if it is intolerably painful, if it no longer sustains bodily life because the patient can no longer absorb the nutrients, or if the patient is in the closing hours or minutes of the dying process when nature can be allowed to take its course and the withdrawal of feeding will not be a cause of death. It is immoral, however, to remove the tube or do to anything else with the intent to kill the patient. In the objective moral sense, that is murder.

"Terri Schiavo is not dying. She has an indefinite life expectancy, she is not in pain and her bodily life is sustained by the feeding tube (the role of that tube is not to cure her PVS but merely to sustain her bodily life). The purpose of removing Terri's feeding may have been to end a life considered burdensome to herself or others, but the specific intent was to achieve that purpose by an intrinsically evil act, i.e., the intentional killing of the innocent.

"But what's the big fuss over Terri Schiavo? Every day uncounted, but surely numerous, people like Terri are murdered, in the moral sense of the term, because their relatives and care-givers are united in deciding to do to them what Michael Schiavo wants to do to Terri. And nobody notices. The lawyers and judges provide us an excuse to ignore in such cases the corporal works of mercy: Feed the hungry. Give drink to the thirsty. But another Lawgiver takes those works more seriously: 'Depart from me . . . for I was hungry, and you did not give me to eat; I was thirsty and you gave me no drink . . . as long as you did not do it for one of these least ones, you did not do it for me.' Matthew 25:41–46.

"That Lawgiver, incidentally, seems to have a habit of holding nations as well as individuals accountable."

PARTIAL-BIRTH ABORTION, Dec. 3, 2003

"Observer Editor's note: Because the late-term abortion procedure is a current political issue and some descriptions of it may contain graphic content and offensive language, the letters discussing this issue may contain such

language as well. In order to foster an intelligent dialogue on this matter, this language must be included. Readers who might be offended by such language are cautioned.

"The new federal law banning 'partial-birth abortion' will not stop a single abortion and it will probably be struck down by the courts. So why did they enact it?

"Most abortions after 12 to 13 weeks are done by dilation and evacuation. The cervix, or entrance to the womb, is dilated, the fetal sac is punctured and drained and the unborn baby's head is crushed. The body is then dismembered and removed with suction and forceps. Abortionist Martin Haskell developed an alternative, dilation and extraction, because 'most surgeons find dismemberment at 20 weeks and beyond to be difficult due to the toughness of fetal tissues' and because dilation and evacuation can involve a risk of perforating the uterus. Dilation and extraction is called 'partial-birth abortion.'

"In partial birth abortion, which is done after 20 weeks, the cervix is dilated to allow removal of the child's body except for the head. The abortionist uses forceps to deliver the baby feet first up to the head which is too large for the opening. He inserts scissors into the back of the baby's skull and opens the scissors to enlarge the hole. He inserts a suction tube and sucks out the brains. The empty skull then collapses enough to fit through the opening. The new law contains Congressional 'factual findings' that 'during [partial birth abortion] the child will fully experience the pain associated with piercing his or her skull and sucking out his or her brain.' The Alan Guttmacher Institute reported this year that 2,200 partial birth abortions were performed in the United States in 2000. In 1996, 650 were performed.

"In *Stenberg v. Carhart*, decided in 2000, the Supreme Court struck down a Nebraska ban on partial birth abortion because it failed to allow partial birth abortion to preserve the 'health' of the mother. 'Health' now includes mental and emotional health and it amounts to abortion on request. In the new law Congress declared that partial birth abortion 'is never medically necessary to preserve the health of a woman.' The Supreme Court is unlikely to defer to Congressional findings on any law restricting abortion.

"The new law allows a partial birth abortion if it is necessary to save the mother's life when it is endangered by a 'physical condition.' This exception can be evaded; it could include a physical condition arising from the mother's asserted disposition to commit suicide. The Congressional findings call partial birth abortion a 'gruesome and inhumane procedure that is never medically necessary and should be prohibited.' If so, how can it be allowed even to save the life of the killer?

"As Ron Fitzsimmons, of the National Coalition of Abortion Providers, said in 1997, 'the real world impact' of a partial birth abortion ban 'is virtually nil.' He said doctors would use an alternative method such as dilation and evacuation, 'making sure the fetus is dead before extracting it.' Or the abortionist could do a hysterectomy, the abortion version of a cesarean section.

"If the partial birth abortion ban will not stop any abortions, why did Congress enact it? Republicans who are soft on abortion voted for the law to obtain 'pro-life' certification from the Beltway pro-life establishment. President Bush signed it, confirming his 'pro-life' credentials for the 2004 election. 'The Republicans got a free vote,' said Judie Brown of the American Life League. 'It was the least they could get away with in order to receive the pro-life vote.'

"The partial birth abortion ban, however, is a pro-life tactical victory because the campaign for it raised awareness of abortion. 'With [partial birth abortion], you cannot miss the baby,' said Senator Rick Santorum (R-PA). Pro-aborts fear that if people focus on partial-birth abortion they might realize that the 'choice' in every abortion, is in the moral but not the legal sense—to murder. Unfortunately, the emphasis on the closeness of partial birth abortion to infanticide might cause people to forget that the use of a morning-after pill is no less a murder than is the debraining of a birthing infant by partial birth abortion.

"The enactment of the partial birth abortion ban is less a triumph than a sign of futility for the establishment pro-life movement. In a civilized society, the issue must be whether innocent human beings may be intentionally and legally killed. Over the past three decades, pro-life leaders, including the bureaucracy of the Catholic bishops, have sought to limit, but not wholly prohibit, abortion, thus framing the issue as which innocents may be killed. The partial birth abortion effort is a further retreat, framing the issue not in terms of whether and not even in terms of which, but in terms of how innocent human beings may be legally executed. It is a confession of moral and political bankruptcy by the establishment pro-life movement.

"Abortion is a legal and political issue, but only incidentally. It presents a non-negotiable moral imperative, that no innocent human being of any age can rightly be classed as a non-person and subjected to death at the discretion of another. The focus on partial birth abortion ought to remind us that the ultimate remedy for legalized abortion is restoration among the American people of the conviction that the right of innocent human life is absolute because it is the gift of God."

THE LOG OF THE TITANIC, Jan. 14, 2004

"'Notre Dame 2010: Fulfilling the Promise' is the provisional strategic plan for the University. This plan follows COUP in 1973, PACE in 1982 and the 1993 Colloquy for the Year 2000. . . .

"Unavoidably, however, this one took the genre to a new level of booster-ism and boredom.

"ND 2010 stresses the need to improve the rankings of 19 programs. It lists four academic goals: 1. 'Provide . . . premier undergraduate education . . . integrating teaching and research better than any other university.' 2. Be 'among leading American research universities.' 3. Be 'the premier center of Catholic intellectual life.' 4. Be 'a diverse and international academic commu-nity.'

"The real goal is research: '[W]e must take the next step—to move for-ward as a center of outstanding research and scholarship.' In the 'allocation of resources,' we 'must focus on those academic areas that give us the greatest opportunity for growth and funding in our research endeavors.' Translation: Get the bucks. ND 2010 hopes to 'increase externally sponsored research expenditures to . . . $100 million a year, . . . double the current levels.'

"ND 2010 says that hiring and promotion should be limited to 'only those faculty for whom superior teaching is a high priority.' Don't bet on it. That same section lists, among the 'Fundamental and Defining Premises,' 'a height-ened sense of urgency for the centrality of research and scholarly publication,' including 'competition for federal, state and private dollars to support the research enterprise.' This 'centrality of research' applies to 'every academic unit.' ND 2010 stresses the importance of hiring new faculty, reducing teach-ing loads, improving research sabbatical support and increasing support for graduate student programs. ND 2010 omits two things:

"1. ND 2010 says not one word about the extent of the costs imposed on students. ND 2010 mentions several times the serious commitment to 'finan-cial aid' by the University and its excellent Financial Aid Office. But the underlying problem is a 'sticker price' continually rising above the inflation rate. In 1978–79, when Notre Dame began its pursuit of Research Greatness, undergrad tuition, room and board totaled $5,180. If it had kept pace with inflation it would now be $14,502. The figure for 2003–2004 is $34,100, a 6.5 percent increase over last year. Notre Dame offers various kinds of aid to stu-dents. The primary form of aid, however, is the student or parent loan, whether federal or private.

"The major universities, including Notre Dame, have built their research enterprises on the backs of borrowing students. The loan burden distorts the career and family options of students, especially if they contemplate grad study. ND 2010 is a detailed analysis of many things. Its failure even to men-tion this problem indicates an astonishing indifference. The main beneficiaries of the University envisioned by ND 2010 will not be the students but the researching professoriate, well paid administrators and striving academics.

"2. ND 2010 is peppered with references to Notre Dame as a 'Catholic' university. But it omits any acceptance of the definition of that term in *Ex*

Corde Ecclesiae, the 1990 apostolic constitution on Catholic higher education. ND 2010 says that the University 'must take into account with . . . sensitivity and respect the formal teaching role of the Magisterium in the life of the Church.' But Notre Dame does not accept the authoritative nature of that role. For example, the bishops' Application of *Ex Corde* to the United States says: 'Catholic students have a right to receive from a university instruction in authentic Catholic doctrine and practice, especially from those who teach the theological disciplines.' Notre Dame accepts that duty neither in theory nor in practice. Notre Dame is servile toward secular academic bodies, the government, the NCAA and others. The only authority it will not accept is that of the Catholic Church to define the 'Catholic university.' As Father James Burtchaell has demonstrated, a 'Catholic' university that severs itself from the defining authority of the Church will predictably follow the secularizing pattern of Vanderbilt, Harvard and other originally Protestant institutions. And there remains a consumer fraud problem in Notre Dame's claim to be 'Catholic' when it does not accept the definition of that term by the Catholic Church.

"ND 2010 chronicles the success of our leaders in transforming Notre Dame's historic character and mission according to their own lights. But it conjures instead an image of the log of the Titanic. The bill-paying students and families deserve better."

THE VAGINA MONOLOGUES: RESIGNATIONS ARE IN ORDER, Jan. 29, 2004

"At least 40 'Catholic' colleges, including Notre Dame for the third time, will sponsor or host public performances of the Vagina Monologues this term. My concern here is solely with the judgment exhibited by our leaders in allowing this play again at Notre Dame. . . .

"One object of the play is to desensitize people to the naming of female sex organs in order to discourage violence against women. The performers deliver monologues focusing on, and personifying, their sex organs. These contributions to literature include a description of a group masturbation in a 'vagina workshop' run by 'a woman who believes in vaginas.'

"It describes how the participants masturbated with the aid of hand mirrors. Other monologists recount conversations with their vaginas. Another talks to her vulva. Others describe lesbian sexual acts. And so on, with abundant description. Apart from this repudiation of modesty and reserve, the personification of a body part destroys the integrity of the person and invites the objectification of women which can generate the violence the play purports to oppose.

"These and other aspects of the play ought to preclude its performance at Notre Dame. The most compelling reason, however, for opposing that performance arises from the sex abuse scandal in the Church.

"The most highly publicized monologue describes the lesbian seduction of a 16-year-old by an adult as a 'salvation' for the victim.

"In 'The Little Coochi Snorcher That Could,' an adult 'Southern woman of color' describes, among other childhood sexual memories, her encounters at age 16 with a 'gorgeous' 24-year-old woman in the neighborhood. The child's mother agrees to the woman's request that the child spend the night with her. (I omit explicit details.)

"'I'm scared but I really can't wait. Her apartment's fantastic . . . the beads, the fluffy pillows, the mood lights. . . . She makes a vodka for herself and then . . . the pretty lady makes me a drink. . . . The alcohol has gone to my head and I'm loose and ready . . . as she gently and slowly lays me out on the bed. . . . Then she does everything to me . . . that I always thought was nasty before, and wow, I'm so hot, so wild. . . . I get crazy wild. . . .

"'Afterward the gorgeous lady teaches me . . . all the different ways to give myself pleasure. She's very thorough. She tells me to always know how to give myself pleasure so I'll never need to rely on a man. In the morning I am worried . . . because I'm so in love with her. She laughs, but I never see her again. I realized later she was my surprising, unexpected, politically incorrect salvation. She transformed my sorry-ass coochi snorcher and raised it up into a kind of heaven.' Eve Ensler, The Vagina Monologues (2001), 77–82.

"On Jan. 6, the Catholic bishops released their report on the efforts of the dioceses to correct the sex abuse problem. The vast majority of cases involved the exploitation by priests of teenage boys in homosexual relations with varying degrees of consent. The monologue recounting the seduction of a trusting 16-year-old girl by a 24-year-old woman she admires is the precise counterpart of the exploitation of male teenagers by priests that has ruined lives and rocked the Church.

"Sexual exploitation of a teenager by an adult is despicable, whether the participants are both male, both female or mixed. No one has a moral right to present such an exploitation as a benefit to the victim. This is a very serious matter.

"In light of the ongoing scandal in the Church, it is totally inexcusable for any 'Catholic' institution, and especially the University of Our Lady, to allow itself to be used as a public forum for a portrayal of the sexual exploitation of a teenager by an adult as a 'salvation' for the victim.

"Regrettably, the Notre Dame President and Provost have responded to complaints about this with academic banalities reflecting a politically correct paralysis of judgment.

"I hope that our leaders will reconsider this failure of judgment and will cancel this third performance. If not, all the responsible administrators, from the top down, should resign their administrative positions. If they do not resign, they should be removed.

"Baseball has it right: Three strikes and you're out."

BENGAL BOUTS AND BANGLADESH, Feb. 11, 2004

"In 1854, Franklin Pierce was president, Notre Dame was 12 years old. And the first Holy Cross missionaries set foot in what is now Bangladesh, one of the poorest countries in the world. Bangladesh is 88.3 percent Muslim and 10.5 percent Hindu. Could these missionaries have foreseen that, 150 years later, Holy Cross priests, brothers and sisters would staff schools, parishes and other activities throughout the country? Maybe. But they could not have imagined that the largest single donation to their apostolate every year would be generated by Notre Dame students majoring in pugilistic science. . . .

"In 1931, Dominic (Nappy) Napolitano organized the Bengal Bouts in the form in which they have continued for 74 years.

"In 2003, the Bouts contributed $44,000 to the Bengal Missions. This year, 143 boxers will try to beat that total.

"The student officers of the Boxing Club run the program under the supervision of Rich O'Leary and Dave Brown of the Club Sports office. The senior captains are Pat Dillon, Tommy Demko, Stefan Borovina, Billy Zizic and Tony Hollowell. The junior captains are Nathan Lohmeyer, Jim Christoforetti and Galen Loughrey. Each boxer is a fund-raiser, selling tickets and program ads. But the brains of the outfit, and the key to its financial success, are the student managers, Kristin Boyd, Ashley Merusi and Rachel Anderson, who are taking the administrative and business end of the Bouts to a new level. . . .

"'We teach traditional stand-up boxing,' said coach Terry Johnson, 'the same way Nappy taught it for 50 years. We approach boxing as a sport, not as a fight. The guys understand this and are dedicated to sportsmanship, camaraderie and boxing for the missions.'

"In a workout led by Tom Suddes, the boxers count push-ups and sit-ups by the hundred and Tom does every one of them himself (almost).

"'The Bouts are special,' notes Suddes, 'because you may end up in the ring with your best friend and after the final bell your relationship and mutual respect are stronger than before you put on the gloves.'

"The assistant coaches, all volunteers, include Sweet C. Robinson, of the Buchanan police department, and former boxers, Ryan Rans, Chip Farrell, Tom Biolchini, Jeff Dobosh and Roland Chamblee, a Superior Court Judge and four-time Bengals champ who may be the only active judge who also serves as corner man in a boxing ring.

"Holy Mother Church is in the act with the chaplains, Fr. Bill Seetch, C.S.C., and Fr. Brian Daley, S.J., who is also a coach. They both work out with the boxers. And the timer is Msgr. John Hagerty, appropriately of Notre Dame parish in Hermitage, Penn.

"The primary emphasis of the program is safety. . . . Dr. James Moriarty, University chief of medicine, closely supervises every phase of the program. EMTs are present at all contact practices. . . .

"The money raised by the Bouts, said Mission Director Fr. David L. Schlaver, C.S.C. 'enables many to earn a living, provide medical care and housing for their families and educate their children for life—and survival— in a difficult society."

LAETARE MEDAL FOR CARDINAL BURKE, Feb. 25, 2004

"Notre Dame should give the 2004 Laetare Medal to Archbishop Raymond Burke of St. Louis. The medal is given to men and women whose lives have 'illustrated the ideals of the Church and enriched the heritage of humanity.' Archbishop (now Cardinal) Burke is a profile in courage who fits that description.

"In Nov. 2003, when he was Bishop of LaCrosse, Wis., Burke decreed that Catholic legislators in his diocese who 'support procured abortion or euthanasia may not present themselves to receive Holy Communion. They are not to be admitted to Holy Communion, should they present themselves, until . . . they publicly renounce their support of these most unjust practices.'

"Burke had privately appealed to the three legislators involved but they essentially told him to get lost. 'The duty of Catholic legislators to respect human life,' said Burke, 'is not [a] personal opinion I have arbitrarily decided to impose. It is not . . . Burke's law, but God's law which Burke, as a shepherd of God's flock, is bound to teach and uphold, also by admonishing . . . those who violate it. As bishop, I am a guardian of the faith and its practice. If I . . . remain silent while the faith, in one of its most fundamental tenets, is . . . openly disobeyed by those who present themselves as sincere adherents of the faith, then I have failed most seriously and should be removed from office.' Whether other bishops will take the same position is a matter for the pastoral judgment of each bishop. But Burke is a bishop who knows how to bish.

"Burke's stand is politically incorrect, which may be the only sin in the 'Church of Where It's At.' But his action is in line with sound reason and the Constitution. He imposed no legal sanction on the legislators. They are free to continue their support for the legalized execution of the innocent by abortion and euthanasia. Burke is simply invoking the principle of truth-in-labeling. If you are going to present yourself to the voters as a Catholic you should act like one. And you should not give the public a scandal.

"Abortion and euthanasia are not wrong merely because the Church says so. Rather, the Church so teaches because the intentional killing of the innocent is always a grave violation of the natural law and of the Commandments. Nor is Burke's action an infringement on conscience. Conscience and freedom have an obligation to the truth. The bishop is obliged to teach that truth in order to assist Catholics of his diocese in the formation of their consciences.

"A legislator takes an oath to uphold the Constitution. But that oath cannot override his obligation, under the natural law and divine law, not to cooperate in the murder of the innocent. Indeed, when the Constitution has been perverted to authorize the execution of the innocent, fidelity to the Constitution requires the effort to restore the right to life. Similarly, Abraham Lincoln insisted on his moral duty to fight to reverse the *Dred Scott* decision, which had decreed that slaves were property and not persons.

"Legalized abortion is the epitome of an unjust law which, as Thomas Aquinas said, is 'no longer a law but a perversion of a law.' Every legislator, Catholic or not, is morally obliged under the natural law to oppose, and to try to change, a law that authorizes the execution of the innocent. A Catholic legislator who openly and persistently favors legalized abortion and euthanasia not only fails in that duty, he also makes himself liable to denial of his right to receive the Eucharist which is the sign of unity in the faith.

"Canon Law requires that 'those . . . who obstinately persist in manifestly grave sin are not to be admitted to Holy Communion' (Canon 915). Burke did not excommunicate the politicians. Rather, he applied Canon 915 as an explicit regulation of the administration of the sacraments. Burke's action, however, was not merely disciplinary. It was pastoral, born of concern for the spiritual welfare of the Catholic legislator as well as of the Catholic people who could be misled or scandalized if the legislator's pro-death position went unchallenged.

"In 1962, Archbishop Joseph Rummel of New Orleans announced that he was going to desegregate New Orleans Catholic schools. Segregationist activists Judge Leander Perez, State Senator E.W. Gravolet and B.J. Gaillot, all Catholics, opposed him. Gravolet threatened to cut off state support to Catholic schools and Perez urged Catholics to withhold financial support from the Church. After reminding them of the danger to their souls in rejecting Church teaching, the archbishop excommunicated all three. Perez was an icon of the legal and cultural mainstream. Rummel was counter-cultural. But he was right. And so is Burke. He would honor Notre Dame by accepting the Laetare Medal."

HOMOSEXUAL CONFUSION, March 26, 2004

"Notre Dame's policies on homosexual issues are a paradigm of incoherence. Our leaders act sincerely in what they see as the best interest of Notre Dame and its students. But in their pursuit of political correctness, they have misled students, especially those with homosexual inclinations, and they have acquiesced in the exploitation of Notre Dame by activist movements hostile to the Catholic Church.

"*Ex Corde Ecclesiae*, the 1990 Apostolic Constitution on Catholic Universities, requires that the 'essential characteristics' of 'every Catholic university' must include: 'Fidelity to the Christian message as it comes to us through the Church.' That message on the homosexual issues is clear:

"1. Persons with 'homosexual tendencies . . . must be accepted with respect, compassion and sensitivity. Every sign of unjust discrimination in their regard should be avoided.' *Catechism*, No. 2358.

"2. Homosexual acts are 'intrinsically disordered. They are contrary to the natural law. They close the sexual act to the gift of life.' 'Scripture . . . presents [them] as acts of grave depravity.' No. 2357.

"3. The homosexual inclination is not a sin. But, as an inclination toward an objectively disordered act, the inclination is itself 'objectively disordered.' No. 2358.

"Notre Dame refuses to recognize student groups which approve homosexual acts. It refuses on the ground that such acts are prohibited by 'official Church teaching.' The University, however, refuses to acknowledge that the inclination toward such acts is disordered. But how can an inclination toward a disordered act be itself anything but disordered? And if an inclination is not disordered why may it not be acted upon? This is important because our leaders wrongly imply that the prohibition of homosexual acts is not rooted in the natural law and the law of God but rather that it is an arbitrary edict of an insensitive Church.

"This misdirection is compounded by the University's readiness to combat other disordered inclinations. Students inclined to eating disorders, smoking and excessive drinking are the object of elaborate programs to control those inclinations. Smokers, especially, have achieved the status of virtual pariahs. Not for them the welcoming solicitude extended to students inclined toward sodomy rather than tobacco.

"To alumni, donors and the public our leaders present an image of fidelity in their refusal to recognize student groups condoning homosexual acts. To the students, however, they offer cognitive confusion. If they are so adamant about refusing to approve homosexual acts, why have they allowed, for three years, University sponsorship of The Vagina Monologues, a play which commends the lesbian exploitation of a teenager by an adult as a 'salvation' for the victim? And why did our leaders allow University sponsorship of the Queer Film Festival which exalted homosexual and transgendered lifestyles so as to hijack the reputation of Notre Dame in support of a politicized agenda hostile to the Catholic Church? Only a liberal academic could imagine that those events were neutral academic exercises.

"Despite their denial of formal recognition to activist homosexual groups, our leaders convey by their actions the message that the legitimacy of the active homosexual lifestyle is at least an open question. While that message accords with political correctness, the de facto official religion of Notre Dame, it poorly serves the members of the University community. The *Letter on the Pastoral Care of Homosexual Persons*, issued with the approval of John Paul II, states: '[D]eparture from the Church's teaching or silence about it, in an effort to provide pastoral care, is neither caring nor pastoral. Only what is true can ultimately be pastoral. The neglect of the Church's position prevents homosexual men and women from receiving the care they need and deserve.'

"The teaching of the Church in this area, rooted in the natural law as well as Scripture, is a hopeful and constructive testimony to the dignity of the person. Notre Dame students are entitled to a coherent affirmation by our leaders of the fullness of that teaching. Here, as in other areas, they are shortchanged."

THE PASSION OF THE CHRIST, April 8, 2004

"Frank Rich of *The New York Times* called it 'a porn movie.' To Christopher Hitchens, it was a homoerotic 'exercise in lurid sadomasochism.' The *New York Daily News* called it 'the most virulently anti-Semitic movie made since the German propaganda films of World War II.'

"How can we explain the hostility of the elites in the media, Hollywood and the academy to Mel Gibson and the Passion of the Christ? Antonio Gramsci can help us understand.

"Gramsci, an Italian Communist who died in 1937, saw that the proletarian revolution of Marxist theory would not happen in western countries because the workers and their oppressors were united by a common bond of Christian culture and belief. The secular, classless paradise, he thought, would be achieved without a revolution, but only if the people were first separated from their Christian roots and conditioned to ignore the transcendent, i.e., God and his truth, and to focus on the immanent, i.e., living day-to-day without reference to God or objective morality.

"Since the 1960s this country has been a Gramscian laboratory. The courts removed any affirmation of God from the schools and public life. Merry Christmas gave way to Happy Holidays. Deconstructionists deprived language of objective meaning. Trendy clerics turned the Commandments into advisories.

"'More than in any other historical period,' said John Paul II, 'one must point to a break in the transmission of moral and religious values between generations.'

"The intentional infliction of death is now an optional problem-solving technique. The contraceptive separation of sex from life provided control over the beginning of life and inevitably over the ending of life through abortion and euthanasia. That separation legitimized sodomy and undermined the status of marriage. Pornography is a bigger business than professional football, basketball and baseball combined. And so on.

"Gramsci wrote approvingly of 'hegemony' as dominance by a ruling class not by the threat of force but by the willing submission of the subordinate classes. The molders of culture have achieved, in recent decades, the cultural hegemony not of a class but of a secular, relativist and individualist code. That code conditions the public to think only of the materialistic here and now, with God excluded or relegated to the margins.

"So why the hostility to 'The Passion?' The protests against it were described by Rabbi Daniel Lapin as 'morally indefensible and ill-advised.'

"'Gibson has complemented the Gospel narrative,' said Vatican Cardinal Dario Castrillon Hoyos, 'with the insights [of] saints and mystics. . . . [The film is] faithful to the meaning of the Gospels, as understood by the church.' Maia Morgenstern, the Jewish actress who played Mary, and whose father is a Holocaust survivor, said, 'Despite the blood and the violence, it's a beautiful film. . . . It brings . . . a peace message.'

"If anything, Gibson understated the sufferings of Christ. St. Alphonsus Ligouri, a Doctor of the Church, relying on St. Bonaventure, St. Anselm and the visions of St. Bridget, said 'the number of the [scourging] strokes amounted to several thousand, the flagellation being administered . . . after the manner of the Romans, with whom there was no [limit]. . . . [T]he bones of his ribs were laid bare . . . St. Peter Damian wrote that the executioners exhausted themselves with fatigue in scourging our Lord.'

"'After the scourging,' wrote St. Alphonsus, '[Pilate showed] him to the people, saying, 'Behold the Man!' [because he was . . . so pitiable . . . that Pilate believed the very sight of him would have moved his enemies . . . to compassion, and hindered them from . . . demanding his death. . . . The appearance of Jesus after his scourging was so shocking . . . as to move to tears even those who hated him.' Ligouri concluded that Christ, a divine person with two natures, human and divine, willed to suffer beyond merely human endurance. The film is a love story.

"Why are the liberal elites so hostile to this film? Because it threatens to upset their applecart, worldwide. 'The Passion'—like a lightning bolt—is a sudden intrusion of the transcendent—God—into the immanent, into the lives of ordinary people.

"A religious renewal had been germinating before 'The Passion.' But 'The Passion' reaches beyond the religiously aware to affect many for whom it is a wake-up call. The elites had already overreached, with the Super Bowl half-time and the arrogance of public officials 'marrying' sodomites in defiance of enacted law. But Mel Gibson is so hated by the elites because he dramatically reintroduced the American—and world—public to the transcendent and specifically to Christ. The fight is not about Mel Gibson. It is about Christ.

"Antonio Gramsci would understand. Pray for him. And go see 'The Passion.'"

BROWN V. BOARD OF EDUCATION AND THE NATURAL LAW, April 26, 2004

"Fifty years ago, in *Brown v. Board of Education*, the Supreme Court outlawed racial segregation in public schools. That anniversary reminds us that even if the Constitution allowed such segregation, it would still be unjust. That leads to two further questions: Why is legalized segregation, or any other evil, morally wrong and unjust? And how do we know that? The answers are in the natural law.

"The natural law is not a Christian invention. Aristotle and Cicero affirmed it. Everything has a law of its nature, prescribed by its maker. If you throw a rock in the lake, it will sink. The natural law that governs human conduct is a rule of reason, implanted by God in man's nature, whereby man (of both sexes) can know how he should act if he is to attain his end of eternal happiness with God.

"The first, self-evident principle of the natural law, in the words of St. Thomas Aquinas, is that 'good is to be done and pursued, and evil is to be avoided.' The good is that which is in accord with the nature of the subject, whether a car or a man. It is good for a car to feed it gasoline, but it not good to feed it to a man. So also it is not good, i.e., it is evil, for a man to steal, since theft is contrary to the natural human inclination to live in community.

"'Moral truth is objective,' Pope John Paul II said, 'and a properly formed conscience can perceive it.' Whether an act, e.g., murder, objectively violates the natural law is a separate question from the subjective culpability of the person who does it. You are morally culpable, i.e., blameworthy, only if you knew the act was wrong and still chose to do it. Apart from special circumstances, such as a juror or confessor, we have neither the right nor the capacity to judge the subjective culpability of anyone.

"The natural law is the standard for the civil law as well as for personal conduct. When Rosa Parks refused to give up her seat on the bus in 1955, she made a natural law statement. A law can be unjust, said Aquinas, 'when burdens are imposed unequally on the community.' Legally enforced racial segregation, whether on a bus or in a school, is unjust because it violates the dignity of the person and undermines community.

"As Aquinas put it, if a human law 'deflects from the law of nature,' it is unjust and 'is no longer a law but a perversion of law.' In his *Letter from Birmingham Jail*, Martin Luther King, Jr. said, 'An unjust law is a code that is out of harmony with the moral law.' We may be obliged to obey an unjust law, as Aquinas said, to avoid a greater evil of 'scandal or disturbance,' but a law that is unjust because it would compel one to violate the Divine law must never be obeyed.

"The question remains: Whose natural law are you going to apply? 'The ideas of natural justice,' said Supreme Court Justice James Iredell in 1798, 'are regulated by no fixed standard; the ablest and the purest men have differed upon the subject.' Reason can attain to moral truth. But if reason were our only guide, we would be doomed to endless and inconclusive debate. Our intellects are weakened by original sin and sincere advocates can be found on both sides of most moral issues. Aristotle sanctioned infanticide. When people disagree, e.g., on the morality of abortion, they can't both be right. As Aquinas tells us, 'If . . . we consider one action in the moral order, it is impossible for it to be morally both good and evil.'

"God gave us the Ten Commandments to spell out the basic obligations of the natural law. But without a visible, authoritative interpreter, how are we to apply the Commandments and the natural law in specific cases?

"Pope John Paul II points to the solution: 'Christians have a great help for the formation of conscience in the church and her Magisterium. As [Vatican II] affirms: "[T]he Catholic Church is by the will of Christ, the teacher of . . . the principles of the moral order which derive from human nature itself." . . . The Church puts herself . . . at the service of conscience, helping it to attain the truth with certainty and to abide in it.' Everyone has a pope, an ultimate authoritative interpreter on moral questions. If it is not the real Pope, it will be the individual himself, or CBS, Katie Couric or whoever.

"It makes sense to recognize that we have only one pope, not six billion, and that he is John Paul II because he is the successor of Peter to whom Christ, who is God, gave the keys. The Church, however, is not an academic 'superteacher' of natural law. Rather, she incorporates the natural law, and especially the teachings of Aquinas, into her teaching of the Truth, who is Christ. The papacy is a gift of God, permitting us to be certain as to what conduct is in accord with our nature and the law of God.

"So, on this anniversary of the *Brown* decision, we ought to remember that all of us, including the state, are subject to what the Declaration of Independence called 'the laws of Nature and of Nature's God.'"

2004–2005

Pastor Sensing Makes Sense, Aug. 26, 2004

"Do you want a different view on same-sex marriage? Take a look at the March 15 *Wall Street Journal* op-ed by Pastor Donald Sensing of Trinity United Methodist Church in Franklin, Tenn.

"'Opponents of legalized same-sex marriage,' notes Sensing, 'say they're trying to protect a beleaguered institution, but they're a little late. The walls of traditional marriage were breached 40 years ago. What we see now is the storming of the last bastion.'

"Marriage, says Sensing, was done in by the contraceptive pill, which severed 'the causal relationships' between sex, pregnancy and marriage, obviating 'the fundamental basis of marriage.'

"Marriage is not merely a contract which the state and the parties have a right to define. Marriage as a man-woman union, Sensing points out, is 'prehistoric' as 'part of a natural law of the creation.'

"The law gives marriage exclusive privileges because the spouses commit to raise children for the future of society and the state. Only a man-woman union can produce new taxpayers. Society, notes Sensing, 'legitimated the sexual union of a . . . man and woman [and] promised structures beneficial to children arising from the marriage. . . . Society's stake in marriage . . . is . . . the perpetuation of the society itself.'

"The pill is decisive because, in a contraceptive society, marriage loses its reason for being. In the natural order, one reason why sex is reserved for marriage, why marriage is permanent and why the man-woman union is privileged by the law is because sex has something to do with babies. But if, through the contraceptive ethic, sex has no intrinsic relation to procreation and man—of both sexes—is the arbiter of whether and when sex shall have that relation, why should sex be reserved for marriage, and why should 'marriage' be reserved to a man-woman union?

"'Sex, child-bearing and marriage now have no necessary connection to one another,' says Sensing, 'because the biological connection between sex and child-bearing is controllable.'

"Since the coming of the pill in the 1960s, the nationwide marriage rate has fallen 43 percent. 'Instead of getting married,' says Sensing, 'men and women are just living together, cohabitation having increased tenfold in the same period. According to a University of Chicago study . . . more than half the men and women who do get married have already lived together.'

"With the dominance of the pill, in Sensing's words, 'weddings become symbolic rather than substantive,' serving 'for most couples [as] the shortest way to make the legal compact [on] property rights and other . . . benefits.'

"The pill undercut the legal basis to deny homosexuals the right to enter the contract of marriage in order to regulate 'their legal and property relationship . . . to mirror exactly that of hetero, married couples.' A contraceptive society cannot deny legitimacy to same-sex unions without denying its own premise that man is the arbiter of whether sex will have any relation to procreation.

"Proponents of same-sex marriage seem to have a more realistic view of what marriage has become in the contraceptive society. The right to separate sex from procreation is an article of faith in our culture.

"Defenders of traditional marriage, unwilling to challenge that article of faith, are defending the 'last bastion.' They would deny the name 'marriage' to a same-sex union. But, in the Federal Marriage Amendment, they would approve Vermont-style 'civil unions' so long as they were legalized by a legislature rather than a court.

"Vermont gives to same-sex 'civil unions' all the legal attributes of marriage except the name. This is symbolism, ignoring the substance of what it means to reduce marriage, as instituted in *Genesis*, to legal parity with same-sex sodomitic unions.

"'Sacred Scripture,' says the *Catechism*, 'presents homosexual acts as acts of grave depravity.' The inclination toward those acts, as with an inclination to any other immoral act, is 'objectively disordered.'

"In its *Considerations* issued last March 25, the Vatican noted 'the difference between homosexual behavior as a private phenomenon and as a relationship in society . . . approved by the law. . . . Legal recognition of homosexual unions would obscure . . . basic moral values and cause a devaluation of . . . marriage.'

"A society where it makes no legal difference whether little boys grow up to 'marry' girls or other boys is past the line of clinical insanity. '[T]raditionalists,' says Sensing, 'need to . . . face the fact that same-sex marriage, if it comes about, will not cause the degeneration . . . of marriage; it is the result of it.'

"Pastor Sensing's essay reflects a growing appreciation by non-Catholics for the traditional Christian teaching on contraception.

"Perhaps it may even occur to cafeteria Catholics and trendy theologians at Notre Dame and elsewhere that the Catholic Church is right in upholding the Christian teaching, unbroken until the Anglican Lambeth Conference of 1930, that contraception is always a social as well as a moral evil."

EXPERIMENTATION—THEN AND NOW, Sept. 9, 2004

"At Reichsfuhrer Heinrich Himmler's suggestion, Dr. Karl Gebhardt, a Nazi physician at the SS hospital in Hohenlychen, specialized in heteroplastic transplantation experiments. If an SS soldier had lost an arm or a leg, a replacement limb would be amputated from a live prisoner at the Ravensbruck concentration camp. The prisoner would be killed in the process and his limb would be rushed to Dr. Gebhardt who would make the futile attempt to attach it to the SS amputee. Leo Alexander, M.D., *New England J. of Med.*, July 14, 1949. Dr. Gebhardt was convicted at Nuremberg and hanged in 1948.

"Dr. Gebhardt's problem is that he was born before his time. The theory of his experiments, the killing of human beings to use their parts for the benefit of others, is precisely the principle that underlies embryonic stem cell research (ESCR). Gebhardt would have been mystified by the technology but otherwise he would have felt at home in listening to Ron Reagan, son of the late president, at the Democratic National Convention.

"First, the background: Your life began at fertilization when your father's sperm joined your mother's ovum. At the one-cell stage you were a zygote. After that you were an embryo until about seven weeks when you were called a fetus. To obtain embryonic stem cells, a woman's ovum is cloned or fertilized in vitro to create a human embryo. Five-to-seven days after fertilization, stem cells are present. They are removed, which kills the embryo. The stem cells are then grown and manipulated to create specific types of human tissue. The hope is that such cells can be used to repair or replace damaged cells.

"Ron Reagan urged the procurement of stem cells by cloning: '[A] doctor . . . takes . . . skin cells from your arm. The nucleus of one of your cells is placed into a donor egg whose own nucleus has been removed. . . . [S]timulation will encourage your cell's nucleus to begin dividing, [generating] embryonic stem cells containing only your DNA, thereby eliminating . . . tissue rejection. These stem cells are then driven to become the . . . cells that are defective in Parkinson's patients. And finally, those cells—with your DNA—are injected into your brain where they will replace the faulty cells whose failure . . . led to the Parkinson's disease. . . . [Y]ou're cured. . . . [T]hese embryonic stem cells, . . . could . . . be induced to recreate virtually any tissue in your body. How'd you like to have your own personal biological repair kit standing by at the hospital?'

"Ron Reagan said that 'no fetal tissue is involved. . . . No fetuses are created, none destroyed.' The process, however, does kill a human being, an embryo who therefore never has the chance to become a fetus, an infant, a law student, etc. You create a DNA-copy of yourself by cloning and then kill that living human being at the embryonic stage so as to use his or her stem cells. You can imagine Gebhardt nodding in approval.

"President Reagan's other son, Michael Reagan, said his father 'opposed the creation of human embryos for the sole purpose of using their stem cells as possible medical cures.' President Reagan's close advisor, Judge William Clark, in a *New York Times* op-ed on the day after the Reagan funeral, quoted the late President's condemnations of the intentional killing of unborn life even at the earliest stage.

"Neither embryonic stem cell research (ESCR) nor human cloning is prohibited by federal law. Both can be legally done with private funding. President Bush, on Aug. 9, 2001, banned federal funding of ESCR except for research on cell lines that had been derived by that date. He sought to avoid 'taxpayer funding that would . . . encourage further destruction of human embryos.' The federal budget in 2003 included $24.8 million for ESCR in accord with the Bush criteria.

"ESCR has not been shown to benefit patients with Parkinson's, Alzheimer's or any other disease. But adult stem cells, taken from bone marrow, the placenta and the umbilical cord, are successfully used to treat some cancers, leukemia, heart attack, stroke, Parkinson's, sickle-cell anemia, and other diseases. Research on adult stem cells presents no moral problem. It attracts private funding because of its success. Proponents of ESCR have to seek federal funding because their lack of success prevents them from attracting private funding.

"Come to think of it, even Gebhardt might be uncomfortable with our 21st century technologists. He used inmates already slated to die, and he agreed with the theory of Nazi Dr. Julius Hallervorden who said, 'If you are going to kill all these people, at least take the brains out so that the material could be utilized.' But even Gebhardt might have been taken aback at our scientists who create new life solely to destroy it for the use of others. Both techniques are diabolic. But the Nazi doctors were comparative amateurs."

FEEDING GRANDMA, Sept. 23, 2004

"Your family can expect to face this problem sooner or later. Grandma is in the hospital, incurably ill. She is comatose or in a persistent vegetative state (PVS). She receives nutrition and hydration through a tube. She is not dying and not in pain. If food and water are continued, she will live for years. Can you turn off that tube and let Grandma go 'home' in peace? Tough question. Fortunately, in his address last March on the care of PVS patients, Pope John Paul II gave a clear answer.

"First, the basic principles: '[T]he direct and voluntary killing of an innocent human being is always gravely immoral.' (*Evangelium Vitae*). This includes euthanasia, which is 'an act, or omission, which of itself or by intention causes death to eliminate suffering.' *Catechism*, no. 2277. We also have a positive, but not absolute, duty to use all ordinary and proportionate means to preserve our own lives and the lives of those in our care.

"The civil law permits, but does not require, some acts and omissions forbidden by the moral law. If a patient is competent he can legally refuse all treatment, including food and water: The law permits withholding of treatment of food and water from an incompetent patient based on the patient's previously expressed intent, or on the decision of his health care agent that the patient would have wanted such withdrawal or that it would be in his best interest. In moral terms that can be euthanasia.

"An advance directive, which the patient had executed when he was competent, can specify the care to be given to him, and it can designate a person to make treatment decisions for him. The basic advance directives are the living will and the power of attorney. A living will is a statement of your intention as to the care you will receive if you become incompetent. It must be interpreted and implemented by the physician and your family. A power of attorney is preferable. It appoints a person you trust to make health care decisions for you if you become incompetent. In moral terms, as the U.S. Bishops put it, that decision-maker 'may not deliberately cause a patient's death or refuse . . . ordinary means, even if he or she believes the patient would have made such a decision.'

"In his March 2004 address, the Pope said 'the administration of water and food, even . . . by artificial means, always represents a natural means of preserving life, not a medical act. Its use [is] ordinary and proportionate, and . . . morally obligatory, insofar as and until it is seen to have attained its proper finality, which . . . consists in providing nourishment to the patient and alleviation of his suffering . . . [W]aning hopes for recovery cannot ethically justify the . . . interruption of minimal care . . . including nutrition and hydration. . . . [I]t ends up becoming, if done knowingly and willingly, true and proper euthanasia by omission.

"As Monsignor Kevin McMahon, of St. Charles Borromeo Seminary, described it, this papal teaching is an 'authoritative interpretation' forbidding Catholic facilities to withhold or withdraw nutrition and hydration from PVS patients as long as it preserves life or alleviates suffering. The law allows religious hospitals to decline to follow instructions in advance directives that conflict with their stated policies.

"Grandma's feeding tube is not supposed to cure her illness but only to sustain her biological life. The fact that it prolongs what some might regard as a pointless existence does not justify its removal. Morally, Grandma's feeding tube may be withheld or withdrawn only in three general situations: 1. If it is useless in sustaining bodily life because her body is unable to absorb the nutrients; 2. In the final dying process when inevitable death is imminent despite the provision of feeding and medical treatments and the removal of the tube would therefore not be the cause of her death; or 3. If the administration of the nutrition and hydration itself causes unreasonably burdensome pain and suffering to the patient. If the tube were excessively painful, which it rarely is, you could remove it if your intent were to relieve the pain and to replace it if and when it could be done without such pain. If your intent in removing it were to cause Grandma's death for her own good, that removal would be euthanasia, a form of murder.

"So Grandma's quality of life may not be so good. But, as John Paul said, the value of her life 'cannot be made subordinate to any judgment of its quality expressed by other men.' Nobody has the right intentionally to starve and dehydrate her to death. The bottom line? Feed the hungry. Give drink to the thirsty."

THE WAR POWER, Oct. 7, 2004

"'I faced the kind of decision that comes only from the Oval Office,' said President Bush. 'Do I forget the lessons of September 11th . . . or do I take action to defend our country? Faced with that choice, I will defend America every time.'

"Campaign rhetoric on both sides implies that the decision for war or peace belongs to one man—the President. The framers of the Constitution saw it differently. On August 17, 1787, they debated whether to give Congress the power to 'make war.' James Madison and Elbridge Gerry successfully 'moved to insert "declare," striking out "make" war; leaving to the Executive the power to repel sudden attacks.' Roger Sherman said, 'The Executive [should] be able to repel and not to commence war.' They left what Justice Robert Jackson called 'a zone of twilight,' with concurrent powers in the President and Congress. The balance is hard to strike.

"The War Powers Resolution of 1973, for example, imposed probably unconstitutional time limits on the President's use of force. Presidents have put forces into combat more than 200 times. Congress has declared war only five times. The last time Congress debated and decided whether to go to war was in 1917.

"The President takes an oath to 'preserve, protect and defend' the Constitution, while other officers swear only to 'support' it. Presidents usually seek Congressional approval before major military action. But no President has admitted that he must do so.

"President Clinton bombed Serbia despite the refusal of the House to authorize it. In the Gulf War, the Afghanistan campaign and the Iraq War,

Congress gave a blank check to the President. In 2002, Congress authorized him to use the armed forces 'as he determines to be necessary and appropriate . . . to defend . . . the United States against the . . . threat posed by Iraq.' The Resolution of September 18, 2001, understandably did not even identify the enemy. It authorized the President 'to use all necessary and appropriate force against those nations, organizations or persons he determines planned, authorized, committed or ordered the . . . attacks . . . on September 11, 2001, or harbored such organizations or persons.'

"In the ongoing war against what the 9/11 Commission called 'Islamist terrorism,' who will decide, for example, whether to use force to prevent Iran from achieving nuclear capability? The citizen, lacking information, must give a benefit of the doubt to the justice and wisdom of a decision to use force, whether made by Congress or the President or both. Congress, however, has a duty to inform itself and to participate in, or perhaps control, decisions to initiate a major use of force.

"The President needs flexibility to fulfill his duty of defense. But if Congress continues its habit of authorizing the President to use force as he thinks 'necessary and appropriate,' Congress may find itself reduced to a merely advisory and funding role. Can there be a situation today in which Congress must go beyond authorization and must itself decide whether to use military force? Was House Speaker Thomas Foley right when he said the Gulf War resolution had 'the moral legal, constitutional, practical consequences of a declaration of war'? Maybe the best we can do is the current pattern of ad hoc cooperation. But the issue compels attention in light of the current expansive concept of defense.

"'The wisest use of American strength,' said President Bush, 'is to advance freedom.' He sees the liberation of Iraq as 'a watershed event in the global democratic revolution.' He views 'our commitment to the global expansion of democracy' and specifically our helping Iraq to build a 'democratic country in the heart of the Middle East' as a way to 'defend our people from danger.' To prevent 'rogue states' from acquiring weapons of mass destruction, he pledges, 'we will not hesitate to act alone, if necessary, to exercise our right of self-defense by acting pre-emptively.'

"This new doctrine of seeking security by advancing a 'global democratic revolution' and by preemptive military action to prevent presidentially defined 'rogue states' from getting WMDs is a presidential creation. And it is light years removed from the framers' quaint idea of 'leaving to the Executive the power to repel sudden attacks.'

"These remarks are not intended to focus criticism on President Bush, for whom I will vote. And Senator Kerry's multiple positions are no less dubious. The point is that, whoever is elected, it ought to be agreed that the decision to initiate major conflict, including separate phases of the 'war on terror,' must involve seriously the elected representatives of the people who will fight that war. Elbridge Gerry was from Massachusetts. But he still got it right when he said he 'never expected to hear in a republic a motion to empower the Executive alone to declare war.'

HOW SHOULD CATHOLICS VOTE? Oct. 28, 2004

"There may be a shortage of vocations to the priesthood. But, as someone said, there is no shortage of vocations to the Papacy. Suppose, however, that you are a believing Catholic, which means, among other things, that you do not feel a vocation to be your own Pope. Instead, you accept the teaching authority of the Church. That opens the question: How should your faith affect your vote? Fortunately, we have clear guidance from the Church. We can summarize that guidance, as found in the writings of the real Pope, in statements issued in 2002 and 2004, with approval of the Pope, by Cardinal Joseph Ratzinger of the Congregation for the Doctrine of the Faith and in statements by the United States Bishops and individual bishops.

"First, abortion, euthanasia and embryonic stem-cell research are qualitatively different from any other issues. All three involve the intentional killing of an innocent human being, which the law is absolutely obliged to forbid. '[N]o one can, in any circumstance, claim . . . the right to destroy directly an innocent human being.' *Evangelium Vitae* (EV). '[T]he law must provide appropriate penal sanctions for every deliberate violation of the child's rights.' *Instruction on Bioethics*. In his 2004 statement, Cardinal Ratzinger said, 'Not all . . . issues have the same moral weight as abortion and euthanasia. . . . There may be a legitimate diversity of opinion even among Catholics about waging war and applying the death penalty, but not . . . with regard to abortion and euthanasia.'

"Second, Catholic lawmakers 'have a grave a clear obligation to oppose any law that attacks human life. For them, as for every Catholic, it is impossible to promote such laws or to vote for them.' Ratzinger, 2002. Under very limited circumstances, a legislator, whose absolute opposition to abortion is well known, could vote for an imperfect law to save lives where it is not possible to abrogate completely a pro-abortion law. EV, no. 73.

"Third, a Catholic voter may never formally cooperate in the wrong committed by a public official who favors legalization of the execution of the innocent. In formal cooperation, which is always wrong, you directly take part in the evil act of another, or you intend to assist that evil act. In his 2004 statement, Cardinal Ratzinger said, 'A Catholic would be guilty of formal cooperation in evil, and so unworthy to present himself for Holy Communion, if he were to deliberately vote for a candidate precisely because of the candidate's permissive stand on abortion and/or euthanasia. When a Catholic does not share a candidate's stand in favor of abortion and/or euthanasia, but votes for that candidate for other reasons, it is . . . remote material cooperation, which can be permitted [for] proportionate reasons.'

"In material cooperation, your act, which is not in itself wrong, helps another to commit sin although you do not intend for it to do so. Material cooperation in evil is not always wrong. Its morality depends on how proximate it is to the evil act and whether there is a proportionate reason for it. A voter who votes for a pro-abortion candidate cooperates in the evil that candidate would commit if elected. What could be a proportionate reason that could justify a vote for that candidate by a voter who does not approve of abortion? The only reason that would make sense would be if that candidate's opponent were even worse on abortion. An alternative would be to vote for neither.

"Archbishop John Myers of Newark, in the Sept. 17 *Wall Street Journal,* explained this in terms that only an academic could misunderstand. He called the toll of 1.3 million abortions each year in the United States 'a tragedy of epic proportions.' He noted that many supporters would worsen the situation 'by creating a publicly funded industry in which tens of thousands of human lives are produced each year for the purpose of being "sacrificed" in biomedical research.' He could have named Senators Kerry and Edwards in that respect. 'Certainly,' said Myers, 'policies on welfare, national security, the war in Iraq, Social Security or taxes, taken singly or in any combination, do not provide a proportionate reason to vote for a pro-abortion candidate.

"As Archbishop Myers concluded, 'Catholics may, in good conscience, support the use of force in Iraq or oppose it. Abortion and embryo-destructive research are different. They are intrinsic and grave evils; no Catholic may legitimately support them. . . . Catholics are called . . . to protect the victims of these human rights abuses. They may not . . . abandon the victims by supporting those who would further their victimization.'

"The premise of legalized abortion is the legal depersonalization of an innocent human being. That was the premise of the Nazi depersonalization and extermination of the Jews and also of the *Dred Scott* decision which defined slaves as property rather than as persons. To vote for a candidate who endorses that premise can be justified neither by hatred of George W. Bush nor by a subordination of the right to life to lesser concerns."

THE YEAR OF THE EUCHARIST, Nov. 11, 2004

"Are you sick of politics? Consider the derivation of the word. Some say that 'poli' means many and 'tics' are little blood-sucking creatures. The profession of politics, of course, is honorable. But, whatever side we were on in the recent election, we can be excused if we suspect that politicians don't have all the answers, neither for what ails the country nor for the issues in our own lives. Maybe it is time to look elsewhere.

"When John Paul II instituted Eucharistic adoration at St. Peter's Basilica in 1981, he said: 'The best . . . way of establishing everlasting peace on the face of the earth is through . . . Perpetual Adoration of the Blessed Sacrament.' For many years, Notre Dame has had the Eucharist exposed for adoration on Friday afternoons in the Basilica. Since 1997, on student initiative and with the aid of Campus Ministry, we have adoration also on Monday through Thursday in the Coleman-Morse chapel.

"Why is this important? First of all, because Christ is really there. 'In the . . . Eucharist, the body and blood, . . . soul and divinity, of our Lord Jesus Christ and, therefore, the whole Christ is truly, really and substantially contained. This presence is called real, by which is not intended to exclude the other types of presence . . . but because it is presence in the fullest sense . . . it is substantial presence by which Christ, God and man, makes himself wholly and entirely present.' *Catechism*, no. 1374.

"This reality will come as a news flash to many Catholics. Surveys show that 70 percent of Catholics in the 18 to 44 age group believe the Eucharist is merely a 'symbolic reminder' of Christ. This is not surprising in light of the pathetic state of 'Catholic' elementary, secondary and higher education. As Father John A. Hardon put it, 'There was never a time when the world needed to be educated in faith in Christ [and] belief in the Real Presence in the Eucharist, more than today. It is the same Jesus who worked miracles in first century Palestine. He is ready to perform miracles of conversion in our day, provided we believe that He is here with us in the Blessed Sacrament.'

"Recent years have seen a resurgence of Eucharistic adoration in parishes and Catholic colleges. When you do it, you will see the reason.

"'People are hungry for God,' said Mother Teresa of Calcutta. 'When the Sisters are exhausted, up to their eyes in work; when all seems to go awry, they spend an hour in prayer before the Blessed Sacrament. This practice has never failed to bear fruit; they experience peace and strength.'. . .

"John Paul II has proclaimed the Year of the Eucharist, from October 2004 to October 2005. 'During this year,' he said, 'take the time to kneel before Jesus present in the Eucharist, . . . to make reparation . . . for the neglect, and even the insults which our Saviour must endure in many parts of the world.'

"'Christians,' continued John Paul, 'should not be afraid to speak about God and to bear proud witness to our faith. The "culture of the eucharist" promotes a culture of dialogue. . . . [O]ur troubled world, which began the new millennium with . . . terrorism and . . . war, demands that Christians learn to experience the eucharist as a great school of peace, forming men and women who, . . . in social, cultural and political life, can become promoters of dialogue and communion.' John Paul encouraged young people to '[b]ring to your encounter with Jesus, hidden in the eucharist, . . . all the enthusiasm of your age, all your hopes, all your desire to love.'

"So if politicians don't have all the answers, it might be a good idea to look to Someone else."

CHRISTMAS—ALWAYS A POLITICAL EVENT, Dec. 2, 2004

"Is Christmas a political event? Yes, in two ways. First, American Civil Liberties Union lawyers can be counted on to rush to court, at the first sign of Christmas, to force communities to remove Nativity crèches from public places, to silence Christmas carols in schools and to prevent public use even of the word, 'Christmas,' from corrupting the 'Holiday Season.' They commonly argue that public recognition of Christmas is politically divisive, although the controversies usually arise only upon the filing of their own lawsuits.

"In a second and more basic way, Christmas is a political event. When the second person of the Trinity became man, he entered the world as a subject of the Roman Empire which recognized no moral limit to the absolute power of its law. Some philosophers, such as the Roman statesman, Cicero, had argued that law was 'the distinction between things just and unjust, made in agreement with . . . Nature.' But the general rule before Christ was that objective justice had nothing to do with the validity of law and therefore that there was no moral limit to what the state could do. The incarnation of the divine person as man, manifested at Christmas, affirmed instead that the power of earthly rulers is subject to the law of God. As Peter told the Sanhedrin, 'We must obey God rather than men.' *Acts* 5:29. The Christian era began with civil disobedience when the Magi, at divine direction, disobeyed the state in the person of Herod and 'went back to their country by another way.' *Matthew* 2:12. And Joseph and Mary rejected the authority of the state when they fled to Egypt with the child to escape from Herod. *Matthew* 2:13–15.

"With the entry of the divine person, Christ, into the world, the absolute claim of the state met a new kind of challenge. Herod tried to kill the child because he wrongly saw him as a contender for political power. Pontius Pilate could not understand why Christ would not make a deal. He asked, 'What is truth?' *John* 18:38, unaware that Truth, with a capital T, was the person standing in front of him.

"Are there moral limits to what the state can do? The answer given by the Soviet Union, Nazi Germany and many regimes in history was: No. The question remains today. The people of California voted last month to fund the creation of human beings for the purpose of killing them and using their parts for the benefit of others. This was an extension of *Roe v. Wade*, in which the Supreme Court decreed that unborn human beings are nonpersons subject to execution at the discretion of others. That power of the state to depersonalize the innocent had been the legal premise of the Nazi depersonalization and extermination of the Jews. It was also the premise of the *Dred Scott* case which declared that slaves were property rather than persons.

"The reigning jurisprudence today is legal positivism, in which none of those deadly decrees can be said to be unjust because no one can know what is just. 'Truth,' said Justice Oliver Wendell Holmes, 'is the majority vote of the nation that could lick all others.' For Holmes, 'the sacredness of human life is a purely municipal ideal of no validity outside the jurisdiction.' As Hans Kelsen, the leading legal positivist of the 20th century, put it, 'justice is an irrational ideal.' Any law is valid if it is effective and enacted according to the prescribed procedures. Kelsen admitted that the Nazi extermination laws were 'valid law' according to positivist theory. In the world of positivist jurisprudence, there is no room for Martin Luther King's conclusion, in accord with Thomas Aquinas, that a law is unjust and void if it 'is not rooted in the eternal law and natural law.' This is not a merely Christian concept. But the natural law makes ultimate sense only if we identify its Lawgiver. The political impact of Christmas arises from its assertion that the infant Christ is that Lawgiver and that his law controls.

"Today, when politicians and judges from the Pontius Pilate school of jurisprudence seek to liberate the state from the moral law, they are trying to relitigate an issue that was explicitly settled by the highest Authority two millennia ago. Every state has a god, an ultimate authority it recognizes. What Christmas tells us is that, whether they like it or not, political leaders derive their rightful authority from the real God and they must exercise that authority in accord with his law. That is why the state can never have authority to legalize murder, to wage war unjustly, to sanction economic, racial or other oppression, or otherwise violate the higher law.

"The courts this year will do their best to extirpate Christmas from public life during the 'Happy Holidays.' From the standpoint of the positivist state that makes sense. That baby in the crib is a threat. Merry Christmas."

WHAT TO DO WITH SCOTT PETERSON? Jan 20, 2005

"If the trial judge approves the jury's recommendation, Scott Peterson will die for the murder of his wife, Laci, and their unborn son, Conner. But don't expect Peterson to check out too soon. The 641 inmates on California's death row wait an average of 16 years to die. Some die of old age rather than lethal injection.

"If the Catholic Church had its way, none of them would be executed. Question: Why is the Church so protective of murderers, even of one like Peterson?

"The 'primary aim' of punishment is 'redressing the disorder introduced by the offense.' *Catechism*, no. 2266. This is retribution, restoring the balance of justice. Other purposes are rehabilitation of the offender and deterrence of the offender and of others.

"Pope John Paul II, in *Evangelium Vitae* (EV) and the *Catechism*, affirmed the traditional teaching that the state has authority to impose the death penalty and that retribution remains the 'primary aim' of punishment. But he has developed the teaching on the use of that penalty, so that neither retribution nor any other purpose will justify the use of the death penalty unless it 'is the only possible way of . . . defending human lives against the unjust aggressor.' In other words, if it is the only possible way of keeping Scott Peterson from killing more people. '[N]on-lethal means,' continued John Paul, 'are more in keeping with . . . the common good and . . . the dignity of the human person. Today, . . . as a consequence of the possibilities which the state has for . . . rendering one who has committed an offense incapable of doing harm—without definitively taking away from him the possibility of redeeming himself—the cases in which . . . execution . . . is an absolute necessity are very rare, if not practically non-existent.' *Catechism*, no. 2267, quoting EV, no. 56.

"This severe restriction arises from the importance of the conversion of the criminal. St. Augustine and St. Thomas agree 'for a just man to be made from a sinner is greater than to create heaven and earth.' S.T., I, II, Q. 113, art. 9.

"Whether execution is such an 'absolute necessity' depends on the ability of the prison system to confine this prisoner securely. That involves a prudential judgment. But John Paul's development of the teaching on the use of the death penalty is a universal, and not a prudential, criterion. It applies everywhere and to all states.

"Even under this teaching, one could still argue for the death penalty in some cases, for example, if a life inmate, already in maximum security, murders another inmate; or if the state is unable to confine inmates securely.

"EV and the *Catechism* discuss the death penalty in the context of 'preventing crime,' and the 'system of penal justice.' Perhaps this teaching might not apply to a military tribunal which applies the 'laws of war' outside the usual criminal process. In a just war, the state has authority to kill intentionally, subject to the restrictions of proportionality and non-combatant immunity. Or perhaps execution of a terrorist leader could be justified even under John Paul's criteria if his continued imprisonment would incite further terrorist attacks. On the other hand, the martyrization of such a leader by executing him might have the same inciting effect. Or, could a terrorist be treated as a spy and rightly executed pursuant to the laws of war? Whatever the answer to such hypothetical cases, John Paul's teaching fully applies to all prosecutions under ordinary criminal law, including that of Scott Peterson.

"This teaching cannot be dismissed as merely John Paul's personal opinion—he put it in the *Catechism*. At the least, it is a teaching of the authentic Magisterium or teaching authority, whether or not the Pope has proclaimed it definitively. As Vatican II declared, 'loyal submission of will and intellect must be given, in a special way to the authentic teaching authority of the Roman Pontiff, even when he does not speak *ex cathedra*.' *Lumen Gentium*, no. 25. The Code of Canon Law, no. 752, codifies this requirement so that such teachings, even if not proclaimed 'with a definitive act' are binding in that 'the Christian faithful are to take care to avoid those things which do not agree with it.'

"This teaching is an aspect of John Paul's advocacy of a 'culture of life.' We have developed instead a 'culture of death' in which the intentional infliction of death is readily accepted as a problem-solving technique, as in the death penalty, war, euthanasia and of course, abortion. Scott Peterson may die for killing the unborn Conner. But Laci could have legally killed Conner to solve a problem or for no reason. John Paul instead appeals 'to each and every person, in the name of God: respect, protect, love and serve life, every human life!' Even the life of a guy like Scott Peterson."

Note: Scott Peterson was convicted of first-degree murder in the death of Laci and second-degree murder in the death of Conner, and sentenced in March, 2005, to death by lethal injection. His case is on appeal and he is on San Quentin's Death Row. To convict someone of fetal homicide for killing an unborn child is of course inconsistent with the holding of *Roe v. Wade* that the unborn child is not a person with respect to the Fourteenth Amendment's guarantee of the right to life and to the equal protection of the laws.

BENGAL BOUTS AND JACK MOONEY, Feb. 3, 2005

"For once, they caught a break. Because of its shallow coastline, Bangladesh suffered only two deaths from the Indian Ocean tsunami. One of the poorest countries in the world, that nation, the size of Iowa with 141 million people (83 percent Muslim, 16 percent Hindu), is usually not that lucky. In 1970, a cyclone killed 500,000 people. Another in 1991 killed 138,000. Ruinous floods, often killing hundreds, are an annual event.

"Since 1853, Holy Cross missionaries have worked in Bangladesh. The

116 Holy Cross priests and brothers, and 55 sisters, run two colleges, nine high schools, eight parishes and numerous ministries. They work especially among the ultra-poor who make up one-fifth of the population. Many families live for a year on far less than we would spend on a football weekend. Those people have depended on money raised by the Bengal Bouts every year since 1931.

"The student-run Boxing Club conducts the Bouts under the guidance of Rich O'Leary and Dave Brown of Club Sports. Last year the Bouts contributed $45,000, a huge sum in Bangladesh terms. The Club aims to do better this year under the leadership of president Galen Loughrey and officers Nathan Lohmeyer, Jim Christoforetti, Mike Panzica, Mark Desplinter, Johnny Griffin, Nathan Schroeder, Greg Schaefer and Mark Basola. The brains of the outfit, however, are the business managers, Kristin Boyd and Ashley Merusi, without whom the whole event would grind to a halt.

"The Club is led by experienced coaches who are former Bengals boxers. The head coaches, Terry Johnson, a Chicago attorney, and Tom Suddes, a Columbus developer, give abundantly of their time and talent, along with coach Pat Farrell, the University pilot. Tom Suddes is sure that his practices will be recalled with pain but also with gratitude.

"Assistant coaches include Sweet C. Robinson, Thad Naquin, and recent Bengals champs Ryan Rans, Chip Farrell, Jeff Dobosh and Tom Biolchini. Judge Roland Chamblee, a four-time Bengals champ, coaches and works the corners at the bouts.

"This 75th anniversary is special because it will be the first program in five decades without Jack Mooney, who died last September at age 92. Jack was literally the paper boy for Knute Rockne, who used to sneak him onto the sidelines for home games. Jack was the trainer and living symbol of the meaning of the Bouts. 'If you never met Jack,' wrote former boxer Jeevan Subbiah, 'think of the old coach Micky from the 'Rocky' movies, and then add an old-school Notre Dame Catholic twist.' The Club aims for a record contribution this year in memory of Jack. His long-time assistant, Jack Zimmerman, has succeeded Jack Mooney as trainer.

"The boxers participate for various reasons: to get in shape, for the experience of climbing into the ring alone and with no excuses, for the friendship and for the fun of it. But you might be surprised at the impressive extent to which they buy into the purpose of the Bouts—to help others who really need it.

"Think of what those Holy Cross priests, brothers and sisters accomplish with sums that we would see as small change. St. Joseph Parish in Srimangal is 60 miles long with 70 villages and 8000 parishioners, almost all from the 'tribal people' who represent 1 percent of the population of Bangladesh, but 65 percent of the Christian population. The parish runs a 'life skills' school for young women from very poor families. With 16 students, it operates for a year on a meager total of $2,000. They also facilitate a primary-grade hostel for poor and isolated children, often from broken families. With only $5,000, they could double the size of the building to accommodate 20 students. In the parish dispensary, the . . . doctors . . . serve for a fee of only $1.50 a visit, but the normal daily income of a family is 40 cents. In Mariamnagar and Chittagong, a common problem is the destruction of crops by rampaging wild elephants and pigs.

"Still, the primary need is education. Each child at Diglakuna Primary Hostel incurs a cost of $32 a year to educate. Each of the 100 teens at Maramnagar High School Hostel requires just $80 per year. So you see why the Bengal Bouts are important.

"Despite ever-increasing political violence and terrorism, the Holy Cross missionaries stay on the front lines. They need our help. So please support the Bengal Bouts."

PERPETUAL WAR FOR PERPETUAL PEACE, Feb. 17, 2005

"'Perpetual War for Perpetual Peace.' Could this title of Harry Elmer Barnes' 1953 book describe the focus of the Bush Inaugural and State of the Union Addresses? The question is not hostile. I voted for President Bush in 2004 and, given the same choice, would do so again. But both speeches raise concerns.

"This Bush Doctrine pledges to 'support . . . democratic movements and institutions in every nation and culture, with the ultimate goal of ending tyranny in the world.' It equates freedom with democracy: '[B]ecause democracies respect their own people and their neighbors, the advance of freedom will lead to peace.' This promotion of democracy 'in every nation and culture' is now 'the urgent requirement of our nation's security.'

"One problem is ambiguity—'Democracy' is not defined. An authoritarian regime need not be an automatic threat to the United States. Nor is a democracy intrinsically incapable of presenting such a threat. Thomas Aquinas listed the 'forms of government' as monarchy, aristocracy and oligarchy as well as democracy. Pope John Paul II has spoken favorably of democracy, but all of those forms can sustain a culture of peace and freedom.

"Does the Doctrine indicate a duty on the part of the U.S. to press every nation to hold elections and to do so according to our standards? What further reforms does it require? We will tell 'other governments . . . that success in our relations will require the decent treatment of their own people [including] human dignity [and] rights . . . secured by free dissent and the participation of the governed.' If the people of a nation elect a leader dedicated to strict Islamic law and supportive of jihad, does the Doctrine imply a right of the U.S. to exert pressure, including the threat or use of force, to negate the results of that election?

"'America,' said the president, 'will not impose our own style of government on the unwilling.' But the system in the West is implicitly a model for 'every nation and culture,' and that model has problems of its own. Thirteen days after September 11, Pope John Paul II reminded the Islamic people of Kazahkstan of 'the danger of a slavish conformity' to Western culture. . . . 'Western cultural models are enticing . . . because of their . . . scientific and technical cast, but . . . there is growing evidence of their deepening human, spiritual and moral impoverishment. The culture which produces such models is marked by the fatal attempt to secure the good of humanity by eliminating God, the supreme good.' The president's personal invocations of God do not change that reality in Western culture.

"The Constitution vested the powers of foreign relations in both Congress and the president. In regard to defense, it created a twilight zone, giving Congress the power to 'declare' war, and in James Madison's words, 'leaving to the president the power to repel sudden attacks.' Presidents have sent forces into combat more than two hundred times. Congress has declared war five times.

"After 9/11, and in 2002 for Iraq, Congress essentially gave the president a blank check to use military force 'as he determines to be necessary and appropriate.' Consequently, Congress recedes here to a merely advisory and funding role. In any event, James Madison and his colleagues would have been surprised at the suggestion that Congress and the President are able to define the defense of the U.S. to require the active promotion of a particular form of government in 'every nation,' regardless of whether that nation had ever attacked or menaced us.

"The president says the promotion of democracy 'is not primarily the task of arms, though we will defend ourselves and our friends by force of arms when necessary.' But if that promotion is now an 'urgent requirement' of U.S. defense, how can the Doctrine categorically rule out the covert or overt use or threat of armed force, secondarily if not 'primarily, 'to meet that defense imperative?'

"The Iraq War was presented as a response to an imminent threat of attack by Saddam's weapons of mass destruction and his support of terrorism. Citizens had a duty to give the president's judgment the benefit of the doubt. But the new Doctrine defines defense in such a way that regime-change could be construed as an 'urgent requirement' of U.S. defense without an attack, or a threat of attack, by the nation involved. A just war requires that it be waged by a competent and lawful authority and that it be a last resort. It is difficult to see how those conditions could be met in the use or threat of force to implement regime-change in such a case. By what right does the U.S. claim the authority to prescribe the form of government appropriate for 'every nation' on earth?

"Congress would do well to scrutinize this new Doctrine. Harry Elmer Barnes may have called it right."

VAGINA MONOLOGUES, March 3, 2005

"In retrospect, . . . the Queer Film Festival and *The Vagina Monologues* were not what they claimed to be. My concern is with the judgment of our leaders in permitting these events again at Notre Dame. These comments, therefore, raise no issues relating to the students involved.

"Liam Dacey, director of the Queer Film Festival, said 'The theme . . . was . . . not a promotion of [a] gay agenda.' The 'gay agenda,' however, is to legitimize homosexual activity as a mainstream lifestyle. The presentation of films that support that objective at a Catholic university serves that 'gay agenda.' Due to space limits, discussion of that will wait for another day.

"With respect to *The Vagina Monologues*, it claims to promote awareness of the problem of violence against women. *The Vagina Monologues*, however, is so inconsistent with that purpose that it could almost qualify as a spoof. In two ways, the play itself promotes violence against women. First, the proceeds of *The Vagina Monologues* went to Sex Offense Services, the rape-crisis center, and to the St. Joseph County YWCA. Both entities provide information on abortion access to pregnant women. Abortion is an act of violence, in which about half of the victims who are killed are women.

"Second, in its context, *The Vagina Monologues* promotes violence against women by glorifying depersonalization that contributes to such violence. The human person, as Pope John Paul II put it, is a 'unified totality' of body and spiritual soul. *The Vagina Monologues* fragments that unity of the woman's body in two ways, by personalizing a part of her body and by identifying the woman herself with that body part.

"Various monologues present the vagina as an entity with which the woman can, and should establish a 'conscious relationship.' I spare the reader the abundant details (believe it—you should thank me). The monologues include such literary gems as, 'If your vagina got dressed, what would it wear?" and "If your vagina could talk, what would it say, in two words?" One monologue recounts a group masturbation in a workshop run by 'a woman who believes in vaginas.' This introduces the Notre Dame community to the concept of organolatry, the deification of a body part. The decisive moment in that monologue came when the workshop participant thought, 'I didn't have to find it. I had to be it. Be it. Be my clitoris. Be my clitoris. My vagina, my vagina, me.' There, the person is reduced to, and equated to, her body part. This fragmentation and objectification of the person facilities violence against women.

"*The Vagina Monologues* includes a monologue, 'The Little Coochi Snorcher That Could,' a detailed recounting of the lesbian seduction of a 16-year-old by a 24-year-old. This seduction is described by the victim as 'my . . . salvation.' This monologue is abominable in a 'Catholic' university in light of the sex abuse crisis in the American Church. The great majority of such cases involve seduction of a teen-aged boy by a homosexual priest, the mirror image of the lesbian seduction portrayed as a 'salvation' for the victim in the monologue.

"Another monologue consists of the repeated utterances of a four-letter expletive used to describe a body part. Other monologues, I guarantee, are better left unmentioned. The intellectual content of the text would suffer by comparison with the transcript of a town meeting of 'Idiot Village.' Maybe you have to be a politically correct academic or administrator to take such material seriously.

"*Ex Corde Ecclesiae*, the Apostolic Constitution on the Catholic University, lists, as one of the 'essential characteristics' of the Catholic university: 'Fidelity to the Christian message as it comes to us through the Church.' Bishop John D'Arcy concluded that The Vagina Monologues violate not only the common good but also 'the truth about women; the truth about sexuality; the truth about male and female; and the truth about the human body.'

"Notre Dame is subservient to the NCAA, accrediting agencies and many other entities. The one entity it will not obey is the Catholic Church, not even to the limited extent required by *Ex Corde*. The University's concept of academic freedom is no different from that at Michigan State, Stanford, etc. In short, Notre Dame's claim to be Catholic violates the principle of truth-in-labeling.

"The effect of the Queer Film Festival and *The Vagina Monologues* was to hijack the reputation of Notre Dame in support of an agenda at war with the Catholic Church. Our leaders who permitted this repeated exploitation of Notre Dame ought to be more than embarrassed. They ought to be ashamed of themselves."

THE QUEER FILM FESTIVAL, March 24, 2005

"Notre Dame rocketed to the top of the political correctness charts with the *Vagina Monologues* and the Queer Film Festival (QFF). That moment of glory is past. It remains only to note some key points regarding the QFF.

"The key strategy of the 'gay' movement is to gain recognition of homosexual activity as a mainstream lifestyle. The sponsorship of QFF by Notre Dame lent important support to that strategy. Our leaders' repeated sponsorship of QFF was the predictable outcome of their refusal to affirm the full and positive Catholic teaching. That teaching, in the *Catechism*, has three points:

"1. Persons with 'homosexual tendencies . . . must be accepted with respect, compassion and sensitivity. Every sign of unjust discrimination in their regard should be avoided.'

"2. Homosexual acts are 'intrinsically disordered. They are contrary to the natural law. They close the sexual act to the gift of life.' 'Scripture . . . presents [them] as acts of grave depravity.'

"3. The homosexual inclination is not a sin. But, as an inclination toward an objectively disordered act, the inclination is itself 'objectively disordered.'

"Notre Dame's Spirit of Inclusion commendably promotes 'an environment of mutual respect . . . in which no one is a stranger and all may flourish.' When it was adopted in August 1997, I asked [Vice-President O'Hara] why it did not specify, in accord with the explicit papal teaching, that the homosexual inclination is disordered. She replied that the 1992 draft of the *Catechism* did not include a statement to that effect. On Sept. 8, 1997, however, the final text revised the *Catechism* to state that the homosexual inclination is 'objectively disordered.' Through an apparent transcription error, incidentally, Bishop D'Arcy's forthright statement on QFF quoted the 1992 text of the *Catechism* on that point rather than the final language.

"Homosexual acts, and the inclination to them, are disordered not because of Church teaching, but because they are contrary to nature. Not even the Faculty Senate could repeal that law of nature. If, as the *Catechism* states, the acts are 'objectively disordered,' how could the inclination to those acts be anything but disordered? But, if, as our leaders imply, the inclination is not disordered, why may it not be acted upon?

"The problem is that Notre Dame still refuses to emphasize that the homosexual inclination is disordered. So why is that a big deal? Because the failure to insist that the inclination is disordered could lead students to conclude that the homosexual lifestyle itself is not disordered and is therefore a legitimate alternative, prohibited only by the teaching of an arbitrary Church.

"This inference is strengthened by the solicitude shown by our leaders to those with homosexual inclinations, beyond that shown to students afflicted with other disordered inclinations. Notre Dame participated, rightly, in the national Eating Disorders Awareness Week. The University offers 'smoking cessation programs to all members of the campus community who desire them.' To treat an inclination to smoking as a disorder is politically correct. To do so with the homosexual inclination is not. This disparity reflects the reality that the de facto official religion of Notre Dame is political correctness.

"*Ex Corde Ecclesiae* lists as one of the 'essential characteristics' of the Catholic university: 'Fidelity to the Christian message as it comes to us through the Church.' It would be contrary to that 'Christian message' for Notre Dame to host an event that portrayed any disordered activity, such as excessive drinking or shoplifting, as a good lifestyle, even if the event included a panel to discuss whether those activities were really good. A Catholic university knows that they are morally wrong. It should not sponsor a program that presents them as debatably moral activities. Nor should it do so with homosexual activity. Moreover, a Catholic university knows that the inclination to any disordered act is itself disordered. It should not mislead its students by omission of that truth.

"The 1986 *Letter to Bishops*, approved by John Paul II, said, "[T]he proper reaction to crimes committed against homosexual persons should not be to claim that the homosexual condition is not disordered . . . [D]eparture from the Church's teaching or silence about it . . . is neither caring nor pastoral. Only what is true can ultimately be pastoral. The neglect of the Church's position prevents homosexual men and women from receiving the care they need and deserve.'

"Notre Dame students are entitled to the truth. All of it."

BEYOND TERRI SCHIAVO, April 7, 2005

"*Schiavo* is more important than *Roe v. Wade*. In *Roe*, the Court cancelled prohibitions of abortion because the Court wrongly said the unborn child is not a person whose life is protected by the Fourteenth Amendment against deprivation by the state. The courts do not themselves order abortions. The mother makes that decision. In *Schiavo* the state itself ordered Terri's execution. Columbia law professor Michael Dorf commented on U.S. District Judge Whittemore's ruling that there was no state action and therefore no Fourteenth Amendment violation in Florida Circuit Judge Greer's ruling: 'Judge Greer issued an order instructing Michael Schiavo to remove Terri's feeding tube, even specifying the exact date and time. . . . The state court did not merely stand idly by while permitting Michael to take such action; the court . . . mandated the disconnection. That ought to have counted as state action by a state actor.'

"In *Schiavo*, the state itself executed an innocent person without the protections mandated for a defendant accused of capital murder or even of shoplifting. Judge Greer found that Terri was in a persistent vegetative state (PVS), in the face of contrary evidence, and that she would have wanted her tube removed. He relied on Michael's testimony despite Michael's conflicting statements and despite his conflict of interest that should have caused his removal as guardian. The Florida courts deferred robotically to Greer's findings which they never would have done in a criminal death penalty case. Nor would a convicted murderer's desire to die be considered by any court as a justification for sentencing him to death. The federal courts refused Terri the stay of execution which is automatic whenever a condemned murderer brings his case from the state courts to a federal court. Governor Bush also abdicated his responsibility by his deference to Judge Greer.

"*Schiavo* is important for reasons beyond judicial abuse. Since the *Bouvia* case in 1986, the law allows a competent adult to starve and dehydrate himself to death. This is a form of suicide. If a person is incompetent, food and water may legally be withheld from him if there is evidence that he would have wanted that withholding or, in some states, if a court decides that the withholding would be in his best interest. Where the family and caregivers agree that food and water should be withdrawn, it is commonly done without court involvement. The intent to deprive a patient permanently of food and water is essentially an intent to kill. In moral terms it is murder. A benevolent motive does not change that reality.

"John Paul II said, 'the administration of water and food, even . . . by artificial means, always [is] a natural means of preserving life, not a medical act.' It is 'morally obligatory' as long as it is achieving its goal of 'providing nourishment to the patient and alleviation of his suffering.' Food and water do not aim to cure the patient's underlying disease or the suffering caused by it. They sustain biological life, nourish the body, and prevent the suffering of hunger and thirst. 'Death by starvation or dehydration,' said John Paul, 'is . . . the only possible outcome . . . of their withdrawal.'

"The only reason anyone heard of *Schiavo* was because Michael wanted to kill Terri and her parents and siblings did not. An impasse arising from such disagreement was inevitable in a legal regime which allows family members, who agree, to kill quietly an incompetent relative.

"In *Schiavo*, the focus on PVS, including Governor Bush's petition to intervene on the ground that Terri might not have been PVS, generated an inference that an indisputably PVS patient would want to end his life. *Schiavo* is precedent for courts to order the starvation of PVS patients in reliance on testimony of hostile, court-appointed guardians even against the wishes of family members who want to care for the patient. With diminished public attention, starvation will give way to the painless injection. And the triggering disability will drop below PVS.

"In late 1938, the Knauer case, in which Hitler authorized euthanasia of a blind and deformed infant, was the 'test case' that 'was pivotal for the two killing programs of children and of adults,' Robert Jay Lifton, *The Nazi Doctors* (1986), 51. Within months the grounds for killing included such

274

defects as cleft palates and 'badly modeled ears.' Those programs evolved into the Holocaust.

"It is useless to criticize the *Schiavo* execution by the state of an innocent, disabled person without confronting the practice that allows family members to starve and dehydrate an incompetent patient to death when they agree that he would so desire. More basically, *Schiavo* is a predictable result of the acceptance of contraception in which man, of both sexes, assumes the role of arbiter of whether and when life shall begin. Inevitably that role will extend to that of arbiter of whether and when life shall end.

"The Nazis, as arbiters of the value and termination of life, brought disaster to Germany. Maybe, because we are Americans, God will consent to be mocked indefinitely. But it might not be a good idea to count on it."

THE PASSING OF JOHN PAUL II, April 21, 2005

"Even with the election of Benedict XVI, it is difficult to put out of mind the symbolisms in the death of Pope John Paul II. He had canonized St. Faustina, a Polish nun to whom Christ had personally committed the devotion of His Divine Mercy. John Paul died on the vigil of Divine Mercy Sunday, which he had established as a special day of grace. His funeral was swept by a wind reminiscent of Pentecost; it flipped over and closed the book of the Gospels on his coffin. And so on.

"John Paul II himself had become a symbol—one of strength as well as sanctity. His human qualities brought him the love and respect of millions. He spoke directly, in person, to more people than anyone else in history. He will merit the title 'John Paul the Great' not only for his impact on geopolitics and culture but because he was, above all, a holy pastor of souls and a teacher of Truth.

"In Benedict XVI, the Holy Spirit, we trust, has given us the pope we need. But a cautionary note may be in order: the human qualities of its leaders are not what ensure the survival of the Church. Benedict XVI will not have the 'star' quality of John Paul II. But the Church will endure because Benedict will be the successor of Peter, the 'Rock.'

"John Paul II was not even in his grave before pundits were giving the unnamed pope their orders: to survive, which means to win the approval of the mainstream media, the Church must drop its opposition to women's ordination, contraception, homosexuality and abortion, for starters.

"Fat chance.

"Those are definitive teachings, not disciplinary rules like Friday abstinence or clerical celibacy which could be changed at the will of the Pope.

"In one of his last public statements, on Dec. 6, 2004, John Paul stressed to American bishops 'the Church's binding obligation to remind the faithful of their duty in conscience to act in accordance with her authoritative teaching.'

"A teaching of the 'authentic Magisterium . . . upon a matter of faith or morals,' even if not proclaimed 'by definitive act,' must be given 'religious submission of intellect and will,' requiring the faithful to 'avoid whatever does not accord' with it.

"The usual Catholic critics, some in unfamiliar clerical collars, materialized on television after John Paul's death to warn the Church that it must change.

"But their day is passing, like an oil slick on a river. John Paul's appeal to youth reflects the reality of the future. That future belongs not to the dinosaurs left over from the 1960s, but to what *The New York Times* reported as the youthful 'Generation John Paul II.' It belongs to the culture of life as presented in the social and moral teachings of the Church. John Paul gave the world, and especially its youth, a believable answer: that there is an objective moral standard. It is not a theory but a person, Jesus Christ, who is himself Truth with a capital 'T.'

"The 'culture of death' sees the intentional infliction of death as an optional problem-solving technique. John Paul identified the error of that culture as the denial of both God and the capacity of reason to know objective moral truth.

"Thirteen days after 9/11, John Paul warned the Muslim people of Kazakhstan not to use the West as a model in rebuilding their country. The West, he said, suffers from a 'spiritual and moral impoverishment' because of its 'fatal attempt to secure the good of humanity by eliminating God, the Supreme Good.'

"He saw that a democratic system without objective truth is a suicide pact: '[I]f there is no ultimate truth to guide . . . political activity, then ideas . . . can easily be manipulated for reasons of power. As history demonstrates, a democracy without values easily turns into open or thinly disguised totalitarianism.'

"John Paul II, however, was no pessimist. The opening phrase of his pontificate, 'Be not afraid!' was 'an exhortation,' he later wrote, 'to all people . . . to conquer fear in the present world situation. . . . Why should we have no fear? Because man has been redeemed by God. . . . The power of Christ's Cross and Resurrection is greater than any evil which man could or should fear.' *Crossing the Threshold of Hope*, pp. 218–19.

"The pope who died as a new spring was emerging had assured us that 'God is preparing a great springtime for Christianity.' His coffin carried an imprint of a cross and the letter 'M' for Mary. His motto was 'Totus Tuus,' affirming his commitment to her to be 'all yours.'

276

"John Paul wrote that when Christ told the apostles and the women, 'Be not afraid!' those words were not addressed to Mary. Strong in her faith, she had no fear. . . . 'Christ will conquer through her, because He wants the Church's victories now and in the future to be linked to her.' 220–21.

"At the University of Our Lady, we ought to keep that in mind. And act accordingly. *Habemus papam. Deo Gratias.*"

2005–2006

WHY NOT A PRINCETON TUITION? Sept. 1, 2005

"The new gateway on Notre Dame Avenue may remind you of the entrance to a national cemetery. But it also reminds students that their University has lots of money, including the 19th largest endowment and a tuition that rises with the best, or worst, of them.

"This year, the Consumer Price Index (CPI) rose 2.5 percent. Notre Dame tuition, room and board (TRB) rose 6.6 percent, from $37,100 to $39,552. Spending from the $3 billion Endowment covers one-sixth of the University's total expenditures. But student tuition and fee income provides nearly 60 percent of the University's operating revenue. Since 1999, TRB increased by 39 percent, while the CPI increased by only 16 percent, but the University increased its financial aid by 151 percent. Notre Dame, through its excellent Financial Aid office, commits to meet the financial needs of every student, but that generally includes the student's commitment to take loans, whether federal or private. A loan is 'financial aid.'

"A 2005 Cato Institute study concluded that increases in federal financial aid enabled universities, beginning around 1980, to expand their research and building programs, relying on federal loans to pass the costs on to students. As federal loan availability rose, the major universities raised their tuition, then lobbied for increased federal loans, then raised tuition, and so on. The loan burden deters non-wealthy students from attending universities that play the tuition game. 'At the most selective private universities across the country, more fathers of freshmen are doctors than are hourly workers, teachers, clergy members, farmers or members of the military combined.' *N.Y. Times*, April 22, 2004, p. A1.

"Notre Dame is far from the worst offender. But it has used federal loan programs to expand its plant and to pursue Research Greatness while shifting the cost to students through tuition rises beyond the inflation rate. During the past 18 years, 27 new buildings were erected and 20 major renovations of other buildings took place. The end of the building binge is not in sight. The inevitable high-rise parking garage will symbolize Notre Dame's conversion to a crowded urban-style campus. We lack empirical evidence of any ability of our leaders to reject any big donation for any building project.

"In 1978–79, when Notre Dame first proclaimed itself 'A National Catholic Research University,' the Notre Dame TRB was $5,180. Adjusted for inflation, using the CPI, the 1978–79 total, in 2005 dollars, would now be $15,420. In real money, the TRB is now more than 2½ times what is was when

Notre Dame began its pursuit of Research Prestige. In 2004–2005, the average need-based University scholarship, given to the 44 percent of undergrads who qualified, was $16,740, bringing the total amount a scholarship student had to pay by cash, loans or work, down to $20,340, or $4,920 more than the 1978–79 TRB in real money.

"The primary historic mission of Notre Dame was undergrad education in the Catholic tradition, with research in an essential, complementary role. Research, especially in the sciences, is an important part of Notre Dame's mission. But the research enterprise ought not to be the tail wagging the dog.

"Our leaders act in what they see as the best interests of Notre Dame. Any criticism here is of policies, not persons. But the burden of loans, required to finance the research enterprise, tends to compel Notre Dame grads to forego graduate education or community service and to defer marriage. It can make it difficult for those who do marry to remain open to having children.

"Notre Dame has been criticized at times for aping the Ivy League. Princeton, however, has a policy that Notre Dame ought to emulate. Princeton informed its incoming class of 2009: 'Since . . . 2001–2002 . . . no Princeton aid student has been required to take out a loan to pay for his or her education. The amount that a student normally would have received is replaced by increased Princeton grant. . . .

"In 2004–2005, 608 students, or 52 percent of the Princeton freshman class, received scholarships averaging $26,100 for a total scholarship aid of $15.9 million. Students can obtain loans to cover unexpected expenses. But the basic aid package is 'no loan.'

"Princeton is not Notre Dame. It is smaller, with 6,836 students, including 4,678 full-time undergrads. Its endowment in 2004 was $9.9 billion, 3 times Notre Dame's. Notre Dame, however, has a unique ability to bring huge sums into its coffers for special purposes. Notre Dame, as a Catholic university, should take the lead to enable its grads to serve the common good, and the good of their families and the Church, without a disabling student debt. To a regrettable degree, Notre Dame is investing instead in bricks, mortar and ostentation. Notre Dame has a higher purpose. Our leaders ought to consider the Princeton approach."

SUPREME COURT NOMINATIONS, Sept. 15, 2005

"Why the fuss over Supreme Court nominations? The Court merely interprets the law. Right? It wields the power neither of the purse nor of the sword. Until the mid-20th century, nominations to the Court were rarely as controversial as they are today.

"The nominations are so important today because the judiciary is no longer, as Alexander Hamilton put it, 'the least dangerous' branch of the government (*Federalist*, No. 78). Rulings by the unelected Supreme Court, with the acquiescence of Congress and the Executive, bear major responsibility for the terminal decline of the Constitution from its character as the charter of a limited government with only enumerated powers apportioned among the executive, legislative and judicial branches.

"The Court interprets the Fourteenth Amendment so as to bind state and local governments by the Court's mandates on personal rights, including rights of the Court's own invention such as abortion. It has made the 'equal protection of the laws' a license for judicial micromanagement of local decisions. The Court imposes on all governments an impossible neutrality between theism and non-theism which establishes an agnostic secularism. The Court's edicts on the commerce clause and on federal subsidies give Congress almost a blank check for regulation, despite some recent limitations. And so on. The replacement of even one Justice, therefore, can have consequences that would have astonished the framers of the Constitution.

"The current debates focus on abortion. But the issue is oversold because of the assumption that the appointment of pro-life Justices will be the magic bullet to end the dominance of the abortion culture.

"A Supreme Court 'overruling' of *Roe v. Wade* would have only a limited impact on abortion. The essential holding of *Roe* is that, whether or not he is a human being, the unborn child is not a 'person' until birth and therefore has no constitutional right to life. He may be executed at any time in the pregnancy at the practical discretion of his mother. Such depersonalization is the principle that underlay the *Dred Scott* case in which the Supreme Court said in 1857 that slaves were property rather than persons, and that underlay the Nazi depersonalization and extermination of Jews and others.

"To really 'overrule' *Roe* would be to hold that every human being, from fertilization, is a 'person' entitled to the constitutional right to life. That would forbid governments to withhold the protection of homicide laws from the youngest persons, i.e. those in the womb, as if a state were to forbid homicide unless the victim were under eight years of age.

"Both political sides define the 'overruling' of *Roe* as returning the issue to the states, allowing them to restrict or permit abortion. The Supreme Court unanimously endorses that approach. As Justice Scalia put it in his dissent, in which Rehnquist and Thomas joined, in the 1992 *Casey* decision: 'The states may, if they wish, permit abortion-on-demand, but the Constitution does not require them to do so.' That would confirm the nonpersonhood holding of *Roe*. If your life is subject to extinction whenever a state legislature so decides, then you are a nonperson in the eyes of 'the supreme law of the land,' the United States Constitution.

280

"This abandonment of principle contributes to the culture of death by fostering the impression that abortion and other 'life' issues are negotiable, like a highway appropriation. In a just and free society, the only legitimate issue is whether innocent human beings can be legally executed. The incremental approach frames the issue in terms, not of whether, but of which innocent human beings may be legally executed. A measure of the bankruptcy of the pro-life movement is the focus on partial-birth abortion, which tactic frames the issue not in terms of whether, and not even in terms of which innocents may be legally executed, but in terms of how the killing is to be done.

"Of most importance, technology is making abortion a private matter beyond the reach of the law. The law treats various pills and devices as contraceptives although they cause abortions by preventing implantation of the embryo in the womb. The law cannot effectively prohibit such abortions.

"So the appointment of a Supreme Court Justice is not the magic bullet that can lift the scourge of abortion from our contraceptive, and therefore anti-life, society. It is important to put good judges on the Supreme Court. But the solution is not in politics or law but primarily in prayer, education and the reconversion of the American people to the conviction that the right to life transcends the power of the state because it is a gift from God."

Two World Youth Days, Sept. 29, 2005

"2005 had two World Youth Days. The first, in April, was spontaneous. The young predominated among the millions in Rome for the funeral of John Paul II. The event, including the homily by the future Pope, was seen, in person or on television, by more people than any other funeral in history. Four days later, at the Mass inaugurating his pontificate, Benedict XVI looked to the future: '[T]he Church is alive. And the Church is young. She . . . shows . . . the way towards the future.'

"In August, Benedict went to the World Youth Day in Cologne to show young people 'how beautiful it is to be Christian.' The event exceeded expectations, with more than a million at the closing Mass. The Pope made the most of it, confirming that relativism, among other issues, would be a major concern of his papacy.

"At the Mass before the conclave that elected him, then-Cardinal Ratzinger had said, 'We are building a dictatorship of relativism that does not recognize anything as definitive and whose ultimate goal consists solely of one's own ego and desires.' He described 'relativism' as 'letting oneself be 'tossed here and there, carried about by every wind of doctrine.' In Cologne, Benedict developed the point, '[F]reedom,' he said, 'is not simply about enjoying life in total autonomy, but . . . about living by the measure of truth and goodness, so that we . . . can become true and good.' He explained that objective, non-relative 'measure' in the context of the Greek and Latin origins of the word, 'adoration.' Adoration of Christ in the Eucharist leads to 'submission, the recognition of God as our true measure. . . . [That] submission liberates us deep within.'

"Papal discussion of relativism is nothing new. John Paul II, in 1991, denied that 'agnosticism and skeptical relativism' are the foundation of democracy. Rather, without an 'ultimate truth to guide . . . political activity . . . ideas . . . can be manipulated' as a means to power. A relativist democracy 'easily turns into open or thinly disguised totalitarianism.' That makes sense. If there is no acknowledged moral truth, political life becomes a power struggle among interests, with no real limits to what the law can do. Similarly, in 1999, then-Cardinal Ratzinger identified as one of the 'crises of law' the determination of what is just by the shifting consensus of the majority.

"Relativism is a problem of special note in the academic world. More than a few professors are absolutely sure that they can't be sure of anything. But relativism itself is absurd. If you say that all things are relative, you must admit that your statement, too, is relative. The jurisprudence of a relativist society will be legal positivism in which any law, whether *Dred Scott*, Auschwitz, or whatever, will be considered valid if it is enacted by the prescribed procedure. A law cannot be criticized as unjust because nobody can know what is unjust. As Hans Kelsen, the 20th century's leading legal positivist, put it, 'justice is an irrational ideal.'

"The answer to relativism, however, is not in the false absolutes of ideology. Instead, Benedict XVI urges a 'true revolution' in contrast to the ideological revolutions of the twentieth century which 'assumed total responsibility for . . . the world in order to change it. . . . [A] human and partial point of view was . . . taken as an absolute guiding principle. Absolutizing what is not absolute is . . . totalitarianism. It . . . takes away [man's] dignity and enslaves him. It is not ideologies that save the world, but only a return to . . . our Creator, the guarantor of our freedom [and] what is . . . good and true.'

"Carrying on the truth-affirming mission of John Paul, Benedict gently but firmly laid it on the line to the young people of Cologne. Without God, he said at the closing Mass, there is frustration and 'dissatisfaction with everyone and everything. People tend to exclaim: 'This cannot be what life is about!' One result is 'a kind of new explosion of religion.' But Benedict cautioned against letting religion become 'a consumer product. . . . [R]eligion constructed on a "do-it-yourself" basis . . . may be comfortable, but at times of crisis we are left to ourselves.' The answer is in Scripture and the teaching Church.

"So what is Benedict all about? He really believes in objective moral Truth. Imagine that. And he capitalizes it because the Truth is a person, Jesus

282

Christ. Like John Paul, Benedict tells it like it is, especially to the young. At his inaugural Mass, he said, 'I say to you, dear young people, Do not be afraid of Christ! He takes nothing away, and he gives you everything. When we give ourselves to him, we receive a hundredfold in return. Yes, open wide the doors to Christ—and you will find true life.'

"Surprising numbers of young people seem to be listening to this man. Even at Notre Dame."

REASON AND GOD, Oct. 13, 2005

"Apart from faith, can we really know through reason that God exists?

"The existence of God is not self-evident to us, and the reach of science is limited here. But can we really know from reason that there must always have been in existence an eternal being, who always was and who had no beginning? The alternative is that there was a time when there was nothing in existence. But if there was ever a time when there was nothing, there could never be anything. This we know from the self-evident principle of sufficient reason—that whatever exists must have a sufficient reason for its existence. As Thomas Aquinas put it, 'that which does not exist only begins to exist through something already existing. Therefore, if at one time nothing was in existence, it would have been impossible for anything to have begun to exist, and thus even now nothing would be in existence—which is absurd.'

"Or consider what the evidence of design in the universe really means. 'The evolution of living beings,' said John Paul II, 'presents an internal finality. . . . This finality which directs beings in a direction for which they are not responsible or in charge, obliges one to suppose a mind which is its inventor, its creator.' Finality, as Cardinal Christoph Schonborn put it, is 'synonymous with final cause, purpose or design.'

"'To all these indications of the existence of God the Creator,' John Paul continued, 'some oppose the power of chance or of the . . . mechanisms of matter. To speak of chance for a universe which presents such a complex organization in its elements and such marvelous finality in its life would be equivalent to giving up the search for an explanation of the world as it appears to us. . . . [I]t would be equivalent to admitting effects without a cause. It would be to abdicate human intelligence.'

"It is true, as John Paul put it, that 'science must recognize its inability to reach the existence of God: it can neither affirm nor deny His existence. . . . [H]owever . . . the scientist . . . can discover in the world reasons for affirming a Being which surpasses it.'

"Not only is belief in God reasonable. It is unreasonable not to believe in

God. Can you really believe that the human eye, in all its complexity, came about by chance rather than by design? If you were walking along a beach and saw traced in the sand the letters, 'Go Irish,' would you think, 'Look at the words the waves traced in the sand?' If you did, your election as mayor of Idiot Village would be assured.

"'[T]he marvelous "book of nature,"' said John Paul in *Faith and Reason*, 'when read with . . . human reason, can lead to knowledge of the Creator.' In abandoning the 'basic rules' of reason, 'the human being . . . ends up in the condition of 'the fool' [and] shows . . . how deficient his knowledge is and just how far he is from the full truth of things, their origin and their destiny.'"

EUTHANASIA: ARE WE AHEAD OF THE DUTCH? NOV. 3, 2005

"'If you allow it to occur,' said Dr. Chris Feudtner of Children's Hospital in Philadelphia, 'it will occur in cases where it is not ethical, period.' Feudtner was referring to the Netherlands' legalization of euthanasia of newborns and infants pursuant to the Groningen University Protocol. The Protocol prescribes the killing procedures. The child must be in 'hopeless and unbearable suffering,' so that 'the parents and the physicians . . . concur that death would be more humane than continued life.' The Protocol codifies the informal Dutch practice under which newborns had been euthanized, usually for spina bifida, with no physicians prosecuted.

"The Netherlands were the first nation to legalize euthanasia for adults, allowing the physician to 'terminate life on request or to provide assistance with suicide.' That law, which took effect in 2002, allows a person of 12 years or older to be killed if he had made an advance written request for termination of his life and if his suffering becomes 'unbearable' with 'no prospect of improvement.' If the patient is between 12 and 16, the parent or guardian must agree to the killing. If the patient is between 16 and 18, the parent or guardian must be consulted.

"The Dutch get undeserved credit for trail-blazers in euthanasia. The United States may be the front-runner, even though our law does not permit a physician to kill the patient. Oregon allows assisted suicide, but that merely allows the physician to give the patient the means by which the patient can kill himself. While the law in the United States stops short of legalizing intentional, direct and active killing of patients, as permitted in Holland (and Belgium), it broadly permits intentional killing by terminal sedation or by withholding food and water.

"In 1997, in *Vacco v. Quill*, the Supreme Court upheld New York's prohibition of assisted suicide but gave the green light to physicians to provide 'aggressive palliative care,' in which the physician is supposed to intend only to relieve the patient's pain. His undisclosed intent, however, may be to kill the patient by 'terminal sedation.' Palliative care can be morally justified even if it unintentionally shortens life. But, in the absence of exceptional proof of intent, the law cannot effectively determine whether the physician acted with the intent to relieve pain or to cause death.

"If the family and physician concur that the patient should die, terminal sedation, under the guise of pain relief, can be a convenient and practically undetectable means of homicide, beyond the effective reach of the law.

"The second, and legal, form of homicide of patients is withdrawal of nutrition and hydration. In American law, a competent adult has the legal right to refuse to take food and water whether administered normally or artificially. Incompetent patients may be denied nutrition and hydration if they had, when competent, expressed their desire to be so denied or, in some states, if such denial is in the best interests of the patient. In cases where the family and the physician agree that the patient should die, the issue never gets to court and the patient can be quietly starved and dehydrated to death.

"We have not formally legalized it, but we are further down the slippery slope of euthanasia than are the Dutch. We have, in effect, legalized homicide of patients by starvation and dehydration, when the family and physicians agree, without even the minimal procedures required in the Netherlands.

"Moreover, we have progressed beyond the allowance of private killing to killing by order of the state. In *Roe v. Wade*, the Court authorized the mother to kill her unborn child. The law does not mandate the killing. In the Terri Schiavo case, the state itself, in the person of Judge Greer, ordered that Michael, her husband, 'shall cause the removal of nutrition and hydration' from Terri. The court mandated Terri's execution. The only reason we heard about the Schiavo case is because Michael Schiavo and Terri's parents disagreed and the court became involved. What Michael did to Terri happens routinely, without public notice, when the 'caregivers' agree that the patient should be killed.

"As this practice becomes embedded in the culture, we can expect judges to rule that defective, incurable or even simply aged patients, can be presumed to desire what the Nazi theorists called a 'merciful release.' We can expect that sedation, starvation and dehydration will give way to the painless injection. And *Schiavo* already established that PVS, the persistent vegetative state, is an accepted excuse for execution of a patient whose consent can be inferred even from the testimony of a hostile witness. We can expect the justifications to go beyond PVS.

"So the Dutch may be the amateurs here. We are smarter, allowing the killing of the burdensome or unwanted without even the paperwork required in Holland. And maybe we will be smart enough to explain it all to our final Judge, who has a soft spot for babies and helpless people."

RIGHTS, Nov. 17, 2005

"The Senate will hit Supreme Court nominee Samuel Alito with a lot of questions about 'rights,' including the right to privacy, to abortion, etc. Before the hearing begins, it might be a good idea to get our own act together on 'rights.'

"The index of the *Compendium of the Social Doctrine of the Catholic Church* lists 197 separate 'rights,' including the 'right to freedom in religious matters,' the 'right to a just wage' and many more. Where did we get all those rights? Who can take them away? According to historian, Arthur Schlesinger, Jr., 'Human rights is not a religious idea. It is a secular idea, the product of the last four centuries of Western history.' Or did the Declaration of Independence get it right when it said that 'all men are created equal,' and 'are endowed by their Creator with certain Unalienable Rights'?

"Does the Constitution give you the freedom of speech? Or does it merely guarantee that freedom which you got somewhere else? Professor Iredell Jenkins, in the *American Journal of Jurisprudence*, three decades ago, described the 'two broad views which have disputed the field for centuries.' One view holds that 'rights have a real metaphysical and moral status. . . . Rights derive directly from God or Nature . . . and they belong to man as part of his intrinsic nature. . . . Law merely recognizes these rights and enforces respect for them. . . . The other view holds that rights . . . owe their being and their nature exclusively to law . . . whose creatures they are. . . . [T]hat legislative or judicial act . . . brings the rights into being and constitutes its content.' Under this second view, the state gives rights and can take them away.

"Whether the person has any absolute rights depends on his origin, nature and destiny. 'I see no reason for attributing to man,' wrote Justice Oliver Wendell Holmes, a patron saint of American jurisprudence, 'a significance different in kind from that which belongs to a baboon or a grain of sand.' What claim to immunity could such an insignificant entity have against the power of the majority or of the state to subject him to slavery or death at the discretion of others? 'The sacredness of human life' Holmes said, 'is a purely municipal ideal of no validity outside the jurisdiction. I believe that force, mitigated so far as may be by good manners, is the *ultima ratio*.' He defined truth as 'the majority vote of the nation that could lick all others.'

"If Holmes is right, if there is no objective truth and no God, the Creator, how can we offer any reason why the human person has more intrinsic rights than 'a baboon or a grain of sand?' As Pope John Paul II said, 'the eclipse of the sense of God and of man . . . leads to a practical materialism, which breeds individualism, utilitarianism and hedonism. . . . The first to be harmed are women, children, the sick or suffering and the elderly. The criterion of personal dignity . . . is replaced by the criterion of efficiency. . . . [O]thers are considered not for what they "are," but for what they "have, do and produce." This

286

is the supremacy of the strong over the weak.' After the experience of the Godless regimes of the 20th century and today, can we doubt the truth of John Paul's assessment?

"'We are not,' said Pope Benedict XVI at the start of his pontificate, 'some casual and meaningless product of evolution. Each of us is the result of a thought of God. Each of us is willed, each of us is loved, each of us is necessary.' That is why, as John Paul put it in *Veritatis Splendor*, 'civil authorities and . . . individuals never have authority to violate the fundamental and inalienable rights of the human person. . . . [O]nly a morality which acknowledges certain norms as valid always and for everyone, with no exception, can guarantee the ethical foundation of social coexistence.'

"The only coherent basis for asserting those exceptionless moral norms and the transcendent rights of the human person is his creation in the image and likeness of God with an immortal destiny. As you read these lines, some child is being born in a hospital somewhere in Indiana. That child's life began some nine months before his birth. There will come a time when there will be no Indiana, no Washington, no Ireland, no Paris, no Rome. Maybe not even a Notre Dame Stadium. It will all be gone. But that child will still be alive. The human person, because of that immortal destiny, has rights that the state, and everyone else, is absolutely bound to respect because those rights come from God.

"The bottom line? Let's stop being apologetic about bringing God into 'rights talk.' Without God, our very existence makes no sense and we have no absolute, inalienable rights. With God, it all makes sense. It might even make sense to the United States Senate."

CHRISTMAS AS REAL HISTORY, Dec. 1, 2005

"As we move into December, how do we handle Christmas? If you are an American Civil Liberties Union lawyer, you might sue some school teacher who tells her kids 'Merry Christmas' instead of 'Happy Winter Solstice.' The Supreme Court's edicts in this area serve mainly to confuse to and drain the 'holiday' of any meaning. Maybe we ought to consider a different approach.

"One approach might be to reflect on Christmas as history, an event involving real persons who can teach us a thing or two about how we should live in the 21st century. First among those characters of Christmas is Christ, who is now the target of a judicial and cultural white-out campaign against even the mention of his name. But for two millennia, Christmas has been a feast of hope and joy because of who that Child is and what he came on earth to do. Red and green, the Christmas colors, are the colors of life and blood.

Christmas commemorates the birth of a Redeemer who restored our supernatural life by his passion, death and resurrection.

"The red of Christmas could also remind us not only of Calvary but also of the Holy Innocents. 'Then Herod, seeing that he had been tricked by the Magi . . . sent and slew all the boys in Bethlehem and all its neighborhood who were two years old or under.' (Matt 2:16).

"Herod commanded the Magi to tell him the Child's whereabouts so he could 'go and worship Him.' Herod, who wanted to murder the Child, was the first, but not the last, lying politician of the Christian era. In the first church-state conflict of that era, the Magi defied his order and Herod responded with the wholesale murder of the helpless. Herod is an important figure in the Christmas event. But Herod was a piker. The abortionists, and practitioners of euthanasia and those who license them to kill, are the Herods of our day. Today, the state sanctions and encourages the murder of millions of babies each year. And now we are moving on to the killing of the disabled and other 'useless eaters.'

"*The New England Journal of Medicine* recently disclosed a new test that can reveal weeks earlier than conventional screening whether a mother is carrying a child with Down syndrome. Columnist Patricia Bauer, in the *Washington Post* on Nov. 8, described how Margaret, her Down syndrome child, 'enriches our lives.' 'In ancient Greece,' says Bauer, 'babies with disabilities were left out in the elements to die. We in America rely on genetic testing to make our selections in private, but the effect on society is the same. Margaret's old pediatrician tells me that years ago he used to have a steady stream of patients with Down syndrome. Not anymore. [T]hey aren't being born anymore.'

"A more noble model than Herod, of course, was Joseph who 'arose, and took the Child and His Mother by night, and withdrew into Egypt.' Joseph, like the Magi, defied the tyrant. He was a strong guy and no wimp. He practiced civil disobedience as a conscientious objector.

"So Christmas has a rich cast of characters, including Christ above all. Christ is a victim of cultural amnesia today. But he is not the only one. Archbishop Fulton Sheen said, 'some of us may forget just how the Child came into the world; [some] speak of the Babe but never a word about the Mother of the Babe. The Babe of Bethlehem did not fall from the heavens into a bed of straw, but came into this world through the great portals of the flesh. Sons are inseparable from mothers, and mothers inseparable from sons. Just as you cannot go to a statue of a mother holding a babe and cut away the mother, leaving the babe suspended in mid-air, neither can you cleave away the Mother from the Babe of Bethlehem. He was not suspended mid-air in history, but like all other babes, came into the world by and through His Mother.

"Archbishop Sheen noted a danger that 'in celebrating a Christmas without the Mother, we may soon reach a point where we will celebrate Christmas without the Babe, and these days are upon us now. And what an absurdity that would be; for, just as there can never be a Christmas without a Christ, so there can never be a Christ without a Mary.'

"On his arrival at the Cologne airport for World Youth Day, Pope Benedict XVI prayed, 'May the Virgin Mary, who presented the Child Jesus to the Magi when they arrived in Bethlehem to worship the Saviour, continue to intercede for us.' We can count on her to do that. And she can help us to remember that, the ACLU notwithstanding, Christmas is a real event with real people."

"REVERSAL" OF *ROE V. WADE*, Jan. 26, 2006

"Since the Jan. 22, 1973 *Roe v. Wade* decision, 47 million unborn children have been legally executed in the United States. The latest Alan Guttmacher Institute report shows 1,293,000 were killed in 2002. . . .

"These figures reflect only surgical abortions and not the uncountable early abortions by pills, including many marketed and sold as 'contraceptives.'

"In *Roe*, the Supreme Court held that the unborn child is a nonperson who has no constitutional right to live and who therefore may be killed at any stage of pregnancy at the virtual discretion of his mother. This is the principle of the Nazi depersonalization of the Jews and of the Supreme Court's declaration, in the 1857 *Dred Scott* case, that slaves were property rather than persons.

"Despite the emphasis on Supreme Court appointments, a 'reversal' of *Roe* will have little effect on the abortion culture we have cultivated. This is so for two reasons.

"First, because even the 'pro-life' justices—Scalia, Thomas and Rehnquist—have accepted the depersonalization principle by defining a 'reversal' of *Roe* as a return of the issue to the states. If you are legally subject to execution at the discretion of another or whenever a state legislature so decides, then you are a nonperson.

"The Court in *Roe* acknowledged that, if the unborn child is a 'person' whose life is guaranteed by the Constitution, the case for any and all abortion 'collapses.'. . . .

"The political pro-life movement, including the Catholic bishops' bureaucracy, actively promotes the 'states' rights' solution. That 'reversal' of *Roe* would make the right of innocent life depend on geography and would imply that anyone and everyone's right to life can be subject to political bargaining like a highway appropriation. . . .

"The second reason why such an illusory 'reversal' of *Roe* will have little effect on the abortion culture is because technology is making abortion a private event beyond the reach of the law. Euthanasia, too, is moving beyond the law. The Supreme Court has given the green light to 'palliative care,' a valid concept in which, however, it can be impossible to tell whether the physician's intent is to relieve pain or to kill. The intentional killing of patients by withdrawing food and water happens routinely in cases where, unlike the Terri Schiavo case, the family members agree that the patient should die.

"Our Culture of Death, in which the intentional infliction of death is an optional problem-solving technique, is a result of the cultural acceptance of contraception. As John Paul II put it, abortion and contraception are 'fruits of the same tree.' If man (of both sexes) makes himself the arbiter, through contraception, of whether and when life will begin, he will predictably make himself arbiter of when it will end. And contraception accepts the idea that there is such a thing as a life not worth living.

"Benedict XVI accurately described abortion as 'an aggression against society itself.' The answer to the Culture of Death is the Culture of Life, which builds on the conviction that innocent life is inviolable because it is a gift from God. To restore that conviction requires uncompromising political, legal and educational activity and the provision of help to those who need it, before birth and beyond. As John Paul and Benedict have urged, however, the most effective weapon is prayer, especially in Eucharistic Adoration and the Rosary.

"A suicidal Culture of Death is intrinsically short-lived. We are on the winning side."

THE "ULTRA-POOR" IN BANGLADESH, Feb. 9, 2006

"Why should you support the Bengal Bouts? Because of people like Father Eugene Homich, a veteran of 50 years in the Holy Cross Missions in Bangladesh. With 131 million people. . . . Bangladesh has only 250,000 Catholics. The per capita income is $1,470, less than some of us spent on the Fiesta Bowl. Homich works among the poorest of the poor. . . .

"With the help of the Bengal Bouts, he has built a medical clinic that treats 9,000 patients per year, including hundreds of snake-bite victims. He has placed over 750 abandoned infants with warm and loving families. These and other works he combines with a full liturgical and catechetical schedule, with the critical aid of the Holy Cross Sisters.

"'My life,' writes Homich, 'has been enriched by working with the poor and marginalized.'

"The 185 Holy Cross brothers, sisters and priests there are mostly natives of Bangladesh. The Bengal Bouts provide the largest single donation for their work every year. 'We rely so much on all of you,' writes Father Stephen Gomez, 'to help us prepare our men in formation, sponsor the social projects for the poor, and support our Tribal parishes.'. . .

"For 75 years, the Bengal Bouts have sent to Bangladesh donations now averaging in excess of $50,000. In a country where the price of a Starbucks coffee could feed a family for a week, the success or failure of the Bouts can actually make the difference between life and death for some of the 'ultra-poor.'

"Under the leadership of Rich O'Leary and Dave Brown of Club Sports, the program is run by the student officers of the Boxing Club—Co-Presidents Mark Basola and Nathan Schroeder and Captains Andrew Breslin, Johnny Griffin, Greg Schaefer, Chris Calderone, Andrew McGill and Stu Styupla.

"'There's a unique camaraderie,' explained Nate Schroeder. 'Boxers help each other, including their own future opponents. And we make a difference in the lives of many people in Bangladesh.'. . . . Everyone knows, however, that the entire enterprise is kept afloat by the competent and organized student managers—Erika Meyer, Megan O'Farrell and Melanie Rodarte. . . .

"The Bengal Bouts would not exist without the leadership of the volunteer head coaches. . . . The chaplains of the Club, who participate in the workouts, are Father Bill Seetch, and Father Brian Daley, who also coaches. Even the upper echelons of Church hierarchy are involved through the timer, Monsignor John Hagerty from Notre Dame Parish in Hermitage, PA.

"In 75 years, the Bouts has never had a participant sustain a serious injury. That impressive statistic is no accident. The Emergency Medical Technicians—Terri Engel and Mike Ude—are present at all sparring matches, and Doctor James Moriarty, the University chief of medicine, keeps close tabs on every aspect of the program. . . .

"Real people, in very real need, depend on the annual successes of the Bengal Bouts. If you have never attended the Bouts, give it a chance. You will not only enjoy it, but your hearts will be touched, for the spirit, inspiration and good will are undeniable."

DEUS CARITAS EST, Feb. 23, 2006

"Pope Benedict XVI's first encyclical, *Deus Caritas Est* (God is Love), signed on Christmas Day, packs a lot of instruction into 25 readable pages. Part I of *Deus Caritas Est* (DCE) analyzes human and divine love in terms of eros and agape. . . . But DCE is loaded with cultural, political and legal implications, arising from its assertion that '[l]ove of God and love of neighbor' are 'inseparable.'

"Part II of DCE is a discourse on 'Caritas,' the 'practice' of love of neighbor. '[N]o one ought to go without the necessities of life.' That 'service of charity' is 'first and foremost a responsibility for each . . . member of the faithful' but it is also a duty of the Church at every level.

"'Christian charity' is not abstract. It is 'first of all the . . . response to immediate needs . . . .: feeding the hungry, clothing the naked, caring for . . . the sick, visiting those in prison, etc.' But people 'need something more than technically proper care. . . . They need heartfelt concern.' Charity therefore cannot be 'just another form of social assistance.' Nor is charity a means of 'proselytism,' using aid to induce conversions. Charity is an act of love and '[l]ove is free; it is not practiced as a way of achieving other ends.'

"Charity must not be at the service of 'parties, ideologies' or 'worldly stratagems.' Benedict responds to the Marxist claim that the poor 'do not need charity but justice.' Charity, they claim, serves injustice by making an 'unjust system . . . appear . . . tolerable' and thus blocking 'the struggle for a better world.' Benedict rejects that approach as 'an inhuman philosophy,' sacrificing people of the present to 'the Moloch of the future. . . . One does not make the world more human by refusing to act humanely here and now. We contribute to a better world only by personally doing good now.'

"But what about justice? Doesn't the Church care about it? Yes, it does. But the 'just ordering' of society and the State is the role of 'politics' and not of the Church.

"The 'direct duty' to work for a just society belongs to the 'lay faithful' rather than to the Church itself. 'Fundamental to Christianity,' says DCE, 'is the distinction between Church and State.' The Church should not be in politics, but it does have an educative role. To define justice is the job of practical reason. But to do its job, reason needs 'purification. . . . Here politics and faith meet.' Faith liberates reason from its 'ethical blindness caused by the dazzling effect of power and special interests.' DCE traces Catholic social teaching from Leo XIII's *Rerum Novarum* in 1891 through John Paul II. That teaching offers guidelines that are valid for everyone. It does not, however, seek to impose on others 'ways of thinking and . . . conduct proper to faith.' It aims 'to help purify reason' by arguing 'on the basis of reason and natural law' so as 'to help form consciences in political life' and to 'reawaken the spiritual energy' needed for justice to prevail.

"So the Church has a role to play in the fight for justice. DCE urges the State to follow the principle of subsidiarity by supporting efforts of social forces, including the Church, to achieve justice. Civil justice, however, is not enough. 'Love—caritas—will always prove necessary even in the most just society.' The claim that 'just social structures would make works of charity superfluous,' says DCE, 'masks a materialist conception . . . that man can live "by bread alone."'

"DCE encourages 'cooperation' between State and Church agencies but insists that the State 'must guarantee religious freedom.' Three days before he signed DCE, Benedict addressed the Curia on the teaching of Vatican II that religious freedom is required because 'the human person is capable of knowing the truth about God' and because such truth 'cannot be externally imposed' and 'can only be claimed with God's grace in freedom of conscience.'

"A recurrent theme of Benedict's papacy is his criticism of the 'dictatorship of relativism' to which he called attention in his homily to the Cardinals before the Conclave in which they elected him. DCE continues this theme in its insistence on religious freedom and on the role of the Church as moral educator. Both rest on the reality that the truth about God and morality is objective and knowable. That Truth, with a capital T, is a person, Christ.

"These are only a few of the points in this innovative and challenging encyclical. Read it. It could change your way of thinking. And your life."

CATHOLIC SOCIAL TEACHING, March 9, 2006

"It may come as a news flash, but Catholic teaching is about more than sex and the right to life. It covers the entire range of human experience. But how much do you, yourself, really know about Catholic social teaching? If the answer is, 'Not much,' don't feel so bad. You have plenty of company.

"'[M]ore than in any other historical period,' said Pope John Paul II, 'there is a breakdown in the process of handing on moral and religious values between generations.' Over the past four decades, religion classes at Catholic schools have focused on making collages or imparting the gospel of political correctness. The students, when they become parents, cannot pass on to their children what they never received. But now, help is at hand.

"In his first encyclical, *Deus Caritas Est* (God is Love), Pope Benedict includes a reading list which could be a remedial study assignment.

"After affirming the need to build 'a just social order in which all receive their share of the world's goods and no longer have to depend on charity,' *Deus Caritas Est* (DCE) listed the interventions of 'the papal magisterium' in response to the changing 'social problems' resulting from industrialization and later developments including 'the growth of a globalized economy.' Several great popes have developed this teaching, starting with Pope Leo XIII's *Rerum Novarum*, in 1891. Pope Pius XI followed with *Quadragesimo Anno* (1931) and Pope John XXIII with *Mater et Magistra* (Mother and Teacher) (1961). Pope Paul VI contributed *Populorum Progressio* (1967) and *Octogesima Adveniens* (1971), addressing especially the social problems in Latin America. John Paul II left a trilogy of social encyclicals, *Laborem Exercens* (1981) on the dignity of work, *Sollicitudo Rei Socialis* (1987), and *Centesimus Annus* (1991) which cautioned against the acceptance of a materialist capitalism as an alternative to the failed prescriptions of Marxism. . . .

"Even a Notre Dame student would find it a daunting task to plow through all those papal teachings. Benedict, however, comes to the rescue by recommending the *Compendium of the Social Doctrine of the Church*, published in 2004 by the Pontifical Council on Justice and Peace. In 255 pages of text, with a detailed index, the *Compendium* synthesizes all those teachings, beginning with the foundational principle of the dignity of the person which arises from his creation in the image and likeness of God. From that dignity arise the organizing principles of solidarity and subsidiarity, both of which are stressed in DCE. The *Compendium* covers the family, human work, economic life, the political and international communities, the environment and war and peace.

"The *Compendium* provides a useful overview of the social teachings. But if you want a really short, but excellent, introduction, take a look at *Citizens of the Heavenly City: A Catechism of Catholic Social Teaching*, by Dr. Arthur Hippler, director of the Office of Justice and Peace in the diocese of LaCrosse, Wisconsin. In 154 pages, including notes, Hippler covers it all in a format suitable for individual or group study. The foreword, by Most Rev. Raymond L. Burke, now Archbishop of St. Louis, praises the book for its 'attention to the totality of the Church's social teaching, beginning with the sources . . . and then progressing to a study of the social implications of the love of God and the love of neighbor.' Hippler covers, concisely and accurately, the what and the why of the teachings on family, life, capital punishment, the environment, war and peace, free speech and the common good as well as the just wage and economic justice.

"The social and moral teachings of the Catholic Church provide the only coherent response to the dominant utilitarian culture. If you want to be clear about those teachings, Hippler's book will do it for you. Its format is attractive. It is reliable and easy to read.

"With Benedict's emphasis on the social teachings in DCE and elsewhere, with the convenient *Compendium* and with the appearance of accurate, reader-friendly books like Hippler's, no one, especially at Notre Dame, has any excuse for ignorance of the rich and comprehensive social teachings of the Church. So take a look. You might be surprised at what you will find."

IMMIGRATION: POLITICIANS AS "ILLEGALS," April 13, 2006

"'This country has lost control of its borders.' Three years after President Reagan said that, a 1986 amnesty covered 2.7 million 'illegals' amid promises of border control. Two decades later, 'illegals' have quadrupled to 11 or 12 million. Let's look at this issue in light of Catholic teaching.

"The 'original gift of the earth to the whole of mankind' entails a 'universal destination of goods' which applies to the earth itself. *Catechism*, No. 2403. This gives rise to the right of a person, in the words of Pope John XXIII, 'to enter a country in which he hopes to . . . provide more fittingly for himself and his dependents.' That right is not absolute. '[P]rosperous nations are obliged, to the extent that they are able, to welcome the foreigner.' For the 'common good,' they may condition 'the right to immigrate.' And 'immigrants are obliged to respect with gratitude the . . . heritage of the country that receives them, to obey its laws and to assist in carrying civic burdens.' *Catechism*, No. 2241. We can note here three points:

"1. The United States has a right and a duty to regain control of its borders, north and south, so that persons can enter only with permission. '[I]llegal immigration,' said Pope John Paul II, 'should be prevented [and it is] essential to combat . . . criminal activities which exploit illegal immigrants.'

"2. 'Governments,' said John Paul II, have a duty 'to regulate the migratory flows with full respect for the dignity of the persons and . . . families . . . mindful of the requirements of the host societies.' Once the borders are secured, reasonable criteria must be set for future admissions. That involves debatable issues, including doubtfully enforceable 'guest worker' proposals to admit immigrants for a limited period. Nor is there any obligation to admit political agitators with no credible prospect of supporting themselves. In any event, as John Paul II said in *Ecclesia in America* in 1999, 'the Church in America must [defend] against any unjust restriction the natural right of . . . persons to move freely within their own nation and from one nation to another.'

"3. What about the 'illegals' now in this country? Whenever you see a problem that cries out for a government solution, look for the government program that caused the problem. For two decades and more, presidents, senators and representatives of both parties have abdicated their duty to control the borders. Enforcement personnel are too few to protect the borders and to detect illegals within the states. When they are detected, too often nothing happens. Some members of Congress have pressured officials to overlook violations by influential constituents who employ illegals.

"In tort law, if you knowingly allow persons to use your land, you may confer a license, or even an invitation, on them, especially if you dismantle the fence that formerly prevented their entry and if you stand by and watch them enter.

"The politicians' refusal to enforce the border is, at least in major part, for the benefit of employers who want cheap labor and who support the politicians who enable them to get it. This is the flip side of outsourcing jobs to foreign countries. You can't readily outsource an onion field, a construction or restaurant job or poultry processing. Non-enforcement of the border brings the cheap labor to the employers, with the medical and other needs of those 'illegals' possibly shifted to the taxpayers. This is 'neoliberalism' which, as John Paul II described it, 'considers profit and the law of the market as its only parameters, to the detriment of the dignity of and respect due to individuals and peoples.'

"The politicians' refusal to enforce the borders has impliedly invited not only honest aliens seeking better pay but also criminals, security risks and committed terrorists. Such persons, on detection, should be deported if not imprisoned. But otherwise law-abiding 'illegals,' who were impliedly invited by our own officials' dereliction of duty, should be allowed to remain as long as they otherwise obey the laws. They should have a chance for permanent residence and citizenship, but only at the end of the line after those who came here legally. As the Catholic Bishops urge, immediate family members, including at least parents, spouses and minor children, should be allowed to join them.

"Popular wrath, on talk shows and elsewhere, should be directed, not at those otherwise law-abiding 'invitees,' but at the politicians who subordinate the common good to their own benefit and to the bottom-line interests of influential employers. The politicians and those they serve are the real 'illegals.'"

FR. JENKINS ON *THE VAGINA MONOLOGUES*, April 25, 2006

"University President Father John Jenkins, in his April 5 closing statement, delivered the name of Notre Dame to validate 'The Vagina Monologues' movement, including the book of that name, and the Queer Film Festival, with the movement of which it is a part. He distorted the meaning of a Catholic university. And he did it all with persistent incoherence.

"Jenkins ignored the substantive defects of the Queer Film Festival and gave it a license as long as it goes by its new name. That is like dealing with a soiled diaper by changing the pins. That validation of the Queer Film Festival may be more significant, but 'The Vagina Monologues' was the focus of his statement.

"Jenkins fell for the lie that the 'Monologues' oppose violence against women. 'The Vagina Monologues' promotes that violence. First, the proceeds go to the YWCA, which informs pregnant women about abortion, in which about half of those murdered are women. Second, the 'Monologues' encourage such violence by objectifying women. The human person, as Pope John Paul II put it, is a 'unified totality' of body and soul. 'The Vagina Monologues' fragments that unity by personifying a body part and equating the woman to that part.

"The 'Monologues' present the vagina as an entity with which the woman should 'establish a conscious relationship.' It includes such gems as, 'If your vagina got dressed, what would it wear?' and 'If your vagina could talk, what would it say, in two words?' The 'Monologues' recount the lesbian seduction of a 16-year-old by a 24-year-old, which the victim describes as 'my . . . salvation.' Another monologue consists of the repetition of a four-letter expletive describing a body part. Other monologists recount conversations with their vaginas or vulvae. Others describe lesbian sexual acts. One monologue recounts a group masturbation, with the aid of hand mirrors, in a workshop run by 'a woman who believes in vaginas.' The decisive moment came when a participant thought, 'I didn't have to find it. I had to be it. Be my clitoris. My vagina, my vagina, me.' This moronic equation of a woman with her body part facilitates the violence the 'Monologues' claims to oppose.

"Jenkins would 'suppress speech' only if it were 'overt and insistent in its contempt for the values and sensibilities of this University, or of any of the diverse groups that form part of our community.' Those, including Bishop John M. D'Arcy, who rightly see 'The Vagina Monologues' as a 'contempt for [their] values and sensibilities,' do not count, in the Jenkins world, as one of those 'diverse groups.' Bishops, incidentally, 'should be seen not as external agents but as participants in the life of the Catholic university' (*Ex Corde Ecclesiae*, Application, III).

"Jenkins' Jan. 23 address said, of an anti-Semitic play, 'I don't' believe that such a performance could be permitted at Notre Dame.' He got that right: 'Its anti-Semitic elements are clearly and outrageously opposed to the values of a Catholic university.' But what about 'The Vagina Monologues' and the Queer Film Festival? The Jenkins Statement says that '[The Monologues'] portrayals of sexuality [are] in opposition to Catholic teaching.' So they should be banned, right? Guess again:

"'It is essential,' said Jenkins, 'that we hear a full range of views . . . but . . . we must . . . bring these . . . views into dialogue with the Catholic . . . tradition. This demands balance . . . and the inclusion of the Catholic perspective. . . . [T]his year's [Monologues] was brought into dialogue . . . through panels which . . . taught me . . . that the creative contextualization of a play like ['The Vagina Monologues'] can bring certain perspectives on important issues into a constructive and fruitful dialogue with the Catholic tradition.' Translating this jargon, his bottom line is, 'I see no reason to prohibit ['The Vagina Monologues.']'

"So Jenkins, correctly, would bar the anti-Semitic play, even with a panel. Such a play is a lie. But so are the 'Monologues' and the Queer Film Festival. Jenkins would allow 'The Vagina Monologues' if it is followed by a panel including the Catholic 'perspective' as a debatable alternative. The Catholic university 'guarantees academic freedom . . . within the confines of the truth and the common good' (*Ex Corde Ecclesiae*, no. 12). That truth, a unity of faith and reason, includes the ennobling Catholic teaching on women and sexuality. It is objective and normative, not one of the 'perspectives' that that might be nonjudgmentally included in a panel at Michigan State.

"Why do the 'Monologues' and the Queer Film Festival get an easy pass at Notre Dame? In our politically correct culture, it is open season on Catholic sexual morality. That teaching can be advanced only as one 'perspective' without any serious claim to objective validity. Jenkins, playing that game, confirms that political correctness is the operative official religion of Notre Dame. His statement patronized faculty and students with a self-centered concept of freedom, divorced from any duty to objective truth. That concept corresponds to the 'relativism' which, in Pope Benedict's XVI's words, 'recognizes nothing as absolute and . . . leaves the I and its whims as the ultimate measure.'

"Incidentally, Jenkins' encouragement of 'Loyal Daughters,' a proposed play of uncertain content, his creation of a diverse and predictably useless committee to discuss things and his announcement of porous guidelines for events, all amount to a fig leaf to cover an accommodation to the relativist, homosexual culture.

"President Brian J. Shanley, O.P., got it right in banning 'The Vagina Monologues' at Providence College. 'A Catholic college' said Shanley, 'cannot sanction the performance of works of art that are inimical to the teaching of the Church in an area as important as female sexuality and the dignity of women.' Jenkins should have borrowed the Shanley statement.

"The Closing Statement is well named. It closes the effective phase of the Jenkins presidency. It involves no animosity or disrespect toward Jenkins to conclude, with regret, that he should resign or be removed."

Student Loans Again, Aug. 29, 2006

"The student loan problem has gotten so bad that several major universities, not including Notre Dame, are finally doing something dramatic about it. . . .

"The most creative is Princeton University. In 2001, Princeton became the first university to replace loans with grants and a campus job for all students qualifying for aid. Six hundred seventy-four members (or 55 percent) of the entering class of 2009 received such aid. The average scholarship was $28,100, with $18,900,000 in total scholarship aid. The average family income of aid recipients was $93,950, with 225 below $40,000 and 124 more below $60,000.

"Princeton is smaller than Notre Dame and has a much bigger endowment. Notre Dame's excellent Financial Aid Office tries to help students, including an effort to reduce the loan portion of need-based aid by replacing loans with scholarships. But a major element continues to be the student loan. It is fair to suggest that Notre Dame should emulate the no-loan concept openly and aggressively. Notre Dame's undergraduate tuition rate for 2006–2007 rose 5.8 percent over last year for a new total of tuition and average room and board (TRB) of $42,137. The rate of increase is lower than in the previous three years, but it is higher than the 4.2 percent rise in the Consumer Price Index (CPI) from 2005 to 2006. While some belittle the use of the CPI to evaluate the rise of college tuition, the CPI does measure what it costs the students and their families to live. In 1978–79, before Notre Dame began its pursuit of Research Prestige, TRB was $5,180. Adjusted for inflation by the CPI, the TRB now would be $16,255 instead of $42,137. . . .

"Recent studies, including one from last December by Allan Carlson of the Howard Center, document the obvious impact of student debt on marriage and childbearing. A national Creighton University study of young married couples, published in 2000, asked respondents to state 42 issues that 'might be problematic during the early years of marriage.' For all respondents, 'debt brought into marriage' ranked third. Among respondents under age 30 and among those married one year or less, it ranked first.

"For very Catholic reasons, Notre Dame should be in the forefront in the war on student-loan debt. Heavy loans narrow a graduate's career, marriage and family options. Examples abound of young lawyers compelled by debt to forego, or leave, lower-paying positions as public defenders, disability advocates and prosecutors. Alumni in other occupations could tell similar stories.

"Our leaders' pursuit of a Research Reputation has unjustly inflicted this loan burden on non-wealthy alumni of Notre Dame. Our leaders have a duty to relieve that burden at least for present and future Notre Dame students. Notre Dame should be a leader, not a follower, in affording its grads the freedom to choose to contribute to the common good in their career and family choices."

THE FLAG AMENDMENT, Sept. 12, 2006

"'Old Glory lost today,' said Senate Majority Leader Bill Frist (R-Tenn.) when the Senate rejected, for the fourth time, the Flag Desecration Amendment. The vote, 66-34, fell one short of the two-thirds needed to send it to the states for approval.

"The amendment states: 'The Congress shall have power to prohibit the physical desecration of the flag of the United States.' Contrary to Frist, this amendment is an election-year scam. It could be Exhibit A on 'How Not to Mess with the Constitution.'

"The amendment was a response to Supreme Court decisions in *Texas v. Johnson* (1989) and *U.S. v. Eichmann* (1990). In *Johnson*, the Court denied that 'a State may foster its own view of the flag by prohibiting expressive conduct relating to it.' In *Eichmann*, the Court struck down, on free speech grounds, a federal statute punishing flag desecration. Neither case prevents punishment of a breach of the peace involving flag desecration.

"Both cases are dubious in their interpretation of the freedom of speech. The invalidation in *Johnson* of the flag laws of 48 states also illustrates the rigidity created by the incorporation doctrine, the misinterpretation of the Fourteenth Amendment's guarantee of 'due process of law' so as to bind every state and local government strictly and uniformly by the Court's interpretations of the Bill of Rights.

"The flag amendment, however, is an imprudent response. It affirms the power of Congress only and withdraws from the states any power to protect the flag as a symbol of national unity. It concedes that *Johnson* and *Eichmann* have the same status, as 'the supreme law of the land,' as does the language of the Constitution itself, so that the only way to undo it is another amendment. The amendment is also unclear as to whether it would give Congress power to criminalize a person's 'physical desecration,' in his home, of a flag he owns.

"The amendment disregards an alternative remedy provided in the Constitution itself. Congress has power to control the entire jurisdiction of the lower federal courts and the appellate jurisdiction of the Supreme Court. Article II, Section 2 provides that the Supreme Court shall have appellate jurisdiction 'with such exceptions, and under such regulations as the Congress shall make.' Legal scholars debate it. But the 1869 case of *Ex Parte McCardle*, and other precedents and statements in later Supreme Court opinions, indicate that Article III, Section 2, means what it says. 'As respects our appellate jurisdiction,' said Justice William O. Douglas in 1968, 'Congress may largely fashion it as Congress desires by reason of the express provisions of Section 2, Article III.' If a federal statute were enacted depriving the lower federal courts and the Supreme Court of jurisdiction in cases involving federal and state flag desecration statutes, the state courts could rule on such cases without fear of being overruled by the Supreme Court.

"A statute withdrawing Supreme Court appellate jurisdiction in flag cases would affirm that the constitutional checks and balances work. It would not overrule *Texas v. Johnson* or *U.S. v. Eichmann*. It would not change the Constitution, as would an amendment. The jurisdiction of the Court could be restored whenever Congress so chose.

"The State is not God, and the flag is not an object of religious veneration. But, Congress and the states ought to be held to have a sufficient interest to protect the flag, as the unique national symbol, from public and contemptuous physical desecration even when that act is intended as political expression. The amendment, however, is phony electoral posturing that would deny the rightful power of the states and ignore the remedy provided by Article III, Section 2."

BENEDICT AT REGENSBURG, Sept. 26, 2006

"The original *New York Times* story on the Pope's University of Regensburg address was headed, 'Pope Calls West Divorced from Faith, Adding a Blunt Footnote on Islam.' That footnote, three paragraphs in a 30-minute academic speech, prompted the violent response in the Muslim world.

"Let's look at what Benedict XVI actually said. The address was essentially on the West's divorce of reason from religion. Benedict first noted that when he began teaching at the University of Bonn in 1959, it was 'accepted without question,' within the university as a whole, that one could 'raise the question of God through the use of reason . . . in the context of . . . the Christian faith.' He said that he was 'reminded of all this recently' when he read the fourteenth= century dialogue between the Byzantine emperor Manuel II Paleologus and 'an educated Persian on the subject of Christianity and Islam, and the truth of both.'

"[T]he emperor,' said Benedict, 'touches on the theme of the jihad (holy war). The emperor must have known that sura 2:256 reads: "There is no compulsion in religion." It is one of the suras of the early period, when Mohammed was still powerless and under [threat]. But naturally the emperor also knew the instructions, developed later and recorded in the Koran, concerning holy war.'

Benedict stated that the emperor put to the Persian, 'in these words . . . the central question on the relationship between religion and violence: "Show me just what Mohammed brought that was new, and there you will find things only evil and inhuman, such as his command to spread by the sword the faith he preached."'

"'The emperor,' continued Benedict, 'goes on to explain . . . why spreading the faith through violence is . . . unreasonable. Violence is incompatible with the nature of God and the nature of the soul. "God is not pleased by blood, and not acting reasonably . . . is contrary to God's nature. Faith is born of the soul, not of the body. Whoever would lead someone to faith needs the ability to speak well and to reason properly, without violence or threats. . . . To convince a reasonable soul, one does not need a strong arm, or weapons of any kind or any other means of threatening a person with death. . . ." The decisive statement in this argument against violent conversion is this: Not to act in accordance with reason is contrary to God's nature.'

"Benedict then stated that Theodore Khoury, editor of the dialogue, observed that 'for Muslim teaching, God is absolutely transcendent. His will is not bound up with . . . rationality.' Benedict did not state this, or the emperor's view, as his own opinion.

"Benedict went on to note that God acts with 'logos,' which 'means both reason and word.' God is reason, which is not the same as saying that reason (our reason) is god. From 'Christian faith' and . . . 'Greek thought now joined to faith,' said Benedict, 'Manuel II was able to say: Not to act "with logos" [with reason] is contrary to God's nature.'

"The dialogue between Manuel II and the Persian was relevant to Benedict's main theme, a critical analysis of the Western divorce, dating from the late Middle Ages, of reason from faith and religion. Benedict discussed the 'sola scriptura' approach of the Reformation; the later distinction between 'the God of the philosophers and the God of Abraham, Isaac and Jacob'; the presentation of Jesus as merely 'the father of a humanitarian moral message'; and the 'modern concept of reason' with 'mathematical and empirical' certainty as the measure even of the 'human sciences, such as history, psychology, sociology and philosophy.' That method 'excludes the question of God [as] unscientific or pre-scientific.' Therefore questions of religion and ethics have nothing to do with 'reason as defined by 'science.' They are 'subjective.'

"Benedict's intent is one of 'broadening our concept of reason and its application. . . . We will succeed in doing so only if reason and faith come together in a new way, if we overcome the self-imposed limitation of reason to the empirically verifiable. . . . [T]heology rightly belongs in the university and within the . . . dialogue of sciences . . . as inquiry into the rationality of faith.'

"Pope John Paul II described *Faith and Reason* as 'like two wings on which the human spirit rises to the contemplation of truth.' Benedict's address

302

gave a new dimension to that insight. 'I am deeply sorry,' Benedict said, 'for the reactions in some countries to a few passages . . . which were considered offensive to the sensibilities of Muslims. These were a quotation from a medieval text which do not in any way express my own personal thought. . . . [M]y address . . . in its totality was and is an invitation to frank and sincere dialogue, with mutual respect.'

"Those who react with violence to this address validate Emperor Manuel II's opinion of Islam. Benedict, as the Vicar of Christ, has done the world an important service. It would be a good idea to read this address. And anything else Benedict says. *Habemus papam. Deo gratias.*"

How Should a Catholic Vote? Oct. 10, 2006

"Are you trying to decide how to vote this November? Benedict XVI can help, whatever your religion or lack thereof.

"In a little-noticed March 30 address to European parliamentarians, Benedict spelled out three 'non-negotiable' principles for the public arena. They are not 'truths of faith,' but rather 'are inscribed in human nature' and are therefore 'common to all humanity,' including candidates and voters in the United States. Achieving a 'just society,' said Benedict, is the job of 'politics, not of the Church.' As he said in his first encyclical, *Deus Caritas Est* (God is Love), the job of the Church is 'to help form consciences in political life.' She does not seek to impose 'ways of thinking and . . . conduct proper to faith' but argues 'on the basis of reason and natural law' so as to reawaken spiritual energy.

"The first principle stated by Benedict requires 'protection of life in all its stages, from the first moment of conception until natural death.' That recommendation was dead-on-arrival in the United States.

"Abortion and euthanasia are moving beyond the practical reach of the law. Early abortion technology is making abortion-by-pill a private event. At the other end of life, the legitimate technique of palliative care can be misused with the intent to kill a patient. The law also permits in some cases the intentional killing of a patient by starvation and dehydration where family and caregivers agree.

"In abortion the law authorizes, but does not require, a mother to kill her unborn child who is defined by the Supreme Court as a nonperson. In the Terri Schiavo case, Judge George Greer took legalized murder to a new level. He did not merely authorize Terri's killing. He ordered that Michael Schiavo 'shall cause the removal of nutrition and hydration from Theresa Schiavo, at 1:00 p.m. on Friday, March 18, 2005.' That was as much a scheduled execution as the ones they do at the Florida state prison in Raiford. This is the first time ever that an American court ordered the execution of a concededly innocent person accused of no crime. On this the Pope, to say the least, is out of sync with American law and culture. But, regardless of what the law says, 'all Catholics,' as the American bishops said last March, 'are obliged to shape their consciences in accord with the moral teaching of the Church.' And vote accordingly.

"Benedict's second principle requires 'recognition and promotion of the natural structure of the family—as a union between a man and a woman based on marriage—and its defense from attempts to make it juridically equivalent to radically different forms of union.' In the United States as well as the European Union, a homosexualization of culture results from the acceptance of contraception which separates sex from any connection to procreation. The main political issue is whether to confer the name or legal incidents of marriage on same-sex unions. In 2003, then-Cardinal Ratzinger, now Benedict XVI, described the family as 'the primary unit in society' and said 'married couples ensure the succession of generations and . . . therefore . . . civil law grants them institutional recognition.' Putting homosexual unions on the same level as marriage would approve 'deviant behavior' . . . making it a model [and would] obscure basic values which belong to the common inheritance of humanity.' You won't hear anything like that on the Sunday morning talk shows.

"Benedict's third principle requires 'the protection of the rights of parents to educate their children.' Parents, and not bureaucrats, are the primary educators of their children. '[M]ore than in any other historical period,' said John Paul II, 'there is a breakdown in the process of handing on moral and religious values between generations.' The Supreme Court promotes that breakdown by imposing a religion of secularism on public schools. Justice requires that the law must protect the religious freedom, including freedom of expression, of students in public schools as well as the freedom of parents to choose home schools or authentic religious schools for their children.

"Benedict works at his job, taking stands on many issues, including war, migration, globalization and others. But, as John Paul II said, 'a family policy must be the basis and the driving force of all social policies.' The three policies noted here relate to the family. Since they are 'common to humanity,' Benedict's teaching is addressed to 'all people.' That includes politicians and voters in the United States. Benedict is counter-cultural. And he is serious about it. But so was his Boss."

Plan B, Oct. 31, 2006

"In August, the FDA approved over-the-counter sales of Plan B, the morning-after pill, without a prescription, by pharmacists (including pharmacy departments at Wal-Mart and similar stores), to men and women who can prove that they are over 18. Some states had already allowed such sales through procedures such as 'open prescriptions' given by physicians to pharmacists.

"Plan B is a higher dose of the birth control pill which can be sold only by prescription. Plan B is marketed as an 'emergency contraceptive,' but that is a misnomer. Like most oral 'contraceptives,' Plan B operates in three ways: it prevents ovulation; it prevents fertilization, the union of the sperm and the ovum; or, if fertilization occurs, it alters the lining of the womb so as to prevent the embryo (i.e., the new human being) from implanting in the womb. Implantation, five to seven days after fertilization, is necessary for the embryo to draw nutrition and survive.

"That embryo is a human being. Beyond any rational doubt, the life of each human being begins at fertilization. When Louise Brown, the world's first 'test-tube baby,' was born in 1978, the whole world knew when her life began—at the *in vitro* fertilization. Even with identical twins, we know there is at least one life present at fertilization.

"Since the mid-1960s, 'pregnancy' has been widely redefined so as to begin not at fertilization but at implantation. That made it possible to market birth control pills as contraceptives despite the fact that most of them prevent implantation and are therefore abortifacients. Plan B, in preventing the implantation of the new human being in the womb, perpetrates a homicide.

"Proponents claim that easy access to Plan B will reduce unwanted pregnancies and abortions. Recent studies from Washington State and Scotland, however, draw that assumption into question. The security blanket of the 'morning-after pill' can reduce barriers to a girl's consent to sexual relations. The authorization for over-the-counter sale of the morning-after pill can also facilitate sexual relations between minors and adults. A girl under 18 cannot go to a pharmacist and get the morning-after pill. But her over-18 male 'partner' can get it. In 2002 the California Center for Health Statistics reported that a 'slight majority' of pregnancies of girls ages 10 to 14 resulted from sex with an adult. And, of course, the morning-after pill can provide an added means to induce the consent to sexual relations of a female of any childbearing age.

"Plan B, incidentally, is not free from its own complications. The package insert notes the following possible reactions: nausea, vomiting, stomach pain, tiredness, diarrhea, dizziness, heart pain, headache and menstrual changes.

"So why is the over-the-counter sale of Plan B an important cultural indicator? The over-the-counter approval of Plan B reflects the decadence of a culture in which the intentional infliction of death upon the innocent is seen as an optional problem-solving technique. Legalized surgical abortion, of course, provides the primary example. Another is the acceptance of the killing of some kinds of patients by starvation or excessive sedation, when the family and caregivers agree that the patient would want, or perhaps ought to want, to depart. The *Schiavo* case moved this allowance of homicide to a new and compulsory level—Judge George Greer ordered, rather than merely authorized, Michael Schiavo to remove all 'nutrition and hydration' from his wife, Terri.

"Ideas have consequences. The Columbine High School massacre in 1999 was the first of many comparable incidents. If one has a personal problem, homicide is now on the table as a culturally, if not always legally, acceptable solution.

"The over-the-counter sale of Plan B brings us down to a new level. You can buy an instrument of homicide, such as a knife or a hammer, in any hardware store. But Plan B is different. To use Plan B, unlike a hammer, according to the manufacturer's directions, necessarily involves a conditionally homicidal intent. The intent is to 'prevent pregnancy,' including by homicide if the life of the child has already begun. The message is that innocent life is so cheap that its termination can be included in your shopping list, over-the-counter. We can predict the expansion of providers beyond pharmacies to convenience stores, gas stations, mail order, etc. And we can hardly expect that this cultural and legal verdict that innocent life is so cheap will be confined to the unborn.

"As Mother Teresa said at the 1994 National Prayer Breakfast, '[I]f we accept that a mother can kill even her own child, how can we tell other people not to kill one another?' Especially if the potential mother can buy the murder weapon over-the-counter at CVS or Wal-Mart."

DEMOGRAPHIC WINTER, Nov. 14, 2006

"The United States population reached 100 million in 1915, 200 million in 1967 and, according to the Census Bureau, 300 million on Oct. 17, 2005 at about 7:45 a.m. The Bureau sees a net increase of one person every 11 seconds, reaching 400 million around 2043.

"We have no idea whether the 300 millionth was a newborn or an immigrant. But it led some to revive the warning of Paul Ehrlich, in *The Population Bomb*, in 1960, that we will 'breed ourselves into oblivion.' The reality is more complicated.

"The economic and social problems of the world are not due to an absolute excess of people. If you took all 6.6 billion people in the world and gave each one six square feet to stand on, you could fit them all (I am not suggesting this) into 35 percent of the land area of Los Angeles County and you would have 2641 square miles of that county left over. Advocates of 'zero population growth' regard each new life as a threat. As Julian Simon, Colin Clark and other demographers have shown, each new human being is not only a consumer but also a potential producer with an intellect and will as well as an appetite. Overcrowding, poverty and disease are attributable more to political and other causes than to overpopulation.

"The emerging problem is the 'demographic winter' in Europe, Japan, Russia and some other nations. A fertility rate of 2.1 is needed for a population to replenish itself. The rate for the 25 nations of the European Union is 1.5. Only France is increasing, with a rate of 1.94, second only to Ireland's falling rate of 1.99. Islamic and other immigrants to the E.U. exceed 2 million a year.

"The decline in fertility is widespread. The rate in India is down to 2.85, China 1.69, and 1.38 in Japan which in 2005 experienced its first recorded decline in population. Russia is projected to decline from 140 million people today to about 104 million in 2050. The United Nations Population Division estimates that the population of affluent nations will remain stable at 1.2 billion through 2050 while the population of comparatively poor nations will triple to about 7.8 billion.

"'The problem with low fertility,' warned Peter McDonald, of Australian National University, in 2001, 'is that it reduces population size . . . only among the young [and] . . . creates a momentum for future population decline. . . . The longer low fertility is maintained, the harder it becomes to reverse population decline. . . . [Governments] will need to deal with . . . impacts of low fertility, namely shrinking labor forces.'

"The United States fertility rate is 2.07, with 1.8 for non-Hispanic whites, 2.2 for blacks and 2.9 for Hispanics. The U.S. population over age 65 will rise from 12.3 percent today to 20.6 percent by 2050. Those who are age 80 or over will rise from 3.6 percent to 7.3 percent. 'Our worker-to-retiree ratio is already at a dangerous three to one,' notes Joseph D'Agostino of the Population Research Institute. 'By 2050 it will be two to one. And those retirees will be living much longer than they do today.' As Stephen Mosher, president of PRI, put it: 'America's baby boomers didn't have many children on average, and as a result, our country faces a gray dawn. Even . . . high immigration levels haven't made up the difference.'

"The aging will not be limited to affluent nations. Elderly dependants per 100 working-age people worldwide will go from 17 today to 37 in 2050. In less developed countries, the figures are 13 today and 34 in 2050. One result of this aging will be the legalization or toleration of euthanasia of elderly dependants.

"Pope Benedict XVI put all this in context: '[We] are witnessing on a planetary level, and in developed countries in particular, two . . . interconnected trends: . . . an increase in life expectancy and . . . a decrease in birthrates. . . . [M]any nations . . . lack a sufficient number of young people to renew their population. The situation is the result of . . . complex causes. . . . But its ultimate roots can be seen as moral and spiritual; they are linked to a . . .

deficit of faith, hope and, indeed, love. To bring children into the world calls for . . . a creative [love] marked by trust and hope in the future. By its nature, love looks to the eternal. Perhaps the lack of such creative and forward-looking love is the reason why many couples today choose not to marry, why so many marriages fail, and why birthrates have significantly diminished.'

"Some may agree with Benedict. 'It's barely a blip on the nation's demographic radar,' said the *Washington Times*, 'But there seems to be a growing openness to having more than two children, in some cases more than four. The reasons are diverse—from religious to . . . 'Why not'?'."

CHRISTMAS AS A POLITICAL EVENT, Nov. 28, 2006

"As we move into the Christmas season, maybe you think it has nothing to do with the political season we just survived. If so, think again.

"The Magi were latecomers to the Christmas narrative. But they tell us a lot about Christmas as a political event. According to tradition their names were Melchior, Gaspar and Balthasar. They got some good press from Benedict XVI last year at World Youth Day in Cologne. In 1164 the relics of the Magi were formally transferred from Milan, across the Alps to Cologne where, in the words of Benedict, the people 'produced the most exquisite reliquary of the whole Christian world and raised above it an even greater reliquary: Cologne Cathedral.'

"So what do the Magi have to do with politics? In their day there was no recognized moral limit to the power of the state. The Magi proclaimed one by defying Herod's command that they tell him where the Child was so 'that I too may go and worship him' (Matthew 2:8). He was, of course, a lying politician, which some may regard as a redundancy. When the Magi had departed for home, Joseph was warned by an angel to take the Child into Egypt because Herod wanted to kill him. Joseph obeyed and he and Mary joined the Magi as the first practitioners of civil disobedience in the Christian era.

"What got into the Magi to make them challenge the King? At World Youth Day, Benedict explained that the Magi had come seeking the prophesied 'King who would be intimately united with God, a King who would restore order to the world, acting for God and in his Name.' That King turned out to be 'quite unlike what they were expecting.' Still, 'they knelt down before this child and recognized him as the promised King. But they still had to . . . change their ideas about power, about God and about man, and in so doing, they also had to change themselves. Now they were able to see that God's power is . . . the power of love . . . which constitutes the new divine intervention that opposes injustice and ushers in the Kingdom of God.'

"Christmas made visible the Incarnation in which the second person of the Trinity became man. When that Child became an adult, he spelled it out for Pilate, that the power of the state is given by God and is subject to his law: 'Thou wouldst have no power over me were it not given to you from above.' (John 19:11). This juridical impact of the Incarnation had become reality at Christmas in the civil disobedience of the Magi and then of Joseph and Mary.

"Benedict asked the youth at Cologne, 'what does all this mean for us?' He answered his own question by giving them a short course on the nature of true revolution. 'The saints,' he said, 'are the true reformers. . . . In the last century, we experienced revolutions with a common programme—expecting nothing more from God, they assumed total responsibility for the cause of the world in order to change it. [This] meant that a human and partial point of view was always taken as an absolute guiding principle. Absolutizing what is . . . relative is . . . totalitarianism. It does not liberate man, but takes away his dignity and enslaves him. It is not ideologies that save the world, but only a return to the living God, our Creator, the guarantor of our freedom, the guarantor of what is really good and true. True revolution consists in simply turning to God who is the measure of what is right and who at the same time is everlasting love.'

"The Magi sent a news flash to the world that there is a law higher than the state. That higher law, however, like any law, makes ultimate sense only if we can identify its lawgiver and discern his intent. That Lawgiver is the Child whom the Magi adored. As Benedict, the Vicar of that Child, told the youth at Cologne, 'Here in the Sacred Host he is present before us and in our midst . . . as he was then in Bethlehem.'

"So Christmas tells us a lot about how to keep politics in perspective. That is so because that Child himself is still a current event."

Notre Dame and the March for Life, Jan. 23, 2007

"The seats, about 250, on the buses were sold out almost immediately. The riders subjected themselves to a 10-hour trip each way. In between, they had to sleep on a gym floor, spend long hours out in the cold and do what they could for food, etc. Where were they going? A concert? The Motor City Bowl? Not quite. They are Notre Dame and Saint Mary's students going to the March for Life in Washington. It marked the 34th anniversary of *Roe v. Wade* on January 22.

"A reasonable observer might ask, 'Why bother?' Maybe students just don't have enough to do. The reality, however, is that those students are doing something real and important.

"For most readers of these words, *Roe v. Wade* is ancient history. Since that ruling in 1973, more than 43 million unborn children have been legally executed by surgical abortion through 2002. That is the last year for which the Alan Guttmacher Institute, the source of the most complete statistics, has reported. Since the early 1990s the totals have leveled out and declined somewhat. In 2002, the total was about 1.29 million. Those figures do not include the uncountable but increasing number of early abortions by chemicals, intrauterine devices and other means. The legalized execution of unborn children is a fixed reality in our law and culture. Victims from the first decade of *Roe* would have already attended, had they lived, their tenth college reunions.

"You have rights under the Constitution because you are a person. In any civilized society where personhood is the condition for possessing rights, every innocent human being should be entitled to be treated as a person. The theory of *Roe* is simple. The Court declined to decide whether the unborn child is a living human being. The Court held instead that, whether or not he is such, he is not a person. The ruling is the same in effect as a ruling that an acknowledged human being is a nonperson and therefore has no rights. That depersonalization principle of *Roe* is the principle that underlay both the Nazi extermination of the Jews and the depersonalization of slaves in the *Dred Scott* case of 1857.

"If the students in the March seek to accomplish a restoration of legal rights to the unborn child they are embarked on an exercise of futility. The most the Court will do is to let the states decide whether to allow or prohibit abortion. That would confirm the nonpersonhood of the unborn child, because if an innocent human being is subject to being executed whenever a legislature authorizes it, he is a nonperson.

"The Court will soon rule on the federal prohibition of partial-birth abortion. That case, however, is a sideshow. The issue there is not whether innocent human beings may be legally executed and not even which ones may be so killed, but rather how the killing is to be done. In any event, the restoration of legal rights to that child will not happen because early-abortion technology is irrevocably moving abortion beyond the effective reach of the law.

"For these reasons, abortion is now essentially not a legal problem but one that is cultural and—dare we say it?—religious. Here is where the March for Life becomes a big deal and the students are doing something real and important.

"The students from ND/SMC Right to Life are joining other thousands at the March for Life in giving witness not only to justice but also to peace. In his message for the World Day of Peace, Jan. 1, 2006, Benedict XVI said, '[t]he right to life . . . is not subject to the power of man. Peace requires . . . a clear boundary between what is at man's disposal and what is not. . . . As far as the right to life is concerned, we must denounce its widespread violation. . . . Alongside the victims of armed conflicts, terrorism and the different forms of violence, there are the silent deaths caused by hunger, abortion, experimentation on human embryos and euthanasia. How can we fail to see in all this an attack on peace?' Benedict described abortion and embryonic experimentation as 'a direct denial of that attitude of acceptance of others that is indispensable for . . . peace.' The evils named by Benedict prevent peace because they deny what he called 'the requirements of the nature bestowed on man by the Creator.' Legalized abortion is part of the bigger picture.

"Benedict entrusted his prayer for peace to 'the Queen of Peace' who is, of course, Notre Dame. As Right to Life chairman Mary Elizabeth Walter described it, the journey to the March for Life is 'not so much a demonstration but a prayer.' Those students embody Notre Dame at its best. They have their act together, evidently more than some faculty."

A Serious Piece of Business: Bengal Bouts, Feb. 6, 2007

"Let me tell you about a serious piece of business we do every year at Notre Dame. It's the Bengal Bouts. How can that be serious? Because every year since 1931, the Bouts have given to the Holy Cross Missions in Bangladesh donations averaging in the past decade over $50,000 a year. The annual per capita income of the 141 million people in Bangladesh is $1,470. Among the ultra-poor tribal people (1% of the population) served by the Holy Cross priests, brothers and seminarians (126 of whom are Bangladeshi) and the 60 Holy Cross sisters, a family of four could eat for two weeks on what we would casually pay for a pizza. The Bengal Bouts literally provide a lifeline for the poor.

"Bangladesh is 88.3 percent Muslim and 10.5 percent Hindu. Catholics are fewer than 300,000. Holy Cross conducts over 200 primary schools and 12 secondary schools, all serving the very poor. Fr. Tom Smith, C.S.C., recently returned from Bangladesh, described the ministry as 'evangelization, health care, education and hostels.' The hostel—a bamboo and thatched-roof room with a dirt floor and platforms for sleep and study—provides children from remote villages their only chance for education. If we grumble about having to walk from North Quad to South Quad, it might help for us to think about the 14-year-old boy who told Smith that he walked three days through the jungle to reach the hostel in a Chittagong Hill parish near the border with Myanmar (formerly Burma.) The education, the boy said, was his 'only hope.' Smith visited a pastor in another jungle parish where four teenage girls were lying on a hostel platform 'burning up with malarial fever.' When Smith asked the pastor why he had too few mosquito nets in the hostel, the pastor replied: 'We do give nets, but at the first opportunity they take them home for their infant brothers and sisters. They consider themselves able to survive the malaria but they worry about their weaker siblings in the village. They care for the little ones first.'

"The Tripura tribe, incidentally, 'is embracing Christianity, whole villages at a time, with 600–700 Easter baptisms in each parish each year.' In one village in Kalipur, 86 were baptized this last Christmas.

"So the Bouts have a purpose. The program, under the sponsorship of Rich O'Leary and Dave Brown of RecSports, is run by the student officers, president Andrew McGill, and captains Stu Stypula, Stephen Hansen, Mike Hennig, Dan Ward, Chris Calderone, Hunter Land, Lawrence Sullivan and Jesse Brawer. The officers run every aspect of the training but they agree that it would all come to a grinding halt without the student managers, Erika Meyer, Meghan O'Farrell and Melanie Rodarte. Working with Jimmy Rogers of RecSports, the managers maintain impeccable financial, medical, sparring and other records. . . .

"If you want to know why this program has not had a serious injury in 76 years, give credit to Dr. James Moriarty, the University chief of medicine, and the Emergency Medical Technicians, led by Terri Engel, who attend every sparring session along with two of the Notre Dame Fire Department paramedics, Jordan Lacy, Baker Jones, Gordon Martinczak, Wayne Bishop and Damien Cruz. Safety is the controlling concern of the medical staff as well as of long-time trainer Jack Zimmerman. . . .

"St. Joseph Parish in Srimangal is 60 miles long with 70 villages. To finish a hostel to house and educate 50 girls, grades 3–5, from those tribal villages, they need a well, latrines, wiring, fixtures, equipment and furnishings. The cost: $2,800. In Fatima Rani parish in Bandarban, an area infested with malaria and also typhoid and jaundice they need $1,500 to cover medical care for one year. King of Peace parish in Thanci, the most rural and remote parish in Bangladesh, needs to build a medical dispensary. The parishioners will do the labor but they need $1,500 for materials. The list could go on. These may be trifling amounts to us. But not to them. Those people need the Bengal Bouts. Be there."

CONGRESS AND WAR, Feb. 20, 2007

"Ready for a surprise? A member of Congress has introduced, on the Middle East, a bill embodying common sense and constitutional principle. No kidding. H.J. Res. 14, introduced by Congressman Walter B. Jones (R-NC), with two Republican and four Democratic co-sponsors, provides that no previously enacted law 'shall be construed to authorize the use of military force by the

United States against Iran.' The punch line is in the next section: 'Absent a national emergency created by attack by Iran, or a demonstrably imminent attack by Iran, upon the United States, its territories or possessions or its armed forces, the President shall consult with Congress, and receive specific authorization pursuant to law from Congress, prior to initiating any use of military force against Iran.'

"Substantial evidence supports a description of the Iraq war as a mistake in its inception and flawed in its execution. H.J. Res. 14 seeks to prevent a worse replay in Iran by requiring that a new war must be initiated pursuant to constitutional process.

"On Aug. 17, 1787, according to James Madison's notes of the debates, the Constitutional Convention gave Congress the power to 'declare' rather than to 'make' war, 'leaving to the Executive the power to repel sudden attacks.' 'The Executive,' Roger Sherman said, '[should] be able to repel and not to commence war.' Elbridge Gerry said he 'never expected to hear in a republic a motion to empower the Executive alone to declare war.' George Mason 'was against giving the power of war to the Executive, because [he was] not safely to be trusted with it.'

"The Constitution created, in Justice Robert Jackson's words, 'a zone of twilight,' with concurrent war powers in the President and Congress but no bright line of separation. Presidents have put forces into combat more than 200 times, all with explicit or implicit Congressional approval before or after the fact. As Alexander Hamilton noted even in 1787, 'the ceremony of a formal denunciation of war has of late fallen into disuse.' Congress has declared war only five times. But it is still true that Congress should decide whether to go to war, with or without a formal declaration, and the President should conduct it.

"The President is 'Commander in Chief of the army and navy' because, as Hamilton said, 'the direction of war . . . demands . . . exercise of power by a single hand.' Congress has no right to forbid the 'surge' of more troops to Iraq or to cut off funds for that 'surge.' Congress, however, has the power of appropriation and could cut off funds for continuation of the entire war, as was done in Cambodia and Vietnam. If the President vetoed a cut-off of funds, an override of that veto would require a two-thirds vote in the House and Senate. And impeachment of the President for his position on the war would require a two-thirds vote in the Senate to convict him. The President, incidentally, is 'Commander in Chief of the army and navy,' not of the country. . . .

"In 2002 Congress gave the President authority to decide whether to go to war against Iraq 'as he determines to be necessary and appropriate.' That sort of blank check should not be given again. The members of Congress should make the actual decision whether or not to go to war, and account for it to their constituents.

"'Too many times,' said Congressman Jones, 'Congress has abdicated its
. . . duty. . . . [W]hile the Commander in Chief has the power to conduct wars—
only Congress has the power to authorize war. . . .

"The military personnel of the United States are relatively few. But they
are the very best among us. They have a moral and legal right to have military
power used, and themselves put at risk, only through a decision made in accord
with the Constitution and therefore made with proper authority. H.J. Res. 14
should be enacted to achieve that end."

EUCHARISTIC ADORATION: ON THE RISE, March 6, 2007

"Let's look at a new phenomenon you may know very little about. It is the
remarkable rise of Eucharistic Adoration in Catholic parishes and institutions
in every part of the world. Why is it happening? And what is it?

"'The Catholic Church,' says the *Catechism*, 'offers to the . . . Eucharist
. . . adoration, not only during Mass, but also outside of it, reserving the consecrated hosts . . . exposing them to the solemn veneration of the faithful, and
carrying them in procession' (No. 1378).

"But why do we do this? 'In the . . . Eucharist, the body and blood, . . .
soul and divinity, of our Lord Jesus Christ and, therefore, the whole Christ is
truly, really and substantially contained. This presence is called real, by which
is not intended to exclude the other types of presence . . . but because it is
presence in the fullest sense . . . it is substantial presence by which Christ,
God and man, makes himself wholly and entirely present' (*Catechism*, no.
1374.)

"This conversion of the bread and wine into the body and blood of Christ,
promised in the sixth chapter of John's gospel and fulfilled at the Last Supper,
is called transubstantiation.

"'Substance,' as Cardinal Avery Dulles put it, 'denotes the basic reality of
the thing, i.e., what it is in itself.' A change in appearance does not affect the
substance of the thing. When the angel Raphael stood before Tobiah, his
appearance was that of a 'young man,' but his substance was that of an angel
(*Tobit*, 5:5, 12:15).

"'Christ is present,' wrote Cardinal Dulles, 'by his dynamic power and
action in all his sacraments, but in the Eucharist, His presence is, in addition,
substantial. For this reason, the Eucharist may be adored. It is the greatest of
all sacraments.' (Feb. 15, 2005).

"You are in the real presence of Christ every time you step into a Catholic
church with the lighted lamp or candle indicating that the Blessed Sacrament
is in the tabernacle. At any such time one can be with Christ in adoration. The

term Eucharistic Adoration, however, is usually applied to the Exposition of the Blessed Sacrament.

"When Pope John Paul II instituted Eucharistic Adoration at St. Peter's Basilica in 1981, he said, 'The best . . . way of establishing everlasting peace on the face of the earth is through . . . Perpetual Adoration of the Blessed Sacrament.' Why is this so? 'Above all,' said Pope Benedict XVI, 'the Eucharist is the great school of love.'. . . .

"Benedict XVI has insisted on this point: 'Eucharistic Adoration is an essential way of being with the Lord. . . . In the Sacred Host, He is present, the true treasure, always waiting for us. Only by adoring in this presence do we learn how to receive him properly. . . . Let us love being with the Lord! There we can speak with Him about everything. We can offer Him our petitions, our concerns, our troubles, our joys. Our gratitude, our disappointments, our needs and our aspirations. . . . ' (Sept. 11, 2006).

"What can we at Notre Dame do to fix a world in cultural meltdown? The greatest event in the history of the world is the Incarnation, when God became man. It's just possible that Christ, the God who became man for us, can give us some answers. Why don't you go ask him? Maybe you don't feel like it. Then pray for the desire to see him. Maybe you have too much to do. As Peter Kreeft put it, 'That's why you can't afford not to give God give loaves and two fishes of your time so that he can multiply it.' In short, we need to go meet with the Boss."

IMMIGRATION: WHO ARE THE ILLEGALS? March 27, 2007

"In 'Operation Return to Sender,' ICE (Immigration and Customs Enforcement) is deporting thousands of illegals, including 1,282 workers arrested in raids at Swift meatpacking plants in six states. Of 424 deported from Miami in January, 131 had criminal convictions. The raids also netted many non-criminal parents of small children.

"Are the raids justified? Yes. And no.

"1. The government has a duty to regain control of its borders and impose reasonable criteria for admission. 'The Church in America,' said Pope John Paul, 'must [defend] against any unjust restriction to the natural right of . . . persons to move freely within their own nation and from one nation to another.' 'Governments,' he said, must 'regulate the migratory flows with full respect for the dignity of the persons and for their families' needs, mindful of the requirements of the host societies.' Nevertheless, '[i]llegal immigration,' said John Paul II, 'should be prevented [and it is] essential to combat . . . criminal activities which exploit illegal immigrants.'

"If a steel fence is the most practical means to secure the border, it ought to be built, for the safety of Border Patrol agents as well as immigrants. Those agents, who confront the heavily armed drug gangs which, according to ICE, are 'ravaging border communities in South Texas,' are persons with dignity equal to that of immigrants.

"2. At least 11 million illegals are in this country. Efforts should focus on deporting those involved in gang or other criminal activities. In 2005, 26,000 were deported under the inadequate 'aggravated felony' standard of federal law.

"Undocumented immigrants who are otherwise law-abiding should not be deported. Many entered legally and overstayed or otherwise became illegal. Many live with minor babies, including 'anchor babies' who are citizens because they meet the Fourteenth Amendment's criterion that 'persons born . . . in the United States' are citizens.

"To expel millions of otherwise law-abiding illegals would be unjust as well as an administrative nightmare. Other considerations are raised by the failure of the government to secure the borders, especially but not exclusively with respect to the Mexican border. For the past two decades, the notorious failure of the government to enforce the border has implicitly invited people to cross it illegally. Enforcement personnel have been undermanned and hampered by the failure of successive Presidents, with Congressional acquiescence or complicity, to provide them with the means to secure the border. That dereliction of duty benefits employers who seek cheap labor with the medical and other needs of the laborers shifted to the taxpayers.

"Every person has a right, in the words of Pope John XXIII, 'to enter a country in which he hopes to provide more fittingly for himself and his dependents.' While that right is subject to restriction, it would be unjust to deport otherwise law-abiding persons who accepted an implied invitation to enter. They are invitees. Congress ought to enable them to regularize their status as residents and perhaps as citizens.

"3. We brought this problem upon ourselves through the refusal of non-Hispanic whites, and to a lesser extent blacks, to reproduce themselves. The United States fertility rate is 2.07. The replacement level is 2.1 at which a population would replenish itself. We are almost there only because of the Hispanics whose rate is 2.9; blacks are at 2.2 and non-Hispanic whites are 1.8. Since 1973, more than 45 million persons who would have been citizens at birth have been killed by surgical abortion, not including the uncountable numbers killed by chemical and other abortifacients. The endemic practice of contraception multiplies the shortage. As University of California Professor Franz Shurman put it, 'America needs the South's babies. . . . American civilization wants sex, but does not want children.'

"4. One cause of this problem is neoliberalism, described by John Paul II

316

as 'a purely economic conception of man [which] considers profit and the law of the market as its only parameters, to the detriment of the dignity of and respect due to individuals and peoples.' In the 1980s, to profit from the devaluation of the Mexican peso, U.S. companies abandoned their U.S. employees and moved assembly plants to maquiladoras in Mexico just south of the border. Many of those later closed as the companies found cheaper labor in Asia. The resulting unemployment and the stagnation of the Mexican economy and government, both totally corrupt, led many to enter the U.S. illegally. Companies in the U.S. employ them as an outsourcing in reverse. You can't outsource a restaurant job to a foreign country. So Presidents, Congressmen and officials send the cheap labor to the employers. This is applied neoliberalism. The real 'illegals' are those politicians and those for whose benefit they betray their oath to enforce the law.

"5. The Church offers guidance here. Archbishop Charles Chaput of Denver said it well in his comment on the ICE raids: 'The Catholic Church respects the law, including immigration law. We respect those . . . who have the difficult job of enforcing it. We do not encourage or help anyone to break the law. . . . Americans have a right to solvent public institutions, secure borders and orderly regulation of immigration. . . . We . . . need . . . reform that will address our economic and security needs, but also regularize the status of the many decent, undocumented immigrants who help our society to grow."

NATURAL LAW: NOT REPEALED, April 24, 2007

"How do we decide whether we are doing right or wrong? Jack Bauer and the '24' counterterrorism unit might say the test is utility, a point that might be disputed by their torturees. Others might ask whether the act makes you feel good.

"There is a better way. Through the natural law, we can know the right and wrong of our own actions and we can set moral limits to the power of the state.

"Everything has a law of its nature, built into it by its maker. A rock will sink. And your Chevy will run if you put gasoline, but not sand, in the tank. When we talk about the natural law, we mean the law inscribed in the nature of human beings by their Maker. The natural law is not a Christian invention. Aristotle and Cicero, the Roman statesman, affirmed it. Saint Thomas Aquinas, however, provided the most comprehensive exposition of it.

"The natural law is a rule of reason by which man (of both sexes) can know how he should act in order to achieve his final end of eternal happiness with God. The 'first and general principle' of that law, as Pope Benedict XVI recently put it, is 'to do good and to avoid evil.' The good is that which is in accord with the nature of the thing we are talking about. It is good to feed your Chevy gasoline.

"As for man, Aquinas said, 'all those things to which man has a natural inclination are naturally apprehended by reason as being good.' From those inclinations we reason to conclusions. From the inclination to preserve oneself, we reason that it is good to eat a balanced diet and not to gorge on Big Macs. We know that theft is wrong because it is inconsistent with the inclination to live in community. From the inclination to unite sexually and raise our offspring, we conclude that sex should be reserved for marriage and marriage should be permanent. And so on. We make these judgments though our conscience, a faculty of our intellect. 'Moral truth is objective,' said Pope John Paul II, 'and a properly formed conscience can perceive it.' However, to declare that theft, etc., is objectively wrong is not to judge the subjective culpability of the person who does it. To be morally culpable, one must know it is wrong and yet choose to do it. We generally have neither the right nor the capacity to judge the subjective culpability of anyone.

"But whose natural law are you going to apply? Supreme Court Justice James Iredell, in 1798, rejected natural law because 'the ideas of natural justice are regulated by no fixed standard: the ablest and the purest men have differed upon the subject.'

"People may sincerely disagree, as they have on slavery, abortion, etc. But they can't both be right. 'If . . . we consider one action in the moral order,' said Aquinas, 'it is impossible for it to be both good and evil.'

"Our intellects are weakened by original sin. But the Lawgiver of the natural law came to the rescue of wounded human nature by giving us the Commandments, which are specifications of that law, so we would have sure guidance. And Christ, who is God and the Lawgiver, founded one Church, headed by his Vicar who is the authoritative interpreter of the natural law and the Commandments. The Magisterium, or teaching authority, of the Church is possessed by the Pope and the bishops in union with him. 'Christians,' said John Paul II, 'have a great help for the formation of conscience in the Church and her Magisterium. . . . The Church puts herself . . . . at the service of conscience . . . helping it not to swerve from the truth about the good of man.'

"Everyone has a pope, a visible authority on moral questions. If it is not the real Pope, it will be a pope of the individual's own choosing—whether Bill Clinton, Sean Hannity or the individual himself. It makes sense that we have one Pope rather than seven billion, which would involve the natural law and its Lawgiver in a chaos of contradictions.

"The natural law is a standard for human law as well as for personal conduct. Martin Luther King echoed Aquinas when he said that 'an unjust law is a human law that is not rooted in eternal law and natural law.' As Aquinas put

318

it, if a human law 'deflects from the law of nature,' it is unjust and 'is no longer a law but a perversion of law.' Rosa Parks affirmed the natural law when she refused to give up her seat on the bus in Montgomery in 1955. A law mandating racial segregation is unjust and void. Aquinas said that we may be obliged to obey an unjust law 'to avoid scandal or disturbance,' but that a law that is unjust because it would compel one to violate the divine law must never be obeyed.

"The alternative to natural law is some form of legal positivism, which is based on the idea, as Hans Kelsen put it, that 'justice is an irrational ideal.' If we cannot affirm any knowable, objective norms of justice, we cannot define any moral limits to what the state can do. '[I]f there is no ultimate truth to guide and direct political activity,' said John Paul, 'then ideas and convictions can easily be manipulated for reasons of power.' We all know that by experience.

"The natural law has not been repealed. Think about it. Even Jack Bauer might find it of interest."

NATURAL LAW AND SLAVERY, LETTER TO THE EDITOR, April 30, 2007

"In response to my column on the natural law and the Magisterium of the Church (April 24), Professor Christian Moevs claims that 'until 1888' the popes were 'condoning slavery' ('Natural law proves fallible,' April 25). Normally, a reader who comments on a column should have the last word. But the Moevs comment is inexcusably simplistic and misleading.

"Slavery antedated the Church by centuries. The Latin *servitus* can mean either 'slave' or 'servant.' It embraced servitude by 'just title,' as in punishment for crime or by voluntary contract, as well as the unjust servitude which we know as slavery. The 1866 Holy Office document to which Moevs apparently refers, recognized that distinction—a point which Moevs fails to mention. In 1866, the Pope over the Holy Office was Pius IX who, in beatifying Peter Claver in 1850 for his work among slaves, had called slavery 'supreme wickedness.'

"For more information I suggest Rev. Joel Panzer's book, *The Popes and Slavery* (Alba House, 1996). Panzer analyzes 12 explicit papal condemnations of slavery, dating from the 1400s when the modern age of slavery arose. Prior to the Civil War, some American bishops taught that, although trading in slaves was immoral, owning slaves was not. Panzer demonstrates that this erroneous teaching contradicted the teaching of the popes. The fact that some bishops fail to do their duty should not surprise us today.

"The teaching authority of the Church, exercised by the Pope and the bishops in union with him, has been consistently right on slavery as it has been on contraception, homosexual activity, economic injustice and other issues that bother today's cafeteria Catholics."

2007–2008

WHY CAN'T NOTRE DAME BE LIKE PRINCETON?
August 29, 2007

"Do you wonder how you are going to pay those student loans? Two University announcements last spring might give you heartburn. Or encouragement.

"First, undergrad tuition, room and board (TRB) will increase 5.4 percent for 2007–2008, up nearly $2,500 from 2006–2007. The TRB for 2007–2008 is $44,477, including $35,187 for tuition and $9,290 for average room-and-board. In 1978 when Notre Dame first described itself as 'A National Catholic Research University,' TRB was $5,180. If the rise in that 1978 TRB had kept pace with the rise in the Consumer Price Index (CPI), the 2007–2008 TRB would be $16,368. The rise beyond the CPI is partly due to factors beyond University control. The main reason, however, is Notre Dame's drive for acceptance as a Great Research University. The traditional focus of Notre Dame had been on undergrad education, with research and grad studies playing an important but balanced role. The drive for Research Greatness involves reduced teaching loads for faculty, more grad students as teachers and other effects including the paving and building mania that has converted the formerly pastoral Notre Dame into an imitation urban campus.

"Like other universities, Notre Dame has financed its research ambition by raising tuition. Its budget, as a former Provost observed, is 'tuition driven.' Notre Dame's excellent Office of Financial Aid does an admirable job of distributing aid to students who could not attend Notre Dame without it. Unfortunately, loans are an integral part of the typical aid package. Heavy loan burdens can distort the career and family choices of Notre Dame grads.

"Which brings us to the second announcement. In May, the University announced the largest fund-raising program in the history of Catholic higher education. The Spirit of Notre Dame campaign seeks $1.5 billion, of which $887 million had been raised at the time of the announcement.

"The campaign allots $250 million for undergrad scholarships and $40 million for graduate fellowships. 'We would like,' said Vice President John Affleck-Graves, 'to move every student who is on one loan to no loan, and every student who's on two loans to one loan. The worst case for a student in need at Notre Dame at the moment is a two-loan package.'

"About two dozen major universities have moved to replace loans with university grants for low-income students. Princeton University, however, in 2001 expanded its 'no loan' policy beyond low-income students to all students entitled to aid. Princeton's tuition of $33,000 did not increase for 2007–2008 although room-and-board did increase. Princeton's TRB is $43,980—less than Notre Dame's.

"Princeton's total 'no loan' program belongs at Notre Dame. No Princeton student is required to take a loan as part of his or her aid package. The amount a student normally would borrow is replaced with an increase in the Princeton grant. The full need of every undergrad is met through Princeton grants, scholarships from external sources and a campus job. In 2006–2007, 52% of all undergrads received financial aid, with an average aid package of $30,750, including $2,200 in campus jobs. The total scholarship budget is $71.9 million. About $52 million comes from endowed scholarship funds and the rest through annual giving and other current-use support. Students can borrow for personal needs. The median family income of students receiving financial aid is $90,400.

"Compared to the national average of $20,000 of debt for graduating seniors, Princeton grads have an average total debt of $2,360. Two-thirds of the class of 2005, the first to enroll under the no-loan policy, reported that graduating with little or no debt 'had a significant impact' on their ability to pursue further studies and seek teaching or other service-oriented jobs. 'Since I have no debt,' said one grad teaching in a high school, 'I have time to make wise decisions about my future after Princeton and to pursue my true interests. I probably would not have chosen to become an educator if I was burdened with loans.'

"A Catholic university is uniquely obliged to free its grads from onerous debt. The only middle-class students now at Notre Dame tend to be ROTC students, scholarship athletes, faculty and staff children, recipients of academic or special scholarships and those who are willing to come to Notre Dame at the price of crippling debt. Princeton has about 5,000 undergrads with an endowment of $13 billion compared to about $3 billion for Notre Dame. To emulate the Princeton plan here would be a daunting task. But it is difficult to imagine that Notre Dame alumni would not respond abundantly to a commitment, as part of the Spirit of Notre Dame campaign, to adopt the Princeton no-loan program. Notre Dame grads should be a leaven in society. Notre Dame should not consign them to life as loan serfs to the government or to Sallie Mae or other private lenders whose interest rates can approach the confiscatory. This is one case where we ought to imitate the Ivy League."

A CIVILIZATION IN DECLINE? Sept. 12, 2007

"Can we tell when a civilization is in decline? Consider two recent events.

"Leona Helmsley, the New York real estate developer known in the tabloids as 'The Queen of Mean,' left a 12 million dollar trust fund for the care and feeding of Trouble, her Maltese terrier. She gave nothing to two of her grandchildren, but she did leave her chauffer $100,000. As John Gapper commented in the *Financial Times*, Trouble is in the same league as 'Incitatus, Caligula's horse, which slept in a marble stable and was fed oats mixed with gold flakes.' Caligula wanted to make Incitatus a consul of Rome. 'Perhaps,' said Gapper, noting a parallel between ancient Rome and today's America, 'the rich and powerful treating animals as if they were humans is a symptom of the decadent last days of empire.'

"Compared with Trouble, the unborn child is really in trouble. Last April, in *Gonzales v. Carhart*, the Supreme Court upheld the federal Partial-Birth Abortion Ban Act of 2003. Justice Anthony Kennedy wrote the majority opinion, joined by Chief Justice John Roberts and Justices Antonin Scalia, Clarence Thomas and Samuel Alito. Partial-birth abortion is used in the second trimester or later. As described in the Act, the partial-birth abortionist 'delivers a living fetus until, in the case of a head-first presentation, the entire fetal head is outside the body of the mother, or, in the case of breech presentation, any part of the fetal trunk past the navel is outside the body of the mother, for the purpose of performing an overt act that the person knows will kill the partially delivered living fetus; and . . . performs the overt act, other than completion of delivery, that kills the partially delivered fetus.'

"The *Gonzales* ruling upholds a prohibition of only one method of executing an unborn child. It will not stop a single abortion. Abortionists easily avoid the Act by killing the child inside the womb by a lethal injection.

"The Kennedy opinion portrayed the homicidal reality of partial-birth abortion in such graphic terms that none of the Justices could possibly have had any doubt about the humanity of the victim. Yet they all agree that the unborn child is a nonperson and therefore has no right to life.

"The Fourteenth Amendment protects the right of a 'person' to life and to the equal protection of the laws. In *Roe v. Wade*, the Court stated that if the personhood of the unborn child were established, the pro-abortion case 'collapses.' The *Roe* Court held, however, that 'the word "person," as used in the Fourteenth Amendment, does not include the unborn,' whether or not that unborn child is a human being. *Roe* is therefore the same as a ruling that an acknowledged human being is a non-person. The principle that an innocent human being can be defined as a non-person and deprived of the right to life is the principle that underlay the Nazi extermination of the Jews and the 1857 *Dred Scott* case in which the Court said that slaves were property rather than persons.

"Every Justice now on the Court accepts the *Roe* holding that the unborn child is a nonperson. Even the 'pro-life' Justices, Thomas and Scalia, agree that, in Scalia's words, 'The states may, if they wish, permit abortion-on-demand, but the Constitution does not require them to do so.' That position confirms that, as far as the U.S. Constitution is concerned, the unborn child is a nonperson. If an innocent human being can be subjected to death at the discretion of another whenever a state legislature so decides, he is a nonperson in the eyes of both state law and that Constitution.

"If the unborn child can be treated as a nonperson so can anyone else. The law is an educator. The highest Court proclaims the constitutional legitimacy of the intentional infliction of death on the innocent as an optional problem-solving technique. It does so with respect to the youngest. Why are we surprised when it is applied to others, as in Columbine, Virginia Tech, Terri Schiavo's case, etc.?

"In 1974, Cardinals Krol, Manning, Cody and Medeiros insisted before a Senate committee that a constitutional amendment 'should clearly establish that, from conception onward, the unborn child is a human person in the terms of the Constitution. . . . Protection of human life should not depend upon geographical boundaries.' The Cardinals had it right. A pro-life position should insist not only on effective prohibitions of abortion but also on the treatment of all innocent human beings as persons entitled to the right to life.

"The object is to restore among the American people the conviction that life is inviolable because it is a gift from God. A civilization might survive the pampering of a horse or a dog by people with more money than brains, but it cannot survive the systematic depersonalization of its own innocent human beings."

CHRISTIANS IN IRAQ, Sept. 26, 2007

"The Assyrians have lived in Iraq since 5,000 B.C. Ethnically distinct from Arabs and Kurds, they are Christians and speak neo-Aramaic, similar to the language of Christ. They include Chaldean Catholic, Apostolic Catholic and Syriac Orthodox churches.

"'In Iraq,' Chaldean Archbishop Louis Sako, of Kirkuk, said last April, 'Christians are dying, the Church is disappearing under . . . persecution, threats and violence . . . by extremists who are leaving us no choice: conversion or exile.'

"Last June, the Assyrian International News Agency (AINA) issued a report, 'Incipient Genocide: The Ethnic Cleansing of Assyrians in Iraq.' In 2003, Christians and smaller non-Muslim groups were about one million of Iraq's 26 million people. Probably 50 percent have now fled the country. Persecution began after the Gulf War and escalated after the fall of Baghdad in 2003. AINA reported that from 1995 to 2002 there were 19 murders of Assyrians in Iraq, with none in 1996, 2000, and 2001. From 2003 to June 2007 there were 370. Assyrians and other Christians have been attacked by Sunnis, Shiites, Kurds and al-Qaeda in every part of Iraq. The Assyrians, with no tribal structure, military or militia, are defenseless. Since the coming of Islam in 630 A.D., noted AINA, Assyrians have suffered thirty 'genocides at the hands of the Muslims,' several in the 20th century. They experienced comparative safety and tolerance under the oppressive but secular regime of Saddam Hussein.

"Since the fall of Saddam, the persecution has intensified, with the added motive that many Iraqi Christians who speak English have worked for Americans. The AINA study, however, confirms that the persecution is primarily religious. Last October, for instance, Ayad Tariq, a 14-year-old Assyrian in Baquba, was accosted at his place of employment by insurgents who asked if he was a 'Christian sinner.' 'Yes,' he replied, I am a Christian, but I am not a sinner.' The insurgents quickly pronounced him a 'dirty Christian sinner' and, shouting 'Allahu akbar!' beheaded him. Also last October, Father Paulos Iksander was kidnapped in Mosul. His head, arms and legs were severed from his body.

"AINA graphically described many attacks since 2003, which we can only summarize here. Five priests have been kidnapped and released after ransom was paid. 33 churches have been attacked or bombed since June 2004. At least 13 young women have been abducted or raped, causing some of them to commit suicide. Female students have been targeted in Basra and Mosul for not wearing veils; some had nitric acid squirted on their faces. Elders of a village in Mosul were warned not to send females to universities. The Mahdi Army circulated a letter warning all Christian women to veil themselves. Al-Qaeda moved into an Assyrian neighborhood and began collecting the jizya tax and demanding that females be sent to the mosque to be married off to Muslims. Assyrian businesses have been targeted, especially stores selling alcohol, radios, TVs and music. On the night of Sept. 7, 2005, a fire, with arson suspected, destroyed or damaged more than 500 Assyrian shops in Dora. The fire trucks did not arrive for hours. The owners had to watch from their homes. If they violated curfew, they would be shot. Property of Christians has been confiscated by Kurds and Shiites. The Kurds blocked foreign aid for Assyrian communities and diverted water and other resources from Assyrians to Kurds. Kurdish forces blockaded Assyrian villages. Children have been kidnapped and transferred to Kurdish families.

"The Assyrians and their supporters urge, in the words of Doctor Nina Shea of the Center for Religious Freedom, the 'establishment of a new autonomous district,' in the Nineveh Plains 'that would be jointly governed' by Assyrians and smaller religious groups. Unfortunately, as Shea stated on Aug. 27, 2007, 'there has been no progress' on creating 'a Nineveh province' and 'U.S. policy . . . runs counter to the initiative. When asked about such a haven, the State Department's

Iraq policy coordinator, David Satterfield, told me that it is 'against U.S. policy to further sectarianism.' The administration has not even brought together . . . leaders of Iraq's non-Muslim minorities to discuss solutions.'

"Meanwhile the mayhem continues. Father Ragheed Ganni and three deacons were assassinated by gunmen as they drove from a church in Mosul after Mass on June 3, 2007. Their car was booby-trapped by the gunmen to prevent retrieval of the bodies. On June 19, at a Mass for Father Ganni and the deacons in Southfield, Michigan, Chaldean Catholic Bishop Ibrahim N. Ibrahim called for the withdrawal of U.S. troops from Iraq. Bishop Ibrahim has a point. One result of the Iraq War has been to expose the Assyrians and other Christians to genocidal repression by all the major Muslim groups who appear to be of one mind on this. But the U.S. should not leave Iraq without ensuring the safety of those minorities in their homeland.

"Bishop Ibrahim is entitled to make his point, because in December, 2002, he warned the United States against 'going to war, which will be a disaster for the whole region, not only for the Iraqi people.' Nor was he the only Chaldean prelate to do so. On Jan. 9, 2003, Chaldean Bishop Shlemon Warduni of Baghdad warned that 'the war threatens our children, our elderly, our sick, and our young.' We can now add to that list the Christians who are about to disappear from Iraq. As Shea put it, 'The very existence of these non-Muslims within Iraq may soon be extinguished under pervasive persecution that the U.N. High Commissioner on Refugees says is targeted against them due to religion.' President Bush should have listened to the Chaldeans."

WHO DECIDES ON WAR? Oct. 10, 2007

"What constitutional and moral issues could arise if President Bush orders an attack on Iran? General David Petraeus' report to Congress concluded that 'Iran plays a harmful role in Iraq . . . by providing lethal capabilities to the enemies of the Iraqi state.' President Bush has increased American naval and air forces in the region. It would be no surprise if he ordered an attack on Iran, not only to prevent Iranian aid to Iraq's insurgents, but also to prevent Iran from acquiring nuclear weapons in a more remote future. Such an attack would be primarily a Presidential, rather than a Congressional, initiative.

"The Constitutional Convention, on Aug. 17, 1787, gave Congress power to 'declare' rather than 'make' war and left 'to the Executive the power to repel sudden attacks.' 'The Executive,' said delegate Roger Sherman, '[should] be able to repel and not to commence war.' The result was what former Supreme Court Justice Robert Jackson called a 'twilight zone' of concurrent powers of Congress and the president.

"Even in 1787, the formal declaration of war was becoming outmoded. Congress has declared war only five times. The president has put forces into combat more than 200 times, almost always with prior or later Congressional approval. But no president has admitted that he must have such approval. The courts would probably stay out of a controversy between the President and Congress on this issue, treating it as a nonjusticiable political question.

"According to the Constitution, therefore, Congress decides whether to go to war. The president, as 'Commander in Chief of the Army and Navy of the United States,' decides how to fight the war. Congress has no power to tell the president how to fight a war. Congress could, of course, refuse to appropriate funds for the war; a two-thirds vote would be needed in each house to override a presidential veto of such a refusal. Or the House could impeach the president, but a two-thirds vote in the Senate would be required to convict and remove him from office.

"Congress, in its response to 9/11 and in 2002 on Iraq, surrendered to the President its power to decide whether to go to war. It gave the President a free pass to use military force 'as he determines to be necessary and appropriate.' An attack on Iran would be covered by that blank check if the President, in his discretion, judges that attack to be necessary to accomplish the mission in Iraq. Thus, in his Aug. 20 address to the American Legion, President Bush said, 'I have authorized our . . . commanders to confront Tehran's murderous activities. . . . We've conducted operations against Iranian agents supplying lethal munitions to extremist groups.' In accord with that presidential authority, the bills introduced by Congressman Walter Jones (R-NC), Senator James Webb (D-VA) and others to require Congressional approval for an attack on Iran properly make exceptions to that requirement for an actual or imminent attack by Iran, hot pursuit of combatants into Iran and intelligence gathering activities in Iran.

"A different issue would arise if the attack on Iran were alleged to be necessary to forestall Iran's development of nuclear weapons in the comparatively remote future. That would involve 'the dreadful alternative' posed by French Foreign Minister Bernard Kouchner on Sept. 20, 'the Iranian bomb or the bombing of Iran.' Such an attack to prevent 'the Iranian bomb' could fairly be regarded, not as a proximate incident of the war in Iraq, but as a new war. The constitutional reservation, in principle, to Congress of the decision whether to go to war could raise not only a constitutional issue, but also a moral one as to whether such an attack on Iran would satisfy two requirements of the just-war doctrine—that the war be waged by proper governmental authority and that it be 'the last recourse,' as Pope John Paul II put it, 'after having exhausted every other peaceful solution.'

"The citizen, lacking the necessary information, is obliged to give a strong benefit of the doubt to Congress and the executive, as to whether a war is both lawful and just. But at some point, if the attack on Iran were clearly a new war rather than a necessary incident of the Iraq war, and if that attack were clearly a Presidential rather than a Congressional initiative, a reasonable person could regard that attack as unjust because not initiated by the proper authority and perhaps also because not initiated only as a last resort.

"Congress in 2002 had the duty to examine the reasons alleged for the war on Iraq and to make the decision itself. Instead, it surrendered to the president its most awesome responsibility: to decide whether the U.S. shall go to war. To be sure, Congress has ratified the Iraq war by appropriations and otherwise. But that ratification does not excuse the failure of Congress to decide the issue of war in the first place. Nor would it justify a repeat abdication by the conferral on the president of a blank check for a new war on Iran. In any event, having given the president a blank check to decide on war with Iraq, Congress will find it difficult, if not impossible, to resist the expansion of that authorization beyond Iraq and to reclaim its rightful power in this case.

"The framers gave us a republic, not a monarchy. They did well in reserving the decision on war to the elected representatives of those who would fight it. Congress owes it to the members of the volunteer armed forces, the best among us, and to the American people, to reclaim its role through hearings and other processes by which Congress itself would make the decision as to whether an attack on Iran would be a new war and, if so, whether the U.S. should wage it. As Elbridge Gerry said in the Constitutional Convention, he 'never expected to hear in a republic a motion to empower the Executive alone to declare war.'"

STUDENT LOAN FORGIVENESS, Oct. 31, 2007

"Borrowing students ought to note the College Cost Reduction and Access Act, signed into law on Sept. 27. Georgetown Law Professor Philip Schrag analyzes the Act in the Fall 2007 *Hofstra Law Review.* . . .

"'Congress,' notes Professor Schrag, 'significantly reduced the period (10 years rather than 25) after which public servants' educational loans were partly forgiven. It also reduced monthly payments for all high debt/ low income borrowers . . . with a new 'income based' repayment (IBR) program.'

"Borrowers with eligible Federal Direct Loans will have the unpaid balance of principal and interest forgiven after they have made 120 monthly payments after Oct. 1, 2007, provided that all of those payments have been made while the borrower was employed in a 'public service job.' Employment in such a job does not have to be for 10 consecutive years nor does it have to be with the same employer. But the borrower has to be so employed at the time the loan is forgiven. A public service job is defined as:

"'A full-time job in emergency management, government, military service, public safety, law enforcement, public health, public education (including early childhood education), social work in a public child or family service agency, public interest law services (including prosecution or public defense or legal advocacy in low-income communities at a nonprofit organization), public child care, public service for individuals with disabilities, public service for the elderly, public library sciences, school-based library sciences and other school-based services, or at an organization that is described in section 501(c)(3) of the Internal Revenue Code of 1986 and exempt from taxation under 501(a) of such Code: or

"'Teaching as a full-time faculty member at a Tribal College or University as defined in section 316(b) and other faculty teaching in high-needs area, as determined by the Secretary.'

"'The Act defines an 'eligible Federal Direct Loan' as '[a] Federal Direct Stafford Loan, Federal Direct PLUS Loan, or Federal Direct Unsubsidized Stafford Loan, or a Federal Direct Consolidation Loan.'

"A borrower with government-guaranteed loans that are not federal direct loans may consolidate such loans into a Federal Direct Consolidation Loan that qualifies for the loan forgiveness program. A federal 'direct' loan is made by the U.S. Department of Education as the lender. Loans that are not already guaranteed by the federal government are not eligible for consolidation and eligibility for loan forgiveness.

"Effective in July 2009, borrowers of most government-guaranteed loans, including Stafford and Grad PLUS loans, can reduce their monthly payments of principal and interest if they qualify, by reason of 'partial financial hardship,' for the new 'income-based repayment' option.

"Professor Schrag recommends that borrowers consolidate non-qualifying government-guaranteed loans into federal direct loans and then reduce their monthly payments by using the current income-contingent repayment plan and, when it becomes available in July 2009, the income-based repayment plan if they qualify for it. According to Schrag, a borrower who has $100,000 in college loans and who works in a 'public service job' with a starting salary of $40,000 and annual salary increases of 3 percent could have more than $125,000 in principal and interest forgiven under the combined programs at the end of 10 years of public service.

"The Act will benefit some student borrowers. It remains true, however, that whenever you see a problem that cries out for a government solution you should look for the government program that caused the problem in the first place. As Professor Gary Wolfram concluded in his Cato Institute study in 2005, 'both theoretical analysis and empirical evidence indicate that the federal government's financial aid programs cause higher tuition costs.' That conclusion applies to the research universities, including Notre Dame, which have financed their quest for research greatness on the backs of students who could pay the rising tuition only by borrowing. Student borrowing has about reached its realistic limit. The new Act offers an out through the IBR reduction of payments for high debt/low income borrowers and through loan forgiveness for grads who spend 10 years in a 'public service job.'

"The Act, however, also gives to the striving research universities an enhanced ability to raise tuition. Those who can afford to pay that tuition will do so. Non-wealthy students can borrow and now they can use the Act to pass much of that cost on to the taxpayers.

"Notre Dame makes commendable efforts to reduce borrowing by students. . . . Neither such University efforts nor the new Act, however, lessen the urgency of Notre Dame's adoption of the Princeton no-loan program, in which all students who would otherwise have to borrow have their needs met by University grants. Notre Dame ought to set an example of using its own resources to remove the crippling debt burden from its students. Nor should Notre Dame exploit the new Act by further raising tuition and using the new Act to pass the costs of research greatness on to the taxpayers."

CATHOLIC FACULTY AND THE MISSION, Nov. 14, 2007

"'The Catholic identity of the University,' says the Notre Dame Mission Statement, 'depends upon . . . the . . . presence of a predominant number of Catholic intellectuals.' *Ex Corde Ecclesiae* (ECE), the 1990 apostolic constitution on Catholic universities, requires more explicitly that 'the number of non-Catholic teachers should not be allowed to constitute a majority within the institution.' Notre Dame's pursuit of recognition as an elite research university has coincided with a severe drop in the percent of faculty who identify themselves as Catholic. Retirements and other factors portend an irreversible decline, far below 50 percent. That can be averted, as the Project Sycamore analysis shows, only by an immediate change to the hiring each year of a strong majority of Catholics. . . .

"It will be useful to reflect on the Oct. 11 address, 'Catholic Colleges and Universities Today,' by Cardinal Avery Dulles at Assumption College.

"A convert and the son of John Foster Dulles, President Eisenhower's Secretary of State, the Cardinal has rendered distinguished service to Catholic higher education. Using as his 'primary guides' ECE and Cardinal John Henry Newman's *The Idea of a University*, Cardinal Dulles addresses bluntly the hiring of Catholic faculty. He does so in the context of culture and the relation of the university to the Church and its magisterium or teaching authority. A 'Catholic institution,' he said, 'must be founded on three principles: that there is a God, that he has made a full and final revelation of himself in Jesus Christ and that the Catholic Church is the authorized custodian and teacher of this body of revealed truth.'

"The Cardinal proposed 'that all disciplines involving human values should be taught at a Catholic institution with due attention to their religious implications.' 'Graduates,' he said, 'should not go forth with an advanced education in literature and science, while remaining at grade school level in their knowledge of religion,' including 'the interplay between faith and reason.' He reminds us that '[w]e live in a consumerist society, in which colleges tend to shape their policies according to the demands of the market, as though the measure of success were to construct more buildings and increase student enrollment . . . Our colleges and universities must . . . guard against being coopted into this culture, which is . . . anti-Christian and dehumanizing.'

"The cardinal's remarks are relevant to Notre Dame in his treatment of religious diversity and the marginalization of religion by the academic establishment. He questioned the pursuit of diversity as a goal in itself: 'Postmodern students . . . imagine that change and diversity are desirable for their own sakes. . . . [S]tudents should be educated for the world of today [and] a variety of cultures may be a source of enrichment. But for nations to live together in peace and friendship, they must share common convictions regarding . . . the basic norms of morality.'

"'Religious diversity,' he said, 'is not desirable in itself. It appeals chiefly to those who believe there is no truth in religion anyway. If we believe that God is one, and that Jesus is his incarnate Son, we will hope that all peoples, with their different voices and idioms, may someday unite in praising him. To make this goal persuasive in the contemporary atmosphere of subjectivism and relativism is a serious challenge. Still another challenge comes from the academic establishment in America today. In secular circles there is a virtual consensus that no courses ought to be taught from a distinctive religious point of view. Faith is generally held to have no place in the classroom, at least on the level of higher education. If this only means that the faith should not be imposed in the classroom, we can agree. But if it means that professors should not manifest their religious beliefs or seek to defend them, the objection is unsound.'

"Cardinal Dulles went on to relate the hiring of all faculty to mission without limitation to percentages. 'A Catholic institution,' he said, 'has to be clear about its mission. An essential step . . . is that faculty be hired for mission. If the teachers are hostile to the mission of the college or indifferent about it, the college will suffer. It does not suffice to hire faculty who are nominally Catholic. If teachers are angry with the Church or unsympathetic toward her doctrines, no changes in the curriculum will succeed in making the institution truly Catholic.'

"The Cardinal stressed that the Catholic university 'participates . . . in the mission of the universal Church,' and that the teaching authority of the Church should be welcomed: 'Cardinal Newman . . . points out the advantages that the guidance of the magisterium gives for the . . . university itself. Just as we turn to professors to teach us disciplines in which they are expert, so we turn to the . . . Church to give secure guidance in matters of religion. For it is to the Church that God has entrusted the deposit of faith . . . for answering important questions that . . . arise in the human heart. . . . Without the helping hand of the Church, Newman contends, the human mind gravitates toward infidelity. . . . The Catholic . . . university . . . should gratefully acknowledge the mercy of God who has provided an institution that has for two thousand years kept the Christian revelation complete and unsullied. Whatever the latest theories of professors or the inclination of students may be, the college should not forsake its Catholic allegiance. While offering its students a vast panoply of skills and learning, it gathers up the fragments of knowledge under the luminous aegis of Christian faith, proclaimed today as always by the successor of Peter and the bishops in union with him.'

"Meeting the challenges facing a Catholic university, Cardinal Dulles said, 'cannot be the task of the president alone. He must have backing from the trustees and cooperation from the faculty and administration.' The Notre Dame administration and the ad hoc committee seek to build such cooperation. The proportion of Catholic faculty at Notre Dame is declining, however, not because suitable candidates cannot be found, but because of the obstacle course any seriously Catholic candidate faces in obtaining departmental approval.

"The University mission is subordinated to the contrary will of component departments. The Academic Articles, however, vest the power to appoint faculty in the president himself. The existing processes will produce only marginal and fruitless tinkering. The president has power, in effect, to govern by veto. In support of the mission, he ought to use that power."

THE REALITY OF CHRISTMAS, Nov. 28, 2007

"A 1659 law of the Massachusetts Bay Colony levied a fine of five shillings on '[w]hosoever shall be found observing any such day as Christmas.' Christmas, to them, was a 'popish' frivolity at best.

"We don't fine people anymore for celebrating Christmas, a legal holiday. But local governments can go to curious lengths to purge the observance of winter holidays, Winter Solstice, or whatever, of any recognition of the Christmas reality that gave rise to the 'holidays' in the first place. This year, in

Fort Collins, Colo., a 'Holiday Display Task Force' recommended using white lights instead of red and green ones. The objective was to recognize the diversity of 'a variety of winter holidays, such as Christmas, Hanukkah, Diwali, Birth of Baha'u'llah, Bhodi Day, the Winter Solstice, Kwanzaa and more.'

"'Throughout history,' the task force said, 'the most common theme of winter celebration is light at a time of darkness.' The 'holiday displays' can include 'Symbols of Winter: snowflakes, snowmen, snow balls, ice skates, skis, penguins, polar bears, white lights, etc.' Christmas was singled out for special depreciation by the exclusion of red and green lights which could remind people of something. Presumably, that exclusion would not apply to traffic signals. On Nov. 20, sanity prevailed. The City Council rejected the proposal.

"Such controversies over Christmas reflect changes in the posture of government toward religion dictated by Supreme Court decisions which lack coherence as well as fidelity to the meaning of the Constitution. Those decisions affect the culture.

"In 1984, in *Lynch v. Donnelly*, the Court upheld the inclusion of a nativity crèche in a Pawtucket municipal display because the display also included 'A Santa Claus house, reindeer pulling Santa's sleigh, candy-striped poles, a Christmas tree, carolers, cutout figures [of] a clown, an elephant, and a teddy bear, hundreds of colored lights [and] a large banner that reads 'Seasons Greetings." The purpose of the display, said the Court, was not to endorse religion, but to promote shopping. This has come to be known as the 'Three Plastic Animals Rule.' As Justice Harry Blackmun accurately said, it reduces the crèche 'to the role of a neutral harbinger of the holiday season, useful for commercial purposes, but devoid of any inherent meaning.' Five years later, in *County of Allegheny v. ACLU*, the Court held that a crèche standing by itself on a courthouse staircase, with a sign saying the crèche was donated by the Holy Name Society, was an unconstitutional endorsement of religion. The Court found no such endorsement in the placement of a Hanukkah menorah, a Christmas tree and a 'salute to liberty' sign outside the building.

"It is difficult to see any objective and predictable principle in such rulings. But what neutrality toward religion was the Constitution intended to require?

"The Establishment Clause of the First Amendment forbade Congress both to create an official, established church for the nation and to interfere with the established churches that existed in six states, the last of which ended in 1833. The Clause required neutrality among religious denominations. We lack the space to explain here the process by which the Court has wrongly interpreted the Clause to require governmental neutrality, not among denominations, but between theism and non-theism.

"As Justice William Brennan put it, the words 'under God' can remain in the pledge of allegiance only because those words 'may merely recognize the historical fact that our Nation was believed to have been founded 'under God." Under the Court's theory, a statement by a public official that the four affirmations of God in the Declaration of Independence are in fact true would be an unconstitutional preference of theism.

"This suspension of judgment on the existence of God implicitly establishes an agnostic secularism as the official religion. Government cannot affirm Christmas as a fact because, according to the Court, it cannot affirm even the existence of God as a fact. That would have surprised the members of the First Congress. On Sept. 24–25, 1789, they approved the First Amendment and directed President Washington to declare a day of 'public thanksgiving and prayer . . . acknowledging the . . . favors of Almighty God.' Washington did so, stating that 'it is the duty of all Nations to acknowledge the providence of Almighty God, to obey his will, to be grateful for his benefits, and humbly to implore his protection and favor.'

"We have come a long way since 1789. But not even the Supreme Court can change the reality of Christmas. As Cardinal Ratzinger agreed, before he became Pope Benedict XVI, the Christmas event 'is infinitely more important than the creation of the world.' 'The birth of Christ,' he said, 'is an event of a far greater order of significance. God himself comes into the world and becomes a man.'

"The trend today, he said, is 'to separate this festival from Christianity and to reject its Christian beginnings. . . . In America, . . . in commercialization and . . . sentimentality, the display windows of large shops, which in former years were decorated with crèches . . . are now equipped with mythical representations, with deer and stags and Santa Clauses, whereby what is truly mythical is set side-by-side with what is Christian. Of course a lingering echo still remains of what touched people when they learned that God became a man. But this is an attempt to keep what is beautiful and touching and to get away from anything that makes demands upon us.'

"And Christ does make 'demands upon us.' The birth of Christ, unlike that of, say, Aristotle or Jeremy Bentham, is controversial because, unlike all others, Christ makes a continuing claim, in the words of Monsignor Luigi Guissani, the founder of Communion and Liberation, to 'absolute importance in our lives. . . . If an individual rejects this . . . then a fundamental aversion sets in.' The continued and focused opposition to public recognition of Christmas is a back-handed recognition of its unique reality and significance.

"Benedict XVI recently reminded a conference on the future of Europe that '[a] community that is built . . . without remembering that every person is created in the image and likeness of God, ends by doing no one any good.' Christmas recalls us to that reality. If we pay attention. Merry Christmas."

334

ABORTION FROM CONTRACEPTION, Jan. 23, 2008

"Would you call it an exercise in futility? On Jan. 22, Notre Dame and Saint Mary's students joined the annual March for Life in Washington, D.C., calling for reversal of *Roe v. Wade*, the Supreme Court ruling on that date in 1973 which mandated, in effect, elective abortion at every stage in pregnancy. The Court defined the unborn child as a nonperson who is therefore not entitled to the right to life guaranteed by the Constitution to persons.

"The Supreme Court will not reverse that holding of *Roe*. Even the Justices who say that *Roe* should be 'overruled' define that as a 'states' rights' approach that would allow the states to permit or forbid abortion. That would affirm the holding of *Roe*. If your life is subject to extinction whenever a state legislature so decrees, then, so far as the United States Constitution is concerned, you are a nonperson.

"Depersonalization is the theory of the Nazis' treatment of the Jews and of the Supreme Court's 1857 *Dred Scott* case in which the Court held that freed slaves could not be citizens and said that slaves were property rather than persons.

"Abortion . . . is embedded in American culture. The Alan Guttmacher Institute reports that from 1973 to 2005, more than 45 million surgical abortions occurred in the United States, with 1.21 million in 2005, down from 1.31 in 2000. Twenty-two percent of all pregnancies in the United States end in abortion. These figures do not include the uncountable number of early abortions by abortifacients, including most 'contraceptive' pills.

"Abortion is a symptom of what Pope Benedict XVI called 'a dictatorship of relativism . . . that recognizes nothing as absolute and which only leaves the "I" and its whims as the ultimate measure.' The secularism, relativism and individualism of that culture affect the most fundamental human activity, the generation of life.

"Abortion is a product of the contraceptive ethic. '[D]espite their differences,' said John Paul II, 'contraception and abortion are often closely connected, as fruits of the same tree . . . rooted in a hedonistic mentality unwilling to accept responsibility in matters of sexuality, and . . . a self-centered concept of freedom, which regards procreation as an obstacle to personal fulfillment.'

"Until the Anglican Lambeth Conference of 1930, no Christian denomination had ever said that contraception could ever be objectively right. Contraception deliberately separates sex from procreation. It affirms that there is such a thing as a life not worth living, and that man (of both sexes), rather than God, is the arbiter of whether and when human life shall begin. If you claim the right to decide when life begins you will predictably claim the right to decide when it ends, as in abortion and euthanasia.

"With the marketing of the pill in the 1960s, *Roe v. Wade* was inevitable. A contraceptive culture needs abortion as a back-up. The meltdown of that culture is accelerating.

"Francis Fukuyama called the introduction of the contraceptive pill *The Great Disruption* in relations between men and women. In the nature of things, sex is reserved for marriage, and marriage is permanent, because sex has something to do with babies. The contraceptive separation of sex from life leads to the separation of sex from marriage and to the irrelevancy of marriage. In 2006, as reported by the Centers for Disease Control, a record 36.9 percent of all births were out of wedlock. Out-of-wedlock births are 80 percent of births to teens and 60 percent to mothers in their early 20s. In 2006, they were 26.6 percent among non-Hispanic whites, 70.7 percent among non-Hispanic blacks and 49.9 percent among Hispanics.

"Government officials, including educators, throw fuel on the fire by promoting contraception even among pre-teens. Not surprisingly, the birth rate to teens rose three percent in 2006, the first rise since 1991. Cases of gonorrhea, chlamydia and syphilis, the STDs for which reporting is required, continue to rise.

"In such a Copulation Explosion, you have to expect a rise in pregnancies and that many will end in abortion. The 'morning-after pill,' an abortifacient, is available over-the-counter and is easily, if illegally, obtainable by minors without parental knowledge.

"Neither the law nor politics can get us out of this mess. Contraception and abortion are a subset of the question: Who is God? Who decides whether and when life begins and when it ends? Abortion is an aspect of our contraceptive rejection of God's gift of life. Before he became Benedict XVI, Cardinal Joseph Ratzinger said, '[T]he ultimate root of hatred for human life . . . is the loss of God. When God disappears, the absolute dignity of human life disappears as well. . . . Only this divine dimension guarantees the full dignity of the human person. . . . In the struggle for life, talking about God is indispensable.'

"The March for Life is not a futile exercise. It focuses on abortion, the ultimate secular sacrament. The March is an in-your-face, on-site reminder to the Executive, the Court and the Congress of their derelictions and of what they ought to do. Under the leadership of Washington attorney Nellie Gray, the March, from its inception, has also been an act of prayer. The message: Human life is sacred because it is a gift of God. The students in the March bring honor to the Notre Dame community."

BENGAL BOUTS: ARE THEY NUTS? Feb. 6, 2008

"Are they nuts? 237 students returned from Christmas to go into training for the Bengal Bouts. In addition to endless push-ups, sit-ups, running, etc., they invite the rearrangement of their own facial landscapes.

"No, they are not crazy. Let me tell you why. A family of four among the ultra-poor served by the Holy Cross missions in Bangladesh would live for at least a week on the $3.87 we casually drop for a latte at Starbuck's. In 2007, the Bouts contributed $60,000 to those missions. The Holy Cross Brothers had run a boxing program at Notre Dame in the mid-1920s, but the Bengal Bouts began in 1931, with all proceeds going to the missions as they have every year since then.

"Bangladesh has 140 million people in a country the size of Iowa. It is 88.3 percent Muslim, 10.5 percent Hindu and 0.3 percent Christian. The per capita annual income is $1,470. Holy Cross missionaries came there in 1854. There are 145 Holy Cross priests, seminarians and brothers (133 of them Bangladeshi) and 70 Holy Cross sisters there. They run two colleges, eight high schools and 10 parishes as well as other apostolates. In addition to political violence and corruption, they have to deal with the effects of Cyclone Sidr last November, which killed at least 5,000 people, injured 40,000, destroyed or damaged 1.2 million homes and 1.6 million acres of cropland and killed 1 million livestock.

"The missions depend on the Bengal Bouts, according to Father Tom Smith of the Holy Cross Mission Center. The needs are basic: sanitation, clean water, safe shelter, electricity, etc. In Khalippur Parish, 20 villages of poor tribal people need for each village a latrine, costing $25 each and a tube well at $150 each. . . .

"Space limits prevent mention of many other urgent needs. But the next time you interview for a job after graduation, give a thought to Holy Cross Parish in Dhaka which needs to hire a full-time teacher-catechist to work among the Telegu, a people of the lowest caste, many of whom are joining the Church. The teacher's annual salary will be $1,000.

"The participants in the Bouts take their purpose seriously. The program, under the sponsorship of Rich O'Leary and Dave Brown of RecSports, is run by the officers of the Boxing Club, president Hunter Land and captains Jesse Brawer, Patrick O'Brien, Patrick Ryan, Lawrence Sullivan, Michael Lee, Leo Rubinkowski, Mark Weber and Andres Villalba. 'We run a tough program,' Hunter Land said, 'but the rewards are great, including the camaraderie and friendships and especially the certainty that we are helping those who need it most.'

"The toughness of the program is largely the doing of Tom Suddes, a Columbus developer who runs practices guaranteed to reduce the number of participants. Tom describes the practices as 'character building.' Those who survive tend to agree. 'The boxing alumni,' notes Tom, 'say that what they remember above all about Notre Dame is the Bengal Bouts and the resulting friendships.' Tom and the other head coaches—Chicago attorney Terry Johnson and University pilot Pat Farrell—are former Bengals champs and volunteer their time. The assistant coaches include Sweet C. Robinson of the

Buchanan Police Department, former boxers Ryan Rans, Chip Farrell, Thad Naquin, Judge Roland Chamblee and Father Brian Daley. Jimmy Rogers, of RecSports, doubles as coach and supervisor.

"The emphasis is on safety, with no serious injuries in 77 years. Dr. Jim Moriarty, the University physician, and his staff keep that record going with strict testing and safety rules. Emergency Medical Technician Terri Engel attends every sparring session along with EMTs Eva Chu, Baker Jones, Jordan Lacy, Wayne Bishop, and Gordon Martinzak of the Notre Dame Fire Department.

"If you think that no one is indispensable, let me introduce you to the student managers, Melanie Rodarte, Meghan O'Farrell, Kelly Garvey, Ashley Mensch and Katherine Johnston. They maintain the financial, sparring, equipment and other records. They organize, they solve problems and they leave no doubt in anyone's mind that if they faltered, the operation would descend into chaos. They share the view expressed by Melanie when asked why she gives so much time to this. 'One word,' she said, 'Bangladesh. When I graduate, I want to know that I did something special here that helped real people in real need.'. . . .

"One final word, from Father Louis Cruge, who runs the Nevin Clinic for the Sick Poor in Dhaka: 'So many sick people are coming to us from the city slum area, the budget is always in the red. Most expensive is our care for cancer patients. We never have enough to care for all the sick who come. The patients can offer very little. Please pray for us so that we can do something good for the poor and needy sick people and show God's kindness and mercy to them.'

"Please support the Bengal Bouts. They are fun to watch. And they are one of the very best things we do at Notre Dame."

SPE SALVI, Feb. 20, 2008

"'What is most embarrassing to the world today,' said Georgetown professor James Schall, S.J., 'is that the most intelligent voice it confronts, or deliberately refuses to confront, is that coming from the papacy.' Fr. Schall has a point. He was commenting on Pope Benedict XVI's second encyclical, *Spe Salvi*, which drew its title from its opening words. '*SPE SALVI facti sumus*—in hope we were saved.' The message is simple: 'A world without God is a world without hope.' No. 44.

"Benedict admits that 'we need the . . . hopes that keep us going day by day. But these are not enough without the great hope which . . . can only be . . . the God who has a human face and who has loved us to the end, each one of us and humanity in its entirety.' No. 31. A secularist culture, he insists, can offer no hope for anything after death. No future. In contrast, their 'encounter with Christ' gives Christians their 'distinguishing mark' which is 'the fact that they have a future: it is not that they know the details . . . but they know in general terms that their life will not end in emptiness. Only when the future is certain as a positive reality does it become possible to live the present as well.' No. 2.

"A point of interest to a university community is the relation between the lack of hope and what Benedict had described at Regensburg in 2006 as 'the self-imposed limitation of reason to the empirically verifiable' so that 'questions of religion and ethics no longer concern it.' When reason is so limited, affirmations of God and objective morality are dismissed as non-rational. No one can know anything about God. And 'justice' becomes, in the words of Hans Kelsen, the foremost legal positivist of the last century, 'an irrational ideal.'

"Benedict describes as 'presumptuous and false,' the idea that '[s]ince there is no God to create justice . . . man himself is now called to establish justice.' 'It is no accident,' he said, 'that this idea has led to the greatest forms of cruelty and violations of justice. . . . A world which has to create its own justice is a world without hope.' No. 42. Justice will be whatever man decrees. Thus Kelsen said that Auschwitz and other Nazi exterminations were 'valid law.' In accord with his 'philosophical relativism,' he could not reasonably criticize them as unjust.

"*Spe Salvi* traces 'the foundations of the modern age' to Francis Bacon and others who thought that 'man would be redeemed through science.' Nos. 16, 25. '[U]p to that time, the recovery of what man had lost through the expulsion from Paradise was expected from faith in Jesus Christ. . . . Now, this 'redemption,' the restoration of the lost Paradise, is no longer expected from faith, but from the newly discovered link between science and praxis [practice, action or conduct]. It is not that faith is simply denied; rather it is displaced onto another level—that of purely private and otherworldly affairs—and . . . it becomes . . . irrelevant for the world. . . . This . . . vision . . . shapes the present-day crisis of faith which is . . . a crisis of Christian hope. Thus hope too . . . acquires a new form. Now it is called: faith in progress. . . . [T]hrough the interplay of science and praxis . . . a totally new world will emerge, the kingdom of man.' No. 17.

"Benedict affirms the achievements and potential of science, but he cautions that '[i]f technical progress is not matched by . . . progress in man's ethical formation . . . it is not progress at all, but a threat for man and for the world.' No. 22. The problem is that ethical formation is impossible unless reason can offer answers on moral right and wrong. But reason cannot do that if it is limited to the empirical, without 'integration through . . . openness . . . to the differentiation between good and evil . . . [R]eason . . . becomes human only if it is capable of directing the will along the right path and it is capable of this only if it looks beyond itself. . . . Let us put it very simply: man needs God, otherwise he remains without hope . . . God truly enters into human affairs only when, rather than being present merely in our thinking, he himself comes towards us and speaks to us. . . . Reason . . . and faith need one another in order to fulfill their true nature and their missions.' No. 23.

"Because of protests, Benedict XVI cancelled an address last month at La Sapienza University in Rome. In the address he had prepared, he said, 'the danger for the western world . . . is that . . . because of the greatness of his knowledge and power, man will fail to face up to the question of truth.'

"That comment is pertinent to the United States, where the Supreme Court has misinterpreted the First Amendment to impose an impossible neutrality between 'religion and irreligion.' In theory, that 'neutrality' forbids any public official to affirm that the Declaration of Independence is in fact true when it identifies God as the author of rights. Similarly, public education is founded on a non-theistic religious proposition, that moral questions can—and must in the public sphere—be decided without reference to any controlling role of God and His law. Instead, each person creates his own moral truth. He is his own god. The result is not neutrality but an established agnosticism devoid of ultimate hope.

"*Spe Salvi* is part of Benedict's ongoing project to rescue reason by integrating it with faith and objective morality, so that it can address questions beyond the empirical. He would have told the Sapienza students that 'if reason, out of concern for its alleged purity, becomes deaf to the great message that comes to it from Christian faith and wisdom, then it withers like a tree whose roots can no longer reach the waters that give life to it.'

"Fr. Schall described Benedict XVI as 'the only universal voice in the world.' He is that. His vindication of reason should be taken seriously, especially in universities that claim to be Catholic."

LAETARE MEDAL: WHY MARTIN SHEEN? March 12, 2008

"'The Laetare Medal has been worn only by men and women whose genius has ennobled the arts and sciences, illustrated the ideals of the Church, and enriched the heritage of humanity.' Citation for Laetare Medal given to General William Rosecrans in 1896.

"The 2008 recipient, Martin Sheen, a self-described 'peace and justice activist,' has been arrested at least 65 times for nonviolent obstructions and trespasses at military installations and other sites. Mr. Sheen's many pronouncements on public issues merit discussion, including his views on homosexual rights, his 'doubts' about the *9/11 Commission Report*, and his personal but guarded opposition to abortion. . . .

"This column, however, is concerned with Sheen's attitude toward military service. In a 2003 interview with David Kupfer, Sheen denied the accusation 'of not supporting the military.' 'Nothing could be further from the truth,' Sheen said. 'The leaders . . . make the decisions. . . . I support the soldiers as human beings.'

"One manifesto, however, that Sheen signed on January 5, 2005, described 'military training' as 'schooling body and spirit in the art of killing. . . . It is the perpetuation of war spirit. It hinders the development of the desire for peace.' The manifesto called for 'non-violent resistance to the military system,' including not only conscientious objection 'by conscripts and professional soldiers, in war and peace time,' but also 'Civil Disobedience, War Tax Resistance, Non-Cooperation with military research, military production and arms trade.' The Laetare award to Sheen could generate confusion as to whether military service is consistent with 'the ideals of the Church.' Let's try to set the record straight.

"'All those who enter the military service in loyalty to their country,' the Second Vatican Council said, 'should look upon themselves as the custodians of the security and freedom of their fellow countrymen; and when they carry out their duty properly, they are contributing to the maintenance of peace.' *Gaudium et Spes*, no. 79.

"The *Catechism* affirms that 'governments cannot be denied the right of lawful self-defense, once all peace efforts have failed.' No. 2308. Such defense must satisfy 'just war' analysis. The requirements for jus ad bellum, justice in going to war, are proper authority, just cause and right intention. The *Catechism* lists further details: '[T]he damage inflicted by the aggressor . . . must be lasting, grave and certain;' war must be a last resort, with 'all other means impractical or ineffective;' 'there must be serious prospects of success;' and 'the use of arms must not produce evils . . . graver than the evil to be eliminated.' 'The evaluation of these conditions,' however, 'belongs to the prudential judgment of those who have responsibility for the common good.' No. 2309. Citizens are obliged, in effect, to give a benefit of the doubt to the decisions of those in lawful authority.

"*Jus in bello*, justice in fighting a war, requires proportionality and discrimination (non-combatant immunity from intentional attack). What Sheen, and other politicized critics, appear to overlook is the fact that the Uniform Code of Military Justice, the very restrictive Rules of Engagement and other binding military policies effectively protect noncombatants and otherwise conform to the requirements of jus in bello. Some military personnel violate the law but their record is far better than that of corporate executives. And the

armed services are diligent, perhaps to the point of excess, in prosecuting puta-
tive offenses.

"The universal pacifist refuses to take part in any and all wars. 'Those
who renounce violence . . . and, in order to safeguard human rights, make use
of those means of defense available to the weakest, bear witness to evangelical charity, provided they do so without harming the rights and obligations of
other men and societies. They bear . . . witness to the . . . risks of resource to
violence.' No. 2306. However, a universal pacifism which denies the right of
the state ever to use force in defense, is inconsistent with the teaching of the
Church.

"The selective pacifist refuses to take part in a particular war he regards
as unjust. Citizens are obliged to support a just war. 'Public authorities, in this
case, have the right and duty to impose on citizens the obligations necessary
for national defense.' No. 2310. The law of the United States allows exemp-
tions from military service only for universal, and not selective, pacifists. The
Catechism urges, but does not require, exemption for all conscientious objectors. No. 2311. It is difficult, however, to see how an exemption for selective
objectors could be administered without inviting fraudulent evasion.

"Granting the sincerity of universal pacifists, their claim to moral superiority is flawed. One can well 'bear witness to evangelical charity' by renouncing force in defending himself. The universal pacifist, who denies that force
can ever be used in defense of the common good, would refuse to defend not
only himself but others. He would deny to his fellow citizens their right to have
the state provide what the *Catechism* calls 'legitimate defense by military
force.' No. 2309.

"Selective pacifism, on the other hand, is required by the teaching of the
Church. We should all be selective pacifists, insisting, with prudence, that any
war—or any other act of state—is subject to the higher standard of the natural
law and the law of God. A strong presumption of validity attaches to the decisions and acts of those entrusted with the care of the common good. But that
presumption is not conclusive.

"All wars are debatable, including the Iraq War. Hostility to President Bush
should not be allowed to distort the principles involved. In full disclosure, permit me to note the view that, although he has competitors for the honor, George
W. Bush, for various reasons foreign and domestic, may be the worst president
ever. But, subject to the legitimate authority of Congress, the president has the
duty to defend the nation and his decisions are entitled to a strong benefit of the
doubt. To participate in that defense is an honorable calling. Those who do so
deserve appreciation and respect. They ought not to be subjected to disparagement no matter how politically correct that disparagement might be. The Laetare
award to Mr. Sheen implicitly and unjustifiably denigrates those who serve in
the armed forces, including alumni and present students of Notre Dame."

EUCHARISTIC ADORATION, March 26, 2008

"Elsewhere, this is Easter Week. At Notre Dame it appears to be The Week of the Vagina Monologues. To the reader's relief, this column will defer discussion of that production. Instead, we suggest a better way to spend your time these next few days and beyond.

"One impact of the papacies of John Paul II and Benedict XVI is a dramatic rise in the practice of Eucharistic Adoration in parishes and other venues throughout the world, including Notre Dame. What is it? And why is it such a big deal?

"The Eucharist was instituted by Christ at the Last Supper, fulfilling the promise he made as recorded in the sixth chapter of John's Gospel: 'In the . . . Eucharist, the body and blood, . . . soul and divinity, of our Lord Jesus Christ and, therefore, the whole Christ is truly, really and substantially contained. This presence is called 'real,' . . . not . . . to exclude the other types of presence . . . but because it is presence in the fullest sense . . . it is a substantial presence by which Christ, God and man, makes himself wholly and entirely present' (*Catechism*, no. 1374). This is called transubstantiation because the substance of the bread and wine changes while the appearances of the bread and wine remain the same. The distinction between substance and appearance is familiar. When the angel appeared to the women at the tomb on Easter, his appearance was that of a man but his substance was that of an angel. Mark 16:1–8.

"Adoration of the Blessed Sacrament is possible whenever the consecrated hosts are reserved in the tabernacle, as indicated by the lighted lamp near the tabernacle. The term, Eucharistic Adoration, however, commonly refers to adoration when the Sacrament is exposed to view on the altar. Such exposition is available at Notre Dame. . . . In his apostolic exhortation, *Sacramentum Caritatis* (Sacrament of Love) (2007), Benedict XVI . . . said, 'adoration outside Mass prolongs and intensifies all that takes place during the liturgical celebration itself. Indeed, 'only in adoration can a profound and genuine reception mature. And it is precisely this personal encounter with the Lord that then strengthens the social mission contained in the Eucharist, which seeks to break down not only the walls that separate the Lord and ourselves, but also and especially the walls that separate us from one another.' No. 66.

"Adoration of the Eucharist, therefore, is not some kind of sterile, self-centered devotion. Rather, it has a social impact. . . . 'The union with Christ brought about by the Eucharist,' Benedict said, 'brings a newness to our social relations [and] is social in character.'. . . .

"The Lord Jesus . . . spurs us to be mindful of the situations of extreme poverty in which a great part of humanity still lives: these are situations for which human beings bear a clear and disquieting responsibility.'. . .

"Mother Teresa of Calcutta spoke often of Eucharistic Adoration as a source of power. 'When the Sisters are exhausted, up to their eyes in work, when all seems to go awry,' she said, 'they spend an hour in prayer before the Blessed Sacrament. This practice has never failed to bear fruit: they experience peace and strength.'. . . .

"When he was ordained a priest, Archbishop Fulton J. Sheen promised that he would spend an hour in adoration before the Blessed Sacrament every day. He kept that promise and described the 'holy hour' as not merely a devotion but 'a sharing in the work of redemption. He [Jesus] asked for an hour of reparation to combat the hour of evil; an hour of victimal union with the cross to overcome the anti-love of sin.'

"So adoration of the Eucharist is a very big deal. But no one can cram it down your throat. We are free to accept it or reject it. If you are not convinced that it is true, it might still be worth a visit to check it out. There is no set formula. You don't have to contact anybody. Just show up. Stay for as long or as short a time as you wish. You can pray, read or just think. If you fall asleep, don't worry about it. Archbishop Sheen recounts the time in a church in Paris when he knelt down, promptly fell asleep and 'woke up exactly at the end of one hour.' He wondered if he had made his promised Hour until he realized 'that's the way the Apostles made their first Holy Hour in the Garden.'

"If you want to do something real for Notre Dame and for yourself, don't waste your time on anything like the Vagina Monologues. Go instead to spend some time with the Person who himself really is Truth. And Love."

ANOTHER TERRI SCHIAVO? April 8, 2008

"'[T]hese crimes . . . started . . . with . . . the attitude . . . that there is such a thing as life not worthy to be lived. This attitude in its early stages concerned itself merely with the severely and chronically sick. Gradually the sphere . . . was enlarged to encompass . . . the radically unwanted and finally all non-Germans. But . . . the infinitely small wedged-in lever from which this entire trend of mind received its impetus was the attitude toward the nonrehabilitable sick.' That summary is from Dr. Leo Alexander's classic analysis of the Nazi euthanasia program.

"One wonders what Dr. Alexander would think of the treatment of the 'nonrehabilitable sick' in American law and culture today. This comes to mind because of Lauren Richardson, a 23-year-old Delaware woman who may become the new Terri Schiavo. In 2005, Terri, a disabled, brain-damaged woman on a feeding tube, was starved and dehydrated to death by order of a Florida court. Her parents and siblings wanted to keep her alive and care for her but her estranged husband wanted to remove the tube in accord with what he claimed were her wishes. After years of litigation that gained world attention, the husband prevailed and Terri died.

"In August 2006, Lauren Richardson overdosed on heroin, with resulting brain damage, while she was three months pregnant. On a respirator and feeding tube, she gave birth to a healthy girl in February 2007. She is off a respirator but remains on a feeding and hydration tube in a nursing home. Lauren's parents divorced when she was an infant and each has remarried. Both parents seek to be Lauren's guardian. The mother, Edith Towers, who has custody of Lauren's baby, would terminate Lauren's feeding. The father, Randy Richardson, would keep her alive, bring her home and provide treatment for her. Both sides agree that Lauren is in a persistent vegetative state, which is sort of an awake unconsciousness. Lauren did not execute an advanced directive indicating whether she would want to be kept alive on a tube.

"On January 24, 2008, a Master in the Delaware Court of Chancery appointed the mother as guardian because he found that Lauren, while a competent adult, had orally 'expressed her wish not to be artificially sustained by medical treatment, including hydration and nutrition, in a persistent vegetative state.' The appeals could take years.

"Cases like *Schiavo* and *Richardson* are dramatic but they are like the tip of an iceberg. Such cases come to court and public view only because the family members disagree. More ominous is the acceptance by American law and culture of the quiet execution of incompetent patients when the family and caregivers agree that it is time for the patient to die.

"A competent adult has the legal right to refuse any and all medical treatment. Since the 1980s that legal right has included the refusal of food and water whether naturally or artificially provided. A refusal of food and water with the intent to die is a form of suicide. 'Suicide,' as John Paul II put it, 'is always as morally objectionable as murder.'

"If a patient is incompetent and on a feeding tube, the law permits the tube to be removed if the patient had expressed such a desire when he or she was competent, or, in some states, if such removal is in the best interest of the patient. In moral terms, as John Paul said on March 20, 2004, 'the administration of food and water, even . . . by artificial means, [is] a natural means for preserving life, not a medical act. Its use [is] morally obligatory.' As long as it achieves its purpose of 'providing nourishment to the patient and alleviation of his suffering.' Nutrition and hydration are not intended to cure the cancer or other disease; the suffering they are designed to relieve is the suffering from hunger and thirst.

"Morally, a feeding tube can be removed from a patient when it is excessively painful, when the patient cannot absorb the nourishment and in the closing of the dying process when the lack of nourishment would not contribute to the death. When such factors are not present, if you remove a feeding tube from a patient with the intent not to put it back, the act and your intent are homicidal. It is, as John Paul put it, 'euthanasia by omission.' But the law permits such removal, when the parents and caregivers are in agreement that the incompetent patient would want to die or that it is in his best interest to die. Similarly, palliative sedation, which can be morally justified even if it shortens life, can be used with the intent not to relieve pain but to kill; it is ordinarily difficult, if not impossible, to prove such intent.

"Starvation and dehydration can be an unpleasant way to go. 'I watched my own sister anguish through 13 days without food or water,' Terri Schiavo's brother, Bobby Schindler, recently said, 'and there are no words that can properly describe this inhumanity. . . . If you did the same thing to a dog, you would rightly join Michael Vick in jail for animal abuse.' We can, however, expect starvation and dehydration of incompetents to give way to the lethal injection as the method of killing.

"'Euthanasia,' said John Paul, 'is a grave violation of the law of God.' One reason we accept the intentional killing of the innocent as an optional problem-solving technique, in abortion and now euthanasia, is that we have forgotten that life comes from God and that it comes on his terms. In the nearly universal practice of contraception, we have claimed 'a power that belongs solely to God: the power to decide . . . the coming into existence of a human person.' John Paul II, Sept. 17, 1983. If, through contraception, you make yourself the arbiter of whether and when life shall begin, you will predictably make yourself the arbiter of when life shall end, as in abortion, euthanasia, etc. Contraception also affirms that there is such a thing as a 'life not worthy to be lived,' i.e. the life you prevent. Ideas do have consequences.

"Let Terri Schiavo's brother have the last word: 'Persons with disabilities . . . are just that—persons. They should be treated as our most precious treasures reflecting who we should be as a nation—not as damaged goods to be discarded when they outlive their 'usefulness.' Dr. Leo Alexander would agree."

NOTE: In November 2008, the litigation was settled by agreement between Lauren's parents to share joint guardianship of Lauren and to cooperate in caring for her at Randy Richardson's Maryland home. Lauren "wept emotionally when her mother informed her of the settlement and the reconciliation of her parents." "This change of heart and settlement has profoundly affected everyone involved," said Matt Bowman, the Alliance Defense Fund attorney who handled the effort to save Lauren. www.telladf.org.

BENEDICT XVI ON CATHOLIC SCHOOLS, April 23, 2008

"Pope Benedict XVI's address in Washington to Catholic educators requires extensive analysis. We can mention here only a few of the aspects pertinent to Notre Dame.

"The Pope rejected a merely statistical concept of Catholic identity: 'A university or school's Catholic identity is not simply a question of the number of Catholic students. . . . Catholic identity is not dependent upon statistics. Neither can it be equated simply with orthodoxy of course content.' Some at Notre Dame will spin those statements to minimize concern about the sinking of the number of Catholic faculty below the fifty percent mark or about the haphazard exposure, if any, of Notre Dame students to orthodox course content. For Benedict, however, the irrelevancy of mere statistics evidently means that it is not enough to count the faculty who, for whatever reason, check the 'Catholic' box. 'Catholic identity,' he said, 'demands and inspires much more: namely that each and every aspect of your learning communities reverberates within the ecclesial life of the faith. Only in faith can truth become incarnate and reason truly human, capable of directing the will along the path of freedom (cf. *Spe Salvi*, 23). In this way our institutions make a vital contribution to the mission of the Church and truly serve society.'

"This obviously means that a Catholic university cannot isolate itself from the 'ecclesial life' of the Church: 'A particular responsibility therefore for each of you, and your colleagues, is to evoke among the young the desire for the act of faith, encouraging them to commit themselves to the ecclesial life that follows from this belief. It is here that freedom reaches the certainty of truth. In choosing to live by that truth, we embrace the fullness of the life of faith which is given to us in the Church.'

"On this point, that 'the fullness of the life of faith . . . is given to us in the Church,' Notre Dame has a problem of its own making. The President, Fr. Jenkins, and the Provost, Dr. Burish, initiated a new process of dialogue in their April 2 'statement on the rationale for hiring faculty who will enhance our Catholic mission.' The statement went on for six pages about keeping Notre Dame 'truly Catholic' without once mentioning the Catholic Church. That is like explaining how to play baseball without mentioning the ball. The new dialogue process will be interminable and fruitless, as have been all its predecessors.

"The incoherence of this dialogue project arises from Notre Dame's dogged adherence to an abstract relic of 1960s ideology. In 1967, officials of the leading Catholic universities met at the Notre Dame retreat at Land O'Lakes, Wisc., and declared that: 'To perform its teaching and research functions effectively, the Catholic university must have a true autonomy and academic freedom in the fact of authority of whatever kind, lay or clerical, external to the academic community itself.'

"That claim of autonomy from external authority is phony. Notre Dame, like all universities, willingly submits to dozens of governmental and non-governmental authorities including, of course, the NCAA. The only 'external authority' Notre Dame will not recognize appears to be the Catholic Church. The Notre Dame brand of academic freedom, for example, is hardly consistent with Benedict's: 'I wish to reaffirm,' he said, 'the great value of academic freedom. In virtue of this freedom you are called to search for the truth wherever careful analysis of evidence leads you. Yet it is also the case that any appeal to the principle of academic freedom in order to justify positions that contradict the faith and the teaching of the Church would obstruct or even betray the university's identity and mission; a mission at the heart of the Church's *munus docendi* [teaching office or function] and not somehow autonomous or independent of it.'

"Interestingly, Benedict reaffirmed, without explicit mention of it, the principles of *Ex Corde Ecclesiae*, the 1990 Apostolic Constitution on Catholic Universities. *Ex Corde* requires of the Catholic university 'a recognition of and adherence to the teaching authority of the Church in matters of faith and morals.'

"A final quote from Benedict causes regret that no one asked him about the Vagina Monologues: 'Teachers and administrators, whether in universities or schools,' said Benedict, 'have the duty and privilege to ensure that students receive instruction in Catholic doctrine and practice. This requires that public witness to the way of Christ, as found in the Gospel and upheld by the Church's Magisterium, shapes all aspects of an institution's life, both inside and outside the classroom.' It would be difficult to imagine the man who spoke those lines finding academic merit in the Vagina Monologues.

"The problem is truth-in-labeling. Notre Dame, in its fundraising, professes to be Catholic. But it defines that term by its own interpretation. An appropriate name for that mindset is Protestantism, except that Protestants have the integrity not to call themselves Catholic."

2008–2009

HUMANAE VITAE AT FORTY, Sept. 2, 2008

"Notre Dame should, but probably won't, commemorate this anniversary. Forty years ago, July 25, 1968, Pope Paul VI, in *Humanae Vitae* (HV), reaffirmed the traditional Christian position on contraception. Until 1930, no Christian denomination had ever said that contraception could be objectively right. Luther, Calvin and Wesley rejected it.

"The 1930 Anglican Lambeth Conference gave cautious approval to contraception. Pope Pius XI replied that 'any use . . . of matrimony . . . in such a way that the act is deliberately frustrated in its natural power to generate life is an offense against the law of God and of nature . . . and a grave sin.'

"When the Pill came on the market in the 1960s, the Catholic Church came under pressure to abandon its solitary stand against it. HV's disapproval of the Pill brought a storm of dissent and ridicule on Paul VI, e.g., 'he no play-a the game, he no make-a the rules.' Four decades later, nobody in his right mind is laughing.

"Experience has validated the prediction of the *Washington Post* on March 22, 1931, that the approval of contraception 'would sound the death knell of marriage as a holy institution by establishing degrading practices which would encourage indiscriminate immorality.'

"Contraception deliberately separates sex from procreation by acting to make procreation impossible; it makes man, of both sexes, the arbiter of whether and when life will begin; and it prevents the total mutual self-donation that ought to characterize the conjugal act. It also accepts the idea that there is such a thing as a life not worth living, i.e., the life that might have resulted had not contraception prevented it. If, through contraception, man makes himself (or herself) the arbiter of whether and when life shall begin, he will predictably make himself the arbiter of when it shall end, as in abortion and euthanasia. John Paul II described abortion and contraception as 'fruits of the same tree.'

"In HV, Paul VI foretold three evils that would result from the acceptance of 'artificial methods of birth control':

"1. '[C]onjugal infidelity and the general lowering of morality.'

"One reason why sex should be reserved for marriage is that sex has something to do with babies. But if it is entirely up to man (of both sexes) whether sex will have any relation to procreation, why should it be reserved for marriage, why should marriage be permanent and why should marriage be heterosexual?

"As Methodist Pastor Donald Sensing wrote in 2004, the legalization of 'homosexual marriage' became inevitable when the Pill severed '[t]he causal connection between sex, pregnancy and marriage.' A contraceptive culture will legitimize not only homosexual activity, but also promiscuity, pornography, divorce, in vitro fertilization, cloning, etc. President R. Albert Mohler, Jr., of the Southern Baptist Theological Seminary said in 2005, 'The . . . separation of sex from procreation may be one of the most important defining marks of our age—and one of the most ominous . . . [T]he pill gave incredible license to everything from adultery and affairs to premarital sex.' From 1960 to 2000, the percentage of children born out of wedlock in the United States rose from 5 percent to 33 percent. Over half of all first marriages are now preceded by cohabitation. The 2008 Gallup Values and Beliefs poll showed that 61 percent of Americans approve of sex between an unmarried man and woman. And so on.

"2. Woman as an object, so that man considers the woman 'as a mere instrument of selfish enjoyment, and no longer as his respected and beloved companion.'

"The objectification of women is evident in the prevalence of pornography, especially on the Internet. Women are the big losers in the contraceptive culture. Francis Fukuyama, in *The Great Disruption*, said the Pill and abortion liberated men from responsibility and put the burden on women, allowing 'many . . . ordinary men . . . to live fantasy lives of hedonism and serial polygamy formerly reserved only for a tiny group of men at the very top of society.'

"3. '[A] dangerous weapon would thus be placed in the hands of . . . public authorities.'

"Since 1970 the federal government has promoted population control through contraception, with a focus on minorities and third-world countries. Planned Parenthood and other publicly funded entities promote all forms of birth control among minorities to the extent that 37 percent of all abortions are on black women although blacks, at 36 million, are only 13 percent of the U.S. population. Since 1973, 10 to 13 million black babies have been aborted.

"'Contraception,' said John Paul II, is 'so profoundly unlawful as never to be, for any reason, justified.' That conclusion is not disturbed by the legitimacy of natural birth regulation. As HV put it, 'If . . . there are serious motives to space out births. . . . it is . . . licit to take into account the natural rhythms . . . for the use of marriage in the infecund periods only, and in this way to regulate birth without offending the moral principles.'

"HV was a defining event because Paul VI refused to follow an insane world over the cliff into an abyss of nihilism. He stood for the Truth of love and life. Conjugal love, he said, 'is total . . . a very special form of personal friendship, in which husband and wife generously share everything, without undue reservations or selfish calculations.'

"Members of the Notre Dame community could best commemorate HV by a prayerful consideration of its Truth."

GUN CONTROL, Sept. 16, 2008

"Since 1982, Kennesaw, an Atlanta suburb, has required every head of a household to own a gun and ammunition, with an exemption for those who conscientiously object. One effect of the enactment was the appearance of yard signs: 'Never Mind the Dog—Beware of Owner.' Another was that the Kennesaw crime rate dropped and remains well below the national average.

"What brings Kennesaw to mind is *District of Columbia v. Heller*, decided last June, the Supreme Court's first in-depth examination of the Second Amendment. That amendment provides: 'A well-regulated Militia, being necessary to the security of a free State, the right of the people to keep and bear Arms, shall not be infringed.' The Court held, 5-4, that the District of Columbia's 'ban on handgun possession in the home violates the Second Amendment, as does its prohibition of immediate self-defense.' The *Heller* ruling was hailed by many as the decisive victory for 'gun rights.' First impressions, however, can be misleading.

"One lesson here is that saying too much can get you into trouble. The Second Amendment is the only one in the Bill of Rights with a prefatory clause stating its purpose. That 'militia' clause, over the years, gave rise to endless debate, which the Court settled in *Heller*. In the majority opinion, written by Justice Antonin Scalia, the Court held that the amendment 'protects an individual's right to possess a firearm unconnected with service in a militia, and to use that firearm for traditionally lawful purposes, such as self-defense within the home.' The dissenters argued that the Amendment protects only the right to possess and carry a firearm in connection with militia service. The ruling, however, did not settle much beyond that point.

"'[T]he Second Amendment,' said the Court, 'codified a pre-existing right' which developed in England as a protection against government. '[T]he Stuart Kings Charles II and James II,' said Scalia, suppressed political dissent 'in part by disarming their opponents. . . . [T]he Catholic James II had ordered . . . disarmaments of [Protestant] regions.' The English Bill of Rights of 1689, the predecessor of the Second Amendment, reacted by providing 'That the subjects which are Protestants may have arms for their defense suitable to their conditions and as allowed by law.' This was, said the Court, 'clearly an individual right, having nothing whatever to do with service in a militia.'

"When the Second Amendment was adopted, the 'militia,' said the Court, consisted of 'those who were male, able-bodied, and within a certain age range.' The Amendment, wrote Scalia, 'helped to secure the ideal of a citizen militia, which might be necessary to oppose an oppressive military force if the constitutional order broke down. . . . [T]he . . . prefatory clause announces the purpose for which the right was codified: to prevent elimination of the militia. [I]t does not suggest that preserving the militia was the only reason Americans valued the ancient right; most undoubtedly thought it even more important for self-defense and hunting. But the threat that the new Federal Government would destroy the citizens' militia by taking away their arms was the reason that right—unlike some other English rights—was codified in a written Constitution. . . .

"[T]he [Heller] ruling left the door open for restrictive regulation rather than prohibition. The Court said the Second Amendment 'does not protect those weapons not typically possessed by law-abiding citizens for lawful purposes, such as short-barreled shotguns.' The Court also noted approvingly the 'longstanding prohibitions on the possession of firearms by felons and the mentally ill, or laws forbidding the carrying of firearms in sensitive places such as schools and government buildings, or laws imposing conditions and qualifications on the commercial sale of arms.'

"'The gun issue is far from settled. The District of Columbia reacted to *Heller* by imposing a regulation practically as restrictive as the one the Court struck down. A new appeal is underway. The Supreme Court has held that most of the protections in the Bill of Rights are binding on the states and local governments as well as on the federal government. But in *Heller* the Court interpreted earlier cases to establish that 'the Second Amendment applies only to the Federal Government.' Future litigation may turn on provisions in state constitutions comparable to that amendment. Justice Breyer's dissent in *Heller* highlighted also the uncertainty that still surrounds the level of juridical scrutiny that must be applied in Second Amendment cases.

"So what can we learn from *Heller*? It is far from a mandate that every American community become a Dodge City or even a Kennesaw. On Supreme Court decisions, and everything else, don't jump to conclusions without reading the fine print."

NOTE: In *McDonald v. Chicago*, on June 28, 2010, the Supreme Court ruled that the states are bound by the Second Amendment. The Court struck down laws of the City of Chicago and Oak Park, IL, that effectively banned handgun possession by almost all private citizens.

40 DAYS FOR LIFE, Sept. 30, 2008

"Are you 'pro-life' but tired of the way abortion becomes a political football every four years? The politicians make their points on one side or the other. And then they forget it—for another four years.

"If you are looking for a positive and non-political approach, consider 40 Days for Life, an interfaith initiative. . . . The campaign, organized by local residents, is part of a rapidly growing national effort. It includes local residents and Notre Dame students, faculty and staff. . . . The campaign has three components. If you can't do them all, do what you can:

"1. Most important: Personal prayer and fasting for an end to abortion. . . .

"2. Peaceful, lawful witness for life, 24/7, outside the Women's Pavilion at 2010 Ironwood Circle, South Bend, between Edison and Rte. 23. This constant vigil is neither a demonstration nor a protest. It is primarily a prayer, reminding ourselves and the community that the legalized execution of the innocent is an evil that cannot be overcome by politics as usual but indispensably through the grace of God. You can sign up for a particular time but you don't have to. Just come when you can, if only for a few minutes. You will make a difference.

"3. Community outreach, taking a positive pro-life message to individuals and the community in every constructive way we can. . . .

"Why take part in this unique testimony for life? Because the reality of legalized abortion requires each of us to take a personal stand. Evasions won't work. When Louise Brown, the first 'test-tube baby,' was born in 1978, the whole world knew exactly when her life began—at the union of the sperm and the ovum in the *in vitro* fertilization. To deny this reality of another human life inside the mother, at every stage from that fertilization, can today be the product only of ignorance or willful denial. . . .

"The new technology of morning-after pills and other abortifacients is making abortion a private matter beyond the effective reach of the law. Surgical abortions, such as those performed at Ironwood Circle, are decreasing in frequency. The 40 Days of Life vigil at Ironwood is not therefore to infer that the existence of such execution centers is the only problem. Rather, the abortuary on Ironwood is one sign of a malignant culture in which the intentional infliction of death on the innocent is accepted as an optional problem-solving technique. The 'greatest destroyer of peace today,' said Mother Teresa at the 1994 Prayer Breakfast in Washington, 'is abortion, because it is a war against the child, a direct killing of the innocent child, murder by the mother herself. And if we accept that a mother can kill her own child, how can we tell other people not to kill one another?' We were appalled at the random killings at Columbine, Virginia Tech and elsewhere. But, except for the age and visibility of the victims, how were those murders essentially different from the thousands more that are legally committed each day in abortuaries throughout the land?

"The 40 Days for Life are a reminder of the reality of every abortion, whether surgical or chemical. Abortion, now moving beyond the reach of the law, is the first sacrament of the militant, agnostic secularism which is our dominant public religion. The only remedy for abortion is the voluntary reconversion of the American people to the conviction that every human life is precious because it is a gift of God. The 40 Days for Life campaign is a positive way of asking for the grace of increasing that conviction in the minds and hearts of all of us."

HOW SHOULD CATHOLICS VOTE? Oct. 14, 2008

"How does a Catholic voter decide? If you are uncertain, you have plenty of company. But you also have clear guidance from the Church.

"In *Forming Consciences for Faithful Citizenship*, the U.S. Catholic bishops affirmed in 2008, in accord with Vatican statements, a 'consistent ethic of life [which] neither treats all issues as morally equivalent nor reduces Catholic teaching to one or two issues.'

"Abortion, however, is a defining issue. The Church has always taught that abortion is a grave evil. In 2004, Cardinal Joseph Ratzinger, now Pope Benedict XVI, in a letter to the American bishops, said: 'Not all moral issues have the same weight as abortion and euthanasia. For example, if a Catholic were to be at odds with the Holy Father on the application of capital punishment or on the decision to wage war, he would not for that reason be considered unworthy to present himself to receive Holy Communion. While the Church exhorts civil authorities to seek peace, not war, and to exercise discretion and mercy in imposing punishment on criminals, it may still be permissible to take up arms to repel an aggressor or to have recourse to capital punishment. There may be a legitimate diversity of opinion even among Catholics about waging war and applying the death penalty, but not however with regard to abortion and euthanasia.'

"In other words, there can be a just war, but there can never be a just abortion. In a postscript, Ratzinger said: 'A Catholic would be guilty of formal cooperation in evil, and so unworthy to present himself for Holy Communion, if he were to deliberately vote for a candidate precisely because of the candidate's permissive stand on abortion and/or euthanasia. When a Catholic does not share a candidate's stand in favor of abortion and/or euthanasia, but votes for that candidate for other reasons, it is . . . remote material cooperation, which can be permitted in the presence of proportionate reasons.'

"What could be such 'proportionate reasons?'

"Archbishop John J. Myers, of Newark, in response to the 2004 Ratzinger letter, gave a clear analysis: '[F]or a Catholic citizen to vote for a candidate who supports abortion and embryo-destructive research . . . either (a) both candidates would have to be in favor of embryo killing on roughly an equal scale or (b) the candidate with the superior position on abortion and embryo-destructive research would have to be a supporter of objective evils of a gravity and magnitude beyond that of the 1.3 million yearly abortions plus the killing that would take place if public funds were made available for embryo-destructive research. Frankly, it is hard to imagine circumstance (b) in a society such as ours. . . . [P]olicies on welfare, national security, the war in Iraq, Social Security or taxes, taken singly or in any combination, do not provide a proportionate reason to vote for a pro-abortion candidate.' The Myers analysis makes sense because legalized abortion involves explicit legal authorization of the intentional killing of innocent human beings, with a toll to date of 48.5 million surgical abortions since 1973, not including the uncountable victims of the morning-after pill and other chemical abortifacients.

"Senator Obama regards the question of when babies get human rights as 'above my pay grade.' In the Illinois Senate, despite his disclaimers, he voted, in committee and on the floor, against the Born-Alive Infants Protection Act that would have guaranteed the rights of a person to a child born alive in a botched abortion. Obama supports *Roe v. Wade*. He supports federal funding of abortion and embryonic stem cell research. He co-sponsored the federal Freedom of Choice Act which would establish a 'fundamental right' to abortion and would ban practically every federal or state law restricting abortion. He is a persistent and comprehensive supporter of legalization of the right of any mother to execute her unborn child.

"Senator McCain has adopted a pro-life position during this campaign. He opposes *Roe*, affirms that life begins 'at the moment of conception,' and says that he 'will be a pro-life president.' His pre-campaign record is mixed, including, among other points, his leadership of the 'Gang of 14' which prevented Senate confirmation of pro-life judges. McCain's pro-life position today, however, is clearly superior to Obama's.

"Can a Catholic vote for Obama? Some Catholics, who oppose abortion, support Obama on the ground that the effort to 'reverse' *Roe* is futile and Obama will reduce abortions by fostering pro-life attitudes. Abortion is moving beyond the reach of the law because chemical and other abortifacients are making it a truly private matter. That cultural reality is all the more reason to form the culture by insisting that the law protect the right to life of all innocent human beings. The notion that an administration staffed by Obama activists would promote 'pro-life' attitudes is beyond fantasy. Obama promises to set in concrete the principle that innocent persons can be legally depersonalized and subjected to execution at the discretion of others. That is the principle, not only of *Roe v. Wade* but also of the 1857 *Dred Scott Case*, where the Supreme Court said that slaves were property rather than persons, and of the Nazi extermination of the Jews.

"Opposition to the current wars cannot justify a vote for Obama. The toll

355

from legalized abortion dwarfs the toll of military and civilian casualties in the current wars. In legalized abortion, government explicitly authorizes the intentional killing of innocent human beings. American law does not authorize intentional killing of the innocent in war. The killing of innocents can occur in war as an unintended 'double effect' of justified military action. If United States forces, however, intentionally kill the innocent in war, they are subject to prosecution.

"If a voter's opposition to war cannot justify a vote for Obama, he clearly cannot justify that vote because he thinks Obama's position is superior on economic or social issues where innocents are not subjected to death by government authority.

"A strong, indeed compelling, reason to vote for McCain is to keep Obama out of the White House. But to say that a Catholic cannot vote for Obama is not to say that Church teaching requires that he must vote for McCain. That is up to the voter's prudential judgment. If he can't morally vote for Obama and he won't vote for McCain, he can vote for one of the minor candidates. Or he can skip the presidential ballot. A refusal to vote for President when you have voted on the other offices is still a vote, for 'none of the above.'. . .

"For now, suffice it to say that a Catholic who supports Obama, despite his record, ought at least to refrain from claiming that his position is consistent with the teaching of the Church."

The "Catholic Vote," Nov. 4, 2008

"In this presidential campaign, why did so many Catholics . . . reject the teaching of the Church on . . . abortion and voting? 'Not all moral issues,' said Cardinal Joseph Ratzinger, now Pope Benedict XVI, 'have the same weight as abortion. . . . There may be a . . . diversity of opinion . . . among Catholics about . . . war and . . . the death penalty, but not [on] abortion and euthanasia. . . . A Catholic would be guilty of formal cooperation in evil. . . . if he were to . . . vote for a candidate . . . because of the candidate's permissive stand on abortion. . . . When a Catholic does not share a candidate's stand in favor of abortion . . . but votes for that candidate for other reasons, it is . . . remote material cooperation, which can be permitted in the presence of proportionate reasons.'

"With over 48 million surgical abortions and uncountable millions more by pill or other abortifacients, all authorized by law, Archbishop John J. Myers of Newark accurately concluded that 'policies on welfare, national security, the war in Iraq, Social Security or taxes, taken singly or in any combination, do not provide a proportionate reason to vote for a pro-abortion candidate.'

"The Obama campaign, as the *Washington Post* put it, reached out 'aggressively' to Catholics, arguing 'that the church's teachings on social justice and . . . poverty, the environment, health care and unjust warfare should guide Catholic voters as much as abortion. . . . The Democratic effort includes antiabortion Catholic scholars who . . . favor . . . Obama [and] progressive Catholic organizations that have sprung up.' Some Catholic professors described Obama as the 'pro-life' candidate, because he would reduce abortions by promoting pro-life attitudes and providing social services. You probably have to be an academic to believe that.

"The readiness of some Catholics to put abortion on a par with issues of lesser gravity and so find a 'proportionate reason' to support a pro-abortion candidate could be an unintended consequence of a decision the bishops themselves made nearly three decades ago.

"In *Roe v. Wade*, the Supreme Court ruled that, whether or not the unborn child is a human being, he is not a 'person' and therefore has no right to life. The Court acknowledged that if he is a 'person' the case for abortion 'collapses, for the fetus' right to life is then guaranteed by the [Fourteenth] Amendment.'

"The National Conference of Catholic Bishops (NCCB) promptly condemned the decision and urged 'legal and constitutional conformity to the basic truth that the unborn child is a "person" in every sense of the term from conception.' When four cardinals, Krol, Manning, Cody and Medeiros, testified before the Senate in 1974, they insisted that a constitutional amendment 'should clearly establish that, from conception onward, the unborn child is a human person in the terms of the Constitution' It should restore the 'right to life . . . to the unborn, just as it is provided to all other persons in the United States.' Cardinal Medeiros said 'A States rights' amendment which would simply return jurisdiction over the abortion law to the States, does not seem to be a satisfactory solution. . . . Protection of human life should not depend upon geographic boundaries. . . . Therefore, the prohibition against the direct and intentional taking of innocent taking of innocent human life should be universal and without exceptions.' If the unborn child were recognized as a 'person' with respect to his right to life, abortion would still depend on state legislatures for its prohibition but those legislatures would be bound by 'the supreme law of the land' not to deprive the unborn child of that right to life.

"During the late 1970s support for the cardinals' position eroded. In 1981, the bishops endorsed a states' rights amendment which, . . . the NCCB acknowledged, . . . 'places the extent of restriction and prohibition [of abortion] entirely in the discretion of the federal and state legislatures.' The Senate Committee on the Judiciary agreed that, under the amendment, a state legislature or Congress 'could . . . prohibit abortion or . . . maintain . . . abortion on demand [or enact] reforms that fall somewhere between these . . . propositions.' Report, June 8, 1982.

"The 'states' rights' approach affirms the holding of *Roe* that the unborn child is a nonperson. If your life is subject to termination at the discretion of a state legislature or Congress, you are, in terms of the Constitution, a nonperson. That goes beyond the limited recognition in *Evangelium Vitae*, no. 73, that a legislator 'could licitly support' an imperfect law on abortion when it is 'not possible to overturn or to abrogate a pro-abortion law.' Nor is 'states' rights' a return to the situation prior to *Roe*. Before *Roe*, there had never been a ruling by the Court on personhood. Once the Court ruled in the negative, the only coherent response was, and is, to insist on the personhood of the unborn with respect to his right to life. That does not preclude the advocacy also of effective restrictions on abortion.

"The bishops continue in their support for 'states' rights.' One of the most eloquent statements by bishops in the 2008 campaign undermined its affirmation of the right to life by saying, '*Roe* is bad law. As long as it stands, it prevents returning the abortion issue to the states where it belongs, so . . . the . . . people can decide its future through fair debate and legislation.'

"It is no surprise that some Catholics interpret, or use as a pretext, the bishops' consignment of abortion to the evaluation and 'discretion' of state legislators as an invitation to them, as voters, to make that same political evaluation with abortion as one issue on a par with others.

"The technology of early abortifacients is making abortion a truly private matter beyond the reach of the law. To promote what John Paul II called a 'culture of life,' it is more essential than ever to insist on the entitlement of every human being to be respected and treated as a person from the moment of conception. It would be appropriate for [the bishops] to [adopt] the cardinals' 1974 insistence on the entitlement of the unborn child to the right to life guaranteed to persons by the Constitution."

THE DEATH PENALTY AND RECANTING WITNESSES, Nov. 18, 2008

"When former President Jimmy Carter and Bob Barr, the 2008 Libertarian candidate for President, agree on anything, we should take notice. Both recently urged the Georgia Board of Pardons and Parole to reverse its decision to deny clemency to Troy Anthony Davis, sentenced to death for the 1989 murder of police officer Mark MacPhail.

"Davis was charged with two counts of aggravated assault, one for shooting Michael Cooper at a party, the other for striking, two hours later, a homeless man, Larry Young, on the head with a pistol. Davis with charged with murder for shooting Officer MacPhail, moonlighting as a security guard at a bus station. As charged, MacPhail chased Davis after the assault on Young. Davis fired at MacPhail who was shot in the face and fell. Davis, it was charged, walked over to MacPhail and shot him twice again. The pistol was never found, but shell casings at the scenes showed that the same pistol was used to shoot Cooper and MacPhail. The jury convicted Davis on all counts.

"Davis has sought a new trial on the grounds that he is innocent, that seven of the nine witnesses who testified against him have recanted their testimony and that evidence implicates another person as the killer. The George Supreme Court, in a 4-3 ruling in April 2008, denied Davis a new trial. The Supreme Court of the United States denied review. Further proceedings are pending.

"Courts properly give less weight to a recantation, whether sworn or unsworn, than to the witness' testimony before the judge and jury at the trial. The George Supreme Court majority last April found the recantations insufficient to overturn the jury's verdict because they lacked materiality as to innocence or failed to show the witness' testimony at trial to have been the 'purest fabrication.' The three dissenters said the majority's approach 'is overly rigid and fails to allow an adequate inquiry' into the question of whether an innocent person might have been convicted and might be put to death.

"An innocent person should not be imprisoned for a day, let alone executed. The finality of execution adds urgency to any claim that a person sentenced to death is innocent. On the entire facts, Davis' entitlement to a new trial is . . . doubtful at best. But whatever the outcome, his claim should prompt us to ask: Does it make sense to impose the death penalty even for an aggravated murder such as this? Thirty-six states, plus the United States government, have the death penalty, with 1,129 executions since 1976. As of Jan. 1, 2008, 3,350 persons were on death row in the United States. The passage of two decades and more between the crime and the execution is not unusual. Numerous studies show that the imposition of the death penalty costs taxpayers far more than it would to imprison the defendant for life without parole.

"Since 1973, at least 130 persons have been released from death row with evidence of their innocence of the crime for which the death penalty was imposed. The death penalty, however, should be reconsidered for reasons more basic than the possibility of executing the innocent. The clearest exposition of those reasons is in the recent teaching of the Catholic Church.

"No one, including the state, ever has authority intentionally to kill the innocent. The state, because it ultimately derives its authority from God, has authority to kill intentionally in two cases, the just war and the death penalty.

"The 'primary aim' of punishing a criminal is retribution, 'redressing the disorder introduced by the offense.' *Catechism*, no. 2266. The other purposes of punishment are rehabilitation of the offender and deterrence of the offender and others.

"In *Evangelium Vitae* (EV) and the *Catechism* (CCC), John Paul II reaffirmed the authority of the state to impose the death penalty. But he gave us a new criterion for the use of that penalty. Neither retribution, nor another purpose, will justify the use of the death penalty unless it 'is the only possible way of . . . defending human lives against the unjust aggressor.' In other words, it has to be the only way to keep this criminal from killing again. The fact that the death penalty may deter others from killing is not enough. Nor does the horrific nature of the crime justify execution.

"This restriction arises from the importance of the conversion of the criminal. As St. Augustine and St. Thomas agree, 'for a just man to be made from a sinner is greater than to create heaven and earth.' *S.T.* I, II., Q. 113, art. 9.

"'[N]on-lethal means,' said John Paul, 'are more in keeping with . . . the common good and . . . the dignity of the human person.' Today, . . . as a consequence of the possibilities which the state has for . . . rendering one who has committed an offense incapable of doing harm—without definitively taking away from him the possibility of redeeming himself—the cases in which . . . execution . . . is an absolute necessity 'are very rare, if not practically non-existent.' *Catechism*, no. 2267, quoting EV, no. 56.

"Whether execution is an 'absolute necessity' depends on a prudential judgment as to the ability of the prison system to confine this prisoner securely. But the Church's limitation on the use of the death penalty is a universal, and not a prudential criterion. It applies everywhere and in all states. Use of the death penalty could be permitted under this criterion in some cases, for example, if a life inmate, already in maximum security, murders another inmate or a guard; or if the state is unable to confine inmates securely.

"In our culture the intentional infliction of death has become an optional-problem solving technique. The ultimate perversity is seen in those who oppose the death penalty for criminals and support it for the innocent unborn child. As John Paul said, '[I]n the name of God, respect, protect, love and serve life, every human life!' EV, no. 5.

"If Troy Anthony Davis is innocent of murder, he should not be executed or imprisoned for that crime. For the more basic reasons advanced by the Vicar of Christ, he should not be executed even if he did murder Officer MacPhail."

NOTE: Troy Anthony Davis was executed on September 21, 2011, in the Georgia state prison in Jackson.

CHRISTMAS AND OBAMA, Dec. 9, 2008

"Each Christmas Day, the Pope delivers a message *Urbi et Orbi* to the City and the World. Last year, Benedict XVI said that at Christmas, 'the great hope that brings happiness entered the world.' Perhaps in his *Urbi et Orbi* this year, Benedict will sound again the Christmas note of hope. It would be familiar to the American people who have just elected a President who promises 'change' through 'the audacity of hope.' That political hope, however, is different from the hope Benedict sees in the Christmas event.

"In his 2007 Christmas address to Rome's university students, the Pope urged them to reflect on 'the hope of the modern age' as described in his encyclical *Spe Salvi* (In Hope We Were Saved.) From the 17th century on, he said, 'human progress' was seen as the work only of 'science and technology.' Reason and freedom were separated from God so as to construct the 'kingdom of man . . . in opposition to the kingdom of God.' In this 'materialistic concept . . . changing the economic and political structures . . . could finally bring about a just society where peace, freedom and equality reign.' The 'fundamental error' in this, said Benedict, is that man is not merely the product of economic and social conditions. '[W]ithout ethical principles, science, technology and politics can be used, as . . . still happens . . . for . . . the harm of individuals and humanity.'

"Some changes promised by our president-elect could serve as Exhibit A for the truth of that last comment. Barack Obama not only pledges that 'the first thing I'd do as President is sign the Freedom of Choice Act,' which would remove all restrictions on the 'fundamental right' to abortion. He also strongly supports, and co-sponsored as a Senator, federal funding of embryonic stem-cell research (ESCR) beyond the limited funding allowed heretofore. Each embryo is a living human being. In ESCR, human embryos are produced, by cloning or otherwise, for the purpose of killing them by removing their stem cells which are then used for biomedical research. This is not only wrong in itself. It opens the door to the mass production of human beings as objects of science, the creation of 'designer' human beings, etc.

"In his 2002 book, *God and the World*, Cardinal Joseph Ratzinger, now Benedict XVI, discussed the description in Genesis 3 of the posting of angels east of Eden with flaming swords to keep man, after the Fall, from eating of the Tree of Life (p. 133–38). After the Fall, man was forbidden to eat of that tree which gave immortality, 'since to be immortal in this [fallen] condition would . . . be perdition.' People are now, Ratzinger said, 'starting to pick from the tree of life and make themselves lords of life and death, to reassemble life.' '[P]recisely what man was supposed to be protected from is now actually happening: he is crossing the final boundary. . . . [M]an makes other men his own artifacts. Man no longer originates in the mystery of love, by . . . conception and birth . . . but is produced industrially, like any other product.'

"This is serious business. '[W]e can,' said Ratzinger, 'be certain of this: God will take action to counter an ultimate crime, an ultimate act of self-destruction, on the part of man. He will take action against the attempt to demean mankind by the production of slave-beings. There are indeed final boundaries we cannot cross without turning into agents of destruction of creation itself, without going far beyond the original sin and the first Fall and all its negative consequences.'

"In this presidential interregnum we already know that the 'hope' offered by our political messiah includes the utilitarian abuses described above. In that 'hope,' . . . the intentional killing of the innocent is an optional problem-solving technique. Perhaps some Catholics, especially in the professoriate, will come to reconsider the enormity—and frivolity—of their voting into power a politician committed to the implementation of such a 'hope.'

"Christmas tells a different story. Christmas overturned 'the world-view of that time, which . . . has become fashionable . . . again today. It is not . . . the laws of matter and of evolution that have the final say, but reason, will, love—a Person. . . . who in Jesus has revealed himself as Love.' *Spe Salvi* (SS), no. 5.

"The smart guys of the media, the academy, and the political world can't tell you where you came from, where you are going and how you get there. But 'Christians . . . have a future: it is not that they know the details of what awaits them, but they know in general terms that their life will not end in emptiness. Only when the future is certain as a positive reality [is it] possible to live the present as well.' SS, no. 2. We know this by experience. We ask ourselves, 'What's it all for?' We look for answers here but we know there has to be more. '[W]e need,' said SS, 'the greater and lesser hopes that keep us going day by day.' But 'anyone who does not know God, even though he may entertain all kinds of hopes, is ultimately without hope, without the great hope that sustains the whole of life.' SS, no. 27.

"So what is the lesson of Christmas? As Pope Benedict said last year, it gives us the 'great hope' that is true. That hope transcends political counterfeits because the Person born at Christmas is, himself, Truth with a capital T. In him we 'have a future.' Merry Christmas."

NOTRE DAME'S CATHOLIC IDENTITY, Jan. 19, 2009

"Three decades ago, in 1978, Notre Dame proclaimed itself a 'Research University.' Notre Dame's mission had been the provision of affordable

362

education, in the Catholic tradition, to undergrads, with research and graduate education in an important, complementary role.

"The major universities went heavily into the research business in the 1970s as income limits were raised by Congress on eligibility for federally supported student loans. As limits were repeatedly raised, the universities repeatedly raised tuition to finance their research programs and buildings. The federal programs were a Big Rock Candy Mountain for the universities. They financed their research enterprises on the backs of borrowing students.

"Notre Dame was far from the worst offender but it was in on the action. In 1978–79, undergrad tuition, room and board at Notre Dame was \$5,180. In 2008–2009, it is \$46,680. If it had kept pace with the Consumer Price Index, it would now be \$17, 042. Notre Dame's financial aid office does excellent work in reducing the debt burden of students, but the student or parent loan remains the major form of 'financial aid.'

"In pursuing research repute, our leaders act in what they see as the best interests of Notre Dame. Any criticisms here relate to policies and not persons. The research fixation, however, has unintended consequences. One is the escalation of tuition and student debt. Another is the 'building binge' which has irrevocably transformed the formerly pastoral Notre Dame into a crowded, urban-style campus. One wonders where they will put the inevitable parking garage and which lucky donor will get to put his or her name on it. Another result is a diminished emphasis on undergrad teaching. As one tenured liberal arts professor put it, 'You don't really need to have any impact on the undergraduates' to get promoted. 'You just need [to have written] a book.'

"One overlooked result is the decrease of Catholic faculty. In the 1970s more than 80 percent of the Notre Dame faculty identified themselves as Catholic. In 1986 it was 64 percent. Now it is 53 percent and going south.

"17 years ago, Dr. David W. Lutz, then a Notre Dame Ph.D. candidate and now professor of philosophy at the Catholic University of Eastern Africa in Nairobi, identified the 'real danger' to Notre Dame's Catholic identity as those 'who believe that Notre Dame can strive for ever-higher standards of academic excellence—and use the same criteria . . . by which . . . secular universities . . . are judged to be excellent—without forfeiting [its] Catholic character.' *First Things*, January 1992. 'Elite universities,' Dr. Lutz later wrote, 'are ranked by . . . the research they produce. One . . . problem with emphasizing research is that teaching may be de-emphasized but a far more important, though less-noted, danger is that emphasizing research causes Catholicism to be de-emphasized. This is true, not because there is any problem with doing excellent Catholic research, but because it is more difficult to publish such research in prestigious journals and with elite university presses than to publish the kind of scholarship respected by secular universities.' *Observer*, Feb. 17, 1993. [In August 2011, Dr. Lutz joined the faculty of Holy Cross College, Notre Dame, IN.]

"Notre Dame benefits greatly from the presence of faculty who are not Catholic. The Administration, in accord with *Ex Corde Ecclesiae*, the Apostolic Constitution on Catholic Universities, is trying to increase the Catholic faculty. One obstacle is the insistence, as the Ad Hoc Committee put it, that those efforts 'cannot be allowed to compromise the University's academic quality.' The false dichotomy between faith and academic quality distorts reason as well as faith. It ensures the obliteration of the Catholic character of the University.

"In 'The Decline and Fall of the Christian College,' in *First Things* in 1991, Fr. James T. Burtchaell, C.S.C., said the Christian college 'must have a predominance of committed . . . communicants of its mother church. This must be regarded, not as an alien consideration, but as a professional qualification. . . . [A]cademic qualifications can be . . . traded off . . . but when any one of them is systematically subordinated . . . it will shortly disappear from the institution.'

"Commitment to the Catholic faith is not a non-rational preference irrelevant to suitability for the academic life of a Catholic university. John Paul II affirmed the 'unity between the knowledge of reason and the knowledge of faith. . . . [T]he world and . . . history cannot be understood in depth without professing faith in the God who is at work in them.' *Fides et Ratio*, no. 16. He described the 'knowledge which is peculiar to faith' as 'surpassing the knowledge proper to human reason.' No. 8.

"In his 2005 Address at Notre Dame, Archbishop J. Michael Miller, of the Congregation for Catholic Education, addressed the relation between faith and research. He quoted John Paul II: 'In carrying out its research, a Catholic university can rely on a superior enlightenment which, without changing the nature of this research, purifies it, orients it, enriches it and uplifts it. . . . This light is not found 'outside' rational research, as a limitation or an impediment, but rather 'above' it, as its elevation and an expansion of its horizons.' As Miller noted, 'the Catholic tradition has unremittingly held that the more we probe the mystery of God with the help of faith, the more we understand reality. . . . The gift of faith empowers the intellect to act according to its deepest nature.

"Our leaders ought not to subordinate Catholic faith as a professional qualification for the academic life of Notre Dame. The President has authority to appoint faculty. He could solve the 'Catholic' problem by executive veto of appointments. It is a question of will."

RATS, ELEPHANTS, AND THE BENGAL BOUTS, Feb. 10, 2009

"'We are being overrun by rats that have come into the jungle and the hills because of the flowers and the seeds/fruits of the bamboo. They are destroying the crops of the people. And a group of 41 elephants has destroyed crops, banana trees and homes in a number of villages. And now is the time of drought. The people are suffering a lot, with very little food (surviving on wild roots and new bamboo plants as their daily food), and they cannot afford the school fees for their children. They come to us everyday asking for money for food and treatment or medicine. I am sorry for telling you the present situation of our people, but as a pastor I think and feel for them and I just needed to share with someone.'

"Those lines, in a recent letter from Fr. Robi Gomes, C.S.C., to Fr. Tom Smith, C.S.C., tell you more about the need for the Bengal Bouts than I ever could. Since 1931 the Bouts have become the largest single contributor to the Holy Cross missions in Bangladesh. Now the relation has moved to a new level. Last summer, Boxing Club president Mark Weber, boxers Tomas Castillo, Patrick Martin, Leo Rubinkowski, Mike Lee and Patrick Ryan raised money to go to Bangladesh with Professor William Donaruma and cinematographer John Klein, '06. They made a film, 'Strong Bodies Fight,' depicting the realities of the missions. The premiere will be on campus on the Navy weekend in November. See www.strongbodiesfight.org. A student service project in Bangladesh may result from the effort. More about the film and project in a later column.

"Since 1854, Holy Cross priests, brothers and sisters have labored in Bangladesh, especially among the tribal people in remote areas. Of the 140 priests and brothers and the 70 sisters now in Bangladesh, all but 19 are Bangladeshi. The country has more than 140 million people in an area the size of Wisconsin. 89.7 percent are Muslims, 9.2 percent are Hindus, with the rest Buddhists, Christians and others. The nationwide per capita income is $1400, but the ultra-poor served by Holy Cross have far less. When you go to a basketball game at the JACC and drop $3.50 for some ice cream creation, you will spend what would feed a family of four among those ultra poor for almost a week. In 2008, the Bouts contributed more than $50,000 to the missions, a comparatively huge sum.

"The needs are pressing. Fr. Alex Rabanol, C.S.C., in St. George's Parish in remote Mariamnagar, has 50 children, grades one through five, and two teachers in his boarding school. The children have no money and they board because they live far away. Fr. Alex needs money to feed those kids.

"Corpus Christi Parish is in Mymensingh diocese, a hilly area where the water is putrid for at least half of the year. Fr. Schusanto Gomes, C.S.C., needs at least 50 tube wells, at a total cost of $3,500, to relieve the disease caused by the bad water.

"Fatima Rani Parish in Bandarban is in a very poor and remote, forested area. Holy Cross has served it since 1957. The priests always carry medicines to treat the many adults and children afflicted with malaria and dysentery. They also have the rat and elephant problems described above by Fr. Gomes, the pastor. He needs about $4,000 for a badly needed dispensary.

" The list of needs could go on and on. The Bengal Bouts are literally a lifesaving operation. The program is run by the boxers themselves, under the supervision of Rich O'Leary and Jimmy Rogers of Rec Sports. The captains are Mark Weber, Mike Lee, Kris Perez, Dan Rodgers, Leo Rubinkowski, Diego Villalba, Brian de Splinter, Patrick Burns and Chris Cugliari. Tom Suddes, Chicago attorney Terry Johnson and University pilot Pat Farrell are the head coaches. The assistant coaches include Sweet C. Robinson of the Buchanan Police Department, Mike Hurley, former boxers Ryan Rans, Chip Farrell, Thad Naquin, Judge Roland Chamblee, and Father Brian Daley.

"Dr. Jim Moriarty oversees the medical and safety program which has prevented serious injury for 78 years. Emergency Medical Technician Terri Engel attends every sparring session along with EMTs Erica Daley, Sean Bradley and Steve Serbalik, along with Bonnie Chow, Bert Williams and Myisha Eatmon of RecSports whose official title, on their T-shirts, is (no kidding) 'professional rescuers.'

"The real indispensables, however, are the managers, Kelly Garvy, Katherine Johnson, Ashley Mensch, Catherine Cooney, and Meghan Rolfs. They not only keep impeccable sparring, advertising, equipment and other records. They are the brains of the outfit, day to day. Without them, things would grind to a halt. And they know why they do it. 'The work is challenging, the people are great,' said Ashley Mensch, 'but most important, we are doing something real for people who need it.'

"On Jan. 13, more than 300 athletic (some might say masochistic) young men began their final training for the Bouts. Probably half will survive the training imposed, not offered, by volunteer coach Tom Suddes, a Columbus developer, who matches his victims push-up for push-up. Why do the boxers do this? One reason is to get in shape and experience the challenge of stepping into the ring, alone, and putting yourself on the line. But the other reason, as any of us involved with the boxers can guarantee, is that they really want to 'give back' to help the poor on those missions. . . .

"'The Bengal Bouts,' said Fr. Tom Smith, C.S.C., director of the Holy Cross Mission Center, 'are a vital support as our Holy Cross community seeks to show God's love and compassion to the hungry and sick, and offers hope through education efforts throughout Bangladesh.' Beyond that, the Bouts are fun to watch. If you go once, you'll be hooked. Please support them."

GRANDMA AND THE FEDS, Feb. 24, 2009

"Grandma has a problem. The Feds, it appears, are about to ration her health care. That could turn out her lights. The Obama stimulus package creates a new bureaucracy under a National Coordinator for Health Information Technology. . . . The Coordinator is mandated to develop an infrastructure that 'reduces health care costs resulting from inefficiency [and] inappropriate care. . . .' [Sec. 3001 (b) (3).]. Medicare currently pays for treatments that are safe and effective. The stimulus opens the door to a cost-effectiveness standard pursuant to guidelines set by the bureaucracy. Under such a standard the availability of care could turn on Grandma's age, her productivity, etc. The recession will intensify pressure to reduce medical spending on non-productive persons. In that game a 75 year-old woman seeking a substantial medical procedure will be a predictable loser.

"A later column will discuss the stimulus in detail. For now, let's ask: If Grandma is denied a needed operation and is home in bed with no hope of recovery, can you put her out of her misery? If she is on a feeding tube, can you withdraw it? Suppose she wants to die? The stimulus provides an added reason to address these issues, but they already arise with patients of all ages who are incurable, incompetent, or both.

"The legal and moral principles are clear. A competent adult has the legal right to refuse any and all medical treatment, including the right to refuse food and water whether naturally or artificially provided. If a patient is incompetent, the law permits withholding of treatment, including food and water, based on the patient's intent previously expressed in an advance directive or otherwise, or based on his health care agent's opinion that the patient would want such withdrawal or, in some states, that it would be in his best interest.

"The moral principles are clearly presented in Catholic teaching. First, you never have the right intentionally to kill the patient. '[T]he direct and voluntary killing of an innocent human being is always gravely immoral.' *Evangelium Vitae* (EV), 57. This includes euthanasia, 'an act or omission which, of itself or by intention, causes death in order to eliminate suffering.' *Catechism* (CCC), 2277. The *Catechism* calls it 'murder.'

"With respect to medical treatments, we have a duty to use all ordinary and proportionate means to preserve our own lives and the lives of those in our care. See CCC, 2276–79. '[M]edical procedures that are "burdensome, dangerous, extraordinary or disproportionate" are not morally obligatory.' CCC, 2278.

"The main issues involve palliative care and the withdrawal of nutrition and hydration. In *Vacco v. Quill*, in 1997, the Supreme Court said a State 'may permit palliative care' of patients to relieve their pain, even though it 'may have the foreseen but unintended "double effect" of hastening the patient's death.' According to Catholic teaching, palliative care may be so administered to relieve pain even though it hastens the unintended death of the patient. But it cannot be used with the intent to kill the patient. The law, however, cannot ordinarily determine whether the palliative care was given to relieve pain or to cause death. Where the family and caregivers agree that it is time for the patient to die, the administration of morphine and other palliatives can be a mode of homicide effectively beyond the reach of the law.

"On nutrition and hydration, if a patient refuses food and water with the intent to die, it is a form of suicide which 'is always as morally objectionable as murder.' EV, 66.

"In the Terri Schiavo case, Judge Greer ordered, and not merely authorized, Michael Schiavo to remove not only the feeding tube but all forms of 'nutrition and hydration' from his wife. The only reason you heard about Terri Schiavo was because the family members disagreed. When the family and caregivers agree that the patient should die, he can be legally executed by withdrawal of food and water. There are no statistics but it is fair to assume that such executions are numerous and perhaps routine.

"The Congregation of the Doctrine of the Faith (CDF), with the approval of Pope Benedict XVI, issued a statement on August 1, 2007, on 'the nutrition and hydration of patients in . . . a "vegetative state."' The principles apply to all patients in whatever condition. The CDF posed and answered two questions:

"First question: Is the administration of food and water (whether by natural or artificial means) to a patient in a 'vegetative state' morally obligatory except when they cannot be assimilated by the patient's body or cannot be administered to the patient without causing significant discomfort?

"Response: Yes. The administration of food and water even by artificial means is, in principle, an ordinary and proportionate means of preserving life. It is therefore obligatory to the extent to which, and for as long as, it is shown to accomplish its proper finality, which is the hydration and nourishment of the patient. In this way suffering and death by starvation and dehydration are prevented.

"Second question: When nutrition and hydration are being supplied by artificial means to a patient in a 'permanent vegetative state' may they be discontinued when competent physicians judge with moral certainty that the patient will never regain consciousness?

"Response: No. A patient in a 'permanent vegetative state' is a person with fundamental human dignity and must, therefore, receive ordinary and proportionate care which includes, in principle, the administration of food and water even by artificial means.'

"A feeding tube is not intended to cure the cancer or other disease. Its purpose is nourishment and the prevention of suffering from hunger and thirst. Grandma's feeding tube may morally be removed only when she cannot assimilate the food and water or when it is disproportionately painful and the removal is intended only to relieve the pain, with the implicit intent to replace it as soon as it can be done without causing such pain. One could apparently also be justified in removing the tube in the closing minutes before death when the lack of food and water will not cause discomfort and will not contribute to the death, subject to the duty to put it back if the expected death does not occur. The fact Grandma is incurable or will never recover consciousness does not justify starving or dehydrating her to death. To remove a feeding tube with the intent to end Grandma's life is 'murder.' CCC, 2277.

"Whatever President Obama does to ration health care, each of us ought to be aware of the principles that govern our own care and the care of those for whom we are responsible."

Octomom, March 17, 2009

"The California hospital where they were born calls them 'Suleman Babies A to H.' Their mother, Nadya Suleman, an unmarried, unemployed 33-year-old grad student, already had six children, ages two to seven, all through in vitro fertilization (IVF). She was surprised when the octuplets appeared after six embryos, conceived by IVF, were placed in her womb. She instantly became Octomom. Reaction, mostly critical, focused on Nadya's 'irresponsibility' and the 'professional negligence' of a physician who would perform IVF on a single mother of six.

"The case, however, should prompt a reappraisal of the effects of IVF and related techniques on the human dignity of all those involved. On Sept. 8, 2008, the Congregation for the Doctrine of the Faith issued, with the approval of Pope Benedict XVI, an instruction on bioethics, *Dignitatis Personae* (*The Dignity of a Person*) (DP). DP presents the principles governing IVF and other types of artificial fertilization, as well as new techniques including gene therapy, therapeutic and reproductive cloning, the use of stem cells, both embryonic and adult, and the attempted hybridization of human and animal genetic elements. Space permits discussion here only of DP's treatment of IVF.

"The opening sentence of DP states the theme: 'The dignity of a person must be recognized in every human being from conception to natural death.' DP builds on *Humanae Vitae*, the 1968 encyclical of Pope Paul VI which affirmed the inseparability on human initiative of the unitive and procreative meanings of the conjugal act. 'The transmission of life,' said DP, 'is inscribed in nature and its laws stand as an unwritten norm to which all must refer.' (6). The acceptance of IVF is a predictable result of the acceptance of contraception. Contraception seeks to take the unitive without the procreative, while IVF takes the procreative without the unitive.

"Hormonal or surgical techniques, however, that remove obstacles to natural fertilization, such as surgical repair of fallopian tubes, are encouraged by

DP because none of them 'replaces the conjugal act.' (13) But techniques 'which substitute for the conjugal act' (12) are unacceptable, including artificial fertilization, both heterologous (using the sperm of a third party) and homologous (using the husband's sperm). IVF, followed by transfer of the embryo to the womb, is such a technique.

"In IVF, more embryos are produced than are intended to be placed in the womb. Some may be frozen for future use. Those with defects are 'discarded.' (15) More embryos are then placed in the womb than the number of children desired, 'to increase the chance that at least one will implant in the uterus.' (15) If, however, more implant than are desired, the answer is 'embryo reduction' in which the extra children in the womb are 'exterminated [by] selective abortion.' (21)

"Such a 'purely utilitarian treatment' of human life is seen clearly in the genetic diagnosis made before transfer into the womb. '[A]n embryo suspected of having . . . defects, or not having the sex desired, or having other qualities that are not wanted [is destroyed].' (22). Such reflects 'a eugenic mentality that [measures] the value of a human being only [by] 'normality' and physical well-being, thus opening the way to . . . infanticide and euthanasia.' (22). 'The acceptance of the enormous number of abortions involved in IVF illustrates how the replacement of the conjugal act by a technical procedure . . . leads to a weakening of the respect owed to every human being.' (16.)

"Remember that each embryo is a living human being. IVF affronts the human dignity of the embryo and of Octomom herself. One is treated as an industrial product, subject to quality control, and the other as a receptacle for that product subject to further quality control.

"'The Church,' said DP, 'understands the suffering of couples struggling with problems of fertility. [T]he desire [for a child], however, should not override the dignity of [a] human life,' nor can it 'justify the 'production' of offspring.' (16). And the desire not to have a child cannot justify the abandonment or destruction of a child once he or she has been conceived.' (16.)

"IVF often requires repeated attempts to achieve success. Multiple oocytes (unfertilized eggs) can be taken from the woman and frozen for future use in 'artificial procreation.' Such is 'morally unacceptable' (19), as are proposals to use frozen embryos for research or treatment of disease; such 'would treat the embryos as mere 'biological material' and result in their destruction.' (19)

"Adoption of frozen embryos, who could be implanted in the adopted woman's womb and carried to term, could give them a chance to live. On the other hand, it would encourage, and materially cooperate with, the IVF industry by making adoption a profitable outlet for its 'products.' DP does not address these concerns, although it describes 'prenatal adoption' as 'praiseworthy [in its] intention of respecting and defending human life.' (19). But

370

then it concludes that, 'all things considered, . . . the . . . abandoned embryos represent a situation of injustice which in fact cannot be resolved.' Therefore John Paul II made an 'appeal . . . that the production of human embryos be halted, taking into account that there seems to be no morally licit solution regarding the human destiny of the 'frozen embryos,' which . . . should . . . be protected by law as human persons.' (19). A more detailed discussion by the Magisterium of the 'prenatal adoption' issue would be helpful.

"The 'Suleman Babies A to H' ought to make us think. We can proceed down the path laid out by the contraceptive separation of life from conjugal love. That path leads not only to IVF but to other techniques discussed in DP, including embryonic stem cell research which taxpayers will now fund by order of President Obama, cloning and other refinements. They involve the acceptance of utilitarian murder on a mass scale. The alternative is to return to the natural law and the recognition of every human being, from conception to natural death, as a person who has, from God, a right to life that transcends the state."

Notre Dame and Obama, March 31, 2009

"Notre Dame is not a public utility. It has no commitment to honor at its capstone ceremony every politician whom the political process deposits in the Oval Office. Nor is there an unbroken custom that, if a president is invited, it must be in his first year.

"Our leaders had to know that their invitation to President Obama would imply a general commendation of the man and his policies. In the conflicts over those policies, our leaders have committed, in perception but also in fact, the name and prestige of Notre Dame to the side that is hostile to the imperatives of faith and reason affirmed by the Catholic Church. Our leaders are not only dismissive but also contemptuous toward the Church. The first thing Bishop D'Arcy knew about it was when he was told that Obama had accepted the invitation.

"President Obama is a relentless advocate of unrestricted abortion, including the Freedom of Choice Act, which would abrogate all state laws restricting abortion. . . .

"At the other end of life, the Stimulus Package foreshadows the rationing of health care for the elderly and unproductive. '[T]he Obama Administration,' said Cardinal Francis George, 'intends to remove a . . . rule for the Department of Health and Human Services [HHS] that [protects] doctors, nurses and others . . . who have objections in conscience to . . . abortion and other killing procedures . . . [S]uch . . . would be the first step in moving our country from democracy to despotism.' Not surprisingly, Obama's nominee for Secretary of HHS, Governor Kathleen Sebelius, a Catholic, has a strongly pro-abortion record, including persistent vetoes of restrictions on late-term abortions. The abolition of conscience protection could spell the end of Catholic hospitals and drive Catholics out of much of the medical profession. That prospect raises our leaders' honoring of Obama to a new level of scandal and betrayal.

"The definitive 'life' issue arises from Obama's authorization of HHS 'to fund and conduct human embryonic stem cell research' (ESCR). Adult stem cells, derived from bone marrow and other sources, have been used successfully in relieving various injuries and medical conditions. Embryonic stem cells have never successfully treated a human patient for anything. But federal funding would make ESCR a profitable, if useless, industry.

"No moral problems arise in the use of adult stem cells. But every embryo is a living human being. To remove the stem cells kills that embryo. It is, in moral terms, a murder.

"ESCR can be performed on embryos left over from in vitro fertilization. The excuse that 'they are going to die anyway' does not justify intentionally killing them any more than it would justify involuntary lethal experiments on condemned criminals.

"ESCR can also be performed on embryos created by cloning. In cloning, the nucleus of a somatic cell, which is any cell of the body other than a sperm or egg cell, is inserted into an egg (ovum) cell from which the egg cell's nucleus has been removed. The egg is then electrically stimulated to react as if it had been fertilized by a sperm cell. The result is a one-cell zygote which divides and develops. For the first eight weeks it is called an embryo. The cloned embryo is genetically identical to the donor of the somatic cell.

"Cloning can be reproductive, in which the embryo is implanted in a woman's womb and carried to term, or therapeutic, in which the embryo is killed by removal of the stem cells for use in research. Both types are condemned by Catholic teaching. See *Dignitas Personae* (2008), nos. 28–30.

"'[W]e will ensure,' Obama said, 'that our government never opens the door to the use of cloning for human reproduction. It is dangerous, profoundly wrong, and has no place in our society, or any society.' He opened the door for the worse evil of therapeutic cloning. The Dickey Amendment, which has denied funds for 'creation of a human embryo . . . for research purposes' or for 'research in which a human embryo is destroyed,' is being removed. So the Obama Administration will fund the creation of new human beings by cloning for the purpose of killing them and using their stem cells for research. The experiments performed by Nazi doctors on concentration camp victims were unimaginative and primitive by comparison. Our leaders ought not to act like the 'good Germans,' who were submissive to their Fuhrer, by conferring Notre Dame's highest honors on the perpetrator of such an atrocity.

"Apart from the 'life' issues, our leaders were reckless to commit Notre Dame to Obama in the face of mounting and well-grounded opposition to other Obama policies, including his fiscal deficits and such a stunning expansion of executive power and of federal control over private entities and states that it amounts to a constitutional coup. Unmentioned in the background are the pending lawsuits—not yet decided on the merits by the Supreme Court—that raise serious questions as to Obama's eligibility for the office.

"Our leaders act in what they think are the best interests of Notre Dame. But that is no excuse. The invitation should be withdrawn. It implies no personal animosity to suggest that Fr. Jenkins and the other Fellows and Trustees responsible for this fiasco should resign or be removed.

"What would be a proper response? On-site demonstrations would be counterproductive. You can petition or write to our leaders. But the appeal should be made instead to a higher authority. An alumnus has suggested that students, faculty, staff and friends of Notre Dame ought to—and we will—pray a continuous Rosary of reparation at the Grotto during the time of the Commencement, from two to four on Sunday, May 17th. This would not interfere with Commencement which is on the other side of campus. It would not be a demonstration or protest. No signs, marches, or disruption. Just peaceful prayer, in silence or aloud, by individuals and families. If you can't make it to the Grotto, pray the Rosary during that time wherever you are. Incidentally, Professor Mary Ann Glendon, the Laetare Medal recipient, would make better use of her time at the Grotto than as a warm-up or wind-up act at Commencement.

"Parking is limited, but you can park off campus and walk to the Grotto. There should be no objection by Notre Dame officials to students, faculty, staff and friends of Notre Dame peacefully going to the Grotto to pray. It makes no difference how many show up. The objective is simply a union of prayer to make reparation and to petition Notre Dame, Our Lady, for Notre Dame, our University."

THE GOVERNANCE OF NOTRE DAME, April 28, 2009

"Notre Dame's honoring of President Obama is no surprise. It is a predictable result of a change of course that Catholic universities made four decades ago. In 1967, officials of the leading Catholic universities met at the Notre Dame retreat at Land O'Lakes, Wisconsin, and declared that: 'To perform its teaching and research functions effectively, the Catholic university must have a true autonomy and academic freedom in the face of authority of whatever kind, lay or clerical, external to the academic community itself.' Most Catholic universities, including Notre Dame, soon severed their juridical connection with the Church and transferred control to lay-dominated boards of trustees. As Fordham President Leo McLaughlin had earlier observed, one reason was to 'make them eligible for federal and state aid.'

"At Notre Dame the Fellows have the leading role. 'From 1842 to 1967 [Notre Dame] was owned by the Congregation of Holy Cross. In 1967, governance . . . was transferred to a predominantly lay Board of Trustees [and] the Statutes of the University created a body . . . known as the Fellows. They have . . . all power and authority granted by [the charter of the University]. The Fellows are a self-perpetuating body, 12 in number, six . . . are [Holy Cross priests] and six . . . are lay persons . . . [T]he establishment of the Fellows was intended to be a protective mechanism for the University.' The Holy Cross priests who are six of the 12 Fellows, if united, can prevent any University action of which they disapprove. The Fellows also have the duty to maintain the 'essential character of the University as a Catholic institution.'

"*Ex Corde Ecclesiae*, the 1990 Apostolic Constitution on Catholic Universities, does not require the Catholic university to have a juridical connection with the Church. But the university does have an 'essential relationship' to the Church which 'includes a recognition of and adherence to the teachings of the church in matters of faith and morals.' It is difficult to imagine a more flagrant disrespect for those teachings than Notre Dame's bestowal of its highest honors on a person with the record and stated purposes of Obama.

"The problem is 'truth in labeling.' For four decades, Notre Dame has promoted itself as a 'Catholic university,' according to its own private definition rather than that of the Church which alone has authority to define that term. ND 2010, the strategic plan, says the University 'must take into account with . . . sensitivity and respect the formal teaching role of the Magisterium in the life of the Church.' But Notre Dame does not accept Church teaching as binding on the University. The Magisterium is practically irrelevant. Thus, in their April 2, 2008, 'statement on the rationale for hiring faculty who will enhance our Catholic mission,' Fr. Jenkins and the Provost, Dr. Burish, went on for six pages about keeping Notre Dame 'truly Catholic' without once mentioning the Catholic Church. That is like explaining the game of baseball without mentioning the ball.

"Our leaders' pursuit of autonomy from the Church fosters a relativism which has eroded Catholic identity, as in the reduction of Catholic faculty. In the 1970s, before Notre Dame, in 1978, proclaimed itself a 'research university' more than 80 percent of the Notre Dame faculty identified themselves as Catholic. In 1986 it was 64 percent. Now it is 53 percent and going south with little prospect for change.

"The Land O'Lakes 'autonomy . . . in the face of [external] authority' is a fake. Notre Dame accepts the authority of the federal government and dozens of other entities, such as the NCAA, as well as the secular academic establishment. One authority it will not accept is that of the Catholic Church to define the meaning of a 'Catholic university.' This problem is not peculiar to Notre Dame. 'In the United States,' said the late Cardinal Avery Dulles, 'Catholic universities have been very apologetic, almost embarrassed, by their obligation to adhere to the faith of the Church. For [Cardinal John Henry] Newman and John Paul II, any university that lacks the guidance of Christian revelation and the oversight of the Catholic magisterium is . . . impeded in its mission to find and transmit truth. It fails to make use of an important resource that God in His providence has provided. Surrounded by powerful institutions constructed on principles of metaphysical and religious agnosticism, the Catholic universities . . . have too long been on the defensive. . . . They should proudly reaffirm the essentials of their own tradition.' The first step in that reaffirmation would be to repudiate Land O'Lakes.

"Our leaders do not own Notre Dame. They are temporary fiduciaries with a duty to preserve its Catholic character. They violated that duty by severing it from the Church. And now, as the nation finds itself with a president who, through cloning and embryonic stem cell research, will fund the creation of human beings to kill them, who will end conscience rights for health care personnel, etc., our leaders have a duty to witness to truth. Instead, they have assumed the role of the sycophant by conferring Notre Dame's highest honors on that man in defiance of the mandate of the U.S. bishops.

"The trajectory from Land O'Lakes to honoring Obama is a straight line. The stakes are high. Cardinal Joseph Ratzinger, now Benedict XVI, discussed in 2002 the posting of angels east of Eden with flaming swords to keep man, after the Fall, from eating of the Tree of Life which gave immortality. '[T]o be immortal in this [fallen] condition would . . . be perdition.' People are now, Ratzinger said, 'starting to pick from the tree of life and make themselves lords of life and death, to reassemble life. . . . Precisely what man was . . . to be protected from is now . . . happening: he is crossing the final boundary. . . . [M]an makes other men his own artifacts. Man no longer originates in the mystery of love . . . but is produced industrially, like any other product.'

"'We can,' said Ratzinger, 'be certain of this: God will take action to counter an ultimate crime, an ultimate act of self-destruction, on the part of man. He will take action against the attempt to demean mankind by the production of slave-beings. There are . . . final boundaries we cannot cross without turning into agents of destruction of creation itself.'

"Our last column presented the suggestion of an alumnus that our best response to the honoring of Obama would be a continuous Rosary of reparation and petition at the Grotto during the time of Commencement, from 2–4 p.m., on May 17. If you can't be there, pray the Rosary wherever you are at that time. Either way, pray to Notre Dame, Our Lady, for our country. And pray that she will bring Notre Dame, her University, back to the Church of her Son."

2009–2010

END OF LIFE AND OBAMACARE, Sept. 8, 2009

"The main health care bill, H.R. 3200, 'America's Affordable Health Choices Act of 2009,' has 1,017 pages. I read it, which gave me some, but not much, sympathy for House members who admit that they voted for it in committee, or endorsed it, without reading it.

"Section 1233 (pages 424–34), on 'advanced care planning consultation,' expands the physician services that Medicare will reimburse, to include consultations regarding end-of-life decision-making. Senator Chuck Grassley (R-IA) says the Senate Finance Committee has removed 'the end-of-life provisions' from its bill because they would pay physicians to 'advise patients about end-of-life care and rate physician quality of care based on the creation of and adherence to orders for end-of-life care.' But that bill is only one of several on the subject. It is too early to count the end-of-life consultations out. As Health and Human Services Secretary Kathleen Sebelius said on August 16, 'I'm hoping that at the end of the day' the consultation provisions 'will be part of the overall package.'

"Let's look at what Section 1233 says and, more important, what it does not say and thus leaves to bureaucratic, implementing regulations which could make the 1,017 pages of the bill look like a telegram. An 'advanced care planning consultation' is between 'the individual and a practitioner' who does not have to be the individual's own physician. A 'practitioner' can be a physician or a 'nurse practitioner or physician's assistant who has the authority under State law to sign orders for life sustaining treatments.' The bill does not state whether the consultation will be initiated by the practitioner or by the individual. Nor does it state that the individual is compelled to have a consultation. 'Though not mandatory,' wrote Charles Lane of the Washington Post editorial board, 'the consultations . . . aren't quite "purely voluntary." To me,' he said, "purely voluntary" means "not unless the patient requests one."' Section 1233 . . . lets doctors initiate the chat and gives them an incentive—money—to do so. Indeed, that's an incentive to insist. Patients may refuse without penalty, but many will bow to white-coated authority. Once they're in the meeting, the bill does permit 'formulation' of a plug-pulling order right then and there. Regulations could, in effect, make the consultations mandatory, to be initiated by the individual or the practitioner with penalties on the individual who fails to initiate it.

"A consultation shall include: 'An explanation by the practitioner of advanced care planning . . . and . . . advance directives, including living wills and durable powers of attorney . . . the role . . . of a health care proxy . . . [t]he provision by the practitioner of a list of . . . resources to assist . . . with advanced care planning. . . . [a]n explanation . . . of . . . end-of-life services . . . available, including patient care and hospice . . . an explanation of orders regarding life sustaining treatment . . . which shall include . . . the reasons why . . . such an order is beneficial to the individual and the individual's family and the reasons why such an order should be updated periodically as the health of the individual changes.' Note that the consultation 'shall include' an explanation of only one side of the question of whether such an order would be beneficial.

"'A consultation . . . may include the formulation of an order regarding life sustaining treatment . . . [which is] an actionable . . . order relating to the treatment of that individual that (i) is signed and dated by a physician . . . or another health care professional (as specified by the Secretary) . . . in a form that permits it to stay with the individual and be followed by health care professionals . . . across the continuum of care; (ii) . . . communicates the individual's preferences regarding life sustaining treatment, including an indication of the treatment and care desired by the individual; (iii) is . . . standardized within in a given locality . . . (as identified by the Secretary); and (iv) may incorporate any advance directive . . . if executed by the individual.'

"'The level of treatment indicated' by the order 'may range from . . . full treatment to an indication to limit some or all or specified interventions. Such . . . levels of treatment may include indications respecting, among other items—(i) the intensity of medical intervention if the patient is pulse-less, apneic, or has serious cardiac or pulmonary problems; (ii) the individual's desire regarding transfer to a hospital or remaining at the current care setting; (iii) the use of antibiotics; and (iv) the use of artificially administered nutrition and hydration.'

"This 'actionable' order becomes part of the individual's permanent record, available to the government and health care professionals who are required to follow it. Opponents of end-of-life consultations were derided by President Obama and the media for raising the prospect of 'death panels.' But note that the order does not have to be signed by the practitioner who conducts the consultation. Regulations, consistent with Section 1233, could provide that the order would be signed by a 'health care professional' other than that practitioner who formulated it. There is no mandate that the professional who signs the order ever saw the individual involved. Could the signer be a member of a panel reviewing such orders without ever seeing the patient? Apparently so.

"The order 'communicates the individual's preferences . . . including . . . the treatment . . . desired by the individual.' But it does not specify that the order must comply with those preferences. If the individual had executed an advance directive, the order 'may incorporate' it but does not have to include it or even refer to it.

"Section 1233 does not state whether the individual's personal physician, lawyer or family members may be present at the 'advance care planning consultation.' Nor does it specify that the order will be subject to judicial review.

"An 'advance care planning consultation' may be held 'if the individual . . . has not had such a consultation within the last 5 years.' A consultation 'may be conducted more frequently . . . if there is a significant change in the health condition of the individual, including diagnosis of a chronic, progressive, life-limiting disease, a life-threatening or terminal diagnosis or life-threatening injury, or upon admission to a skilled nursing facility, a long-term care facility . . . or a hospice program.' The bill imposes no limit on the number or frequency of such consultations, raising the prospect of repeated pressuring of patients to forego treatment.

"'Obamacare' seeks to increase those who are covered and to reduce costs. The only way to achieve both objectives is to ration the health care provided to the elderly and disabled. Half of a person's medical expenses generally occur in the last six months of life. The rationing, at first, will be technically voluntary. Grandma will be told that she is not eligible for that hip replacement. She will be given the option of taking pain pills. But she will be encouraged to relieve the burden on her family through legal means of achieving 'death with dignity.' Section 1233 is evil in its effect and potential."

ABORTION IN OBAMACARE, Sept. 22, 2009

"When Congressman Joe Wilson (R-NC) shouted 'You lie!' to President Barack Obama's denial, in his address to Congress that his health care reforms 'would insure illegal immigrants,' Obama retorted, 'It's not true.' Wilson later properly apologized to the president for disrupting the session but he reaffirmed his accusation. In the very next sentence of his speech, however, the president lent credibility to Wilson's accusation by claiming that 'under our plan, no federal dollars will be used to fund abortions.' Amherst Professor Hadley Arkes fairly described that statement as 'a manifest lie' (www.catholic.org, Sept. 15). Let's evaluate it by looking at the main health care bill, H.R. 3200, which Obama has endorsed.

"The Capps Amendment to H.R. 3200, approved by the House Energy and Commerce Committee by a 30-28 vote, states: 'The public health insurance option shall provide coverage for . . . abortions for which the expenditure of Federal funds appropriated for the Department of Health and Human Services is permitted.' That limitation refers to the Hyde Amendment, a rider to the annual Labor/Health and Human Services Appropriation, which prohibits use of those funds to pay for abortions except to save the life of the mother or where the pregnancy is the result of rape or incest. The Hyde Amendment, however, is not itself a restriction on the use of funds under H.R. 3200 which itself appropriates the funds for its own operation. The Capps Amendment further states that 'Nothing in this Act shall be construed as preventing the public health insurance option from providing for or prohibiting coverage of . . . abortions for which the expenditure of Federal funds appropriated for the Department of Health and Human Services is not permitted.' That refers to elective abortions other than those for life of the mother, rape or incest.

"The Capps Amendment further requires that, among the health benefit plans 'offered in each premium rating area of the Health Insurance Exchange . . . there is at least one such plan that provides coverage' and 'at least one such plan that does not provide coverage' of the abortion services permitted, and also those forbidden, by the Hyde Amendment.

"Obama has proposed no 'plan' of his own separate from the bills he has endorsed, including chiefly H.R. 3200 and other bills which allow federal funding of abortion. The question remains: Is he correct in claiming that 'under our plan, no federal dollars' will be used to fund abortions? The Capps Amendment is complicated. It provides that the federally funded subsidy for individual public option health care premiums known as an 'affordability credit,' H.R. 3200, Sec. 241, 'may not be used for payment for' abortions for which the Hyde Amendment forbids federal payment. However, the Health Care Commissioner 'shall estimate the basic per enrollee, per month cost, determined on an average actuarial basis, for including coverage' for such elective abortions. The premium charged to all enrollees in the federally operated public option would be increased by the proportional amount (at least $1 a month) required to pay for all those elective abortions. The abortionists would bill the federal agency for such abortions performed on subscribers to the public option. The abortionists would be paid by checks drawn on the United States Treasury. Everyone subscribing to public option health insurance would be required to pay the premium surcharge to support all the abortions for which the Treasury would pay the abortionists. The dollars paid to the federal government under that surcharge would obviously become 'federal dollars' which would then be disbursed by the Treasury to the abortionists. Obama's flat statement to Congress and the American people that 'under our plan no federal dollars will be used to fund abortions,' is either evidence of an inconceivable ignorance of what is in H.R. 3200 and similar bills or it is knowingly false, that is, to borrow the words of Congressman Joe Wilson, 'You lie!'

"The nation's Catholic bishops, including principally Cardinal Justin Rigali and Bishop William Murphy of Rockville Center, New York, view health care 'as a basic right' and 'have long supported health care reform that respects human life and dignity from conception to natural death; provides access to quality health care for all, with a special concern for immigrants and the poor; preserves pluralism, with respect to rights of conscience; and restrains costs while sharing them equitably.' The bishops rightly insist that payment for abortion must be excluded from any health care reform.

"It would be a mistake, however, to conclude that merely excluding abortion coverage would make the proposed 'reforms' acceptable. Other problems are involved. One is the definition of abortion. Many so-called contraceptive pills can operate as abortifacients. The 'morning-after pill,' which can cause abortion, is sold over-the-counter as an 'emergency contraceptive.' A prohibition of funding for 'abortion' would not prevent funding of such abortifacient 'contraceptives.' On another point, consider H.R. 3200, Sec. 1713, page 768, which provides funding for 'home visits by trained nurses to families with a first-time pregnant woman, or a child (under 2 years of age), who is eligible for medical assistance.' One of the preconditions for such home visits is that they 'are effective' in '[i]mproving maternal or child health and pregnancy outcomes or increasing birth intervals between pregnancies.' A federal functionary, therefore, would come into a low-income home to improve 'pregnancy outcomes,' one of which could be abortion, and to 'increase birth intervals between pregnancies.' By the time the bureaucrats get through writing the regulations for this, it could operate as a covert version of China's 'one-child policy.'

"In a joint statement, 'Principles of Catholic Social Teaching and Health Care Reform,' the Kansas City bishops, Archbishop Joseph F. Naumann and Bishop Robert W. Finn, emphasized that the principle of subsidiarity requires that 'health care ought to be determined at the lowest level rather than at the higher strata of society. . . . The writings of recent Popes have warned that the neglect of subsidiarity can lead to an excessive centralization of human services, which in turn leads to excessive costs, and loss of personal responsibility and quality of care.'

"'The right of every individual to access health care,' said Naumann and Finn, 'does not necessarily suppose an obligation on the part of the government to provide it. Yet in our American culture, Catholic teaching about the 'right' to healthcare is sometimes confused with the structures of 'entitlement.' The teaching of the Universal Church has never been to suggest a government socialization of medical services. Rather, the Church has asserted the rights of every individual to have access to those things most necessary for sustaining and caring for human life, while at the same time insisting on the personal responsibility of each individual to care properly for his or her own health.'

"Here, as elsewhere, the social and moral teachings of the Church offer principles supportive of human dignity, freedom and common sense as well as the right to life."

FEDERAL TAKEOVERS, Oct. 6, 2009

"The health care debate makes sense only in the context of the transformation of our constitutional system. So let's do a quick review of Constitution 101.

"The Constitution of the United States was the first creation in history of a national government with only limited, delegated powers. Magna Carta, the English Bill of Rights and other documents involved only limitations on the otherwise unlimited power of government. The Articles of Confederation, under which the United States functioned from 1781 until the Constitution took effect in 1789, created essentially a confederation of semi-autonomous states. The Constitution created a real government of the nation, but a government limited to specified powers.

"Under the Constitution, neither Congress, nor the Executive nor the Judiciary, had unlimited jurisdiction. Article I, Sec. 8, specified that 'The Congress shall have Power' to legislate only on specified subjects. Incidentally, no power was granted to Congress to regulate health care as such. Nor was Congress granted a power over education, apart from special situations such as land-grant schools. The states retained all powers not delegated by the Constitution.

"That constitutional system has gone the way of the bronze axe and the spinning wheel. One transformative event was the Supreme Court's definition in *U.S. v. Butler* (1936), that Congress' power to tax and spend for the 'general welfare of the United States' was not limited to spending on the subjects on which Article I, Section 8, authorized Congress to legislate. But Congress' spending had to be for the 'general welfare.' Congress, however, has wide latitude to determine what is the 'general welfare.' While the Court said that the spending power was not a general power to regulate for public purposes, the Court has held that Congress can impose conditions on the subsidies it grants. *South Dakota v. Dole* (1987). That power to regulate recipients of federal money is, to put it mildly, very broad, as General Motors, banks, and other recipients of bailout money have learned. And as all of us will learn when the likely terms of Obamacare go into effect in 2013 (after Obama's reelection), there is no such thing as a free lunch. If you take the money, you take the controls.

"Many factors contributed over the years to the centralization of power in Washington. But in the past eight months, Congress' use of its spending power, and President Obama's unprecedented executive edicts, have so expanded federal power that it amounts to an extraconstitutional coup. The federal takeover of health care, one-sixth of the economy, is essential to the success of that coup. It would open the door to federal controls not only on what medical care you can receive but potentially also on what you eat, how much you weigh, your exercise regime, the level of heat and noise in your home and whatever else might affect your health and therefore the cost of your health care to the taxpayers. The framers of the Constitution would be surprised, to say the least.

"Health care, however, is not the only centralizing initiative in Congress. Another example is H.R. 3221, the Student Aid and Fiscal Responsibility Act of 2009 (SAFRA). It advanced under the radar while everyone was talking about health care. SAFRA reduces the financial options of students seeking higher education. It passed the House and now is in the Senate Health and Education Committee.

"The federal government now subsidizes student loans through the Federal Family Education Loan (FFEL), which offers subsidized loans to students from private lenders at low interest rates, and through the Direct Loan program (DL), in which the Department of Education is the lender and the funds come from the U.S. Treasury. The Higher Education Act sets the terms and conditions on FFEL and DL loans. FFEL was created in 1966. More than 2,000 lenders participate in FFEL, serving 4,400 institutions, with $70 billion in loans this year. The DL program, established in 1993, serves 1,700 institutions, with $22 billion in loans this year.

"SAFRA would terminate FFEL and shift all federal student loans, including Federal Direct Perkins Loans, to the DL program. SAFRA would also create nine new programs and otherwise increase federal involvement in early education, school construction, etc. On September 10, 40 current and former presidents of state, regional and national financial aid associations alerted House and Senate committees to problems involved in implementing SAFRA as early as the 2010–11 school year.

"Beyond those implementation issues, SAFRA would be a huge expansion of the DL program. It would dismantle a system that has worked fairly well for four decades. It would eliminate private sector jobs as well as consumer choice, competition among lenders, and existing programs to reduce defaults. For non-wealthy high school seniors, SAFRA would make their potential for federal student loans depend entirely on approval by government bureaucrats or contractors retained by government. One concern is that the predictably voluminous SAFRA regulations could provide openings for covert political or other illicit discrimination against borrowers or recipient schools. A more obvious concern is that 'Congress,' in the words of Representative Paul C. Broun (R-GA), 'has no business putting taxpayers on the hook for defaulted student loans when the private sector would gladly bear this risk.'

"The objections to federal takeovers of the private sector do not arise from constitutional archeologism. Those takeovers violate the social principle of subsidiarity: 'Just as it is wrong to withdraw from the individual and commit to the community at large what private enterprise and industry can accomplish, so too, it is an injustice, a grave evil, and a disturbance of right order for a larger and higher organization to arrogate to itself functions which can be performed efficiently by smaller and lower bodies. This is a fundamental principle of social philosophy, unshaken and unchangeable, and it retains its full truth today . . . The true aim of all social activity should be to help individual members of the social body, but never to destroy or absorb them.' Pius XI, *Quadragesimo Anno*, no. 79.

"'Subsidiarity,' said Benedict XVI, 'is the most effective antidote against any form of all-encompassing welfare state.' *Love in Truth*, no. 57.

"When they elected Notre Dame's most obsequiously honored alumnus, the American people voted for both hope and change. They are, indeed, getting one of those. Congressman Broun asked the question about the change that, so far, has no answer: 'When will the massive spending and Federal takeover end?'"

NOTE: The Health Care and Reconciliation Act of 2010 included the SAFRA requirement that, starting July 1, 2010, all new federal education loans, including Stafford, PLUS and Consolidation Loans, must be made through the Direct Loan program. For passage of SAFRA in the Senate a 60-vote majority would have been necessary to overcome a Republican filibuster; 60 votes would have been required also to pass Obamacare, the Patient Protection and Affordable Care Act. A parliamentary alternative called "budget reconciliation" permits passage of a bill with only a simple majority of 51 votes. However, only one "reconciliation" bill is allowed in each budget cycle. The Democratic leadership in the Senate therefore combined most elements of SAFRA, and also Obamacare, in one "budget reconciliation" bill, the Health Care and Reconciliation Act of 2010, which passed the Senate, 56 to 43, and the House of Representatives by 220 to 207. Council on Law in Higher Education, www.clhe.org, Special Report, May 4, 2010.

CARITAS IN VERITATE, Oct. 27, 2009

"Our first three columns this term discussed the Obama administration's takeover of the American private sector, including the automotive industry, banking, health care, student loans, etc. To avoid getting lost in the details, let's note some controlling principles offered by Pope Benedict XVI in his third encyclical, *Love in Truth* (*Caritatis in Veritate*) (CIV), issued June 29. CIV builds upon his first two encyclicals, *God is Love* (*Deus Caritas Est*, 2006), and *In Hope We Were Saved* (*Spe Salvi*, 2007). It carries forward Benedict's assertion in his first World Day of Peace message, on Jan. 1, 2006, that 'Any authentic search for peace must begin with the realization that the problem of truth and untruth is the concern of every man and woman; it is decisive for the peaceful future of our planet.' His first three encyclicals emphasize that love and acceptance of the truth about man and God offer the only hope for peace. 'Jesus,' said Benedict in that message, 'defined himself as the Truth in person, and . . . states his complete aversion to 'everyone who loves and practices falsehood.'

"CIV focuses on 'integral human development,' as urged by Paul VI in *Populorum Progressio* in 1967. CIV's opening words note the spiritual as well as material character of such development: 'Charity in truth, to which Jesus Christ bore witness . . . is the . . . driving force behind the . . . development of every person and of all humanity.'

"CIV deserves attention, especially within the Beltway and in the media. Don't hold your breath waiting for that. Let us, rather, note some unfashionable truths offered by CIV:

"1. Solidarity. We are relational by nature. John Paul II described 'the full meaning of freedom' as 'the gift of self in service of God and one's brethren.' *Veritatis Splendor*, no. 87. 'The human being,' said CIV, 'is made for gift.' No. 34. 'Economy and finance . . . can be used badly where those at the helm are motivated by purely selfish ends. . . . [I]n commercial relationships . . . gratuitousness and the logic of gift as an expression of fraternity . . . must find their place within normal economic activity.' No. 36.

"2. Subsidiarity. '[I]t is an injustice for a larger and higher organization to arrogate to itself functions which can be performed efficiently by smaller and lower bodies.' Pius XI, *Quadragesimo Anno* (1931), No. 79. This principle insists on 'the autonomy of intermediate bodies . . . and is the most effective antidote against [an] all-encompassing welfare state.' No. 56. Obamacare and other takeovers are at war with this principle.

"3. The moral law applies to all human activity. 'The conviction that man is self-evident and can . . . eliminate . . . evil . . . by his own action alone has led him to confuse happiness and salvation with material prosperity and social action. [T]he conviction that the economy must be autonomous [and] shielded from "influences" of a moral character [has] led to economic, social and political systems that trample upon personal and social freedom.' (No. 34). Integral human development requires more than self-interest. It requires 'upright . . . financiers and politicians whose consciences are . . . attuned to . . . the common good.' No. 71.

"4. Consistent ecology. 'The Church . . . must defend not only the earth, water and air as gifts of creation. . . . She must above all protect mankind from self-destruction . . . [T]he decisive issue is the . . . moral tenor of society. If there is a lack of respect for the right to life and to a natural death, if human conception, gestation and birth are made artificial, if human embryos are sacrificed to research, the conscience of society [loses] the concept of human ecology and, along with it, that of environmental ecology. It is contradictory to insist that future generations respect the natural environment when our educational systems and laws do not help them to respect themselves. The book of nature . . . takes in not only the environment but also life, sexuality, marriage, the family, social relations: in a word, integral human development. Our duties toward the environment are linked to our duties towards the human person . . . It would be wrong to uphold one set of duties while trampling on the other. Herein lies a grave contradiction in our mentality and practice.' No. 36. Exhibit A for that contradiction is the pro-abortion politician who told Notre Dame's graduates last May that they 'must decide how to save God's creation from a changing climate that threatens to destroy it.'

"5. Population growth is good. '[O]penness to life,' CIV states, is 'a rich social and economic resource. Populous nations have [emerged] from poverty thanks not least to the size of their population and [their] talents . . . [F]ormerly prosperous nations are [in] decline . . . because of their falling birth rates; this [is] a crucial problem for highly affluent societies. The decline in births . . . puts a strain on social welfare systems, increases their cost, eats into . . . financial resources needed for investment, reduces the availability of . . . labourers, and narrows the "brain pool." . . . [S]maller . . . families run the risk of impoverishing social relations, and failing to ensure . . . solidarity. These situations are symptomatic of a scant confidence in the future and moral weariness. It is . . . a social and even economic necessity . . . to hold up to future generations the beauty of marriage and the family, and the fact that these institutions correspond to the deepest needs and dignity of the person. . . . States are called to enact policies promoting the centrality and the integrity of the family founded on marriage between a man and a woman . . . and to assume responsibility for its . . . needs, while respecting its . . . relational character.' No. 44.

"6. Respect for life is essential to development. 'In . . . developed countries, legislation contrary to life [contributes] to the spread of an anti-birth mentality. . . . [A]ttempts are made to export this mentality to other States as if it were a form of cultural progress. Some . . . [o]rganizations work . . . to spread abortion [and promote] sterilization in poor countries, in some cases not even informing the women concerned. [D]evelopment aid is sometimes linked to the . . . imposition of strong birth control measures. Further grounds for concern are laws permitting euthanasia as well as pressure . . . in favor of its juridical recognition.' No. 28.

"'Openness to life,' CIV concludes, 'is at the center of true development. When a society moves towards the denial or suppression of life, it ends up no longer finding the . . . motivation and energy to strive for man's true good.' No. 28.

"The Pope is the one universal voice showing the way to a Culture of Life built on love, Truth and hope. It is time even for politicians to give him a listen."

EUCHARISTIC ADORATION AT NOTRE DAME, Nov. 10, 2009

"St. Thomas Aquinas defines peace, in one aspect, as the 'tranquility of order.' However you define it, we are not doing too well in achieving peace in domestic and international as well as cultural matters. Maybe we are missing something. Let me suggest a practice that can help.

"When John Paul II instituted Eucharistic adoration at St. Peter's Basilica in 1981, he said, 'The best . . . way of establishing everlasting peace on the face of the earth is through . . . Perpetual Adoration of the Blessed Sacrament.'. . . .

"[C]onversion of the bread and wine into the body and blood of Christ, promised in the sixth chapter of John's Gospel and fulfilled at the Last Supper, is called transubstantiation, 'a change of the whole substance of the bread into the substance of the body of Christ . . . and of the whole substance of the wine into the substance of his blood.' *Catechism*, no. 1376. 'Substance,' as Cardinal Avery Dulles put it, 'denotes the basic reality of the thing, i.e., what it is in itself.' A change in appearance does not affect the substance of the thing. When the angel Raphael stood before Tobiah, his appearance was that of a 'young man,' but his substance was that of an angel (*Tobit*, 5:5, 12:15).

"'Christ is present,' wrote Cardinal Dulles, 'by his dynamic power and action in all the sacraments, but in the Eucharist, His presence is, in addition, substantial. For this reason, the Eucharist may be adored. It is the greatest of all sacraments.' (Feb. 15, 2005).

"You are in the real presence of Christ every time you step into a Catholic church where the lighted lamp or candle indicates that the Blessed Sacrament is in the tabernacle. At any such time one can be with Christ in adoration. The term Eucharistic adoration, however, is usually applied to the exposition of the Sacrament to view. Christ is as fully present in the closed tabernacle as he is in the monstrance during exposition. It helps devotion to be able also to look upon him in the host in which 'the whole Christ is truly, really and substantially contained.'

"Eucharistic adoration is a part of Notre Dame, in history as well as practice. 'Our great consolation here,' wrote Fr. Edward Sorin, C.S.C., from the wilds of Indiana, 'is the Perpetual Adoration in our midst, and the perpetual daily Mass. . . . Upon these two wide spreading wings may we not, each and all, daily rise above the dense and thick fogs of this dreary land of exile? When we die, this double insurance against forgetfulness will prove to be a rich investment, a precious solace—aye, a source of joy for our last hours, but especially for those whose life is moulded after the Divine precept—always to pray and never to faint.'. . . .

"The practice of Eucharistic adoration complements the liturgy of the Mass. 'One of the most moving moments of the Synod [of Bishops],' wrote Benedict XVI, 'came when we gathered in St. Peter's Basilica, together with a great number of the faithful, for Eucharistic adoration. In this act of prayer, and not just in words, the . . . Bishops wanted to point out the intrinsic relationship between Eucharistic celebration and Eucharistic adoration. [An] appreciation of this . . . has been important . . . in the years following the liturgical renewal desired by the Second Vatican Council. . . . [A]doration outside Mass prolongs and intensifies . . . the liturgical celebration. . . . Indeed, 'only in adoration can a profound and genuine reception mature. And it is precisely this personal encounter with the Lord that then strengthens the social mission contained in the Eucharist, which seeks to break down not only the walls that separate the Lord and ourselves, but also and especially the walls that separate us from one another.' Benedict XVI, Apostolic Exhortation, *Sacrament of Love* (2007), no. 66, quoting his address, Dec. 22, 2005.

"So why should we consider Eucharistic adoration? One reason is that it works. 'People are hungry for God,' said Mother Teresa of Calcutta. 'When the Sisters are exhausted, up to their eyes in work; when all seems to go awry, they spend an hour in prayer before the Blessed Sacrament. This practice has never failed to bring fruit; they experience peace and strength.'

"Eucharistic adoration at Notre Dame is essentially a student initiative, with the support and encouragement of Campus Ministry. It is one of the very best things about Notre Dame."

RIGHT-TO-LIFE TUNNEL VISION ON OBAMACARE, Nov. 24, 2009

"The health care debate shows the limits of single-issue abortion politics. Obamacare, in its several versions, is objectionable for reasons beyond the funding of abortion and of euthanasia through rationing of care. It would transform the economy and culture. Its centralization and pervasive reach violate the principle of subsidiarity. The takeover of health care invites bureaucratic control of everything that affects your health, including what you eat, how you heat your home, etc.

"Individual bishops and the U.S. Conference of Catholic Bishops (USCCB) have objected to federal funding of elective abortion. They rightly insist that any reform must improve access to health care and protect conscience rights and the rights of the elderly, the disabled, immigrants and other vulnerable persons. Major pro-life entities, however, including the National Right to Life Committee (NRLC) and the USCCB, have stressed the restriction of abortion to such an extent as to generate the impression that the lack of such a restriction is the only decisive objection to Obamacare. That impression contributed to the House approval of Obamacare.

"On Saturday night, Nov. 7, the House passed H.R. 3962, the Affordable

Health Care for America Act, by a vote of 220 to 215. Its passage was secured by the approval that night of the Stupak-Pitts Amendment, which made H.R. 3962 subject to the Hyde Amendment, the restriction on other appropriations that forbids federal funding of abortions except to save the life of the mother or where the pregnancy resulted from rape or incest.

"Stupak-Pitts was adopted, 240 to 194, with one 'present.' The Member voting 'present' was John Shadegg, a pro-life Republican from Arizona. He had obtained commitments from numerous Republicans to vote 'present' so as to defeat Stupak-Pitts and ensure the defeat of H.R. 3962 itself. At noon Saturday, Nov. 7, however, the National Right to Life Committee (NLRC) informed all members of the House that 'NRLC will regard a "present" vote as equivalent to a negative vote on the Stupak-Pitts Amendment.' Faced with that threat of NRLC opposition to their re-election, those who might have supported the Shadegg strategy voted 'yes' on Stupak-Pitts.

"Shadegg's strategy of voting 'present,' so as to defeat Stupak-Pitts, was designed to kill H.R. 3962 itself since, if Stupak-Pitts were defeated, enough Democrats would have voted against H.R. 3962 to ensure its defeat. His strategy would have stopped Obamacare and would have cleared the way for a genuinely deliberative consideration by Congress of health care reform. H.R. 3200, the original House proposal, had 1,017 pages. H.R. 3962 has 1,990. The main Senate bill, which funds abortion, has 2,074. The accelerated votes on those and other bills, which very few, if any, members of Congress have read, is a mockery of legislative process.

"Not even a total prohibition of abortion funding would make Obamacare worthy of support. Pro-life entities, therefore, should have supported the Shadegg strategy instead of reacting to the Stupak-Pitts approval by virtually endorsing Obamacare. 'Over the weekend,' said the USCCB Monday, Nov. 9, 'the US House of Representatives advanced major legislation to provide adequate and affordable health care to all.' None of the versions of Obamacare deserves that description. Stupak-Pitts incidentally, in addition to funding abortion in life-of-the-mother, rape and incest cases, would not restrict funding of abortifacients which can prevent implantation of the embryo in the womb and which are wrongly defined as contraceptives.

"At the other end of life, Sec. 1233 of H.R. 3962 provides Medicare reimbursement to practitioners for 'voluntary advance care planning consultation' between 'the individual and a practitioner' who does not have to be the individual's physician. It does not state whether the consultation will be initiated by the practitioner or the patient. An individual may receive such consultation 'no more than once every five years unless there is a significant change in [his or her] health.' The bill imposes no limit on the number or frequency of such consultations. A consultation may include: an explanation of 'end-of-life services [and an] explanation by the practitioner of physician orders regarding life sustaining treatment.' Such is 'an actionable medical order relating to the treatment of that individual that . . . is signed . . . by a practitioner, and is . . . to be followed by health care professionals across the continuum of care.' The order 'communicates the individual's preferences regarding life sustaining treatment.' But it does not specify that the order must comply with those preferences. The order must be 'signed and dated by a practitioner' who could be someone other than the practitioner who gave the consultation and formulated the order. Nor does the bill require that the signer ever saw the patient. Could the signer by a member of a panel reviewing such orders without ever seeing the patient? Yes. Could that fairly be called a 'death panel'? Yes.

"Speaker Pelosi won approval of H.R. 3962 by exploiting the pro-life focus on restricting funding of abortion. 'The Stupak amendment,' Shadegg said, 'gave political cover to Democrats . . . Before the vote [Pelosi] promised pro-abortion Democrats she would strip the Stupak language [from the final bill.] Obama will help her. She will strip the Stupak amendment in Conference and pass the bill with the votes of Democrats who claim to be pro-life. . . . Republicans who, at the request of Right to Life . . . voted "yes" on Stupak last night defined a "yes" vote as the pro-life vote. But, it wasn't. A "yes" vote increased the votes for [H.R. 3962] and enabled Pelosi to pass it. That means more abortions. . . . If Republicans had voted "present" as a group, we would have defined the "present" vote as the pro-life vote. . . . Now, the Democrats who voted for Stupak will say the "Right to Life" vote was on Stupak and they voted pro-life. Republicans set the standard. Instead of making "present" the pro-life vote, we made "yes" the pro-life vote. . . . When the Stupak language is stripped in Conference (and Nancy Pelosi will strip it), the supposedly pro-life Democrats will be pressured by Pelosi and Obama to vote "yes" on the Conference report. . . . Pelosi and Obama . . . will tell [them] they're safe from attack by Right to Life because they voted for the Stupak Amendment. For real pro-lifers to stop the Conference Report after the Stupak language has been stripped will be nearly impossible. I pray we can, but fear last night was our best chance. . . . Nancy Pelosi caught Republicans off-guard.'

"The Obama Administration has indeed brought change. For a comparable transformation of a constitutional republic to a command economy under a leader with an anti-life agenda, one has to go back a few years. Adolf Hitler was named Chancellor on Jan. 30, 1933. In the following weeks he consolidated his power through decrees and other measures. The decisive event, however, was the Reichstag's approval of the Enabling Act on March 23, 1993, by which it ceded practically full and irrevocable powers to Hitler. The Enabling Act received the needed two-thirds vote only because it was supported by the Catholic party, the Center Party. Eliot Barculo Wheaton, *The Nazi Revolution: 1933–35* (1969), 286–93; William L. Shirer, *The Rise and Fall of the Third Reich* (1959), 88, 276–79. If Obamacare becomes law, it will be permanent lights out for limited government in the United States. It will be pathetically tragic if it becomes law through the misguided tunnel-vision support of Catholic entities and individuals."

NATURAL LAW, Dec. 8, 2009

"'The crisis of . . . democracies,' said Benedict XVI in accepting the credentials of American Ambassador Miguel Humberto Diaz, a Notre Dame alumnus, 'calls for . . . policies respectful of human nature and human dignity,' including 'respect for the inalienable right to life from the moment of conception to natural death.'

"These remarks raise questions we ignore at our peril: Why do we have to be 'respectful of human nature?' And where do we get 'inalienable' rights?

"Do moral issues, in health care and elsewhere, reflect merely personal or sectarian preferences? Or is there an objective moral order—a natural law—that determines whether an act is right or wrong? In 'her interventions in the public arena,' said Benedict to European parliamentarians on March 30, 2006, the Church draws attention to 'principles which are not negotiable [including] protection of life in all its stages. . . . These principles are not truths of faith, even though they receive . . . light and confirmation from faith; they are inscribed in human nature itself and therefore they are common to all humanity.'

"Natural law is neither a merely Catholic teaching nor even a Christian invention. Aristotle and Cicero affirmed it. Everything has a nature built into it by its maker. General Motors built a nature into your Chevy and gave you directions as to how to act in accord with that nature so the car will achieve its purpose. Our 'Maker' has built a nature into us that we ought to follow if we are to achieve our goal of eternal happiness.

"We can know the law of our nature, as St. Thomas Aquinas put it, by 'the light of natural reason, whereby we discern what is good and what is evil.' And our Maker has given us directions in Revelation, including the Ten Commandments which express the 'principal precepts' of that natural law (*Catechism*, No. 1955).

"The first, self-evident principle of the natural law is, in Aquinas' words, that 'good is to be done and promoted and evil is to be avoided.' The good is that which is in accord with the nature of the subject. It is good to feed gasoline to a car. It is not good to feed it to a man. And it is not good, i.e., it is evil, to steal or murder, because such acts are contrary to the natural human inclination to live in community. While we can affirm through reason the objective rightness or wrongness of acts, we generally have neither the right nor the

390

ability to judge the subjective culpability of the person who commits that act. To be culpable, one must know the act is wrong and choose to do it.

"The natural law provides a standard for human law as well as personal conduct. Martin Luther King cited Aquinas when he said, in his *Letter from Birmingham Jail*, that 'An unjust law is a code that is out of harmony with the moral law.' So, when Rosa Parks refused to give up her seat on the bus in 1955, she made a natural law statement. Legally enforced racial segregation is unjust and a civil law that mandates it is void.

"'Moral truth is objective,' said John Paul II at World Youth Day in Denver, 'and a properly formed conscience can perceive it.' But if reason were our only guide we would be in confusion. Our intellects are weakened by original sin and sincere advocates can be found on both sides of most moral issues. Aristotle, who had a pretty good LSAT score, sanctioned infanticide. Some Christians in the last century upheld the morality of slavery. Today people differ on the morality of abortion. They can't both be right. As St. Thomas tells us, 'If . . . we consider one action in the moral order, it is impossible for it to be morally both good and evil.'

"But whose natural law are you going to apply? As Supreme Court Justice James Iredell said in *Calder v. Bull*, in 1798, 'The ideas of natural justice are regulated by no fixed standard: the ablest and the purest men have differed upon the subject.' If Iredell is right, the natural law is indeterminate and relatively useless as a higher standard for law and a guide for human conduct. An authoritative interpreter is needed. 'Christians,' however, said John Paul, 'have a great help for the formation of conscience in the Church and her Magisterium. As the [Second Vatican] Council affirms: . . . "[T]he Catholic Church is by the will of Christ, the teacher of truth. Her charge is to . . . teach . . . that truth which is Christ . . . and confirm the principles of the moral order which derive from human nature itself." . . . The Church puts herself . . . at the service of conscience, helping it to . . . attain the truth with certainty.' *Veritatis Splendor*, no. 64.

"Everyone has a pope, an ultimate visible authority on moral questions. If that authoritative interpreter is not the real Pope, it will be a pope of the person's own choosing, usually the person himself. It makes sense to say that we have only one Pope, not seven billion and that his name is Benedict because he is the successor of Peter to whom Christ gave the keys.

"'[F]undamental rights,' said Benedict, are 'accorded universal recognition because they are inherent in the very nature of man, who is created in the image and likeness of God . . . [A]ll human beings . . . share a common nature that binds them together and calls for universal respect.' May 4, 2009. Every state that has ever existed has gone out of existence or will go out of existence. Every human being who has ever been conceived will live forever. That immortal nature of man, created in the image and likeness of God, is the basis of the inalienable, transcendent rights of man against the state.

"So when the Church speaks out against abortion, euthanasia, contraception and other intrinsic evils, she is not expressing merely some sectarian preference. Rather she incorporates the teaching of the natural law on those and other issues into her teaching of Christ who is the Author of that natural law and whose birth, described by Benedict XVI as 'the central event of history,' we celebrate in a few days."

THE MANHATTAN DECLARATION, Jan. 14, 2010

"One hundred fifty-two Catholic, Orthodox and Evangelical leaders recently issued the *Manhattan Declaration* (MD) in defense of 'the sanctity of human life, the dignity of marriage as a union of husband and wife, and the freedom of conscience and religion.' MD was drafted by Princeton Professor Robert George, Dean Timothy George of Samford University and Chuck Colson, founder of the Center for Christian Worldview. Online signers of MD exceed 400,000.

"MD tells it like it is: '[I]n our nation . . . the lives of the unborn, the disabled, and the elderly are . . . threatened; . . . the institution of marriage, already buffeted by promiscuity, infidelity and divorce, is . . . redefined to accommodate fashionable ideologies; . . . the rights of conscience are . . . jeopardized by those who would . . . compel persons of faith to compromise their deepest convictions.' MD relies on reasoned argument, consistent with Benedict XVI's view that the Church contributes to 'discussion of the . . . questions shaping America's future by proposing respectful and reasonable arguments grounded in the natural law and confirmed by the perspective of faith' (Oct. 2, 2009).

"MD spares neither political party: '[S]ince Roe v. Wade, . . . both . . . parties have been complicit in giving legal sanction to what Pope John Paul II described as "the culture of death."' MD presents a bill of particulars. '[H]uman embryo-destructive research and its public funding are promoted. . . . The President and many in Congress favor . . . funding of . . . "therapeutic cloning" . . . the . . . mass production of human embryos to be killed [to produce] . . . customized stem cell lines and tissues. At the other end of life, [a] movement to promote assisted suicide and "voluntary" euthanasia threatens the lives of "vulnerable" persons.'

"MD, unfortunately, misreads the origins of the 'culture of death.' MD describes 'the cheapening of life that began with abortion' and 'the license to kill that began with the abandonment of the unborn to abortion.' Legalized abortion, however, and the other evils denounced by MD, are not origins. They are symptoms of the contraceptive ethic that dominates our secularist, relativist and individualist culture.

"Until the Anglican Lambeth Conference of 1930, no Christian denomination had ever held that contraception could ever be objectively right. Contraception requires abortion as a backup. And the declining number of young is a factor in promoting euthanasia. If you make yourself the arbiter of whether and when life shall begin, you will predictably make yourself the arbiter of when, as in abortion or euthanasia, life shall end. In *Evangelium Vitae*, John Paul II noted that 'contraception and abortion are often closely connected, as fruits of the same tree. . . . [I]n very many . . . instances such practices . . . imply a self-centered concept of freedom, which regards procreation as an obstacle to personal fulfillment. The life which could result from a sexual encounter thus becomes an enemy to be avoided at all costs, and abortion becomes the only possible decisive response to contraception.' (No. 13).

"MD eloquently affirms that 'the marital relationship is shaped and structured by its intrinsic orientation to . . . procreation.' But it mentions neither contraception nor the defining aggression by which the federal government intruded itself, on the side of preventing life, into private reproductive decisions especially among the poor. During the 1960s, federal funding of family planning was limited. In 1970, Title X of the Family Planning and Population Services Act authorized grants and contracts to provide, in President Nixon's words, 'family planning services . . . to all those who want them but cannot afford them.' Abortifacients that prevent implantation of the embryo in the womb can be defined and funded as contraceptives under Title X and under Medicaid which, according to the Alan Guttmacher Institute, is now 'the primary source of public funding for contraceptive services.' Federal subsidies of birth control are directed primarily toward low-income persons in the United States, and abroad in foreign aid programs. Pending health care and other programs are likely to increase such funding.

"In *Humanae Vitae*, Pope Paul VI predicted that the acceptance of contraception would place 'a dangerous weapon . . . in the hands of . . . public authorities . . . for applying to . . . problems of the community those means acknowledged to be licit for married couples. . . . Who will stop rulers from . . . imposing upon their peoples . . . the method of contraception which they judge to be most efficacious? In such a way men would [place] at the mercy of . . . public authorities the most personal . . . sector of conjugal intimacy.' (No. 17).

"The failure of MD, in its catalogue of legalized promotions of the 'culture of death,' even to mention the entry by government into the business of subsidizing by contraception the rejection of new life, is inexcusable. Once that role of government was conceded, the other evils denounced by MD were predictable. Perhaps the purpose of MD was to put together a coalition of signers that would include proponents of public funding of contraception. If so, MD politicized and trivialized itself.

"On another concern of MD, same-sex marriage, the impact of

contraception was spelled out by Methodist Pastor Donald Sensing of Franklin, Tenn.: 'Since the invention of the Pill . . . human beings have . . . been able to control reproduction. . . . The . . . acceptance of these changes is impelling the move toward homosexual marriage. Men and women living together . . . became . . . the dominant lifestyle in the under-30 demographic. . . . Because they . . . control their reproductive abilities—that is, have sex without sex's results—the arguments against homosexual consanguinity begin to wilt.'

"'When society decided—and we have decided, this fight is over—that society would no longer decide the legitimacy of sexual relations between particular men and women, weddings became . . . symbolic rather than substantive . . . the shortcut way to make the legal compact regarding property rights, inheritance and . . . other . . . benefits. . . . Sex, childbearing and marriage now have no necessary connection to one another, because the biological connection between sex and childbearing is controllable. . . . If society has abandoned regulating heterosexual conduct of men and women, what right does it have to regulate homosexual conduct, including the regulation of their legal and property relationship with one another to mirror exactly that of hetero, married couples? I believe that this . . . is contrary to the will of God. But . . . same-sex marriage, if it comes about, will not cause the degeneration of . . . marriage; it is the result of it.' (*Wall Street Journal*, March 15, 2004).

"The signers of MD commendably pledge, in accord with St. Thomas Aquinas and Martin Luther King, to disobey any edict that would compel them or their institutions to participate in 'any . . . anti-life act,' treat 'immoral sexual partnerships . . . as marriages or . . . refrain from proclaiming the truth.' They also voice a prayer for their own perseverance: 'May God help us not to fail in [our] duty' to proclaim the Gospel.' Regrettably, MD did not go further and call upon the American people to pray for their country.

"MD forthrightly calls attention to evils that transcend the political as a challenge to reason, nature and God himself. MD itself would have transcended the political if it had called on the American people to put their primary reliance on prayer. Without a confrontation of contraception and its promotion by government, and without a serious call to prayer, MD invites dismissal as just another syncretistic manifesto cast in powerful prose that misses the point."

"Strong Bodies Fight," Feb. 2, 2010

"The Notre Dame community responded with characteristic generosity to the earthquake disaster in Haiti. Every year at this time, however, we remind ourselves of another nation, comparable in some respects to Haiti, in which Notre

Dame is involved. That is Bangladesh, roughly the size of Wisconsin with a population about half that of the United States. In Bangladesh, 57.45 infants die out of every 1,000 live births; in Haiti, 62.33; in the United States, 6.3. The per capita income in 2008, in U.S. dollars, in Bangladesh was $1,500; in Haiti, $1,300; in the United States, $47,000. Cyclones and other natural disasters are frequent and severe in Bangladesh including, in September 1998, the most severe flooding in modern world history. It destroyed 300,000 houses, killed over 1,000 people and made 30 million homeless. Two-thirds of the country was underwater.

"Since 1853, Holy Cross missionaries have labored in Bangladesh. Today they include 140 priests and 63 brothers. All but 19 are Bangladeshi. More than 70 Holy Cross sisters also serve there. Bangladesh is 89.7 percent Islam, 9.2 percent Hindu, 0.7 percent Buddhist and 0.3 percent Christian. Because conversion from Islam, the state religion, is illegal, the missionaries work among tribal groups who had never embraced Hinduism, Buddhism or Islam and are predominantly Catholic. The missionaries serve the spiritual needs of all the Christian faithful and the dire material needs—especially educational—of all Bangladeshis.

"The 'tribal groups,' said Fr. Frank Quinlivan, Class of 1966, the Holy Cross provincial of Bangladesh, 'are often neglected, isolated and marginalized. Holy Cross is in eight tribal parishes in four dioceses. Those children who pass Class 5 come to the parish center for high school. There are no high schools in the villages. The parish provides a hostel, one for the boys and one for the girls. Only in this way can they attend school. The children are able to eat regularly and to get medical care they cannot get in the villages. Parents, however, can almost never afford the hostel costs, a little over $20 a month. Finding the money to educate these children is a constant concern in all our parishes: Education is essential for the very survival of these tribal groups.'

"Since 1931, Bengal Bouts has become the largest single contributor to those missions. The boxers themselves run the program, under the supervision of Boxing Club Administrator Vince Voss and the director, Terry Johnson, a Chicago attorney and former Bengals champ. Seniors Patrick Burns and Chris Cugliari are co-presidents of the Boxing Club. The senior captains are Will Burroughs, Michael Sayles, Tim Thayer, John Maier and Nic Ponzio. The junior captains are Bobby Powers, Dominic Golab and John Tchoula. The captains organize and run the practices, a major job since, for the second year in a row, more than 300 boxers are in the program. That number will decline as the boxers experience the creatively onerous workouts imposed by Tom Suddes, a Columbus developer and former Bengals champ who donates several weeks each year to the program. This can be unnerving because Tom does the workouts himself, a potentially embarrassing motivator for the much younger boxers. Tom and Notre Dame pilot Pat Farrell are the head coaches.

The assistant coaches include Sweet C. Robinson of the Buchanan Police Department and former boxers Pat Ryan, Pete Ryan, Kevin Smith, Thad Naquin, Ryan Rans, Chip Farrell and Superior Court Judge Roland Chamblee, who also exercises judicial restraint as a corner man at the Bouts. Holy Mother Church and the Jesuits are involved through Fr. Brian Daley who coaches and, like Tom Suddes, works out with the boxers.

"Dr. Jim Moriarty runs the medical and safety program which has avoided serious injury for the entire 80 years since the Bouts were first organized by Dominic 'Nappy' Napolitano. Emergency Medical Technical Terri Engel attends every session and maintains the sparring and medical records. The two practice rings are closely monitored by Notre Dame Fire Department EMTs, including Steve Serbalik, Lee Anne Feher, Nadeem Haque, Sean Bradley, Zinaida Peterson, Olivia Mahon, Brian Bush, and Frannie Rudolph, and by Bonnie Chow, Bert Williams and Serene Cuenco who work for Rec Sports as 'professional rescuers' (no kidding; their shirts say so). They are all very effective.

"The Indispensables, without whom the entire Boxing Club would implode, are the managers, Ashley Mensch, Katherine Johnston, Kelly Garvey, Catherine Cooney, and Meghan Rolfs. They cheerfully handle, with impressive efficiency and ease, an endless array of financial, administrative and other details.

"Over the past two years the boxers themselves have raised the program to a new level. Several boxers raised travel money to go to Bangladesh where, with the help of Notre Dame film professor and former Bengals boxer William Donaruma, Class of 1989, and cinematographer John Klein, Class of 2006, they made a full-length film, *Strong Bodies Fight*, detailing the realities and needs of the mission. 'Our goal,' said Mark Weber, last year's president and producer of the film, 'is to transform the connection [with Bangladesh] from sending them an annual check to an actual relationship. It went from an abstract mission to something we could see and touch.' Tom Suddes oversaw the project and raised the needed money to finance it by simply writing a letter to Bengals alumni who, as Tom put it, 'want to give back for what the Bengal Bouts did for them.' The Center for Social Concerns is developing a summer service program for Boxing Club members to go to Bangladesh and work in the missions. The Autumn 2008 edition of Notre Dame Magazine carried a feature article on the film. To view a trailer and learn more about the film, see www.strongbodiesfight.org. . . .

"Last year Bengal Bouts contributed $50,000 to the missions in Bangladesh. Compared to the federal budget, that may seem like chump change. But among the 'ultra poor' served by the Holy Cross missionaries in Bangladesh, the $10.49 you casually spend for a Papa John's large pizza would feed a family of four for three weeks. Those people need the Bengal Bouts. And they need our support."

RALPH MCINERNY, Feb. 16, 2010

"Ralph McInerny, a member of the Notre Dame philosophy department since 1955, died on Jan. 29. Author of more than 40 scholarly books, Dr. McInerny was justly regarded as the preeminent exponent of the philosophy of St. Thomas Aquinas. He also wrote poetry and more than 80 novels and mysteries.

"The many testimonials by friends and colleagues, available online, recount Ralph's life and achievements. They give a glimpse of his personal side. Ralph McInerny, a man of total integrity, was a kind and happy guy with a drily unique sense of humor, a master of the pun and a family man who devoted over 49 years of marriage to Connie who was his match and whom he would occasionally introduce as 'my first wife, Connie.'

"This column is neither an obituary nor a eulogy. Rather the point is twofold. First, to note that Notre Dame students are now disadvantaged, whether they realize it or not, by their inability to study under Ralph McInerny and to know him in person. We will never see his like on this campus again.

"The second point is to state the obvious. Ralph McInerny still lives—in Heaven (spelled with a capital H because it is a place) as we trust and pray—but also in his writings. Notre Dame students and others can still connect with his thought and wisdom. Reading McInerny on Aquinas has a practical payoff. The philosophy of Thomas Aquinas is called 'realist' because it systematically affirms that there is a real world which we can know and understand through our senses and reason. The study of Aquinas is the study of how to integrate faith and reason, which, as John Paul II said, 'are like two wings on which the human spirit rises to the contemplation of truth.' (*Fides et Ratio*, preamble.) To advance that integration was Ralph's mission. He accomplished it, without intimidating or boring the reader, because he wrote easily on two levels. He operated without peer in the highest reaches of Thomistic philosophy, drawing out its implications and significance. But he also had a rare facility, a gift, for writing with such clarity as to reach and inspire the rest of us. Those of us who are gratefully 'content to retail,' as Ralph put it (*I Alone Have Escaped to Tell You*, 93), the teachings of Aquinas, had—and have—a lodestar in Ralph McInerny. If what we thought was consistent with Ralph's position, we had a surety (not infallible, he would insist) that we were on the right track.

"We all continue to need the guidance of Ralph McInerny. This is especially true for Notre Dame students. Through no fault of their own, they exist in an epistemological free-fire zone where the daily horoscope in The Observer predictably serves a large constituency. McInerny, instead, gave Notre Dame students and others a chance to connect with the real world, known to faith and reason, including the identification of objective right and wrong. Now that Ralph himself is gone, we can connect with those realities by reading his writings, especially on Aquinas. Out of many that could be chosen to provide an introduction to philosophy in general and to Aquinas in particular, I suggest five for openers. They are systematic, readable, and perhaps most important, short:

A Student's Guide to Philosophy (Intercollegiate Studies Institute, 1999, 75 pages). A good refresher for anyone. The beginner should read this first. Everyone 'does philosophy' in that he thinks. McInerny introduces the reader to what passes for modern philosophy and its contrast with the perennial philosophy of Aristotle and Aquinas. He includes one-paragraph biographical inserts on 14 players in the philosophical game, from Socrates to Edith Stein. The reader will learn about the fact-value split between the is and the ought, scientific and pre-scientific analysis, and the essence of our post-Christian era. The book concludes with a remarkable bibliographical essay, by Joshua Hochschild, describing dozens of books the reader can use to go more deeply into the subject.

"A First Glance at St. Thomas Aquinas: A Handbook for Peeping Thomists" (Univ. of Notre Dame Press, 1989, 208 pages). This primer explains Aristotle's common sense approach to philosophy, and Aquinas's use of those ideas to create a common sense foundation for theology. Realities such as form (what a thing is), matter (what a thing is made of), art and nature, causation, creation and the soul are introduced philosophically and theologically. This book easily explains one of McInerny's great contributions: his explanation of the role of analogy for St. Thomas. Incidentally, McInerny's mastery of the pun as a high art form is a use of analogy.

"Ethica Thomistica: The Moral Philosophy of Thomas Aquinas" (Catholic University of America Press, 1982, 129 pages). 'This book attempts to lay out in its main lines the moral philosophy of St. Thomas Aquinas' (ix). McInerny explains the relation between the good and nature in Aristotle and Aquinas. He shows the origin and application of the first principle of practical reason and the natural law: 'The good is to be done and pursued and evil avoided.' (43) He examines the structure of voluntary and other human acts, what makes an action good or evil, prudence, conscience and the relation between religion and morality. St. Thomas' 'conception of man as a rational agent' (124) is countercultural today. Which is a good reason to read this book.

"Characters in Search of Their Author: The Gifford Lectures, Glasgow, 1999–2000" (Univ. of Notre Dame Press, 2001, 138 pages). 'Natural theology,' McInerny says, 'means the philosophical discipline which proves that God exists and that he has certain attributes.' (5). McInerny's Gifford Lectures are presented here in two parts. The first, 'Whatever Happened to Natural Theology?', examines the eclipse of the reality that reason can know God in a skeptical age that has lost the very concept of truth. Part two, 'The Recovery of Natural Theology,' examines the proofs for the existence and attributes of

God. It addresses the reality that the fact that knowing that there is a God does not guarantee that one's conduct will be good. It discusses the different kinds of faith, including 'the faith of scientists,' (124) and the compatibility of reason and religious faith. In short, there is a 'Christian philosophy' (129–32) and McInerny sees himself as a Christian philosopher. He explains how that can be.

"*I Alone Have Escaped to Tell You: My Life and Pastimes*" (Univ. of Notre Dame Press, 2006, 167). This autobiography tells us about many things, Ralph included. 'I picked this book up during a spare hour,' said Michael Novak, 'and hours later have scarcely been able to get back to anything else.' Each chapter includes a personal narrative set in a fast-moving cultural commentary on a lot of things, including universities, the academics who inhabit them, seminaries, the writing trade, Europe and its decline, Notre Dame, the Vatican, and so on. I have listed this book last, but you may want to read it first.

"We can profit from any of McInerny's books, including his fiction, all of which is entertaining and has a Catholic tone. In any event, it's kind of nice to know that Ralph McInerny, in his writings, is still around for us as a mentor. Pray for him and, while you're at it, pray for Notre Dame. Requiescat in pace.."

FINIS: THE COLUMN THAT NEVER WAS

I submitted the following column on March 1, 2010:

"A big issue at Notre Dame a few weeks ago was 'sexual orientation' and the status of the Notre Dame Gay/Lesbian/ Bisexual/Transgender (GLBT) community. Enough time has passed to make it useful to review some of the governing principles as found in the teaching of the Catholic Church. That teaching includes four pertinent elements:

"1. Homosexual acts are always objectively wrong. The starting point is the *Catechism*: 'Homosexuality refers to relations between men or between women who experience an exclusive or predominant sexual attraction to persons of the same sex. It has taken a great variety of forms through the centuries and in different cultures. Its psychological genesis remains largely unexplained. Basing itself on Sacred Scripture, which presents homosexual acts as acts of grave depravity, Tradition has always declared that 'homosexual acts are intrinsically disordered.' They are contrary to the natural law. They close the sexual act to the gift of life. They do not proceed from a genuine affective and sexual complementarity. Under no circumstances can they be approved.' No. 2357.

"Homosexual acts are doubly wrong. They are not only contrary to nature. They are wrong also because they are extra-marital. *The Letter on the Pastoral*

Care of Homosexual Persons, issued in 1986 with the approval of John Paul II, said, 'It is only in the marital relationship that the use of the sexual faculty can be morally good. A person engaged in homosexual behavior therefore acts immorally. To choose someone of the same sex for one's sexual activity is to annul the rich symbolism and meaning, not to mention the goals of the Creator's sexual design.' No. 7.

"2. Since homosexual acts are 'intrinsically disordered,' the inclination toward those acts is disordered. An inclination to commit any morally disordered act, whether theft, fornication or whatever, is a disordered inclination. 'The number of men and women who have deep-seated homosexual tendencies,' says the *Catechism*, 'is not negligible. This inclination, which is objectively disordered, constitutes for most of them a trial.' No. 2358. That inclination, however, is not in itself a sin.

"3. '[M]en and women who have deep-seated homosexual tendencies,' says the *Catechism*, 'must be accepted with respect, compassion and sensitivity. Every sign of unjust discrimination in their regard should be avoided.' No. 2358. In a culture which tends to marginalize and disrespect those with physical or psychological disorders, it will be useful to recall the admonition of the 1986 *Letter* that 'The human person, made in the image and likeness of God, can hardly be adequately described by a reductionist reference to his or her sexual orientation. . . . Today the Church provides a badly needed context for the care of the human person when she . . . insists that every person has a fundamental identity: the creature of God and, by grace, his child and heir to eternal life.' No. 16. The prohibition of 'unjust' discrimination, however, does not rule out the making of reasonable and just distinctions with respect to military service, the wording of university nondiscrimination policies and other matters including admission to seminaries. As the Congregation for Catholic Education said in its 2005 Instruction on the subject, 'the Church, while profoundly respecting the persons in question, cannot admit to the seminary or to holy orders those who practice homosexuality, present deep-seated homosexual tendencies or support the so-called "gay culture."' No. 2.

"4. '[M]en and women who have deep-seated homosexual tendencies . . . are called to fulfill God's will in their lives, and, if they are Christians, to unite to the sacrifice of the Lord's Cross the difficulties they may encounter from their condition. . . . Homosexual persons are called to chastity. By the virtues of self-mastery that teach them inner freedom, at times by the support of disinterested friendship, by prayer and sacramental grace, they can and should gradually and resolutely approach Christian perfection.' *Catechism*, nos. 2358, 2359.

"The positive, hopeful teaching of the Church on marriage, on family and the transmission of life is founded on the dignity of the person as a creature made in the image and likeness of God. The 'gay rights' movement is, instead, a predictable consequence of the now-dominant contraceptive ethic. Until the Anglican Lambeth Conference of 1930, no Christian denomination had ever said that contraception could ever be objectively right. The Catholic Church continues to affirm the traditional Christian position that contraception is intrinsically an objective evil.

"Contraception, said Paul VI in *Humanae Vitae* in 1968, is wrong because it deliberately separates the unitive and procreative aspects of the sexual act. If sex has no intrinsic relation to procreation and if, through contraception, it is entirely up to man (of both sexes) whether sex will have any such relation, how can one deny legitimacy to sexual acts between two men or between two women? The contraceptive society cannot deny that legitimacy without denying itself. Further, if individual choice prevails without regard to limits of nature, how can the choice be limited to two persons? Polygamy (one man, multiple women), polyandry (one woman, multiple men), polyamory (sexual relations between or among multiple persons of one or both sexes) and other possible arrangements, involving the animal kingdom as well, would derive legitimacy from the same contraceptive premise that justifies one-on-one homosexual relations.

"It would be a mistake to view the homosexual issue as simply a question of individual rights. The militant 'gay rights' movement seeks a cultural and legal redefinition of marriage and the family, contrary to the reality rooted in reason as well as faith. Marriage, a union of man and woman, is the creation not of the state but of God himself as seen in *Genesis*. Sacramento coadjutor bishop Jaime Soto, on Sept. 26, 2008, said, 'Married love is a beautiful, heroic expression of faithful, life-giving, life-creating love. It should not be accommodated and manipulated for those who would believe that they can and have a right to mimic its unique expression.' Space limits preclude discussion here of the same-sex marriage issue, which we will defer to a later column."

"Professor Emeritus Rice is on the law school faculty. He may be reached at 574-633-4415 or rice.1@nd.edu."

THE REJECTION (FROM MATT GAMBER TO CHARLES E. RICE, March 2, 2010, 1:24 A.M.)

"Dear Mr. Rice,

"I wanted to first introduce myself as Matt Gamber, the new Editor-in-Chief of *The Observer*. Thank you for your continued hard work and contributions to The Observer's Viewpoint section.

"Second, I wanted to let you know why we chose not to run your most recent submission in Tuesday's *Observer*. First, it far exceeded our word limit guidelines, which I understand our Viewpoint Editor, Michelle Maitz, had shared with you in the past. Our daily space limitations require that we enforce the word limit, and we would appreciate your attention to this limit in the future.

"Also, I personally had some concerns with the content of the column, particularly considering The Mobile Party comic incident earlier in the semester at *The Observer*. While your piece was well-researched and I trust the information was factually correct, I did not feel it lent itself to creating a productive discussion, all things considered. I was a bit concerned with certain language as well.

"In the future, if you would like to examine this topic, we thought it might be beneficial to do so in a point-counterpoint format, perhaps with an author of an opposing or differing viewpoint. That way, each 'side,' so to speak, would have the opportunity to present relevant facts, evidence and analysis to define its position.

"As I began, I again thank you for your contributions to The Observer. Please let me know if you have any questions regarding this decision, and I look forward to working with you in the future."

THE RESPONSES

"On Tuesday, Mar 2, 2010 at 3:04 PM, Charles E. Rice wrote:

"Dear Mr. Gamber:

"Thank you for your email informing me that my column presenting the teachings of the Church on homosexuality will not be published. Since 1992, I have been privileged to publish every two weeks a column, entitled 'Right or Wrong?' in the *Observer*. I emphasize my appreciation for the unfailing professionalism and courtesy of the Observer editors with whom I have had contact over those years.

"You mention the column 'far exceeded our word limit guidelines.' It is in fact significantly shorter than each of the three previous columns published this semester in the *Observer*. I was not asked to shorten any of them. The rejected column accurately presented relevant teachings of the Catholic Church on homosexuality. I understand why you are concerned over the content of the column. You further propose that if I examine the topic of homosexuality in the future, 'we thought it might be beneficial to do so in a point-counterpoint format, perhaps with an author of an opposing or differing viewpoint. That way, each 'side,' so to speak, would have the opportunity to present relevant facts, evidence and analysis to define its position.'

"In a university that claims to be Catholic, I am not willing to restrict my presentation of Catholic teaching to a format that treats the authoritative teaching of the Church as merely one viewpoint or 'side' among many. If you require that future columns of mine on homosexuality comply with a format such as you propose, it will be inappropriate for me to continue writing the column for the Observer.

"Sincerely,

"Charles E. Rice

"Professor Emeritus, Notre Dame Law School."

"On Tuesday, March 02, 2010, 5:29 PM, Matt Gamber wrote:

"To: Charles E Rice

"Dear Dr. Rice,

"Thank you for your response. I appreciate your contributions to *The Observer* and I hope that we will continue to work together. I do not wish to question the Church teachings or argue the points you presented in your essay, but rather, because the paper is still recovering from the incident with The Mobile Party comic, we would prefer to examine this issue at a later time.

"I sincerely appreciate your understanding of our concerns, and I hope you will not hesitate to contact me with any further questions or concerns you may have.

"Sincerely,

"Matt Gamber"

APPENDICES

Rev. John I. Jenkins, C.S.C.
President
University of Notre Dame
Notre Dame, Indiana 46556

Dear Father Jenkins:

Professor Fred Freddoso has shared with me the response on Sept. 17th by Dr. Frances L. Shavers, Chief of Staff and Special Assistant to the President, to Fred's email of that date to you asking that Notre Dame request dismissal of the charges against the persons arrested for trespass on the campus in relation to the honoring of President Obama at Commencement. Dr. Shavers responded on your behalf to Fred's email because, as she said, "the next few days are rather hectic [for Fr. Jenkins]." I don't want to add to the hectic burden of your schedule by sending you a personal message that could impose on an assistant the task of responding. I therefore take the liberty of addressing to you several concerns in the form of this open letter to which a response is neither required nor expected.

First, permit me to express my appreciation for the expressions of support for the pro-life cause in your September 16th "Letter concerning post-commencement initiatives." I know, however, that in a matter as significant as this, you will appreciate and welcome a respectful but very candid expression of views. In my opinion, the positions you have taken are deficient in some respects.

In your Letter of Sept. 16th, you rightly praise the work of the Women's Care Center (WCC) and of its superb leader, Ann Murphy Manion. I commend you on your statement that the WCC "and similar centers in other cities deserve the support of Notre Dame clubs and individuals." Your praise of WCC and similar efforts, however, overlooks a practical step that Notre Dame, as an institution, ought to take. That would be for you, on behalf of Notre Dame, to issue a standing invitation to the WCC to establish an office on the Notre Dame campus to serve students, faculty and staff if, in the judgment of the WCC, that would be desirable and effective. Such would give practical effect, right here at Notre Dame, to your words in support of the WCC and similar efforts.

Your Letter announced your formation of the Task Force on Supporting the Choice for Life. Rather than offer a detailed evaluation of my own, I note my agreement with the personal analysis of William Dempsey, ND '52, President of the Sycamore Trust, calling attention to 'the obviously deliberate exclusion from Task Force membership of anyone associated with the ND organizations that have been unashamedly and actively pro-life: the Center for Ethics & Culture and the ND Fund for the Protection of Human Life. Nor was the student representative chosen from the leadership of the student RTL organization or from anyone active in last year's student alliance protesting the honoring of the President, ND Response. It is hard to resist the inference that this is as a move toward marginalizing the Center and the Fund, neither of which receives any University support the way it is. . . . Finally, it is unsettling but instructive that this announcement comes a day after Fr. Jenkins' annual address to the faculty in which he described his goals for the year, which included increasing female and minority faculty representation but not a word about the most crucial problem facing the university, the loss of Catholic identity through the failure to hire enough Catholics to restore the predominance required by the Mission Statement. This is a striking falling away from [Fr. Jenkins'] wonderful inaugural address. The fact that ND did nothing to serve the pro-life cause ought to be regarded with suspicion.

My main concern in this letter arises from your statement in your Letter that "Each year on January 22, the anniversary of the Supreme Court's Roe v. Wade decision, the March for Life is held in Washington, D.C. to call on the nation to defend the right to life. I plan to participate in that march. I invite other members of the Notre Dame Family to join me and I hope we can gather for a Mass for Life at that event." I understand that Notre Dame students have invited you to participate with them in the March. The problem arises from an aftermath of Commencement. On this I refer back to Chief of Staff Shavers' response to Professor Freddoso's request that Notre Dame ask dismissal of the charges against those arrested. Dr. Shavers states that "these protesters were arrested for trespassing and not for expressing their pro-life position." That is misleading. This is not an ordinary case of trespass to land such as would occur if a commuter walks across your lawn and flower bed as a short-cut to the train station. Notre Dame is ordinarily an open campus. Those 88 persons, 82 of whom are represented by Tom Dixon, ND '84, ND Law School, '93, were arrested not because they were there, but because of who they were, why they were there, and what they were saying. Other persons with pro-Obama signs were there but were not arrested and not disturbed. Serious legal and constitutional questions are involved, arising especially from the symbiotic relationship between the Notre Dame Security Police, who made the arrests, and the County Police. This letter is not a legal brief. Rather I merely note that it is disingenuous for Notre Dame to pretend that this is merely a routine trespass case.

The confusion is compounded by Dr. Shavers' statement that "Under Indiana law, however, Notre Dame is not the complainant in these matters and so is not in any position to drop or dismiss the charges." That sentence is half-true and half-false. Notre Dame is the complaining victim of the alleged trespass. Whether to dismiss the charges, of course, is for the prosecutor to decide.

Dr. Shavers states that "Notre Dame officials have been in regular contact with the prosecutor's office on these matters, and, in consultation with the University, the prosecutor has offered Pre-Trial Diversion to those for whom the May incident was a first-time offense. As described by the prosecutor, this program does not require the individual to plead guilty or go through a trial; rather, the charges are dropped after one year so long as the individual does not commit another criminal offense. We understand that most of those arrested have chosen not to take advantage of this offer and obviously we cannot force them to do so. In essence, the choice of whether or not to go to trial belongs to the defendants."

Pre-trial diversion could change their status as convicted criminals. But it is only because of the actions of Notre Dame that they are treated by the law as criminals in the first place. Notre Dame continues to subject those defendants to the criminal process. If they entered pretrial diversion they would each have to pay hundreds of dollars in costs, which would amount in effect to a fine imposed on them, with the concurrence of Notre Dame, for praying. Most of the 88 are in straitened financial circumstances. The imposition on them of such a fine would be a serious hardship. Instead, Notre Dame ought to state publicly that it has no interest in seeing those prosecutions proceed in any form and that it requests the prosecutor to exercise his discretion to dismiss all those charges unconditionally. Given the prospect of 88 or so separate jury trials, probably not consolidated, in cases involving potentially serious legal and constitutional issues, such a request by Notre Dame would surely be appreciated by the taxpayers of St. Joseph County.

Those 88 defendants were on the other side of campus, far removed from the site of the Commencement. They are subjected by Notre Dame to the criminal process because they came, as individuals, to Notre Dame to pray, peacefully and non-obstructively, on this ordinarily open campus, in petition and reparation, as a response to what they rightly saw as a facilitation by Notre Dame of various objectively evil policies and programs of Notre Dame's honoree, President Obama. Those persons, whom Notre Dame has subjected to legal process as criminals, are neither statistics nor abstractions. Let me tell you about a few of them.

Fr. Norman Weslin, O.S., 79 years old and in very poor health, was handcuffed by Notre Dame Security Police as he sang "Immaculate Mary" on the campus sidewalk near the entrance. He asked them, "Why would you arrest a Catholic priest for trying to stop the killing of a baby?" The NDSP officers put

406

him on a pallet and dragged him away to jail. St. Joseph County Police were also there. I urge you to watch the readily available videos of Fr. Weslin's arrest. If you do, I will be surprised and disappointed if you are not personally and deeply ashamed.

Such treatment of such a priest may be the lowest point in the entire history of Notre Dame. You would profit from knowing Fr. Weslin. Notre Dame should give Fr. Weslin the Laetare Medal rather than throw him in jail. Norman Weslin, born to poor Finnish immigrants in upper Michigan, finished high school at age 17 and joined the Army. He converted from the Lutheran to the Catholic faith and married shortly after earning his commission. He became a paratrooper and rose to the rank of Lieutenant Colonel in the 82nd Airborne Division, obtaining his college degree en route. After a distinguished career, he retired in 1968. As the legalization of abortion intensified, he and his wife Mary Lou, became active pro-lifers in Colorado. In 1980, Mary Lou was killed by a drunk driver. Norman personally forgave the young driver. Norman Weslin was later ordained as a Catholic priest, worked with Mother Teresa in New York and devoted himself to the rescue of unborn children through non-violent, prayerful direct action at abortuaries. In 1990 at Christmastime, I was privileged to defend Fr. Weslin and his Lambs of Christ when they were arrested at the abortuary in South Bend. One does not have to agree with the tactic of direct, non-violent action at abortuaries to have the utmost admiration, as I have, for Fr. Weslin and his associates. At Notre Dame, Fr. Weslin engaged in no obstruction or disruption. He merely sought to pray for the unborn on the ordinarily open campus of a professedly Catholic university. The theme of Notre Dame's honoring of Obama was "dialogue." It would have been better for you and the complicit Fellows and Trustees to dialogue with Fr. Weslin rather than lock him up as a criminal. You all could have learned something from him. His actions in defense of innocent life and the Faith have been and are heroic. Notre Dame's treatment of Fr. Weslin is a despicable disgrace, the responsibility for which falls directly and personally upon yourself as the President of Notre Dame.

The other "criminals" stigmatized by Notre Dame include many whom this university should honor rather than oppress. One is Norma McCorvey, the plaintiff in *Roe v. Wade*, who has become pro-life and a Catholic actively trying to spread the word about abortion. Those "criminals" include retired professors, retired military officers, mothers of many children, a Catholic nun in full habit, Christian pastors, several Ph.Ds, and Notre Dame grads. They are, in summary, "the salt of the earth." They came, on their own, at their own expense, and not as part of any "conspiracy," from 18 states. They came because they love what Notre Dame claims to represent. They themselves do represent it. But one has to doubt whether Notre Dame does so anymore.

Clearly, Notre Dame should do all it can to obtain the dismissal of those criminal charges. This has nothing to do with one's opinion of the tactics of rescue at abortuaries. It is simply a matter of you, as President, doing the manifestly right thing.

Please permit me to speak bluntly about your announced purpose to participate in the March for Life and to "invite other members of the Notre Dame Faculty to join me." Notre Dame should have had an official presence at every March for Life since 1973. But until now it never has. Notre Dame students, with the encouragement of Campus Ministry, participate in the March but the University, as such, has not done so. To put it candidly, it would be a mockery for you to present yourself now at the March, even at the invitation of Notre Dame students, as a pro-life advocate while, in practical effect, you continue to be the jailer, as common criminals, of those persons who were authentic pro-life witnesses at Notre Dame. When the picture of Fr. Weslin's humiliation and arrest by your campus police was flashed around the world it did an incalculable damage to Notre Dame that can be partially undone only by your public and insistent request, as President of Notre Dame, that the charges be dropped. In my opinion your attachment to the March for Life, including your offering of a Mass for Life, could give scandal in the absence, at least, of such an insistent request to dismiss those charges. Your decision to present an official Notre Dame presence at the March could be beneficial, but not in the context of an unrelenting criminalization by Notre Dame of sincere and peaceful friends of Notre Dame whose offense was their desire to pray, on the campus, for the University and all concerned including yourself. If you appear at the March as the continuing criminalizer of those pro-life witnesses, you predictably will earn not approbation but scorn, a scorn which will surely be directed toward Notre Dame as well. As long as you pursue the criminalization of those pro-life witnesses, your newest pro-life statements will be regarded reasonably as a cosmetic covering of the institutional anatomy in the wake of the continuing backlash arising from your conferral of Notre Dame's highest honor on the most relentlessly pro-abortion public official in the world.

In conclusion, this letter is not written in a spirit of contention. It is written rather in the mutual concern we share for Notre Dame—and for her university. I hope you will reconsider your positions on these matters. Our family prays for you by name every night. And we wish you success in the performance of your obligations to the University and all concerned.

Sincerely,

Charles E. Rice
Professor Emeritus
Notre Dame Law School

Notre Dame's Mistreatment of the ND88.
Published in the *Irish Rover*, the alternative student
newspaper at Notre Dame, Sept. 30, 2010

Fr. Norman Weslin, O.S., at the complaint of Notre Dame, was arrested in May 2009 and charged as a criminal for peacefully entering the Notre Dame campus to offer his prayer of reparation for Notre Dame's conferral of its highest honor on President Obama, the most relentlessly pro-abortion public official in the world. The University refuses to ask the St. Joseph County prosecutor to drop the charges against Fr. Weslin and the others arrested, still known as the ND88 although one, Linda Schmidt, died of cancer this past March. Judge Michael P. Scopelitis, of St. Joseph Superior Court, recently issued two important orders in this case.

The first order denied the State's motion to consolidate the cases of multiple defendants. That motion would have denied each separate defendant his right to a separate jury trial. The order did permit consolidation of the trials of twice-charged defendants on the separate offenses with which that defendant was charged; a defendant charged, for example, with trespass and disorderly conduct would therefore not have to appear for two trials. Judge Scopelitis also denied the prosecution's attempt to force each defendant to return to South Bend for each proceeding in the case, which would have coerced the defendants to abandon their defense. Instead, the Judge permitted the defendants to participate by telephone in pre-trial conferences.

The second order upheld the subpoena issued by Thomas Dixon, ND '84, ND Law School, '93, the able attorney for the ND88, to compel the pre-trial testimony by deposition of William W. Kirk, who was summarily fired by the University on June 14th from his position as Associate Vice-President for Residence Life. The details of Bill Kirk's firing were analyzed by Prof. David Solomon in the *Irish Rover* of August 31st. Judge Scopelitis' order is limited and permits defendants to "inquire as to why William Kirk no longer holds the position of Associate Vice-President, Residence Life, at the University of Notre Dame." The University and the prosecution had strenuously resisted any attempt to have Mr. Kirk deposed although he is willing to testify under subpoena and at the eventual trials of the ND88. Nor is the University willing to have the President, Fr. John I. Jenkins, C.S.C., and relevant senior officials, above the Notre Dame Security Police, deposed. Mr. Dixon wants such pretrial testimony to explore the seriously discriminatory, illegal and unconstitutional character of the University's actions against the ND88.

Judge Scopelitis' orders move the case along. But they unavoidably leave a few questions unresolved. Why did the University try to prevent the deposition of Bill Kirk and why is it unwilling to agree to such testimony by senior University officials? What is the University trying to hide? Perhaps it is the unprecedented and discriminatory character of the University's treatment of the ND88. In his statement of April 30, 2010, Fr. Jenkins reiterated Notre Dame's position that, "the University cannot have one set of rules for causes we oppose, and another more lenient set of rules for causes we support. We have one consistent set of rules for demonstrations on campus—no matter what the cause." That statement is untrue.

On March 8–9, 2007, the Soulforce Equality Ride conducted a "gay rights" demonstration on the Notre Dame campus. Six demonstrators were "arrested," taken to the campus security building and photographed. They were then driven by campus police to their hotel. "We never heard another word," said Delfin Bautista, one of the demonstrators. "It was just a setup to get us off campus." Their trespass notices, incidentally, were stamped with the signature of William Kirk. On March 26, 2007, Catholic Worker protestors demonstrated on campus against ROTC. Nine trespass citations and three trespass notices were issued. One demonstrator, George F. Arteaga, was taken to the county jail. The next morning he was told by a guard, "We're letting you go," and was released. The trespassing and disorderly conduct charges against him were dismissed by the prosecutor's office and no further proceedings occurred against any of the demonstrators.

Those 2007 events were recounted in the *South Bend Tribune*, May 1, 2010, and in several very extensive letters written in February and March, 2010, to Fr. Jenkins and Dennis Brown, University Spokesman, by William H. Dempsey, President of the Sycamore Trust. "I tracked down," wrote Mr. Dempsey to Fr. Jenkins on March 11, 2010, "four persons who had been involved: two Catholic Workers (one a priest) and two Soulforce members. They confirmed that the demonstrators had in fact been arrested—one read the citation to me—and that this was the last they had heard of the matter."

Mr. Dempsey's conclusion is an undeniable indictment of Notre Dame's position:

"The short of it, then, is that Notre Dame is not enforcing 'one consistent set of rules for demonstrations on campus—no matter the cause.' Heretofore, it evidently has exercised a discretion appropriate to the circumstances. The result of adopting an inflexible stance respecting the ND88 is truly bizarre. The University acts with tolerance toward pro-gay and anti-military supporters but severity toward pro-life supporters."

Let us assume that Fr. Jenkins had been unaware of what happened in 2007 on his watch. But when he restated on April 30th the University's claim of equal treatment for all, he was aware of Mr. Dempsey's investigation and his demonstration of the falsity of that claim. Yet he restated that claim without qualification and without any mention of those 2007 events. Neither Fr. Jenkins nor any other University official has apologized to Fr. Weslin and the ND88 for its misrepresentation of the University's policy and for its disparate treatment of them. Nor has Notre Dame sought to rectify that injustice by asking the prosecutor to drop the charges.

How can we explain this vindictive treatment of the ND88? Permit me, first, to tell you a little about those targets of the University's wrath. Fr. Weslin was 79 and in very poor health when he was arrested at Notre Dame and literally dragged off the campus on a pallet. Born to poor Finnish immigrants in upper Michigan, he joined the Army after high school. He converted from the Lutheran to the Catholic faith and married Mary Lou before earning his commission. He became a paratrooper and rose to Lieutenant Colonel in the 82nd Airborne Division, earning his college degree en route. When he retired in 1968, he and Mary Lou became active pro-lifers in Colorado. In 1980, Mary Lou was killed by a young drunk driver whom Norman personally forgave. Norman later was ordained as a Catholic priest, worked with Mother Teresa and devoted his life to the rescue of unborn children through peaceful, prayerful direct action at abortuaries. In December, 1990, I was privileged to defend Fr. Weslin when he and his Lambs of Christ were arrested at the South Bend abortuary. One does not have to agree with the tactic of direct, non-violent action at abortuaries to have the highest admiration, as I have, for Fr. Weslin and his associates. He is a hero of the Faith. Notre Dame should have given Fr. Weslin the Laetare Medal rather than throw him in jail.

"The other 'criminals' stigmatized by Notre Dame include many whom this university should honor rather than oppress. One is Norma McCorvey, the plaintiff in *Roe v. Wade*, who had become pro-life and a Catholic actively trying to spread the word about abortion. The ND88 include retired professors, retired military officers, mothers of many children, a Catholic nun in full habit, Christian pastors, several Ph.Ds, and Notre Dame grads. They are 'the salt of the earth.' They came at their own expense, and not as part of any 'experience,' from 18 states. They came because they love what Notre Dame claims to represent. They themselves do represent it. But it is doubtful that Notre Dame does so anymore. The leaders of Notre Dame ought to be deeply ashamed of their continuing persecution of such people.

In response to criticism of its honoring of Obama and its persecution of the ND88, Notre Dame has commendably taken pro-life initiatives, including Fr. Jenkins' leading of a Notre Dame delegation to the March for Life. It was the first official Notre Dame participation in that event since its inception in 1974. In a discordant note, however, Fr. Jenkins went to the March while he was, by his own choice, the intransigent jailer, in effect, of pro-life witnesses whose "crime" was that they sought to pray, peacefully, at and for the University of Notre Dame.

Nothing in this article is meant to disparage those reactive pro-life initiatives Notre Dame has taken, including the recent appointment of Mary Daly as coordinator of University Life Initiatives. Fr. Jenkins and other relevant Notre

Dame officials are acting in what they see as the best interests of Notre Dame. But to what extent is Notre Dame serious about its pro-life commitments? Why do they impose such unrelenting persecution—an apt word—on pro-life witnesses, especially in light of their non-prosecution of pacifist and "gay rights" protestors and their reliance on the brazen falsehood that they "have one consistent set of rules for demonstrators on campus"?

Perhaps a clue may be found in Angelo Codevilla's new book, *The Ruling Class*. Dr. Codevilla, who received his M.A. at Notre Dame and is professor emeritus at Boston University, demonstrates that we are governed by a political and cultural "ruling class," characterized by its "insistence that people other than themselves are intellectually and hence otherwise humanly inferior." (57–58). A comparable ruling class dominates the academic world. Since the misbegotten 1967 Land O'Lakes Declaration which asserted the autonomy of "Catholic" universities from Church teaching authority, Notre Dame has striven to become an accepted player on the periphery of that academic "ruling class." As former president Fr. Edward A. Malloy, C.S.C., said at the 1993 Board of Trustees meeting, "we think we should have greater input into national policy discussions and into ethical preparations for decisions. We think we're capable of operating in the same world as the Ivys, Stanford, Vanderbilt, Duke, Southern Cal and Northwestern." *South Bend Tribune*, Feb. 15, 1993, p. B1.

Notre Dame appears to be governed by academic ruling class wannabes. The operative religion of the academic and political establishments, however, is political correctness. Activist opponents of ROTC and activist advocated of "gay rights" are politically correct. Activist pro-lifers, such as Fr. Weslin and the ND88, are not. For Notre Dame's leaders to show respect for the ND88, let alone apologize to them and seek an end to their prosecution, as they ought, would be to touch a third rail of academic respectability. It would not play well in the ruling academic circles. What would they think of us at Harvard, Yale, etc? Notre Dame has expressed a worthy desire to be a pro-life champion. If they really mean it, the first step must be a public request by Notre Dame to the prosecutor to dismiss unconditionally the charges against the ND88. Without such a rectification of an injustice inflicted by the University, Notre Dame's otherwise commendable pro-life activities are merely cosmetic, a defensive covering of the institutional anatomy. The ND88—and Notre Dame itself—deserve better.

NOTE: On May 5, 2011, Notre Dame and the ND88 announced a settlement pursuant to which the criminal charges against the ND88 were dismissed. Several of the ND88 had intended to file civil actions against the University if the University continued to insist on pursuing the criminal prosecutions. The time limit for filing such civil actions was about to expire when the University agreed to the settlement. The agreement to dismiss the prosecutions therefore protected Notre Dame against potential civil liability in those cases. The very effective lead attorney for the ND88 is Thomas M. Dixon, ND '84, NDLS '93, dixon3902@comcast.net. The Sycamore Trust, a Notre Dame alumni group, is an excellent source of information on the ND88 and other University matters. www.projectsycamore.com.

AFTERWORD

In *America* magazine after the Obama Commencement, Bishop John M. D'Arcy laid out three "critical questions" for "Catholic universities":

> As bishops, we must be teachers and pastors. In that spirit, I would respectfully put these questions to the Catholic universities in the diocese I serve and to other Catholic universities.
>
> Do you consider it a responsibility in your public statements, in your life as a university and in your actions, including your public awards, to give witness to the Catholic faith in all its fullness?
>
> What is your relationship to the church and, specifically, to the local bishop and his pastoral authority as defined by the Second Vatican Council?
>
> Finally, a more fundamental question: Where will the great Catholic universities search for a guiding light in the years ahead? Will it be the *Land O'Lakes Statement* or *Ex Corde Ecclesiae*? The first comes from a frantic time, with finances as the driving force. Its understanding of freedom is defensive, absolutist and narrow. It never mentions Christ and barely mentions the truth. The second text, *Ex Corde Ecclesiae*, speaks constantly of truth and the pursuit of truth. It speaks of freedom in the broader, Catholic philosophical and theological tradition, as linked to the common good, to the rights of others and always subject to the truth. Unlike *Land O'Lakes*, it is communal, reflective of the developments since Vatican II, and it speaks with a language enlightened by the Holy Spirit.
>
> On these three questions, I respectfully submit, rests the future of Catholic higher education in this country and so much else."[1]

In response, Richard C. Notebaert, Chairman of the Notre Dame Board of Trustees, artfully said, in effect, Thank you, Bishop, but we'll stick with Land O'Lakes: "From Father Hesburgh to Father Malloy and now Father Jenkins," he said, "Notre Dame has been blessed with great leadership. I would also like to thank Bishop John M. D'Arcy for his leadership and counsel. For 24 years he has served the diocese and supported Notre Dame. We are saddened by his disappointment in Notre Dame and other Catholic colleges throughout the world that subscribed to the landmark *Land O'Lakes Statement* on academic freedom and institutional autonomy. As the bishop has stated, 'Notre Dame is a splendid place.'"[2]

1   John M. D'Arcy, "The Church and the University," *America*, August 31, 2009.
2   Letters, *America*, Sept. 14, 2009.

Land O'Lakes and *Ex Corde Ecclesiae* cannot be reconciled. As long as Notre Dame adheres to the false "autonomy" of Land O'Lakes, its Catholic character will continue to erode. That is why the compilation of columns in this book might evoke an image of "the log of the Titanic." Notre Dame, however, has more than salvage value. It can be raised to resume its true mission. But "[t]he strengthening of Catholic identity," as Bishop D'Arcy said five years ago, "must be done within the university and by the university, according to the university's statutes and we accept that."[3]

Under the University's Statutes, the Fellows run Notre Dame. The Fellows are a "self-perpetuating body." They elect the Trustees and "have and exercise all power and authority granted by" the State of Indiana to the University. Six of the twelve Fellows must be "members of the Priests Society of the Congregation of Holy Cross, Indiana Province." Four of the Fellows "hold their office *ex officio*, namely the Provincial of the Priests Society of the Congregation of Holy Cross, Indiana Province, the Religious Superior of the Holy Cross Religious at Notre Dame, the President of the University, and the Chairman of the Board of Trustees." One of the prescribed "duties" of the Fellows is to maintain "[t]he essential character of the University as a Catholic institution of higher learning."

Notre Dame's description of itself as "Catholic" is dependent on episcopal permission. Canon Law provides that, "Even if it really be Catholic, no university... may bear the title or name *Catholic university* without the consent of the competent ecclesiastical authority."[4] In *Veritatis Splendor*, John Paul II cited that canon in saying, "It falls to [bishops], in communion with the Holy See, both to grant the title 'Catholic' to Church-related schools, universities, health care facilities and counseling services and, in cases of a serious failure to live up to that title, to take it away."[5] The exercise, or suggestion of the exercise, of that power is, of course, a matter for the pastoral judgment of the bishop.

Since the Obama Commencement, criticisms from alumni and others have caused the University to modify some policies, on pro-life and other matters, toward positions more favorable to Catholic teaching.

Those changes in policy, however, are essentially marginal. This is so for one reason. The main problem at Notre Dame is personnel. Land O'Lakes adherents have governed Notre Dame for the last four decades. The Fellows, Trustees and other officers of Notre Dame, are acting in what they see as the best interest of Notre Dame. They believe in Land O'Lakes' "autonomy." They are driving Notre Dame over the cliff, not because they wish the

3   *So. Bend Tribune*, June 28, 1996, p. D1.
4   Canon 808 (Emphasis in original.)
5   *VS*, no. 116.

University ill, but because Land O'Lakes is, for a Catholic university, a suicide pact. Notre Dame's leaders, in response to alumni and other pressure, will make only marginal or cosmetic changes. They will not abandon Land O'Lakes because they actually believe in it. And, over the past four decades, they have made the University so dependent financially on foundations, corporations, and especially government, that a retreat from Land O'Lakes could be seen as a threat to the symbiotic relation between the University and its governmental and other benefactors. A bursting of a bubble, perhaps.

In short, a genuine abandonment of Land O'Lakes by the present leaders of Notre Dame is, to say the least, highly improbable. Apart from an unlikely episcopal intervention, the only thing that will prevent Notre Dame from following the secularizing course of Harvard, Vanderbilt and other originally Protestant universities, is a change in personnel. Notre Dame needs, without delay, a total changing of the guard.

Beyond these considerations, a curious factor is the anomalous role of the Congregation of Holy Cross. In the 1960s, the Congregation got public relations credit for turning Notre Dame over to "lay control." The problem is that they didn't. They created a "lay board," but that board is totally controlled as to its membership and its every substantial action, by the twelve Fellows, six of whom must be Holy Cross priests of the Indiana Province. No policy can be adopted, or significant action taken, to which those six Holy Cross Fellows object.

The "duties" of the Fellows include:

e) The essential character of the University as a Catholic institution of higher learning shall at all times be maintained....

f) The University's operations shall be conducted in such manner as to make full use of the unique skills and dedication of the members of the Priests of Holy Cross, Indiana Province, Inc.

The Congregation here has set up for itself a perfect storm of power and privilege divorced from institutional responsibility. Priests who are members of the Congregation are six of the twelve Fellows who effectively control Notre Dame. And the Fellows are mandated "to make full use of the unique skills and dedication" of the Holy Cross priests of the Indiana province. Although members of the Congregation effectively control Notre Dame, the Congregation itself is insulated from responsibility for the actions of those Holy Cross priests. The privileged position of the Congregation, however, is not likely to survive the continued implementation of Land O'Lakes and the pursuit of secular prestige.

One might fairly ask whether the Congregation, consistently with Canon Law and its own constitutions and statutes, has, at some level, the power and authority to bring about the replacement of the Holy Cross priests on the

Fellows and Board of Trustees with Holy Cross priests who actually believe in *Ex Corde* rather than in Land O'Lakes. Let us leave it to the Canon lawyers and ecclesiastical experts to analyze the labyrinthine detail that might be involved in answering that question. But it is not wholly inconceivable that such power and authority, whether explicit or implicit, formal or informal, might be found. If so, the question becomes one of will, of institutional as well as personal fortitude, i.e., guts.

In any event, the most important thing any of us can do here is to pray that Notre Dame, Our Lady, will bring her University back into full communion with the Catholic Church, which is the body of her Son.

Index

NOTE: Where a name or subject is mentioned or discussed on consecutive pages of the text, the first such page is stated in the Index.